Health Care
and the Law

HEAD OFFICE: 100 Harris Street PYRMONT NSW 2009
Tel: (02) 8587 7000 Fax: (02) 8587 7100
For all sales inquiries please ring 1800 650 522
(for calls within Australia only)

INTERNATIONAL AGENTS & DISTRIBUTORS

CANADA
Carswell Co
Ontario, Montreal,
Vancouver, Calgary

SINGAPORE
Sweet & Maxwell Asia
Albert Street

HONG KONG
Sweet & Maxwell Asia
Hennessy Road, Wanchai

UNITED KINGDOM & EUROPE
Sweet & Maxwell Ltd
London

Bloomsbury Books Ltd
Chater Road, Central

UNITED STATES
Wm W Gaunt & Sons, Inc
Holmes Beach, Florida

MALAYSIA
Sweet & Maxwell Asia
Petaling Jaya, Selangor

William S Hein Co Inc
Buffalo, New York

NEW ZEALAND
Brooker's Ltd
Wellington

JAPAN
Maruzen Company Ltd
Tokyo

Health Care and the Law

by

Meg Wallace

RN (ACT), B Soc SCI (Waikato), LLB (Hons) (Auck)
*Senior Legal Adviser, Australian Capital Territory
Department of Justice and Community Safety*

THIRD EDITION

*Foreword to the third edition by the Chief Minister
for the Australian Capital Territory, Gary Humphries MLA*

Lawbook Co. 2001

Published in Sydney by

Lawbook Co.
   100 Harris Street, Pyrmont, NSW

First edition 1991
Second edition 1995
Third edition 2001

National Library of Australia
   Cataloguing-in-Publication entry

Wallace, Meg.
   Health care and the law.

   3rd ed.
   Includes index.
   ISBN 0 455 21752 1

   1. Medical care – Law and legislation – Australia.
   2. Medical personnel – Malpractice – Australia. I. Title.

344.94041

© 2001 Thomson Legal & Regulatory Limited ABN 64 058 914 668
   trading as Lawbook Co.

This publication is copyright. Other than for the
purposes of and subject to the conditions prescribed under
the Copyright Act, no part of it may in any form or by
any means (electronic, mechanical, microcopying,
photocopying, recording or otherwise) be reproduced,
stored in a retrieval system or transmitted without prior
written permission. Inquiries should be addressed to
the publishers.

Publisher: Karolina Kocalevski
Senior Editor: Jessica Perini
Product Developer: Georgie Pringle
Marketing Manager: Sherlyn Moynihan

Typeset in Stone, 9 point on 11 point, by Mercier Typesetters
   Pty Ltd, Granville, NSW
Printed by Ligare Pty Ltd, Riverwood, NSW

FOREWORD

There can be few areas of human endeavour where the law is making itself more acutely felt than health care.

This is fuelled by dramatic change in consumer knowledge and expectation as well as the rapid advance of biomedical technology. Much more is now possible. Much more is now expected.

These changes have put substantial pressure on politicians to ensure that the laws governing practice in health care keep pace with community values and expectation. That's why we are likely to see legislation governing health care practice continue to mushroom. There will be more and more laws governing what you do and how you do it—not less.

A sound understanding of the law is, therefore, essential for health care practitioners.

While most medico-legal works address the concerns of doctors, *Health Care and the Law*, now in its third edition, provides for a broader audience of health care practitioners and workers, from nurses to ambulance officers, dentists to physiotherapists. It contains examples and cases that apply to various health care situations. It continues the practice of using checklists and case summaries, with more extensive use and discussion of cases.

The 18 chapters cover core issues, from an introduction to the legal system through to consent, negligence, contract and employment, patient rights and property to reporting to the state of births, deaths, infectious diseases and child abuse.

Chapter 19 explores the difference between law and ethics, and discusses some fundamental principles of ethics, with a guide to practical ethical decision making.

Now, more than ever, those involved in health care need to be familiar with the law that increasingly governs their working lives.

Health Care and the Law should be kept as handy as stethoscope and bandages.

GARY HUMPHRIES MLA

Chief Minister, Australian Capital Territory
June 2001

PREFACE

The first edition of *Health Care and the Law* was written especially for nurses, with illustrations drawn from both my own and my students' experiences. I have attempted to expand the relevance to other health care professionals in later editions.

The book is not intended to be a comprehensive study of all areas of law relevant to health carers. It is an introductory text, which aims at serving the role of a chart of the territory, giving an overview and understanding of the basic layout of the law, with directions to further sources of legal information. It is hoped that it will prove to be a stimulus to health carers to develop their understanding of the law as it relates to their work, and a useful tool for those who want to delve more deeply into the complexities of a system that is becoming increasingly important in the delivery of health care.

This, the third edition, maintains the approach of the past. I have outlined and illustrated the basic principles of law relating to health care, explaining how the legal system works as well as pointing to specific legislation and case law related to health care issues. Health professionals should find the book useful in their work, whether they specialise in one area, such as obstetrics, orthopaedics, community health services or emergency care, or deal with a wide variety of health care needs. In this sense the book is general in its approach.

The ever rapid development of modern biomedical technology, as well as the many sometimes controversial uses to which it is put have provided many legal challenges to both medical professionals and legislators. This book sets out the basic legal principles so that they can be applied by health care practitioners to the many novel situations that arise in everyday practice.

Most of the chapters have been expanded to deal more fully with the issues involved, particularly the chapters on consent, negligence and regulation of the health care professions. Although it has not been possible to set out in detail the whole body of law of each of the States and Territories, as well as federal legislation, I have described the legislation of the different jurisdictions in more detail in this edition. However, Chapter 19 has been revised, but not updated.

I wish to thank friends and colleagues who have offered encouragement and advice, those at the Lawbook Co. who have helped in the production of this book, in editing and organising. Most appreciated of all, however, is the invaluable assistance and support of my husband Max.

MEG WALLACE

Canberra
May 2001

Basic Sources for Research

Each chapter has references to specifically useful material. There are many more books and articles that are available. Some basic general references and sources of law that students will find useful, and that are not referred to at the end of each chapter, as they are useful for all or most of them, are listed below.

General References

Some general references on the law with chapters on both medical and other matters are: *The Laws of Australia*, a series of looseleaf volumes, an encyclopedia of current Australian law, published by Lawbook Co., dealing with different subject areas by volume. *Halsbury's Laws of Australia* is another looseleaf encyclopedia, with different chapters covering the topics, rather than volumes and the Australian version developed from the original *Halsbury's Laws of England*. These are both available on CD-ROM, kept by university and some larger libraries, which can be searched using key-words and indexes. They have an exposition of the law and references to case law. For those who wish to get seriously involved in researching and updating the law, a guide to using these sources is Cooke, C, Creyke, R, Geddes, R and Holloway, I, *Laying Down the Law* (Butterworths, Sydney, 1996), Ch 11.

Medical Law

The two most useful looseleaf services dealing with health care and the law are *Australian Health and Medical Law Reporter* (CCH, Sydney), which comprehensively covers most areas of health law, and *Professional Negligence (Medical)* (CCH, Sydney), which is devoted to medical negligence issues.

Journals

There are two main Australian journals dealing with health care issues. These are the *Journal of Law and Medicine*, general editor Ian Freckelton, published by the Lawbook Co., the *Health Law Bulletin*, senior editor Lynne Smith, published by Prospect Publishing, Sydney. Mainstream law journals and medical journals, as well as journals devoted to medical ethics contain the occasional relevant article. Consulting an index of journals will yield results.

Electronic Databases

There are many commercial legal information services that are available for conditional access from libraries. As noted above these include *Halsbury's Laws of Australia*, and *The Laws of Australia*. The following are free services accessible through the internet.

One of the most useful pages on the internet is:
http://www.austlii.edu.au

It contains legislation in all Australian jurisdictions, case reports from all courts and many tribunals, and links to secondary sources as well as many useful links to other legal material from other countries. It also has material on researching the law on the Web.

High Court of Australia information, cases, transcripts can be found at:
http://www.hcourt.gov.au

Law databases obtained and/or prepared by Federal Attorney-General's Department are at:
http://scaleplus.law.gov.au

This contains Commonwealth legislation and court and tribunal decisions, and legislation for the Australian Capital Territory, the Northern Territory, Queensland and South Australia, and Decisions of the Supreme Courts of Australian Capital Territory (1987+); Victoria (1995+); Tasmania (1987+); Queensland (1993+); South Australia (1989+); New South Wales (1995+); and the Northern Territory (1987+).

Federal, State and Territory government home pages provide links to legal resources such as Acts, Bills and other documents. They can be accessed at
http://www.fed.gov.au/
http://www.act.gov.au/
http://www.nsw.gov.au/
http://www.nt.gov.au/
http://www.qld.gov.au/
http://www.sa.gov.au/
http://www.tas.gov.au/
http://www.vic.gov.au/
http://www.wa.gov.au/

British and Irish case law and legislation etc can be accessed at:
http://www.bailii.org/

House of Lords information, case law etc can be accessed at:
http://www.courtservice.gov.uk/judgments/judg_home.htm

US legal information, case law, legislation etc can be accessed at:
http://www.findlaw.com

Findlaw also has an Australian site:
http://www.au.findlaw.com

TABLE OF CONTENTS

Foreword	v
Preface	vii
Table of Cases	xiii
Table of Statutes	xxv

1	What is law?	1
2	The legal structure	19
3	The legal process	41
4	Consent to care by a competent adult	63
5	Consent for those who cannot legally do so	123
6	Negligence	185
7	Recording, communicating and accessing client information	259
8	Drugs	297
9	Clients' property	319
10	Contract	331
11	Contracts to provide health care services	361
12	Accidents and injuries related to health care	389
13	Registration and practice	417
14	Criminal law and health care	455
15	State involvement in birth and death: registration and coronial enquiries	515
16	State involvement in threats to health or welfare	537
17	Human tissue transplants and reproductive technology	565
18	Expanding recognition of human rights	591
19	Decision making, law and ethics: a discussion	625
Appendix 1	A guide to abbreviations used in law report citations	645
Appendix 2	More cases on negligence	649
Appendix 3	Summary of the national privacy principles	653
Appendix 4	Summary of selected provisions of the Drugs of Dependence Act 1989 (ACT)	657
Appendix 5	Client rights	673
Index		677

TABLE OF CASES

[References are to paragraph numbers]

Where a summary of a case is reproduced, the name of the case and the paragraph on which the reproduction commences are shown in **bold** type.

**A (Children), Re (unreported, Court of Appeal,
 No B1/2000/2969, 22 September 2000)** .... [4.71], [14.76], [14.126],
 [14.132], [14.136], **[14.139]**, [14.144]
AWA Test Case (unreported, 26 September 1997, AIRC) .... [11.76]
Abernethy v Deitz (1996) 39 NSWLR 701 .... [15.47]
Adam v Ward [1917] AC 309 .... [7.104], [7.106]
**Ahern v Burra Burra Hospital (unreported, 22 March 1982, Sex
 Discrimination Board SA)** .... [18.69]
Airedale NHS Trust v Bland [1993] AC 789 .. [4.67], [4.71], [14.76], [14.80],
 [14.93], [14.98], [14.104], **[14.106]**, [14.111], [14.144]
Akerele v The King [1943] AC 255 .... [14.154]
**Albrighton v Royal Prince Alfred Hospital [1980] 2 NSWLR
 542** .... [2.86], [6.37], [6.71], [6.183], [6.187], [6.189], **[7.26]**
Alexandrou v Oxford [1993] 2 All ER 328 .... [6.115]
American Home Assurance v Saunders (1987) 11 NSWLR 363 .... [12.31]
**American National Bank & Trust Company, Special
 Administrator of the Estate of Renee Kazmierowski v City of
 Chicago (Cook County Circuit Court, 10 August 2000)** .... [6.117]
Andrew Thackray v Phillip Hardcastle (unreported, 28 April 1999,
 District Court WA) .... [App 2]
Andrews v Parker [1973] Qd R 93 .... [10.91]
Andrzej Domeradski by his tutor Robert Domeradski v Royal Prince
 Alfred Hospital (unreported, 11 May 1994, SC NSW) .... [App 2]
Appleson v H Littlewood Ltd [1939] 1 All ER 464 .... **[10.12]**
Appleton v Garrett (1997) 8 Med LR 75; CCH ¶16-950 .... [4.37], [4.38]
Argyll v Argyll [1967] Ch 302 .... [7.65], **[10.51]**
Attorney-General v Able [1984] 1 All ER 277 .... [14.78]
**Attorney-General v Garry David (aka Garry Webb) [1972] 2 VR
 46** .... **[5.147]**
Attorney-General v Mulholland [1963] 2 WLR 658 .... **[7.73]**
Attorney-General (Qld) (Ex rel Kerr) v T (1983) 46 ALR 275; [1983] 1
 Qd R 404 .... [5.72], [14.171], [14.184]
Auckland Hospital v Attorney General [1993] 1 NZLR 235 .... [14.110]
Australian Red Cross v BC (unreported, 7 March 1991, Supreme
 Court of Victoria) .... [7.77]
Australian Safeway Stores Pty Ltd v Zaluzna Pty Ltd (1987) 61 ALJR
 80 .... [12.69]

B v Croydon District Health Authority [1955] All ER 683 .... [4.44]
B v Islington Health Authority [1991] 1 All ER 825 .... **[6.55]**
B v Marinovich [1999] NTSC 127 .... [App 2]
B (A Minor), Re [1981] 1 WLR 1421 .... [14.76], [14.95], **[14.133]**

BP Refinery (Westernport) Pty Ltd v Hastings Shire Council (1977)
  180 CLR 266 .... [10.43]
Baby M, Matter of 537 A 2d 1227 NJ (1988) .... [10.92]
Balfour v Balfour [1919] 2 KB 571 .... [10.6]
Balmain New Ferry Co Ltd v Robertson (1906) 4 CLR 379 .... [4.166]
**Barnett v Chelsea and Kensington Hospital Management
  Committee [1969] 1 QB 428** .... [3.25], [6.125], **[6.159]**, [6.211]
Basser v Medical Board of Victoria [1981] VR 953 .... [13.102]
Battersby v Tottman (1985) 37 SASR 524 .... [4.51], [4.52], [4.85], [4.109],
                                                           [4.116], [4.118], **[5.94]**, [8.67]
Bear v Norwood Private Nursing Home (1984) EOC ¶92-019 .... [18.60]
**Beausoleil v La Communitie des Soeurs de la Providence (1964)
  53 DLR 65** .... [4.39]
Becker and Minister for Immigration and Ethnic Affairs, Re (1977)
  32 FLR 469 .... [2.79]
Bill Williams Pty Ltd v Williams (1972) 126 CLR 146 .... [12.54]
**Boerema v Medical Board of Western Australia (unreported, 10,
  19 June 1998, SC WA)** .... [13.85]
Bolam v Friern Hospital Management Committee [1957] 1 WLR
  582 .... [4.51], [4.99], [4.100], [6.67], [6.73], [6.87], [6.103], [13.82]
Bolton v Stone [1951] AC 850 .... [6.25], [6.68], [6.92], [6.96]
Boughey v The Queen (1986) 16 CLR 10 .... [4.24]
Bouvia v County of Riverside (unreported, 16 December 1983,
  Riverside County Cal, No 159780) .... [4.67]
Bouvia v Supreme Court 179 Cal App 3d 1127; 225 Cal Rptr 297
  (1986) .... [4.67]
Boyle v Ishan Ozden (1986) EOC ¶92-165 .... [18.65]
Bratty v Attorney-General (Northern Ireland) [1963] 3 All ER 386 ...... [14.52]
Breen v Williams (1996) 186 CLR 71 ... [7.2], [7.60], [7.111], [10.1], [10.46],
                                                                                                [10.47]
Briginshaw v Briginshaw (1938) 60 CLR 336 .... [13.71]
Brockman v Harpole 444 P 2d (1968) .... [6.220]
Brooks v Blount [1923] 1 KB 237 .... [10.94]
Brown v Brooks (unreported, 18 August 1988, SC NSW) .... [7.72], [7.76]
**Buckman v Electricity Commission of New South Wales [1975]
  WCR 128** .... [12.43]
Bugden v Harbour View Hospital [1947] DLR 338 .. [6.215], [6.222], [8.55]
Bull v Devon Area Health Authority (unreported, CA UK, 1989) .... [App 2]
Bull v Devon Area Health Authority [1993] 4 Med LR 22 .... [App 2]
Burnett v Kalokerinos (unreported, 22 March 1995, SC NSW) .... [App 2]
**Burnett v Mental Health Tribunal (unreported, SC ACT, No 84 of
  1997)** .... [5.175]
Byrne v Australian Airlines Ltd (1995) 185 CLR 410 .... [10.44]

C (A Minor), Re [1998] Lloyd's Law Reports (Medical); [1998]
  FamD 1 .... [14.136]
C (A Minor) (Wardship: Medical Treatment) [1989] 2 All ER 782 ...... [14.136]
C (A Minor) (Wardship: Surrogacy), Re [1985] FLR 846 .... [10.94]
C (Refusal of Medical Treatment), Re .... [4.44]
CES v Superclinics Australia Pty Ltd (1995) 38 NSWLR 47 .... [14.168]
Cam & Sons Pty Ltd v Sargent (1940) 14 ALJ 162 .... [11.5]
Campbell v Dental Board of Vic [1999] VSC 113 .... [App 2]
Canterbury v Spence (1972) 464 F 2d 772 .... [4.109]
Canterbury Hospital v Cappelletto (unreported, 17 May 1991, CA
  NSW) .... [App 2]

Capital & Counties Plc v Hampshire County Council [1997] QB
    1004 .... [6.117]
Causer v Browne [1952] VLR 1 .... [10.24]
Cavan v Wilcox [1975] SCR 663 .... **[8.62]**
Cavanagh v Bristol & Weston Health Authority (1992) 3 Med LR
    49 .... [App 2]
Chapelton v Barry Urban District Council [1940] 1 KB 532 .... [10.24]
Chaplin v Dunstan Ltd [1938] SASR 245 .... [6.197]
Chapman v Hearse (1961) 106 CLR 112 .... [6.35], **[6.49]**
Chappel v Hart (1998) 256 ALR 518 .... [4.106], **[4.111]**, [6.165]
Chapple v Cooper (1844) 153 ER 105 .... [10.56]
Chasney v Anderson [1950] 4 DLR 23 .... **[6.88]**
Chatterton v Gerson [1981] 1 QB 432 .... **[4.49]**, [4.128]
**Childs v Walton (unreported, 13 November 1990, CA
    NSW)** .... **[13.58]**, [13.70], [13.74]
Chin Keow v Government of Malaysia [1967] 1 WLR 813 .... **[8.65]**
Christopher Payne v Dr Jane Antony and Dr Simon Clarke
    (unreported, District Court NSW, No 8083 of 1995) .... [App 2]
Cole v Turner 6 Mod 149 .... [4.24]
Collins v Hertfordshire County Council [1947] KB 598 .... **[6.99]**, [8.49],
                                                                                                 [8.56]
**Commercial Bank of Australia Ltd v Amadio (1983) 151 CLR
    447** .... **[10.85]**
**Commonwealth v Human Rights and Equal Opportunity
    Commission (1998) EOC ¶92-909** .... **[18.48]**, [18.98]
Commonwealth v Oliver (1962) 107 CLR 353 .... [12.36]
Commonwealth v Tasmania (Tasmanian Dam Case) (1983) 46 ALR
    625 .... [1.30]
**Coroner's Act 1975, In matter of application pursuant to s 28a;
    Crowe, Ex parte (unreported, 20 February 1992, SC SA)** .... **[15.83]**
**Cranley v Medical Board of Western Australia (unreported, ,
    21 December 1990, SC WA)** .... [8.38], **[13.98]**
Crawford v Bailey (unreported, 28 February 1992, SC NSW) .... [App 2]
Crotch v Miles (1930) BMJ 620 .... [App 2]
Csomore v Public Service Board (NSW) (1987) 10 NSWLR 587 .... [11.37]

**Daborn v Bath Tramways Motor Co Ltd [1946] 2 All ER
    333** .... [6.97], **[6.100]**
**Daniels v Burfield (unreported, 17 October 1991, SC SA, [1991]
    SASC 3072)** .... [4.84], **[4.94]**
**Daniels v Queensland Nursing Homes Pty Ltd [1995] HREOCA
    2** .... **[18.53]**
Darley v Shale (CA NSW, 4 Med LR 161) .... [App 2]
**Darling v Charlston Community Memorial Hospital 211 NE 2d
    253 (1965)** .... **[6.106]**, [19.10]
Demers v Gerety 515 P 2d 645 (1973) .... **[5.64]**
Dismissal of Fitters by BHP, Re [1969] AR (NSW) 399 .... [11.18]
DoCS v Y [1999] NSW SC 644 .... **[5.30]**
Donoghue v Stevenson [1932] AC 562 ... [3.63], [6.14], [6.15], [6.38], [6.66]
Dorset Yacht Co v Home Office [1970] AC 1004 .... **[6.17]**
Doughty v General Dental Council [1987] 3 All ER 843 .... [App 2]
Dryden v Surrey County Council [1936] 2 All ER 535 .... [App 2]
Dulieu v White & Son [1901] 2 KB 669 .... [6.158]
Dunning v Scheibher (unreported, 15 February 1998, SC NSW) .... [App 2]
Dutton v Bognor Regis Urban District Council [1972] 1 QB 373 ...... **[3.66]**

E v Australian Red Cross Society (1991) ATPR ¶41-085 .... [App 2]
EO v Mental Health Review Board [2000] WASC 203 .... [5.177]
**Ellis v Wallsend District Hospital [1989] Aust Torts Reports
¶80-259** .... [4.101], [6.182], **[6.183]**
English v English (1986) FLC ¶91-729 .... [16.91]
Evelyn, Re (1988) FLC ¶92-807 .... [10.95]
Eyre v Measday [1986] 1 All ER 488 .... [4.94]

F, Re [1990] 2 AC 70 .... [5.19]
F, Re; F v F (unreported, 2 July 1986, SC Vic) .... [14.126], [14.132]
F v F (1989) FLC ¶92-031 .... [5.72], **[14.182]**, [14.186]
F v R (1983) 33 SASR 189 .... [4.94], [4.100], [4.101], [4.118], [4.125], [5.97]
F v West Berkshire Health Authority [1989] 2 All ER 545 .... [4.49]
F (In Utero), Re [1988] 2 All ER 193 .... [4.148]
F (Mental Patient: Sterilisation), Re [1990] 2 AC 1 .... [4.24], [4.71]
FWW and CMW, Re [1997] FLC ¶92-748 .... [5.20]
**Fagan v Metropolitan Police Commissioner [1969] 1 QB 439;
[1968] 3 All ER 422** .... [14.17]
Favelle Mort Ltd v Murray (1976) 8 ALR 649 .... [12.29]
Female Poisoner's Case (1634) Kelyng 53; 84 ER 1079 .... [14.29]
**Ferguson v Central Sydney Area Health Service (1990) EOC
¶92-272** .... [18.97]
Fisher v Bell [1961] 1 QB 394 .... [3.34]
**Fitzgerald, Ex parte; New South Wales Medical Board, Re (1945)
46 SR (NSW) 111** .... [13.95], [13.98]
Fontin v Katapodis (1962) 108 CLR 177 .... [4.76]
Fox v Glasgow South Western Hospitals [1955] SLT 337 .... [App 2]
Furniss v Fitchett [1958] NZLR 396 .... [7.67], [19.11]
Fussell v Beddard (1942) 2 BMJ 411 .... [App 2]

G v L (1995) EOC ¶92-712 .... [18.98]
Gilbert v Castagna (unreported, 25 March 2000, SC NSW) .... [App 2]
Gilchrist Watt and Sanderson Pty Ltd v York Products Pty Ltd
[1970] 3 All ER 825 .... [9.9]
**Gillick v West Norfolk and Wisbech Area Health Authority
[1985] 3 All ER 402** .... [4.89], **[5.23], [5.27], [5.28], [5.38]**
Gold v Essex County Council [1942] 2 KB 293 .... [App 2]
Goode v Nash (1979) 21 SASR 419 .... [6.26]
Goss v Nicholas [1960] Tas SR 133 .... [4.79]
Gover v South Australia (1985) 39 SASR 543 .... [4.117], [4.120]
Greco v Arvind (unreported, 13 December 1994, SC NSW) .... [App 2]
Grey v Pearson (1857) 6 HLC 61; 10 ER 1216 .... [3.35]

H v Royal Alexandra Hospital for Children [1990] Aust Torts Reports
¶81-000 .... [4.101]
Hackshaw v Shaw (1984) 155 CLR 614 .... [12.69]
Haley v London Electricity Board [1965] AC 778 .... [6.93]
Hall v Lees [1904] 2 KB 602 .... [App 2]
Harmer v Cornelius (1858) 5 CN (NS) 236; 141 ER 94 .... [11.61]
Harrington v Macquarie Pathology Services [1998] Aust Torts
Reports ¶81-489 .... [6.52]
Harry v The Mental Health Review Tribunal (1994) 33 NSWLR 315 ... [5.179]
Hart v Herron [1984] Aust Torts Rep ¶80-201 .... **[4.27], [4.167], [6.209]**

Hatzimanolis v ANI Corp Ltd (1992) 173 CLR 473 .... [12.24]
Haughton v Smith [1975] AC 476; [1973] 3 All ER 1109 .... **[14.33]**
Hawkins v Clayton (1988) 164 CLR 539 .... [10.44]
Haynes v Harwood [1935] 1 KB 146 .... **[3.59]**
Heath v Commonwealth (1982) 151 CLR 76 .... [12.24]
**Heathcote v New South Wales Nurses Board (unreported,
    12 April 1991, Dist Ct NSW)** .... **[13.63]**
Hedley Byrne & Co v Heller Partners [1964] AC 465 .... **[3.49]**, [3.53],
                                                                                                                [4.116]
**Henson v Board of Management of Perth Hospital (1939) 41
    WALR 15** .... **[8.53]**
Heydon's Case (1584) 3 Co Rep 7; 76 ER 637 .... [3.29]
Hill v Water Resources Commission (1985) EOC ¶92-127 .... **[18.67]**
Hillyer v St Bartholomews Hospital [1909] 2 KB 821 .... [App 2]
Hockey v Yelland (1984) AWCCD ¶73-555 .... [12.29]
Hoile v Medical Board of South Australia (1960) 104 CLR 157 ...... **[13.89]**
Holgate v Lancashire Mental Hospital Board [1937] 4 All ER 19 .... [6.40]
Holmes v Northern Territory of Australia (1999) 57 ALD 85 .... [7.4]
Honeywell v Rogers 251 F Supp 841 (1966) .... **[8.63]**
Hotson v East Berkshire Area Health Authority [1987] 2 All ER
    909 .... [6.162], [6.212]
Household Fire Insurance Co v Grant (1879) 4 Ex D 216 .... [10.32]
Howden v City of Whittlesea (1990) 32 AILR 392 .... **[11.46]**, [13.25]
Humphrey Earl Ltd v Speechley (1951) 84 CLR 126 .... [12.37]
Hunter v Hanley [1955] SC 200 .... [6.88]
Hunter v Mann [1974] 2 WLR 742 .... [7.46]
Hutton & Co v Jones [1910] AC 20 .... [7.96]

Inspector Callaghan v De Sandre [1989-92] Australian Industrial
    Safety, Health and Welfare Cases 48,966 (¶52-864) .... [12.11]
Inspector Callaghan v Longley [1989-92] Australian Industrial
    Safety, Health and Welfare Cases 48,967 (¶52-865) .... [12.11]

J (A Minor), Re [1990] 3 All ER 930; [1992] 4 All ER 614 .... [14.136]
JLS v JES (unreported, SC NSW Equity Division, No 1871/1996) ... **[5.214]**
Jackson v Vercoe (unreported, 29 May 1990, SC SA) .... [App 2]
**Jacobsen v Nurses Tribunal (unreported, 3 October 1997, SC
    NSW)** .... **[13.59]**, [13.74]
Jaensch v Coffey (1984) 155 CLR 549 .... [6.19], [6.46], **[6.51]**, [6.150]
**Jemielita v Medical Board of Western Australia (unreported, SC
    WA, No 1106 of 1992)** .... **[13.81]**, [13.85], [13.86]
**John Edwin Caley v Northern Regional Health Board [1997] Aust
    Torts Reports ¶81-429** .... **[6.82]**
**John James Memorial Hospital Ltd v Keys (unreported, 21 May
    1999, Federal Court of Australia)** .... **[6.187]**
Jones v Padavatton [1969] 2 All ER 616 .... [10.8]
Jordan v The Queen (1956) 40 Cr App R 152 .... [6.213]

K v Minister for Youth and Community Services [1982] 1 NSWLR
    311 .... [4.64], [5.3], [5.36], [5.92], [14.183]
**Kahler v Nurses Registration Board (unreported, 21 February
    1995, SC NSW)** .... **[13.69]**
Kahn v West [1999] VSC 530 .... [15.75]

Kavanagh v Commonwealth (1960) 103 CLR 549 .... [12.33]
Kent v Griffiths [2000] EWCA 16 .... [6.115]
Kimler v Lort Smith Animal Hospital [1995] HREOCA 20 .... [18.62]
Kinney, Re (unreported, 23 December 1988, SC Vic) .... **[14.118]**
Kirby v Leather [1965] 2 All ER 441 .... [5.85]
Kirumba v Walton (unreported, 4 October 1990, CA NSW) .... [13.53]
Kite v Malycha (unreported, 10 June 1998, SC SA) .... [4.186]
Kitson v Playfair (*The Times*, 23-28 March 1896) .... [7.91]
Koowarta v Bjelke-Petersen (1982) 56 ALJR 625 .... [1.32]
Kosky v Trustees of the Sisters of Charity [1982] VR 961 .... **[6.60]**, **[6.205]**
Kyriakidas v Rondo Building Services Pty Ltd [1974] WCR 62 .... **[12.39]**

Laidlaw v Lion's Gate Hospital (1969) 70 WWR 727 .... [6.169]
Lamphud Marchlewski, Roman Marchlewski and Dolores
  Marcklewski v Hunter Area Health Service (unreported,
  14 August 1998, SC NSW) .... **[6.52]**
Langley v Glandore Pty Ltd (unreported, 3 October 1997, CA Qld) ... [App 2]
Latimer v AEC [1953] AC 643 .... **[11.38]**
Lavelle v Glasgow Infirmary [1932] SC 247 .... [App 2]
Leaf v International Galleries [1950] 2 KB 86 .... [10.73]
Lee v Wilson (1934) 51 CLR 276 .... [7.96]
Levi v Regional Health Authority (1980) 7 Current Law 44 .... [4.55]
Lim Chin Aik v The Queen [1963] 1 All ER 223 .... [14.23]
Lindsey County Council v Marshall [1937] 1 AC 97 .... [App 2]
Lipovac v Hamilton Holdings Pty Ltd (unreported, 13 September
  1996, SC ACT) .... [App 2]
Lloyd's Bank Ltd v Bundy [1974] 3 WLR 501 .... **[10.78]**
Lowns v Woods [1996] Aust Torts Reports ¶81-376 .... **[6.43]**, **[6.80]**
Luck v Blamey & Associates [2000] VSC 77 .... **[6.111]**
Lunn v Giblin (unreported, 30 July 1998, SC NT) .... [App 2]
Lynch v Lynch and the GIO [1991] Aust Torts Reports ¶81-117 ...... **[6.56]**

MB, Re [1997] 8 Med LR 21; [1997] 2 FCR 541 .... [4.21], [4.145], [4.147]
MN v AN (1989) 16 NSWLR 525 .... [5.150]
Mabo v Queensland (No 2) (1992) 107 ALR 1 .... [1.56]
McCabe v Auburn District Hospital (unreported, 31 May 1989, SC
  NSW) .... [6.52], [6.150]
McCleod v Cockatoo Docks [1971] WCR 313 .... [12.54]
McDermott v St Mary's Hospital 133 A 2d 608 (1957) .... [6.70]
Macfarlane v Tayside Health Board [1994] 4 All ER 961 .... [App 2]
McGregor v McGregor (1888) 20 QBD 529 .... **[10.7]**
McKay v Essex Area Health Authority [1982] 2 All ER 771 .... **[6.58]**
McLelland v Symons [1951] VLR 157 .... [4.21]
Macpherson v Beath (1975) 12 SASR 174 .... [4.21]
Mahon v Osborne [1932] 2 KB 14 .... **[6.68]**, **[6.90]**
Malette v Shulman (1991) 2 Med LR 162 .... **[4.24]**, **[4.62]**, **[4.64]**, **[5.101]**
Marshall v Curry (1933) 3 DLR 260 .... [4.60]
Martignoni v Harris [1971] 2 NSWLR 102 .... [12.79]
Martin v East Yorkshire Health Authority, *The Times*, 12 January
  1993 .... [App 2]
Martin v London County Council [1947] 1 All ER 783 .... [9.11]
Massey v Crown Life Insurance Co [1978] 2 All ER 576 .... [11.8]
Maynard v West Midlands Regional Health Authority [1984] 1 WLR
  634 .... [6.72], [App 2]

Medical Board of Queensland v Bayliss (unreported, 6 & 8 February
    1995, Queensland Medical Assessment Tribunal) .... [13.57]
**Medical Board of South Australia v Christpoulos (2000) SADC
    47** .... **[13.61]**
Meehan, Ex parte; Medical Practitioners Act, Re [1965] NSWR
    30 .... [13.54]
Meering v Grahame-White Aviation Co Ltd (1919) 122 LT 44 .... [4.166]
Melvin v Northside Community Service Incorporated [1996]
    HREOCA 20 .... [18.43]
Mendelssohn v Normand [1970] 1 QB 177 .... [9.31]
Methodist Hospital v Ball 362 SW 2d 475 (1961) .... [6.128]
Metropolitan Health Service v King [1999] WASCA 236 .... [6.165]
Miller v Royal Derwent Hospital Board of Management [1992]
    Aust Torts Reports ¶81-175 .... [6.150], [6.151]
Millicent and District Hospital Inc v Kelly (unreported,
    10 September 1996, SC SA) .... [6.153]
Mohr v Williams 104 NW 12 (1905) .... **[4.24]**, **[4.55]**
Morris v Winsbury-White [1937] 4 All ER 494 .... [App 2]
Mt Isa Mines v Pusey (1970) 125 CLR 383 .... [6.149], [6.150], [12.5]
Murray v McMurchy [1949] 2 DLR 442 .... **[4.24]**, **[4.59]**
Mutual Life and Citizens' Assurance Co Ltd v Evatt [1971] AC 793 .... [3.51]

National Workforce Pty Ltd v Australian Manufacturing Workers'
    Union (unreported, 6 October 1997, SC Vic) .... [11.73]
Neale v Merrett [1930] WN (NSW) 189 .... [10.28]
New Biloxi Hospital v Frazier 146 So 2d 882 (1962) .... **[6.129]**
Niles v City of San Rafael 42 Cal App 3d 320 (1974) .... **[4.186]**, **[6.131]**
Northbridge v Central Sydney Area Health Service [2000] NSW SC
    1241 .... [5.56], [14.110]
Norton v Argonaut Insurance Co 144 So 2d 249 (1962) .... **[8.43]**, [8.47]

OLL Ltd v Secretary of State for Transport [1997] 3 All ER 897 .... [6.115]
O'Brien v Cunard SS Co 28 NE 266 (1891) .... [4.32]
O'Shea v Sullivan & Macquarie Pathology Services Pty Ltd [1994]
    Aust Torts Reports ¶81-273 .... [App 2]
**Overseas Tankship (UK) Ltd v The Miller Steamship Co Pty Ltd
    (The Wagon Mound) (No 2) [1967] 1 AC 617** .... **[6.22]**, [6.26], [6.96]

P, Ex parte; Hamilton, Re (1957) 74 WN (NSW) 397 .... [15.71]
P v P (1994) 181 CLR 583; 120 ALR 545 .... [5.21], [5.211]
Pallister v Waikato Hospital Board [1975] 2 NZLR 725 .... **[6.41]**
Paris v Stepney Borough Council [1951] AC 367 .... [11.41]
Parker v British Airways Board [1982] QB 1004 .... [9.4]
Parry-Jones v Law Society [1969] 1 Ch 1 .... [10.49]
Pasminco Australia Ltd v Fairchild [1990] Tas R (NC 18) 262 .... [12.31]
Paterson v Miller [1923] VLR 36 .... [9.31]
Paton v British Pregnancy Advisory Service Trustees [1979] 1 QB
    276 .... [4.139], [4.148], [5.72], [14.183]
Pearce v South Australian Health Commission (1996) 66 SASR 486 .... [17.68]
Pennsylvania v Youngkin 427 A 2d 1356 (1981) .... [14.152]
Perceval v Mater Misericordiae Hospital (unreported, NSW SC, 7
    March 2000) .... [App 2]
Percival v Rosenberg (unreported, 25 May 1999, SC Appeal WA) .. **[4.105]**

Periowsky v Freeman (1866) 176 ER 873 .... [App 2]
Petrie v Dowling [1989] Aust Torts Reports ¶80-263 .... [6.52], [6.150]
Pillai v Messiter (No 2) (1989) 16 NSWLR 197 .... **[8.50]**, [13.92]
Pole v Leask (1863) 33 LJ (Ch) 155 .... [11.12]
Powell v Streatham Manor Nursing Home [1935] AC 243 .... [App 2]
Practitioners Society in Australia v Commonwealth (1980) 54 ALJR
    487 .... [1.35]
**Prendergast v Sam and Dee Ltd, Kozary and Miller (*The Times*,
    London, 14 March 1989)** .... **[8.41]**
Prior v Sherwood (1906) 3 CLR 1054 .... [3.39]
Proudfoot v ACT Board of Health (1992) EOC ¶92-417 .... **[18.76]**
Proudman v Dayman (1941) 67 CLR 536 .... [14.23]

QFG v JM (1997) EOC ¶92-902 .... [17.70]
Qidway v Brown [1984] 1 NSWLR 100 .... [13.56]
Quinlan, Re 355 A 2d 647; revg 348 A 2d 807 (1976) .... [5.92], **[14.127]**,
                                                                                                                 [14.133]
Qumsieh v Guardianship and Management Board and Pilgrim (SC
    Vic, No 5656 of 1998; High Court of Australia, No M 98 of
    1998) .... [4.36], [4.47], [4.52], [5.89], [5.101], [17.14]

R v Adams (*The Times*, 9 April 1957) .... [14.82], [14.91]
R v Adams (*The Times*, 5 November 1981) .... **[7.9]**
R v Adomako [1994] 2 All ER 79 .... [14.154]
R v Arthur (*The Times*, 6 October 1981) .... **[14.93]**, [14.99]
R v B (unreported, SC Vic, 1995) .... [16.35]
R v Bateman (1925) 19 Cr App R 8 .... **[14.151]**
R v Bayliss and Cullen (unreported, 31 January 1986, District Court
    Brisbane) .... [14.171]
R v Bourne [1938] 3 All ER 615 .... **[14.158]**, [14.164]
R v Bournewood Community and Mental Health NHS Trust [1999]
    1 AC 458 .... [4.71]
R v Clarence (1888) 22 QBD 23 .... [16.35]
R v Clarke (1927) 40 CLR 227 .... **[10.17]**
R v Coleman (1990) 19 NSWLR 467 .... [14.56]
R v Coney (1882) 8 QBD 534 .... **[14.11]**
R v Coroner; Alexander, Ex parte [1982] VR 731 .... [15.73]
R v Cox (*The Age*, 15 May 1992) .... **[14.82]**
R v Davidson [1969] VR 667 .... [4.69], [14.164], [14.165], [14.166]
R v Dawson [1978] VR 536 .... [14.59]
R v Duffy [1949] 1 All ER 932 .... [14.66]
R v F (unreported, CA NSW, No 60773/95 1996) .... [6.58]
R v Fennell [1971] 1 QB 428 .... [4.80]
R v Hallett [1969] SASR 141 .... [14.97]
R v Huggins (1730) 2 Ld Raym 1574; 92 ER 518 .... **[14.26]**, [14.31]
R v Hutty [1953] VLR 338 .... [14.71]
R v Jackson [1891] 1 QB 671 .... [16.82]
R v Jenkin (unreported, SC Townsville, June 1993) .... [2.15], **[14.82]**
R v Keite (1697) 1 Ld Raym 138; 91 ER 989 .... [11.44]
R v Larkin [1943] 1 All ER 217 .... **[14.152]**
R v Larsonneur (1933) 24 Cr App R 74 .... **[14.24]**
R v Lawrence [1980] NSWLR 122 .... [14.59]
**R v M (unreported, 15 July 1999, Royal Courts of Justice, Family
    Division, UK)** .... **[5.33]**

R v Medical Council of Tasmania; Blackburn, Ex parte
    (unreported, 26 February 1998, SC Tas) .... [13.28]
R v Miller [1982] 3 All ER 386 .... [14.18]
R v Mobilio [1991] 1 VR 339; 50 A Crim R 170 .... [4.38]
R v Nuri [1990] VR 641 .... [16.35]
R v O'Connor (1980) 54 ALJR 349 .... **[14.55]**
R v Quick and Paddison [1973] 3 All ER 347 .... **[14.53]**
R v Reid [1973] QB 299 .... [16.82]
R v Roberts (1971) 56 Cr App R 95 .... [14.19]
R v Russell [1933] VLR 59 .... [14.1133]
R v Wald (1971) 3 DCR (NSW) 25 .... [14.165], [14.166]
**R-B (A Patient) v Official Solicitor [2000] Lloyd's Law Reports
    (Medical) 87** .... **[5.214]**
Rajagopalan v Medical Board of South Australia (unreported,
    11 September 1997, SC SA) .... [App 2]
Ramsey v Larsden (1964) 111 CLR 16 .... [11.10]
Rand v East Dorset Health Authority [2000] Ll Law Rep (Medical)
    181 .... [6.157]
Regan v Gladesville Hospital [1977] WCR 107 .... **[12.49]**
Reich v Client Server Professionals of Australia Pty Ltd (2000) 49
    NSWLR 551 .... [11.51]
Richards v State of Victoria [1969] VR 136 .... [6.30]
Robinson v Post Office [1974] 1 WLR 1176 .... [8.67]
Roe v Minister of Health [1954] 2 QB 66 .... [6.2], [6.72], **[6.79]**, [6.194],
    [App 2]
Rogers v Whitaker (1992) 109 ALR 625 .... [2.85], [4.49], [4.51], [4.71],
    [4.72], [4.83], [4.89], [4.92], [4.96], **[4.97]**, [4.101], [4.107],
        [4.109], [4.110], [4.111], [4.114], [4.115], [4.116], [6.82], [6.134], [7.2]
**Royal Melbourne Hospital v Mathews (unreported, 9 December
    1992, SC Vic)** .... **[7.84]**
Royall v The Queen (1990) 172 CLR 378 .... [14.18]
Ryan v The Queen (1967) 121 CLR 205 .... **[14.20]**

S (Adult: Refusal of Medical Treatment), Re [1992] 4 ALL ER 671 .... [4.141]
Sayers v Harlow Urban District Council [1958] 2 All ER 342 .... **[4.166]**
Schloendorff v Society of New York Hospital (1914) 211 NY 125 .... [4.2]
Schneiderman v Interstate Transit Lines Inc (1946) 394 ILL 569 .... [6.118]
Seager v Copydex [1967] 1 WLR 923 .... [7.44]
**Secretary, Department of Health and Community Services v JBW
    and SMB (Marion's Case) (1992) 1745 CLR 218; 106 ALR
    385** .... [5.3], **[5.16]**, [5.19], [5.21], [5.27], [5.30], [5.38], [5.58], [5.156],
        [5.199], [5.212]
Seidler v Schallhofer [1982] 2 NSWLR 80 .... [10.91]
Sellers v Cook (1990) 2 Med LR 16 .... [App 2]
Senka Benkovic v Dr Eng Pen Tan (unreported, 5 February 1999,
    District Court NSW) .... [10.52]
Sharman v Evans (1977) 138 CLR 563 .... [6.148]
Shulman v Lerner 141 NW 2d 348 (1966) .... **[4.32]**, [17.15]
**Sidaway v Governors of the Bethlem Royal Hospital [1985] 1 All
    ER 643** .... [4.50], [4.85], [4.99], [4.109], [6.88], [7.60]
Simon Patrick Ward v Aspi Sahukar (unreported, 3 May 1999,
    District Court NSW) .... [App 2]
Skinner v Beaumont [1974] 2 NSWLR 106 .... **[13.100]**
Smith v Auckland Hospital Board [1965] NZLR 191 .... **[4.114]**
Smith v Austin Lifts [1959] 1 All ER 81 .... [11.42]

Smith v Brighton and Lewes Hospital (*The Times*, 2 May
  1958) .... [8.58], [App 2]
Smith v The Queen [1959] 2 QB 35 .... [6.215]
Sonja Harp v Andrew Campbell (unreported, March 1998, District
  Court WA) .... [App 2]
Spence v Percy [1991] Aust Torts Reports ¶81-116 .... [6.52]
Spivey v St Thomas' Hospital, 21 Tenn App 12; SW 2d 450
  (1947) .... [4.190], [6.69], [6.86]
Sroka v Ridge Park Private Hospital (1981) 28 SASR 15 .... [11.39]
St George's Healthcare NHS Trust v S; R v Collins; S, Ex parte
  [1997] 3 All ER 673 .... [4.141]
State of New South Wales v Seedsman [2000] NSWCA 119 .... [12.4]
Stepanovic, Denis v ACT (unreported, 3 November 1995, ACT SC) .... [App 2]
Stevens v Brodribb Sawmilling Co Pty Ltd (1986) 160 CLR 16; 60
  ALJR 194 .... [6.181], [11.2]
Stevenson v Medical Board of Victoria (unreported, 27 June
  1986, SC Vic) .... [13.96], [13.99]
Stewart v Ng [1999] NSWCA 387 .... [App 2]
Stone v Taffe [1974] 1 WLR 1575 .... [12.64]
Strangways-Lesmere v Clayton [1936] 2 KB 11 .... [App 2]
Strelee v Nelson (unreported, 13 December 1996, SC NSW) .... [6.52], [App 2]
Superintendent of Belchertown State School et al v Saikewicz
  Mass 370 NE 2d 417 (1977) .... [14.130], [14.135]
Sweet v Parsley [1970] AC 132 .... [14.23]
Sydney City Council v West (1965) 114 CLR 481 .... [9.31]
Symes v Mahon [1922] SASR 447 .... [4.161]

T (Adult: Refusal of Treatment), Re [1992] 4 All ER 649 .... [4.32], [4.37],
                                                                                   [4.47], [5.101]
Tai v Hatzistavrou [1999] NSWCA 306 .... [App 2]
Talbot v Lusby (unreported, 14 July 1995, SC Qld) .... [App 2]
Tarasoff v Regents of the University of California 551 P 2d 334
  (1976) .... [7.74]
Tasker v Algar [1928] NZLR 529 .... [10.78]
Tasmanian Dam Case *see* Commonwealth v Tasmania
Teenager, Re a [1989] FLC ¶92-006 .... [5.212]
Thake v Maurice [1986] 1 All ER 497 .... [4.94]
Thomas National Transport (Melbourne) Pty Ltd v May & Baker
  (Australia) Pty Ltd (1966) 115 CLR 353 .... [9.33]
Thompson v Commonwealth (1969) 70 SR (NSW) 398 .... [12.65]
Thompson v Lewisham Hospital [1978] WCR 113 .... [12.38]
Thornton v Shoe Lane Parking [1971] 2 WLR 585 .... [9.31]
Tolley v Fry [1930] 1 KB 467 .... [7.95]
Tucker v Hospital Corporation Australia Pty Ltd (unreported,
  18 February 1998, SC NSW) .... [App 2]
Twentieth Century Blinds Pty Ltd v Howes [1974] 1 NSWLR 244 .... [12.79]

Uldale v Bloomsbury Area Health Authority [1983] 2 All ER 522 ...... [14.170]
Ultzen v Nichols [1894] 1 QB 92 .... [9.11]
Unchango, Re; Unchango, Ex parte (1997) 95 A Crim R 65 .... [15.48]
Urry v Bierer, *The Times*, 15 July 1955 .... [App 2]

Vabu v Federal Commissioner of Taxation (1996) 33 ATR 537 .... [11.6]

Vacwell Engineering Co v BDH Chemicals [1971] 1 QB 111 .... [6.29]
Van Wyck v Lewis [1924] ADSA 438 .... [App 2]
**Versteegh v Nurses Board of South Australia (unreported,
4 December 1992, SC SA)** .... [13.93]
Vievers v Connelly (1994) Aust Torts Reports ¶81-309 .... [14.171]
Viro v The Queen (1976) 141 CLR 88 .... [14.62], [14.70]
Voller v Portsmouth Corp (1947) 203 LT 264 .... [App 2]

W v Edgell [1990] 1 All ER 855 .... [7.75]
W (a Minor) (Consent to Medical Treatment), Re [1993] 1 FLR 381 ...... [4.71]
**W (a Minor) (Medical Treatment), Re [1992] 4 All ER
627** .... [5.28], [5.35]
W B Anderson & Sons Ltd v Rhodes (Liverpool) Ltd [1967] 2 All ER
850 .... [3.51]
Wagner v International Railway Co 232 NY Rep 176 (1921) ...... [6.50], [6.76]
Wakim, Re; McNally, Ex parte (1999) 165 ALR 270 .... [2.8]
Walker v New South Wales (1994) 182 CLR 45 .... [1.56]
**Wang v Central Sydney Area Health Service [2000] NSWSC 515;
[2000] Aust Torts Reports ¶81-574** .... [4.186], [6.131]
Wardley v Ansett Transport Industries Pty Ltd (1984) EOC ¶92-002 ... [18.36]
Watson v Marshall (1971) 124 CLR 621 .... [4.164]
Watt v Rama [1972] VR 353 .... [6.54], [6.57]
Weld-Blundell v Stephens [1919] 1 KB 520 .... [11.30]
Wendover v State, 313 NYS 2d 287 (1970) .... [6.88]
Western Suburbs Hospital v Currie (1987) 9 NSWLR 511 .... [12.66]
Wheat v E Lacon & Co Ltd [1966] AC 552 .... [12.63]
Whitehouse v Jordan [1980] 1 All ER 650 .... [6.208], [6.210]
Whitree v New York 290 NYS 2d 486 (1968) .... [7.15]
**Wilsher v Essex Area Health Authority [1988] 1 All ER
871** .... [6.100], [6.161]
Wilson v Wilson's Tile Works Pty Ltd (1960) 104 CLR 328 .... [12.24]
Wolmar v Travelodge Australia Ltd (1975) 8 ACTR 11 .... [12.46]
Woolmington v Director of Public Prosecutions [1935] AC 462 ..... [14.40]
Workers Rehabilitation and Compensation Corp v James (1992) 57
SASR 365 .... [12.24]
Wyong Shire Council v Shirt (1980) 146 CLR 40 .... [6.84]

X v Pal [1991] Aust Torts Reports ¶81-098 .... [6.211]
X v Sattler (unreported, 31 May 1989, SC WA) .... [7.83]
X v Y [1988] 2 All ER 648 .... [7.79]

Yelds v Nurses Tribunal [2000] NSWSC 755 .... [13.71]
Young v Northern Territory (1992) 107 FLR 264 .... [4.96]

Ziems v Prothonotary of Supreme Court of New South Wales (1957)
97 CLR 279 .... [13.105]
Zuijs v Wirth Bros Pty Ltd (1955) 93 CLR 561 .... [6.182]

TABLE OF STATUTES

[References are to paragraph numbers]

Commonwealth

Acts Interpretation Act 1902
  s 15AA: [3.29]
  s 15AB: [3.29]
Administrative Decisions (Judicial Review) Act 1977: [2.74], [2.75], [7.53]
Aged Care Act 1997: [18.73]
Australia Act 1986: [2.29]
Commonwealth of Australia Constitution Act 1901: [1.23]
  s 51: [1.24], [1.26]
  s 51(i): [1.26]
  s 51(ii): [1.26]
  s 51(ix): [1.26]
  s 51(xi): [1.26]
  s 51(xix): [1.26]
  s 51(xvi): [1.26]
  s 51(xxi): [1.26]
  s 51(xxii): [1.26]
  s 51(xxiiiA): [1.34]
  s 51(xxix): [1.26], [18.11]
  s 51(xxxv): [11.50]
  s 51(2): [1.25]
  s 51(3): [1.25]
  s 52: [1.25]
  s 67: [1.23]
  s 71: [2.6]
  s 77: [2.8]
  ss 90-93: [1.25]
  s 107: [1.23]
  s 109: [1.27], [5.22], [17.68]
  s 111: [1.25]
  s 112: [1.25]
  s 122: [1.33], [14.85]
  s 128: [1.25]
Crimes Act 1914: [14.6]
Crimes (Forensic Procedures) Act 2000: [14.195]
Disability Discrimination Act 1992: [18.43], [18.72], [18.78], [18.91]
  s 15(4): [18.45], [18.46]
Disability Services Act 1986: [5.93]
Equal Opportunity for Women in the Workplace Act 1999: [18.93]
Euthanasia Laws Act 1997: [1.33], [14.85]
Family Law Act 1975: [1.28], [2.7], [2.39], [2.40], [2.42], [3.22], [5.2], [5.22], [5.31], [10.4], [16.61], [17.89]
  Pt VII: [5.213]
  s 60B: [17.44]
  s 69W: [17.9]
  s 78: [3.24]
  s 114: [16.89]
Freedom of Information Act 1982
  s 11: [7.113]
  s 41(3): [7.113]
  s 48: [7.113]
Health Insurance Act 1973: [13.45]
Human Rights and Equal Opportunity Commission Act 1986: [5.63], [14.196], [16.40], [18.13], [18.14], [18.40], [18.41], [18.50], [18.91]
  s 3: [18.15], [18.41]
  Sch: [2.71]
Judiciary Amendment Act (No 2) 1984: [2.27]
Migration Act 1958: [18.16]
Mutual Recognition Act 1992: [13.4]
Narcotic Drugs Act 1967: [8.5]
National Health Act 1953: [18.73]
National Health and Medical Research Council Act 1992: [4.151]
National Occupational Health and Safety Commission Act 1985: [12.6], [12.12]
Occupational Health and Safety (Commonwealth Employment) Act 1991: [12.6]
Privacy Act 1988: [7.48], [7.49], [7.54], [7.86], [7.117]
Privy Council (Appeals from the High Court) Act 1975: [2.29]
Privy Council (Limitation of Appeals) Act 1968: [2.29]

Racial Discrimination Act 1975: [18.40],
    [18.52], [18.59], [18.72], [18.78],
    [18.91]
  s 5: [18.59]
  s 6: [18.59]
  s 9: [18.52], [18.59]

Safety, Rehabilitation and
    Compensation Act 1988: [12.6],
    [12.19]
  s 6: [12.42], [12.45]

Sex Discrimination Act 1984: [17.68],
    [17.69], [18.40], [18.59], [18.64],
    [18.76], [18.78], [18.91]
  s 28: [18.64]
  s 33: [18.77]

Therapeutic Goods Act 1989: [8.5], [8.6],
    [8.34]

Therapeutic Goods Regulations 1990:
    [8.5]

Trade Practices Act 1974: [18.21]

Workplace Relations Act 1996: [11.63],
    [11.65], [11.67], [11.71], [11.73],
    [11.86], [11.89], [11.96], [11.97],
    [18.50]
  Pt VIA: [11.79]
  Pt VIB: [11.71]
  Pt VID: [11.70]
  s 170CK: [11.81], [11.89]
  s 170CM: [11.79]
  s 170LJ: [11.70]
  s 170LK: [11.70], [11.72]
  s 170LL: [11.70]

Australian Capital Territory

Administrative Decisions (Judicial
    Review) Act 1989: [2.74]

Adoption Ordinance 1965: [18.16]

Age of Majority Act 1974
  s 5: [5.2]

Archives Act 1983: [7.6]

Artificial Conception Act 1985: [17.44]

Artificial Conception Act 1986: [17.87]

Births, Deaths and Marriages
    Registration Act 1997: [15.2]

Blood Donation (Transmissible
    Diseases) Act 1985: [17.17]
  s 4: [16.33]
  s 5: [16.33]

Children and Young People Act 1999:
    [5.45], [5.47], [16.62]
  ss 156-163: [16.64]
  s 159: [16.72]

Children's Services Act 1986: [16.80]

Compensation (Fatal Injuries) Act 1968:
    [6.141]

Coroners Act 1956: [15.19]

Coroners Act 1997: [15.30]
  s 48: [15.70]
  s 79: [15.70]
  s 80: [15.70]
  s 86: [15.70]

Crimes Act 1900: [14.6], [16.48], [16.49]
  s 18: [4.66]
  s 345: [14.32]
  s 346: [14.32]
  s 347: [14.32]

Crimes (Forensic Procedures) Act 2000:
    [14.195]

Criminal Injuries Compensation Act
    1983: [3.3]

Defamation Act 1901: [7.90]

Disability Services Act 1992: [5.93]

Discrimination Act 1991: [18.82]

Domestic Violence Act 1986: [16.81],
    [16.90]
  s 14(1): [16.95]
  s 27: [16.96]

Drugs of Dependence Act 1989: [8.5],
    [8.10], [8.18], [16.48], [16.49]
  s 114: [8.20]
  s 115: [8.20]

Evidence Act 1971
  Pt 6: [7.26]

Fair Trading Act 1992: [18.21]

Health and Community Care
    Complaints Act 1998: [18.25]

Health Professionals (Special Events
    Exemptions) Act 2000: [13.16]

Health Records (Privacy and Access) Act
    1997: [7.115]

Health Regulation (Maternal Health
    Information) Act 1988: [14.176]

Interpretation Act 1967
  s 11A: [3.29]
  s 11B: [3.29]

Law Reform (Miscellaneous Provisions)
    Act 1955: [6.53], [6.156], [6.199],
    [12.62]
Limitation Act 1985: [6.204], [9.36]
Medical Practitioner Act 1930: [13.45]
    s 35(3): [13.47]
Medical Treatment Act 1994: [5.123],
    [14.123]
    s 6: [5.115]
Mental Health Ordinance 1983: [18.16]
Mental Health (Treatment and Care) Act
    1994: [5.143], [5.161]
    Pt 5: [5.161]
    Pt 7, Divn 1: [5.188], [5.194]
    Pt 7, Divn 2: [5.188]
    Pt 7, Divn 3: [5.194]
Motor Traffic (Alcohol and Drugs) Act
    1977: [17.9]
Mutual Recognition Act (ACT) 1992:
    [13.4]
Nurses Act 1988
    s 61: [13.48]
Occupational Health and Safety Act
    1989: [12.6]
Poisons Act 1933: [8.5]
    s 17: [8.20]
Poisons and Drugs Act 1978: [8.5]
Poisons Regulations 1990: [8.5]
Powers of Attorney Act 1956: [5.123]
Public Health Act 1997: [16.6]
    Pt 6: [16.19]
Public Health (Cancer Reporting)
    Regulations 1994
    reg 4: [16.11]
Public Health (Infectious and Notifiable
    Diseases) Regulations 1930
    reg 4: [16.38]
    reg 13: [16.37]
    reg 14: [16.37]
Public Health (Infectious and Notifiable
    Diseases) Regulations 2000
    reg 4: [16.57]
    reg 5: [16.57]
    reg 8: [16.57]
    reg 9: [16.57]
    regs 11-14: [16.57]
    reg 17: [16.57]
    reg 19: [16.57]

Registration of Births Deaths and
    Marriages Act 1963
    s 27: [15.38]
Substitute Parent Agreements Act 1994:
    [10.92], [17.87]
Substitute Parent Agreements
    (Consequential Amendments) Act
    1994: [17.87]
Transplantation and Anatomy Act
    1978: [17.1]
    s 6: [17.22]
    s 8: [17.21], [17.25]
    s 10: [17.21], [17.25]
    s 12: [17.22]
    s 13: [17.22]
    ss 15-18: [17.26]
    s 20: [17.8]
    s 21: [17.8]
    s 23: [5.5], [17.16]
    s 30: [17.37]
Uncollected Goods Act 1996: [9.36]
Workers' Compensation Act 1951:
    [12.6], [12.19]
    s 7: [12.45]
    s 8: [12.42]

New South Wales

Administrative Decisions Tribunal Act
    1997
    Sch 1: [2.55]
Anti-Discrimination Act 1977: [2.55],
    [11.95], [18.83], [18.93]
    s 63(1): [2.55]
    s 64: [2.55]
Artificial Conception Act 1984: [17.44]
Births, Deaths and Marriages
    Registration Act 1995: [15.2]
Children and Young Persons Act 1998
    s 24: [16.65]
    s 27: [16.73]
    s 103: [16.65]
Children (Care and Protection) Act
    1987: [5.45], [5.48], [16.65]
    s 10: [16.62]
    s 20A: [5.6], [17.16]
    s 20B: [5.216], [5.217]
    s 23(1): [16.80]
Community Services (Complaints,
    Appeals and Monitoring) Act 1997:
    [18.26]

Community Services (Complaints, Reviews and Monitoring) Act 1993: [2.55]

Compensation Court Act 1984: [12.6]

Compensation to Relatives Act 1897: [6.141]

Contracts Review Act 1980: [10.87]

Conveyancers' Licensing Act 1995: [2.55]

Coroners Act 1980: [15.19], [15.31]

Crimes Act 1900: [14.6], [16.81]
  s 36: [16.35], [16.36]
  s 52A: [6.58]
  s 345: [14.32]
  s 346: [14.32]
  s 357G: [16.95]
  s 562: [16.96]
  s 562(1): [16.95]
  ss 562A-562R: [16.90]
  s 574B: [4.66]

Crimes (Forensic Procedures) Act 2000: [14.195]

Criminal Injuries Compensation Act 1967: [3.3]

De Facto Relationships Act 1984: [16.81]
  ss 53-55: [16.90]

Defamation Act 1974: [7.90], [7.107]

Defamation (Amendment) Act 1909: [7.90]

Disability Services Act 1993: [5.93]

District Court Act 1972: [2.20]

Drugs Misuse and Trafficking Act 1985: [16.48]
  s 11(1A): [16.50]
  s 11(1B): [16.50]

Drugs Misuse and Trafficking Regulations
  reg 5: [16.50]
  reg 6: [16.50]

Education Reform Act 1990: [2.55]

Employees' Act 1991
  s 66: [6.200]

Employees (Indemnification of Employer) Act 1982: [11.26]

Evidence Act 1971
  Pt 6: [7.26]

Evidence Act 1995: [7.47]

Fair Trading Act 1987: [18.21]

Freedom of Information Act 1989: [2.55]
  s 7: [7.113]
  s 16: [7.113]
  s 31(4): [7.113]
  s 39: [7.113]

Guardianship Act 1987: [5.22], [5.75], [5.124]
  s 35(1): [5.213]

Health Administration Act 1982: [7.54], [7.58]

Health Care Complaints Act 1993: [18.26]

Health Professionals (Special Events Exemptions) Act 1997: [13.16]

Human Tissue Act 1983: [17.1], [17.17]
  Pt 3A: [16.33]
  s 6: [17.22]
  s 7: [17.21]
  s 9: [17.21]
  s 10: [17.22]
  s 11: [17.22]
  s 12: [17.21], [17.26]
  s 16(2)(a)(iii): [17.27]
  s 19: [17.8]
  s 20: [17.8]
  s 28: [17.37]

Human Tissue Amendment Act 1983
  s 21D: [16.33]

Human Tissue Regulations: [17.17]

Industrial Relations Act 1996: [11.50], [11.92]
  s 106: [11.51]

Interpretation Act 1987
  s 33: [3.29]
  s 34: [3.29]

Law Reform (Miscellaneous Provisions) Act 1944: [6.53], [6.156], [6.199]

Legal Profession Act 1987: [2.55]

Limitation Act 1969: [6.204], [9.36]

Local Government Act 1991: [2.55]

Lunacy Act 1898: [13.95]

Medical Practice Act 1992
  s 36: [13.32]
  s 37: [13.33]

Medical Practitioners Act 1958: [6.43]
  s 27(2): [6.45]

Medical Practitioners (Emergency Medical Treatment) Amendment Act 1983: [17.16]

Mental Health Act 1990: [5.143]
  Ch 4, Pt 2: [5.162]
  Ch 7, Pt 1: [5.195]
  Ch 7, Pt 2: [5.189], [5.201]
  s 156: [4.93]
  s 183: [4.93], [4.93], [5.186]
  Sch 1: [5.143]

Minors (Property and Contracts) Act 1970: [5.2]
  s 20B: [5.14]
  s 49(2): [5.2]

Mutual Recognition Act (NSW) 1992: [13.4]

Notification of Births Act 1915
  s 3: [15.7]

Nurses Act 1991: [13.19], [13.72]
  s 4: [13.34]
  s 4(2)(a): [13.72], [13.73], [13.75], [13.76], [13.79]
  s 4(2)(a)(iv): [13.76]
  s 4(2)(a)(v): [13.76]
  s 4(2)(e): [13.72], [13.77], [13.79]
  s 10: [13.19]
  s 13: [13.19]
  s 17: [13.19]
  s 19A: [13.19]
  s 24: [13.19]
  s 32(1): [13.19]
  s 78A: [13.19]

Nurses Amendment (Nurse Practitioners) Act 1998: [13.19]

Nurses Registration Act 1953
  s 19: [13.63]

Nursing Homes Act 1988: [7.58]

Occupational Health and Safety Act 1983: [12.6]

Occupational Health and Safety (Committees in Workplaces) Regulation 1984: [12.6]

Ombudsman Act 1974: [2.55], [16.73]

Poisons and Therapeutic Goods Act 1966: [8.5], [13.19], [13.20]
  s 10: [13.20]
  s 16: [13.20]

Poisons and Therapeutic Goods Regulations 1990: [8.5], [8.18]
  reg 7: [8.20]
  reg 8: [8.20]
  reg 30(1): [8.20]
  reg 55: [8.20]
  reg 67: [8.20]
  reg 67(a): [8.20]

Private Hospital and Day Procedures Centres Act 1988: [7.58]

Private Hospital and Day Procedures Centres Regulations 1996: [7.6]

Public Health Act 1986: [2.55]

Public Health Act 1991: [7.58], [7.87], [16.6]
  ss 11-16: [16.24]
  s 11: [16.37]
  s 13: [16.35], [16.37]
  s 14: [16.13]
  s 16: [16.38]
  ss 42A-42D: [16.57]
  ss 42E-42P: [16.11]
  s 500A(1): [16.45]
  Sch 1: [16.13]

Public Health Regulations 1991: [16.6]
  reg 4: [16.24]
  reg 5: [16.24]
  reg 9: [16.24]
  reg 10: [16.24]
  reg 10C: [16.57]
  reg 81(a): [16.11]

Public Hospitals Act 1929: [9.37]
  s 40A(1): [9.36]
  s 40A(2): [9.36]

Registration of Births, Deaths and Marriages Act 1973
  s 23: [15.38]

Status of Children Act 1996
  ss 26-31: [17.9]

Therapeutic Goods and Cosmetics Act 1972: [8.5]

Traffic Act 1909: [17.9]

Unclaimed Money Act 1982: [9.36]

Uncollected Goods Act 1995: [9.36]

Workers' Compensation Act 1987: [12.6], [12.19]
  s 3(1): [12.26]
  s 10: [12.42], [12.45]

Workers Compensation (Benefits) Amendment Act 1989: [11.35]

Workplace Injury Management and Workers Compensation Act 1988: [2.38], [12.6], [12.19]

Youth & Community Services Act 1973: [2.55]

Northern Territory

Age of Majority Act 1974
s 4: [5.2]

Anti-Discrimination Act 1992: [18.84]

Births, Deaths and Marriages Registration Act 1996: [15.2]

Cancer (Registration) Act 1988: [16.6], [16.38]
s 5: [16.11]

Cancer (Registration) Regulations 1988: [16.6], [16.38]
reg 3: [16.11]

Community Welfare Act 1983: [5.45], [5.50]
s 4: [16.62]
s 14: [16.74]
s 15: [16.80]

Compensation (Fatal Injuries) Act 1974: [6.141]

Consumer Affairs and Fair Trading Act 1990: [18.21]

Coroners Act 1974: [15.19]

Coroners Act 1993: [15.32]

Crimes Compensation Act 1967: [3.3]

Criminal Code Act 1983: [14.6], [14.162]
s 7: [14.32]
s 8: [14.32]
s 9: [14.32]
s 170: [14.187]
s 174: [14.162]
s 174(1)(b): [14.187]

Defamation Act 1957: [7.90]

Disability Services Act 1993: [5.93]

Disposal of Uncollected Goods Act 1976: [9.36]

Domestic Violence Act 1992: [16.81]

Emergency Medical Operations Act 1973
s 2: [5.7], [17.16]
s 3: [5.7], [17.16]

Evidence Act 1996
s 29: [7.26]

Health and Community Services Complaints Act 1998: [18.27]

Human Tissue Transplant Act 1979: [17.1]
s 10: [17.21]
s 11: [17.26]
s 12: [17.21], [17.26]
s 16(2)(a)(iii): [17.27]

Justices Act 1928: [16.90]
s 100: [16.93], [16.95]
s 100(1): [16.96]

Law Reform (Miscellaneous Provisions) Act 1956: [6.53], [6.199]
Pt IV: [6.156]
s 22A(1): [11.26]

Law Reform (Miscellaneous Provisions) Amendment Act 1984
s 22A: [6.200]

Limitation Act 1981: [6.204], [9.36]

Medical Act 1995
s 38: [13.49]

Mental Health Act 1996: [5.143], [13.49]
Pt III: [5.163]

Misuse of Drugs Act 1987: [16.51]

Misuse of Drugs Act 1990: [16.48]

Mutual Recognition Act (NT) 1992: [13.4]

Natural Death Act 1988: [5.110], [14.122]

Notifiable Diseases Act 1981: [16.6], [16.38], [17.17]
Pt II: [16.19]
s 7: [16.37]
s 8: [16.19]
s 26A(2)(a): [16.33]
Sch 6: [16.33]

Nursing Act 1999
s 21: [13.50]

Poisons and Dangerous Drugs Act 1983: [8.5], [8.18]
s 51: [8.20]
s 52: [8.20]

Poisons and Dangerous Drugs Regulations: [8.5]

Public Health Act 1997: [16.6]

Public Health (Cervical Cytology Register) Regulations 1996: [16.11]

Registration of Births, Deaths and Marriages Act 1962
s 26: [15.38]

Rights of the Terminally Ill Act 1995: [1.33], [14.85]

Status of Children Act 1979: [17.44]
ss 13-15: [17.9]

Traffic Act 1987: [17.9]

Work Health Act 1986: [12.6], [12.19]
s 4: [12.42], [12.45]
s 52: [11.35]

Queensland

Age of Majority Act 1974
s 5: [5.2]

Age of Majority (Reduction) Act 1970
s 3: [5.2]

Anti-Discrimination Act 1991: [18.85]

Children's Commissioner and Children's Services Appeals Tribunals Act 1996
s 19: [16.66]

Children's Services Act 1965: [5.45], [5.51]
s 46: [16.62]
s 47: [16.66]

Children's Services Regulations 1965: [16.66]

Coroners Act 1958: [15.19], [15.33]

Criminal Code 1899: [14.171]
Ch XXXV: [7.90]
Ch LXVA: [3.3]

Criminal Code Act 1899: [14.6]
s 7: [14.32]
s 8: [14.32]
s 9: [14.32]
s 282: [14.177]

Defamation Act 1889: [7.90]

Disability Services Act 1992: [5.93]

Disposal of Uncollected Goods Act 1967: [9.36]

District Court Act 1967: [2.20]

Domestic Violence (Family Protection) Act 1989: [16.81], [16.90]
s 31(1): [16.95]
s 32: [16.95]
s 69(1): [16.93]
s 80: [16.96]

Drugs Misuse Act 1986: [16.48]
s 10(2): [16.52]
s 10(3): [16.52]

Drugs Misuse Regulations 1986
reg 9: [16.52]
reg 10: [16.52]

Electricity (Continuity of Supply) Act 1985: [18.16]

Evidence Act 1977: [7.26]
s 92: [7.26]

Fair Trading Act 1989: [18.21]

Health Act 1937: [5.45], [5.51], [7.58], [8.5], [16.6], [16.15], [16.24]
s 32: [16.38]
s 48: [16.37]
s 48(2): [16.35]
s 76K: [16.75]
s 76L: [16.75], [16.80]
s 100C: [16.11]
s 100D: [16.11]

Health (Drugs and Poisons) Regulations 1996: [8.5], [8.18]

Health Professionals (Special Events Exemptions) Act 1998: [13.16]

Health Regulations 1996
ss 16-21: [16.11]
Sch 2: [16.15]
Sch 3: [16.15]

Health Rights Commission Act 1991: [18.28]

Health Services Act 1991: [7.58]

Industrial Relations Act 1990: [11.50], [11.97], [18.85]

Judicial Review Act 1991: [2.74]

Law Reform Act 1995: [6.199]

Law Reform Act 1996
s 16: [6.47]

Libraries and Archives Act 1988: [7.6]

Limitation of Actions Act 1974: [6.204], [9.36]

Medical Act 1939: [7.6]
s 35: [13.36]

Mental Health Act 1974: [5.143], [5.164]

Mutual Recognition Act (Queensland) 1992: [13.4]

Nursing Act 1992
s 102: [13.37]

Poisons Regulations 1973: [8.120]

Poisons Regulations 1974: [16.48]

Powers of Attorney Act 1998: [5.125], [14.125]
s 35: [5.113]

Public Trustee Act 1978: [9.36]

Registration of Births, Deaths and Marriages Act 1962: [15.2]
s 30(1): [15.38]

Status of Children Act 1978: [17.44]
s 11: [17.9]

Supreme Court Act 1995: [6.141]

Surrogate Parenthood Act 1988: [10.92], [17.84]

Traffic Act 1949: [17.9]

Transplantation and Anatomy Act 1979: [14.145], [17.1], [17.30]
s 10: [17.21]
s 12: [17.21]
ss 12A-12E: [17.22]
s 13: [17.21], [17.26]
s 17: [17.8]
s 18: [17.8]
s 20: [5.8], [17.16]
s 26: [17.37]
s 48A: [16.33]

WorkCover Queensland Act 1996: [12.6], [12.19]
s 37: [12.42], [12.45]

Workplace Health and Safety Act 1995: [12.6]

South Australia

Acts Interpretation Act 1915
s 21: [3.29]
s 22: [3.29]

Births, Deaths and Marriages Registration Act 1996: [15.2]
s 29: [15.38]

Blood Contaminants Act 1985: [17.17]
s 4: [16.33]
s 5: [16.33]

Children's Protection Act 1993: [5.45], [5.52]
s 6: [16.62]
ss 10-18: [16.76]
s 12: [16.67]
s 26: [16.76]

Community Welfare Act 1972: [16.80]
s 112: [17.9]

Consent to Medical Treatment and Palliative Care Act 1995: [5.15], [5.109], [5.126], [14.120]
s 6: [5.2]
s 13(5): [5.9], [17.16]
s 17: [14.101], [14.105]
s 17(1): [14.105]
s 17(2): [14.105]

Controlled Substances Act 1984: [8.5], [16.48]

Controlled Substances Act (Exemptions) Regulations 1989
s 2a: [16.53]

Controlled Substances (Poisons) Regulations 1996: [8.5]

Controlled Substances Regulations 1993: [8.18]
reg 65: [8.20]

Coroners Act 1975: [15.19]

Criminal Injuries Compensation Act 1978: [3.3]

Criminal Law Consolidation Act 1935: [4.66], [14.6]
s 82a: [14.160]
s 82(1): [14.161]

Criminal Law (Forensic Procedures) Act 1998: [14.195]

Disability Services Act 1993: [5.93]

Drugs Act 1908: [8.5]

Drugs of Dependence (General) Regulations 1985: [8.18]

Drugs Regulations 1978: [8.5]

Equal Opportunity Act 1984: [18.86]

Evidence Act 1929
s 45: [7.26]

Fair Trading Act 1987: [18.21]

Family Relationships Act 1975: [17.44], [17.48]

Family Relationships Act Amendments Act 1988: [10.92], [17.83]

Food Act 1985: [8.5]

Guardianship and Administration Board Act 1993: [5.126]

Health Professionals (Special Events Exemptions) Act 2000: [13.16]

Industrial and Employee Relations Act 1994: [11.50], [11.98]

Justices Act 1921
  s 99: [16.90]
  s 99(4): [16.95]
  s 99(6): [16.96]
Limitation of Actions Act 1936: [6.204], [9.36]
Medical Practitioners Act 1983
  s 5: [13.38]
Mental Health Act 1993: [5.143]
  Pt 3: [5.165]
  s 22: [5.190], [5.196]
Mutual Recognition Act (SA) 1993: [13.4]
Nurses Act 1984
  s 3: [13.38]
  s 41: [13.93]
Occupational Safety, Health and Welfare Act 1986: [12.6]
Public and Environmental Health Act 1987: [7.58], [16.6], [16.16], [16.24]
  s 33: [16.16], [16.35]
  s 36: [16.16]
  s 37: [16.37]
Public and Environmental Health (Cervical Cancer Screening) Regulations 1993: [16.11]
Racial Vilification Act 1996: [18.86]
Reproductive Technology Act 1988: [17.49], [17.58]
  s 13: [17.66]
Reproductive Technology Code of Ethical Clinical Practice 1988: [17.66], [17.68]
  Pt 2: [17.66]
  Pt 5: [17.77]
  cll 17-19: [17.72]
  cl 20: [17.72]
  cll 22-30: [17.77]
Road Traffic Act 1961: [17.9]
South Australian Health Commission Act 1976: [7.54], [7.58]
South Australian Health Commission (Cancer) Regulations 1991: [16.6], [16.11]
Summary Procedures Act 1921: [16.81]
Transplantation and Anatomy Act 1983: [17.1]
  s 7: [17.22]
  s 9: [17.21]
  s 12: [17.25]
  s 13: [17.22]

ss 15-17: [17.26]
s 18: [17.8]
s 19: [17.8]
s 25: [17.37]
Unclaimed Goods Act 1987: [9.36]
Unclaimed Moneys Act 1891: [9.36]
Workers Rehabilitation and Compensation Act 1986: [12.6], [12.19]
  s 30: [12.42], [12.45]
  s 54: [11.35]
Wrongs Act 1936: [6.141], [6.199], [11.26], [12.62]
  Pt 1: [7.90]
  s 27: [6.204]

Tasmania

Age of Majority Act 1973
  s 3: [5.2]
Anti-Discrimination Act 1998: [18.87]
Blood Transfusion (Limitation of Liability) Act 1986: [17.17]
  s 4: [16.33]
  s 5: [16.33]
Child Protection Act 1974: [5.45], [5.53]
  s 2: [16.62], [16.77]
  s 8: [16.68], [16.77]
  s 17: [5.53]
Child Welfare Act 1960: [16.80]
  s 2: [16.62]
  s 31: [16.62]
Coroners Act 1957: [15.19]
Coroners Act 1995: [15.34]
Criminal Code Act 1924: [14.6], [18.10]
  s 7: [14.32]
  s 8: [14.32]
  s 9: [14.32]
Criminal Injuries Compensation Act 1976: [3.3]
Defamation Act 1957: [7.90]
Disability Services Act 1992: [5.93]
Disposal of Uncollected Goods Act 1968: [9.36]
Evidence Act 1910
  Divn 2A: [7.26]
Fair Trading Act 1990: [18.21]
Fatal Accidents Act 1934: [6.141]

Guardianship and Administration Act 1995: [5.127]

Health Act 1997: [9.36]

Health Complaints Act 1995: [18.29]

Health Professionals (Special Events Exemptions) Act 1999: [13.16]

HIV/AIDS Preventative Measures Act 1993: [7.58], [7.87], [16.32], [16.44], [16.46]
Pt 3: [16.54]
s 8(3): [16.33]

Human Tissue Act 1982
s 24: [5.11]

Human Tissue Act 1985: [17.1]
s 6: [17.22]
s 7: [17.21]
s 9: [17.21]
s 11: [17.22]
s 12: [17.22]
s 13: [17.22]
s 14: [17.21], [17.26]
s 18: [17.8]
s 19: [17.8]
s 21: [17.16]
s 30: [16.33]

Industrial Relations Act 1984: [11.50], [11.100]

Industrial Safety, Health and Welfare (Employees' Safety Representatives) Regulations 1982: [12.6]

Justices Act 1959: [16.81]
s 100: [16.95]
s 106(1): [16.93], [16.96]
ss 106A-106F: [16.90]

Limitation Act 1974: [6.204]

Limitation Act 1981: [9.36]

Mental Health Act 1996: [5.166]

Mutual Recognition Act (Tasmania) 1993: [13.4]

Nursing Act 1995
s 56: [13.39]

Nursing Code (Medical Practitioners Registration) Act
s 45: [13.39]

Perinatal Registry Act 1994: [15.16]

Poisons Act 1971: [8.5], [16.48]

Poisons List Amendment Order 1990: [8.5]

Poisons Regulations 1975: [8.5], [8.18]
reg 18: [8.20]
reg 19: [8.20]
reg 22: [8.20]
reg 31: [8.20]
reg 37: [8.20]

Public Health Act 1962
s 30: [16.37]

Public Health Act 1997: [16.6]
Pt 3: [16.19]
ss 40-60: [16.32]

Public Health Amendment (Cervical Cytology) Act 1993
s 53A: [16.11]

Public Health (Notifiable Diseases) Regulations 1989: [16.6]
reg 4(3)(b): [16.11]

Public Health (Notifiable Diseases) Regulations 1995
reg 5: [16.38]

Registration of Births and Deaths Act 1895: [15.2]
s 23: [15.38]

Road Safety (Alcohol and Drugs) Act 1970: [17.9]

Status of Children Act 1974: [17.44]
s 10: [17.9]

Surrogacy Contracts Act 1993: [17.85]

Tasmanian State Service Act 1984: [7.54], [7.58]

Tortfeasors' and Contributory Negligence Act 1954: [6.199]

Unclaimed Moneys Act 1918: [9.36]

Workers Rehabilitation and Compensation Act 1988: [12.6], [12.19]
s 25: [12.42], [12.45]

Workplace Health and Safety Act 1995: [12.6]

Victoria

Accident Compensation Act 1985: [12.6], [12.19]
s 135(1): [11.35]

Accident Compensation (WorkCover Insurance) Act 1993: [12.6]
s 83: [12.42], [12.45]

Administrative Law Act 1978: [5.108]
  s 4: [5.108]
Administrative Review Act 1978: [2.74]
Age of Majority Act 1977
  s 3: [5.2]
Births Deaths and Marriages Registration Act 1996: [15.2]
Cancer Act 1958: [16.6]
  ss 59-62: [16.11]
Cancer (BreastScreen Register) Regulations 1994: [16.11]
Cancer (Reporting) Regulations 1992: [16.6], [16.11]
Children and Young Person's Act 1989: [5.45], [5.54]
  s 63: [16.62]
  s 64: [16.69], [16.78]
Commonwealth Powers (Industrial Relations) Act 1992: [11.50]
Community Protection Act 1990: [5.147]
Community Welfare Services Act 1970: [11.47], [16.80]
Coroners Act 1958: [15.19]
Coroners Act 1985: [15.35]
Crimes Act 1958: [14.6]
  s 19A: [16.35], [16.36]
  s 323: [14.32]
  s 463B: [4.66]
Crimes (Capital Offences) Act 1975: [14.6]
Crimes (Family Violence) Act 1987: [16.81], [16.90]
  s 8: [16.95]
  s 16: [16.95]
  s 22: [16.96]
Crimes (Theft) Act 1975: [14.6]
Criminal Injuries Compensation Act 1972: [3.3]
Disability Services Act 1991: [5.93]
Disposal of Uncollected Goods Act 1961: [9.36]
Drugs, Poisons and Controlled Substances Act 1981: [8.5], [13.21], [16.48]
  s 80(5): [16.55]

Drugs, Poisons and Controlled Substances Regulations 1985: [8.5], [8.18], [16.55]
  reg 401: [8.20]
  reg 402: [8.20]
  reg 404: [8.20]
  reg 910: [8.20]
  reg 1110: [8.20]
  reg 1126: [8.20]
Equal Opportunity Act 1995
  s 17: [18.88]
Evidence Act 1958: [7.47]
  s 55: [7.26]
Fair Trading Act 1999: [18.21]
Freedom of Information Act 1982
  s 13: [7.113]
  s 33(4): [7.113]
  s 39: [7.113]
Guardianship and Administration Act 1986: [5.81], [5.129]
Health Act 1958: [7.58], [15.6], [16.6], [17.17]
  s 7: [16.17]
  s 120(2): [16.35]
  ss 124-128: [16.17]
  s 144: [16.57]
  s 145: [16.57]
  s 160: [15.5]
Health (Blood Donations) Act 1985
  s 133: [16.33]
Health (General Amendments) Act 1988
  Divn 4: [16.47]
Health (Immunisations) Regulations 1999
  regs 5-9: [16.57]
  Sch 1: [16.57]
  Sch 2: [16.57]
Health (Infectious Diseases) Regulations 1990: [16.6], [17.17]
  reg 7: [16.37]
  Sch 2: [16.17]
  Sch 3: [16.38]
  Sch 6: [16.33]
  Sch 7: [16.33]
Health Professionals (Special Events Exemptions) Act 2000: [13.16]
Health Services Act 1988: [7.54], [7.58], [7.84]
Health Services (Conciliation and Review) Act 1987: [18.30]
Human Tissue Act 1982: [17.1]
  s 5: [17.22]

Human Tissue Act 1982 — *continued*
  s 7: [17.21]
  s 9: [17.21]
  s 10: [17.26]
  s 11: [17.26]
  s 14: [17.25]
  s 15: [17.22]
  s 16: [17.26]
  s 18(2)(a)(iii): [17.27]
  s 21: [17.8]
  s 22: [17.8]
  s 24: [17.16]
  s 28: [17.37]

Infertility (Medical Procedures) Act 1984: [17.48]

Infertility (Medical Procedures) Regulations 1988: [4.93]

Infertility Treatment Act 1995: [17.57], [17.61], [17.69], [17.82]
  Pt V: [10.92]
  s 7: [17.50]
  s 8: [17.68], [17.69]
  s 8(1): [17.69]
  ss 51-55: [17.73]
  ss 62-70: [17.76]

Infertility Treatment Regulations 1997
  reg 12: [17.73]
  regs 13-18: [17.76]
  Sch 1: [17.76]
  Sch 2: [17.76]

Intellectually Disabled Persons Services Act 1986: [5.93]

Interpretation of Legislation Act 1984
  s 35: [3.29]

Limitation of Actions Act 1958: [6.204], [9.36]

Medical Practitioners Act 1992: [13.40]

Medical Treatment Act 1988: [5.82], [5.111], [5.129], [14.117], [14.119]

Mental Health Act 1986: [5.143], [5.147]
  Pt 3: [5.167]
  Pt 5, Divn 1: [5.197]
  Pt 5, Divn 1AA: [5.191]
  Pt 5, Divn 2: [5.191]
  Pt 5, Divn 4: [5.202]
  s 72: [4.93]
  s 81: [4.191]
  s 82: [4.175], [4.191], [5.205]
  s 83: [4.175], [5.205]

Mutual Recognition Act (Victoria) 1993: [13.4]

Nurses Act 1993: [13.21]
  s 3: [13.40]

s 8B: [13.21]

Nurses Amendment Act 2000: [13.21]

Occupational Health and Safety Act 1985: [12.6]

Occupational Health and Safety Regulations 1989: [12.6]

Public Records Act 1973: [7.6]

Registration of Births, Deaths and Marriages Act 1959
  s 18(1): [15.38]

Road Safety Act 1986: [17.9]

Status of Children Act 1974: [17.44]

Therapeutic Goods (Victoria) Act 1994: [8.5]

Therapeutic Goods Regulations 1994: [8.31]

Unclaimed Moneys Act 1972: [9.36]

Victorian Civil and Administrative Tribunal Act 1998: [2.59]

Wrongs Act 1958: [6.141], [6.199], [12.62]
  Pt I: [7.90]

Western Australia

Age of Majority Act 1972
  s 5: [5.2]

Artificial Conception Act 1985: [17.44]

Births, Deaths and Marriages Registration Act 1998: [15.2]

Blood and Tissue (Transmissible Disease) Regulations 1985
  reg 5(1): [16.33]
  reg 6(1): [16.33]
  reg 9(1): [16.33]
  reg 10(1): [16.33]
  reg 11: [16.33]

Blood Donation (Limitation of Liability) Act 1985: [17.17]

Child Welfare Act 1947: [5.45], [5.55]
  s 4: [16.62]

Child Welfare Act 1972: [16.80]

Coroners Act 1920: [15.19]

Coroners Act 1996: [15.36]
  s 47: [15.70]

Criminal Code 1913: [14.6], [14.172]
  Ch XXXV: [7.90]

Criminal Code 1913 — *continued*
  s 7: [14.32]
  s 8: [14.32]
  s 9: [14.32]
Criminal Injuries Compensation Act 1985: [3.3]
Disability Services Act 1993: [5.93]
Disposal of Uncollected Goods Act 1970: [9.36]
Equal Opportunity Act 1984: [18.89]
Evidence Act 1906
  s 79C: [7.26]
Fair Trading Act 1987: [18.21]
Fatal Accidents Act 1959: [6.141]
Guardianship and Administration Act 1990: [5.130]
Health Act 1911: [16.6]
  s 264: [16.37]
  s 276: [16.18]
  s 289B: [16.11]
  s 289C: [16.11]
  s 310: [16.37]
Health (Cervical Cytology Register) Regulations 1991: [16.6], [16.11]
Health (Infectious Diseases) Order 1993: [16.6]
Health (Notification of Adverse Event after Immunisation) Regulations 1995: [16.6]
Health (Notification of Cancer) Regulations 1981: [16.6], [16.11]
Health Professionals (Special Events Exemptions) Act 2000: [13.16]
Health Services (Conciliation and Review) Act 1995: [18.31]
Human Reproductive Technology Act 1991: [17.48], [17.51], [17.58], [17.67]
  s 7: [17.67]
  s 23: [17.68]
  ss 24-26: [17.74]
  ss 44-50: [17.79]
Human Tissue and Transplant Act 1982: [17.1]
  s 1: [17.25]
  s 6: [17.22]
  s 8: [17.21]
  s 11: [17.22]
  s 13: [17.22]
  ss 15-17: [17.26]

  s 16: [17.21]
  s 17: [17.21]
  s 18: [17.8]
  s 19: [17.8]
  s 21: [5.11], [17.16]
  s 25: [17.37]
Industrial Relations Act 1979: [11.50], [11.99]
Interpretation Act 1984
  s 8: [3.29]
  s 18: [3.29]
  s 19: [3.29]
Justices Act 1902: [16.81]
  ss 172-174: [16.90]
  s 173(1): [16.96]
Law Reform (Contributory Negligence and Tortfeasors' Contribution) Act 1947: [6.199]
Library Board of Western Australia Act 1951: [7.6]
Limitation Act 1935: [6.204], [9.36]
Medical Act 1894: [8.27], [13.4], [13.98]
  s 13: [13.42]
Mental Health Act 1996: [5.143]
  Pt 3: [5.168]
  Pt 5, Divn 4: [5.198]
  Pt 5, Divn 5: [5.192]
  Pt 5, Divn 6: [5.203]
  Pt 5, Divn 8: [5.206]
  Pt 5, Divn 9: [5.206]
Misuse of Drugs Act 1981
  ss 5-9: [16.56]
Mutual Recognition (Western Australia) Act 1995: [13.4]
Nurses Act 1992
  s 61: [13.44]
Occupational Health and Safety Act 1984: [12.6]
Occupiers Liability Act 1985: [12.62]
Poisons Act 1964: [8.5], [16.48]
  s 36A: [16.56]
Poisons Regulations 1965: [8.5], [8.18]
  reg 35: [8.20]
  reg 36: [8.20]
Registration of Births, Deaths and Marriages Act 1961
  s 33: [15.38]
Road Traffic Act 1974: [17.9]
Unclaimed Moneys Act 1918: [9.36]

Workers' Compensation and
    Rehabilitation Act 1981: [12.6],
    [12.19]
  s 19: [12.42], [12.45]

Workplace Agreements Act 1993:
    [11.99]

United Kingdom

Aliens Order 1920: [14.24]

Colonial Laws Validity Act 1865: [1.21]

Family Law Reform Act 1969: [5.29]

United States

Constitution: [1.34]

International

Convention on the Elimination of All
    Forms of Discrimination: [1.32]

Convention on the Rights of the Child:
    [18.15]
  Art 24: [18.12]

Declaration on the Rights of Disabled
    Persons: [18.14]
  Art 6: [18.12]

Declaration on the Rights of Mentally
    Retarded Persons: [18.14]
  Art 2: [18.12]

Declaration on the Rights of the Child:
    [18.14]
  Art 4: [18.12]

European Convention on Human
    Rights: [5.214]

Family Responsibilities Convention:
    [11.81]

International Convention Concerning
    Discrimination in Respect of
    Employment and Occupation:
    [11.81], [18.14]

International Convention on the
    Elimination of all Forms of
    Discrimination against Women:
    [18.59]

International Convention on the
    Elimination of all Forms of Racial
    Discrimination: [18.52]

International Covenant on Civil and
    Political Rights: [18.14]
  Art 7: [18.12]
  Art 14: [2.71]

International Covenant on Social,
    Economic and Cultural Rights
  Art 12: [18.12]

Termination of Employment
    Convention: [11.81]

UNESCO Convention Concerning the
    Protection of the World Cultural
    and Natural Heritage: [1.30]

United Nations Declaration of Human
    Rights: [1.59]

United Nations Declaration on the
    Rights of Mentally Retarded
    Persons: [5.63]

Chapter One

WHAT IS LAW?

INTRODUCTION

[1.1] People obey ethical and moral rules because these are based on what ought to be done according to general opinion, accepted social and cultural values, and a person's own conscience. Breaking these rules invites a feeling of guilt, shame or embarrassment, and the disapproval of others. One may be ruled by the governing board of one's profession as being unfit to practise. People obey the demands of the law, however, because a breach of the law invites more tangible consequences such as imprisonment or a court order either to pay compensation or to carry out some act.

[1.2] Law is the embodiment of what is considered desirable for some social good, in rules which can be enforced. Rules may be desirable because they are considered the morally or socially "right" thing to do, or best for the good government of the country, or simply a means of benefiting some members of society. Although all laws may be considered to be ethically acceptable (though this is often debatable), not all ethical principles are covered by law; for example, people may feel morally obliged to help someone they come across in the street who is injured, but they are not legally required to do so (see Ch 6). There may be great conflict between the law and what some believe to be morally acceptable, for example, the law allowing abortion in certain circumstances, prohibiting euthanasia, and the use of certain drugs, and the law's lack of control of in vitro fertilisation programmes. This book does not discuss the controversies, but does set out the law on these and other bioethical dilemmas. Recent and topical books on the subject of bioethics for health carers in Australia are Johnstone (1999), Kuhse (1997), Freckelton (1999), Darvall (1993), and McLean (1999).

[1.3] There are many ways in which the law affects health carers, either by creating obligations or by conferring rights. Some examples follow, but the list is not exhaustive:

[1.3] SOME WAYS IN WHICH HEALTH CARERS CAN BE FOUND RESPONSIBLE AT LAW

negligence	for example, failing to provide adequate information for a patient's informed consent (Ch 4) or to report a change in a patient's vital signs; giving the wrong drug (Ch 6)
assault/ battery	for example, giving care without consent, threatening a client; forcing a patient to ambulate without her or his consent (Ch 4)
defamation	for example, telling friends harmful details about a client (Ch 7)
crime	for example, wrongly handling drugs; falsifying documents; unlawfully causing death (Ch 14)
other offences	for example, failure to report child abuse in some jurisdictions, or infectious disease in all jurisdictions (Ch 16)
other liability	for example, mishandling of clients' property (Ch 9); failure to carry out an employer's instructions (Ch 11); failure to obtain registration (Ch 13); discrimination against clients in some cases (Ch 18)

SOME RIGHTS CONFERRED ON HEALTH CARERS BY LAW

the right not to be unfairly dismissed or punished	Chapter 11
the right to question an employer's instructions	Chapter 11
the right to receive compensation for work-related accidents	Chapter 12
the right to a fair hearing before any adverse action is taken	Chapters 1, 11, 14
the right not to be discriminated against on the grounds of race or sex (and other grounds in some jurisdictions)	Chapter 18

Understanding Law

[1.4] Law can be studied at two levels. It can be seen in its broadest sense, as a means of creating some order in our society by the evolution of rules, mores and customs. The study at this level considers the nature of society, of "right", "justice", "common good", and other concepts which are [1.6] involved in a consideration of the nature of law. This study, involving philosophical and sociological perceptions, is called *jurisprudence*. The other level of study is that in which lawyers are mainly involved and is the dominant concern of this book: the actual content of our laws (*substantive law*), and the mechanics of making and enforcing them (*procedural law*) (see below, Figure 1.1).

Classifications of Law

[1.5] There are two main branches of law, and sub-branches of those. The first branch is substantive law, or that part of the law which tells us what we can do, must do, or must not do, as well as the interpretation of the law, setting out rights and obligations, etc. It is divided into two sub-branches: civil law and criminal law. Civil law in turn has many sub-branches such as constitutional law, commercial law, contract law, bankruptcy law, administrative law and family law. The second branch is procedural law. This tells us how to go about putting the law into action. It includes such sub-branches as the law of evidence and court rules.

▌▌▌ FIGURE 1.1

CLASSIFICATION OF LAW

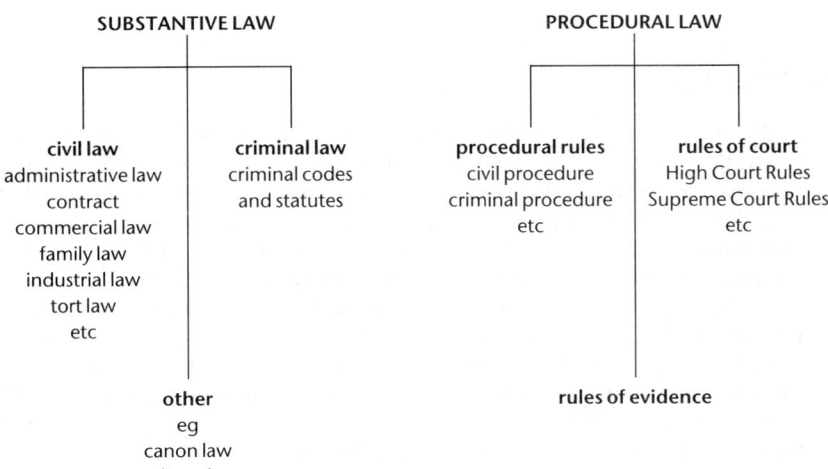

Legal Theory

[1.6] Straddling these two levels of study is an approach to understanding law which considers both the content and process of law in our society. It studies their effects and their ability to fulfil the purposes and goals that may have been recognised at the more fundamental,

[1.6] jurisprudential level. What, for example, is the purpose of the law on drugs, and is it effective? Could it be improved? Are our goals realistic and/or appropriate, acceptable, or worthwhile? Versions of this approach to law have been variously called "critical legal theory", the "realist school of legal theory", or "sociological legal theory". There are some subtle differences in these approaches. Some useful references for an understanding of legal philosophies are Harris (1980), Davies (1994) and Hunter et al (1995). This perspective is used at times in this book to evaluate the law as it applies to health carers, and to consider desirable change.

Natural Law

[1.7] Early jurisprudential theories, propounded by such philosophers as Aristotle and Cicero, and later developed by St Thomas Aquinas, were based on the principle of natural law. This holds that the fundamental source of law is nature, and this source is higher and more binding than any laws made by human beings. It is closely linked with morality (Hunter et al (1995), p 50, Davies (1994), Ch 3). Natural law, it states, is fixed and unchangeable, and it can be discovered by reason and an understanding of human nature. Natural law still underlies much of the western world's legal policies, particularly in the area of human rights (Harris (1980), Ch 2). Some natural law principles still underlie our law today, such as the right to be heard in one's defence before suffering punishment (see [1.59]).

Positive Law

[1.8] An important development in law in our western society was its separation from religion and the subsequent predominance of "positivism", that is, the removal of legal authority from God, or nature, to the state. The recognised founders of this approach are Jeremy Bentham and John Austen. Law is seen, in this perspective, as being a set of commands which result in certain goals being attained or evils prevented, made by someone with the recognised authority to require compliance (Harris (1980), Ch 3, see also Hunter et al (1995), p 50). This then separates the "moral" from the "legal" in the expression of our obligations: something is not part of our law simply because it is morally right. Authority for law is placed in the state, and so the law is what the state says it is, whether it is morally right or not.

[1.9] Davies (1994), p 76 points out that to explain why a law is valid, positivists can only point to another law. It has no more fundamental basis. But because eventually there has to be some non-legal reason for saying that something is law, we come to a political or ideological basis for making the law. The people who dominate society, who really have the means of social control, are those who make the laws.

Legal Systems

[1.10] Throughout the world there are several broad legal systems. Some of the main ones are briefly listed below.

Common Law

[1.11] This is based on the development in England of law common to the many communal systems operating throughout the country. The system was extended to the various colonies and is therefore the basis of the Australian, New Zealand, United States and Canadian legal systems, among others. It is explained more fully below (see [1.37]). The term "common law" is also used to:

- .....differentiate judge-made law from statutory law (see [1.19]–[1.22]); and
- .....differentiate common law from equity (see [1.49]).

[1.12] It is thus important to determine the context in which the term is used. The common law system is based on the adversarial approach to resolving disputes. This means that the parties involved in disputes present their cases and argue their merits before a judge and/or jury, the latter being unable to take an active part in instigating the acquisition of knowledge about the case, or determining what information is put before them.

Civil Law

[1.13] This is the system of law in those European countries which inherited either the French or Roman cultural influence. It is based mainly on a code (which means the law is almost entirely enshrined in statutes), and the approach to dispute resolution is inquisitorial rather than adversarial. This means that the judiciary takes the initiative in seeking the facts, and is not confined to dealing only with what is put before it. The judge's role is investigatory (the role assigned in our common law system to lawyers and police (Easton et al (1985))—the lawyers for each party playing the role of an assistant to the judge rather than the role of advocate for the party, which they adopt in the adversarial system. The term "civil law" may also be used in our common law system to discriminate a matter from criminal law, so the context in which the term is used must be considered.

Socialist Law

[1.14] This system, originally adopted by Russia in the 1920s and still in use in some other countries, is based on the ideology of socialism. This affects both the content of the laws which are enacted (substantive law), as well as rules for the conduct of legal procedures (procedural rules).

Islamic Law and Some Eastern Legal Systems

[1.15] These systems concentrate more on internal religious beliefs and motivation and their perceived moral superiority as the source of authority for law than on mere external control as a means of social ordering, although religious beliefs and values are readily enforced by the laws of the land. They are more patriarchal in nature than the laws of our society, and this is reflected in laws that grant the right to political and legal participation unequally, according to status conferred by gender or religious beliefs.

Customary Law

[1.16] Customary law, as its name implies, is a system of rules generated by the customs of a society. They have not been established by governmental processes similar to those recognised today as law-making. Two forms of customary law that affect the Australian legal system are international customary law and indigenous (that is, Aboriginal and Torres Strait Islander) customary law. The former affects our international relationships and will not be discussed here. Indigenous customary law is discussed at [1.56] below.

Sources of Australian Law

[1.17] Australian law is, as mentioned, a form of the common law system. An understanding of our law is probably best gained by considering the nature and development of our sources of law.

[1.18] There are three main sources of law in Australia: legislation, judge-made law and indigenous customary law.

Laws Made by a Recognised Authority—Legislation

[1.19] These are documents setting out obligations and rights, penalties and procedures. The bodies which make these laws are the federal Parliament, and the Parliaments of the States, the Australian Capital Territory and the Northern Territory. These bodies pass laws in the form of *statutes* (otherwise called Acts of Parliament) which are then binding on all citizens, or a particular class of citizens nominated in the legislation. Copies of all legislation can be purchased from the relevant government publisher, and most can also be downloaded from the internet (see Preface). Statutes can delegate the right to make further legislation to other designated bodies or people (for example, a Minister of a government or a statutory body) which are more detailed in their content. These are in the form of rules and regulations, and are called *delegated legislation*. Statutes (made by Parliament) and rules and regulations (made by a designated person or body) can all be equally binding on people. However, if rules or regulations have provisions which contradict

provisions of a statute in the same State or Territory, the provisions of the [1.21]
rules or regulations are invalid insofar as they contradict the statute. If
State legislation contradicts federal legislation the federal legislation
prevails (see [1.27]).

▌▌▌ FIGURE 1.2

INTER-RELATIONSHIP OF DIFFERENT LEVELS OF LEGISLATION

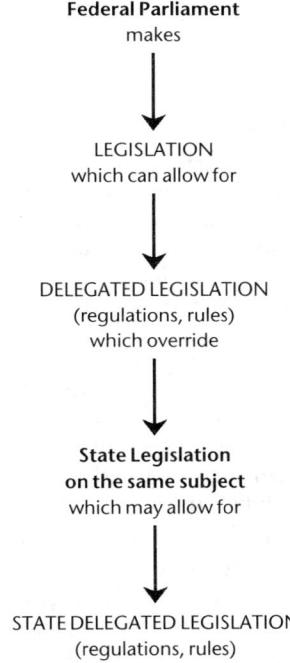

[1.20] Because Australia was originally a colony of Britain, all legislation to apply in Australia prior to Federation was at first enacted in the British Parliament. Thus all laws in force in England applied in the Australian colonies so far as was practicable, with pronouncements by the colonial governors on the advice of the Legislative Council in England on matters of doubt.

[1.21] Self-governing colonies, however, such as New South Wales, Queensland, South Australia, Tasmania, Victoria and Western Australia (although not necessarily as we know them today) were later established. In 1865 the *Colonial Laws Validity Act* was passed by the British Parliament giving the colonies power to make their own laws for their "peace, order and good government", while reserving some powers for the Imperial Parliament of England. Ties to England since then have been weakened.

[1.22] **[1.22]** By the enactment in Britain of a Constitution for Australia, which provided for Federation in 1901, the English monarch remained the head of state of Australia, represented here by the Governor-General (a state of affairs which continues after the 1999 referendum, in which Australians voted to retain the monarchy). Federal and State Parliaments were established and acquired the power to legislate for their respective areas (from 1901). This Constitution differentiates between matters on which the federal government can legislate (for example, regulation of currency, overseas trade, family law) and matters on which State Parliaments can legislate (for example, education, roads, criminal law). This was because at the time it was believed that the Commonwealth could better manage matters where a common policy and practice was desirable throughout the country.

The Australian Constitution

[1.23] Each State has a Constitution which vests power in the State government to make whatever laws are deemed fit for the "peace, order and good government" of that State. This power is limited only by the narrowly defined powers of the federal government set out in the *Commonwealth of Australia Constitution Act* 1901 (Imp) (the Australian Constitution) which is an Act of the United Kingdom Parliament. It established the federation of the States, created the federal government, and defined the legal relationship between the federal government and the States. Section 107 of the federal Constitution provides that every power the State governments had prior to Federation, which the Constitution established, was to remain vested in them unless "it is by this Constitution exclusively vested in the Parliament of the Commonwealth or withdrawn from the Parliament of the State".

[1.24] To determine whether the federal government has the power to make legislation on any matter one turns first to the federal Constitution, where the matters on which the federal government can legislate are listed, especially in section 51. States can legislate on any other matter. If a State refers one of its powers to the federal government, then the federal government can legislate on that matter.

[1.25] Powers vested in the federal government include matters dealing with the seat of government and other Commonwealth places (s 52); customs and excise duties (ss 51(2), (3) and 90-93); the Commonwealth Public Service (ss 52, 67); Commonwealth Territories (ss 111, 122) and initiating constitutional referenda (s 128).

[1.26] Some other powers are granted to the Commonwealth, but are not stated to be exclusive. These are known as *concurrent* powers, and are set out in section 51 of the federal Constitution. There are 39 placita (decrees) in that section. These include such matters as trade and commerce with other countries (pl i); external affairs (pl xxix); nationalisation and aliens (pl xix); quarantine (pl ix); taxation (pl ii); census and statistics (pl xi); bills of exchange and promissory notes (pl xvi); marriage (pl xxi); and divorce and matrimonial causes (pl xxii).

[1.27] In fact the States may make laws in these areas as well as the Commonwealth, but section 109 of the federal Constitution provides that where they do, and there is inconsistency between State law and Commonwealth law, Commonwealth law applies, and the State law is rendered invalid: "When a law of a State is inconsistent with a [valid] law of the Commonwealth, the latter shall prevail, and the former shall, to the extent of the inconsistency, be invalid."

[1.28] *Referral of powers*: States may formally *refer* a power which they have to the Commonwealth, thus permitting the federal government to legislate on the matter involved. This has occurred, for example, on the matter of ex-nuptial children, normally a matter not included among those on which the federal government can legislate. Recognition of the value of allowing the Family Court to deal with custody and access issues relating to ex-nuptial children (as well as those born within a marriage) has led to most of the States referring their power to make laws relating to custody of, and access to, such children. This means that these powers are now included in the *Family Law Act* 1975 (Cth).

Statutory Interpretation

[1.29] The reader may realise that there arises the problem of just how the Constitution and, for example, the powers it vests in the federal government, are to be interpreted. The law as written may be ambiguous or unclear, and language is never so clear and absolute that its meaning is not open to debate. The issue of statutory interpretation, whether it involves the Constitution or any other written legislation, gives rise to a basic task for lawyers and is discussed below (see Ch 3). Interpretation of statutes is also a major function of the courts, the High Court being the court which has the jurisdiction (power) to interpret the Constitution.

[1.30] An example of the need for the High Court to interpret the Constitution occurred in the *Tasmanian Dam Case* (*Commonwealth v Tasmania* (1983) 46 ALR 625). The issue arose because the federal government legislated to prohibit the Tasmanian government from building a dam on the Gordon River, in order to protect the surrounding forest from destruction. Normally the federal government could not do this, but it invoked the fact that Australia is a signatory to the *UNESCO Convention Concerning the Protection of the World Cultural and Natural Heritage*. This, it argued, gave it the right to legislate on the matter as it came under the foreign affairs power.

[1.31] The High Court was approached for interpretation of the meaning of "foreign affairs". It was argued by the Tasmanian government that the power only authorised the federal government to legislate about a matter which was inherently international in nature (that is, involving our relationship with another nation). This has been called the "narrow interpretation". The federal government argued that the power was wider because it had signed an international treaty (including a convention) which required it to put the terms of that treaty into effect domestically. These two views are very different in their nature and effect.

[1.32] The High Court held that the wider view was the better legal view. The narrow view certainly could have been what the founders of the

[1.32] nation had in mind, before the days of international conventions and agreements and, of course, such bodies as the United Nations. The wider view also accords with the plain meaning of the words (see below [3.32]) as interpretation of the Constitution takes into account current legal practice and political processes, the Court decided that the wider meaning was more appropriate. The High Court had also to decide whether the Commonwealth could legislate to prohibit racial discrimination (against the wishes of the State of Queensland) as it was a signatory to the *Convention on the Elimination of All Forms of Discrimination*. Again the court agreed with the wider interpretation of the term "foreign affairs", stating that so long as the Commonwealth was a bona fide signatory of an international document, it could legislate on the matter (and therefore contradictory State legislation would be invalid): *Koowarta v Bjelke-Petersen* (1982) 56 ALJR 625.

Legislating for the Territories

[1.33] The Australian Capital Territory, the Northern Territory and Norfolk Island are self-governing territories under the Constitution. That means they have legislative assemblies and can make their own laws similar to the States. However they do not have the same independence as the States. Section 122 of the Constitution states that the Commonwealth can legislate for the territories. This means that the Commonwealth Parliament can legislate on any matter for the territories, thus overriding Territory legislation and potentially depriving them of the right to make their own laws on that matter. This happened in 1998 when the Commonwealth Government passed the *Euthanasia Laws Act* 1997, which prohibited those Territories from providing for voluntary euthanasia, and overturning the Northern Territory's *Rights of the Terminally Ill Act* 1995.

Changing the Constitution

[1.34] The Constitution is entrenched: that is, it cannot be *amended* (changed) or *repealed* (cancelled) unless there is a national referendum in which all citizens must take part, and there must be an overall majority of voters in a majority of States to approve the change or repeal. The latest referendum was in 1988, and involved proposed changes to include various human rights in the Constitution (we do not have constitutional guarantees of such rights as does the United States in its Constitution). The referendum failed, so no changes could be made. In fact people tend to be conservative and reject proposed changes to the Constitution, so most referenda fail (as evidenced in the referendum of 1999 which proposed an Australian head of state). In 1946, however, one referendum succeeded in giving the federal government new powers in the medical area. Placitum (xxiiiA) of section 51 of the Constitution (inserted as a result of that referendum) adds the power for the Commonwealth to legislate for "pharmaceutical sickness and hospital benefits, medical and dental services (but not so as to authorize any form of civil conscription)".

[1.35] This has been recently interpreted by the High Court to mean that the federal government can regulate medical and dental services on a national basis where federal funds are concerned. Thus, although States

can organise the provision of services themselves without federal [1.39]
government interference, if they accept federal funding they must agree to
comply with federal government directives: the Commonwealth has wide
powers to raise revenue and grant funding to the States. The High Court
also said that the federal government cannot compel health care workers
throughout the nation to carry out clinical activities such as caring for
patients (*Practitioners Society in Australia v Commonwealth* (1980) 54 ALJR
487).

[1.36] This is in contrast to legislation other than the Constitution,
which may be repealed or amended by later legislation. Repeal or
amendment may be *expressed* (spelt out by the wording of the new Act) or
implied (a natural consequence of it). There are also State Constitutions
which set out the powers of State Parliaments, courts and bodies, as well as
individuals.

Laws Developed by the Courts—Common Law

[1.37] In the history of Western law in Australia, originally deriving from
the United Kingdom, common law has its origins in the feudal era. In
earlier times, when someone complained of having been wronged by
another, the way of dealing with this was to gather one's clan, descend
upon the wrongdoer, and reap bloody vengeance on that person and her
or his family. This was, of course, rather disruptive, and the establishment
of feudalism was one way of maintaining order. Feudalism was
fundamentally a system of land tenure, with personal service owed by
many to an overlord, who had immense powers including the exercise of
customary law, based on local customs. The very completeness of its
application made feudalism a potent force for law and order.

[1.38] England was a rural society, and later overlordship carried with it
as a further principle the right of every lord to hold a court for his tenants.
There was very little legislation, but the lord enforced obedience to an
existing and settled custom when disputes were to be resolved. This
custom involved settling disputes by such methods as trial by oath, trial
by battle and trial by ordeal. Where one person had caused another
physical harm or loss of property, he or she was said to have an action in
the law of "wrongs" (or to use the ancient French term, imported into our
legal system and still used today, the law of "torts").

[1.39] Initially, wrongs were seen as personal disputes, but as the central
government began to grow, towns and cities developed, and the king
wished to extend his power, some "wrongs" were increasingly seen as
breaches of the king's peace. The "king's peace" grew and flourished with
the extension and consolidation of the power of the king, until it covered
the whole of England at all times and for all seasons. When this had come
to pass no person committed violence without being liable to a fine at the
suit of the king: a precursor of modern criminal law. However, until the
time of Henry II, the enforcement of law, even penal law, remained in
private hands. Today, we still have the offence of "breach of the peace",
with which a person who causes a serious disturbance to the peaceful
activities of those around them may be charged.

[1.40] **[1.40]** Henry II instituted some dramatic changes. He set apart certain wrongs as matters for the interference of the Crown. Others were peculiarly the concern of the private citizen. This was the beginning of the crime/tort dichotomy ("public"/"private" law). Several crimes, such as robbery with violence, were established, which attracted physical punishment, but private vengeance became mostly monetary compensation. Justice became the business of the monarch, not the lords.

[1.41] In order to seek the aid of royal justice, it was usual to purchase a writ from the King's Chancery. This writ was a royal command based upon the king's royal authority. It specified the injury complained of, and directed that whoever had caused the harm should right the wrong or show cause before the king's justices why they should not.

[1.42] It became obvious that a lot of actions would be comparatively similar in nature, if not in detail, and so common wording was used. Writs became standard in form, adapted for the particular category of action involved, for example trespass, personal injury, robbery. In the course of time, each category tended to develop its own peculiarities, for example, the method of proof for supporting or rebutting the claim in any particular category of case would differ from others. If the writ itself did not follow a common form, it was not incorporated in the Clerk's Register of Writs, and so no action would lie for that particular set of events.

[1.43] In this way, then, a common law became increasingly prevalent, and this was aided particularly by a lawyer, Blackstone, who wrote a many-volumed "Commentary" on the law of England, bringing together the common principles he found in the law as practised throughout the land. His "Commentary" became the main authority for later decisions by the courts.

[1.44] What has all this to do with today's law? The answer lies in the fact that the authority of a law is based on the idea of acceptance of a principle (or rule, or standard of behaviour) by a court, from another court higher in the same hierarchy in that jurisdiction. By the establishment of a "common law", then, principles derived from sources with accepted authority were set down as a guide for future decision-making to be changed only by courts with higher authority than the original court. This laid the foundations for one of the fundamental aspects of our legal system, *stare decisis* (meaning, roughly, "the decision binds"), the requirement that a court is bound by legal principles established by courts with higher standing than it has (see [1.50]ff).

Equity—a Development from Common Law

[1.45] Common law could be very harsh, and somewhat rigid. One example of this is the common law principle that the person whose name is on a title deed to land is the person who owns it at law, and can therefore sell it at will and have sole rights to the proceeds of sale. This can cause hardship where someone else, whose name is not on the title deed, has made a contribution to the acquisition of the property by contributing to its purchase price, or enhanced its value by improving or renovating it. An example is where a couple share a house that has been purchased in the name of one of them, where the other contributes to the [1.49] value of the property by maintenance, renovation, decorating, or to the repayments on the mortgage. Many people who had gone to the courts and found tough justice through the common law. Over time a set of alternative approaches developed in some of the specialised courts, such as the Court of Chancery, the ecclesiastical courts and the Court of Admiralty, which were based more on principles aimed at prevention of unjust enrichment at another's expense. The principles that developed were called "principles of equity". Thus, where at common law a person in the situation described above would not be able to reap the reward of her or his contribution to the property, in equity the fact that that person had contributed to its value could lead to a claim on its value in proportion to the contribution.

[1.46] The principles of equity have been incorporated into the jurisdiction of the common law courts. This means that the courts can consider both the common law *and* equitable remedies for which a person may be eligible. Generally, one or the other will be applicable, but where there is a conflict between the rules of equity and the common law, equity is to prevail.

[1.47] The term "common law" is used in several, potentially confusing ways. It may refer to:

- .....common law principles exclusive of the principles of equity where the writer is drawing a distinction between common law principles, strictly speaking, and principles of equity; or
- .....both traditional common law and equity, to differentiate these from statutory law.

The meaning is to be deduced from the context of the use of the term.

Inter-relationship between Statutory Law and Common Law (including Equity)

[1.48] Parliament creates an enormous amount of law each year and has the power to enact statutes on any and every facet of our lives. Obviously it is impossible to cover everything, so where there is a gap in statutory law judges and lawyers turn to the common law, as discovered through the cases, in an attempt to find enlightenment there. Sometimes cases referred to may be very old.

[1.49] If a judge is faced with a matter where:

- .....there is no statutory provision governing a particular matter before the court; or
- .....the matter has not been the subject of a judicial decision,

he or she will look at cases with the most similar fact situations that can be found, and, using the principles used in those cases, develop principles for the matter now before the court. New law will be developed for future reference where this new situation arises again. This is how the common law adapts to a changing society.

Precedent

[1.50] This is the word used to describe the system by which the common law is passed on to influence later decisions. Courts are arranged in a hierarchy, from the lowest courts (courts of petty sessions, or magistrates' courts), to the highest courts (in Australia—the High Court; in England—the House of Lords). This hierarchy will be considered in more detail in Chapter 2. Decisions made in the higher courts have precedence over decisions made in the lower courts. This means that under some circumstances, when one has received a judgment of a lower court, one can appeal to a higher court to have the lower court's judgment quashed, and either a different judgment may be made or a new hearing may be granted. The decision of the higher court then applies, and it, and the reason for its decision, is binding on all courts lower in the same hierarchy in that jurisdiction.

[1.51] It is important for lawyers to know which court a decision comes from, for a decision is only binding on a lower court in the same hierarchy. Decisions from a court in another hierarchy are of *persuasive precedent* only, that is, not binding on the court, but, depending upon the status of the court from which it comes, worth considering to the extent that a judge would feel obliged to justify not following it. For example, an English court decision is persuasive precedent in Australia, and a New South Wales court decision persuasive precedent in South Australia. As its name implies, persuasive precedent is not binding on a judge and can only be used if no binding precedent can be found. The decisions of the Australian High Court are binding on all Australian courts, unless they are specifically applied only to a particular State or Territory.

[1.52] What this means for practical purposes is that when considering their judgment in a case, judges will look to the decisions of the higher courts, and a lawyer arguing before the judge will attempt to outdo the opposing party's argument by offering a precedent from those cases which have more authority than the opponent's.

[1.53] It may be that the only precedent for a particular fact situation is a fairly lowly court's decision from the last century or it could even come from an earlier case in England. In this case the lawyers get down their dusty old tomes and offer them as *persuasive* precedent to the judge. This sort of situation is not so frequent today.

[1.54] The idea, then, is to follow precedent established by earlier courts, but only those of a court which is higher in one's hierarchy (*stare decisis*). If such a precedent can be found (or adduced from analogous situations), then the court is absolutely bound by that earlier decision. Thus a sort of rigidity is established, which also gives some certainty to the law, otherwise we would be subject to the whims and opinions of individual judges and would never know whether what we were doing was right or not. This is one of the factors which may lead people to complain that at times the law is never flexible enough to accommodate itself to changing times.

New Law [1.56]

[1.55] If there is no legislation on a particular matter, and also no precedent, then the law on that matter is uncertain, and cannot be known until the matter is taken to court and a ruling is made. Sometimes, to establish the law on an issue which is becoming a frequent matter of confusion and concern, a "test case" will be brought: when lawyers see a good opportunity, and funds are available, a case is taken to court, not merely because the particular parties want to settle the matter, but also to establish the law for future reference.

Indigenous Customary Law

[1.56] Indigenous customary law has developed over the thousands of years of occupation of Australia by Aboriginal and Islander peoples of Australia. Evidence is that specific groups have spiritual and physical connections with particular areas of land, which gave rise to well defined rules governing their relationships within the group and between groups and strangers. While customary law has most likely changed over time, there are still groups which operate according to customary law, which they consider meaningful and binding on them.

Some features of Aboriginal customary law are:

- .....no abstract rules separating law from religion or other modes of conduct;
- .....different people know different laws, which are passed on orally;
- .....many laws are secret;
- .....it evolves from custom, or comes from spirits or the Dreaming;
- .....people are judged by relatives, ceremonial leaders and elders or the whole tribe;
- .....it is enforced mostly by relatives or the tribe;
- .....there is no concept of individual ownership; and
- .....the tribe is responsible for the care of the land.

Two principles apply in relation to Aboriginal people and the law introduced at the time of colonisation:

1) .....Aboriginal people are subject to that law in the same way as non-Aboriginal people. They are not a free and independent people who are entitled to any rights or interests other than those created or recognised by the laws of the Commonwealth, States or the Territories or by the common law (*Walker v NSW* (1994) 182 CLR 45 at 48-49; citing *Mabo v Queensland (No 2)* (1992) 107 ALR 1), however,
2) .....there is provision for some recognition by courts of Aboriginal customary law (Law Reform Commission of Australia, *The Recognition of Aboriginal Customary Laws* (1986, AGPS, Canberra)). This has occurred in the criminal law, particularly when courts are sentencing. For example, where an Aboriginal person has been convicted of an offence which is also a tribal offence subject to tribal punishment, courts may in some cases take the tribal punishment into account. Other aspects of customary law have also been given statutory recognition. These include traditional interests in land, items of cultural heritage, traditional marriages for certain purposes and traditional hunting, fishing and gathering rights.

How Does the Law Change?

[1.57] In fact, there is some scope for change in the common law, despite *stare decisis*, as well of course, as the ability of Parliament to change statutes and bring in new ones. First, it will be recalled that the case cited by a lawyer as being applicable to a particular situation must be analogous to the case being decided. This means that a lot of time is spent in court by the lawyers who represent different parties arguing over whether the cases really are analogous. As there are an infinite number of possible variations of any situation, and as times change and statutes are introduced to cover more and more activities, it is surprising how often apparently similar situations are eventually considered by the judges to be different enough in the circumstances to warrant distinguishing the earlier case from the current situation under scrutiny. If one can thus distinguish the cases, then the legal principle(s) established in the earlier case do not bind the court. This results in a gradual and slow development of the law to adapt to a changing society. There is further discussion on the way common law changes below (see [3.56]ff).

Some Basic Principles of Our Legal System

[1.58] English law, which we have inherited in Australia, has several fundamental principles and presumptions which underlie all specific legislation and common law.

Principles of Natural Justice

[1.59] These were formulated in early times by the Greek philosophers, and sought to vest some authority beyond the state, in the very nature of our humanity (if not in a god). These principles underlie the concept of human rights, and so inform such documents as the *United Nations Declaration of Human Rights* and subsequent conventions outlining human rights in more detail, and in procedural law in our country. There are two main principles: first, that no one may be deprived of her or his liberty, livelihood or goods without being given timely notice of the reasons for so doing, and without being given the opportunity to be heard in their own defence, and secondly, that no one may sit in judgment of another who has a vested interest in the outcome of the judgment. It was later recognised that these principles should apply to all citizens regardless of their individual characteristics (see below, Ch 18).

Rule of Law

[1.60] This body of principles establishes two things. First, it says, a person can only be found guilty of a criminal offence that existed at the

time it was allegedly committed: that is, the state cannot create an offence [1.63]
after it has been committed. Secondly, it states that the executive branch
of the government is subject to the law just the same as a citizen is, so that
the citizen is protected from arbitrary action by public officials and
members of Parliament. Further protection from unfair or ill-considered
decisions by administrative bodies has been created by administrative law.

Presumption of Innocence

[1.61] This presumption requires the law to treat any accused person as
innocent until they have been proved guilty (see Ch 14).

Common Law Protection of Human Rights

[1.62] We do not have a Bill of Rights in Australia, and indeed the
United Kingdom has a very basic one, passed in 1688. Most human rights,
such as freedom from arbitrary arrest and imprisonment, freedom of the
press and speech, are protected by the common law as it has developed
over the centuries (see below, Ch 18).

[1.63] These principles are not immutable, however, and can be eroded.
Commentators point to the fact that Parliament may legislate them out of
existence, or that administration of the law may result, even
unintentionally, in debasement of the principles. An example is the often
long period of imprisonment spent by those on remand (awaiting trial for
alleged criminal offences) which, it is argued, erodes the principle that
one may not be jailed without trial, or presumed guilty until proved
innocent. Also, the law of defamation is cited as a way of curtailing free
speech, and it is pointed out that discrimination against people because of
their sex, race, age, or handicap, among other factors, is not prevented by
common law.

■ ■ ■

REFERENCES AND FURTHER READING

Chisholm, R and Nettheim, G, *Understanding Law* (3rd ed, Law Book Co, Sydney, 1988)

Darvall, L, *Medicine Law and Social Change* (Darmouth Publishing Co, UK 1993)

Davies, M, *Asking the Law Question* (Law Book Co, Sydney, 1994)

Derham, D P, Maher, F K H, and Waller, P L, *An Introduction to Law* (8th ed, LBC, Sydney, 2000)

Enright, C, *Studying Law* (Macarthur Press, Sydney, 1991)

Freckelton, I and Petersen, K, *Controversies in Health Law* (The Federation Press, Sydney, 1999)

Harris, J W, *Legal Philosophies* (Butterworths, London, 1980), esp Chs 2, 4, 8, 11

Heilbronn, G, Kovacs, D, Latimer, P, Nielsen, J and Pagone, T, *Introducing the Law* (5th ed, CCH, Sydney, 1996)

Hunter, R, Ingleby, R and Johnstone, R, *Thinking about Law* (Allen & Unwin, Sydney, 1995)

Johnstone, M, *Bioethics: A Nursing Perspective* (3rd ed, W B Saunders/Bailliere Tindall, Sydney, 1999)

Kuhse, H, *Caring: Nurses, Women and Ethics* (Blackwell, Oxford, 1997)

McLean, S, "Law Ethics and Medical Progress: Allies or Adversaries?" (1999) 7 *Journal of Law and Medicine*, p 25

Chapter Two

THE LEGAL STRUCTURE

INTRODUCTION

[2.1] In the Australian legal system, there is a division between the federal courts (those courts which deal with interpretation and application of the federal Constitution and laws made by the federal Parliament), and the State courts (which deal with State Constitutions and State law). The system is outlined in the following paragraphs.

Courts

What is a Court?

[2.2] A court is a gathering, presided over by a judge or other person invested with judicial power, who follows the rules of procedure prescribed for that court, and is in some cases assisted by a jury. Courts are different from tribunals and other dispute-resolution bodies (see [2.44]ff) in that they are independent from the executive government, and judges and magistrates who preside over them have tenure. The judge, or where there is a jury, the judge and jury, exercising different responsibilities as outlined in Chapter 3, determine such matters as:

- whether certain facts have been established;
- whether a person is guilty or not guilty of an offence;
- whether a person is liable or not for harming another;
- where required, the legal obligations and rights of a party or parties;
- the punishment appropriate for criminal or other offences; and
- the interpretation of statutory provisions, the provisions of a will, or of a contract.

A court may make orders, for example, requiring a person to do something, not to do specified things, pay fines, be detained and/or medically assessed, and treated.

Jurisdiction

[2.3] The concept of jurisdiction is central to the court system. It can apply to:

[2.3] 1)..... **geographical jurisdiction**, that is, the geographical district or limits within which the judgment of a court or orders of a court can be enforced or executed. This may be State, Territory or federal jurisdiction; or
2)..... **scope of jurisdiction**, that is, the authority of a court or judge to entertain an action, petition or other proceeding (see below [2.31]); or
3)..... **type of jurisdiction**, that is, whether it is original jurisdiction (initial hearing) or appellate jurisdiction (see below [2.32]).

Geographical Jurisdiction

[2.4] Australia is divided into nine jurisdictions: Federal jurisdiction (covering the whole of Australia), the six States, which have sovereign jurisdiction over State matters, and three Territories have a more limited form of self-governance (the Australian Capital Territory, the Northern Territory and Norfolk Island). State and Territory courts can only deal with people who live within, or events that take place within, that particular State or Territory's boundaries, and orders made by the court will normally be limited to those boundaries. A court may take notice of events that have occurred outside the area of its jurisdiction, but in general a defendant must be within the jurisdiction of the court at the time a writ is served, except in circumstances where leave may be granted to serve the writ out of the jurisdiction. This is generally a matter of discretion for the court, to be exercised in the interests of justice, subject to the rules of the particular court.

[2.5] Where a State (State A) wishes to execute a criminal prosecution against a person who has allegedly committed a crime against that State, but is at the time of prosecution present in another State (State B), the court in State A can apply to the courts of State B for extradition of the accused (power to remove the person from State B and bring that person before a court in State A). State A would have to prove it has a prima facie case against the person. Extradition of a person from one country to another for the purposes of facing trial can also be granted, but this is dependent upon the existence of an extradition treaty between the countries concerned.

Federal Jurisdiction

[2.6] Laws made by the federal government are administered by the federal courts and those State courts invested with federal jurisdiction. Section 71 of the Constitution establishes the High Court as the supreme court of the judicial power of the Commonwealth, and invests federal jurisdiction in such other courts as determined by federal Parliament. The Federal Court was established in 1976 to relieve the workload of the High Court. Many more minor federal matters have been dealt with by State Magistrates Courts in the past, however the Federal Magistrates Court was established in 1999 to deal with these.

[2.7] Another federal court system is the Family Court (see [2.39]ff), established by the *Family Law Act* 1975 (Cth). This is a special court with its own rules and Court of Appeal. Family law matters may originate in the

State or Federal Magistrates Court, or the Family Court, depending on their nature. [2.8]

■■■ FIGURE 2.1

THE FEDERAL COURT SYSTEM OF AUSTRALIA

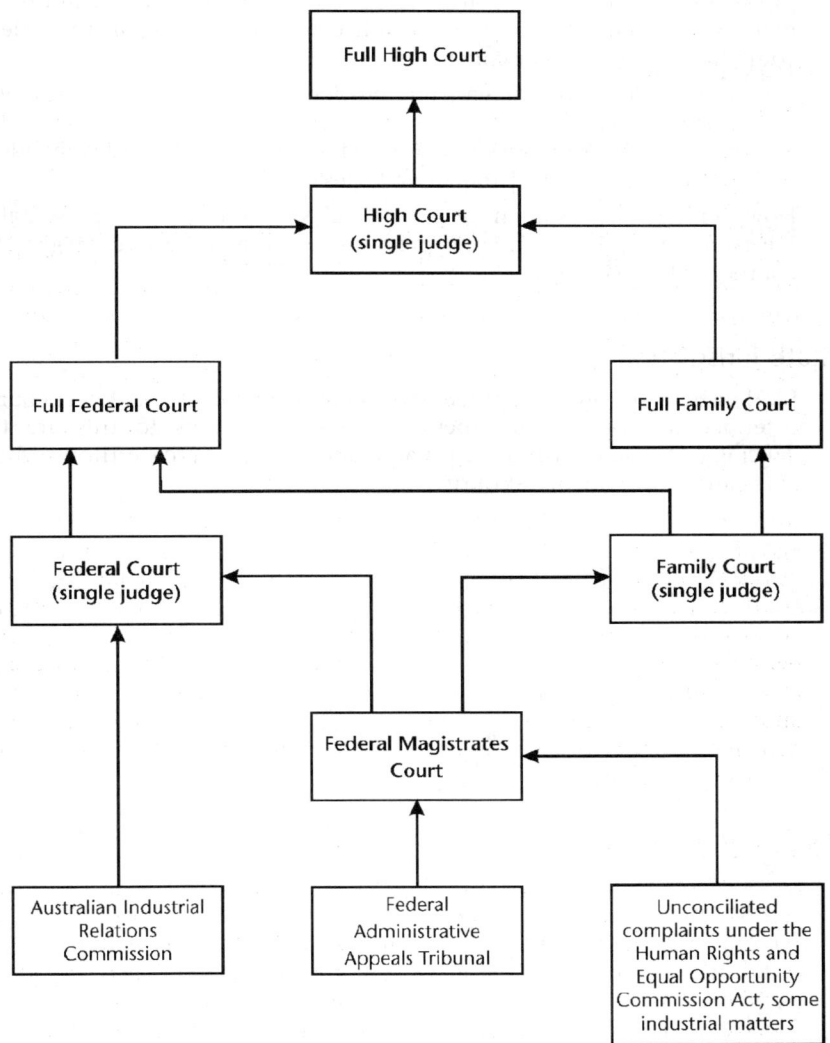

[2.8] Federal matters may be heard in State courts, starting with the Magistrates' Court in some instances. To simplify complex matters that may come before the courts, and to prevent the need for expensive repetition of actions if they are found to have been commenced in the

[2.8] wrong court, in 1988 the Commonwealth and the States enacted legislation "cross-vesting" jurisdiction in some circumstances. This means a State court may hear a federal matter and vice versa, (applying the appropriate law) where it would be either impractical or unjust to refer the matter directly to the correct court. However, the recent High Court case of *Re Wakim; Ex parte McNally* (1999) 165 ALR 270 has held that cross-vesting is invalid to the extent that it purports to confer State jurisdiction on a Federal Court. The Constitution, section 77, limits the matters on which the Commonwealth can confer power on the federal court, and thus the Court concluded:

(a) the federal government *can't* provide for federal courts to deal with state matters;

(b) States and Territories *can* provide for their courts to deal with federal matters, or matters from other States and Territories.

However, the establishment of the Federal Magistrates Court, presumably means that most federal matters previously dealt with by State Magistrates courts will be heard by it.

State Jurisdiction

[2.9] There are generally three tiers of courts in each State: lower courts, intermediate courts and superior courts. Exceptions to this are the Australian Capital Territory, Tasmania and the Northern Territory, where there are no intermediate courts.

FIGURE 2.2

THE STATE AND TERRITORY COURT SYSTEM OF AUSTRALIA

[2.9]

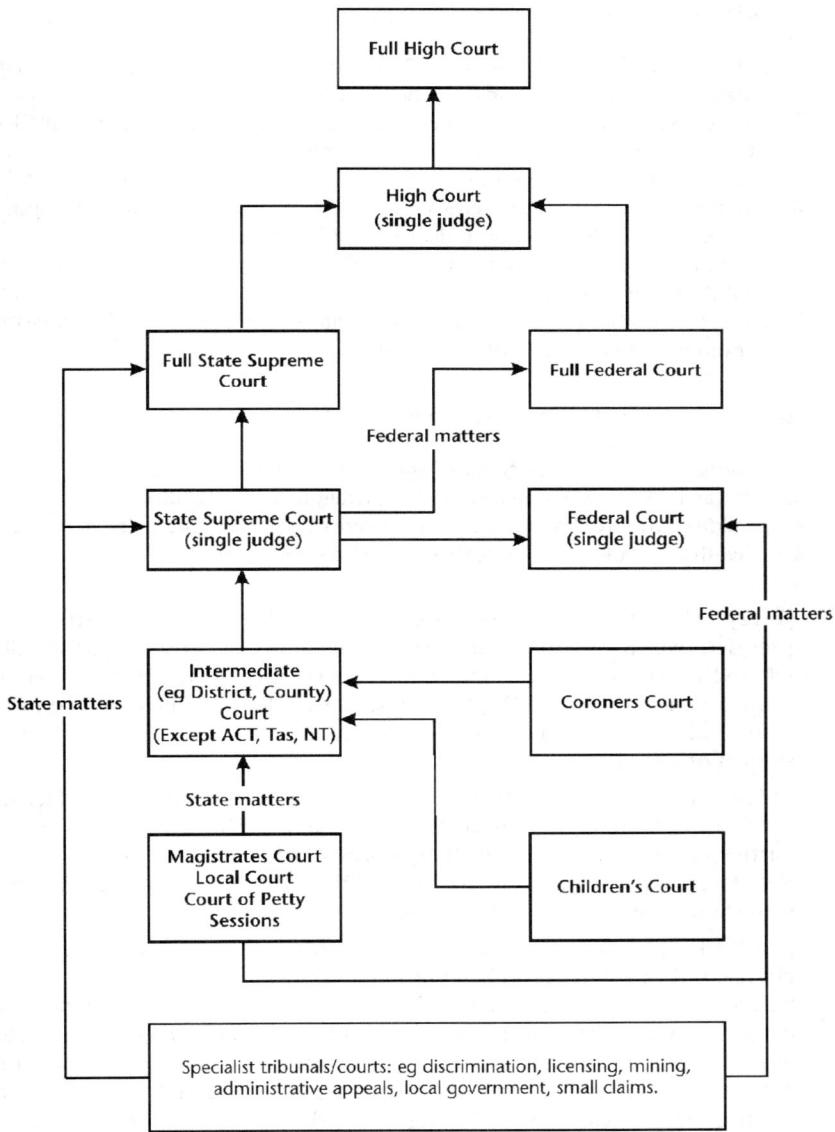

Lower Courts

Magistrates Courts

[2.10] These courts deal with less serious matters. The titles of these courts vary across the States:

- .....in the Australian Capital Territory, Queensland, South Australia and Victoria they are called Magistrates Courts and they deal with both civil and criminal cases;
- .....in New South Wales they are called Local Courts which includes the Small Claims Court and they deal with both civil and criminal cases. Appeals may be made to the District Court or Supreme Court;
- .....in the Northern Territory civil cases are dealt with by Courts of Summary Jurisdiction, while Local Courts deal with minor criminal cases;
- .....in Tasmania Local Courts deal with civil cases, and Courts of Petty Sessions deal with criminal cases; and
- .....in Western Australia Local Courts deal with civil cases, while Courts of Petty Sessions deal with both civil and criminal cases.

[2.11] Matters dealt with at this level are:

- .....minor criminal offences, traffic offences and failure to pay fines;
- .....civil actions below a stipulated sum (generally up to $100,000);
- .....children who are charged with crime, or are neglected (Children's Court); and
- .....investigation of a person's death or fires (Coroner's Court).

[2.12] This court is the lowest court in the hierarchy of courts, and is presided over by a stipendiary (paid) magistrate, or, in some jurisdictions where there is no available magistrate, two justices of the peace. There is a limit on the severity of the fine or sentence it can impose in a criminal case, and on the amount of money involved in a matter which is the subject of a civil case.

[2.13] An important feature of Magistrates Courts is that most decisions therein are summary, that is, they are made without a jury, after both parties involved have made their representations to the magistrate. The decision is usually made at the time of the hearing. There is provision in some States for a jury in some coronial hearings.

[2.14] People charged with an indictable offence (usually a serious charge, but one which has been designated as such), have a right to a trial before a jury if they plead not guilty. However, they must first appear before a magistrate, at a committal hearing. The magistrate decides whether there is a case to answer, that is, whether the evidence against the person is such that a jury *could* (not would) find them guilty of the offence. This is called the finding of a prima facie case. The committal hearing is not a trial, in that, there is no finding of guilt or non-guilt. If there is a finding of a prima facie case, the accused is committed for trial in a higher court. If the finding is that there is no prima facie case, the charge is dismissed and the accused goes free.

Is a "Not Guilty" Verdict Proof of Innocence?

[2.15] The term "non-guilt" is used above to illustrate the fact that a finding of "not guilty" does not mean a person has proved their innocence, but rather the prosecution has not proved their guilt (see *R v Jenkin*; see also [14.83]). The person may well be either innocent or guilty. However the principle has been established at law that a person is presumed innocent until proven guilty.

[2.16] It is also necessary for a jury to determine that a person is guilty as charged. That is, guilty of the precise offence for which they have been charged and no other, even if they did break the law. There are exceptions in several circumstances, such as murder and serious sexual assault, where, if the jury believe the person committed an offence, but is guilty of a lesser offence than that charged (for example, manslaughter, less serious sexual assault) they can find the person guilty of the lesser offence.

[2.17] If a person pleads guilty to an indictable offence at the committal proceeding, and the magistrate is satisfied that the plea is genuine, the accused is committed to the appropriate superior court for sentencing. In some jurisdictions there may still be a trial where the charge is one of murder, to ensure that there is indeed proof of the offence.

[2.18] Where the subject of a hearing is an inquest into a death or an inquiry into a fire under the *Coroner's Act*, the magistrate presiding is designated a coroner, and the court becomes the Coroner's Court (see below, Ch 15). Where a person under 18 years of age is the subject of a hearing under the *Crimes Act* or child welfare legislation, the lower court may become the Children's Court. In both of these cases the hearing will be carried out under the special rules laid down by legislation covering those particular courts.

Appeals from the Magistrates Court

[2.19] Where one of the parties before the magistrate believes that a wrong decision has been made because of an error in the application of the law, or unreasonable findings by the magistrate, given the facts, they may appeal to a higher court, depending on which State they are in and the nature of the matter. Appeals are dealt with in more detail at [2.33].

Intermediate Courts

[2.20] In New South Wales, Queensland, South Australia and Western Australia, these courts are called District Courts; in Victoria they are called County Courts. The Australian Capital Territory, the Northern Territory and Tasmania do not have them at all. These courts hear matters involving more serious crimes, and civil claims involving larger amounts of money than those dealt with by magistrates (the limit to the amount of money differs from State to State). Examples of monetary limits in civil cases in the District Courts are: *District Court Act* 1972 (NSW) $250,000; *District Court Act* 1967 (Qld) $200,000. District Courts hear appeals from the magistrates' courts in some cases.

[2.21] [2.21] Trials in these courts are presided over by a judge, and sometimes also a jury. Where the matter is an appeal from a magistrate's court, or where the law precludes a jury (as it does in most non-criminal claims) a judge will sit alone. Appeals may be made from this court to the next highest court in the hierarchy—the Supreme Court.

Superior Courts

The Supreme Court

[2.22] As its name suggests, this court is the highest court in each State. The most serious crimes (such as murder, rape, serious assault, armed robbery) are dealt with here, after the committal hearing, and also non-criminal matters involving unlimited sums of money. Again, a jury may hear the case, depending on the action being brought before the court.

[2.23] State Supreme Courts are courts of "general jurisdiction", that is, they are not limited in what they can deal with by statute, but can hear any matter at all, except a federal matter or one which is specifically allocated to another court.

[2.24] Appeals from the lower courts and from the findings of Supreme Court trials make up a large amount of work of the Supreme Court. The court may then become the "Court of Appeal" or Full Bench of the Supreme Court, and three Supreme Court judges specially nominated, will hear the case. In rare circumstances an appeal can be made directly to the High Court.

[2.25] Under some circumstances the magistrates' courts and the Supreme Courts are empowered to hear cases coming under federal law, even though they are State courts. Appeals will then go to the Federal Court rather than the State Court of Appeal.

The High Court

[2.26] This is the highest court in Australia. It is now based in Canberra, in its own imposing building, but the judges still go on circuit in some circumstances. The costs of hearings can be reduced by the use of video conference technology. Most of the High Court's work is hearing appeals from the lower courts of the different States, which have worked their way up the hierarchy of courts, sometimes (rarely) all the way from a magistrate's court. In most cases this is the last resort for those involved in a court case (litigants).

[2.27] To limit the workload of the High Court, the *Judiciary Amendment Act (No 2)* was enacted in 1984. This Act gave expression to the principle that in the interests of finality and manageability, an appeal to the High Court following an appeal to a State Court of Appeal should only occur where special leave is granted by the High Court. This is to be where:

■ ..... the appeal involves a question of law of public importance; or

▌.....there are differences of opinion between courts as to the law, and it is in the interests of justice that the High Court hear the matter.

[2.28] The other part of the High Court's work is to hear at first instance cases involving the Constitution (this is the High Court's exclusive jurisdiction), and other federal matters as established by Parliament, for example, matters involving the Commonwealth or an officer of the Commonwealth, and matters where the State governments are the litigants. A jury is not involved (except in very rare cases, for example, treason), and a "Full Bench" consists of seven judges. In many cases only five are required, and in some only one.

The Privy Council

[2.29] The Privy Council sits in England and advises the Monarch. One of its functions is to deal with appeals from the Commonwealth countries. Judges from the House of Lords are appointed to this duty. In the past this was yet a further and higher step one could take either from the High Court on a Federal matter, or the State Courts of Appeal on a State matter, and was thus the highest court in the Australian legal system. Its decisions bound the High Court of Australia and State courts. Over the last 20 years the Privy Council has been gradually removed from the Australian court system. Appeals to the Privy Council from all Australian courts on Commonwealth law were abolished by the *Privy Council (Limitation of Appeals) Act* 1968 (Cth). Appeals to the Privy Council from the High Court on matters of State law were abolished by the *Privy Council (Appeals from the High Court) Act* 1975 (Cth). Finally, appeals to the Privy Council from state courts were abolished by the *Australia Act* 1986 (Cth).

[2.30] This makes the decisions of the Privy Council no longer binding precedent on federal courts, but where that court has no binding Australian precedent a Privy Council decision will be of persuasive precedent, that is, one to which the judge will give great weight in making a decision, with a perceived need to justify not following it.

Scope of Jurisdiction

[2.31] When a court goes beyond its power by, for example, making an order or dealing with an issue it is not empowered to make or deal with, an aggrieved party can seek an order from a higher court to remedy this situation. Such an order may be one of *mandamus* (an order to do something), *certiorari* (a declaration in relation to the wrong) or *prohibition* (an order restraining the lower court from taking specified action).

Type of Jurisdiction

Original Jurisdiction

[2.32] This is exercised when a case first comes to court, and the basic facts and legal issues are determined. It is sometimes called "trial jurisdiction" or "first instance" jurisdiction. Matters are heard for the first time, facts are determined and those involved found guilty or not guilty in a criminal case, or liable or not liable to pay compensation or take other action in a civil case. Witnesses and exhibits are used for this purpose. A decision as to the facts and the legal position of those involved is made, with any appropriate orders authorised by statute being issued by the judge, magistrate or other person presiding.

Appellate Jurisdiction

[2.33] If a decision by the court in its original jurisdiction can be challenged, an appeal from that decision might be made to either a higher court, or to the original court exercising its appellate jurisdiction. For example, the Supreme Court of a State may hear a criminal trial in its original jurisdiction. This would be before one judge and a jury: see the explanation of criminal procedures below. If an appeal is made it will most likely be to the same court, but with three judges (without the original judge or a jury). Appeal courts do *not* hear the matter all over again. They do *not* re-examine the witnesses or exhibits. The parties cannot simply have another go if they think it wasn't done properly the first time. It is considered that the facts have been determined, and the appeal court takes them as established in the lower court. Thus appeals can only be brought by arguing that, for example:

- ..... the court did not have jurisdiction to hear the case;
- ..... the judge in the trial hearing erred as to what the law is;
- ..... the rules of evidence were not properly followed and evidence was wrongly admitted or withheld;
- ..... given the facts that were established, no one could reasonably have come to the decision arrived at by the judge or jury (unreasonable finding); and
- ..... in some cases, fresh evidence has come to light which was not available at the time of trial, and its absence has most likely caused a miscarriage of justice.

Appeal on the Basis of Unreasonable Finding

A nurse in a country town was found guilty of misconduct for her treatment of a patient by the New South Wales Nurses' Registration Board. She appealed to the New South Wales District Court, which found that, while the facts were not in dispute, the Board's finding of misconduct, based on those facts, was unreasonable (*Heathcote v NSW Nurses Board* [13.63]).

[2.34] The appeal court may order a *retrial* (for example, where evidence was wrongly admitted), or quash the verdict or finding (for example, where it considers that the trial judge erred in law and the result is thus wrong at law, or a reasonable judge or jury could not have come to the [2.39] decision arrived at, given the facts).

Rules of the Courts

[2.35] Each court in the hierarchy has its own set of rules, which govern its jurisdiction (matters it may hear), and its procedure. In Australia the decisions of the High Court are binding (that is, courts below it must follow its decisions), and the same principle applies for each of the courts below the High Court. Obviously, the magistrate's decision is binding on no one other than the parties to whom it applies.

Specialist Courts

[2.36] As well as the mainstream system of courts, there are special courts, bodies and tribunals for some areas of law. Examples are:

New South Wales Drug Court

[2.37] The New South Wales Drug Court was established in 1998. It provides a scheme under which drug dependent persons charged with criminal offences which would attract a prison sentence can be diverted into the Drug Court. The Court requires those before it to undertake a program designed to eliminate, or at least reduce their dependency on drugs, and monitors their progress. If they fail to undertake the requirements of their program may be required to serve the prison sentence. If a person comes before a Local or District Court and is assessed as eligible for this program, they can be referred to the Drug Court, which then deals with the matter.

New South Wales Compensation Court

[2.38] This court has the jurisdiction to hear matters arising under the *Workplace Injury Management and Workers Compensation Act* 1988 (NSW). The Act covers workplace injuries for New South Wales employees.

Family Court

[2.39] An example of a federal specialist court is the Family Court, which administers the *Family Law Act* 1975 (Cth), and which deals with dissolution of marriage (formerly called divorce), parenting orders (custody, maintenance and welfare of, and access to, children) in Australia, and the division of matrimonial property during, or after the dissolution of, a marriage. It can also issue injunctions, which are orders stopping someone harming or harassing a family member, or dealing with matrimonial property until appropriate arrangements can be made.

[2.40] The *Family Law Act* 1975 (Cth) is based on the principle that people should be encouraged as far as possible to make their own decisions and to sort out their own problems. Encouragement is given to avoid lawyers and court proceedings, and for couples to come to agreement over such issues as child custody, maintenance arrangements, and property. Its emphasis is on helping, rather than judging. The imposition of court orders is a last resort. Importance is placed on counselling and advising, with, in some applications, the parties being required to undertake this process, and judgment by a court is resorted to only where this is unsuccessful. Priority is given to seeking common ground between the parties and to helping them come to agreement, which the court can then sanction, rather than the imposition of court-generated orders. There are some things the court will not countenance, however, such as agreements that conflict with the interests of any child, and any agreement that is manifestly unjust to any person. More than 80 per cent of matters which arise between couples who divorce are sorted out between them, either with the help of the court or on their own.

[2.41] In keeping with its basic philosophy, the Family Court has less formal procedures than other courts. The judge and lawyers are not robed, the courtrooms are more informal. More importantly, in many matters the Court is given the power to make whatever orders it thinks fit, rather than orders based on strict legal requirements, or precedent. This does not mean that no consideration is given to precedent, but that, where the judge or judges think justice or the interests of the parties (with the welfare of children given paramount consideration) requires it, precedent will not be rigidly followed.

[2.42] The *Family Law Act* 1975 (Cth) was based on the intention that family law matters would be dealt with the least formality necessary and as simply as possible, and that lawyers would be conspicuously absent from proceedings. However, lawyers are now more likely to appear in court as family law legislation has become more voluminous and complex. To some extent this could be explained by the issue of property becoming more complicated and vital, with parties more likely to engage legal advice and fight cases more vigorously. This has led to long delays in finalising matters.

The Federal Magistrates Court

[2.43] The Federal Magistrates Court has recently been established to deal with family law matters among others, and is intended to be even more informal in how it deals with cases. It has a mandate to be "user-friendly" in both its structure and process.

Tribunals

[2.44] Tribunals are other decision-making and dispute-resolution bodies, whose decisions are enforceable at law. They exercise jurisdiction within the administrative law system (which is outlined in more detail below at [2.68]) as administrative decision-makers at first instance, or appeal bodies from such decisions. Examples of tribunals that make first-instance decisions are planning authorities, welfare agencies, licensing bodies, decisions by government departments under freedom of information legislation and Discrimination Commissioners. Tribunals also provide a forum where citizens have an opportunity to challenge decisions which administrators have made, and have them reviewed for fairness and proper procedure. [2.47]

[2.45] It is difficult to generalise about the nature and work of tribunals, as each is a creature of statute, with specified jurisdiction and powers. Some bodies exercise the function of tribunals while not being named as such, for example, health professionals' disciplinary boards, and health complaints commissions. However, some features are common to most tribunals. Like courts, they resolve conflicts, make decisions and review them. Despite their name, they may consist of one or more members.

[2.46] Tribunals differ from courts in the following ways:

- they may not be permanent (that is, they may be established to deal with a particular matter);
- they need not be presided over by the judiciary, but the president at least is usually a judge, magistrate or legal practitioner;
- other members may be lay persons and specialists, their area of specialty depending on the matter before the tribunal;
- they generally are not bound by the rules of evidence;
- the parties may represent themselves, and the tendency is to exclude lawyers unless necessary in the circumstances; and
- precedent is not necessarily followed by all tribunals though most will do so for the sake of convenience and justice.

Jurisdiction of Tribunals

[2.47] Tribunals may have a general jurisdiction, that is, deal with a wide variety of matters, sometimes having specialist Divisions (for example, see discussion of New South Wales below). Apart from Commonwealth and State Ombudsmen, there are tribunals of general jurisdiction in some States and Territories, exercising jurisdiction in a variety of areas. These are:

- the Commonwealth (Administrative Appeals Tribunal);
- Australian Capital Territory (Administrative Appeals Tribunal);
- New South Wales (Administrative Decisions Tribunal); and
- Victoria (Victorian Civil and Administrative Tribunal).

New South Wales and Victorian Tribunals have specialist Divisions (for example, the Equal Opportunity Division). Most States have free-standing specialist Tribunals (for example, the Discrimination, Mental Health, and Guardianship and Management of Property Tribunals in the Australian Capital Territory). See further discussion below.

Types of Tribunals

[2.48] Three are three main types of tribunals; they are adjudicative tribunals, investigative tribunals and review tribunals.

Adjudicative Tribunals

[2.49] These make primary decisions allocating services, providing law enforcement or regulatory functions. Examples are health professionals' disciplinary boards, Mental Health Tribunals or Boards.

Investigative Tribunals

[2.50] These Tribunals include ombudsmen, royal commissions and law enforcement agencies. Examples are the Independent Commission Against Corruption (NSW), National Crimes Authority, Commissioner for Taxation (Cth) and State Directors of Public Prosecutions, and regulatory agencies (for example, the Broadcasting Tribunal). Although, like adjudicative tribunals, they make decisions relating to individuals, they may also have extensive investigative powers and capacity to make decisions with a larger element of policy affecting a wider range of individuals.

Review Tribunals

[2.51] These Tribunals review decisions made in an administrative capacity either by bodies or individuals. These may be decisions relating to social security, licensing of builders, architects etc, which are specified as being reviewable by that particular Tribunal.

[2.52] Generally, a merits review body can take into account facts which it has before it at the time of review. Where facts arise that were not known to the original decision-maker, the review body will generally refer the matter back to the original decision-maker, to review its decision in the light of the new facts, rather than making a substitute decision. An exception is where more efficient and speedy resolution can occur if the review body makes a decision and both parties agree.

Alternative Dispute Resolution (ADR) in Tribunals

[2.53] Most review tribunals require the parties to attempt alternative dispute resolution procedures, such as conciliation, mediation and independent arbitration.

[2.54] It is argued that ADR may be consistent with some of the objectives of administrative review such as improving relations between individual citizens and government departments through informality and the generation of "ownership" of the outcome by the parties contributing to resolution of the dispute. However it may be inconsistent with other objectives, such as improving departmental decision-making and accountability, because of the confidential and individual nature of the proceedings. [2.57]

[2.55] In New South Wales the *Administrative Decisions Tribunal Act* 1997 Schedule 1 (which came into force 1 October 1998) is a model of recent tendencies in the development of the administrative law system. It amalgamates smaller specialist tribunals to create the:

- **Community Services Division** which deals with matters under the *Community Services (Complaints, Reviews and Monitoring) Act* 1993; *Youth & Community Services Act* 1973;
- **Equal Opportunity Division** which hears matters under the *Anti-Discrimination Act* 1977;
- **General Division** which deals with matters under the *Local Government Act*; *Education Reform Act* 1990; *Freedom of Information Act* 1989; *Ombudsman Act* 1974 and *Public Health Act* 1986;
- **Legal Services Division** which deals with matters under the *Conveyancers' Licensing Act* 1995; *Legal Profession Act* 1987; and
- **Occupational Regulation Division**: which deals with matters relating to various occupations such as architects, motor dealers, builders, security personnel, surveyors and veterinary surgeons.

The Tribunal can:

- make an original decision where power to do so is conferred by legislation, or review decisions which are designated as reviewable by legislation;
- affirm, vary, set aside or substitute a reviewable decision with its own, or remit the decision to the original decision-maker with directions or recommendations of the Tribunal;
- decide "what the preferable decision is having regard to the material (any relevant material or any applicable written or unwritten law then before it") (s 63(1));
- give priority to ADR as the method for resolution of disputes, including neutral evaluation and the use of assessors to assist inquiries and assist members in hearings (Ch 2 Part 5). This means that a more non-adversarial approach is being accepted and incorporated into the Tribunal's procedures;
- give force to government policy unless it is contrary to law or will result in an unjust decision in the particular case (s 64);
- exercise its discretion in appointing a legal representative or agent, depending on such matters as the complexity of the case, the parties' capacities, the type of proceedings and any other matter considered relevant; and
- disregard rules of evidence and may inform itself on any matter as it sees fit.

[2.56] The Commonwealth has also established the Commonwealth Administrative Appeals Tribunal to deal with administrative decisions made under Commonwealth Acts.

[2.57] In Queensland the Electoral and Administrative Review Commission *Report on Review of Appeals from Administrative Decisions*

[2.57] (1993) Brisbane (EARC) has proposed an independent Commission for Administrative review.

[2.58] In South Australia the District Court has an Administrative and Disciplinary Division which deals with such matters. The court acts much as a tribunal in that it may bypass rules of evidence, and must act with equity, good conscience and within the substantial merits of the case without regard to technicalities and legal forms except in disciplinary proceedings and proceedings related to contempt of court.

[2.59] In Victoria the *Victorian Civil and Administrative Tribunal Act* 1998 has established the Victorian Civil and Administrative Tribunal ("VCAT"), which amalgamates smaller specialist tribunals, with specialist Divisions and similar procedures to New South Wales. However, the prevalence of legal personnel in VCAT may inculcate the Tribunal with a court-like culture, thus undermining the traditional rationale for the creation of tribunals in the first place, namely, to provide a cheap, quick and informal alternative to litigation in the courts.

[2.60] In Western Australia the fourth Report on Commission on Government of WA (1996 Report No 4) recommended the creation of a Western Australian Administrative Review Tribunal. It recommended that the Tribunal should start from the position that every administrative decision should be reviewable unless specifically exempted by legislation.

Specialist Tribunals

[2.61] Examples of such tribunals are the Social Security Appeals Tribunal, Equal Opportunity or Anti-discrimination Tribunals and Commissions.

The Social Security Appeals Tribunal

[2.62] This Tribunal was set up as an ad hoc tribunal in 1975, and it was intended that it would be taken over by the Administrative Appeals Tribunal, but it still remains as a body of appeal from a decision regarding social security payments. It can only make recommendations to the Director of Social Security, who makes the final decision. However, this decision can be the subject of an appeal to the Administrative Appeals Tribunal.

Equal Opportunity or Anti-discrimination Tribunals

[2.63] These are attached to Anti-discrimination Boards or Commissions, which exist in all jurisdictions. They hear complaints under those States' anti-discrimination legislation, and determine compensatory action which they recommend. Their determinations are generally enforceable, but if they are not, the party concerned may take the determination to court to have it enforced. The other party may also challenge the determination in court.

Commissions [2.69]

[2.64] These generally have a wider mandate than other tribunals and may include among their activities the carrying out of research, education programs, conciliation and arbitration of disputes, and scrutiny of legislation and government policy.

Examples include Health Care Complaint Commissions, the Human Rights and Equal Opportunity Commission and the Australian Industrial Relations Commission.

Health Care Complaints Commissions

[2.65] These Commissions exist in some States (see for example, the Health Services Commission of Victoria and the Health Rights Commission of Queensland). These bodies have powers to receive complaints about health care, and carry out such processes as investigation, mediation, conciliation of a complaint, determinations in some circumstances, or reference to professional disciplinary bodies. They are described in more detail in Chapter 18.

Human Rights and Equal Opportunity Commission

[2.66] This Commission is charged with the above responsibilities in dealing with the promotion and protection of human rights. It is dealt with in more detail in Chapter 18.

Australian Industrial Relations Commission

[2.67] The Australian Industrial Relations Commission has a fairly narrow (but complex) mandate which concerns the conciliation and arbitration of industrial disputes, and the registration of industrial awards. This is explained in more detail in Chapter 11.

Administrative Law

[2.68] A rapidly increasing amount of decision-making that is the government's responsibility has been delegated to administrators. Examples have been given above, including decision-makers with quasi-judicial power such as health professionals' registration boards. A body of law has been developed by which the decisions of administrators may be regulated and subjected to the scrutiny of a court or tribunal as described above. The court or tribunal may reverse the effect of abuse, misuse, or mistake in the making of decisions, which may have an enormous effect on the lives of individuals.

What is Quasi-judicial Power?

[2.69] Quasi-judicial power is described as "executive powers or functions which involve the exercise of discretion and the making of a decision in a judicial manner; for example where a Minister makes an

[2.69] order after consideration of the findings of an inquiry which involves the hearing of evidence" (*Osborn's Concise Law Dictionary* (1983)).

[2.70] Such decisions may involve penalties, demotion, reprimand, or other disciplinary action. See below, Ch 13, where the disciplinary powers of registration boards is discussed. Further examples of legislation granting such powers are social security legislation which gives the Director of Social Welfare the power to make decisions regarding allocation of social welfare benefits, and Licensing Boards which decide on the giving or withdrawal of liquor licences.

[2.71] In his Introduction to Flick (1983), J Daryl Davies pointed out that Article 14 of the *International Covenant on Civil and Political Rights*, which is incorporated in the Schedule of the *Human Rights and Equal Opportunity Commission Act* 1986 (Cth), ensures that "everyone is entitled to a fair and impartial hearing within a reasonable time by an independent and impartial tribunal by law", and goes on to argue: "This article requires review on the merits. It is not satisfied by procedures . . . which permit an examination only of the technical legality and not of the substantial correctness or propriety of a decision or action."

[2.72] Administrative law is aimed at remedying this problem, providing for the review of decisions of administrators on their merits. Complaints may be that actions taken or decisions made are:

- .....contrary to law;
- .....not in accordance with the rule of law (see [1.60]);
- .....carried out for an improper purpose or for improperly stated reasons; and
- .....made on the basis of mistake of law or fact.

[2.73] There are various means for the questioning of these decisions.

Judicial Review

[2.74] The law has broadened to deal with many types of administrative decisions which it formerly would not have dealt with. These include decisions by a State Governor, the Ministers, and price fixing bodies, as well as individuals and bodies acting under governmental authority. These decisions can be reviewed by courts where there is no specific legislative provision for review by a tribunal. Decisions by federal decision-makers not covered by specific provisions are covered under the *Administrative Decisions (Judicial Review) Act* 1977 (Cth), the *Administrative Decisions (Judicial Review) Act* 1989 (ACT), the *Judicial Review Act* 1991 (Qld), and the *Administrative Review Act* 1978 (Vic).

[2.75] In contrast to tribunals, the court cannot consider the merits of a decision itself—that is, it cannot determine whether the actual decision was right or wrong, good or bad. It can only consider whether the process of making the decision was correct—whether, for example, the rules of natural justice were followed, or whether an error of law was made. The *Administrative Decisions (Judicial Review) Act* 1977 (Cth) was enacted to simplify and clarify the grounds and the remedies for judicial review, thereby streamlining access to the courts and review of administrative [2.79] decisions by them. The grounds for review and remedies under the Act are limited, however, to questions of law.

Orders a Court can Make in Reviewing Administrative Decisions

[2.76] A court in response to an application for review of an administrative decision can make the following orders:

- **A declaration that a decision is wrong** (for example, through error of law or improper procedure by the decision-maker);
- **Injunction:** an order to do something, or more commonly, not to do it. This may be a temporary order where a further hearing into the matter is required, to suspend activities to prevent possible injustice;
- **Mandamus:** an order requiring a body or person to perform a public duty (for example, where action is specified in legislation, but the decision-maker has failed to carry it out);
- **Certiorari:** an order applying to a body having legal authority, requiring it to set aside a decision it has made; and
- **Prohibition:** an order to stop proceedings because the court holds they are in breach of natural justice or subject to error at law.

The Ombudsman

[2.77] There are State, Territory and Federal Ombudsmen. The Ombudsman is a channel for complaint by individuals about the conduct of government departments and prescribed authorities. This may involve investigating practices or decisions by individuals in those departments and authorities, and results in a report, recommending appropriate action if required. The Ombudsman cannot enforce such action, but if it is not carried out, this can be the subject of an adverse report to the Premier of the State, for State matters or the Prime Minister, for federal matters.

Administrative Appeals Tribunal

[2.78] This Tribunal hears complaints from decisions made by federal Ministers or officers of prescribed Commonwealth bodies. The Tribunal is informal and does not have to adhere to the rules of evidence. Health carers can, in some cases, appeal to this body from decisions relating to registration and practice made by nursing registration bodies (see below, Ch 13).

[2.79] Unlike the courts, the Administrative Appeals Tribunal *can* review decisions on their merits, and can therefore review government and administrative policy. It can substitute its own decision. Recently, the Federal Court established that the Administrative Appeals Tribunal is not bound to follow ministerial policy, and can determine whether a decision was correct or preferable based on the demands of justice. It can be seen

[2.79] that this development is an extensive (and controversial) one in the growth of control of administrative decision-making (*Re Becker and Minister for Immigration and Ethnic Affairs* (1977) 32 FLR 469). See also Mason, "Administrative Review: The Experience of the First 12 Years" (1989) 18 *FL Rev* 122.

The English Courts

[2.80] The House of Lords is the ultimate English law-making body, presided over by judges who are members of the House of Lords. Australian courts were bound by its decisions failing a decision of the Privy Council until appeals to the Privy Council were abolished (see [2.29]–[2.30]). Today it is of persuasive precedent only, although Australian courts will generally follow its decisions if there is no Australian precedent.

[2.81] Another important court in England, and one which is often quoted in our courts, is the English Court of Appeal, a court directly inferior to the House of Lords. Its decisions are treated with great respect in our courts, because of the eminent judges who preside over it.

[2.82] These courts are mentioned because much of the law regarding health carers, particularly negligence law, has been developed through these two courts, and so they are quite frequently referred to in discussions of the law.

Judicial Decisions from Other Countries

[2.83] The court systems of the United States, Canada, New Zealand and other common law countries are too complex to outline here. They have a court hierarchy which is roughly similar to ours, and which are a source of many decisions on medical matters. These decisions may be offered as persuasive arguments before our courts where the matter has not been decided in Australia or the United Kingdom.

Law Reporting

[2.84] As precedent is so important in the legal system, reporting of cases accurately and easy reference to them is crucial. Official reports of appeal cases are reported by recognised bodies (which may include law book publishers), and series of reports covering each court level in each jurisdiction are published. Cases are cited by giving, after the name of a case, the year of volume (square brackets) or volume number (round brackets), the report series and the page number. A list of the most commonly cited series of reports is given in Appendix 1. An excellent tool for looking up law reports is the Appendix "Using the Law Library" in Derham et al (2000).

Australia

Federal Courts

[2.85] Cases from the High Court and formerly the Privy Council deciding matters from Australia are reported in the *Commonwealth Law Reports* (CLR), and another series called the *Australian Law Reports* (ALR). Thus the important High Court case on consent to medical treatment of *Rogers v Whitaker* which is to be found in volume 109 of the *Australian Law Reports* at page 625, and was reported in the year 1992, is cited *Rogers v Whitaker* (1992) 109 ALR 625 (see [4.98]). Decisions from the federal courts are reported in the *Federal Law Reports* (FLR) and the *Federal Court Reports* (FCR) and are similarly cited.

State Courts

[2.86] Reports of State cases appear in series named for the State: see Appendix 1. For example New South Wales Court of Appeal cases are reported as the NSWLR (*New South Wales Law Reports*). As these reports are bound by the year of the report, the identifier of the volume is the year, and this appears in square brackets. Thus, the case of *Albrighton v Royal Prince Alfred Hospital*, which deals with medical negligence, the judgment of which is reported in the second of the 1980 volumes of the *New South Wales Law Reports* at page 542, is cited as *Albrighton v Royal Prince Alfred Hospital* [1980] 2 NSWLR 542. This case is discussed at [6.37].

■ ■ ■

REFERENCES AND FURTHER READING

Ardagh, A, *Administrative Law* (3rd ed, Butterworths student companions series, Butterworths, Sydney, 1997)

Derham, D P, Maher, F K H and Waller, P L, *An Introduction to Law* (8th ed, LBC, Sydney, 2000)

Flick, G, *Federal Administrative Law* (Law Book Co, Sydney, 1983)

Flick, G, *Natural Justice* (2nd ed, Butterworths, Sydney, 1984)

Heilbronn, G, Kovacs, D, Latimer, P, Nielsen, J and Pagone, T, *Introducing the Law* (5th ed, CCH, Sydney, 1996)

Morris, G, Cook, C, Creyke, R, Geddes, R, *Laying Down the Law* (3rd ed, Butterworths, Sydney, 1992)

Osborn's Concise Law Dictionary (7th ed, Sweet & Maxwell, London, 1983)

Streets, S, *Administrative Law* (2nd ed, Butterworths casebook companions series, Butterworths, Sydney, 2000)

Chapter Three

THE LEGAL PROCESS

INTRODUCTION

[3.1] The legal system (that is the operation of lawyers, courts and police) is concerned with two main processes. The first is that of resolving disputes, whether they are between the State and a citizen or citizens, or between two individuals. It is also concerned with prosecuting offences. The second is concerned with establishing a person's status or rights and obligations.

Dispute Resolution

Civil or Criminal Action?

[3.2] Disputes at law arise when a person or body claims that another has done them a wrong. Criminal actions are instigated by the Crown (in the guise of the State, through the police) claiming a person has committed a wrong against it by committing a crime. A civil action is instigated by an individual, who claims that another person has wronged (harmed) them, either physically, mentally or economically, or is likely to cause such harm by their proposed actions.

[3.3] Criminal cases are prosecuted by the State. They are officially designated, for example, *R v Bloggs* (pronounced "the Queen and Bloggs"). If the prosecution is successful, the convicted person is punished. The Crown is not interested in compensating the victim in these cases, only in punishing the offender. However more attention is being paid to victims by the development of criminal injuries compensation legislation in the States and Territories, which provides the opportunity for victims of crime to apply to the appropriate court or tribunal for compensation for their injuries.[1] Jurisdictions throughout Australia are also allowing "victim impact statements" by the victims of crime at the time of sentencing a person convicted of an offence involving personal injury. The court may take the effects of the crime on the victim into account when considering

---

[1] *Criminal Injuries Compensation Act* 1983 (ACT); *Criminal Injuries Compensation Act* 1967 (NSW); *Crimes Compensation Act* 1967 (NT); *Criminal Code Act* 1899 (Qld), Ch LXVA; *Criminal Injuries Compensation Act* 1978 (SA); *Criminal Injuries Compensation Act* 1976 (Tas); *Criminal Injuries Compensation Act* 1972 (Vic); *Criminal Injuries Compensation Act* 1985 (WA).

[3.3] the sentence, and may require reparation by the offender where appropriate. For a recent discussion see the Community Law Reform Committee of the Australian Capital Territory, *Report No 6: Victims of Crime* (Australian Capital Territory Government Printer, Canberra, 1993).

[3.4] Civil cases, on the other hand are brought about mainly by:

- ..... one person against another, claiming damage wrongfully inflicted on her or him, or a debt owing to her or him, and seeking compensation from that person. In this type of case the first person is suing (not prosecuting) the other. The person suing is called the *plaintiff*, the person being sued is called the *defendant*; or
- ..... a person seeking endorsement of a claim to certain rights and privileges as against another. That person is called an *applicant* to the court and any person or body opposing the claim is called the *respondent*.

(The term "person" in law includes the plural, and refers to individuals, male or female, so long as they are born alive, and also to corporations and statutory bodies. Often the word "party" is used to refer to someone involved in a legal action.)

[3.5] The Crown's only interest here, through the judges, is that the contest in court is carried out according to the established procedure and rules of evidence; it acts as a kind of referee in both types of case (the judges of course have the added role of interpreting the law and determining the facts). Civil cases are designated, for example, *Smith v Jones* (pronounced "Smith and Jones") the name of the plaintiff or applicant first, followed by that of the defendant or respondent.

Appeals

[3.6] As mentioned in previous chapters, one can often appeal from an adverse judgment, but not simply because one does not like it. It must be shown that a judge or magistrate made a legal mistake in the way the case was conducted, or in the way the jury was instructed, or that the trial was for some reason carried out in such a way that it was unjust or unfair to the person appealing (appellant). The case would then be designated with the appellant's name first and the name of the defendant (who is now called the respondent) second. For example, if the defendants in the hypothetical cases cited above appealed, they would become the appellants, and the prosecutor and plaintiff respectively would become the respondents (*Bloggs v The Queen* and *Jones v Smith*).

[3.7] Court action, or litigation, is the last resort for actions other than criminal ones. The prospective expense to those concerned, as well as to the State, means that where a dispute arises those involved will attempt to resolve it before an approach to the courts is made. Negotiations are therefore made under the shadow of the law, so to speak, with the possibility of court action ever present. This strengthens the hand of whoever has the law clearly on their side, but where the law is unclear, those involved may feel that they are dragged into litigation because of someone else hoping to chance their luck by having a favourable court judgment. The threat of expensive litigation can be used as a bluff, to frighten people into compliance: for example, threats to sue another in defamation if they disclose certain information, when in fact one would not really have a case. This may prevent that person from disclosing the information out of fear of being dragged through the courts. Using the threat of legal action as a response to a legitimate disclosure, of incompetence or dangerous practices by a colleague, or hospital management, or of sexual harassment by another at work, may frighten a person into silence (see Chapter 7 for an outline of the law regarding disclosure of information).

[3.8] In fact, most issues between disputants at law are resolved out of court. No more than about three per cent of all claims for compensation for alleged negligence end up in court. The other 90-odd per cent are abandoned or settled by negotiation, called "out-of-court settlement". Insurance companies, of course, prefer to settle claims out of court, and put great emphasis on doing so. One must also consider that many possible actions are never even started. It is estimated by writers that over 30 per cent of injuries and deaths on the roads go uncompensated because no action is commenced, either through insurance companies or an action in negligence. See also the Interim Report of the Review of Professional Indemnity Arrangements for Health Care Professionals, *Compensation and Professional Health Indemnity in Health Care* (AGPS, Canberra, 1994).

[3.9] Most legal disputes are resolved by the parties themselves, through negotiation by their lawyers, with avoidance of court action being a high priority. Such negotiations are usually classified as "without prejudice", meaning that one party to the dispute will not be able to rely on what is contained in the documents as an admission of fault by the other party if they refuse an offer to pay damages and decide to go to court. There is always the threat of one party taking the other to court if the matter is not resolved, and both parties have in mind the possible outcome if the matter does go to court.

Cost of Legal Action

[3.10] Legal advice is not cheap. In Australia a client must pay for a lawyer's advice and other legal expenses in a criminal matter and a family law matter, whatever the outcome. The exception is where a party is eligible for, and is granted, legal aid, which is subject to a person's income and the likelihood of success. In civil matters the general principle is that the "loser" pays their own plus the "winner's" costs. This is a deterrent to legal action in many cases, and is a reason for the dearth of matters which go to court. In the United States lawyers operate on the principle of the contingency fee, which means that they are only paid if they win the case, and payment is a proportion of the compensation paid to their client. An indirect result of this principle is that people are more likely to sue, knowing they have nothing (financially) to lose. Some Australian jurisdictions are adopting various versions of the contingency fee principle.

Functions of the Legal Dramatis Personae

Solicitors

[3.11] Solicitors can be likened in the legal profession to the general practitioner in the medical profession. The solicitor is the person to whom one takes a problem in the first instance. The solicitor determines whether it is in fact one that can be solved by the legal profession, and what action to advise the client to take. If litigation (taking the matter to court) is advised, the matter is referred to a barrister who is like the medical specialist, expert in the particular matter and in presenting it in court.

Barristers

[3.12] Once the solicitor refers a client to a barrister, the barrister prepares all the arguments available in favour of the client. The other party, of course, also has a barrister arguing for it. When appearing in court barristers are called counsel. If one recalls that the modern law case developed out of the trial by battle, where the parties originally fought each other to see who would win the point, and later paid professional fighters to go in and fight for them, one can understand the verbal battle that takes place in our courtrooms. The decision makers decide the winner.

[3.13] Barristers on both sides may attempt to negotiate a settlement (acting under the instructions of their prospective clients), even while the matter is in court, for at any time in the progress of legal action, right up to the court judgment, the parties may come to an agreement. It may be that at a particular point in the trial a barrister may consider it in her or his client's best interest to accept an offer from the other side, and will advise the client accordingly. The decision to do so, however, is up to the client.

The Jury

[3.14] Juries have the task of listening to witnesses and deciding on the facts presented to them as to what must have actually happened. They are guided by the judge, who explains the law to them. For example, if a person is accused of murder, the judge will tell the jury just what constitutes murder at law (for example, what intention the accused must have had) and the jury then decides whether the actions of the accused actually did amount to that legal definition.

The Judge

[3.15] A judge sitting with a jury has the task of ensuring that the person who is complained against has a "fair" trial as prescribed by procedural law and thus that procedural and evidential rules are complied with. Judges rule on what evidence can be admitted and on any other legal questions which arise, including the instructing of the jury as to their tasks. A judge sitting alone, which happens in most civil cases, must act as both judge and jury. In a criminal case, where the defendant has been found guilty by the jury, the judge determines the sentence to be imposed.

Proof

The Burden of Proof

[3.16] A very important fact to keep in mind is that the party bringing the action has the burden of proving its case. This means that defendants or respondents do not have to prove their innocence. They need only raise a doubt as to the validity of the case brought by the applicant/plaintiff. Where that doubt exists, the court must find in the defendant's favour.

The Standard of Proof

[3.17] In criminal cases the prosecution has to convince the jury *beyond a reasonable doubt* that the accused is guilty. This means that unless the prosecution has left no reasonable doubt in the jury's mind as to the accused's guilt, despite the accused's attempts to create that doubt, they must acquit. In a civil case the burden on the plaintiff or applicant amounts to convincing the court *on the balance of probabilities*. This is not as difficult as the standard of proof for a criminal case. The court must find a defendant not liable unless the plaintiff has proved her or his case to that standard.

Outline of a Criminal Action

[3.18] The following main steps of a criminal and civil action are necessarily sketchy and general. They will, it is hoped, give at least a basic idea of the legal process.

Step 1	Alleged criminal behaviour takes place.
Step 2	It is reported to the police if they are not present at the scene.
Step 3	The police arrest the suspect (after obtaining a warrant from a magistrate where that is required). States vary on how much evidence the police must have. Some States require that they have enough evidence to reasonably believe the person committed the crime. Others allow arrest for a limited amount of time before police are prepared to lay charges. Once arrested a person is referred to as "the accused".

[3.18]

Step 4	The accused may be released on bail, which is an agreement or "recognisance" to appear in court when required, or may be remanded in custody, in which case he or she must be brought before a magistrate as soon as practicable. The magistrate may allow bail in the latter case. Where bail is allowed a surety may be required and conditions may be placed on the accused to ensure he or she will turn up for trial. A surety is a sum of money pledged on failure to appear for trial, or a person who undertakes the appearance in court of another (on pain of forfeiture of a sum of money).

Summary Offence

[3.19] Summary offences are generally minor offences (such as petty theft, drunkenness or not paying a fine), and are to be tried summarily (that is, on the spot, by a magistrate without a jury). Summary offences are those which are defined in the legislation as such.

Step 5	The accused (now also called the defendant) appears in a magistrate's court and pleads either guilty or not guilty. If the plea is guilty, sentence is passed and the matter concluded. If the plea is not guilty—
Step 6	The prosecution presents evidence. Each witness for the prosecution is: ■ ..... "examined" by the prosecution (that is, led through their evidence); ■ ..... cross-examined by the defence to test their evidence; ■ ..... re-examined by the prosecution to reinforce their contribution to the case and repair any "damage" done to their testimony by cross-examination.
Step 7	The defence presents its evidence in a similar way.
Step 8	The magistrate makes a decision as to a verdict—guilty or not guilty. If not guilty, the accused is released and the matter concluded; if guilty, he or she is the subject of some form of penalty in the light of the maximum penalty set by law and any submissions made to the magistrate on that matter by either party.
Step 9	An appeal may be made to a higher court by either party.

Indictable Offence

[3.20] Indictable offences are generally serious offences (such as serious assault, murder or sexual assault), and the accused is entitled to trial by judge and jury unless he or she seeks to have a trial without a jury. Indictable offences are defined in the legislation.

Step 5	The accused appears in a magistrate's court for committal hearing, and pleads guilty or not guilty. If the plea is guilty, the accused is committed to the appropriate court for sentencing.
Step 6	If the plea is not guilty, the prosecution presents its evidence as above.
Step 7	The defence is not required to present any evidence at this stage.

Step 8	The magistrate decides whether there is enough evidence on which a jury could find the defendant guilty (a prima facie case). If not, the case is dismissed and the defendant goes free. If the magistrate does find a prima facie case, the defendant is committed for trial by judge and jury. Depending on the seriousness of the offence, this may be in an intermediate court in those States which have them or the Supreme Court.	[3.21]
Step 9	The accused appears before judge and jury for trial and pleads. If the plea is guilty, and the judge is satisfied that the defendant is genuine and mentally competent to so plead, sentence is passed, and the case concluded. If the plea is one of not guilty both prosecution and defence cases are presented by examination of witnesses and exhibits as before, only this time before a jury who are guided in matters of law by a judge, and who must decide on the facts presented whether the offence the accused is charged with amounted to a crime or not. The jury bring in their verdict of guilty or not guilty which must be accepted by the judge, whose task then is to either release the accused, if not guilty, or to pronounce sentence. The maximum punishment for any particular offence is set by the legislation, but the judge has some discretion within that limit to impose anything from a token punishment (suspended sentence) to the maximum provided by the legislation. In making this decision the judge considers arguments on behalf of the parties as to what the sentence should be.	
Step 10	An appeal may be made to a higher court by either party.	

Outline of a Civil Action

[3.21] A civil action is similar to a criminal one in many ways, but has some significant differences:

Step 1	Harm occurs to a person (the plaintiff) or that person's property.
Step 2	The plaintiff sends the other party a letter of demand, stating the party's case and demands. If the claim is not met by the other person, or a settlement not negotiated, the plaintiff sends a letter stating that if there is no resolution within a set time, the matter will be taken to court.
Step 3	The plaintiff issues, through the appropriate court, a writ (a claim to have been wronged and a command to appear in court to answer the allegations), along with a statement of claim (a detailed list of allegations and statement of compensation claimed). The wrong must be one recognised by law and named accordingly (for example, battery, negligence: see below, Chs 4 and 6).
Step 4	The person accused (the defendant) has a set period of time (for example, 30 days) to lodge a statement of defence with the court, setting out an answer to the claim. The defendant may in fact make a counter-claim, alleging that he or she has been harmed by the plaintiff; this must be duly answered by the plaintiff in a similar way.

[3.21]

Step 5	Either party may seek further information through processes called "interrogatories" and "discovery" and be required, under certain circumstances, to provide the other side with answers to questions and documents.
	At any stage the defendant may offer the plaintiff a settlement—that is, a sum less than that demanded (or of course the full amount) and the matter may be resolved by the plaintiff accepting it (settlement out of court). This option may be very tempting to the plaintiff, as it relieves the hardship and anxiety associated with this sort of case, and, as explained above, happens in most cases.
Step 6	If both parties intend to proceed, they notify the court when they are ready and set a date for the hearing. Legislation has provided that juries rarely appear in civil cases, especially those concerning negligence, so that the case is usually before a judge alone.
Step 7	Evidence is presented in a similar way as that described for criminal trials. A decision is made and an award of compensation is ordered if the plaintiff's case is successful.
Step 8	A party may be ordered to pay the other's legal costs by the judge.
Step 9	An appeal may be made by either party to a higher court.

Applications

[3.22] At common law and under some statutes, a person may apply to the appropriate court for a ruling in that person's favour on particular matters. In these cases the person bringing the application is the applicant, and anyone opposing it is the respondent. Some examples of applications are:

- ..... Under statutory law a person brings an application for dissolution of marriage (contrary to popular terminology, that person does not sue for divorce!), custody of children, property distribution on dissolution and declaration of property interests etc, under the *Family Law Act* 1975 (Cth).
- ..... A person also applies to have a guardian appointed for certain people under State legislation (see [5.84]ff).
- ..... A person can also apply for an injunction from the court, in some circumstances, which is an order of a court by which a party to an action is ordered either to refrain from doing an act (restrictive injunction), or to carry out an act (mandatory injunction). The court must be satisfied that the applicant would suffer harm unjustly if the injunction is not issued, and that various rules regarding the petitioner's eligibility to apply, and the worthiness of the action are met (for an example see [1.84]ff).

[3.23] A person can apply for a declaration, in some circumstances. A declaration is:

- ..... a formal statement by a court intending to create, assert, preserve or testify to a right of a person; or
- ..... a finding on a question of law.

[3.24] An example of an application for a declaration is section 78 of the *Family Law Act* 1975 (Cth), where a party to a marriage can seek a declaration from the Family Court in relation to their property rights.

Legal Reasoning

[3.25] The law is given to us by statute or precedent, and we interpret it for ourselves in everyday life. However where there is a dispute as to the meaning of the law, or how it is to be applied, the courts use legal reasoning to come to an answer. It is important to remember that:

- ..... Legal reasoning is not the same as common sense, although common sense is invoked as the approach to use in some circumstances.
- ..... Legal reasoning does not necessarily aim at what we would consider morally just or fair. An example of this is where the court found that a doctor who did not bother to examine a man who was desperately ill was found not liable in negligence despite the fact that the man later died of arsenic poisoning. One might think that justice would decree the doctor be somehow found responsible, but the court found that he did not fulfil all the requirements for being found liable in negligence (see [6.11]; *Barnett v Chelsea and Kensington Hospital Management Committee* [1969] 1 QB 428, discussed below, Ch 6 esp [6.159]). One could argue, of course, that this is justice according to law.

[3.26] How, then, do courts reason? This question is addressed in examining statutory interpretation and the use of precedent separately.

Statutory Interpretation

[3.27] As mentioned in Chapter 1, statutory provisions are subject to the same problems as all language: they are not always absolutely clear. Words may be unclear, vague or ambiguous. One provision of an Act may appear to contradict another, or, despite clear language, appear ambiguous in its overall construction.

[3.28] Courts, in interpreting statutes, are guided by rules, which have been developed by statute or common law. Thus we have Acts Interpretation Acts (both State and federal), which set out some rules as to how to interpret words (for example, the meaning of "ten days"; does it include weekends and/or the day on which the action takes place? When does the period finish—5 pm?, midnight?). We also have some common law principles which apply to terms in general, or specific terms in specific statutes.

Rule 1: Serve the Object and Purpose of the Act

[3.29] In the Australian Capital Territory, New South Wales, South Australia, Victoria and Western Australia the Interpretation Acts have a

[3.29] dominant and mandatory rule of interpretation. The court must, in determining the meaning of a word, consider the purpose of the Act.[2]

The other States have a common law rule, the "purpose" or "mischief" rule. The purpose of an Act is the purpose Parliament had in bringing about the Act, and is generally discernible in the Second Reading Speech given by the Minister who introduces the Act into Parliament, but may also require consideration of other sources, such as documentation of Parliamentary debates, Parliamentary Committee reports, or Law Reform Commission reports. It is up to the discretion of the court what materials (given they are not prohibited from consulting them) they will use. The "mischief rule" is derived from *Heydon's Case* (1584) 3 Co Rep 7; 76 ER 637. This ancient case has been endorsed repeatedly. It stated that the courts should, when interpreting a statutory provision, consider:

1)......what the common law was before the Act was passed;
2)......what the mischief or defect was for which the common law did not provide;
3)......what remedy Parliament resolved was required; and
4)......the "true reason" for the remedy.

The court's answer is to "suppress subtle inventions and invasions of the mischief".

[3.30] This is not the end of the story; there may be further problems in determining the meaning of a statutory provision. Other maxims have been developed which courts may use to help with interpretation. They do not have any particular order, and do not have the mandatory effect of the purposive rule, but should be considered in the light of the purpose rule.

[3.31] An exception to this rule occurs where the words used are specifically defined, either in the applicable Interpretation Act, or in the specific Act itself. Most Acts have an interpretation section at the beginning, or in a "dictionary" at the end, where key words are defined specifically for that Act. This, of course, is the first place to look in determining a word's meaning.

Rule 2: The Literal Rule

[3.32] Another ancient, but time-honoured rule, is that, in the absence of specific provision to the contrary, words are to be given their ordinary everyday meaning. This applies unless, they are specific legal terms, when they must be given their legal meaning, for example, the word "negligence" has a common meaning which is much more restrictive in its legal sense (see below, Ch 6); the word "invitee" has a special meaning in law (see below, Ch 12), as does "publication" (see below, Ch 7).

---

[2] *Acts Interpretation Act* 1901 (Cth), ss 15AA, 15AB; *Interpretation Act* 1967 (ACT), ss 11A, 11B; *Interpretation Act* 1987 (NSW), ss 33, 34; *Acts Interpretation Act* 1915 (SA), ss 21, 22; *Interpretation of Legislation Act* 1984 (Vic), s 35; *Interpretation Act* 1984 (WA), ss 8, 18, 19.

[3.33] If the literal meaning is clear, and the statute makes sense, and by giving that interpretation the purpose of the statute is fulfilled, one looks no further. If the purpose of the Act is not fulfilled by giving a word its ordinary and popular meaning, another meaning must be sought under the more dominant "purpose" rule. Sometimes the everyday meaning of a word may have changed since the time the Act was passed. The purpose rule predominates, and the meaning that Parliament intended the word to have must be used, as far as is practicable, to give effect to the purpose of the Act.

[3.34] Examples of the conflict between these two rules can be seen in the case of *Fisher v Bell* [1961] 1 QB 394. In that case the legislation provided that anyone who "sells, lends or gives" a flick-knife to another is guilty of an offence. Parliament meant to prevent the presence of flick-knives in the community. A policeman saw flick-knives in a shop window and proceeded to prosecute the shopkeeper. The court considered the words of the statute literally, and said that the shopkeeper did not commit an offence, as he did not actually sell them to anyone, which was required for an offence by the statute. Another instance is where a car mechanic who was under a car asked a colleague to turn the motor on. The colleague did, and as a result the mechanic was injured. For purposes of litigation the court had to decide if the colleague was a "driver". Despite the fact that the colleague was not in the driver's seat, nor did he intend to "drive" the car anywhere, the court decided he was the driver because he was in control of the means of propulsion.

Rule 3: The Golden Rule

[3.35] The ordinary meaning must be given to a word, unless that would lead to absurdity or some repugnancy or inconsistency with the rest of the Act, in which case the grammatical and ordinary sense of the word may be modified to avoid absurdity and inconsistency, but no further (Lord Wensleydale in *Grey v Pearson* (1857) 6 HLC 61 at 106; 10 ER 1216 at 1234).

[3.36] This rule gives the court further leeway to alter the actual wording of an Act if it were otherwise to make the meaning of the section absurd or repugnant to common sense and justice.

Rule 4: Statute to be Read as a Whole

[3.37] A further basic principle is that, in determining the purport of a word or a provision, the whole statute must be considered to give meaning to its general intention. For example, a statute which is intended to regulate the poultry industry and which was devoted to the raising and dealing in hens, ducks and geese, which referred in one of its provisions to "eggs" which was not otherwise defined, would most likely *not* be referring to pigeon or fish eggs! This principle is associated with the noscitur a sociis (coincidentally called the "birds of a feather") rule, described below.

Presumptions of Interpretation

[3.38] There are several presumptions that courts bring to the interpretation of statutes. The main ones are:

Noscitur a Sociis ("Birds of a Feather Stick Together", or "One is Known by One's Associates") Rule

[3.39] This rule is applied where a general term is interpreted according to its more restrictive neighbours. In the case of *Prior v Sherwood* (1906) 3 CLR 1054, the court held that a prohibition on bookmaking in any "house, office, room or place" did not include a public lane. The word "place" was to be interpreted in the light of the other words, and thus limited to indoors.

Ejusdem Generis ("of the Same Kind") Rule

[3.40] This is similar in its effect, but refers to things of the same class. It has been suggested, for example, that where a ferry is prohibited from carrying horses, cows, sheep and other animals, it is not prohibited from carrying tigers, as the list of animals, being only domestic ones, indicates the intention only of prohibiting domestic animals. That would be a decision to be made in the light of the intention of the Act, derived from other means, as outlined. If the intention of the Act is clearly to keep ferries completely animal-free, then the lack in the wording can be remedied by the wider interpretation. The often somewhat arbitrary nature of statutory interpretation can be seen from these examples.

Expressio Unius Exclusio Alterius ("Naming one Thing Excludes Others") Rule

[3.41] If specific reference is made to a particular member of a class, then, unless it causes absurdity, injustice or does not carry out the intention of the Act, all other members of that class are excluded. For example, a statute which makes it an offence for any person to sell intoxicating liquor to a minor or for any person to purchase intoxicating liquor intended for consumption by a minor, will catch only the seller of such liquor, not someone who gives it to a minor. Also it excludes the manufacturer who produces the liquor, even if it is intended for minors, so long as they do not actually sell it to a minor.

Some Statutes are to be Interpreted in Favour of the Citizen

[3.42] When the question of the meaning of a statutory provision in, for example, criminal statutes and tax statutes, involves a decision either in favour of, or against, a citizen, and there is no reason for favouring one meaning rather than the other, courts have adopted the approach of applying the meaning that will favour the citizen rather than the State.

Common Law should not be Altered

[3.43] As the common law is the source of human rights, the protection of liberty and courts are the source of the exercise of such rights, there is a presumption, all being equal and in the absence of any clear indication otherwise, that interpretation of statutory provisions should not alter common law or limit access to the courts.

Statutes should not be Retrospective

[3.44] In the absence of clear intention to the contrary in a statute's provisions, courts will not construe a statute to take effect before it was passed by Parliament.

[3.45] The court's interpretation of a statute becomes common law, and is precedent for the future interpretation of that statute. The precedent only applies to the statute interpreted and to identical provisions in other statutes in the same jurisdiction. So when deciding on the meaning of a word or provision, a lawyer will look for any case law involving interpretation of the statute. There are special publications which "annotate" statutes, pointing to cases where particular provisions have been interpreted by the courts, and there is also a publication *Words and Phrases Judicially Considered* which is regularly updated.

[3.46] Useful publications for researching the meaning of words are *Subject Index to the Acts and Regulations of the Commonwealth of Australia* (Lawbook Co.) (giving an alphabetical list of topics and the relevant legislation on that topic), the *Commonwealth Statutes Annotated* (Lawbook Co.) and *Annotations to the Acts and Regulations of the Australian Parliament* (Butterworths), which contain references to case law on specific sections of federal legislation. These are updated regularly. Similar publications exist for New South Wales (for example, *Annotations to the New South Wales Acts with Regulations* (Butterworths)); Queensland (for example, *The Statutes of Queensland Annotations* (Butterworths)); and Victoria (for example, *Victorian Statutes Annotations* (Butterworths)). Indexes of Statutes are only available for the Australian Capital Territory, Tasmania and Western Australia to the author's knowledge. There is the *Australian Digest* (Lawbook Co.), which provides a brief summary and index of case law by topic. It is supplemented annually. There is also the *Australian Legal Monthly Digest* (Lawbook Co.), a looseleaf service, which gives developments in statute law, case law, delegated legislation and legal publications by the month. The Digests can be consulted by topic name to get an updated summary of the law.

54 ■ HEALTH CARE AND THE LAW

[3.46] ■■■ **CHECKLIST**
INTERPRETATION OF STATUTES
- Is the word defined in the Act itself, or in a relevant *Acts Interpretation Act*? If so, use that definition.
- Has this particular provision been the subject of judicial interpretation? Is that decision binding?
- If not, what is the purpose of the Act, and what meaning would give effect to it?
- Is that meaning the ordinary meaning of the word (or the legal meaning if it is a legal term)?
- If not, is the purpose of the Act so clear as to warrant this unusual meaning of the word?
- Is the purpose of the Act clear enough to override any of the rules and presumptions mentioned above? If not, they should be applied in a way to give effect to the purpose of the Act.

■■■ **EXAMPLE**
Using the checklist above and the following section from the *Nursing Act* 1996 (NT) how would you go about determining whether the following people are entitled to practise or attempt to practise midwifery under that Act?
- A naturopath;
- A male doctor;
- A person rendering assistance when contractions are 15 minutes apart and no-one else is available;
- A local nurse residing 10 kilometres away who has applied for, and is awaiting, registration as a midwife.

■■■ **STATUTE**
Section 28: Unregistered Person Not to Act as Midwifery Nurse
A person who is not a midwifery nurse shall not practise or attempt to practise as a midwifery nurse or practise midwifery, unless she is—
(a) a legally qualified medical practitioner;
(b) a person rendering assistance in a case of emergency; or
(c) a person acting as a midwife, whether for reward or not,
in a case where there is no legally qualified medical practitioner or midwifery nurse, able and willing so to act if requested, residing within a distance of 20 kilometres of the place where the person so acts.
Penalty: Imprisonment for 2 years.

Common Law

[3.47] Judges decide cases before them, with their primary concern being the issues as they affect the actual parties involved. Unlike statutory law, which is concerned with future behaviour and applies to all designated

Chapter 3—The Legal Process **■** 55

people for all time (until it is changed), courts are concerned with past [3.51]
events and those who appear before them. As our society values fairness
and stability, and this is not attainable without some degree of certainty as
to how cases will be decided, judges decide them by applying the
principles of common law, as described in Chapter 1.

Determining the Reason for a Decision

[3.48] When declaring a decision in a case a judge explains the legal principle or principles which have been applied when coming to the decision. This is part of the official reason for the decision, or *ratio decidendi* (or if there is more than one reason, *rationes decidendi*); often called "ratio". Where the court is an appeal court, the ratio decidendi then becomes binding on courts which are lower in the court hierarchy of the particular jurisdiction, or of persuasive value to courts in other jurisdictions (that is, they are treated with respect, but following them is not mandatory). There are many medical issues which have been considered in courts overseas but not in Australia, so the rationes from those cases are used here when such issues arise, but are of persuasive value only.

Other Observations in a Case

[3.49] A judgment may contain more than the reason for the decision, such as observations and general comments. These are known as obiter dicta—"said by the way", or obiter, and are not binding on any court, although they may be followed anyway.

[3.50] An example of the distinction between ratio decidendi and obiter dicta can be seen in a brief outline of the following case on negligent advice (dealt with in more detail in Ch 6).

■■■ CASE
> **Hedley Byrne & Co v Heller & Partners [1964] AC 465 (House of Lords England)**
>
> Advertising agents (the plaintiffs) were concerned about the creditworthiness of a client. They requested the client's bank (the defendant) to provide them with an assessment of the client's financial position. The bank responded in a letter headed "Private. For your private use and without responsibility on the part of the bank or its officials", and stated that the client was good for its ordinary business engagements, but that the enterprise mentioned was bigger than it was "accustomed to see". The advertising agency took this as a sign of approval and went ahead with the proposed deal. In fact the deal fell through when the client went bankrupt, and the advertising agency sued the bank in negligence for not giving them reasonable advice.

[3.51] The court in fact relied on the law relating to the disclaimer of responsibility by the bank, and held that this protected the bank from any

[3.51] action, as it disclaimed any responsibility as to the validity of its comments. That was straightforward, and formed the ratio decidendi of the case. However, five of the judges went on to consider the giving of professional advice in general, where no disclaimer is made, and set out principles of law to cover such situations. These comments were obiter dicta, the result of the concern of the Law Lords to establish the fact that negligence could extend to cases where professional advice was badly given, although this was not such a case. Although such statements were obiter dicta, as five judges agreed on them it is generally considered they should be followed. In *W B Anderson & Sons Ltd v Rhodes (Liverpool) Ltd* [1967] 2 All ER 850, Cairns J commented that although the statements in *Hedley Byrne* are obiter, when five members of the House of Lords say something a single judge in a lower court should follow it. However, as they were only obiter dicta, they would not be held as laying down the "metes and bounds" of the law on negligent advice (*Mutual Life and Citizens' Assurance Co Ltd v Evatt* [1971] AC 793 at 805-809 per Lord Diplock).

[3.52] Where more than one judge gives judgment, there may be disagreement as to the decision which should be made. The majority decision is the one which is binding. There may be dissension, however, among these judges as to *why* they have come to that decision. The lawyer's task is to determine whether there are similar reasons given by the majority judges. These may not constitute a ratio decidendi, as there may not be a majority who have used the same reasons for their decision, as described above, but they have the qualified authority of obiter dicta. If there is a majority decision as to the verdict, but no common reason for it, the case is said to have no ratio, and is thus of no use as precedent for other cases.

Distinguishing Cases

[3.53] Given that in a particular type of situation the law is established by precedent, counsel for one of the parties may argue that the facts in the previous case under consideration were significantly different from the facts in the case before the court in this instance, and therefore the precedent cannot be applied. If, for example, in *Hedley Byrne & Co v Heller & Partners* the plaintiff's counsel pointed to a previous case where careless advice had been given, and argued from precedent that the statement given by the bank as to the client company's creditworthiness was negligent at law (indeed the court did this itself in its obiter dicta), the defendant could argue that the waiver of responsibility in the bank's statement was a significant fact which distinguished this case from the previous one, and so the principle of law developed in that case should not apply here.

[3.54] The common law has inbuilt flexibility, however, in several ways:

- .....the facts themselves may be under dispute;
- .....where the facts are not under dispute, those facts which are to be considered *material* (significant) may be under dispute;

▌.....just what the ratio decidendi of a previous case is may be under dispute; and [3.55]
▌.....the wording of legal principles may be vague and open to various and changing interpretations, so that over time the meaning of a particular principle may be modified.

[3.55] It can be seen that the process of legal reasoning is complex. The apparently simple theory of considering the facts, determining the relevant law, applying it to them, and then declaring judgment, is not what it seems. Thus, when asked for advice on a particular issue, lawyers can, by going through the process, and considering arguments for both sides, only come up with an educated opinion as to which party may have a better legal argument. No result is guaranteed, though many may be assured.

▌▌▌ **CHECKLIST**

Applying Precedent
▌.....Establish the importance of the case being applied. Is it binding or persuasive precedent?

Analysing Each Case
▌.....What seem to be the important facts in the case under consideration?
▌.....What other cases deal with similar facts?
▌.....In those cases what was the decision; who won, and what order was made by the court?
▌.....What propositions of law were relied on by the judge(s) as essential to the decision which was reached?*
▌.....What facts were essential in linking those legal propositions to the decision?*
▌.....What propositions put forward in the judgment were *not* essential to the decision?†

Establishing Any Distinctions Between the Precedent Cases
▌.....In arriving at an overall statement on what the law is, are there any differences between the facts of the precedent cases?
▌.....Are there any important differences in the legal principles applied to the facts?

Considering a Situation of Your Own
▌.....Compare the facts of the situation with those of the precedent cases, noting differences and similarities.
▌.....Are there enough similarities to apply a principle of law to your situation?
▌.....Would you need to know more facts to reach a definite conclusion? If so these must be established.

* The answers to these questions identify the ratio of the case.
† The answer to this question identifies obiter dicta.

What do Judges do Where there is no Legislation or Precedent?

[3.56] Sometimes there are situations before the court in which the facts are so novel there is no precedent case in which the facts are analogous. Such a case is called *res integra*, or a case of first impression.

[3.57] In the absence of binding precedent, a judge is free to choose which of three approaches to take: arguing from analogy, following persuasive precedent, or considering public policy.

Argument from Analogy

[3.58] This involves taking binding precedent cases with similar but distinguishable facts, extracting broad principles from them, and adapting the principles to the fact situation currently before the court.

Following Persuasive Precedent

[3.59] Cases from other jurisdictions are considered and applied. Often United States cases are cited in judgments on issues not previously litigated in English or Australian courts.

▮▮▮ CASE

Haynes v Harwood [1935] 1 KB 146 (Court of Appeal (England))

The employee of the defendant left his horse-drawn van unattended in the street while he went about his deliveries. A child mischievously threw a stone at the horses, which panicked and bolted. A policeman nearby saw a woman and some children were endangered by the runaway horses and van, and succeeded in stopping them. He was injured, and sued the owner of the horses in negligence, as their servant had acted without due care in leaving them. The defendant appealed to the Court of Appeal from a finding of liability against them.

[3.60] The court accepted that the delivery man had acted without due care, but the defendant argued that it was not liable because the policeman had voluntarily undertaken the risk of harm when he decided to stop the horses, and *"volenti non fit injuria"* (freely undertaking a risk prevents one from claiming when one is harmed by it).

[3.61] In fact there was no case with similar facts to provide a precedent for the Court of Appeal, so the judges turned to United States law on similar rescue scenarios. In one paragraph Lord Greer said at p 156:

The third ground was [treated as if it was a separate ground, namely,] that the principle of volenti non fit injuria applied. . . . The effect of the American cases, although we are not bound by them, is, I think, accurately stated in Professor Goodhart's article: 'Rescue and Voluntary Assumption of Risk' (1934) 5 Cam LJ 192. In accurately summing up the American authorities . . . the learned author says (at 196): 'The American rule is that the doctrine of the assumption of risk does not apply where the plaintiff has, under an exigency caused by the defendant's wrongful misconduct, consciously and deliberately faced a risk, even of death, to rescue another from imminent danger of personal injury or death, whether the person endangered is one to whom he owes a duty of protection, as a member of his family, or is a mere stranger to whom he owes no such special duty.' In my judgment, that passage not only represents the law of the United States but I think it also accurately represents the law of this country.

For further discussion of the duty of care mentioned here see below, Chapter 6.

[3.62] Lord Greer went on to argue (loc cit) that a general principle from a different but similar set of facts could be applied. The cases discussed in United States precedent involved rescue by passers-by:

> [The above principle] is all the more applicable to this case because the man injured was a policeman who might readily be anticipated to do the very thing which he did, whereas the intervention of a mere passer-by was not so probable.

Public Policy

[3.63] Judges are conscious of the fact that they are supposed, in the absence of clear legal directives, to dispense justice as recognised by the society in which they are operating. Thus public policy is a basis of legal judgments although judges are reluctant to be too open in applying it. Public policy serves a purpose, however, and its most famous application was in the case of *Donoghue v Stevenson* [1932] AC 562 (discussed more fully at [6.14], where the facts and judgment are given). This case involved the decision of the court in the light of precedent which the judges did not in fact believe was fair and just. In that case Lord Atkin said (at 582):

> It is said that the law of England and Scotland is that the poisoned consumer has no remedy against the negligent manufacturer. If this were the result of the authorities, I should consider the result a grave defect in the law, and so contrary to principle that I should hesitate long before following any decision to that effect which had not the authority of this House.

[3.64] He went on to say (at 583) that the law should not be "so remote from the ordinary needs of civilised society . . . as to deny a legal remedy where there is so obviously a social wrong".

[3.65] Policy is a nebulous thing, however, and depends very much on individual opinion, as demonstrated by the fact that in the same case Lord Buckmaster came to the conclusion (at 678) that the "poisoned consumer" should not be able to recover damages on the ground of public policy, as it would make the manufacturer liable for every bottle which issues from their works, and that they might be "called on to meet claims of damages which they could not possibly investigate or answer".

[3.66] In the end the approach by Lord Atkin was adopted by the majority of the judges, Lord Buckmaster being a dissenting judge. The

[3.66] majority was by a 3/2 margin, so one can see the uncertainty of relying on policy!

[3.67] In a later case Lord Denning explained his approach to policy as follows.

■ ■ CASE

Dutton v Bognor Regis Urban District Council [1972] 1 QB 373 (Court of Appeal England)

Mrs Dutton bought a house which developed serious defects owing to the fact that it had been built on an old rubbish dump and the foundations were not adequate. Mrs Dutton was the third owner of the house. When it was being built the council carried out a routine inspection of the foundations and passed them as satisfactory. The court found that the inspection was negligently carried out, but had to decide, in the absence of any precedents, whether the council should be held liable.

[3.68] Lord Denning was confronted with the argument that liability on the part of the council would "open the floodgates" to numerous claims which, if successful, would place an unfair burden on the ratepayers. He decided to invoke public policy and expressed the questions he should ask, in coming to a decision, in the following way:

- ..... First, who is responsible in fact for the harm to the plaintiff? In the case before him he found that the council shared the blame with the builder, as its job was in fact to prevent the very thing which happened.
- ..... Secondly, is there any reason in law why the council should *not* be held liable? He found that there was not.
- ..... Thirdly, if the council was found liable, would this have an adverse effect on the council's work, that is, would it deter it from carrying out inspections at all, or to be so cautious that inspections would be unnecessarily held up? In fact he decided that if liability were found, it would simply tend to make the council carry out the work more carefully.
- ..... Finally, is there any economic reason why the council should not be liable? The danger of unlimited liability through frequent claims, and subsequent inability to meet the costs, is one that causes the courts to limit the liability of potential defendants. However, Lord Denning argued that as in this particular case the council had the resources to pay, and that in nearly every expected similar case the builder would be primarily liable and would be insured, cases where a council would be expected to compensate a plaintiff would be rare.

[3.69] There has been some criticism of this approach, and one can see that opinions may differ, but it is suggested that this is a good basis for reasoning in those cases where there is no clear direction from legislation or case law.

▌▌▌ CHECKLIST [3.69]
LEGAL REASONING WHERE THERE IS NO CLEAR LAW

▌.....Is there binding precedent on a different but similar fact situation which established a broad enough principle to apply to this situation?
▌.....If not, is there persuasive precedent on this issue?
▌.....If not, using public policy (for example, Lord Denning's approach) what is the most just decision?

▌▌▌

REFERENCES AND FURTHER READING

Introductory texts on law and some books on health care and the law should provide some guidance. They include:

Disney, J, et al (eds), *Lawyers* (2nd ed, Law Book Co, Sydney, 1986)

Enright, C, *Studying Law* (Macarthur Press, Sydney, 1991)

Frazer, S A, *How to Study Law* (Law Book Co, Sydney, 1993)

Gillies, P, et al, *The Law in Action* (3rd ed, CCH, Sydney, 1990)

Heilbronn, G, Kovacs, D, Latimer, P, Nielsen, J and Pagone, T, *Introducing the Law* (5th ed, CCH, Sydney, 1996)

O'Sullivan, J, *Law for Nurses* (Law Book Co, Sydney, 1983), Chs 2, 14, 18

Pearce, D C, and Geddes, R, *Statutory Interpretation in Australia* (4th ed, Butterworths, Sydney, 1996)

Sawer, G, *The Australian and the Law* (Pelican, Sydney, 1972)

Wallace, J and Pagone, T (eds), *Civil and Legal Rights Handbook* (Collins Dove, Melbourne, 1983)

Also texts listed at the end of Chapter 6 (tort law) and Chapter 14 (criminal law) should be useful.

Chapter Four

CONSENT TO HEALTH CARE BY A COMPETENT ADULT

Autonomy and Consent

[4.1] Historically, medical practice has been based on the Hippocratic Oath, with its principle of beneficence and paternalism, but this has changed:

> Changes in societal values, the changing relationship between doctor and patient, abuse of position and misconduct on the part of practitioners, the great importance accorded to individual freedom of action and personal autonomy, along with advances in medical techniques which provided a greater range of patient choice, brought about a shift from paternalism to personal autonomy [Mason (2000), p 13].

[4.2] This has led to the development in law of the principle that health care must not be given without the client's consent. The words of Cardozo J, a most articulate American judge, are quoted in *Schloendorff v Society of New York Hospital* (1914) 211 NY 125 at 126 as the classic expression of the principle of medical autonomy:

> Every human being of adult years and sound mind has a right to determine what shall be done with his own body; and a surgeon who performs an operation without his patient's consent, commits an assault.

[4.3] The right to autonomy is not simply a right to make decisions for oneself: it is a right to a relationship based on trust and dignity, trust that the health carer will be honest and act only for the well-being of clients, and dignity, that the client's wishes in relation to how they handle their illness will be both respected and supported. This may mean that cultural or religious practices and beliefs are explored and followed. Some clients may want others to decide for them, believe that others have the right to do so, or reject information altogether. It may be a matter for waiting until the client has come to terms with his or her life story and is *ready* to decide, to review the story and rewrite the next chapters according to new and perhaps catastrophic circumstances.

[4.4] Autonomy thus requires good communication, and good communication requires a dialogue between health carer and client, and understanding by each of the views, values and expectations of the other. Written information about a specific proposed medical treatment can result in variable and selective interpretations (Sutherland et al (1992)). This makes it all the more important that the health carer state his or her

[4.4] position and seeks to involve the client in determining how to proceed, for example,

> I need to understand how you want to go about this. I can tell you what I think is wrong with you, possible treatments and their effects and side-effects. I can make a recommendation as to the care you should have. I can then let you make a decision so that we can plan your progress together. You have the right to that. How do you feel about it?

—here exploring the person's fears, concerns, wishes and ability to decide. This approach to decision-making is in accordance with the law. It is based on what Brody ((1989), pp 7-8) calls the "transparency model":

> The key to reasonable disclosure is not adherence to existing standards of other practitioners, nor . . . to a list of risks that a hypothetical reasonable patient would want to know. Instead, disclosure is adequate when the physician's basic thinking has been rendered transparent to the patient. . . . [it is] to engage in the typical patient-management thought process only to *do it out loud in language understandable to the patient.*

The above model ideally involves health carers as a team in the process of caring for a client. There is an increasing recognition of the need to place more emphasis in case management of communication, with one person being responsible for forging a link between all health carers and the client in a co-ordinated and co-operative approach to discussion and information-giving. Consent in this expanded form is properly an *ongoing process*, part of the client's progress through life (or death). It is not just a one-off act, such as the signing of a form.

[4.5] Whilst this is an ideal approach, this chapter sets out the basic requirements of the law in relation to consent.

[4.6] Autonomy is recognised as a basic legal and human right of all competent adults. It has been the basis of many judicial decisions, some from highest courts of the land, and is set out in numerous declarations of patients' rights. While this legal principle may be simple in its formulation, that is, that an adult of "sound" mind can determine absolutely what is done with his or her body, the genuine dilemmas, personal turmoil and heartbreak that can arise from complex and difficult situations have caused some muddying of the waters. Health carers find the principle in its application is often vague and uncertain, raising some serious legal and ethical problems. Cases in Australia, England and the United States have demonstrated the conflict between the perspectives of client autonomy and medical paternalism. Autonomy is based on the principle of the right of the client to knowingly make decisions regarding medical treatment, no matter how unwise others may consider them, or how disastrous the effects on the person. It also fails to take account of limits on resources, and consequent undisclosed rationing of services by providers:

> Decisions to treat kidney patients are being taken by doctors all the time. Usually the patient does not understand that he could have been treated and goes away to die quietly [Schwartz and Grubb (1985), p 23].

Recent revelations have also indicated that it is the policy of some health care institutions not to provide various services to clients who smoke.

Paternalism is another factor limiting autonomy, based on the desire to allow the medical professional, and not the client to judge what is in his or her interest.

[4.12]

[4.7] Tension has developed between ethical schools of thought, some of which promote the concept of autonomy as paramount, others portraying this as resulting in abandonment and lack of care of the client—endorsing what is claimed to be the more compassionate aim of beneficence (Andrews, K, "The Medical Treatment Act and the Incompetent Patient", 8 *St Vincent's Bioethics Centre Newsletter* 1990, p 1 at p 3). For a more comprehensive view of the issue see Kuhse (1997). Many attitudes are based on the simplistic and erroneous characterisation of others' viewpoints, and generalisations have led to conflicting approaches to the care of those considered to be making the wrong decisions. It is the author's view that a mistaken assumption that the conflict outlined above is a conflict between two equally applicable legal principles: autonomy on the one hand, and a legal duty of care on the other. There is no legal duty of care to a competent person who does not want that care. This means that legally, when there is a conflict between autonomy and beneficence, beneficence should always yield to the right of a competent person to consent to, or refuse, health care.

[4.8] Despite the legal principle of autonomy, relatives, health carers, and even lawyers and judges have undermined the independence of clients by substituting their own opinions as to what is in their interests, whether the client wants it or not. Thus, for example, judges had fallen back on ill-defined and vague concepts, such as "necessity" and "therapeutic privilege" (see Ch 5). This has resulted in numerous daily breaches of clients' legal right to autonomy in the name of beneficence. In practice it means that health carers may well be risking liability for acting in this way.

Summary of the Law of Consent

[4.9] To assist in understanding, a summary of the law on consent is presented here, and explained more fully below.

[4.10] In law, there are two possible actions that can be taken against a health carer where consent to health care was absent: *trespass to the person* (including assault and/or battery or unlawful detention) or *negligence*.

[4.11] *To avoid an action in trespass to the person* the health carer must ensure that the client understands the broad nature and effects of the proposed procedure or intervention, and consent to it (here called *"general consent"*).

[4.12] *To avoid an action in negligence* the health carer must ensure that the client is at least aware of the material risks associated with the proposed procedure (here called "informed consent").

[4.13] **[4.13]** It can be seen that both elements should be present for lawful consent. In both cases:

- .....the client must be capable of understanding the information; and
- .....the health carer must have taken reasonable steps to ensure understanding.

What Constitutes Understanding?

[4.14] The client must:

- .....understand and retain the information;
- .....believe the information (that is, he or she must not be divorced from reality or unable to comprehend what is being said);
- .....understand that a choice can be made; and
- .....be able to reason (however "unreasonably") and make a choice.

What Constitutes "Broad Nature and Effects"?

[4.15] Briefly, this involves a description of the physical intervention proposed and its intended outcome (for example, how it is intended to benefit the client, and its overall effects on the client).

What are "Material Risks"?

[4.16] A risk is material if the health carer knows or should know that, if it occurred:

- .....a person in this client's situation; or
- .....this particular client,

would be likely to attach significance to it.

Trespass to the Person

[4.17] It is part of a health carer's work to touch a client and to carry out procedures on her or him, be it washing, giving medication, open heart surgery, resuscitation or sustenance. According to the law no such action whatsoever may be taken without the patient's consent to it.

[4.18] The common law, has, for hundreds of years maintained that any unwanted interference with a person's body, or creation of fear of such interference, is an actionable wrong at law, and the remedy is based on the law of trespass: in this case, trespass to the person.

It has been established in the courts that a competent person has an absolute right to refuse to consent to medical treatment for any reason, rational or otherwise, or for no reason at all, even where that decision may [4.21] lead to his or her own death (*Re MB* [1997] 8 Med LR 21). This includes medical procedures, whether therapeutic or experimental, thus the concern of hospitals to gain patients' consent before medical procedures are undertaken. However, the action in trespass covers all activity affecting another's physical integrity, so it applies to all health care workers, as well as the public in general. There are several grounds for an action in trespass to the person: assault, battery and false imprisonment are the main ones.

Assault

[4.19] The term "assault" is often used to mean the beating up of a person, and certainly that is its colloquial use in criminal law. In fact, strictly speaking, assault is carried out simply by intentionally creating in the mind of another the apprehension of unwanted physical contact. This does not have to be harmful contact. The indication that one is going to kiss another against their will is technically an assault. If a health carer, for example, threatens a patient with medication, loss of privileges or restraint if the patient does not behave (unless there is a real risk of harm from their actions (see [4.79]ff)), this can constitute assault. The threat does not have to be explicit, it only needs to be inferred from the carer's words or actions. Any fear of unwanted contact placed in the mind of a client through the carer's actions can constitute assault, however, so that the implication that he or she will be treated in such a way if he or she does not conform, or that treatment will be given regardless of the person's wishes, can be considered assault.

[4.20] In everyday practice health care staff may pressure patients to agree to do what they want where they believe it is in the patient's interest, or feel the need to maintain a smooth, uncomplicated routine by so doing. When the workplace is understaffed and workers feel the need to get things done in a hurry, the client who wants to question what is happening, or (worse!), refuses to co-operate with the staff, may be a barrier to what staff may consider to be proper and necessary treatment, efficient ward organisation, getting to much needed morning tea on time, or pleasing the staff nurse or supervisor. However hospitals are issuing charters of patients' rights as they are being increasingly recognised (see below, Ch 18), and apart from the ethical issues involved in the bullying and domineering of patients, such behaviour may amount at law to either assault or battery, depending on the circumstances.

[4.21] The elements of assault involve what a reasonable person with the patient's characteristics would make of the situation. That is, the defendant need not intend to carry out the threat, it may be a joke. So long as someone is made to believe that they will be touched against their will, and:

- ..... the means for such touching are reasonably available; or
- ..... the perpetrator ought to have foreseen that the person would be likely to believe this,

[4.21] they may be able to sue in assault (*Macpherson v Beath* (1975) 12 SASR 174 per Bray CJ at 177). For example, it has been held that pointing an unloaded gun at a person who reasonably believes it is loaded was an assault (*McLelland v Symons* [1951] VLR 157 at 164). Such an act is, of course, a criminal as well as a civil assault.

Battery

[4.22] When the threat is carried out, that is the patient or other person is touched against their will, that may be, in law, battery.

Damage Need not be Caused

[4.23] While assault and battery can be considered a crime (a man has been prosecuted for kissing a policewoman who was directing traffic at a street intersection), it is also the basis of a civil action, for which the aggrieved person may claim damages. An important distinction between an action in assault and battery and an action in negligence is that in assault and battery the plaintiff need not show that any harm was suffered, whereas in negligence they must do so. The developers of our law have put such a premium on the personal integrity of the individual, that one is liable to compensate for the breach of that integrity, even where one has caused no physical or mental harm to someone.

Battery may Occur even Where the Intent is to Benefit

[4.24] In the ancient case of *Cole v Turner* 6 Mod 149, it was held that "the least touching of another in anger is battery". However later courts have held that it has never been the common law that actual hostility or hostile intent is necessary (*Boughey v The Queen* (1986) 16 CLR 10). The intent may be to assist the person, even save life (see, for example, *Malette v Shulman* below, [4.62]). The invasion to the person's autonomy itself is harm enough. It has been held that a prank that gets out of hand, an over-friendly pat on the back, surgical treatment where it is mistakenly thought that the patient has consented may constitute battery (*In Re F (mental patient)* [1990] 2 AC 1 (HL)). As stated above, the person who unlawfully touches another may thus do so with the best of intentions.

▌▌▌ CASE
Mohr v Williams 104 NW 12 (1905) (Minnesota SC United States)

A surgeon was operating on a woman's right ear, by her consent. While she was under anaesthesia, he discovered that the left ear was much more seriously diseased. After consulting her general practitioner, who by her request was present at the operation, the surgeon proceeded to carry out an ossiculectomy on her left ear. See also *Murray v McMurchy* [1949] 2 DLR 442 at [4.59].

[4.25] Even at that early date the court was in no doubt that the operation on the woman's left ear was battery, despite the good intentions of the surgeon. Given that the operation was not an emergency, as described below, the court held that there was no justification in carrying out the operation, even though permission had been given for surgery on the right ear. Thus the surgeon was found liable in battery for carrying out the ossiculectomy. Carers should keep in mind that there may be all sorts of reasons, rational or irrational, unknown to them, that might cause a patient to come to a decision they would believe improbable, impossible or unthinkable! In that case they can attempt to persuade, but they cannot, without invoking legal liability, impose their views on a reluctant patient. There is obviously a need to ensure one is not placing pressure on clients, and consideration of allowing them to nominate another person to be with them when they make decisions if they wish to do so.

The Patient Need not be Aware of Battery

[4.26] Battery may take place when the subject is asleep, comatose or anaesthetised. The patient does not have to know that the unwanted act is taking place, nor does he or she have to have specifically stated an objection to it. If no permission for the act has taken place, and there is no necessity for the action to preserve or save the person's life or limb, then he or she has the right to sue the perpetrator of the act in battery. It is quite clear that any act that is not consented to and that is unnecessary, is unlawful. Examples include the pelvic examination by students of anaesthetised patients, or practice in the insertion and removal of inter-uterine devices on them. Cases involving unnecessary and unauthorised surgery are discussed below.

Implications for Health Carers

[4.27] It can be seen that consent issues do not simply apply to the medical profession: all health carers are required to ensure they do not deal with people without their consent. Carers may also become agents in the administration of treatment without the patient's consent. An example of this occurred at Chelmsford Hospital, Sydney, in the 1960s and 1970s. A Royal Commission into practices during that time at the hospital found that treatment, often in the form of "deep-sleep" treatment, was rarely if ever fully explained to patients:

> There was evidence patients were often tricked into accepting treatment ... [the treating physician] stated they were not to know what the treatment was and they must have it. Some patients were deceived by staff ... the staff were exhorted to keep up the pretence. Some patients were given the treatment when they had expressly stated that they did not want it [Parliament of New South Wales, *Report of the Royal Commission into Deep Sleep Therapy* (NSW Government Printer, Sydney, 1990), Vol 1, p 171].

[4.27] ■■■ **CASE**
Hart v Herron [1984] Aust Torts Rep ¶80-201 (SC NSW)

The plaintiff argued that on arrival at hospital, he expressed concern about the procedure he was to receive and asked to see his doctor. He said he was offered medication to "calm him down" and was subsequently given "deep sleep treatment" and electroconvulsive therapy. He sued in battery, as he alleged he had not consented to treatment. The defence argued, among other things, that the fact that he presented himself at the hospital and did not leave when he expressed concern about the treatment was an indication of his consent to it. The court's ruling on matters of law in relation to consent was sought.

[4.28] The jury found that the plaintiff had not consented to the treatment and that the doctor was liable in battery. The hospital, through its staff, was found not liable in battery as the plaintiff had not made out his case against it. However, the court rejected the argument that attendance at a hospital is necessarily consent to subsequent treatment, and the hospital was found liable for false imprisonment. A distinction was drawn between "genuine" consent (negated by trickery or fraud) and consent, which may be "genuine" consent, but which is based on inadequate information regarding the procedure, and was thus rather a matter of negligence (see discussion at [4.83]ff). In determining whether the consent was "genuine" the court considered the evidence of one of the nurses who testified that the general nature of the procedures that were carried out on Mr Hart had been explained to, and accepted by, him. Although the plaintiff argued that the nurse's evidence should be disregarded because it was discredited on cross-examination, the court was not convinced that the plaintiff had made out his case against the hospital. The court said that the jury had to be satisfied on the evidence that the hospital staff were liable for assault and/or battery, and on the evidence before the court the only arguments substantiated appeared to be that the treatment was inappropriate and unnecessary, and could thus not amount to assault or battery (allegations of negligence against the hospital had in fact been dropped).

[4.29] In circumstances where consent has not in fact been given, however (see the report on Chelmsford Hospital cited above, which was based on a fuller inquiry), carers who know consent has not been given may be responsible for their part in battery, and cannot point to the fact that they have been told to act this way. Staff are not required to follow unlawful orders of their employer (see Ch 11), and may be individually responsible for acts of battery they carry out. Where a health carer is expected to assist in a procedure to which the client has not consented, before refusing to assist he or she must consider whether to refuse would result in harm to the client.

▮▮▮ CASE [4.32]
Re T (Adult: Refusal of Treatment) [1992] 4 All ER 649

T, who was 34 weeks pregnant, was involved in a car accident and doctors told her she would require a caesarian section. After a conversation with her mother, who was a Jehovah's Witness (T was ambivalent in her views, but still did not believe in transfusions) T told the doctors that she did not want a blood transfusion. She was assured that a caesarean could be performed without blood transfusion, so she signed a form refusing transfusions in the process of giving birth. She was not told that a transfusion could be required for other reasons. A caesarean section was performed without a transfusion, but T later required one for haemorrhage. The doctor would have given it except for the purported refusal, and instead T was put on life support. T's father and partner applied to the court for assistance.

[4.30] The court authorised a transfusion, holding that T had neither consented to, nor refused, a blood transfusion, and that it was therefore lawful to go ahead and give her life-saving treatment. There was also doubt as to whether T's refusal was voluntary, or the result of undue influence of her mother.

[4.31] The court also held that misinforming a patient (whether or not innocently) and the withholding of information which is expressly or impliedly sought by a patient may well vitiate a consent or refusal.

[4.32] Health carers, however, must not carry out any procedure to which a client has not consented. It should not be presumed that because someone has entered hospital or some other health facility they have given a blanket consent to whatever might be done to them. They have the right to refuse any treatment at any time, and indeed to leave the institution at any time. Consent, however, may be implied from a person's words or actions, for example, if a client waits in line for treatment or rolls up her sleeve when she sees a nurse approach with an injection, the nurse can presume consent (*O'Brien v Cunard SS Co* 28 NE 266 (1891)). In that case the plaintiff had plenty of time after joining a queue to watch the procedure being carried out on others waiting to be vaccinated, to find out what was going on and leave if she wished, according to the court. Outward behaviour, not inner thought, is what is taken into account by the courts, so that, if a client indicates consent by some action, and the person carrying out the procedure has no reason to doubt that they are knowingly doing so, consent may be presumed. However, one should take care to ensure that that is the case, and that the client understands the nature and effect of the procedure (including drugs to be given) to avoid an action in trespass, and any risk that is involved in the health care, to avoid an action in negligence.

▮▮▮ CASE
Shulman v Lerner 141 NW 2d 348 (1966) (Michigan CA United States)

A dentist with an infected eyelid attended his doctor's surgery. Previously the condition had been dealt with non-surgically, but on this occasion the doctor removed the gland surgically, presuming the dentist's consent. The dentist sued in battery.

[4.33] **[4.33]** The doctor argued that consent could be implied by the fact that the dentist was familiar with surgical technique and would have understood by the preparation of instruments and draping of the eye that some sort of surgical procedure was to follow. The court rejected this argument, stating that the dentist had been fully conscious, the procedure was neither life-saving nor urgent, and the opportunity for obtaining consent was available. The dentist was awarded $12,500.

[4.34] This case has a most important message for health carers. It indicates that the presumption should be that a person does not want treatment unless they specifically agree to it, not that they want it unless they specifically decline it. Passivity is not necessarily consent, and the onus is on the health care worker to actively determine that the client consents, not on the client to express her or his refusal.

Elements of Consent

[4.35] It is important that there must be effective consent to health care procedures, and that that consent must be "real" in the eyes of the law. Simply having something in writing is not enough. Consent must have at least three elements:

- .....it must be *voluntary and freely given* (consent given under threat or duress, or the effect of stupefying drugs is not valid) and the client must understand that it can be withdrawn at any time;
- .....it must be *specific* (the act carried out must be the act consented to); and
- .....it must come from a *competent person,* in other words the client must be capable of understanding the nature and effect of the proposed care, and of making a choice in relation to having the care.

Consent must be Voluntary

[4.36] Consent must be given without undue influence, or coercion. There must be no misrepresentation (whether deliberate or mistaken) as to the nature or necessity of a procedure, nor must there be threats, bribes, or other attempts to get the desired results. The fact that medical personnel believe that treatment is for the patient's own good, even if it is to save life, is not enough to override a reasoning (not necessarily *reasonable*) adult's right to refuse treatment. When health carers, in the interests of beneficence, disregard this right in such circumstances, the patient may sue in battery. This could leave the court with the dilemma of upholding the right to refuse treatment on the one hand, or punishing those who rendered what they considered to be a benefit to the client on the other, perhaps substantially improving the quality of their life (see the case of *Qumsieh* at [5.108]).

Misrepresentation will Vitiate Consent to Treatment [4.39]

Misrepresentation as to Need for Treatment

[4.37] Where a dentist induced clients to agree to extensive procedures, including fillings and root canal treatment which were not necessary, he was held liable in battery. The court said that despite purported agreement by the plaintiffs, the dentist failed to provide sufficient information for a decision to be made. Indeed, such information was withheld in bad faith as he knew they would not consent if they understood the work was unnecessary (*Appleton & Ors v Garrett* (1997) 8 Med LR 75; CCH ¶16-950; see also *Re T* at [4.29]).

Misrepresentation as to Nature of Treatment

[4.38] Another situation resulting in the question of consent arose in the case of *R v Mobilio* [1991] 1 VR 339; 50 A Crim R 170. The appellant, a radiographer, in carrying out ultrasound examinations on three women, represented to them that the examination would require a vaginal probe with the transducer, and they agreed to this action. In fact the probes were completely unnecessary, and carried out solely for the purpose of sexual gratification. The radiographer was convicted of rape and appealed to the Victorian Court of Criminal Appeal. That court upheld the appeal, finding that the appellant did no act which was essentially different from the act to which the women knew he proposed, and to which they consented. It must be remembered that this was a prosecution for rape (the law has since been amended). It was based on the need for the jury to be convinced beyond a reasonable doubt that a specific offence had been committed. If the case had been one of battery, based on vitiation of consent through fraud, the result may have been quite different. Thus the question of whether there was a battery in terms of the provision of health care was not properly addressed, and it is considered that the better approach would have been that of the court in *Appleton* (above). Certainly such conduct is also a breach of professional standards, and would be the basis of disciplinary action by the relevant licensing body (see Ch 13).

Medication and Consent

[4.39] The question of consent to treatment arises in cases where harm has occurred to the person through medication, as in the following example.

▋▋▋ CASE

Beausoleil v La Communitie des Soeurs de la Providence (1964) 53 DLR 65 (CA Quebec)

A patient asked to have a general anaesthetic rather than a spinal anaesthetic for a surgical procedure, as her mother had had serious adverse effects from a spinal anaesthetic. After she received her pre-medication, she was pressured into having a spinal anaesthetic by medical staff. As a result she became a paraplegic. She sued, claiming that her apparent consent had not been valid, as it had not been voluntary.

[4.40] **[4.40]** The court agreed that the fact that she had been given the pre-medication and its potential sedative effects meant that legally the plaintiff was not in a condition to agree voluntarily to the procedure. This principle indicates that any consent given after or during the giving of medication which might cause a person to be incapable of making a reasonable decision is suspect. The legal position is not so clear if a person who is groggy from medication refuses treatment after having consented to it beforehand. The law requires that a change of mind under these circumstances is to be treated seriously. Where the treatment is not urgent, health carers have the options of going ahead and carrying out the procedure, or postponing the treatment until the person is no longer affected by the drugs and can express his or her wishes. Where they go ahead, there is the risk that the person will bring an action in battery. It could be argued in defence that the health carers were of the honest and reasonable belief that the person was, at that time, not competent to make the decision to refuse the treatment. Health carers wishing to protect themselves from an action in battery can postpone the procedure until either:

- ..... the client is restored to a state of competence; or
- ..... it is established that he or she is in a permanent state of incompetence. In this case consent should be sought from the appropriate decision-maker. If there is no person authorised at law, an application should be made to the appropriate court or tribunal for the appointment of one (as outlined in Ch 5).

Consent Does Not Have to be in Writing

[4.41] As long as it is quite clear to a reasonable person that the client consents, and the procedure is legal, treatment may be given. Consent may thus be given by implication, by some kind of clear indication, verbally, or in written form. A consent form is merely *evidence* of that consent (see [4.127]). Legally recognised consent is the valid agreement of the client to the treatment, however they convey this. Evidence of consent may also be provided by witnesses (a written consent is preferable of course, signed by the patient and witnessed). Where a patient refuses consent to treatment, this should also be evidenced in writing or by witnesses, to avoid any claims of neglect (negligence) by the client or relatives.

Legal "Competence"

What is Competence at Law?

[4.42] At law, every adult is to be presumed to be competent to make decisions unless there is clear evidence or knowledge that they are not. These people have at law the right to accept or refuse treatment, for whatever reason they like, despite the consequences, subject of course to the exceptions and defences mentioned. Staff cannot assume that patients would not really wish to put their health in jeopardy if they were in their right mind and that therefore this could not be their real wish. Except in an emergency, where: [4.46]

- ..... a person has not made a valid and current enduring power of attorney or advance directive (see Ch 5);
- ..... he or she is not competent to make decisions about proposed care (whether temporarily or permanently); and
- ..... the care is urgently necessary to save his or her life, or avert serious danger to health,

consent of an adult is required.

[4.43] There have been differences of opinion as to what constitutes competence (or the capacity) to consent to health care. Is it evidenced by the fact that a person makes a choice, or only when a reasonable choice is made? Is it evidenced simply by the making of a choice (no matter what it is)? Does it have to be a *reasonable* choice, or a *reasoned* one (that is, where the person has consciously chosen a course of action, no matter how irrational that choice may seem)? Or is it an *ability* to understand (whether one does or not) or *actual* understanding? Very little attention has been given to just what capacity is (McHale (1997), p 268). This is surprising given the number of decisions which are made every day as to the capacity of clients to consent to treatment.

[4.44] The question of just what is required for someone to be held to have the capacity to consent to treatment was first addressed in detail by Thorpe J in *Re C (Refusal of Medical Treatment)*, a case where a man who suffered from schizophrenia refused to agree to a clinically indicated amputation of the leg. The judge stated that he found helpful the suggestion that the decision-making process follows three stages:

- ..... comprehending and retaining treatment information;
- ..... believing it (that is, they must not be "impervious to reason, divorced from reality or incapable of judgment after reflection" (*B v Croydon District Health Authority* [1955] All ER 683)); and
- ..... weighing it in the balance to arrive at a choice.

[4.45] It is suggested that the third criterion above has, in fact, two elements:

- ..... the ability to weigh something up (that is, consider respectively the effects of having or not having the care); and
- ..... making a decision based on that ability.

[4.46] Buchanan and Brock ((1989), p 19) propose the view that the necessary degree of understanding depends on the nature of the treatment and thus decision-making tasks vary substantially in the capacities they require of the decision-maker. They believe that some will demand a higher level of competence and higher level of understanding. The crucial question is how defective a person's capacity and skill to make a particular

[4.46] decision must be in order for that individual to be deemed to lack the capacity to make that particular decision. Also the person must be able to make a choice and communicate it.

[4.47] In the case of *Re T* (see [4.29]) the court held that there was no clear evidence that T had not been unduly influenced by her mother. Consultation with relatives might reveal some insight into the personal circumstances of the client, and what he or she would have wanted. Neither the personal circumstances of the client, nor consideration of what he or she would have chosen, can be binding on the health carer in determining whether or not, or how to provide treatment, or justify actions contrary to a clearly established anticipatory refusal via an advance directive (see [5.99]ff) of treatment. However, they are factors to be taken into account in forming an opinion as to what the client would have considered to be in his or her best interests. For example, the court held, if the treating doctor learnt that the patient was a Jehovah's Witness, but had no evidence of a refusal to accept a blood transfusion, he could avoid or postpone any blood transfusion as long as possible. It is instructive to see how such a clearly pronounced principle has been passed over by health carers and judges, as the inclination to paternalism and beneficence is very strong, as occurred in the recent case of *Qumsieh* (see [5.108]).

Fluctuating and Reversible Loss of Competence

[4.48] Whilst there has been no judicial ruling directly on the point, the principle of autonomy would indicate that where a person's lack of competence is episodic, fluctuating, limited or reversible, there is an obligation to take reasonable measures to remove any barriers to their gaining adequate capacity to make decisions about their bodily integrity and health. In a Report *Assessment of Mental Capacity: Guidance for Doctors and Lawyers,* published by the British Medical Association in 1996, principle 12.7 states that "Doctors should be aware both that medical disabilities can fluctuate and that there are many factors extraneous to a person's disorder which may adversely influence capacity. It is the duty of the assessing doctor to maximise capacity." Ways in which capacity can be enhanced are set out, and include:

- treating any condition which may be affecting capacity;
- waiting for a period of lucidity where capacity fluctuates;
- assisting the condition (such as short-term memory) through therapy where appropriate;
- ensuring that the difficulty is not one of *communication*;
- eliminating factors that may make capacity difficult, such as stress, anxiety, insecurity;
- sensitivity in approach and presentation of issues;
- ensuring adequate education, explanation and sufficient time for understanding; and
- ensuring the presence of a third party where that would help, and absence of a person where their presence causes stress.

What Must a Person Understand? [4.51]

[4.49] It has been held that a client must understand the nature of the treatment, and be able to weigh the risks and benefits (*F v West Berkshire Health Authority* [1989] 2 All ER 545). This is where it is most important to be clear that for the purposes of consent to health care (that is, to avoid an action in battery) the person need only understand "in broad terms, the nature of any procedure proposed to be performed upon them" (*Rogers v Whitaker* (1993) 175 CLR 479 at 484; see [4.98]).

❙❙❙ CASE
Chatterton v Gerson [1981] 1 QB 432

A woman suffering from pain from a post-operative scar underwent an unsuccessful intrathecal block, with the result that the pain became almost unbearable. The procedure was competently performed, but the woman sued the specialist in battery and negligence. As to the battery allegation, she argued that because she had not been informed of the risks of the procedure, she had not given a valid consent to the surgery.

[4.50] The court rejected Ms Chatterton's claim in battery, stating that once a person has been informed in broad terms of the nature of the procedure, that is sufficient for their agreement to the procedure to be consent. Any allegation that he or she should have been given information about risks of the health care is a question of negligence, not battery.

❙❙❙ CASE
Sidaway v Governors of the Bethlem Royal Hospital [1985] 1 All ER 643 (House of Lords (England))

Mrs Sidaway was an elderly patient who underwent an operation on her cervical vertebrae. There was a one to two per cent risk of paralysis occurring inherent in this operation, but she was not informed of this. Unfortunately she did suffer some paralysis, and sued, alleging that it was the surgeon's duty to inform her of the risk.

[4.51] The House of Lords rejected this claim, re-affirming the decision of the case of *Bolam v Friern Hospital Management Committee* [1957] 1 WLR 582, which gave medical staff the discretion to decide what disclosure is proper and in the patient's interest. But, while the court kept for itself the right to review such a decision, it would only do so where the discretion has fallen patently below what is deemed to be reasonable in the circumstances. Thus, the issue of informed consent comes under the category of negligence rather than trespass. In the Australian case of *Battersby v Tottman* (see [5.95]), the court endorsed this approach strongly. At that time it held that courts should not doubt the judgment of doctors, nor refuse them the right to make decisions, unless convinced they are wrong. *Bolam's* case was further restricted by the Australian High Court in *Rogers v Whitaker* (see [4.98]).

[4.52] **[4.52]** The majority of the Full Court of the Supreme Court held in the *Battersby* case that the patient's condition was such as to render her consent unnecessary, basing its finding on the evidence of the medical profession. Zelling J, who dissented, held that a patient must be allowed to make her or his own decision, no matter whether the doctor thinks them well enough or not, unless they are too young or too mentally ill to understand the risks involved. He did not believe that Ms Battersby was too mentally ill. His was a voice of protest against the overwhelming tendency of the courts at the time to favour the opinion of doctors.

[4.53] In practice, a patient's wishes are often disregarded and no legal action is taken when they are. It has been found that the majority of patients want information, no matter how negative it may be, while the majority of doctors control the information they give to patients. In a Victorian Law Reform Commission Report it was found that less than two-thirds of doctors could explain the meaning of "informed consent" and less than 50 per cent thought that an informed consent was necessary or important ("Informed Decisions about Medical Procedures" (1989), pp 23-26). The courts have, in the past often countenanced the paternalism of medicine, and still sometimes do (see *Qumsieh v Pilgrim* at [5.108]). However, at least in the UK, they are increasingly recognising patients' right to refuse treatment they do not want, even to their serious detriment, and that of an unborn (see *S v St George* at [4.141]).

[4.54] People who are considered not competent to decide are dealt with in Chapter 5.

Consent must be Specific

[4.55] No treatment is consented to at law unless the person giving consent knows just what the treatment is. Thus, consent for surgery or other procedure will not be of any value unless the precise form of surgery or procedure is determined. Forms should specify the treatment, for example, "left tympanoplasty". That procedure is all that the surgeon is allowed to perform (see *Mohr v Williams* at [4.24] above). Many surgeons (and other medical personnel in different circumstances) breach the patient's right by sterilisation, appendectomies or other procedures when these are not necessary to save the patient's life. Generally, no legal action is taken, for such behaviour is accepted by patients or unknown to them. However, acceptance of a legal wrong after the event does not make it a legal right. Courts have held, for example, that consent to an operation on the womb is not consent to sterilisation (see at [4.59]; *Levi v Regional Health Authority* (1980) 7 *Current Law* 44). Consent may also specify who is to carry out the procedure.

Defences to an Action in Battery

[4.56] It is a defence to a claim of assault and battery that:

- .....any apparent threat or physical contact was unintended or an accident;
- .....the situation was an emergency, and measures used were to save life or health;
- .....the action taken was in self-defence when faced with imminent danger, by the use of no more force than was necessary to prevent that danger (self-defence);
- .....the action taken was for the protection of another (including the victim), from danger, again using no more than reasonably necessary force;
- .....the action taken was for the protection of property, with no more than reasonably necessary force (given the relative value of the welfare of those involved, compared with the value of the property); and
- .....there was statutory power to do so.

[4.57] There is tension in the law between the principle of freedom to refuse treatment and freedom to try to save someone's life and health as expressed above, which has not been satisfactorily resolved. It is the author's view that the law will not permit a person to sue another in battery for attempting to save them from acts of self-destruction or suicide (see [4.66]). This applies only to emergency measures. Long-term forceful treatment is subject to mental health law (see below, Ch 5).

Emergencies

[4.58] As indicated above, presumption of consent allows staff to carry out treatment in an emergency. "Emergency" has not been defined by the courts, but it has been described variously as being:

- .....a situation where a medical or surgical procedure is immediately necessary to save the life of a person: "Such would require the patient to be in grave danger, with death imminent in the sense of hours or days as against weeks or months" (Dix et al (1988), p 102);
- .....a situation requiring treatment necessary in order to save a person's life or to prevent serious injury to their health (*Australian Health and Medical Law Reporter* at ¶17.150).

[4.59] When consent is an issue it is suggested that neither of the above definitions is entirely satisfactory. Rather, it is suggested that the question of whether an emergency exists in relation to consent for a person who is unable to do so is based on whether serious harm would occur if attempts were made to seek consent from whomever is authorised to give it. That is, the word "immediate" should be applied literally. Whether the term "necessary to save life" should be interpreted strictly is unclear and statutory references to emergencies do not help to clarify the meaning either. They mention "emergency" but do not define it in uniform or precise terms. Certainly it is clear that any treatment which is simply thought to be desirable, or which may preserve life later, cannot be

[4.59] considered as necessary for the purposes of acting without consent. The action contemplated must be action to save life at the time of making the decision.

▌▌▌ CASE
Murray v McMurchy [1949] 2 DLR 442 (SC British Columbia)
A surgeon carrying out a caesarean section noted that the woman had a number of uterine fibroids, which were capable of causing harm to the woman, foetus or both in a later pregnancy. He carried out a hysterectomy to prevent such an occurrence.

[4.60] The court held that, as the harm was avoidable and not imminent, his performance of a tubal ligation was battery. Note the opposite result in a case where, in a hernia operation the surgeon removed a diseased left testicle which posed a risk of death from septicaemia (*Marshall v Curry* (1933) 3 DLR 260).

[4.61] Saving of a limb or the function of a part of the body which would be lost without the treatment would most likely be considered necessary treatment, on the basis that the law allows one to presume that people would consent to such treatment if they knew or fully understood its necessity to maintain bodily function.

Refusal of Emergency Treatment

[4.62] Where adults of apparently sound mind require emergency treatment, and are conscious, they can, according to common law, refuse it.

▌▌▌ CASE
Malette v Shulman (1991) 2 Med LR 162 (CA Ontario)
Ms Malette was seriously injured in a car accident and taken to hospital unconscious. She was carrying a card, unsigned and unwitnessed, which stated that she was a Jehovah's Witness and refused any blood transfusions. She deteriorated and was bleeding profusely from severe facial injuries, severed nose and internal bleeding. Dr Shulman gave her a blood transfusion. She sued him, and he argued that as she had been unconscious he had been unable to inform her properly for her "informed refusal" and he was thus under a legal and ethical duty to give emergency treatment. The trial court found in the plaintiff's favour and the doctor appealed.

[4.63] The Ontario Court of Appeal denied the appeal, stating that the card did impose a valid restriction on the treatment that could be given. The plaintiff did foresee this sort of situation, the court said, and that was the very reason for her carrying it. The court went on to state that it recognised the dilemma in which the doctor was placed, however he would not have violated his legal duty, or his professional responsibility if he respected the plaintiff's right to control over her body. He had no right to judge the rationality of her decision, so long as the instructions were

valid. It was her responsibility if harmful consequences arise from her [4.65]
decision. It is important to note that Ms Malette received what in terms of
today's figures could only be considered to be nominal damages, and also
had to pay her own legal costs. This is an indication of the legal approach
to cases where a doctor may have technically breached the patient's legal
right to autonomy, but has nevertheless acted in what he or she believed
to be the interests of the patient. Readers should contrast this case with
Qumsieh v Pilgrim (see [5.108]).

Uncertainty About Refusal of Emergency Treatment

[4.64] Given that an emergency requires legal action, where health
carers are unsure as to whether a patient's refusal of emergency treatment
is valid, they are entitled to presume that the person consents to
life-saving treatment. However, it should not be presumed that an
emergency by its very nature automatically renders a person unable to
make health care decisions. In less urgent situations they should seek
assistance to ensure their actions are lawful. This may require application
to the appropriate court or tribunal for emergency guardianship (compare
Malette v Shulman, above) or reference to a person responsible (see Ch 5).
Where there is no time for this, and the refusal is genuinely in doubt, then
the consent of the client can be presumed. The Supreme Court has
inherent jurisdiction, called *"parens patriae"* jurisdiction, to make any
ruling affecting the well-being of any child or incompetent adult citizen
who is in need. Decisions can be made urgently, with consequent legal
protection of medical personnel in carrying out the court's ruling. An
example of resort to the Supreme Court is the case of *K v Minister for Youth
and Community Services* [1982] 1 NSWLR 311, which involved differences
of opinion over whether a minor could have an abortion (see below,
Chapter 5). Corresponding jurisdiction for children other than those in
State care now also vests in the Family Court (see [5.20]).

Emergency Services

[4.65] Paramedics, ambulance officers, rescuers and firefighters are
subject to the law as outlined above. A competent person may refuse care
even in an emergency. It is often the case that such refusal is considered
not competent, and emergency workers may consider that they can ignore
refusals. This could leave them open to action for assault and battery.
However where their work involves sudden accidents and catastrophes, it
could well be that both emergency workers and victims are not in a state
to assess or know:

- ..... the true gravity of the person's injuries;
- ..... the precise nature of any health care (as this may change from moment to moment); and
- ..... given the circumstances of the event, the risks involved in any procedure undertaken.

[4.65] In the face of this uncertainty, emergency workers may act in the interests of preserving life and health. Sometimes relatives or those around may seek to assure ambulance officers that a person, now unconscious or otherwise incompetent, has expressed a clear wish that treatment not go ahead. In the absence of any real evidence of this, such as a written advance directive, those rendering care may reasonably consider there is enough doubt as to the person's refusal for them to disregard such a claim, and that their duty of care overrides such doubt. Whilst there is no definitive case law on the matter, it is the author's view that this would be a good defence to any claim that they should not have gone ahead. Reasonable action may also be taken, as described elsewhere, for the protection of oneself or of others, or of property.

Suicide

[4.66] Where people have attempted suicide, the overwhelming practice in Australia has been to provide emergency treatment to preserve their lives, in the face of evidence that they do not want this. One justification used for so doing is a generalised belief that most attempted suicides are really attempts to attract attention rather than genuine attempts to end life. No one in Australia who has been "rescued" from a suicide attempt has successfully sued their "saviours" in battery to the author's knowledge, and it is doubtful whether such a suit would succeed. This is because of the court's ready acceptance of the medical opinion that there is uncertainty that suicide attempts are genuine (which is a generalisation adopted by most health carers). The law, when in doubt, opts for life rather than no life, and treatment rather than no treatment. This is also reflected in the fact that some jurisdictions have provided in their Crimes Acts that it is not assault or battery at criminal law to restrain or attempt to stop a person from committing suicide.[1]

[4.67] In the case of Elizabeth Bouvia and the Riverside Hospital the trial court refused Bouvia an injunction ordering the hospital to cease force feeding her to prevent her carrying out her wish to be allowed to die. The court agreed with the hospital that the injunction would require it to assist suicide, against ethical and professional standards, and also that it had the right to decide how to treat patients "taking up its space". On appeal the Superior Court of California held that the patient's motives for refusing treatment were not relevant. It also considered relevant her dependency on the hospital and lack of alternative health care institutions that would care for her as she wished. The court concluded: "It is not illegal or immoral to prefer a natural albeit sooner death than a drugged life attached to a mechanical device ... [having accepted her the hospital] may not deny her relief from pain and suffering merely because she has chosen her fundamental right to protect what little privacy

---

[1] *Crimes Act* 1900 (ACT), s 18; *Crimes Act* 1900 (NSW), s 574B; *Criminal Law Consolidation Act* 1935 (SA), s 13(a); *Crimes Act* 1958 (Vic), s 463B.

remains to her." It overturned the lower court's decision (*Bouvia v County of Riverside* (unreported, 16 December 1983, SC Riverside County Cal, No 159780); *Bouvia v Supreme Court*, 179 Cal App 3d 1127; 225 Cal Rptr 297 (1986)). It has been recently held by the House of Lords that those who accede to a person's refusal of treatment are not aiding and abetting suicide (*Airedale NHS Trust v Bland*; see [14.104]). [4.71]

Necessity

[4.68] There has developed, in criminal law, the defence of "necessity". It is used to argue that the defendant was justified in breaching the law as the action was taken to avert a harm which was much more severe. The defence has two elements:

- .....the defendant must have had a reasonable and honest belief in the need to act in this way to avert the harm (and that there is no better means of doing it);
- .....the harm to be avoided must be proportionately more severe than that which is caused.

[4.69] Originally necessity applied to acts taken to prevent the commission of felonies, to apprehend offenders, or in self-defence. It was applied by the Supreme Court of Victoria in the case of *R v Davidson* [1969] VR 667 in which a doctor was tried for unlawful abortion. The court there decided that:

> for the use of an instrument with intent to procure a miscarriage to be lawful . . . the accused must have honestly believed on reasonable grounds that the act done by him was (a) necessary to preserve the woman from a serious danger to her life or her physical or mental health (not being merely the normal dangers of pregnancy and childbirth) which the continuance of the pregnancy would entail; and (b) in the circumstances not out of proportion to the danger to be averted.

[4.70] The doctor was found not guilty. This was a criminal case, but some commentators suggest that the defendant in a civil case of battery involving medical procedures could argue that he or she honestly believed a procedure was necessary because otherwise the person would suffer serious danger to life or health, and the procedure was not out of proportion to the danger to be averted.

[4.71] Mason ((2000), p 8) describes the doctrine as having, after lurking at the outer margins of medical law, "recently burst into new life in England". It was referred to in *Re F (mental patient: sterilisation)* [1990] 2 AC 1; *Airedale NHS Trust v Bland* [1993] AC 789 at 867; *Re W (a minor) (consent to medical treatment)* [1993] 1 FLR 381. In *R v Bournewood Community and Mental Health NHS Trust* [1999] 1 AC 458 at 490 the House of Lords held that care could be given to a compliant incompetent person on the basis of necessity. More recently, in the case of *Re A (the "Siamese Twins Case")* [2000] (see [14.138]) the doctrine of necessity was considered and accepted as a basis for the carrying out of a procedure that would cause the death of one of the Siamese twins to save the life of the other,

[4.71] when both would otherwise die. "Necessity" was referred to by the Australian High Court as a possible basis for treatment without consent in *Rogers v Whitaker* (see [4.98]). However, given the unquestionable principle of competent patient autonomy, and the specific laws in Australia relating to the care of those who are not competent, it is suggested that there is no clear exposition of any legal principle of "necessity" that provides for treatment of a competent person without their consent. It is considered that requirements of a concept of necessity are in effect no different to those of emergency, and reference to "necessity" is apt to cause confusion amongst health carers. As a clear definition has not been accepted for civil cases, it should be approached with caution (see Mason, p 9).

[4.72] Skene ((1998), p 83) argues:

> Although there is no authority on point, there would seem to be no reason why a broad principle of necessity should not be accepted by an Australian court [as indicated in *Rogers v Whitaker*], with the court, rather than medical practice, ultimately determining whether the principle of necessity justified the doctor's action in a given case.

[4.73] To do this, however, would in the author's view severely limit, if not remove, the principle of autonomy. It would also leave health carers in great doubt as to when necessity applies and when it does not.

[4.74] The gravity of the situation would be of crucial interest in determining any justification of necessity: for example, consideration would be given to what state the client was in, the urgency for action, the seriousness of the potential harm, etc. Where the client was lucid and determined to refuse treatment, the law would not consider lightly a lack of regard for that refusal. Where a person is competent, but requires multiple procedures and treatments in an emergency, to seek their consent to these may well be impracticable in preserving life and limb. In such a case courts may accept actions based on necessity, but the law is far from clear at present.

Best Interests of the Client

[4.75] Another approach some English cases have introduced is the principle that a patient may be treated in the absence of consent when it is in his or her best interests. It has been recognised that a person is entitled to determine their own best interests, and that this approach will only arise where the person is not competent to do this. This is discussed at [5.100].

Self-defence

[4.76] Action may be taken which is necessary for self-protection, the protection of others, or the protection of property, even where this results in harm to the person.

■ ■ ■ CASE [4.80]
Fontin v Katapodis (1962) 108 CLR 177 (High Court of Australia)

Katapodis (K) sued Fontin (F), a hardware shop assistant, in battery. K had purchased goods at the shop, and some days later returned. F accused him of failing to pay for the goods. K produced a receipt after some argument, and the manager apologised. Not F, however; the argument between him and K continued, and K seized a wooden T-Square, hitting F with it twice. F threw a piece of glass at K, who dropped the T-Square and raised his hand to protect his face. He suffered serious and permanent damage as a result of severance of the ulnar nerve at the base of the thumb. F claimed, on the basis of these facts, that his action was self-defence under the attack of K.

[4.77] The court agreed that K had assaulted F, and that F was entitled to protect himself. However, it was decided by the court that F's action was in excess of that necessary to so do. A piece of glass can do a lot of harm, the court said, and aimed at the face, it is a very dangerous weapon—far more dangerous than that used by K. The court stated that while K might have caused more harm if F did not prevent him from doing so, F's action in throwing a piece of glass was out of all proportion to the danger confronting him. He could easily have moved away.

[4.78] Health carers may take measures, even severe ones, to protect themselves from harm from others, for example, disoriented or aggressive patients. Avoidance of contact (backing off) should be the first consideration of anyone in the face of an attack, seeking help the second. If it is not feasible to evade contact, choosing a weapon, striking blows or immobilising someone involves a consideration of what would stop the *attack* rather than what would stop the *person*—unless, of course, stopping the person is the only way to protect oneself or others, which leads to the next defence.

Defence of Another and Defence of Property

[4.79] A similar principle applies where action is required to prevent someone from harming a third person. The amount of force used must be reasonably proportional to the degree of injury to be expected from the assault upon the stranger. As Crawford J said in *Goss v Nicholas* [1960] Tas SR 133 at 144:

> The time factor must also be taken into account, and if it is possible gently to restrain the would-be assailant, then this should be the manner of dealing with him.

[4.80] Of course, it is recognised that such situations may occur in an atmosphere of stress and emergency. A genuine and honest mistake as to the gravity of a situation may occur. If this is the case one court has held that it would be unjust to penalise someone who acted according to that mistaken belief; for example, that a gun is loaded when it is not, or that a person is armed when that is not so (*R v Fennell* [1971] 1 QB 428 (English Court of Appeal)).

[4.81] **[4.81]** Where defence of property is at issue, measures taken to protect it may involve force against another. Indeed, employees have an obligation to take reasonable steps to protect their employer's property (see Ch 10). Reasonable steps in this sort of situation would be calculated on the balancing of harm to a person against harm to property. Obviously one would draw the line in such a situation long before one would when human life and well-being are involved.

Statutory Power to Use Force

[4.82] This can only occur when the client comes under criteria set out by a court order, statutory requirement, mental health legislation (Ch 5) or child welfare legislation (Chs 5 and 16).

Information and Consent

[4.83] It has been stated above that a certain amount of understanding is required before a person can be said to have given "competent" consent to treatment. However, there is general consensus at law that a person who has agreed to health care when they have not been adequately informed as to the nature and consequences of the procedure, and substantial risks (including side effects) should have a remedy at law. The term "informed consent" has a place in US law, where lack of such information gives rise to an action in battery, but this is not the case in English or Australian law. It has been well established by the High Court of Australia that the term "informed consent" has no special legal meaning in our law (*Rogers v Whitaker* at [4.98]). The term "informed consent" is used frequently, in fact so frequently that it often seems to have lost its meaning. Indeed, if health carers were questioned, the author doubts that many would have any clear idea of what it means at all, and what it requires of them as health carers. The result is a confusion over just what one is supposed to be doing when "securing the patient's informed consent".

[4.84] The expression "informed consent" can itself have unfortunate connotations. It can be interpreted as involving the ritual of a one-way flow of information, and the return of agreement to the proposed treatment (the terminology "securing the patient's informed consent", in the author's opinion denotes the attitude of inevitability health carers have to the patient's agreeing to treatment). As Bollen J in *Daniels v Burfield* stated at par 67 at [4.94]:

> The use of the expression "informed consent" may be, like other labels, unfortunate. It may promote a narrow view of a case or too "compartmentalised" a view. Before anyone was clever enough to use the phrase a surgeon, indeed any doctor, owed his patient a duty which included the giving of careful and thorough advice and information.

[4.85] Thus English and Australian courts have considered lack of full information as being a matter of negligence rather than a lack of consent, so long as the patient knew the general nature of the procedure. This was [4.90] established in the English case of *Sidaway v Governors of the Bethlem Royal Hospital* [1985] 1 All ER 643 (House of Lords), where the court drew the distinction between the "ordinary risks" of surgery, about which no information need be given, and "material" risks, which are special to the particular procedure to be undertaken. It has been followed in Australia (see *Battersby v Tottman* (1985) 37 SASR 524, discussed below, Ch 5). However, what can be considered "ordinary" risks as opposed to "material risks" is problematic, and the practice of some health carers in considering *all* risks that may be considered not far-fetched or fanciful as material is recommended.

[4.86] Despite the above, for the ease of recognition, the expression "informed consent" is retained in this book. However it must be understood that this term is not used as a legal term.

Lack of Information as a Ground for Negligence

[4.87] In English and Australian law, where a person makes a decision which is based on unreasonably inadequate information, they must sue the person responsible in negligence, not battery. The action in negligence is outlined in Chapter 6, but, in relation to information, requires that the client show that:

- .....the health carer had a duty of care to provide the information;
- .....that duty was breached by the failure to provide the information;
- .....the client would not have agreed to the health care if adequate information had been given; and
- .....as a result, the client suffered harm.

[4.88] As there is no requirement to prove a duty of care or harm in an action in battery, an action based on lack of adequate information is procedurally more difficult than one in battery.

What Information Should be Given?

[4.89] The court will consider what a reasonable doctor should have told the patient under the circumstances. It would seem that details that may alarm a sensitive patient and unduly influence that person against treatment considered necessary, need not be given; although the House of Lords has recently decided that the courts and not the medical profession will determine what is reasonable information in any particular case (*Gillick's* case [1985] 3 All ER 402, see Ch 5). The High Court of Australia endorsed this principle in *Rogers v Whitaker* (see [4.98]).

[4.90] It is instructive to note that in a survey of 1,158 doctors published in May 1993, 84 per cent of respondents said there were circumstances in which they would be justified in withholding information from patients. Of these 41 per cent said they would withhold information because the patient might refuse the treatment, 53 per cent because they considered

[4.90] the patient a poor decision maker. A significant number also based their decision on judgment as to the patient's anxiety (77 per cent), illness (85 per cent), or lack of interest in knowing (65 per cent). On the other hand, other studies have shown that patients want doctors to give them information, even if it is unfavourable (94-96 per cent), even when they do not ask for it (Hancock, L, *Defensive Medicine and Informed Consent* (Review of Professional Indemnity Arrangement for Health Care Professionals) (AGPS, Canberra, 1993)).

[4.91] There is a growing volume of opinion that the patient should also be informed of alternative treatments that may be available. However, there is little case law on what information on alternative treatment is reasonable and should be given to a client in Australia.

[4.92] There are ethical guidelines relating to the giving of information, and courts will take these into account, but there is no precise legal concept of "informed consent". Although the giving of adequate information is a necessary ingredient of reasonable and professionally accepted treatment, the Australian High Court in *Rogers v Whitaker* (1992) 109 ALR 625 at 632 (see below [4.98]) sought to differentiate between autonomy and negligence:

> The right of self-determination is an expression which is, perhaps, suitable to cases where the issue is whether a person has agreed to the general surgical procedure or treatment, but is of little assistance in the balancing process that is involved in the determination of whether there has been a breach of the duty of disclosure. Likewise, the phrase "informed consent" is apt to mislead, as it suggests a test of the validity of a patient's consent . . . Anglo-Australian law has rightly taken the view that an allegation that the risks inherent in a medical procedure have not been disclosed to the patient can only found an action in negligence and not in trespass; the consent necessary to negative the offence of battery is satisfied by the patient being advised in broad terms of the nature of the procedure to be performed.

[4.93] Some jurisdictions have set out what is "informed consent" for specific purposes, such as for those who have a mental illness (see *Mental Health Act* 1986 (Vic), s 72; *Mental Health Act* 1990 (NSW), ss 156, 183) or those undergoing assisted reproductive services (see Infertility (Medical Procedures) Regulations 1988 (Vic)). The following requirements for "informed consent" to electroconvulsive therapy and psychosurgery are set out in New South Wales:

▌▌▌ STATUTE [4.94]
MENTAL HEALTH ACT 1990 (NSW), SECTION 183
Requirements for obtaining informed consent
183 (1) Before the consent of a person is obtained to the administration to the person of a treatment to which this Division applies:
(a) a fair explanation must be made to the person of the techniques or procedures to be followed, including an identification and explanation of any technique or procedure about which there is not sufficient data to recommend it as a recognised treatment or to reliably predict the outcome of its performance; and
(b) a full description must be given, without exaggeration or concealment, to the person of the possible attendant discomforts and risks (including possible loss of memory), if any; and
(c) a full description must be given to the person of the benefits, if any, to be expected; and
(d) a full disclosure must be made, without exaggeration or concealment, to the person of appropriate alternative treatments, if any, that would be advantageous for the person; and
(e) an offer must be made to the person to answer any inquiries concerning the procedures or any part of them; and
(f) notice must be given to the person that the person is free to refuse or to withdraw consent and to discontinue the procedures or any of them at any time; and
(g) a full disclosure must be made to the person of any financial relationship between the person proposing the administration of the treatment or the medical practitioner who proposes to administer the treatment, or both, and the hospital or institution in which it is proposed to administer the treatment; and
(h) notice must be given to the person that the person has the right to obtain legal and medical advice and to be represented before giving consent; and
(i) any question relating to the techniques or procedures to be followed that is asked by the person must have been answered and the answers must appear to have been understood by the person.
The Act provides that a person is to be taken to have given informed consent to the specific procedure if she or he has given a free, voluntary and written consent after the above information has been given, in a language which can be understood.

[4.94] In situations not covered by legislation, there is a duty to disclose material or substantial risks, and determination of what these are will depend on the circumstances of individual cases. There are some conflicting decisions as to what are material or substantial risks in similar cases. For example, in the case of *Thake v Maurice* [1986] 1 All ER 497 the court held that the risk of recanalisation after vasectomy should be disclosed to a patient, whereas in the cases of *Eyre v Measday* [1986] 1 All ER 488 and *F v R* (1983) 33 SASR 189 the Court of Appeal and the South Australian Court of Appeal respectively held that there was no negligence where surgeons failed to inform patients of the remote chance of reversal of a tubal ligation.

[4.94] ■■■ **CASE**
Daniels v Burfield (unreported, 17 October 1991, SC SA, [1991] SASC 3072)

The plaintiff, Mr Daniels, had a vasectomy, which he later wanted reversed (a "vasovasostomy"). The defendant, Dr Burfield performed a bilateral vasovasostomy, as a result of which the plaintiff suffered loss of use of the right testicle, and extensive pain. The plaintiff sued in negligence, arguing, among other things, that he had not been properly informed of the possibility of loss of use of a testicle.

[4.95] The judge considered what the plaintiff had been told by the defendant. That was:

■ .....that he could not guarantee 100 per cent success, and why this was so;
■ .....that he could not assure the same success rate as with other surgical work;
■ .....that he could estimate a 80-90 per cent success rate for the production of sperm, and a 60 per cent success rate for pregnancy; and
■ .....that there would be more bruising and more discomfort and swelling than after an uneventful vasectomy (paragraph 59).

[4.96] There was no information about the possibility of damage to the testes. Of the several specialists who gave evidence (of which the defendant was one) only one said he warned of this possibility, and then only as a "worst case scenario". Others considered it too uncommon, and the plaintiff said he did not consider it "normally as an accepted risk of the procedure" (paragraph 66). The judge found that the defendant was not in breach of his duty, as the risk of loss of the testicle was much too remote. He invoked a term used in an earlier case adopted by the courts, saying the risk was "far fetched or fanciful", and thus that it was not unreasonable for the defendant not to warn the plaintiff. This approach was also used by Gaudron J in *Rogers v Whitaker* (see [4.98]).

■■■ **CASE**
Young v Northern Territory and Others (1992) 107 FLR 264

The plaintiff, who had a history of mild pelvic inflammatory disease (PID), made a six-weekly post-natal visit to Darwin Hospital. There she was advised that the oral contraception which she was taking would be inappropriate under the circumstances and that she should have an intra-uterine contraceptive device (IUCD) inserted. There was some question in the evidence as to whether the plaintiff's uterus had fully returned to its normal size, but accepted by the court that the notation in the plaintiff's notes that it was "6 weeks" meant that it had not. The plaintiff said she did not want the IUCD, as a previous IUCD had caused her severe pain and excessive bleeding, and resulted in a laparoscopy and scarring. She finally agreed to the insertion, however, with resulting perforation of the uterus (and resulting pain and bleeding) and lodgment of the IUCD in the eploicacae of the sigmoid. The IUCD had to be removed by laparoscopy, and curettage was also required. As a result, she suffered from amenorrhoea, dyspareunia, uterine fibrosis, a diseased uterus and bilateral tubal disease.

[4.97] It was argued among other things, and accepted by the court, that, given the patient's recent delivery, her history in relation to the IUCD and PID and the notation by the doctor that her uterus was still enlarged to some degree, there was an increased risk of perforation of the uterus. The court held that the plaintiff should have been told of the risk of perforation, and of alternative forms of contraception, as she would not have had the IUCD inserted if she had been told.

[4.98] A more comprehensive consideration of what information should be given, which resulted in a restrictive approach, was undertaken by the High Court of Australia in the same year.

CASE
Rogers v Whitaker (1992) 109 ALR 625 (High Court of Australia)

The patient, Ms Whitaker, decided to have elective surgery on her right eye, which was vision-impaired from an accident which had occurred in her youth. Despite the almost total blindness resulting in the right eye, she had led a "substantially normal life", working, marrying and raising children. However on having a check-up, surgery was recommended on the basis that she could benefit, even cosmetically. Subsequent to surgery complications developed in the right eye, spreading to the left eye and resulting in almost total blindness. This is known as "sympathetic ophthalmia", and is a recognised risk of eye surgery. At no stage was Ms Whitaker warned of the probability of this occurring. Ms Whitaker sued in negligence on several grounds, including failure of Dr Rogers to warn her of the risk of sympathetic ophthalmia, performing an ill-advised operation, failure to follow up missed appointments, failure to enucleate the right eye following development of symptoms of sympathetic ophthalmia in the left eye.

[4.99] The defence relied on the principle enunciated in *Bolam v Friern Hospital Management Committee* (see discussion of *Sidaway* above). That case ruled that the decision of what to tell a person is one which the doctor can make, based on medical judgment. That would make a doctor not negligent if he or she acts in accordance with a practice of disclosure or non-disclosure accepted at the time as proper practice by a responsible body of medical opinion, even if some doctors adopt a different practice. They produced evidence from a group of specialists who supported Dr Rogers' actions. They also relied on the fact that the risk of sympathetic ophthalmia was considered to be 1 in 14,000, and therefore too remote to mention to the client. The judge in the trial rejected all but the first ground of complaint, and ruled that the failure to warn of the risk of sympathetic ophthalmia amounted to negligence. He considered the following facts:

- ..... Ms Whitaker had expressed a keen interest in avoiding harm to her good eye, and Dr Rogers was aware of this;
- ..... she repeatedly asked about risks;
- ..... Dr Rogers was aware at the time of the risk, although it was remote;
- ..... the failure to warn of the risk was not contemplated for therapeutic reasons; and
- ..... had Ms Whitaker been advised of the risk, she would not have had the surgery.

92 | HEALTH CARE AND THE LAW

[4.100] **[4.100]** The appeal went first to the New South Wales Court of Appeal where it was dismissed, and then to the High Court of Australia. The High Court said that the principle in *Bolam* is no longer applicable in determining whether a medical practitioner has given adequate information about a medical procedure to a patient. Instead the court followed the judgment of King J in *F v R* (1983) 33 SASR 189 in which he stated that although the court will consider evidence by medical specialists of what is considered proper medical practice, it is ultimately for the court to determine what the appropriate standard of care is, and that the paramount consideration is to be that a person is entitled to make her or his own decisions about her or his life. The court went on to say that the more drastic the proposed procedure, such as major surgery, the more necessary it is to keep the patient informed about the risks.

[4.101] The High Court drew a distinction between *diagnosis and treatment* on the one hand, and *provision of information*, on the other. The former was held to be determined by medical judgment and practice, whereas the provision of adequate information is a *right*. Information is a right. This right is not based on medical judgment, but on legal principles, and it is for the court to decide whether a person's right to be adequately informed about a procedure has been breached or not. This may be based on consideration of medical practitioners as what is considered appropriate practice, but in the final analysis it will be a matter for the court to determine, given the paramount consideration that people are entitled to make their own decisions about their lives.

> The ultimate question, however, is not whether the defendant's conduct accords with the practices of his profession or some part of it, but whether it conforms to the standard of reasonable care demanded by the law. That is a question for the court and the duty of deciding it cannot be delegated to any profession or group in the community [*F v R* (1983) 33 SASR 189 per King CJ at 194: quoted with approval by the High Court in *Rogers v Whitaker*; see also *Ellis v Wallsend District Hospital* [1989] Aust Torts Reports ¶80-259; *H v Royal Alexandra Hospital for Children & Ors* [1990] Aust Torts Reports ¶81-000].

[4.102] The question of what is "reasonable" is a difficult one, and is considered in more detail in Chapter 6.

Client Should be Told of "Material Risks"

[4.103] The High Court stated that the patient should be told of any material risk inherent in the treatment. A material risk is one:

- .....to which a reasonable person in the patient's condition would be likely to attach significance;
- .....to which the health carer knows (or ought to know) the particular patient would be likely to attach significance; and
- .....about which questions asked by the patient reveal her or his concern.

[4.104] The court also established that the fact that a person does not insist on information being provided does not reduce the health carer's duty (or client's right) that it be provided. This means that health carers must be careful to take account of factors associated with the special needs of clients, "be they wishes, anxieties or beliefs" (Kerridge and Mitchell, (1994), p 241). Justice Gaudron stated that where no specific inquiry is made, the duty is to provide the information that would reasonably be required by a person in the position of the client. This requires the health carer to consider what they ought to anticipate as this particular client's needs, wishes etc. For example, where the client is a professional singer or speaker, one could argue that the health carer ought to anticipate that he or she would have a particular interest in any risk of harm to the vocal chords.

[4.105] It was accepted that Ms Whitaker may not have asked the right question to elicit information about sympathetic ophthalmia, but she made clear her concern that nothing should happen to her good eye. The placing of an onus on the patient to ask questions could be considered somewhat unfair, but the matter was not pursued further by the court.

▮▮▮ CASE
Percival v Rosenberg (25 May 1999, SC Appeal WA, WAS 31 FUL 176 of 1997)

> The plaintiff had an underdeveloped jaw, and required a saggital split osteotomy. Postoperatively, she suffered excessive pain and further procedures were undertaken, resulting in "excruciating pain" on attempting to open her mouth. Further procedures were undertaken with the result that the appellant had difficulty opening her mouth, eating and speaking. She claimed she lost her university lecturing position, and enjoyment of life. It was established that she had signs of a condition called tempero-mandibular joint disorder, a condition which caused a small risk of the complications which eventuated after saggital split osteotomy. However, this risk is well documented. The trial judge found in favour of the defendant surgeon because it was not clear that the surgeon should reasonably have concluded that there was a risk. The plaintiff appealed to the Western Australian Supreme Court of Appeal.

[4.106] In this case the patient's condition suggested that there was some risk of complications due to the pathology of the joints, and her long history of illness. The court held that there was ample evidence of possible risk. Also, it was not a question of the resultant harm being a rare occurrence (such as was the case in *Chappel v Hart*, see [4.111]) and not mentioned in textbooks. This risk was known generally to the medical profession.

[4.107] The Court of Appeal reversed this finding, holding that once there is a risk which is generally known to the profession, there is clearly a duty to warn.

Since the above was written the High Court heard an appeal from the Court of Appeal's judgment and upheld the trial judge's finding. The Court held that the two main issues arising from the case were, firstly,

[4.107] whether the appellant was in breach of his duty of care to the respondent, by failing to bring to her notice the risk of the harm that eventuated and secondly, if there had been such a breach of duty, whether it was causally related to the respondent's injuries. That in turn involved the question whether, if she had been made aware of the risk, the respondent would have decided not to undergo the surgery. The Court was not convinced that she would have forgone the surgery, and so it became unnecessary to determine the answers to the first two questions.

The Court, however, undertook a thorough consideration of the law in relation to information.

The Court reiterated the *Rogers v Whitaker* ruling that there are two alternative tests of materiality in determining what are "material risks": the objective test of what risks a reasonable person in the patient's circumstances would consider significant, and the subjective test of those risks the particular patient actually considers to be significant. As Dr Percival had not expressed any particular concerns (except to have the operation), the Court held that, unlike *Rogers v Whitaker*, the issue was one of whether the objective criterion had been met, and determined that it had. It also agreed with precedent that a risk is real and foreseeable if it is not far-fetched and fanciful.

Other principles reinforced by the Court were that:

- ..... the law demands no more than what was reasonable under the circumstances, and that 'reasonable' is the operative word;
- ..... matters such as the severity and likely eventuation of the risk must be weighed up against the need for the surgery and availability of alternative treatment;
- ..... one should not be too quick to discard consideration of the subjective criterion simply because the patient asked no questions.

The Court pointed out that there is a danger in hindsight influencing a person's perception of whether a risk was foreseeable at the time information was given, as the fact that the risk did materialise can convince one it is foreseeable. The word "reasonable" when applied to foreseeability, means that foreseeability is limited to what would have been reasonable for the health carer, with the knowledge of an ordinarily skilled practitioner, to have foreseen as a material risk. Justice Kirby also considered the many reasons given for not setting out all foreseeable risks, such as time, the ability or willingness of the client to understand the details and practicality. He recognised that these factors do affect the communication process, but pointed to the principles laid down by *Rogers v Whitaker*, which have not been changed over time, and which, he said, serve the purpose of "nagging" and "prodding" health carers as best practice in communication and legal insurance against liability.

Implications for Health Carers

[4.108] The case law has developed in the past few years to become more specific in its outline of what information should be given to clients. It would now seem to be clearly articulated that so long as a procedure or medication involves a risk which is known or *ought to be known* to the [4.109] carer, then this should be disclosed to the client. This, of course, applies to all who are able or entitled at law to make a decision about their treatment. Thus where it is proposed that clients, including nursing home residents, should undergo some form of care not in the course of care already agreed to, such as a medicated bath, application of ointment, the taking of medication or involvement in physiotherapy or complementary therapy, they should be given the opportunity to decide whether to undergo that care. Where that care involves a material risk to the client this should be explained. Where it is for a therapeutic purpose and there are reasonably available alternatives, they should be advised of this. If they are unable to understand or decide, then the appropriate person at law (being a relative does not automatically entitle one to consent) should be contacted and informed.

▌▌▌ CHECKLIST
WHEN IS "INFORMED CONSENT" REQUIRED?

All health carers owe a duty of care to clients to consider the need for "informed consent" when any proposed procedure involves:
- ▌.....a recognised risk of side-effects or adverse effects;
- ▌.....any side-effects or adverse effects that the proposed client would consider significant;
- ▌.....alternative procedures that are reasonably available that the health carer can offer; and
- ▌.....the effects on the client of not having the procedure.

A recognised risk can be established by considering:
- ▌.....texts, articles and courses to which the health carer has or ought to have access;
- ▌.....required knowledge;
- ▌.....accepted and widespread practice; and
- ▌.....codes of health care practice.

"Therapeutic privilege"

[4.109] There is a view that information may be withheld on the basis of "therapeutic privilege", which was referred to by the court in *Rogers v Whitaker*. "Therapeutic privilege" has not been clearly defined by the courts, however the High Court referred to a situation where "there is a particular danger that the provision of all relevant information will harm an unusually nervous, disturbed or volatile patient" (at paragraph 14) where special skill is required in advising the patient. Although the majority of judges did not discuss in detail to what extent therapeutic privilege applies, they did describe it as "an opportunity afforded to the doctor to prove that he or she reasonably believed that disclosure of a risk would prove damaging to the patient" (see also *Canterbury v Spence* (1972) 464 F 2d 772 at 789; *Sidaway v Governors of the Bethlem Royal Hospital* [1985] 1 All ER 643 per Lord Scarman; *Battersby v Tottman* (1985) 37 SASR 524 at 527-528, 534-535; Mason (2000), p 7). Gaudron J did make some specific statements which indicated that therapeutic privilege should be very limited. She stated that:

[4.109]   I see no basis for any exception [from the need to inform the client] or "therapeutic privilege" which is not based in *medical emergency* or in *considerations of the patient's ability to receive, understand or properly evaluate the significance of the information* that would ordinarily be required with respect to his or her condition or the treatment proposed. (Emphasis added)

[4.110] The above approach would appear to define "therapeutic privilege" as meaning nothing more than careful consideration as to what and how information is given to a person in an emergency and where he or she has limited capacity. The question of just what circumstances justify withholding information on the basis of therapeutic privilege is thus unanswered by judicial decisions, but it is suggested that it is based on whether the provision of information will actually exacerbate the health problems of particularly at-risk clients (for example, those with a mental illness), or enhance his or her decision-making capacity by withholding information that would impair it, rather than making the expression of consent to a proposed procedure difficult (Freckelton (1999), p 119; Schwartz and Grubb (1985), p 19).

Emergency and Necessity

All the judges in *Rogers v Whitaker* referred to emergency and necessity as being circumstances which presented exceptions to the provision of information. However, as these circumstances were not relevant to the present case, they did not consider what actually amounted to circumstances of emergency or necessity. Emergency and necessity are dealt with at [4.58] and [4.68] respectively.

Effect of *Rogers v Whitaker*

[4.111] *Rogers v Whitaker* was a landmark case in that it cut across frequent confusion and contradictions to establish two main principles:

1).....the client has a legal right to adequate information about the nature of any proposed procedure, and the material risks associated with the procedure; and
2).....that two broad perspectives are used in deciding how to judge the adequacy of information: the doctor-centred perspective (that is, usual practice adopted by the profession) and the patient-centred perspective (what is of importance and use to the patient). Faden and Beauchamp ((1986), p 278) discuss these different approaches and their legal and social effects. *Rogers v Whitaker* quite clearly indicates that the law gives preference to the patient-centred perspective.

■■■ CASE   [4.113]
Chappel v Hart (1998) 256 ALR 517 (High Court of Australia)

The plaintiff, Mrs Hart, was advised by the defendant, Dr Chappel that she required surgery for removal of a pharyngal pouch in her oesophagus (Endoscopic Zenker's Diverticulotomy). The condition was one that was relentlessly progressive, and while she did not have to have the operation at this time, Mrs Hart accepted that it would be necessary at some time in the future. She was assured by Dr Chappel that it was a "common operation". He also mentioned the risk of perforation of the larynx as a recognised complication. Mrs Hart, whose occupation required a degree of public speaking, expressed concern at the possible effect to her voice (she stated that she did not want to end up sounding like Neville Wran—a former New South Wales Premier who had surgery which resulted in his speaking with a rasp). Despite this, Dr Chappel did not warn her of the possibility of perforation of the oesophagus, with resulting contraction of mediastinitis, which could lead to damage to the vocal chords. It was accepted that perforation could occur in between one in 20 and one in 40 procedures, and that consequent infection and damage to vocal chords was very rare. One expert witness testified that he had carried out between 100 and 150 such operations without the occurrence of perforation of the oesophagus. The trial court also accepted evidence that the more experience the surgeon had, the less likely that complications such as these would occur. Dr Chappel was not as experienced as the witness, and Mrs Hart argued successfully that as the operation was not urgent, had she known of the potential result, she would have sought a more experienced surgeon. Dr Chappel appealed to the High Court.

[4.112] The High Court upheld the finding, concluding that Dr Chappel was negligent in not providing the information to Mrs Hart. Given her questions about the possible effect on her voice, the court held, he should have been more forthcoming. Having been put on notice of her concerns, he should have known that such a risk was a material one to her, and provided her with adequate and appropriate information for decision making.

[4.113] Mrs Hart's argument was that if she had been made aware of the risk to her vocal chords, she would have undergone the operation later, after finding someone least likely to cause the harm which in fact resulted. While the facts of the case thus did not require the court to consider precisely what information should have been given to her, Justice Gaudron held that the doctor's duty was to inform her that there were more experienced surgeons practising in the field. Thus, in her view, there is a duty on health carers additional to disclosure of material risks: and that is information related to the competence and skills of the health carer. While it must be noted that the majority finding was based on the failure to advise of a risk, Gaudron J's approach, if adopted by future courts, would seem to require that health carers must advise a client if there is someone more experienced than they are where the client indicates particular concern about the outcome.

Answering Questions

[4.114] Until *Rogers v Whitaker* the courts made few demands on the medical practitioner when giving information other than those resulting from professional discretion. However, the law did require that where the patient asks specific questions, the practitioner must take more care. It was clearly established in *Rogers v Whitaker* that a person's questions should be taken as indicating that he or she may have particular concerns that will require special attention by health carers.

CASE
Smith v Auckland Hospital Board [1965] NZLR 191 (CA New Zealand)

Smith entered Green Lane Hospital, Auckland for aortography—the insertion of a catheter in the femoral artery towards the aorta and injection of dye for the purpose of X-ray. A low probability of gangrene as the result of dislodgment of arterial atheromatous material existed, but when he asked the surgeon "Is there any risk attached to this?" he was told "Old chap, within a couple of days you will be back home". In fact the risk did materialise, and Smith lost a leg through resulting gangrene.

[4.115] The court held that a doctor must use due care in answering the question of a patient where the patient, to the knowledge of the doctor, intends to place reliance on that answer in making a decision. *Rogers v Whitaker* held that a "normal" patient who asks questions which indicate a serious desire for relevant information is entitled to a careful and skilful answer, which should only omit mention of a risk if that risk is too remote ("far-fetched or fanciful"), or for therapeutic reasons (see [4.109]).

[4.116] There are two points to make about this finding:

1)......The court did not require a full and honest response. It adopted a similar approach to *Hedley Byrne & Co v Heller & Partners* [1964] AC 465 which involved advice given to the plaintiff by a bank. The court extended that to the medical field. In *Hedley Byrne* the court held that if any person, acting as a professional with certain skills, is asked a question and he or she knows or ought to know that the questioner is relying on professional advice to make a decision, then the professional has a duty of care to give the advice carefully, bound by the "reasonable person" test (see Ch 6). Thus, the giving of advice is made subject to the law of negligence.

2)......It endorses the favourable approach of the courts to medical discretion, as there is no requirement to tell the client the truth, or all the facts. Indeed, some courts have expressly sanctioned the withholding of information when it is considered that the client may be emotionally unable to cope with it (see "therapeutic privilege", discussed in the case of *Battersby v Tottman* at [5.95] and *Rogers v Whitaker* at [4.98]). Therapeutic privilege has been accepted in England and North America. As stated above, in Australia there appears to be conflicting views among the judiciary.

[4.117] An instructive case as to how the courts consider what information should be given follows.

▌▌▌ CASE
Gover v South Australia (1985) 39 SASR 543 (SC SA)
A client who suffered from thyroid eye disease underwent blepharoplasty and canthoplasty. She had not been told what was involved in the operations, or the risks or dangers of it. She had expected only the left eye to be operated on, and so was surprised when the surgeon told her that he did not know which one it was "so we done [sic] both". These procedures involved some degree of risk of blindness, entropion or trichiasis. In fact the patient did develop trichiasis and entropion. The court had to consider whether the doctor was negligent in failing to warn her of the risks.

[4.118] Cox J held that the duty of care owed by a doctor includes "the whole of the professional relationship" including the provision of information. The next question involved what information should have been given. The judge said that professionals should keep abreast of developments. Thus the professional should be reasonably knowledgeable and up-to-date. Further, it was held that even where a risk may be small, if its effect is likely to be devastating (as blindness would be) then this should be told to the client. In *Battersby's* case Cox J quotes the Chief Justice as saying in an earlier case:

> The more drastic the proposed intervention in the patient's physical make-up, the more necessary it is to keep him fully informed as to the likely risks and likely consequences of the intervention [*F v R* (1983) 33 SASR 189 at 192-194].

[4.119] However, it was stressed that the condition of the patient should be considered. It is argued that this begs the question: does that mean that if it is considered that the patient would not be able to cope emotionally with the information that it need not be given under the principle of therapeutic privilege (see Ch 5)?

Plaintiff Must Prove that Ignorance Affected Decision

[4.120] In the *Gover case* the plaintiff here was not able to convince the court that had she been given the information she would not have had the operation. Thus although she should have been told of the risks, she was unsuccessful in her suit because this critical element was missing.

[4.121] The refusal, in England or Australia, to accept the doctrine of informed consent as a basis for action in trespass has served to limit litigation against the medical profession. This preserves the myth that "doctor knows best", and the paternalism that is the corollary of that myth. It also forces a client who does wish to know all the facts to turn to other sources for that information. This leads to the client's mistrust of health carers and prevents their optimal co-operation and involvement in treatment, which would maximise the effect of that treatment.

[4.122] **[4.122]** It can be seen that while consent to medical treatment does not have to be written, unless it is provided for by statute both verbal and written consent to, or refusal of, health care should ideally be evidenced by detailed patient notes setting out an account of the communication between the health carer and client. Because the law, when matters are to be adjudicated, whether in a court or out of it, relies entirely on present evidence of past facts, verification of conversations is best afforded by a written record, made contemporaneously or as soon after the event as possible. Where verbal agreement to treatment is given and even where a written consent form is completed, a more comprehensive record of the conversation between health carer and patient is advisable.

▌▌▌ CHECKLIST
GUIDELINES FOR GIVING INFORMATION FOR CLIENT DECISION-MAKING

Giving information

▌..... There should be no coercion, patients should be encouraged to be frank, ask questions, and make up their own minds. Provide interpreters and repeat information if required, and look for responses that indicate that information has not been understood.

▌..... Where possible, give the patient adequate time to make a decision, ask more questions, talk to others, think about the matter, etc.

▌..... Advise the patient that he or she can get another medical opinion, and assist the patient to seek it if it is requested.

▌..... Ensure that the patient understands:
— the diagnosis, including the degree of uncertainty in this;
— the prognosis, and any degree of uncertainty in this;
— the anticipated effects of not undergoing the proposed treatment;
— the nature of the intervention, for example, how invasive it is, whether it will be painful, how long it will take, how they will feel before, during and after it;
— any significant long and short term physical, emotional, mental, social, sexual, or other outcome which may be associated with the proposed treatment;
— the time involved in the treatment;
— the costs involved in the treatment; and
— the availability of alternative treatments, the above information about them, and why they are not recommended.

This involves consideration of the patient's personality, beliefs, fears, values and cultural background.

Withholding information

Information should only be withheld in the following circumstances:

▌..... the patient's physical or mental health might be seriously harmed (this involving more than the patient being disconcerted or dismayed, or the health carer's discomfiture at giving the information);

- .....the patient refuses information, and requests the health carer to make the decisions. This does not relieve the health carer from giving basic information, or from first encouraging the client that, on the basis that the client's body is the object of the treatment, he or she should also be the decision maker, may be better able to co-operate with the treatment if he or she is better informed, and that the decision should not be made by someone else; and
- .....it is an emergency and not practicable to give the information.

[4.123] This checklist is based on guidelines produced in pamphlet form by the National Health and Medical Research Council in 1993. Those guidelines were produced following a recommendation by the Australian, Victorian and New South Wales Law Reform Commissions in 1989 that guidelines be drawn up for the medical profession concerning the provision of information to patients. The guidelines are available from the National Health and Medical Research Council.

[4.124] An important caveat should be made about these guidelines. They require more than has been demanded by law. However, in somewhat circular fashion, as they have been established as a "reasonable standard" of care by the medical profession, they may be adopted by the courts as the *legal* standard of care to be demanded of health carers, as such guidelines are considered by the courts when determining that standard of care.

What if the Client does not Want to Know?

[4.125] Some clients will state that they do not want to be burdened with a whole lot of information, and leave the treatment decision to the health carer. The law does not have much to say on this matter. In the case of *F v R* (1983) 33 SASR 189 King CJ stated that the doctor is not required to inflict unwanted information on a client, but the decision that the patient does not wish to be informed should not be made lightly. The Victorian Law Reform Commission ("Informed Decisions about Medical Procedures" (1989), p 18) suggested that, firstly, the client should be sufficiently informed to decide that he or she does not want the information, secondly, that the doctor should determine *why* the client does not want to be informed. It might be because he or she understands broadly what is involved, or is unable to deal with the matter (for example through fear, or a feeling that he or she is not able to even consider the matter). If the latter is the case, the Commission says, the doctor should ensure the client understands at least broadly what is involved. Gutman (2000) argues that this is paternalistic, and that the law has not adequately dealt with this situation.

[4.126] It is suggested that in these circumstances health carers should encourage the client to reconsider, telling them that it is their body, and they can better understand and co-operate with the treatment regime if they are well informed. The client should not be pressed, however, and if there is a continued reluctance the advice above should be followed. It may be that over time, as the client gradually comes to terms with his or

[4.126] her condition, the client will become more ready to understand both it and the treatment proposed.

Consent Forms

[4.127] Much of the contact health carers have with patients will involve verbal or implied consent only. Where medical procedures are major, most health care workers ensure that they have written consent forms, which are signed by the client. These days, where people are much more aware of the law, and more prepared to take legal action than in the past, more and more situations are being covered by written consent forms. However, written consent may be revoked verbally, and at any time prior to the care. Carers may be asked to "secure" a client's signature on a consent form (it is suggested that the word "secure" implies that consent is *required* one way or the other and one doesn't come away without it, rather than considering consent as a matter of a *decision* made by the client). What are their responsibilities when they are seeking to obtain a signed consent form for a procedure to be carried out by someone else?

The Legal Implications of Consent Forms

[4.128] First, the nature of consent forms should be understood. At law, a signed document is a contemporaneous record of a person's intentions or understanding. When one signs a contract, one is bound by its contents, but the law has recognised that evidence of the conditions under which one signs something may be potential evidence that credence should not be given to the document. See, for example, the section on setting aside contracts in Chapter 10. If, for example, one is affected by drugs, then, whatever is said in the document, despite one's signature, is suspect. Similarly, one may sign a form giving permission to others to carry out a procedure without fully understanding what the procedure is. That would be held by the courts as being not valid as a consent. The form is only *evidence* of the consent, not consent itself, and it is poor evidence of the patient knowing adequately what is being consented to if there is also no record of proper advice having been given at, or before, the time of signing.

In *Chatterton v Gerson* [1981] 1 QB 432 Lord Bristow stated that:

> getting the patient to sign a pro forma expressing consent to undergo an operation should be a valuable reminder to everyone of the need for explanation and consent. But it would be no defence to an action in trespass to the person if no explanation had in fact been given. The consent would be expressed in form only, not in reality.

[4.129] Anomalies can occur where there is concentration on getting consent forms signed without sufficient appreciation of the legal implications. An extreme example of this was pointed out in the Royal Commission Report on Chelmsford where:

> consent forms were not filled in . . . consent forms were falsely filled in either by a signature clearly made when the patient was seriously affected

by the drug regime or by a different hand, probably a doctor or a nurse, but now unidentifiable. There were times when Dr Bailey signed to authorise the treatment. There were times when the records showed treatment given even when the very record noted that the patient had expressly refused it [Parliament of New South Wales, *Report of the Royal Commission into Deep Sleep Therapy* (NSW Government Printer, Sydney 1990), Vol 1, pp 57-58].

[4.130] Although health carers can legally witness someone signing a consent form, where the care is to be given by someone else, then the person providing the care is responsible for ensuring the person has been adequately informed. Health carers should be wary of accepting the responsibility of providing such information in such circumstances. They should definitely not be responsible for explaining care that others are going to give the client; legally this is the responsibility of those others and the form should indicate who informed the client. It should be borne in mind that what is said to the patient by a health carer may influence a consent to treatment, and this influence may be misleading. A court could ignore such a document as not indicating proper consent. It is best for carers to be very careful in discussing the nature and effects of treatment others are going to give: suggest that the client discuss it with the provider, and assist in their seeing him or her to do so. Many writers have emphasised that it is the responsibility of the medical practitioner who is treating the patient, not others, to explain treatment and other procedures:

> The duty to disclose to the patient the nature of the treatment being undertaken and the possibility of adverse results remains squarely upon the physician [providing the treatment]. It is a duty that cannot be delegated except to another physician; it may not be delegated to the nurse [Murchison and Nichols (1970), p 131].

[4.131] Whilst there has been no clear legal rulings as yet, it is most likely that these days, with the emergence of allied health care specialities, where, for example, nurses and para-medics are providing care and advice, and technicians are involved in sophisticated diagnostic procedures, this statement applies equally to any person who actually provides the health care.

[4.132] Both the provider of health care who neglects to undertake the responsibility of gaining the knowledgeable consent of a patient and a health carer who takes on the task of informing them run legal risks, the former in trespass or negligence, the latter in negligence for negligent misstatement. Although it may be tempting to reassure the anxious client who needs information and cannot seem to get it, carers are advised under such circumstances to treat consent as not given, and attempt to get the provider concerned to see the client, or at least report the matter to superiors, who may be able to organise responsible communication with the client. This may seem a drain on time and resources, but may result in a happier client, who is more willing and able to co-operate, and prevent successful legal action against those concerned.

[4.133]   **[4.133]** Consent forms should be specific to the procedures involved. "Blanket" or standard forms signed on entry to a hospital or clinic covering any or all (or "appropriate" or "desirable") treatment to be given may be held to be too vague and general to be valid at law. Emergency treatment is covered by the presumption that the client would wish to have treatment to save life and limb (unless otherwise clearly stated by the client). It may be specifically added to the form, but is redundant, so general consent forms are inappropriate.

[4.134] The following checklist is an example of what could be included in a consent form. The more communication between client and health carer is set down, the less chance of both client confusion, dissatisfaction and non-co-operation (and associated legal action) where that communication has been satisfactory, as there is a clear record of what has been said.

▌▌▌ CHECKLIST
ELEMENTS OF A CONSENT FORM

- name and full identification of client;
- name (and brief description*) of procedure agreed to;
- name of place for carrying out of the procedure;
- consent to specified associated treatments (these should have been discussed as part of the procedure);
- *acknowledgement of, and consent to, possible need for emergency treatment (this is presumed at law anyway, but it is good to remind both provider and client of the possibility of such a contingency);
- *statement of what information had been given, for example, what the procedure involves, why it is required, why it is recommended in preference to alternatives (one could add further items as per those in Statute (see [4.56]));
- list of specific risks and advantages which have been discussed;
- name of person who will carry out the procedure, or, if not appropriate, acknowledgement that no specific person will carry it out; and
- agreement to another person carrying out the procedure, or any other necessary procedure, if circumstances require this.

* *Optional items are preferred items.*

[4.135] Some institutions and practitioners may wish to have additional statements to the effect that the client assumes all risks and acknowledges that benefits are not guaranteed or certain. This does not protect health carers from potential liability in negligence.

Specific Situations

Blood Transfusions

[4.136] As has been stated above, adults can validly refuse blood transfusions, even if their lives are in danger. Where a child's life is in danger, and parents refuse a transfusion, legislation in most States

provides that the treating doctor may, if a second doctor's opinion is [4.141]
secured, go ahead with the transfusion in the absence of a parent's or
guardian's permission. See Chapters 5 and 16.

The Pregnant Woman and Consent

[4.137] The development of modern technology which allows examination of the foetus before birth creates a dilemma for health carers—they start to treat the foetus as the patient rather than the woman, and at times this results in a conflict of interests between those of the woman and those of the foetus. "Knowledge of the foetus is no longer purveyed from the woman to her doctor, but the other way around" (Wells C, "Maternal versus Foetal Rights" (1992) Working Paper No 1, Feminist Legal Research Unit, University of Liverpool, p 17 at pp 18-19). Ultrasound pictures "personify" the foetus.

[4.138] Thus the issue becomes what the woman should do in the interests of the foetus. Should health carers place the therapeutic interests of another being, the foetus, above those of the woman? McLean S and Petersen K ((1996), p 230) argue that what has often developed into a "maternal/foetal conflict" is based on several false assumptions: that the woman is a "mother" in relation to the foetus, when in fact she has not yet become one, and that this is a conflict between "persons" (who are equal). In law there is only one person, the woman, the foetus is a potential person only. Further, they say the term "conflict" implies hostility, and again, as the foetus is not a person it cannot be hostile—only the woman can, and the implication is that any decision she makes will be not so much in her interests, but in hostility to the foetus.

[4.139] It is quite clear from legal precedent that a woman retains her right to autonomy when she becomes pregnant (see, for example, Seymour (1995)), and in fact the law has quite clearly established that the foetus has no rights at law (*Paton v BPAS Trustees* [1979] 1 QB 276).

[4.140] To argue differently is to hold that whilst a mother cannot be forced to undergo treatment to save the life of her born child, she may be forced to do so for a non-person.

[4.141] In *Re S (adult: refusal of medical treatment)* [1992] 4 All ER 671 the judge granted a declaration authorising doctors to perform a forced caesarean section even though the woman had expressly refused treatment for religious reasons. Sir Stephen Brown accepted evidence that it was a life and death situation and the woman and the foetus would die if the procedure was not performed. The child was stillborn. However, this is to be compared with the following case.

[4.141] ■■■ CASE
St George's Healthcare NHS Trust v S; R v Collins and Ors, ex parte S [1997] 3 All ER 673 (English Court of Appeal)

S was 36 weeks pregnant and diagnosed with pre-eclampsia. She was advised that she needed to be admitted to hospital for an induced delivery. S fully understood the potential risks but rejected the advice as she wanted her baby to be born naturally. After extensive consultation with doctors and a social worker she was admitted to a mental hospital for assessment on the social worker's application. Subsequently she was transferred to another hospital which applied *ex parte* for the court for a declaration dispensing with her consent. This was granted, and S was delivered of a baby girl by caesarean section. S was returned to the psychiatric hospital, where her detention under mental health legislation was terminated, and she discharged herself.

S later appealed against the grant of declaration dispensing with her consent, and applied for judicial review of her detention under mental health law, her detention and treatment at the second hospital, and her return to the psychiatric hospital.

[4.142] The court re-iterated the right of an individual to autonomy, and to refuse treatment even when his or her life depended on receiving that treatment. It said that in the case of a pregnant woman, that right is not diminished merely because her right to do so may be morally repugnant. The removal of the child from her body amounted to trespass.

[4.143] It also stated that the making of the order had occurred without S's knowledge or attempt to inform her or her solicitor of the application, and without any evidence or provision for her to apply to vary or discharge the order.

[4.144] The court went on to say that the mental health legislation cannot be invoked because a person's thinking process is unusual or bizarre and irrational, and contrary to the views of the overwhelming majority of the community at large. The legislation is only to apply if the case falls within the prescribed conditions. Moreover, people detained under the Act for mental disorder cannot be forced into a medical procedure unconnected with their mental condition unless their mental capacity to consent to such treatment is diminished. In the circumstances, then, S's treatment and transfer were unlawful.

[4.145] The court repeated and expanded on advice given in *Re MB* [1997] 2 FCR 541. Judge LJ at 703 stated that where a competent patient refuses treatment the advice given to the patient should be recorded. This record should include unequivocal assurance from the client that the refusal represents an informed decision: that is, that she understands the nature of, and reasons for, the proposed treatment, and the risks and likely prognosis involved in the decision to refuse or accept it. If the patient is unwilling to sign a written indication of the refusal, this too should be part of a written record. It should be noted that this is merely a record for evidential purposes. It is not a disclaimer of liability, that is, it is still possible for the client to prove that in fact the decision was not properly "informed".

[4.146] If the woman is incapable of giving or refusing treatment, either in the long term or temporarily, she or he must be cared for according to the authority's judgment of her or his best interests. Where the patient has given an advance directive, before becoming incompetent, treatment and care should normally be subject to the advance directive. However if there is reason to doubt the reliability of this, an application to a court for a declaration as to the validity of the directive should be made.

[4.147] The court further stated that while pregnancy increases the personal responsibilities of a woman it does not diminish her entitlement to decide whether or not to undergo medical treatment. Although human, and protected by the law in a number of different ways, an unborn child is not a separate person from its mother:

> Its need for medical assistance does not prevail over her rights. She is entitled not to be forced to submit to an invasion of her body against her will, whether her own life or that of her unborn child depends on it. Her right is not reduced or diminished merely because of her decision to exercise it may appear morally repugnant [at 682].

Butler Schloss LJ stated in *Re MB* [1997] 2 FCR 541 at 561 (albeit obiter dicta):

> The foetus up to the moment of birth does not have any separate interests capable of being taken into account when a court has to consider an application for a declaration in respect of a caesarian section operation. The court does not have the jurisdiction to declare that such medical intervention is lawful to protect the interests of the unborn child even at the point of birth.

[4.148] This approach is supported by the case of *Paton* [1979] 1 QB 276, an unsuccessful application to prevent an abortion by a husband, and *Re F (in utero)* [1988] 2 All ER 193 at 200, where refusing an application that a foetus should be made a ward of the court, Balcombe LJ observed:

> there is no jurisdiction to make an unborn child a ward of court. Since an unborn child has, ex hypothesi, no existence independent of its mother, the only purpose of extending the jurisdiction to include the foetus is to enable the mother's actions to be controlled.

[4.149] Seymour (1995), p 56 notes that the woman and foetus have been approached under two models—the "Not two but one" model, and the "Not one but two". Seymour argues that from the legal viewpoint there is in fact a third model, the "Not one but not two" model:

> The pregnant woman must be the one to decide what intervention should be employed (either for herself or the foetus). In doing so she must recognise that the foetus does have interests and is more than a body part. It is important to understand the full implications of this result. The mother will be in a position to decide not only how the interests of the foetus are to be protected, but also whether they will be protected.

Consent and Research

[4.150] So far the discussion has been restricted to therapeutic treatment, that is, treatment of someone who is ill, with the intention of effecting either cure or relief from the condition. Research, of course, is done with the intention of gathering information. Generally, the two approaches are considered to be mutually exclusive, but in fact it has been argued that all treatment may be considered, at least to some extent, as experimental, as one can never be absolutely sure of the effect of treatment on different people. It should be kept in mind that the role of the carer–client relationship changes; with research the roles become that of researcher–subject. The interest of the carer is consistent with the client in the therapeutic relationship; presumably both want the client to benefit. However the interest of the researcher is not necessarily similar to that of the client—rather than being solely interested in the benefit of the client, the researcher's priority is to gather information. See the excellent discussion of research and ethics in Brody (1981).

[4.151] International recognition of the need for accountability in research was expressed in the Nuremburg Code in 1949, and the Declaration of Helsinki in 1964 (revised in 1975). In Australia, the National Health and Medical Research Council (NH&MRC) was established in 1936 and given statutory recognition by the *National Health and Medical Research Council Act* 1992 (Cth). Its charter is to enquire into, issue guidelines, make recommendations and advise the community on research into public health and medical research.

The NH&MRC has issued a series of studies and guidelines on health and medical research, and it is a condition of funding that those conducting research follow these guidelines. These guidelines require the establishment of ethics committees in institutions conducting research. Breach of these guidelines can lead to "withdrawal of funding, suspension of employment or professional registration, adverse publicity . . . and professional liability in negligence" (Skene (1989), p 34). Liability in battery, and prosecution under fair trading or trade practices legislation can also result (see [4.37]ff vitiation of consent).

[4.152] Codes of ethics which have been developed by the various health professions deal with matters including research, and similar penalties apply to breach of them.

[4.153] When research is undertaken, clients should be told this (that is, there should not be the belief that they are undergoing proven therapeutic health care). No research project should be undertaken unless it has been carefully scrutinised by an independent ethics review committee, which considers, among other things, what information the subjects will be given, and how consent is to be obtained. Some research projects may be reliant upon the person being either misinformed or uninformed. In these cases the committee must give careful consideration to the reasons for the research and its necessity, the risks involved, why alternative methods of seeking the information are not suitable, and to the value of the research to society in general. These reasons must demonstrate clearly that the research cannot be effectively carried out in any other way, that it carries little risk, and is important and valuable enough to warrant the invasion of the physical or mental integrity of the subjects, and/or the use of misinformation. These guidelines are applicable to all health carers.

Research Involving Those who are Incompetent

[4.154] The Nuremburg Code was developed as a result of the horror caused by the Nazi experiments during the Second World War. However it is necessary to maintain vigilance in ensuring adequate protection is given to those who are the subjects of research in all aspects of the project including consent. Brody (1981) gives some examples of scandalous research projects. In Australia an example of research without consent is given in Pappworth (1967), pp 36-37. Bromberger et al (1991) outline the scandal of Dr Harry Bailey's research into "deep sleep". More recently in New Zealand there was the trial over approximately 20 years of the non-treatment of positive pap smears (Coney (1988)). Research involving those who are incompetent is dealt with in more detail in Chapter 5.

Removal of Body Fluids for Testing

[4.155] There is provision in some circumstances for compulsory blood tests which may or must be taken. The removal of body fluids is the subject of the law of consent.

Testing Blood for Alcohol Content

[4.156] Where a person is the victim of a motor vehicle accident, there are provisions for the compulsory taking of blood and urine alcohol tests by a doctor or the doctor's agent, and a person may request such tests be taken after a breath-test or motor vehicle accident in most jurisdictions. Jurisdictions differ in the details of their provisions. A test does not have to be taken if the patient will not co-operate to the extent that the safety of any person or property is in jeopardy.

Testing of Criminal Suspects

[4.157] Crimes legislation in the Australian Capital Territory, New South Wales and Victoria provides for the taking of blood tests of those charged with certain criminal acts. In other jurisdictions police may require a medical examination, which in practice may include samples of body fluids.

DNA Testing

[4.158] All jurisdictions are in the process of legislating for compulsory collection of body fluids, hair or skin for DNA testing. As this procedure can be carried out by those other than health carers, issues relevant to

[4.158] health carers in forensic investigations are dealt with in Chapter 6. The use of hair or skin, and body fluids from the scene of a crime do not constitute an invasive procedure in conventional legal theory, and the issue in these circumstances becomes the use of information arising from that fluid—for example, does the person "own" their genetic information, and do they have any control over it?

Unlawful Restraint or Imprisonment

[4.159] Allied to the action of battery, the action of "false imprisonment" covers situations where a person is unlawfully restrained from leaving a place against their will. This action is a relevant matter of concern to nurses because it covers two main types of situations:

- refusing to allow a person to leave a premises, or preventing them from doing so, where there is no lawful authority to keep them; and
- placing physical, chemical or mental restraints on a person, and thereby preventing them from freedom of movement (restraint).

[4.160] The only time a person may be restrained against her or his will is:

- where there is a legal right to restrain (for example, under mental health, infectious diseases, quarantine or crimes legislation where they may be subject to powers of detention); and
- where a person is likely to harm herself or himself or someone else, or is likely to cause damage to property.

Detention

[4.161] People are falsely imprisoned when they perceive that they are confined to a particular place and believe there is no way of escape, or there will be reprisals if they leave. The confinement or absence of escape need not be fact—it is the person's own perception of the situation which is relevant. Thus a person who is led to believe that he or she cannot leave a hospital until payment for care is made would be falsely imprisoned.

▌▌▌ CASE [4.166]
Symes v Mahon [1922] SASR 447 (SC SA)

> The defendant, a police officer in a country town, told the plaintiff that there was a warrant for his arrest for failing to maintain his child and that he should "come to town [Adelaide] to have matters cleared up". He was asked to undertake to be at the police station the next morning and responded "I suppose I'll have to". He did turn up at the station, and accompanied the police officer in the train to Adelaide. He was not arrested at any stage, the police officer maintaining that he was "taking Mahon up for questioning". In Adelaide he was allowed to leave on two occasions, only after seeking and being granted permission to do so. It turned out that Mahon was not the person who was the subject of the warrant, but a Mr McMahon.

[4.162] The court held that although Mahon had never been in legal custody, and had at all times the freedom to leave, he submitted himself to the defendant's power, reasonably thinking that he had no way of escape which could reasonably be taken by him.

[4.163] This case establishes some important principles. First, giving clients to believe that they have no alternative but to remain in a particular place or submit to the control of others is unlawful and can result in an action for false imprisonment, even though they have the physical means of leaving. A second principle is that police cannot require someone to accompany them anywhere simply for questioning, unless the law specifically allows this.

[4.164] Where there is no power to detain a person, even where it is thought to be for their own good, this may be false imprisonment. For example, in wards where some patients are involuntarily detained but others are voluntary patients, staff should be very careful to ensure that if doors are locked, those who are voluntary patients are not only permitted freedom of movement, but are made to feel that no restraint is being placed on their freedom of movement, and that they are perfectly free to leave if they wish.

▌▌▌ CASE
Watson v Marshall (1971) 124 CLR 621 (High Court of Australia)

> The defendant was a police officer who asked the plaintiff to accompany him to the psychiatric hospital. The plaintiff believed (justifiably, the court held) that if he did not go voluntarily he would be forced into going.

[4.165] The court held that it was the plaintiff's belief that he had no choice which was relevant, nor any objective assessment of the law and the situation. It is thus not legally acceptable to use subterfuge or to trick a person into remaining in a particular place or in the control of someone else, unless one can plead a defence as outlined above.

[4.166] People are also unlawfully detained when they are physically confined to a particular place whether they are aware of this or not.

[4.166] ■■■ CASE
Meering v Grahame-White Aviation Co Ltd (1919) 122 LT 44 (House of Lords)

The plaintiff attended the defendant's office to give evidence relating to some stolen goods. Unbeknown to the plaintiff three detectives were stationed outside the office to prevent his leaving.

[4.167] The House of Lords held that this was false imprisonment. It follows that the unconscious or mentally unaware patient who is detained in a hospital without their consent may be the subject of false imprisonment.

■■■ CASE
Hart v Herron [1984] Aust Torts Reports ¶80-201 (SC)

The plaintiff had been detained and given treatment to which he claimed he had not consented (including electroconvulsive treatment and deep sleep therapy). See facts and commentary at [4.27].

[4.168] The court held that even though he had no recollection of the imprisonment the fact did not prevent him from succeeding in his claim.

[4.169] Restraint must be intentional and complete. Where there is a reasonable way out, even if it is unconventional (for example, windows) there is no "imprisonment".

■■■ CASE
Balmain New Ferry Co Ltd v Robertson (1906) 4 CLR 379 (High Court of Australia)

A man bought a ticket for a ferry to Balmain. The sign over the wharf from which it left said that any person entering or leaving the wharf had to pay a penny whether or not they used the ferry. He entered through the turnstile (paying his penny) and found he had missed the ferry and would have to pay another penny to leave the wharf. Employees prevented him leaving by a small opening beside the turnstile. He sued the company for false imprisonment.

[4.170] The court took into account the fact that the plaintiff had agreed to the terms of entry clearly established, that egress would cost him one penny. He had placed himself in such a position that he could not complain of a certain restraint of liberty. However he was not being denied exit under the terms on which he had entered. Only if he had been denied exit under any circumstances would he have been imprisoned.

❚❚❚ CASE [4.175]
Sayers v Harlow Urban District Council [1958] 2 All ER 342 (CA UK)
A tourist visited the public toilets and found that, due to a faulty lock she was trapped in the cubicle. She failed to attract attention, and so proceeded to stand on the toilet roll holder to climb over the door. She slipped on the holder, injuring herself. Later she brought an action against the Council in false imprisonment and negligence.

[4.171] The court dismissed Ms Sayers claim of false imprisonment because there had been no intention to confine her. It upheld her claim in negligence because of the faulty lock, but reduced the damages because of her contributory negligence in standing on the toilet roll holder.

[4.172] A health carer cannot argue that it is simply for the patient's own good that restraint be used but should have reasonable grounds to believe in the lawfulness of such action. If a patient wishes to leave a hospital or other health-care institution and the exceptions (above, [4.56]) do not apply, they should be allowed to go. Staff should attempt to get a signed statement from the patient, stating that despite advice to the contrary, the patient is leaving of her or his own free will. A witness should sign as well, if possible.

[4.173] It is advisable for staff to carefully warn the patient of the consequences of such a decision, to determine that the person understands what they are doing, and to get, in writing if possible, and witnessed by someone else, a statement signed or acknowledged by the patient to the effect that he or she has been fully informed of the consequences of the decision, and is making the decision voluntarily. Under these circumstances it is unlikely the courts would find staff liable for *not* giving the treatment.

Restraint

[4.174] There are many situations in which it is considered necessary to restrain a patient who is violent, disruptive, difficult to care for or who be mentally dysfunctional and in danger of self-harm.

There is a wide variety of *restraining behaviour*. This includes such activity as:

- ..... yelling or haranguing to restrict movement by fear;
- ..... the use of drugs to restrict movement;
- ..... threats to physically restrict movement;
- ..... threats to use seclusion to restrict movement and influence behaviour;
- ..... actual use of physical or chemical restraint; and
- ..... actual seclusion.

[4.175] Actual restraint has been described as the application of devices such as belts, harnesses, manacles, sheets and straps on the person's body to restrict movement (but do not include the use of cot sides and chairs with tables fitted on their arms). Actual seclusion has been described as

[4.175] the sole confinement of a person at any hour of the day or night in a room of which the doors and windows are locked from the outside (*Mental Health Act* 1986 (Vic), ss 82, 83). It is considered that prolonged use of chairs with tables fitted can amount to wrongful "restraint", and also requires regulation.

[4.176] Chemical restraint is the use of medication to control behaviour.

[4.177] Studies show that clinicians restrain patients to prevent falls, control agitated behaviour and stop patients from disrupting therapy. However these objectives are not being well met by restraint and frequent serious accidents and injuries, even death has been a direct result of physical restraint (Mion et al (1996), p 412). Mason and McCall Smith ((1994), p 271) point out that fear of culpability for accidents to patients, even where these are unavoidable can result in "defensive action" by health carers—that is, unnecessary restraint of patients to avoid liability for accidents.

[4.178] Approximately one in 10 adults and one in five older adults (over 65) are physically restrained at some point during their hospitalisation. Several studies have shown that:

- nurses instigate most requests for physical restraint;
- nurses as well as doctors, vary widely in their reasons for using physical restraint for the same person;
- although the two major reasons for using physical restraint are to prevent falls and stop the patient from disrupting therapy, more than one reason for using physical restraint is frequently given for a single patient;
- health carers seldom discussed restraint;
- documentation of physician's orders was poor;
- restraint was considered benign and rarely worthy of monitoring or evaluation; and
- there was little consensus on the need or value of restraint (Mion et al (1996), p 414).

[4.179] These studies also show that the decision to use physical restraint tends to be based on individual judgment rather than on scientifically validated guidelines or protocols. The patients subjected to restraint or seclusion generally had the following characteristics:

- confusion or cognitive impairment;
- physical impairment leading to difficulty with daily living or mobility;
- increased severity of illness,
  — (presence of one or more of these characteristics increased chance of restraint threefold);
- old age;
- presence of medical devices; and
- use of tranquillisers (indicating that sedation is often used *with* restraint, not instead of it) (Mion et al (1996), p 416).

[4.180] However, other studies provided different results: "younger age, length of stay between 30 and 365 days, involuntary legal status, female gender, and a diagnosis of mental retardation enhanced the probability of a patient's being secluded or restrained" (Way and Banks (1990), p 79). [4.186]

[4.181] Sometimes restraint, particularly with those who are mentally ill or have an intellectual disability, through the act of yelling, haranguing or the threat of physical restraint, seclusion or the use of drugs may be used to induce conformity through fear of unwanted treatment. This may even be done with the well-being of the person in mind, however such a motive of itself does not make such activity lawful. It may constitute either assault or battery. There is a growing awareness of such behaviour as elder abuse.

[4.182] As with an action of assault or battery, a person need not suffer damage, nor need they even be aware of the restraint (for example, a door locked without their knowledge). Restriction of patients, or refusal to allow them to leave hospital, where they are:

- .....competent;
- .....do not consent; and
- .....there is no legal justification,

are examples of false imprisonment. Legal justification to restrain a person would include, for example, self defence, power under the mental health legislation, infectious diseases legislation, and child welfare legislation.

[4.183] It should thus be clear that it is not enough to restrain a person simply for his or her own good. Health carers should have reasonable grounds to believe in the lawfulness of such action. Restraint should be limited to what is required for protection of the patient or others where there is no reasonable alternative: it must not be used as a management aid.

Freedom to Leave Hospital

[4.184] Clients who wish to leave a hospital or other health-care institution where the exceptions described above do not apply should be allowed to go. Staff have a duty of care to:

- .....warn them of the consequences of such a decision;
- .....determine that they understand what they are doing; and
- .....attempt to get a signed statement, stating that despite advice to the contrary, the client is leaving, that s/he has been fully informed of the consequences of the decision, and is making the decision voluntarily.

[4.185] A witness should sign as well, if possible. If the person is considered unable to understand what he or she is doing, and harm is likely to result, he or she should be dealt with as a non-competent person in need of care. If not an emergency, this may involve an application to a court or tribunal under the mental health or guardianship legislation.

[4.186] Where a patient leaves hospital, the general duty of care on the part of staff requires them to consider what will happen to him or her, and

[4.186] to take reasonable steps to ensure that any necessary care to which the person consents is undertaken. It would seem that they should at least provide the patient with information as to what further care he or she will need, and where and how this can be obtained. This was specifically addressed in *Niles v City of San Rafael* 42 Cal App 3d 230 (1974). There is no known Australian ruling directly on this matter, but it is considered that such information would be part of the duty of care under general negligence principles (for example, *Kite v Malycha & Anor* Supreme Court of South Australia, Judgment No S6702 (10 June 1998); *Wang v Central Sydney Area Health Service* [2000] Aust Torts Reports ¶81-574).

Restraint and Seclusion Should be Least Restrictive

[4.187] Restraint and seclusion should be the least restrictive compatible with the care of the patient under the circumstances. There is no legislative guidance or standards as to procedures to be adopted in respect of restraint or seclusion, except in relation to the mentally ill (see [4.204]) although facilities may have protocols for dealing with restraint. The potential for instilling fear and coercing behaviour by improper use of seclusion was raised by the Human Rights and Equal Opportunity Report, "Human Rights and Mental Illness" ((1993), p 271).

"Chemical" Restraint

[4.188] The administration of drugs has been reportedly used for the purpose of restraining patients and keeping them quiet, especially those who suffer from mental illness or dementia. This method of restraint is potentially more devastating and harmful than physical methods. It is important to note that restraint by drugs may also amount to battery or false imprisonment where the restraint is for the convenience of the staff rather than the protection of the client, staff or others. MacFarlane ((2000), p 106) states that:

> The necessity to protect staff or other residents would be difficult to argue where the restraint (without consent) was due to the fact that the resident was being a nuisance or because the restraint was considered desirable in order to speed up recovery from some illness.

The situation is complex because of the need to balance the rights of the individual patient with those of others. Nevertheless it remains unlawful to chemically or physically restrain a person without just cause.

[4.189] It is the author's view that "all health care facilities should have written policies about seclusion and restraint policies". It would follow that health carers should be clear on:

- ..... the identification of those who can be treated without their consent;
- ..... procedures under which such people are to be dealt; and
- ..... any limits on the treatment which can be given to such people.

[4.190] Restraint must be based on the principle of protection for the patient and/or others only (see [4.182]), and not carried out just for the convenience of the staff. A policy should be adopted by health care facilities which clearly set out circumstances under which restraint may be used, and those when it is not to be used.

> In order that justice may be achieved, nurses must assess each case individually as to the benefits and harms of physical restraint, accept the views and values of individual clients, be able to justify the use or non application of physical restraint, and be supported by a philosophy of care in their work place that advocates justice for staff and residents [Koch, S, "Ethical issues in Restraint use", in RMIT Faculty of Nursing, *Nursing Law and Ethics, "Meeting the Challenge of Patient's Rights—Issues for the 1990s" Proceedings of the Conference, November 1992* (Faculty of Nursing, RMIT, Melbourne), p 12].

▌▌▌ CHECKLIST
CONSIDERATIONS FOR POLICY ON RESTRAINT

- All health carers of the patient should be consulted, to see if alternative treatment can be adopted to alleviate the patient's need for restraint.
- Family should be consulted, as they may be able to offer assistance and ideas in relation to controlling the patient's behaviour (see *Spivey's* case at [6.69]).
- Any restraint should be the least restrictive measure to protect the patient—the aim should be to stop the harm, not the patient. Materials used should be such as to cause the least injury to the patient compatible with this aim.
- Authorisation from a person with appropriate authority (for example nursing management, doctor) should be required.
- Management should be notified of the circumstances of any restraint of a patient.
- Family should be notified of any restraint of the patient, if not already consulted.
- Regular assessment of the patient and the reason for restraint should be carried out.
- Full and accurate documentation of the circumstances and type of restraint, as well as the other matters listed here should be made in the nurses' notes.

[4.191] Victoria is the only jurisdiction with comprehensive legislation on restraint and seclusion, and this is limited to those who are mentally ill. The provisions set out what could be considered guidelines for all patients, particularly residents of nursing homes and hostels for those with a disability. The Victorian provisions are summarised in Figure 4.1.

[4.191] ▌▌▌ **FIGURE 4.1**

RESTRAINT AND SECLUSION

Summary of Sections 81 and 82, *Mental Health Act* 1995 (Vic)
These sections apply to a person receiving treatment for a mental disorder in an approved mental health service. Restraint or seclusion may be used in the absence of the person's consent.
Mechanical restraint means the application of devices (including belts, harnesses, manacles, sheets and straps) on the person's body to restrict movement, but does not include the use of cot sides and chairs with tables fitted on their arms. It can only be applied if it is necessary:
- for the purpose of the medical treatment of the person;
- to prevent the person from causing injury to himself or herself or any other person; or
- to prevent the person from persistently destroying property.

Seclusion means the sole confinement of a person at any hour of the day or night in a room of which the doors and windows are locked from the outside. A person may be secluded only where:
- this is necessary to protect the person or any other person from an immediate or imminent risk to his or her health or safety; or
- to prevent the person from absconding.

Mechanical restraint or seclusion of a person can be applied only if they have been:
- approved by the authorised psychiatrist*; or
- in the case of an emergency, authorised by the senior registered nurse on duty and notified to a registered medical practitioner without delay (and the authorised psychiatrist as soon as practicable); and
- applied for the period of time authorised.

Where mechanical restraint or seclusion is used, the person must:
- where restrained, be under continuous observation by a registered nurse or registered medical practitioner, and in all cases the restraint or seclusion be reviewed as clinically appropriate to his or her condition at intervals of not more than 15 minutes by a registered nurse;
- subject to variation of the interval by an authorised psychiatrist, be examined at intervals of not more than four hours by a registered medical practitioner;
- be supplied with bedding and clothing which is appropriate in the circumstances;
- be provided with food and drink at the appropriate times; and
- be provided with adequate toilet arrangements.

Where a doctor or nurse is satisfied, having regard to the above criteria, that the continued application of mechanical restraint or seclusion is not necessary, he or she must without delay release the person from the restraint.

Any person who applies restraint or seclusion in contravention of the law is guilty of an offence.

The authorised psychiatrist must send a monthly report to the Mental Health Review Board and the chief psychiatrist a report of the details of the restraint including the name of the person restrained, the period of restraint or seclusion, who authorised and who applied the restraint or seclusion, and the reason for it.

* an authorised psychiatrist is a qualified psychiatrist appointed in respect of each psychiatric in-patient service by the Chief General Manager of the Department of Health.

REFERENCES AND FURTHER READING

Annas, G, "When Suicide Prevention Becomes Brutality: The Case of Elizabeth Bouvia" (1988), *Judging Medicine* (Havana Press, New Jersey), p 290

Australian Health and Medical Law Reporter (CCH, Sydney, 1991), (CCH, Sydney, 1983)

Betsas, A and Forrester, K, "Consent: Implications for Health Care Practitioners" (1995) 2 *Journal of Law and Medicine* 317

Bochner, S, "Doctors, Patients and their Cultures" (1988) in Hasler, J (ed), *Doctor and Patient Communication* (Academic Press, London)

Brazier, M, *Protecting the Vulnerable: Autonomy and Consent in Health Care* (Routledge, London, 1991)

Brody, H, *Ethical Decisions in Medicine* (Little, Brown & Co, Boston, 1981)

Brody, H, "Transparency: Informed Consent in Primary Care" 19 Hastings Center Report No 5, pp 5-9 (Sep/Oct 1989)

Bromberger, B and Fife-Yeomans, J, *Deep Sleep: Harry Bailey and the Scandal of Chelmsford* (Simon & Schuster, Sydney, 1991)

Buchannan, A and Brock, D, *Deciding for Others: The Ethics of Surrogate Decision Making* (CUP, Cambridge, 1989)

Bunney, L, "A Right to Die—Has Patient Autonomy Gone too Far?" (1993) 2 *Health Law Bulletin* 29

Coney, S, *The Unfortunate Experiment* (Penguin, 1988)

Faden, R and Beauchamp, T, *A History and Theory of Informed Consent* (Oxford University Press, New York, 1986)

Faulder, C, *Whose Body is it?* (Virago, London, 1985)

Freckelton, I, "Malpractice Actions Against Health Care Providers" in Freckelton, I and Petersen, K, *Controversies in Health Law* (The Federation Press, Sydney, 1999), p 119

Freckelton, I and Petersen, K, *Controversies in Health Law* (The Federation Press, Sydney, 1999), p 119

Gutman, J, "The Right Not to Know: Patient Autonomy or Medical Paternity" (2000) 7 *Journal of Law and Medicine* 286

Human Rights and Equal Opportunity Commission, *Human Rights and Mental Illness* (AGPS, Canberra, 1993)

Johnstone, M, *Bioethics: A Nursing Perspective* (W B Saunders/Bailliere Tindall, Sydney, 1989)

Kerridge, I H and Mitchell, K R, "Missing the Point: Rogers v Whitaker" (1994) 1 *Journal of Law and Medicine* 239

Kirby, M, "Patients' Rights—Have we Gone too Far?" (1993) 2 *Health Law Bulletin* 13 and (1993) 2 *Health Law Bulletin* 38

Kushe, H, *Caring: Nurses, Women and Ethics* (Blackwell Publishers, Oxford, 1997)

Langslow, A, "Witness to Battery" (1993) *Australian Nurses Journal*, August, 35-37

Lanham, D, *Taming Death by Law* (Longman Professional, Melbourne, 1993)

Law Reform Commission of Victoria, *Medicine, Science and the Law: Informed Consent*, Symposia 1986 (Globe Press, Melbourne, 1987)

Law Reform Commission of Victoria, *Informed Decisions about Medical Procedures* (1989)

Law Reform Commissions of New South Wales and Victoria, *Informed Consent to Medical Treatment* (NSW Government Printer, Sydney, 1988)

Lidz, C, et al, *Informed Consent: a Study of Decision Making in Psychiatry* (The Guildford Press, New York, 1984)

Luntz, H, Hambly, A and Hayes, R, *Torts: Cases and Commentary* (Butterworths, Sydney, 1985)

Mason, J and McCall Smith, R, *Law and Medical Ethics* (Butterworths, London, 1994)

McFarlane, P, in McCullough, S, *Older Residents' Legal Rights* (Federation Press, Sydney 1992)

McHale, J, Fox, M and Murphy, J, *Health Care and the Law—Text, Cases and Materials* (Sweet & Maxwell, London, 1997)

McLean, S and Petersen, K, "Patient Status: the Foetus and the Pregnant Woman" 2 *Australian Journal of Human Rights* Vol 2, p 229

Milstein, B, "Informed Consent: the Envelope Expands (again)" (1997) 5 *Health Law Bulletin* 65

Mion, L, Minnick, A, Palmer, R, et al "Physical Restraint Use in the Hospital Setting: Unresolved Issues and Directions for Research" (1996) *The Milbank Quarterly* Blackwell, Cambridge MA & Oxford UK

Murchison, I A, and Nichols, T, *Legal Foundations of Nursing Practice* (Macmillan, New York, 1970)

Pappworth, M, *Human Guinea Pigs* (Routledge & Keegan Paul, London, 1967)

President's Commission for the Study of Ethical Problems in Medicine and Biomedical and Behavioural Research, *Making Health Care Decisions* (Government Printing Office, Washington DC, United States, 1982)

Rozovsky, F, *Consent to Treatment: A Practical Guide* (Little, Brown & Co, Boston, 1984)

Scott, R, "Duty to Disclose Risks of Treatment and Procedures" (1993) 2 *Health Law Bulletin* 1

Seymour, J, *Foetal Welfare and the Law* (1995) Report of the Enquiry commissioned by the Australian Medical Association

Skene, L, *Law and Medical Practice: Rights Duties Claims and Defences* (Butterworths, Sydney, 1998)

Sutherland, H, Lockwood, G and Till, J, "Are we Getting Informed Consent from Patients with Cancer?" 11 *Bioethics News* No 2 (1992), p 5

Schwartz, R and Grubb, A, "Why Britain Can't Afford Informed Consent" 15 *Hastings Centre* Report No 4 (August 1985), p 19

Victorian Law Reform Commission, *Informed Decisions About Medical Procedures*, Report No 24 (VGPS, 1989)

Young, P, *The Law of Consent* (Law Book Co, Sydney, 1986)

Wallace, M, "Restraint and the Law" Paper presented at the Royal College of Nursing Australia conference, *Restraint: Exploring the Pathway between Risks and Rights* (National Conference Centre, Canberra 1997)

Way, B and Banks, S, "Use of Seclusion and Restraint in Public Psychiatric Hospitals: Patient Characteristics and Facility Effects" *Hospital and Community Psychiatry* 41:1 (Jan 1990)

Chapter Five

CONSENT FOR THOSE WHO CANNOT LEGALLY DO SO

INTRODUCTION

[5.1] This chapter continues the discussion of consent, looking at the rights of those who are at the time considered at law not to be competent to give their consent to treatment, either by reason of their age, mental capacity at the time, or their status under other legislation. Such persons are called "incompetent" at law.

"Incompetence" by Reason of Age

"The Common Law Principle"

[5.2] It is accepted that a basic principle in law is that a child cannot consent to medical treatment (but see Ch 10 for more detailed discussion of minors and contracts). Generally a person is a minor or "child" at law for most purposes until the age of 18 unless he or she marries.[1] However section 49(2) of the *Minors (Property and Contracts) Act* 1970 (NSW) sets the age at which a child can consent to medical treatment at 14 years and section 6 of the *Consent to Medical Treatment and Palliative Care Act* 1995 (SA) sets it at 16 years. In all the other jurisdictions the right to consent is traditionally vested in:

- .....a parent of the child, or person in whose favour a parenting order has been made under the *Family Law Act* 1975 (Cth);
- .....a person to whom the parent has given the right to make such a decision;
- .....a legally appointed guardian of the child (for example, child welfare officer, foster parent); and
- .....a court with the jurisdiction to make such a decision for the child (that is, the Supreme Court or the Family Court, exercising *parens patriae jurisdiction*).

---

[1] *Age of Majority Act* 1974 (ACT), s 5; *Minors (Property and Contracts) Act* 1970 (NSW); *Age of Majority Act* 1974 (NT), s 4; *Age of Majority Act* 1974 (Qld), s 5; *Age of Majority (Reduction) Act* 1970 (Qld), s 3; *Age of Majority Act* 1973 (Tas), s 3; *Age of Majority Act* 1977 (Vic), s 3; *Age of Majority Act* 1972 (WA), s 5.

"Mature" minors

[5.3] The courts have also recently applied the rule that a child can consent to treatment of which he or she is capable of understanding the nature and consequences ("mature minor"). It has been stipulated by a court that the New South Wales legislation does not cancel a parent's right to consent or refuse medical treatment, in fact it is meant to prevent a child arguing that due to her or his minority, consent to treatment he or she may have given was invalid, and that the medical staff is liable in battery (see *K v Minister for Youth and Community Services* [1982] 1 NSWLR 311). The High Court has ruled that the common law principle does result in the diminishing of parental control as the child matures (*Secretary, Department of Health and Community Services v JWB and SMB (Marion's Case)* (1992) 175 CLR 218; see [5.17]). Just how the High Court principle and the New South Wales legislation interrelate is not certain. In the author's opinion the better view is that, whilst the child's right to consent to particular health care may be present, parents' *general* legal rights and obligations do not cease under such circumstances, and their consent should be sought where this is neither contrary to the wishes of a "mature minor", nor his or her interests.

Exceptions to the Common Law Principle: Emergencies

[5.4] In emergencies, similar principles apply to children as for adults (see [4.58]ff, necessity [4.30]ff, transplants Ch 17). In other circumstances, where a child is not mature enough, or otherwise not competent to decide, parents or legal guardians are at law authorised to make decisions for them. Statutory provisions also allow the State welfare authorities to take children into care when they are considered to be neglected or in danger (Ch 17). In addition, all jurisdictions spell out for doctors the authority to provide life-saving blood transfusions to children regardless of the presence or absence of parental consent.

[5.5] In the Australian Capital Territory blood transfusions may be given to a child without parental consent if the child is in danger of dying, two doctors must agree that it is necessary (*Transplantation and Anatomy Act* 1978 (ACT), s 23).

[5.6] In New South Wales blood transfusions may be given to a child without parental consent if the child is in danger of dying. A doctor may carry out medical treatment without consent of the child or parents to save the child's life or prevent serious damage to the child's health (*Children (Care and Protection) Act* 1987 (NSW), s 20A).

[5.7] In the Northern Territory legislation specifically allows a doctor to carry out an operation (including administration of anaesthesia and blood transfusion in an emergency) without parental consent, where two doctors believe it is necessary and it is not practicable to delay the treatment until parental consent is obtained. This is, of course in addition to the common law principles relating to emergencies (see [4.58], [5.55]; *Emergency Medical Operations Act* 1973 (NT), ss 2, 3).

[5.8] In Queensland blood transfusions may be given to a child without parental consent if the treatment is necessary to preserve the life of the child (*Transplantation and Anatomy Act* 1979 (Qld), s 20).

[5.9] In South Australia blood transfusions may be given to a child without parental consent if the child is in danger of dying. Emergency medical treatment may be given without the parents or the child's consent where there is imminent danger to the child's life or health. A second opinion should be secured unless that is not possible (*Consent to Medical Treatment and Palliative Care Act* 1985 (SA), s 13(5)).

[5.10] In Tasmania blood transfusions may be given to a child without parental consent if two doctors agree that it is necessary to prevent death (*Human Tissue Act* 1985 (Tas), s 21).

[5.11] In Victoria blood transfusions may be given to a child without parental consent if the child is in danger of dying. Two doctors must agree that it is necessary (*Human Tissue Act* 1982 (Vic), s 24).

[5.12] In Western Australia blood transfusions may be given to a child without parental consent if the child is in danger of dying (*Human Tissue and Transplant Act* 1982 (WA), s 21).

Statutory Exceptions

[5.13] Several jurisdictions have legislation which recognise this trend in relation to non-urgent treatment.

[5.14] In New South Wales the *Minors (Property and Contracts) Act* 1970 (NSW), provides that a medical or dental practitioner who provides treatment to a child of less than 16 years with the prior consent of a parent or guardian is protected from liability for assault or battery. Those who give treatment to a child over 14 years with the consent of the child only are also protected from liability. The law requires that some treatments, called "special medical treatment" must have the consent of the Supreme Court (*Children (Care and Protection) Act* 1987 (NSW), s 20B). They are:

- .....treatment that results in permanent infertility;
- .....long-acting injectable contraception;
- .....drugs of addiction (other than for cancer) over 10 days in any 30 days;
- .....experimental procedures not complying with Government guidelines; and
- .....vasectomy or tubal occlusion.

[5.15] In South Australia the *Consent to Medical Treatment and Palliative Care Act* 1995 (SA) permits children of 16 years or more to consent to medical or dental treatment as if they were an adult. Further, the common law principle is set out that a child under 16 may consent to treatment if the person treating them believes they are able to understand the nature and effects of the treatment, and that it is in the best interest of the child's health and well being. This opinion must be supported in writing by a second medical practitioner who has personally examined the client. A person over 16 years may refuse emergency medical treatment.

[5.16] [5.16] Health carers are advised, that where anything other than minor treatment is involved, unless:

- ..... the situation is an emergency and parental consent is impracticable (and can be presumed); or
- ..... they believe it is not in the minor's interests to involve a parent (for example, he or she would be the victim of abuse by that parent);

they should ascertain who the child's decision-maker is, and discuss the treatment with that person. If it is apparent that a child is in need of non-urgent major treatment and involvement of a parent or guardian is not in the child's interests, one can approach the Community or Public Advocate (where available), or the Family Court or the State Supreme Court and seek authority to provide the care. The Family Court of Australia was endorsed as a court with *parens patriae* jurisdiction for all children since it was given this power by all States except Western Australia (where the State Family Court would exercise it).

[5.17] The following case dealt with sterilisation, but also with the legal capacity of a child to consent to medical treatment. It is a comprehensive review of the law in relation to children, incapacity and consent to treatment:

CASE
Secretary, Department of Health and Community Services v JWB and SMB (Marion's Case) (1992) 175 CLR 218; 106 ALR 385

"Marion" was at the time a 14-year-old girl suffering from intellectual disability, deafness, epilepsy and behavioural problems. Her parents and doctors agreed on a hysterectomy to prevent pregnancy and menstruation as these were considered to have adverse psychological and behavioural consequences. Her parents applied to the Family Court of Australia for an order authorising the procedure. Questions arose as to (1) whether parents can legally authorise the sterilisation of their child; (2) whether the Family Court has jurisdiction to authorise the operation; and (3) whether Family Court authorisation is required by law in the Northern Territory. These matters were taken to the High Court.

[5.18] The High Court stated that except where sterilisation is an incidental result of surgery performed to cure a disease or correct a malfunction (that is, carried out for therapeutic reasons) parents do not have the power to authorise the operation. The court importantly also held that parental power diminishes gradually as the child's capacity and maturity grows. A minor can give informed consent when he or she achieves a sufficient understanding and intelligence to comprehend fully what is proposed. It is irrelevant that the child may have an intellectual disability, so long as she or he understands the nature and effects of the proposed treatment. It went on to say that the Family Court does have the jurisdiction to authorise a "non-therapeutic" sterilisation. In such cases the Court's function is to decide whether, in the circumstances of the case, it is in the best interests of the child. Indeed, the jurisdiction of the

Family Court is similar to the *parens patriae* jurisdiction of State and Territory Supreme Courts. [5.21]

[5.19] In *Marion's Case* at 246 the Court quoted Lord Brandon in *Re F* [1990] 2 AC at 70-71 in setting out the reasons for treating sterilisation as a special case:

- .....the operation is not reversible;
- .....it deprives a woman of a fundamental right to bear children;
- .....moral and emotional considerations mean that this right has great importance;
- .....if a court is not involved, there is a greater risk of the matter being decided wrongly;
- .....it may be carried out for improper reasons; or
- .....there is a need to protect those involved from legal action.

When Parents do not Have the Power to Consent to a Medical Procedure

[5.20] It is thus established that parents do not have the legal authority to consent to a procedure for the purpose of sterilisation of a child (or non-competent adult). The Family Court can consider any treatment which is not "therapeutic" (that is, not for the benefit of the person).

CASE
GWW and CMW [1997] FLC ¶92-748 (Family Court of Australia)

The parents of a child of 10, B, applied for an order authorising the collection of bone marrow or peripheral blood stem cells for donation to his aunt, who suffered from leukaemia. The aunt was expected to die within 12 months without the transplant, and B had expressed a strong wish to donate the tissue. It was accepted that whilst B had an understanding of the nature of the procedure, his understanding was not adequate for him to provide informed consent. The questions for the court were whether the parents could lawfully authorise the procedures, and if not, whether it was in B's best interests for the court to intervene and exercise its welfare jurisdiction to authorise the procedures.

[5.21] Hannon J held that the Family Court did have jurisdiction to hear the application pursuant to its welfare jurisdiction. This was a special case outside the scope of parental power to consent. Hannon J stated that passages in the judgment of *Marion's Case* indicated that the approach taken in that case did not only apply to sterilisation, but to other "non-therapeutic" procedures, including "the donation of healthy organs such as a kidney from one sibling to another". He stated that while the procedure proposed here was not irreversible (in that the stem cells can regenerate and blood re-infused into the donor) it was nevertheless an invasive procedure requiring general anaesthetic that was not for the benefit of the child. The paramount consideration was the welfare of the child, and whether the procedure would be in his interests. The close relationship with his aunt, and the value of the continuation of that

[5.21] relationship to the child who wanted to assist her, were factors that outweighed the risk or discomfort of a surgical procedure. It is interesting to note that in weighing up the benefits and disadvantages, the judge also took into account psychological evidence that refusal of the application could be detrimental to B because he would be puzzled by the court not allowing him to help his aunt. This, the court was told, could lead to a lack of respect for authority and especially the court system.

State Supreme Courts are still the courts in all States where a child comes under State welfare law (for example, is a ward of the state or otherwise under the control of State authorities).

CASE
P and P (1994) 181 CLR 583; 120 ALR 545 (High Court of Australia)

This case involved a child who had a mental disability. Her parents believed that it was in her interests to be sterilised. They wanted court authorisation to do this, and decided that, as the New South Wales Guardianship Board requires that such a procedure would have to be either life-saving or for the prevention of serious damage to health (and this case did not fit those criteria) they would apply to the Family Court for authorisation of the procedure. The case went to the High Court as a case stated by the Chief Justice on the application by the Attorney-General of New South Wales.

[5.22] The majority of the High Court stated that the child welfare jurisdiction of the Family Court corresponds with the traditional *parens patriae* jurisdiction of the State Supreme Courts. They pointed out that the Family Court welfare jurisdiction adopted in 1988 (see [1.28]) does not extinguish that of the State Courts, but encompasses the substance of it, freed from the preliminary requirement of a wardship order. The intent of Parliament was that both jurisdictions should exist concurrently. The *Guardianship Act* 1987 (NSW) prohibits sterilisation unless it is necessary to save life or prevent serious harm to health. The *Family Law Act* 1975 (Cth) and approach of the Family Court are much wider in their scope. In the case of a conflict between orders made by the Family Court and those of a State Supreme Court, the Family Court orders would necessarily prevail, as per section 109 of the Constitution (see [1.22], [1.27]). For a more detailed consideration of the case law see Skene (1998), p 116.

When Can a Child Consent to Treatment?

[5.23] The English House of Lords has established the legal category of "mature minor" for those seeking contraceptive advice or contraceptive measures.

▌▌▌ CASE
Gillick v West Norfolk and Wisbech Area Health Authority [1985] 3 All ER 402 House of Lords (England)

A mother sought to have the court rule that parents and guardians have a right to make decisions on behalf of children as to contraceptive advice or treatment. Her children, along with others, had been receiving information about contraception through the family planning clinic without the prior knowledge and consent of their parents. These children were under the age of 16.

[5.24] The majority of the House of Lords held, firstly, that children may authorise medical treatment when they are old enough and mature enough to decide for themselves. It would be arbitrary and unreal, the court held, to draw a line between childhood and maturity at a certain number of years, disregarding human development and social change:

> Provided the patient, whether a boy or a girl, is capable of understanding what is proposed, and of expressing his or her own wishes, I see no good reason for holding that he or she lacks the capacity to express them validly and effectively to make the examination and give the treatment that [the doctor] advises [per Lord Fraser at 409].

[5.25] Secondly, the court held that the rights of parents to control their child are for the child's benefit, and one recognised only so long as they are needed for the protection of the child. Absolute dominion over their child by parents is now a thing of the past and parental rights dwindle proportionately with the child's maturity. Accordingly, there may be occasions when the child's interest indicates that a parent's rights be disregarded.

[5.26] Lord Fraser (at 413) made the useful suggestion that:

> [where a girl] refuses either to tell the parents herself or permit the doctor to do so . . . the doctor will, in my opinion, be justified in proceeding without the parent's consent or even their knowledge provided he is satisfied on the following matters: (1) that the girl . . . will understand his advice; (2) that he cannot persuade her [that parents should be informed]; (3) that she is very likely to begin or to continue having sexual intercourse with or without contraceptive treatment; (4) that unless she receives contraceptive advice or treatment her physical or mental health or both are likely to suffer; (5) that her best interests require . . . advice, treatment or both without the parental consent.

[5.27] This is not the ratio of the case, as there were differences of opinion on this point. However, there was no serious objection to it by the majority judges, so the criteria set out above could well be adopted by health care workers for all major procedures on those under 18 years of age. The principle of *Gillick* was adopted by the Australian High Court in *Marion's Case* (above).

When Can a Child Refuse Health Care?

[5.28] Courts have been reluctant to give a "mature minor" the right to *refuse* (as opposed to *consent to*) health care. In *Gillick* the court indicated a clear tendency to substituting the doctor's views of the interests of the child for that of the parent. In other words, without clear elucidation of the point by the courts, it would seem that the child might be able to refuse, but only if that refusal is reasonable in the eyes of the medical profession rather than in the eyes of the parents. The child cannot make her or his own unreasonable refusal.

CASE
Re W (a minor) (medical treatment) [1992] 4 All ER 627 (CA England)

A teenager suffering from anorexia nervosa who understood her condition but who wished to seek treatment in her own time, refused treatment for her condition. The local authority applied to the court for an order for her treatment. The judge held that although she had sufficient understanding to make an informed decision, he had inherent power under his *parens patriae* jurisdiction to order the treatment be given. W appealed.

[5.29] By the time of the appeal, W was deteriorating, to the point where medical opinion estimated her reproductive capacity could be lost within a week, and her life a short time later. The Court of Appeal made an emergency order that W be removed to a specialist unit for treatment, on the basis that her wishes were outweighed by the threat of irreparable damage to her health. The Court made it clear that it was not considering the importance of a child's views generally, nor the weight it would have given her view earlier on, when she was not so ill. However it later said at a full hearing, that its inherent jurisdiction over children meant that it could override the wishes of a person under 18 years. It also pointed out that although children can agree to treatment they understand (in the UK this is provided for in the *Family Law Reform Act* 1969 (UK)), this does not mean an absolute right of *refusal* of treatment. It simply means that where parents have refused treatment and a child consents to it, the health carer is protected from a suit in battery.

[5.30] Despite the approach of *Re Marion* (see [5.17]) that a "mature minor" can consent to treatment, the New South Wales Supreme Court in *DoCS v Y* [1999] NSW SC 644 (30 June 1999) raises the question of whether the court can make an order, based on the best interests of a child, even where that child is a "mature minor" and refuses (see also Eades (2000), p 54).

■■■ CASE [5.33]
DoCS v Y (unreported, 30 June 1999, [1999] NSW Supreme Court 644)

A teenage girl was diagnosed as suffering from anorexia nervosa. Both she and her parents believed the diagnosis to be wrong and were non-compliant with recommended treatment, which included forced feeding because of her dangerously low body weight. She was considered in danger of death or serious future physical and metal deterioration without this treatment. The attitude and behaviour of both the girl and her parents made voluntary treatment impossible. The Department of Children's Services applied for an order for her treatment. The judge considered whether recent legislation granting the Family Court *parens patriae* jurisdiction (that is, the right to make orders for the welfare of those requiring care), meant that State Supreme Courts were thus stripped of this jurisdiction, as the Family Court, acting under Federal Law, has precedence over State Courts dealing with similar matters.

[5.31] The judge held that the "complex web of provisions" of the *Family Law Act* 1975 (Cth) did not extinguish the *parens patriae* jurisdiction of the Supreme Courts of the States and Territories. The judge made the girl a ward of the Court and placed her in the custody of the New Children's Hospital at Westmead. He also authorised the staff at the hospital to detain her, using reasonable force if necessary, and to treat her. The orders excluded the parents from any say in the medical treatment of their daughter, and countermanded the girl's own wishes as to her treatment. However the judge noted that the court's power to override the wishes of the child should be exercised "sparingly", and that in this case he had considered the wishes of both the girl and her parents carefully. However he had come to the conclusion that her wishes were affected by her medical condition, which appeared to prevent her from understanding the seriousness of her medical condition and from taking proper account of the expert medical advice which is available to her. He went on to say that:

> The justification for overriding her wishes is that on the evidence, her long term health and even her survival are seriously at risk unless steps are taken to give her the medical treatment she needs.

[5.32] The reasoning of the judge makes it uncertain as to whether he is taking the serious consequences of the girl's wishes as evidence of her lack of understanding ("if she was competent she wouldn't make that decision") or is basing his decision on a more objective assessment of her capacity to decide. The former would mean that the decision in fact limits the autonomy of children who understand the nature and consequences of their decision where this would lead to serious or fatal results. If this is to be the basis for our treatment of children, this should be spelled out clearly.

[5.33] A recent case in England, also throws doubt on the right of a minor to refuse treatment.

[5.33] ■■■ CASE
R v M (unreported, 15 July 1999, Royal Courts of Justice, Family Division, UK)

A girl, M, 15 and a half years old, suffered sudden onset of heart failure. It was considered that the only treatment available to save her life was a heart transplant. Her mother consented, but M did not. Despite extensive counselling and explanation M remained steadfast, and the hospital applied to the court for authorisation to operate. Time was limited to a few days if M was to benefit from the surgery. It is interesting to note that the solicitor appointed to represent M, although submitting that M was intelligent and understood her circumstances, rather than advocating her wishes to the court, recommended to the judge that he authorise the transplant.

[5.34] The judge authorised the transplant stating that whilst a child's wishes should be considered seriously, the exercise of the court's overriding power is justified where refusal of treatment would lead to death. He recognised that M would have to live with the effects of his decision, and could well resent it for the rest of her life. Gutman (2000), p 114 concludes that the court failed to give adequate weight to the far-reaching consequences of the decisions, and its serious and life-long consequences, and indeed potential lack of compliance with treatment required of M because of her feelings about the procedure.

Consideration of a Child's Wishes

[5.35] This does not mean that a child's wishes should not be taken into account. The court in *Re W* (see [5.28]) made a strong statement to the effect that the refusal of treatment by a child, although not automatically legally actionable, is nevertheless of great importance for health carers in making clinical judgments, and should reasonably be considered. Lord Balcombe said, at 643:

> In a sense [consideration of the child's wishes] is merely one aspect of the test that the welfare of the child is the paramount consideration. It will normally be in the best interests of a child of sufficient age and understanding to make an informed decision that the court should respect [her or his] integrity as a human being and not lightly override [her or his] decisions on such a personal matter as medical treatment, all the more so if the treatment is invasive.

[5.36] In New South Wales, the Supreme Court has held that a guardian could not insist on having the power to refuse consent to a child having an abortion when her doctor (among others) considered it necessary for her physical and mental well-being (*K v Minister for Youth and Community Services* [1982] 1 NSWLR 311). Uncertain though the law is in this area, there seems to be a trend towards allowing a child to agree to contraception and abortion without parental consent (unless there is a statutory restriction: for example, in the Northern Territory a girl under 16 cannot give valid consent to an abortion). Abortion is dealt with in more detail in Chapter 14.

"Mature Minor"—Disagreement with Parents

[5.37] Despite the capacity at law for a "mature minor" to consent to treatment without reference to an adult in some cases, there is no legislation or case law setting out the position where parents want the child to receive treatment, but the child objects. The following points should be kept in mind:

- ..... Presuming the treatment sought is not emergency treatment, health carers are not obliged to give any treatment they consider unnecessary or unwise.
- ..... To go ahead and give the treatment is to leave oneself open to an action in battery by the child (CCH, *Australian Health and Medical Law Reporter* (1991) ¶17-360).
- ..... To fail to give treatment would be to leave oneself open to an action in negligence by the parents, but this would require their proving direct cause of harm to a child by the failure to act. If the treatment is not urgent and alternatives are possible (although medical staff should consider carefully the consequences failure to give treatment may incur), they should keep the issues in perspective.

[5.38] There is little help from the *Gillick* case on this point. The judges in that case seemed unclear about the status of parental rights where the child is mature enough to make a decision. However the Australian High Court in *Re Marion* (see [5.17]) noted and endorsed the majority view in *Gillick,* and stated (at 237) that:

> parental power to consent to medical treatment on behalf of a child diminishes gradually as the child's capacities and maturity grow and that this rate of development depends on the individual child.

[5.39] Where there is a difference between child and parents and the health carer believes the treatment is necessary for the child's welfare, she or he can approach the appropriate body for an order in relation to the child. However it is important to keep in mind that the consent to health care of a "mature minor" *or* a parent is legal authority to carry out the care, and the health carer may go ahead, so long as he or she can show that the care is indicated. In such circumstances health carers may want to review just how necessary the health care is.

Child Under Care of Third Parties

[5.40] A child may be in the care of someone other than a parent. For example, a guardian, institution, teacher, baby sitter, relatives or neighbours.

[5.41] Where a child in such a person's care requires emergency treatment there is no doubt that this can be given and no consent is necessary (see [4.58]).

[5.42] Minor treatment and first aid can be consented to by the child who understands this.

[5.43] Given that the third person is acting in loco parentis, delegated authority to consent is vested in them. There is no established limit to

[5.43] such authority, but it is suggested that authority would only apply to consent to treatment which is necessary for the continued good health of the child and which would be impractical to delay until a parent or guardian could be contacted. See Figure 5:1.

Child Who is the Subject of Abuse or Neglect

[5.44] When it is suspected that a child is the subject of abuse, some jurisdictions require certain classes of people, such as doctors, nurses, teachers and social workers, to report this to the authorities (see Ch 16).

[5.45] Child welfare legislation may be invoked, permitting welfare officers to take custody of the child and to organise treatment for her or him.[2] Also, some jurisdictions give medical personnel power to detain a child in a hospital, examine and administer treatment necessary for the child's welfare pending further legal action. Health carers should know what can be done, and who to notify when they suspect that a child in their care has been subject to abuse, or is being—or is likely to be—neglected. If in doubt, the State or Territory child welfare authorities can be contacted for assistance.

Children in Need of Health Care

[5.46] The child protection legislation mentioned above provides extensive provision in all Australian jurisdictions providing for welfare officers to take action to remove, detain and arrange for the treatment of children in need of care. Definitions of what is meant by "in need of care" differ (see Ch 16), but generally this includes abuse and neglect, either physically or emotionally. Below is an outline of provisions in relation to the examination and care of children. Generally speaking the relevant authority for consent to care is established by the State's legislation, and that person is the guardian for the child at the time care is authorised. This may be the Minister or Director of Child Welfare. For practical purposes it is the authorised officer who can direct that the care be given on his or her behalf. It should be noted that if a child requires a special examination (vaginal, anal or penile), there are special requirements in relation to those whose consent is required.

[5.47] In the Australian Capital Territory the *Children and Young People Act* 1999 (ACT) provides for family and group conferences and voluntary care agreements as the first consideration when children are in need of care and protection. However if a police officer or the chief executive of children's services believes it necessary, they may take emergency action in relation to a child. They have parental responsibility (that is, the

---

[2] *Children and Young People Act* 1999 (ACT); *Children (Care and Protection) Act* 1987 (NSW); *Children's Services Act* 1965 (Qld), *Health Act* 1937 (Qld); *Community Welfare Act* 1983 (NT); *Children's Protection Act* 1993 (SA); *Child Protection Act* 1974 (Tas); *Children and Young Person's Act* 1989 (Vic); *Child Welfare Act* 1947 (WA).

authority to consent to health care) until the child is returned to a [5.51] responsible person, or the court makes an order placing such responsibility elsewhere. Where a person reasonably believes that a child is in need of care and protection, he or she may apply for a care and protection order. The court may make an interim care and protection order in relation to a child or young person when immediate action is required until a final order is made. The court may make a "therapeutic protection order" in relation to a child or young person if satisfied that there are reasonable grounds for believing that the child is in need of care and protection. Such an order authorises the chief executive to detain the child and take necessary measures for the provision of the required care.

[5.48] In New South Wales the *Children (Care And Protection) Act* 1987 (NSW) provides that the Director-General or a member of the police who believes on reasonable grounds that a child under the age of 16 years has been abused or is in need of care shall take appropriate action. This may include requiring the child to be presented forthwith to a medical practitioner or facility for assessment and care. A person who fails to comply is guilty of an offence. If it is believed that the child is in immediate need of care and protection they may move him or her to a place for care and protection, using such force (including breaking into premises) as is reasonably necessary.

[5.49] An officer or member of the police force who has reasonable grounds for believing that there is in any premises a child in need of care may apply to an authorised justice for a search warrant. Police may enter specified premises, search for and remove the child and present him or her to a medical practitioner for medical examination. Seventy-two hours is allowed for the examination. The Director-General is deemed the minor's Guardian for purposes of examination.

[5.50] In the Northern Territory the *Community Welfare Act* 1983 (NT) provides that an authorised person may remove a child who is reasonably considered to be abused or in need of care. The child in custody may be held for a maximum of 48 hours during which time he or she must be brought before the court for a "holding" order, which means retention in a place of safety for up to 14 days. An authorised person may consent to an urgent medical procedure or treatment. The person in charge of a hospital who reasonably believes a child in the hospital has suffered or will suffer maltreatment may detain him or her in the hospital and conduct a medical examination during 48 hours and apply for a holding order for a maximum of 14 days. The Minister responsible for child welfare may order a medical examination and treatment of a child when in receipt of a report of maltreatment.

[5.51] In Queensland the *Children's Services Act* 1965 (Qld) and the *Health Act* 1937 (Qld) are relevant. Authorised officers and police may take a child reasonably suspected of being in need of care and protection into custody. A care and protection application must be made as soon as possible. A court may order necessary investigation and medical examination, in which case the child is remanded into the custody of the Director. Where a child presents at a hospital and maltreatment is suspected, an authorised medical officer may order his or her admission

[5.51] and detention for a maximum of 96 hours. Assessment and treatment may be carried out without parental consent.

[5.52] In South Australia the *Children's Protection Act* 1993 (SA) provides that a child at risk may be removed from a parent or guardian using reasonable force. The child remains in the custody of the Minister for one working day for assessment. A court order may then be sought, with orders for examination and assessment valid for four weeks, extendible for a further four weeks. Medical examination can be carried out without parental or guardian consent but not without the consent of the child.

[5.53] In Tasmania the *Child Protection Act* 1974 (Tas) provides that an authorised officer may require anyone having care of a child to cause her or him to be taken to the assessment centre to be examined. Where this cannot or does not happen, a warrant may be issued authorising a police officer to remove the child and take him or her to a place of safety. A child may be detained in a place of safety (including a hospital), assessed and treated, for a maximum 120 hours. During any period of detention, the Child Protection Assessment Board may apply to the Magistrates Court for a child protection order. The child may then remain in the place of safety for 30 days, extendible for further 30 days (s 17).

[5.54] In Victoria, the *Children And Young Person's Act* 1989 (Vic) provides that a "protective intervener" (person authorised under the Act) must, as soon as practicable after receiving a notification that a child is in need of care or protection investigate the subject-matter of the notification and take appropriate action in a way that will best ensure his or her safety and well-being. The intervener may, with without warrant, take the child into safe custody pending hearing of an application for a protection order, and serve notice requiring her or him to be brought before children's court for the application. Once application has been made, the child may be medically examined. A child in safe custody must be brought before court for an interim accommodation order, and the Director-General may at any time order that the young person be medically examined. An interim accommodation order may be for up to 42 days, and may include hospital care.

[5.55] In Western Australia the *Child Welfare Act* 1947 (WA) provides that the police or an authorised officer may apprehend a child in need of care and protection. Application must be made for a care and protection order and the child must be brought before the court as soon as practicable for that purpose. Medical assessment may be carried out. Where a child under six years old is admitted to hospital and is reasonably suspected of being in need of care and protection, the medical officer or deputy in charge of the hospital may order the detention of the child in the hospital for a maximum of 48 hours.

FIGURE 5.1 [5.55]

CONSENT TO HEALTH CARE FOR A CHILD

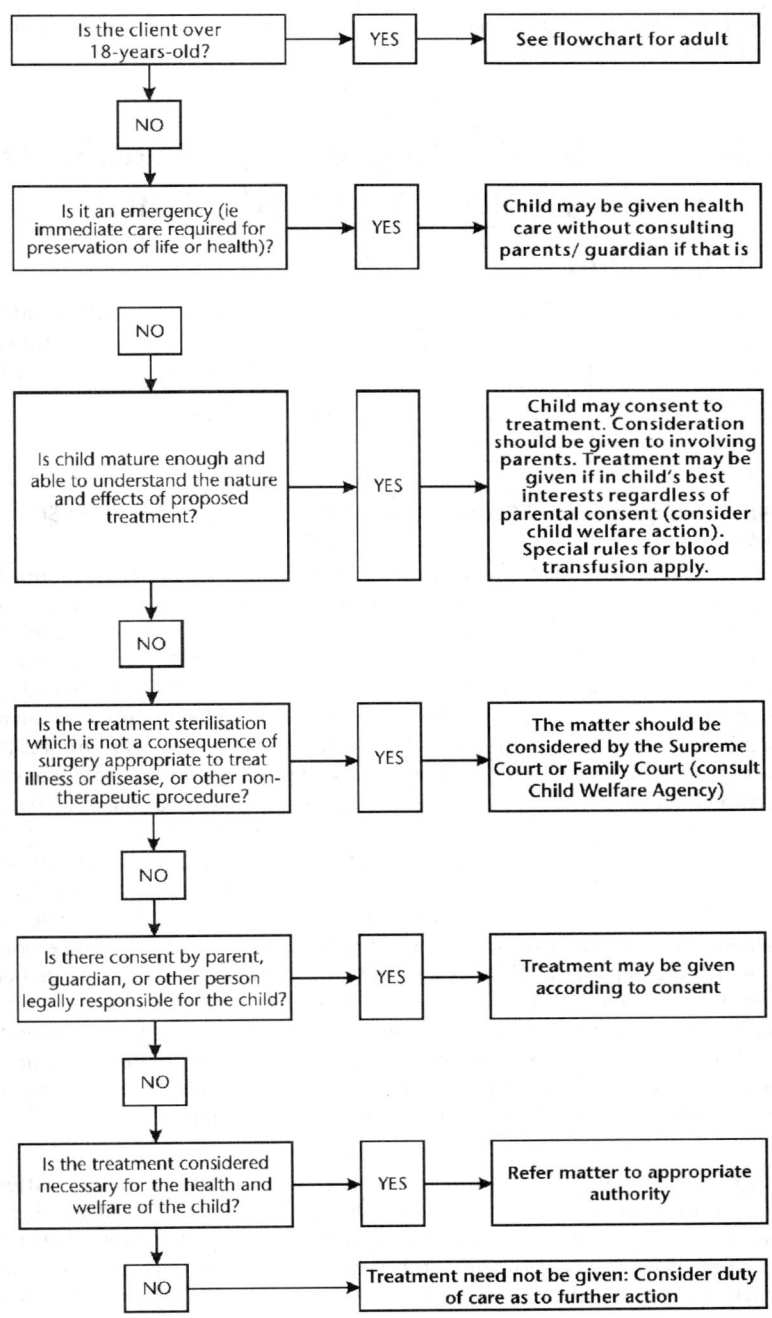

[5.55] **Notes:**
1. Where major treatment is being proposed, it is advisable that the capacity of the child is determined by a specialist (for example, in intellectual disability, child development or psychology). It is also advisable to refer to a specialist for determination of this issue.
2. The Court must be satisfied that all options have been considered, and support for carers has been addressed.

Adults who are Legally Incapable of Consenting to Health Care

Role of the Court

[5.56] The court that has *parens patriae* jurisdiction over adults who are not competent is the State or Territory Supreme Court. The following case dealt with such a person, and also illustrates the urgency with which the Court can act:

CASE
Northbridge v Central Sydney Area Health Service [2000] NSW SC 1241

At 2.56 on a Sunday afternoon the duty judge at the Supreme Court was contacted at home by phone by a security officer at the Court, who advised that Mrs Northbridge had rung seeking an order preventing the administration of a hospital from withdrawing treatment from her brother, a patient at the hospital who was suffering from brain damage and who she claimed would die if not treated. The judge formulated some questions for the purpose of eliciting the facts from Mrs Northbridge, and by 3.25 these were answered by phone. The judge immediately rang the relevant hospital registrar, who advised that the decisions to discontinue treatment of the patient had been made on the basis of neurological examination, which disclosed only some basic brain activity after an overdose of drugs. The patient was considered to be in a persistent vegetative state, and had been taken off all treatment, and was not for resuscitation. The judge requested that unless some accommodation could be reached with the treating medical officers in relation to continuation of treatment, a hearing would be required that evening. The matter was tentatively listed for hearing the following day, and arrangements were made for legal representation of the parties. Mrs N was appointed as "tutor" for her brother (that is, the person acting for him). As a result of this action the doctors agreed to reinstate antibiotics and lift a "not for resuscitation" order. In fact the patient recovered a substantial degree of cognitive ability, and was transferred to a nursing home under a rehabilitation program.

[5.57] To ensure the continued care and rehabilitation of the patient, and that no order against resuscitation be made, the judge finally made an order that the patient remain in a hospital or other institution within the area and under the care of the defendant, be provided with necessary and appropriate medical treatment to preserve life and promote his good health, and that no "not for resuscitation" order be made in respect of the patient.

[5.58] The judge held that one of the prerogatives of the Crown is the right to take care of the person and property of those who through disability are unable to do so for themselves. This is part of the *parens patriae* jurisdiction of the Supreme Court. He pointed to *Marion's Case* (see [5.17]) where Brennan J at 266 stated that:

> The law will protect equally the dignity of the [hale] and hearty and the dignity of the weak and lame: of the frail baby and of the frail aged; of the intellectually able and the intellectually disabled . . . our law admits of no discrimination against the weak and disadvantaged in their human dignity.

[5.59] It was also pointed out by the judge that not only should hospitals have a clear resuscitation policy, doctors and hospital staff doctors must comply with the policy. It may not be unlawful for doctors to withhold futile treatment from patients, but failure to adequately consult with families may well result in an order from the court to continue treatment.

[5.60] The law relating to persistent vegetative state and not for resuscitation orders is considered further in Chapter 14.

[5.61] In considering who can consent on behalf of adults with impaired decision-making capacity, this section deals with those suffering from:

- temporary decision-making incapacity (for example someone who is affected by medication, is suffering from sudden and severe emotional shock or fluctuating dementia, or who is unconscious);
- permanent decision-making incapacity (for example those suffering from intellectual disability, chronic dementia); and
- those suffering from a mental illness.

Temporary Decision-Making Incapacity

[5.62] Where someone is temporarily unable to give permission for treatment, and the treatment proposed is not urgent, health carers should wait until the client has regained the capacity to consent where this is feasible. Where the client's state of lucidity is unstable, staff should, both legally and ethically, take the effort to determine what level of understanding prevails at the particular time, or wait until the person is lucid. Blanket labelling of such a person as "incompetent" is a potential denial of their legal and human rights.

[5.63] These rights are enshrined in the *Human Rights and Equal Opportunity Commission Act* 1986 (Cth), where they are based on international covenants which give those with some kind of mental impairment the same rights as other human beings "to the maximum degree of feasibility" (*United Nations Declaration on the Rights of Mentally Retarded Persons*), and in anti-discrimination legislation in all jurisdictions in Australia (see below, Ch 18). The common law also provides that any

[5.63] person who is competent enough may exercise rights to own property, marry, enter into contracts, and consent to (and refuse) health care.

Impairment Caused by Drugs

[5.64] Consideration should be given to the effect of medication on clients' decision-making capacity, particularly drugs that may not be specifically given for neuroleptic and mind-altering purposes, such as pain relief, hormones, sedatives etc. A common situation that may arise is where the client is asked to sign a consent form for an operation after the pre-medication is given, or after preparations for a procedure have commenced. Any consent purported to be given in such a situation would most likely be rejected by a court where it was considered that the person was incapacitated by drugs, felt some pressure to sign, or did not feel free to receive, question and consider the information necessary.

▮▮▮ CASE

Demers v Gerety 515 P 2d 645 (1973) (New Mexico Court of Appeal United States)

The plaintiff, who did not speak much English, had made it clear he did not want surgery for repair of a ventral hernia if it would affect his ileostomy. Told he could have his wish, he signed a consent form for the hernia repair only. After sedation, with no explanation, and in the dark (he had to be guided as to where to sign, and could not read the form) he signed a form which happened to be a second consent form, permitting revision of ileostomy and repair of hydrocele.

[5.65] The court rejected the argument that it was a valid consent. Obviously several factors were present to make this "consent" invalid; as well as being temporarily incompetent, the client did not voluntarily give consent to the procedure, although he voluntarily signed his name. It would seem that staff were less than frank in giving him information as to the nature of the procedure, and why they thought he should have it. The court referred to the "ritual of the consent form"; the relentless determination to have the document signed, regardless of how that is done. Courts will discount consent forms where it is not convinced the client gave consent at least knowing the nature of the procedure, and freely consenting to it.

Chronic Decision-Making Incapacity

[5.66] "Intellectual disability" is the term generally used to describe those who have a permanent or long-term intellectual deficit which renders them to some extent unable to lead a normal life without some degree of assistance. Their impairment may be mild or severe, but although they may improve with care, their condition is not expected to be rectified with treatment. Those who have an intellectual disability are divided into persons who are capable of understanding the particular medical procedure proposed, despite their handicap, and those who cannot. If they are so capable, they have the same rights as those without an intellectual disability. The first consideration is whether a person is capable of giving consent, as the law presumes that people can consent for themselves, and that presumption is only discarded when it is clear that they are unable to do so.

[5.67] Others in this category are those suffering from chronic dementia and Alzheimer's disease. Their condition is generally progressive, again with no real prospect of cure or significant improvement with treatment.

Who Can Consent for a Person with Decision-Making Impairment?

[5.68] Where a person suffers from the inability to consent to treatment, health care cannot legally be given without with the consent of a substitute decision-maker who is authorised by law to act on their behalf. Who this person is is determined by legislation which differs across jurisdictions. This is outlined below.

[5.69] The following flowchart provides a quick guide to determining who can consent to health care for an adult who is unable to do so. It is explained in more detail below.

[5.69] **FIGURE 5.2**

CONSENT TO HEALTH CARE FOR AN ADULT WITH IMPAIRED DECISION-MAKING CAPACITY

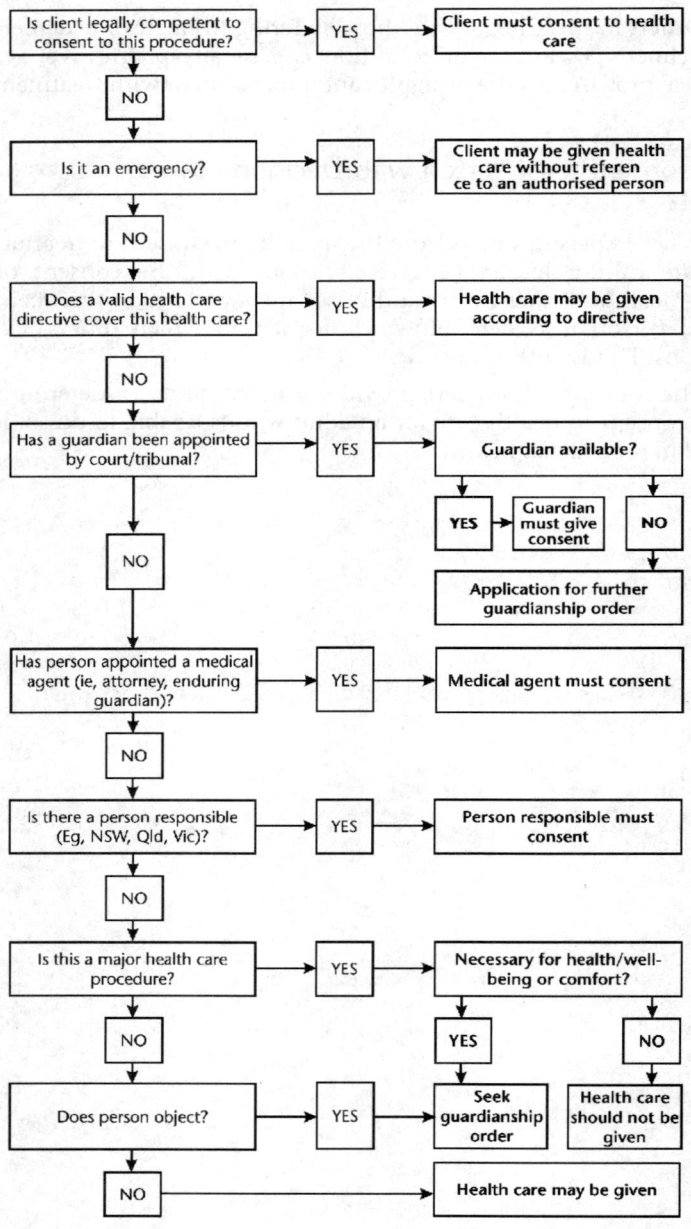

Notes: [5.75]
1   A "prescribed" or non-therapeutic procedure requires the authorisation of a court or tribunal.
2   Where the person has made a directive and there is a guardian or person responsible etc, consent must be given according to the directive.
3   Some jurisdictions provide that where a person responsible is not available, the next person on the prescribed hierarchy may be eligible to give consent. If so, and there is no person left in the hierarchy, there is no person responsible.

[5.70] Where non-urgent treatment is proposed for a person who is not competent, consent must be given by a person who is authorised under law to do so. This may be a medical agent appointed by the person when competent to do so, or a guardian appointed by a court or tribunal. In several jurisdictions it may be given by a spouse, relative or carer.

Consent by Spouse or Relatives

[5.71] It is very often the policy of hospitals to obtain the consent of a spouse or relatives to health care when consent cannot be given by the client. There is a basic legal principle that no one can legally give or withdraw consent to treatment for another legally incompetent adult without a court order, or, where provided for, an enduring power of attorney. Otherwise such consent has no legal standing. In fact the medical staff can only act on implied consent for life-saving measures on the part of the patient; consulting relatives is simply a matter of courtesy.

[5.72] This also means that any belief that a spouse must give consent to, for example, sterilisation or a legal abortion is incorrect. In *Attorney-General (Qld) (Ex rel Kerr) v T* (1983) 46 ALR 275 the court refused the putative father of a foetus the right to prevent the mother from having an abortion, and recently in *F v F* (1989) FLC ¶92-031 the Family Court refused to recognise the right of a husband to restrain his wife from having an abortion. This follows a similar finding by the English court in *Paton v BPAS Trustees* [1979] 1 QB 276.

Exceptions

[5.73] However, legislation regulating reproductive technology in Victoria, South Australia and Western Australia requires a spouse's consent in some circumstances (see [17.68]ff).

[5.74] Some jurisdictions have also provided that spouses, relatives and carers can consent generally to treatment under some circumstances.

[5.75] In New South Wales the *Guardianship Act* 1987 (NSW) provides that the "person responsible" for an adult who is not capable of consenting to treatment may consent to major and minor medical and dental treatment. A "person responsible" includes:

- a legally appointed guardian;
- a spouse with whom the person has a close continuing relationship;
- a carer; and
- a close friend or relative other than a person who is paid for their care.

[5.76] **[5.76]** The President of the Guardianship Board may issue guidelines specifying whether a person is to be regarded as a "close friend or relative". The Act covers medical treatment given by or under the supervision of a doctor, and dental treatment given by or under the supervision of a dentist.

[5.77] A doctor or dentist may also administer minor medical or dental treatment where there is no "person responsible", the patient does not object, and the treatment is necessary for her or his health and well-being. This is expected to reduce significantly the need for medical guardians, "lead to fewer guardianship orders and less need for state bodies like the Guardianship Board or the Public Guardian to come to the assistance of those with disabilities and their families" (Guardianship Board NSW, *The Guardianship Board Report 1993* (NSW Guardianship Board, Sydney, 1993), p 56). On the other hand it may leave a person's medical decisions in the hands of those who do not fully understand her or his wishes, and cause contention among family members.

[5.78] Non-intrusive examinations for diagnosis, first-aid and "over the counter" medications and other treatment declared by regulation not to be medical treatment can be given without a person's consent.

[5.79] The New South Wales Act does not deal with treatment other than that given or supervised by a doctor or dentist. There is no provision for the independent carrying out of health care by other professionals. Whether or not one believes that this legislation puts too much decision-making power in the hands of doctors and dentists, it is quite clear that the role of other carers is not acknowledged at all.

[5.80] In Queensland a statutory health attorney (someone appointed to make decisions) is authorised to make decisions about an incapable person's health care. Next on the list of eligible persons comes:

▌.....the person's spouse;
▌.....an adult carer; and
▌.....a friend or relative.

[5.81] One goes down the list until one finds an eligible person responsible. If there is no person responsible, there is a statutory "adult guardian"—a statutory authority who has power to consent to treatment on behalf of an incompetent person. If there is more than one eligible person and a conflict arises as to what health care should be given, the adult guardian will make the final decision. Health care that is "minor and uncontroversial", but necessary to promote the health and well-being of the person can be given without consent if there is no statutory health carer and no knowledge of any objection from interested persons. However the treatment should not be given if the health care provider knows or ought to be aware that the client has any objection to the treatment (unless he or she cannot understand what is going on, the care is unlikely to cause distress or it will be temporary and outweighed by the benefit). These are broad exceptions.

[5.82] In Victoria the *Guardianship and Administration Act* 1986 (Vic) provides that a "person responsible" may consent to treatment for someone who is no competent to make decisions. A "person responsible" [5.85] is the first person from a list who is willing and able to make a decision. Those on the list, in order of precedence, are:

- .....an attorney appointed under the *Medical Treatment Act* 1988 (Vic);
- .....a person appointed for the purpose by the Civil and Administrative Tribunal;
- .....a guardian appointed by the Tribunal;
- .....an "enduring guardian";
- .....a person appointed in writing to make decisions for the client;
- .....the client's spouse;
- .....the client's primary carer; and
- .....the client's nearest relative (again a list noting the precedence of relatives is set out in the Act).

"Special" Medical Procedures

[5.83] Most jurisdictions provide that only a court or tribunal can agree to the administration of certain procedures to a person who is not competent to consent to them. These procedures are generally:

- .....removal of tissue for donation (again there are some exceptions);
- .....sterilisation or long-acting contraception and abortion;
- .....psychiatric care for psychiatric illness; and
- .....withdrawal of life-sustaining measures.

These are discussed more fully below at [5.211].

Guardianship

[5.84] It can be seen that the law requires that those with some sort of cognitive impairment be given the same fundamental rights as everyone else, and this includes the right to self-determination (see Ch 18 for a discussion of these rights). Where it is considered that an adult is not capable of understanding what is involved, in an emergency the ordinary considerations regarding emergencies apply (see [4.58]ff). Where there is no emergency and it is believed that a person is unable to understand the nature of proposed treatment because of their lack of competence, those proposing it should seek the consent of the appropriate person as set out in that jurisdiction's legislation.

[5.85] The appropriate person may be a guardian designated by law. If there is no other person who is legally authorised to make decisions for the client, an application for a guardianship order should be made to the appropriate court or tribunal for a guardianship order. Each State and Territory has legislation for the appointment and conduct of guardians. Someone simply exercising factual (but not legal) control over the person is not in a position to give or withhold consent. The law simply refuses to recognise that one adult may control the life of another, no matter how retarded, without express statutory or court authority [*Kirby v Leather* [1965] 2 All ER 441, discussed in Hayes (1985), p 58].

[5.85] ▌▌▌ **FIGURE 5.3**

GROUNDS FOR GUARDIANSHIP/MANAGEMENT ORDERS

STATE	GROUNDS FOR GUARDIANSHIP ORDER[1]	GROUNDS FOR MANAGEMENT ORDER[2]
ACT	(Guardianship and Management of Property Tribunal): Person is unable, because of a physical, mental, psychological or intellectual condition, to make reasonable judgments about matters relating to his/her health or welfare, or to do anything necessary for his or her health or welfare, with the result that the person's health or welfare is, or is likely to be, substantially at risk (*Guardianship and Management of Property Act* 1991 (ACT))	(Guardianship and Management of Property Tribunal): a manager may be appointed of the whole or part of a person's property, for the purpose of entering into a transaction, or preventing a disposition, where the subject person is legally incompetent to enter into the transaction. *Guardianship and Management of Property Act* 1991 (ACT)
NSW	(Guardianship Board): Person has a disability and, by virtue of that disability, is totally or partially incapable of managing his or her person (*Guardianship Act* 1987 (NSW))	(Supreme Court/Magistrates Court): Person is incapable of managing his/her affairs (*Mental Health Act* 1990 (NSW), s 51; *Protected Estates Act* 1983 (NSW), s 16(1))
NT	(Local Court): Person is under an intellectual disability and is in need of a guardian (*Adult Guardianship Act* 1988 (NT))	(Supreme Court): Person is, by reason of age, disease, illness or mental or physical infirmity, in a position which renders it necessary in the interests of that person, or in the interests of those dependent upon that person, that the person's estate be protected (*Aged and Infirm Persons' Property Act* 1979 (NT))
Qld	(Guardianship and Administration Tribunal): Order may be made for a guardian for a particular personal matter for a person who has impaired capacity for the matter, and there is a need for a decision, or the person is likely to cause unreasonable risk to his/her health welfare or property and without appointment the person's needs or interests will not be adequately protected (*Guardianship and Administration Act* 2000 (Qld))	Same as for guardianship.

[1] This is an order nominating a person to manage the represented person's day-to-day living arrangements and medical care.

[2] This is an order (very often made in favour of the Public Trustee) for management of the person's estate and financial affairs.

STATE	GROUNDS FOR GUARDIANSHIP ORDER[1]	GROUNDS FOR MANAGEMENT ORDER[2]
SA	(Guardianship Board): Person is unable to look after his or her own health, safety or wellbeing as a result of mental incapacitation (*Guardianship and Administration Act 1993* (SA))	Same as for Guardianship. Also where person is unable, wholly or partially, to manage his/her affairs, susceptible to undue influence or considered to require assistance in relation to his/her estate.
Tas	(Guardianship Board): Person is suffering mental illness or severe subnormality or a guardian of a person under 21 years of age suffering from a psychopathic disorder or subnormality to such a degree that warrants the reception of the person into guardianship. It may be necessary in the interests of the person or for the protection of others that a guardianship order should be made (*Guardianship and Administration Act* 1995 (Tas); *Mental Health Act* 1963 (Tas))	(Guardianship Board): Disability renders the person unable to make reasonable judgments in respect of matters relating to all or any part of his or her estate and is in need of an administrator of his or her estate (*Guardianship and Administration Act* 1995 (Tas))
Vic	(Guardianship and Administration Board): Person is unable by reason of disability to make reasonable judgments in respect of all or any of the matters relating to his or her person or circumstances and who is in need of a guardian (*Guardianship and Administration Board Act* 1986 (Vic))	(Guardianship Board): Disability renders the person unable to make reasonable judgments in respect of matters relating to all or any part of his or her estate and is in need of an administrator of his or her estate (*Guardianship and Administration Board Act* 1986 (Vic))
WA	(Guardianship and Administration Board): Person is: (1) incapable of looking after his or her own health and safety; (2) unable to make reasonable judgments in matters regarding his or her person; (3) in need of oversight, care or control in the interest of his or her own safety or for the protection of others; and (4) in need of a guardian. (*Guardianship and Administration Act* 1990 (WA))	(Guardianship and Administration Board): Person unable, by reason of mental disorder, intellectual handicap or other mental disability, to make reasonable judgments in respect of matters relating to any part of that person's estate (*Guardianship and Administration Act* 1990 (WA))

[5.86] Guardians may be given full (or "plenary") powers, which means they can make decisions covering all aspects of the person's life—for example where they live, education, lifestyle and medical treatment. They may be given limited or conditional powers, with the limits on the matters about which decisions can be made by the guardian set by legislation, and conditions under which the guardian can make decisions

[5.86] specified by the court's or tribunal's order. An order may also be temporary, specifying the period of time or events which determine the existence of the guardianship. A guardian may apply to the Board for directions where guidance is sought as to his or her rights and responsibilities.

[5.87] A guardian must act according to the known wishes of a person and in his or her interests, but cannot consent to a "special medical procedure" (see [5.83], [5.211]) which can only be authorised by a court or tribunal. In most cases parents, friends, "interested persons" or professional health workers are eligible to apply to be a guardian. When necessary an emergency appointment can be made. This raises the question of who is best able to make decisions on behalf of the person concerned.

[5.88] In practice decisions about health care are often made primarily by health care workers in consultation with the family, with no specific guardian appointed at law. Minor health care is often given without even consulting the family. It is very easy to overlook the rights of such people because they can't complain, and they may be difficult to deal with. It is often much easier and quicker to go ahead and carry out procedures without having to determine who is required to consent to them, and negotiating with that person. As stated at the beginning of Chapter 4, all health carers are potentially legally liable for administering care without proper consent. Apart from being unlawful, this custom raises other controversial issues:

- .....the client may have little say in the decision-making, particularly as his or her interests are defined by others, who may be biased by their own concerns and feelings; and
- .....health carers may wield undue influence over the family. Where there is a difference of opinion between members of the family, or between the family and the health team, resolution may be a matter of power wielding or undue influence by one person or group over another.

[5.89] Perhaps health care professionals, who may not be in a position to consider factors other than medical issues, are not the best people for this task, and someone with personal knowledge of the individual and their lifestyle, interests and abilities would more appropriate for the task. Obviously parents or family may also not be best able to decide impartially, and/or according to the person's wishes (see the *Qumsieh* case at [5.108]). Frequently in these situations someone involved may believe that the arrangement is not the best and challenge it.

[5.90] The State Supreme Court can deal with the care and protection of the intellectually impaired under its *parens patriae* jurisdiction.

Guardianship Orders

[5.91] The purpose of Guardianship Boards and Tribunals is to apply varied expertise to the issues of guardianship, to make orders which best suit the needs of the person and the specific circumstances, and allow for as much autonomy as possible. The Board or Tribunal is to give

consideration to the wishes of the person where these are ascertainable [5.93]
when appointing a guardian, as must guardians when they are making
decisions on behalf of the person. Thus the guardian's view and values
must not lead to the making of a decision which is contrary to those of
the person.

Where Guardian and Client Disagree

[5.92] It is important to note that while guardians can consent to
treatment or withhold their consent it is questionable whether they can
order involuntary treatment against a person's will, and whether health
carers can force treatment on an unwilling person without further
authorisation from a court or tribunal. Obviously it is best practice to
avoid distress and alienation through enforced treatment, to ensure both
the comfort, dignity and well-being of the client, and his or her
co-operation with the care for optimum effect. Alternatively, more
acceptable care should be considered if at all practicable. It is suggested
that where the client objects to health care which is:

- .....considered necessary for his or her well-being;
- .....to which there is no reasonable acceptable alternative; and
- .....to which the guardian or the client objects,

application to the appropriate court or tribunal should be considered. In
the case of *K v Minister for Youth and Community Services* [1982] 1 NSWLR
311, the Supreme Court of New South Wales was dealing with an
application by a social worker to override the refusal of permission for
abortion by the guardian of a child who was a ward of the State. The
guardian was therefore the Minister for Youth and Community Services.
However, the Court ruled that it could override his decision as guardian,
and did so. In the famous United States case of Karen Quinlan (*Re Quinlan*
355 A 2d 647; see [14.127]), a 21-year-old who was in a permanent
vegetative state, there was a dispute between her parents, who wished to
cease artificial ventilation, and the hospital administration, which wanted
it maintained. Karen's father sought, and was granted, guardianship ad
litem of her, which gave him the right to decide whether artificial
ventilation should be continued or not.

Other Legal Obligations Towards those with an Intellectual Disability

[5.93] The Commonwealth and all States and Territories have legislation
which specifically requires that health care be made available to those
with an intellectual disability and stipulates the promotion of autonomy
in as much as it allows for the health and well-being of the person.[3]

---

3 *Disability Services Act* 1986 (Cth); *Disability Services Act* 1992 (ACT); *Disability Services Act* 1993 (NSW); *Disability Services Act* 1993 (NT); *Disability Services Act* 1992 (Qld); *Disability Services Act* 1993 (SA); *Disability Services Act* 1992 (Tas); *Intellectually Disabled Persons Services Act* 1986 (Vic), *Disability Services Act* 1991 (Vic); *Disability Services Act* 1993 (WA).

[5.94] [5.94] The lack of what the law calls a "sound mind" may be diagnosed by physicians, but must ultimately be decided by a court when the diagnosis is questioned. Legislative provisions in each State and Territory set out the procedure for appointment of guardians. Bodies have been established by all jurisdictions for this purpose (Figure 5.3). Some States and Territories have a statutory public advocate who, among other functions, can offer information, advice and assistance to those with an intellectual disability, intervene on behalf of a person who lacks capacity, investigate complaints, and apply for guardianship over them (see [5.17]ff, [5.207]).

[5.95] Health carers should always explore the possibility of such a client's capacity to consent before giving treatment. It may in fact take longer, and involve much more careful counselling and explanation, but nevertheless is required by law. However the law is not entirely clear as to how this happens in practice.

CASE
Battersby v Tottman (1985) 37 SASR 524 (CA)

The plaintiff suffered a serious mental illness involving acute depression and suicidal tendencies and was potentially homicidal, according to evidence. She was given very heavy doses of the drug melleril over a prolonged period of time, and as a result suffered serious and permanent damage to her eyes: a predictable outcome of the medication. She sued the doctor in negligence, as he failed to inform her of the risk of serious and permanent eye damage, and failed to arrange monitoring of her eyes, believing that such information would have an adverse effect on her. Thus, she claimed, he failed to obtain her valid consent.

[5.96] Both at the trial and the appeal, the courts held that her condition was such that she would not have been able to have adequately weighed up the relative costs and benefits.

[5.97] King CJ said (at 527), referring to his own statement in an earlier case *F v R* (1983) 33 SASR 189:

> I adhere to what I said [there] at 193: 'Even where all other considerations indicate full disclosure of risks, a doctor is justified in withholding information, and in particular refraining from volunteering information, when he judges, on reasonable grounds, that the patient's health, physical or mental, might be seriously harmed by the information. Justification may also exist for not imparting information when the doctor reasonably judges that a patient's temperament or emotional state is such that he would be unable to make the information a basis for a rational decision.'

[5.98] This approach, called "therapeutic privilege" is also dealt with at [4.109]. It appears to apply to clients of either "sound" or "unsound" mind), and can severely limit the legal right of a client to be fully informed.

Ensuring Autonomy During Future Decision-Making Incapacity

[5.103]

[5.99] There is a way that people can attempt to retain their autonomy even when they are unable to make decisions about their health care. This is by making an advance directive. An advance directive (sometimes, erroneously called a "living will") is a document written in anticipation of the possibility of the writer being in a state of incapacity. The directive is to have effect if, and only if, that person actually becomes incapacitated. This means that the requirements for giving consent apply to the author of a directive *at the time it is made*. An example of an advance directive is a statement, written by a person who is competent, that should illness or accident in the future reduce him or her to a permanent vegetative condition, he or she does not wish to receive artificial ventilation or other life-preserving treatment. Another common request of those who are terminally ill and approaching the end of their life, is that resuscitation not be given when it is otherwise required for survival.

[5.100] As has been stated, and is dealt with in more detail below, when a person is unable to decide on treatment, decisions will be made for them. These will be based on the person's interests (the "best interest" principle; see [4.75]) and welfare (the "substituted judgment" principle); and, to the extent they are known, their wishes. However they will not necessarily reflect the views of the person. In an advance directive, the person's intentions and values can be set out so that these can be known to guide the decision-maker. It is particularly useful where there is no family to consult as to their wishes, or the family's understanding of their wishes is divided or unclear.

[5.101] The question arises as to just what legal force directives have. There have been several decisions in common law jurisdictions which have upheld the validity of directives, and these have mostly involved refusal of blood transfusions (see, for example *Mallette v Shulman*, see [4.62], and *Re T*, see [4.29]). There is no Australian precedent. It is, however, by no means certain that a directive would be legally binding on either a decision-maker or health carer who does not follow it without there being a clear requirement to do so in statutory law (see Foukas (1999), p 2). Otherwise, it seems they are a non-obligatory, although useful, insight to the person's wishes. Some further problems with legal recognition of a person's wishes expressed in advance are discussed in relation to *Qumsieh* (see [5.108]; see also Stewart, (2000)).

[5.102] Those who argue against directives being legally enforceable point to the fact that the person may not have envisaged the type of situation that has arisen, or may have changed their mind (especially if the directive is old, or vague). It is only a guide, they argue, and should be taken into account along with other consideration such as the person's perceived interests. On the other hand, proponents argue that where the directive is clear enough, it should be given the same respect (and legal force) that would be given to a contemporaneous competent decision.

[5.103] Directives are considered by many mental health consumers as a way of their being able to exercise their autonomy when they are well, so

[5.103] that they do not lose it when they suffer a relapse. Little real consideration is given to the wishes of a person with a mental illness if they are not in accord with what is considered to be appropriate treatment by health carers. The benefits of a directive are multiple:

- .....directives are a means by which the person suffering from decreased capacity may be listened to more readily where treatment preferences expressed are consistent with those expressed in a valid directive;
- .....directives encourage dialogue with health carers and friends when they are in the process of making them, and where these set out the values, wishes, and (particularly where mental health care is involved) treatment plans, and encourage a positive relationship between all parties, and consequent willingness for co-operation with health care; and
- .....there is the possibility of earlier intervention in treatment, with less hesitancy and lack of uniformity in approach of the health care team and family. Especially with the mentally ill this can avoid the avoidance of early warning signs of illness, and consequent dramas and distress when the person's condition requires emergency treatment.

[5.104] However, there are potential problems with advance directives. They may be vague, using poorly defined terms such as "heroic measures" or "resuscitation": this may be helped with careful language and medical advice. The person's views may have changed over time: this too may be dealt with by frequent updating of the directive. Kerridge et al ((1999), p 311) argue that advance directives should "be treated in a similar manner to other consent forms—as evidence for effective communication that can be used to guide decision-making within its clinical context". They list matters which should apply to advance directives, including that they be simple and concise, allow for disease-specific statements and treatment-specific directions, include a statement of the person's life values to guide decision-makers, nominate a proxy decision-maker, and allow for periodic review.

Psychiatric Treatment is not Covered by Advance Directives

[5.105] Foukas (1999) considers the nature of a psychiatric directive, in which she suggests that it could include a statement of values, and a treatment plan, noting preferred and rejected treatment and care. She suggests that directives should apply across the board, with no special consideration necessary for mental illness, as there is no reason for not providing the same respect for the autonomy of all clients. However the law currently provides that psychiatric health care to a non-competent person is subject to review by a court or tribunal under mental health legislation.

[5.106] Readers might thus consider whether:

- .....the mentally ill should be able to make legally binding directives about future treatment which they may require later when undergoing an episode where they are not competent to agree to it; and
- .....a person who has made a directive authorising particular treatment should be given that treatment at a later date when, having become incompetent, they violently object to the treatment. Would it make a difference if the directive covered psychiatric treatment, agreed to if the person is suffering a psychotic episode?

What is the "Triggering Event"?

[5.107] Advance directives are not confined to decisions to forego life-sustaining treatment, but may be drafted for use in any health care situation in which people anticipate they will lack capacity to make decisions for themselves. This raises the question of what constitutes the "triggering event", when the directive comes into effect, and this would depend on the nature of the directive. A "general" advance directive is one that anticipates any situation where the person is unable to express his or her choice. It would seem that a general advance directive comes into effect when the person is declared to be incompetent by a prescribed person (or persons). If, however the directive was to apply only to a current condition (see below) or a terminal condition (a "specific" advance directive) then one would have to satisfy the particular requirements set out.

Must Advance Directives be Followed? Qumsieh's Case

[5.108] Despite rulings in cases from the United Kingdom and United States that advance directives should be followed, and legislation in some Australian States and Territories (see below), a recent case has shown that it is difficult for the judiciary in Australia to uphold refusal of life-saving treatment by a competent adult (*Qumsieh v Guardianship and Management Board and Pilgrim* (SC Vic, No 5656 of 1998; High Court of Australia, No M98 of 1998)). In that case, a woman gave birth and then suffered post-partum haemorrhage. Being a Jehovah's Witness, she had made a recent advance directive rejecting blood transfusion, and had appointed an elder of the church as her medical attorney. She had also verbally indicated her wishes, and had written them on a consent form. However her husband was appointed guardian by the Guardianship Board in a hasty decision made in the absence of advice about these moves. The husband gave instructions to the hospital allowing his unconscious wife to receive a blood transfusion. On recovery, the wife sought a review of the Board's order by the Supreme Court. The judge in the Supreme Court dismissed the case out of hand, stating that "the order was made to save her life and no court would contemplate exercising its discretion to grant a remedy". This judgment was appealed in the Victorian Court of Appeal.

[5.108] That Court also dismissed the appeal, holding that the Board was entitled to act on evidence before it, and did not have to "look over its shoulder" to ensure that all the evidence was before it. The judge had been correct in his decision, it held, because of the circumstances of the case, given:

- .....the large number and variety of grounds for the appeal;
- .....the large number of respondents the appellant wanted to make party to her claims;
- .....the fact that the challenged order was now exhausted (that is, it had had its effect and could not be reversed); and
- .....it would "bring the appellant into disrepute with her husband".

Sufficient basis existed for the judge's conclusion that he should exercise discretion under section 4 of the *Administrative Law Act* 1978 (Vic), to refuse application for order for review, since it considered that no matter of substantial importance was involved.

The appellant applied for leave to appeal to the High Court of Australia, arguing that she should have a right to raise a controversy ex post facto, as a declaration of invalidity which the *Administrative Law Act* indicates she is entitled to seek, would assist her in any future decisions in relation to whether or not she would take the matter further, and that while the Board's order was exhausted the matter was one of public importance (that is, the right to refuse treatment). However the High Court also dismissed the case stating that the facts of the case and the fact that the events were in the past militated against the grant of special leave to have the appeal heard.

Jurisdictions Giving Legislative Effect to Advance Directives

[5.109] South Australia was the first State to legislate on this matter. The *Consent to Medical Treatment and Palliative Care Act* 1995 (SA) permits a person to give directions, when he or she may be suffering from a terminal disease, that no extraordinary means (defined as artificial ventilation, intravenous lines, dialysis, artificial heart or the organs of others) are to be used. "Terminal illness" means any illness, injury, degeneration of mental or physical faculties which would indicate that death would be imminent if the extraordinary means were not used, and temporary or permanent recovery is not possible even with extraordinary means being used. The person (an adult) makes the direction, in the presence of two witnesses. This may be at any time either before or after the onset of the illness. The legislation declares that the non-application of the extraordinary measures does not constitute a cause of death. It also protects any medical practitioner who acts in good faith upon the belief that such a statement was made and was not revoked, that the person was able to understand the nature and consequences of the direction, and is suffering from a terminal illness, even though the belief is in fact erroneous.

[5.110] In the Northern Territory the *Natural Death Act* 1988 (NT) is similar to the South Australian legislation.

[5.111] In Victoria the *Medical Treatment Act* 1988 (Vic) goes somewhat further than the legislation described above, but it also has more restrictions. First, it requires that a refusal of treatment statement is signed by the person in the presence of a doctor and one other witness. They must declare they are satisfied that the client:

- .....clearly expressed a decision to refuse treatment *in relation to a current condition*;
- .....made the decision voluntarily;
- .....had adequate information to make the decision and understood it; and
- .....was of sound mind and over 18.

[5.112] The treatment refused may be "any . . . medical procedure", but does not include palliative care (relief of pain, suffering or discomfort, or reasonable provision of food and water). The person also does not have to be terminally ill. Having established these safeguards, the Act establishes the offence of medical trespass for a medical officer who provides treatment which a client has refused in these circumstances. It also provides immunity from civil or criminal action for medical staff who act in good faith and in reliance on a refusal certificate.

[5.113] In Queensland, section 35 of the *Powers of Attorney Act* 1998 (Qld) provides that an adult person may give directions, about health matters and special health matters, for his or her future health care and give information about his or her directions. These may be a consent, in the circumstances specified, to particular future health care of the person when necessary and despite objection by the person when the health care is provided. It may also require, in the circumstances specified, particular life-sustaining measures to be withheld or withdrawn.

[5.114] In Queensland people can also appoint one attorney or more to exercise power for a health matter on their behalf in the event the directions prove inadequate, and provide terms or information about how to go about exercising that power. This may include authorising the attorney to physically restrain, move or manage the person, or have the person physically restrained, moved or managed, for the purpose of health care when necessary and despite objection by the person when the restraint, movement or management is provided. A direction in an advance health directive operates only while the person has impaired capacity for the matter covered by the direction; and is as effective as if he or she was competent and making the decision when the treatment was being given.

The person cannot make a direction to withhold or withdraw a life-sustaining treatment except under certain circumstances.

[5.115] In the Australian Capital Territory, section 6 of the *Medical Treatment Act* 1994 (ACT) provides that a competent adult may make a direction in writing, orally or in any other way in which the person can communicate to refuse, or for the withdrawal of, medical treatment, either generally or of a particular kind. However the Act does not provide that this has any specific legal effect.

Client Refusal of Treatment Agreed to in an Advance Directive

[5.116] It may be the case that a person who has agreed to treatment in an advance directive then refuses violently to it when incapacitated. This may be for example a person who has agreed to specific treatment, having a particular person care for them, or to being moved into particular nursing home. There is no legal precedent for such a case to the author's knowledge, however, it is suggested that in such cases, unless a less distressing and acceptable form of care can be used, and the care is considered necessary for the person's health and well-being, application should be made to the appropriate body for authorisation to carry out the care. It is recommended that no person (no matter what their mental capacity) should be treated in a way to which they seriously object without an order from a court or tribunal.

Recording of, and Access to, Advance Directives

[5.117] There is no provision for recording of, or access to, medical directives, which may be a critical issue where a person is not competent to determine treatment. A person who has multiple or a serious illness may be being cared for by a large number of health carers. They may or may not be in a health care facility, and may be transferred between facilities or discreet treatment areas within the same facility. There is a need to ensure that health carers are at any time aware of the existence of an advance directive. Health carers should treat an advance directive in the same way as they would treat a consent form and ensure its existence is communicated to, or available for, all who may be involved in a person's care.

Appointment of a Medical Agent (Power of Attorney)

Ordinary Power of Attorney

[5.118] The idea of an enduring power of attorney arises out of the legal concept of an ordinary power of attorney. An ordinary power of attorney is a document whereby a person (the donor of the power: for the purposes of this paper referred to as the "client") gives someone else (their "attorney") the power to act on his or her behalf for certain purposes which then binds the client at law. The power of the attorney commences at a time stated by the client, and ceases to have effect when he or she:

- ..... loses the capacity to understand the effect of the power which has been given;
- ..... dies; or
- ..... revokes the power.

Enduring Power of Attorney ("Medical Attorney", "Enduring Guardian", "Medical Agent") [5.125]

[5.119] A person may appoint an agent to make decisions on his or her behalf when he or she is no able to do so through some form of mental or physical impairment. An enduring power of attorney (EPA) differs from an ordinary power of attorney in that it only operates when the client is no longer competent. In all jurisdictions except the Northern Territory, a person can appoint an enduring attorney or enduring guardian to make decisions in relation to health care. This power does not come into effect until the client is declared incompetent. Both a medical attorney and an enduring guardian will be called a "medical agent". The agent is required to act according to his or her understanding of the wishes of the client, and, where a valid consent (or refusal) is given by the attorney, it has the same effect as if it were made by the client.

[5.120] The advantage of appointing a medical agent is that it is an inexpensive and simple way for a person to choose who will make decisions about health care when he or she is unable to do so. The person who acts as attorney may be any adult who is trusted in that capacity by the client. It obviates the need for the appointment of a guardian by a court or tribunal, and can be changed or revoked at any time.

[5.121] An enduring power of attorney generally permits a person to authorise the attorney:

- to consent to medical treatment;
- to refuse medical treatment; or
- consent to the donation of an organ, blood or tissue on their behalf,

if they are unable to do so themselves. The client may nominate specific treatments which may or may not be consented to, and conditions under which this may occur.

[5.122] Some jurisdictions allow for an enduring guardian to make day-to-day decisions about such matters as residence, education, work, etc.

[5.123] In the Australian Capital Territory a competent adult can appoint a person to consent to, or refuse medical treatment under the *Powers of Attorney* Act 1956 (ACT). The *Medical Treatment Act* 1994 (ACT) provides for the appointment of a person to *refuse* medical treatment only. In both cases palliative care cannot be refused.

[5.124] In New South Wales the *Guardianship Act* 1987 (NSW) provides for a competent adult to appoint an enduring guardian. The enduring guardian can make general lifestyle decisions for the person, as well as decisions about health care when they cannot do so for themselves. The powers of the enduring guardian are superseded by a guardianship order.

[5.125] In Queensland the *Powers of Attorney Act* 1998 (Qld) provides that competent adults may appoint an "enduring attorney" to make health care decisions on their behalf on loss of competence. If there is no enduring attorney, a statutory health attorney is authorised to make

158 ■ HEALTH CARE AND THE LAW

[5.125]   decisions. A statutory attorney is the first of those who are readily available to make decisions about the person in the following order:

- .....the person's spouse or de facto spouse;
- .....an adult who has continuing unpaid care of the person; and
- .....an adult who is a close friend or relation of the person.

If a statutory guardian is not available, the "adult guardian", a statutory authority, becomes the relevant authority for making decisions on the person's behalf. There is provision for reviewing a decision by a statutory guardian, but not one by the adult guardian.

An attorney cannot consent to "special medical treatment" (see below [5.211]). Application for this must be made to the Supreme Court.

Health care can be given in an emergency or where the care is:

- .....minor and uncontroversial, but necessary for the health and well-being of the person; and
- .....there is no known objection by the person to the care; or
- .....the person objects; but
   — the health care is unlikely to cause distress; or
   — temporary distress is outweighed by the benefits.

[5.126] In South Australia under the *Consent to Medical Treatment and Palliative Care Act* 1995 (SA) a competent adult can appoint another person (called an "agent") to make decisions about health care on his or her behalf. He or she can also appoint an enduring guardian under the *Guardianship and Administration Board Act* 1993 (SA) to undertake the personal care and welfare (including health care) of the person. An agent is not authorised to refuse:

- .....palliative care or food, water or medication intended to relieve pain or distress; and
- .....medical treatment intended to assist the person gain capacity, unless he or she is in the terminal stage of a terminal disease.

[5.127] A decision can be reviewed by the Supreme Court on the application of a person's medical practitioner or someone who has a "proper interest" in the exercise of powers conferred by the medical power of attorney. An exception is where the person is in the terminal stage of a terminal illness and treatment would only prolong the dying process.

[5.128] In Tasmania under the *Guardianship and Administration Act* 1995 (Tas) a competent adult can appoint an enduring guardian with all the powers of a guardian appointed at law. These include the power to make health care decisions when the person is not competent to do so.

[5.129] In Victoria the *Medical Treatment Act* 1988 (Vic) provides that a competent adult can appoint someone under an enduring power of attorney to make health care decisions necessary for the well-being of the person in the event of incapacity. The *Guardianship and Administration Act*

1986 (Vic) allows for the appointment of an enduring guardian, who can [5.133] make lifestyle decisions as well as health care decisions for the person if "and only to the extent that" the person becomes unable to make these decisions. An appointment may be revoked not only by the person, but by the Victorian Civil and Administrative Tribunal if the appointee is unable or unwilling to operate under the appointment, or has not acted in the best interests of the person.

[5.130] In Western Australia the *Guardianship and Administration Act 1990* (WA) provides for the appointment of an enduring power of attorney for decision-making in relation to health care.

[5.131] The legislation differs in detail across jurisdictions and generally lacks a requirement that a person be given specific medical or legal information before appointing a medical agent (of course this is desirable). Provision for documentation that the person has received such information or a requirement that the person must understand the nature and effect of the power is also generally lacking. Those appointing a medical agent should at least record whether he or she has received independent medical and legal advice, to prevent the validity of an EPA or its terms being brought into question.

Who May Witness the Appointment of a Medical Agent?

[5.132] Most Australian jurisdictions do not require witnesses to the appointment of an agent to possess any particular qualifications except that they be over 18 years of age. Queensland requires a witness to be a lawyer or a Justice of the Peace. Finding such a person may make the document harder to execute, however given the seriousness of the power being conferred, it may be considered that such a requirement should be universal. Such an approach would have to be weighed against the practicality and ease with which a document can now be witnessed. Relatives of the client and the agent are also generally prohibited from witnessing the appointment.

Role of Witnesses

[5.133] Jurisdictions differ in the requirements placed on witnesses to the appointment of a medical agent (for example, Victoria provides for both witnesses to certify that the client is of "sound mind and understands the import" of the document; Queensland, South Australia and Tasmania require witnesses to indicate that the client and the attorney appeared to understand the effect of the document they were signing). It is thus necessary for witnesses to be aware of their obligations. It is recommended that a person who approaches health carers to be witnesses to the appointment of a medical agent be referred to legal advice to ensure the validity of the document.

Obligations and Powers of Person Acting as Medical Agent

[5.134] The law is generally quite clear in relation to the obligations of medical agents in all jurisdictions. They are entitled to consent to, or refuse, treatment according to the terms of their appointment as attorney even if health carers believe the decision is not in the best interests of the client. Most jurisdictions specifically state that in exercising powers under an enduring power of attorney while the client is incapacitated, the medical agent shall act, as far as possible, and can be ascertained, as the client would have acted if the client were not incapacitated. In doing so, he or she must take into account the need for preventing the client from becoming destitute, and the desirability of maintaining, so far as is possible, the client's style of life as it was before the incapacity. Where the client's views on a particular issue are not known the attorney must act in the client's best interests.

Transitory Incapacity

[5.135] The question arises as to what happens when the client regains capacity either permanently or transiently. While presumably the power of the medical agent would no longer be effective (until any further incapacity occurs) there is no clear provision for this in the legislation. Variations in the depth of incapacity may also occur. Victoria requires that an agent's powers are to exercise the powers of a guardians "if, and only to the extent that", the appointor becomes incapacitated. Issues relating to the question of capacity are dealt with in Chapter 4.

Role of Health Carers

[5.136] Questions also arise as to the role of health carers in dealing with consent to, or refusal of, treatment by an attorney. For example there may be uncertainty as to how a health carer is to satisfy him or herself that the power of attorney is made in compliance with legislation. This is not uniformly dealt with in legislation and so it can only be presumed that where a health carer reasonably believes a document to be a valid appointment of a medical agent, he or she can act on it. The Australian Capital Territory, Queensland and Victoria provide that a registered medical practitioner or dentist who, in good faith carries out medical or dental treatment on a person in compliance with the legislation is not guilty of assault, battery or professional misconduct or liable in a civil action for assault or battery. This protection excludes other health carers and other health care—an omission which may particularly affect nurses and other practitioners whose activities can include quite significant care to clients.

Differences of Opinion About Care

[5.137] A further issue which may arise is the action which should be taken if there is a difference of opinion among health carers as to whether the person is incompetent, and thus whether the wishes of the client or his or her attorney are to be followed. There is currently no legislation setting out how to deal with such a situation. Provision in legislation for a procedure for dealing with this issue would be one way to deal with this situation (for example, by providing for recognition of the opinion of the client's most senior treating medical practitioner, the medical superintendent, or appeal to one or more professionals appointed for the task). [5.140]

Revocation of Appointment of a Medical Agent

[5.138] Little specific provision is made across jurisdictions for the revocation of an appointment of a medical agent. The person must specifically revoke an appointment in writing, or tear up all copies of the document.

Those Suffering from a Mental Illness

[5.139] In recent years lawyers have taken more interest in the protection of the rights of the mentally ill. Whereas in the past the retention and treatment of a person involuntarily was considered a medical procedure based on a medical decision, today it is being increasingly recognised that the compulsory retention and treatment of a person should be given full legal consideration, as it is a potential violation of the person's human and legal rights. However, as the following discussion will show, this development is patchy, and fraught with confusion, prejudice and stereotypical thinking.

[5.140] The Australian Government has participated in the development of the *United Nations' Principles for the Protection of Persons with Mental Illness and for the Improvement of Mental Health Care* and these principles have been included in a National Health Plan. The Principles state, among other things, that:

- a mentally ill person is to have all the rights of any other person, and is to be free from discrimination;
- the determination that a person has a mental illness shall be made in accordance with internationally accepted principles;
- a person is to be able to live and work within the community to the extent of her or his capabilities;
- treatment is to be based on the principle of the "least restrictive alternative", to be individualised, discussed with the client and reviewed regularly;
- clients are to be protected from exploitation, abuse and degrading treatment;
- a person is not to be detained involuntarily unless this is necessary for the safety of the person or others, or to prevent serious deterioration in the person's condition;
- where necessary for the above reasons detention may be for a short period pending review; and
- detention should involve the least restrictive measures for the least necessary time, and follow legislatively established procedures.

[5.141] **[5.141]** In 1993 the Human Rights and Equal Opportunity Commission was critical of legislation in every jurisdiction of Australia for its inconsistency with these principles, and as a consequence most States and Territories reviewed their mental health legislation (*Report of the National Inquiry into the Human Rights of People with Mental Illness*, 1993). As can be seen from the outline of the law below, in some cases inadequate attention is given to the need for informed consent, and few protections are provided in relation to treatment of clients. Further discussion of human rights can be found in Chapter 18.

[5.142] Involuntary detention and treatment is a legal act, subject to the rule of law, with those seeking to deprive a person of their liberty being answerable on legal rather than medical grounds. Thus, while there are often medical arguments about whether a person actually suffers from a mental illness, mental disorder or otherwise, legislation is more concerned with establishing criteria that warrants the detention and treatment of a person against their will.

Definition of "Mental Illness"

[5.143] There is no attempt at a precise definition of "mental illness" in any State or Territory legislation,[4] except perhaps for Sch 1 of the *Mental Health Act* 1990 (NSW) (which calls it "mental illness") and the *Mental Health (Treatment and Care) Act* 1994 (ACT) (which calls it "psychiatric illness").

Both Acts use similar terms, and define the illness as:

> a condition which seriously impairs, either temporarily or permanently, the mental functioning of a person and is characterised by the presence in the person of any one or more of the following symptoms:
>
> (a) delusions;
> (b) hallucinations;
> (c) serious disorder of thought form;
> (d) a severe disturbance of mood;
> (e) sustained or repeated irrational behaviour indicating the presence of any one or more of the symptoms referred to in paragraphs (a)-(d).

[5.144] Both Acts go on to differentiate between a mentally ill person (who is suffering from mental illness and requiring care, treatment or control for her or his own or others' protection from serious physical or other harm) and a mentally disordered or dysfunctional person (who is not suffering from mental illness), but whose:

> behaviour is so irrational that temporary care, treatment or control is necessary for his or her protection from serious physical harm ["mentally disordered" person, NSW].

---

[4] Legislation relating to mental health is as follows: *Mental Health (Treatment and Care) Act* 1994 (ACT); *Mental Health Act* 1990 (NSW); *Mental Health Act* 1996 (NT); *Mental Health Act* 1974 (Qld); *Mental Health Act* 1993 (SA); *Mental Health Act* 1996 (Tas); *Mental Health Act* 1986 (Vic); *Mental Health Act* 1996 (WA).

or who suffers from [5.147]

> a disturbance or defect, to a substantially disabling degree, of perceptual interpretation, comprehension, learning, judgment, memory, motivation or emotion ["mentally dysfunctional person", ACT].

Victoria and Western Australia use the latter definition for "mental illness".

[5.145] For the purposes of this book, the following terms will be used:

Mental illness: any illness of the mind, including psychiatric illness or mental disorder, but excluding intellectual disability.

Psychiatric illness: a condition fitting the New South Wales definition of "mental illness" above.

Mental disorder: any impairment fitting the New South Wales definition of "mental disorder", above.

[5.146] The Australian Capital Territory, New South Wales, Victoria and Western Australia provide a list of behaviour which does *not* constitute mental illness. This includes:

- religious, political and philosophical beliefs and practices;
- sexual orientation, preference or promiscuity;
- immoral, illegal or anti-social behaviour;
- drug-induced behaviour; and
- developmental disability of mind.

[5.147] Certification of a person as mentally ill is thus a very serious and sometimes difficult responsibility for the medical profession. Firstly, a proper understanding of what constitutes mental illness in the particular jurisdiction of practice is required, along with the requisite diagnostic skills. There has recently been some controversy over whether those with a personality order whose behaviour is anti-social and actually or potentially harmful should be dealt with by the criminal justice system or the mental health system, particularly as a result of the following case in Victoria.

■■■ CASE
Attorney-General v Garry David (aka Garry Webb) [1992] 2 VR 46 (SC Vic)

> The appellant had been imprisoned following conviction for murder. During his imprisonment he carried out several acts of serious self-mutilation, threatened prison officials with violence and made threats aimed at the public at large when he would be free. Although it was considered that he was not suffering from a mental illness, he was certified under the *Mental Health Act* 1986 (Vic) so that he could be involuntarily detained in a hospital and treated for his injuries, and to relieve the prison staff. He lodged an appeal with the Victorian Mental Health Review Board, arguing that he was not mentally ill under the mental health legislation. As he was due for release, Parliament meanwhile passed the *Community Protection Act* specifically for Webb, which permitted a court to make a preventative detention

[5.147] order to keep him in prison or hospital if it considered him a risk to himself or the community. The Act initially expired in April 1991, but its operation was extended to April 1994.

The Mental Health Review Board ruled that he was not mentally ill, but suffering from a personality disorder, and should be returned to prison. The Attorney-General appealed against this decision to the Administrative Appeals Tribunal. The Tribunal's decision, it was argued, would have some bearing on an application then before the Supreme Court to have David detained under the *Community Protection Act* 1990 (Vic).

[5.148] This case raised both medical and legal issues. Medically, it highlighted differences of opinion as to whether personality disorder constitutes a "mental illness" either medically and/or for the purposes of the legislation. Legally, it raised concerns that Parliament would make legislation to detain a specific person under criteria that do not apply to the community in general, thus breaching a principle of the Rule of Law.

[5.149] The Administrative Appeals Tribunal did not make a determination as to whether Webb suffered from a mental illness or not, and sent him to Pentridge Prison. The matter was later heard by the Supreme Court, which ordered that David be detained in preventive detention in J Ward at Ararat maximum security psychiatric unit for six months as if he were a psychiatric patient. At the end of that time a further order was made by the court that he continue to be held in Pentridge Prison.

[5.150] Some other States have attempted to define aspects of mental illness, such as "social breakdown", or "mental dysfunction", but generally they refer to "disease of the mind", or "mental illness", and leave it to the medical profession to decide if any person is suffering from this. As pointed out in [5.146], it may be specified, in addition, that certain attitudes, beliefs and behaviour will *not* indicate mental illness, such as political or religious beliefs, erratic but harmless behaviour. The New South Wales Supreme Court has ruled that senile dementia, without evidence of psychotic symptomatology, does not justify the making of a detention order (*MN v AN* (1989) 16 NSWLR 525).

Mental Illness or Mental Disability?

[5.151] Legislators have had some difficulty in differentiating mental illness from intellectual disability. Some legislation does not do so. It seems generally accepted by the medical profession however, that mental illness is considered a condition which is potentially treatable, with impaired function reducible or temporary, whereas mental disability is a permanent condition, with no reasonable prospect of recovery. It is also clear from legislation that the law is concerned with drawing a distinction between:

> .....people who are mentally ill and in no actual or potential harm to themselves or others, either because of the nature of the illness or the fact that they are willingly undergoing treatment which allows them to live safely in the community; and

- .....people who are mentally ill and are an actual or potential danger to themselves or others. Legislation may include threats to economic well-being (to include those who may foolishly spend money or place themselves in debt when not in a state to make decisions), or threats to reputation, as being types of danger; and
- .....people who are not mentally ill, but who are, nevertheless, an actual or potential danger to themselves and others. There is some difference of opinion in the various jurisdictions as to how to deal with these people.

When the Law Will Order Treatment

[5.152] The law is not concerned with restricting the freedom of the first category of people. It is only when the mentally ill become part of the second and third categories that they attract this concern. Thus, for legal purposes, most legislation requires something more than simply the presence of mental illness, however defined, for detention. Law makers are more concerned with the danger people pose to themselves or others, than they are with the presence or nature of any mental illness. Thus the legal focus is on behavioural outcomes of mental impairment such as a threat of serious physical harm to themselves or others, rather than the precise nature of the mental impairment itself.

[5.153] Health carers should be aware that because a person is diagnosed as having a mental illness, he or she is not necessarily unable to give or withhold consent to health care at law. Those with a mental illness may sue in battery where they have been given non-urgent treatment to which they are capable of consenting. These people have the right to be treated in the same way as a person who is not mentally ill in all matters except those which relate to an order by a court (see below, Ch 18).

[5.154] Because each jurisdiction has its own legislation, and this can become somewhat complicated, a detailed description of statutory provisions in each State will not be set out here. However, some main aspects of the law and mental illness will be considered. Carers who are dealing with clients who are considered not competent to make decisions should be familiar with the law regarding their powers and responsibilities towards those clients.

Voluntary Patients

[5.155] Victoria and Tasmania have provision for people with a mental illness to appeal against a decision by a hospital to refuse them admission. In Victoria the chief psychiatrist must review the refusal, and in Tasmania the person is to be advised of community services, and the right to seek a second opinion. In Queensland admission is to be denied only if, after psychiatric assessment, alternative care is considered more appropriate.

[5.156] It would appear from common law that voluntary patients in an institution should be treated like any other member of the community, and with the same dignity and respect. They may consent to or refuse treatment as they wish, as they are legally entitled to be considered competent enough to do so. Their property should not be confiscated, nor should they be denied information, services or freedom of movement to

[5.156] any lesser extent than any other competent person. This has been endorsed by the Australian High Court in *Secretary, Department of Health and Community Services v JWB and SMB (Marion's Case)* (1992) 175 CLR 218 (see [5.17]). It is only when they fulfill the requirements for involuntary treatment that their refusal to consent to treatment can be overridden:

> A person (whether or not the person is suffering from mental illness) is a mentally disordered person if the person's behaviour for the time being is so irrational as to justify a conclusion on reasonable grounds that temporary care, treatment or control is necessary:
> (a) for the person's own protection from serious physical harm; or
> (b) for the protection of others from serious physical harm.

[5.157] Voluntary patients should be free to walk around hospital grounds and even leave the hospital if they so wish. There is a distinction between a person leaving hospital and a person being discharged, the latter involving an undertaking by the hospital that their condition is satisfactory for leaving. In Western Australia, a voluntary patient seeking to be discharged is to be referred to be examined by a psychiatrist, and may be detained for up to six hours for this purpose. A voluntary patient (in any jurisdiction) who leaves without being discharged cannot automatically be apprehended and returned. They must fulfill the emergency apprehension provisions described below. They should not be detained in the facility unless legal authority to do so is obtained through the proper legal process.

[5.158] The Australian Capital Territory, New South Wales and Western Australia provide for unrestricted communication with outsiders. However this may be restricted in some circumstances.

Involuntary Patients

Emergency Detention and Treatment

[5.159] At common law a person who has been wrongfully detained can apply for a writ of *habeas corpus*, by which a court requires the person to be brought before it, and the reason for detention considered. There is, however, provision for the lawful detention of those apparently suffering from some sort of mental disorder. These laws are very complex, and it is not possible to give other than a general outline here. Carers of those who are suffering from mental illness should be familiar with the law in their State or Territory as the question of whether they can insist on a client submitting to restraint and treatment, which may be a critical aspect of the client's treatment, may vary from case to case. Subject to variations, most States provide for the apprehension, detention, conveyance to a health facility, examination and treatment of a person who is considered to fulfill prescribed criteria. These generally require that not only is the person considered to have a mental illness in the broad medical sense, in the opinion of those apprehending her or him, but that their continued freedom must be considered to be likely to result in some harm either to themselves or to others. Relatives or friends in some jurisdictions may request the apprehension of someone they believe to be in such a condition. This may involve a magistrate issuing a summons, or an authorised person (for example, a police officer or doctor) taking the person into custody.

[5.160] A doctor may also issue a certificate which allows police or ambulance officers, etc, to detain a person and bring him or her to a hospital. There is generally a deadline set (from four to 24 hours) within which the person must be examined, and in most jurisdictions the person may be kept for up to 72 hours for observation and assessment. The person must then either be released, or further detention maintained under certain circumstances. These are summarised below.

[5.161] The Australian Capital Territory (in Part 5 of the *Mental Health (Treatment and Care) Act* 1994 (ACT)) allows a person who is deemed to be suffering from mental illness and a danger of self-harm or harm to others to be apprehended by the police or person authorised by law. The person must be taken to a prescribed hospital and may be detained for 72 hours, after which time an application must be brought in the Mental Health Tribunal for a treatment order. The Act requires the Tribunal to be satisfied that the person is suffering from a psychiatric illness or a mental dysfunction, is engaging or likely to engage in behaviour significantly harmful to herself or himself or others, and has refused treatment or does not accept or understand the need for necessary treatment. The *Mental Health (Treatment and Care) Act* provides that the minimum necessary treatment and restraint is to be given for the client's and community's safety and well-being.

[5.162] In New South Wales, Chapter 4, Part 2 of the *Mental Health Act* 1900 (NSW) provides that where a doctor or accredited person certifies that a person is mentally ill or disordered, the person may be detained if that is considered necessary and there is no other appropriate means of caring for them. They must be seen within 12 hours by the medical superintendent, and a further opinion obtained as soon as possible. If there is agreement that detention is required, the person is detained pending application before a magistrate for a treatment order. If they are considered mentally ill they may be kept no longer than 72 hours. Pending the appearance before the magistrate, they may be treated as the medical superintendent thinks fit, but due regard must be given to the effects of medication on their ability to communicate adequately with a representative at the inquiry.

[5.163] The Northern Territory (in Part III of the *Mental Health Act* 1996 (NT)) has different requirements depending on the situation. A police officer or doctor may detain, or a magistrate may issue a warrant for the detention of, a person who appears to be mentally ill and requires detention and care. An application must be made to the court to detain the person further. This must be within 24 hours if the person is taken into custody without a warrant, and within three days if detention is with a warrant. The magistrate may make an order for detention and treatment, observation, care or control for up to six months.

[5.164] In Queensland the *Mental Health Act* 1974 (Qld) provides that a police officer may remove a person suspected of suffering from a mental illness to a "place of safety" (for example, hospital or police station). Also

[5.164] a relative or person authorised under the Act may apply for admission of a person to a psychiatric hospital other than a security patients' hospital, and if a medical practitioner provides a recommendation, the person may be detained for up to three days. On further examination by another medical practitioner, the person may be detained for a further period of up to 18 days (21 days in all). The period of detention may be renewed for a further three months, then indefinitely for periods of up to 12 months. Renewal of detention is dependent simply on the examination of a psychiatrist.

[5.165] In South Australia Part 3 of the *Mental Health Act* 1993 (Qld) states that a patient may be detained initially for up to three days on the recommendation of a doctor, and examined by a psychiatrist as soon as possible after admission. He or she may then be detained for further two periods of up to 21 days where detention is "justified" for a period not exceeding 12 months. Two psychiatrists may recommend any further detention "for the protection of others". On application by the patient, a relative, guardian, doctor or the Public Advocate the Guardianship Board may make an order for further detention for up to 12 months.

[5.166] In Tasmania the *Mental Health Act* 1996 (Tas) states that where a person suffers from apparent mental illness, and detention is considered necessary to prevent a consequent significant risk of harm to the person or others, an order may be made by an authorised officer or the person's carer. A medical practitioner may order the emergency detention of the person, who must be further examined by an approved doctor within 24 hours, the person either released or detained for a period of up to 72 hours of admission. The person can then be detained, or subjected to a community care order, on the recommendation of two doctors, one at least of whom must be approved as having relevant specialist qualifications. The order may be renewed from time to time by two approved medical practitioners, or the person discharged by a senior medical practitioner at the hospital. The Mental Health Review Tribunal must be informed of any orders or discharges.

[5.167] In Victoria, Part 3 of the *Mental Health Act* 1986 (Vic) states that a medical practitioner may recommend detention of a person considered mentally ill and in need of treatment. The person must be examined by a psychiatrist within 24 hours of detention. As a result of this examination the person may be detained. Continued detention may be authorised by the chief psychiatrist for a period of three months. Further detention may be authorised by a committee of three psychiatrists. Provision is made for notification to the Secretary of the Department of Human Services and for three-monthly reviews of the detention. The Mental Health Review Board must hear appeals against detention four to six weeks after detention and review the patient at intervals of not more than 12 months.

[5.168] In Western Australia, Part 3 of the *Mental Health Act* 1996 (WA) provides that mental health practitioners (psychologists, nurses or occupational therapists) or medical practitioners who are authorised by the Chief Psychologist can refer clients to a psychiatrist for examination at an authorised hospital where they pose a danger to themselves or others. This includes a danger of serious financial harm, damage to reputation or lasting or irreparable harm to an important personal relationship. The person can be detained for up to 24 hours to be examined by a psychiatrist who may detain the person for up to 72 hours from the time of admission for further assessment. The psychiatrist may order that the person be detained for no longer than 28 days, with a further determination for detention up to six months.

[5.169] For those who, because of mental illness, are unable to exercise the understanding and insight required for autonomous decision-making, the principle applies that they can be given emergency health care or restrained where they place themselves or others in danger without their having consented to it. Under mental health legislation courts and tribunals can go further, and authorise the treatment of a person against his or her will, by force if necessary. Thus in all jurisdictions there is an eventual time limit at the end of which the person must be released, or a court or tribunal order for compulsory treatment sought. Detention periods stated are maximum periods, and the person may be detained for shorter periods, or released at any time by the relevant authorised person or body. The person may appeal the detention to a nominated body, such as the Guardianship Board, Mental Health Tribunal or Court. There must be periodic reviews of a detained person and that person's situation. The person may be entitled to have a nominated representative who is notified of all legal action and who may advise and act for the client, and represent them at a hearing. Other safeguards may also be established, such as the right to communicate to those outside the institution, to be informed about all treatment, and to seek legal review of the involuntary detention at any time. The institution must then justify detaining the person.

Orders for Treatment

[5.170] As stated in Chapter 4 it is erroneous to characterise the principles of autonomy and beneficence as "rights" which can compete in certain circumstances. The first is a right, the second an ethical directive, which must be subject to the first. However when dealing with those who are unable to appreciate their own position, or their need for care, several rights come into conflict: the right of a person to care and protection, their right to dignity and self-determination; their right to freedom from unnecessary detention and the right of the community from protection from harm. These are all legitimate rights (see discussion of rights in Ch 18; Hundert (1990)). Consequently, legislation attempts to strike a balance between them and as seen above, elaborate procedures have been created to do this.

[5.171] Those bodies authorised to order involuntary treatment should give careful consideration to any evidence which may assist in coming to the most appropriate decision when making an order which is coercive. In those jurisdictions that do not require a hearing by a magistrate or tribunal for detention and treatment of a person, there is no specific limit on the nature of treatment which may be given, other than restrictions on psychiatric surgery and electroconvulsive therapy (see below).

[5.172] At the hearing before the court or tribunal the person may be represented by a lawyer or other person, who is entitled access to medical

[5.172] records. Medical practitioners are generally required to explain why the application for detention and/or treatment within the community is sought. The person and/or their representative can challenge this. The court or tribunal then determines if, on a balance of probabilities, the person fits the criteria for an order.

[5.173] Powers to appeal such orders are being made wider and more accessible. Jurisdictions have moved towards vesting in a public advocate oversight of the administration of treatment orders. Increased opportunity for the involvement of a personal representative (who may be a friend or relative of the client), and for notification to the representative of any matters such as treatment decisions and pending applications for treatment orders. Where there is a community advocate or representative, there may be a requirement on those involved to notify him or her of any involuntary detention and treatment, and for review by the advocate of this.

[5.174] The precise criteria for authorising involuntary health care varies between jurisdictions, but generally the person must be suffering from a psychiatric illness to be the subject of psychiatric treatment. Others who are mentally disordered or dysfunctional and a danger to themselves or others may be the subject of treatment and care orders, which involve other kinds of treatment and care. They may be detained, or allowed to live in the community (or other specified place) where they receive that care and support. A difficulty arises from the fact that "care" may cover much more than the administration of psychiatric medication, but legislation is couched in terms that are addressed only to the medical profession. Thus little or no guidance is given to nurses or others involved in the administration of other forms of care.

Mental Illness or Dysfunction Must be Established

[5.175] It is important to establish some form of mental illness or dysfunction before an order can be made.

■ ■ ■ CASE

Burnett v Mental Health Tribunal & Ors (unreported, SC ACT, No 84 of 1997)

> The appellant had a been diagnosed as having a mild psychiatric disorder, and had had a series of disputes with neighbours, behaving aggressively towards them on occasions, which led to her being hospitalised. An order for her involuntary treatment was made by the Tribunal, without explaining its reasons for this. Her psychiatrist's view was that although she had acted in an irrational and distressing way, her illness could not be described as severe in a clinical sense. The appellant questioned whether where there was evidence of psychiatric illness, and showed that she was able to care for herself and generally manage her own affairs, including her financial affairs.

[5.176] The judge held that there was no evidence in the Tribunal's transcript that the appellant was experiencing any of the symptoms referred to in the Act's definition of "psychiatric illness" such as delusions, hallucinations etc. It stated that the Tribunal should not act on unsubstantiated allegations, but should look for clear evidence of mental dysfunction and danger of harm if the order is not made. There must be "clear and persuasive" evidence demonstrating the need for an order, and the person involved should be given an opportunity to be heard, if this is possible. The judge concluded that even if he had been convinced that the appellant suffered from a psychiatric illness as defined in the Act, he would not have been convinced that a detention order was necessary to protect the appellant, the neighbours or the community.

[5.177] Procedural fairness (or "natural justice") is also required (see [1.59]; see also *"EO v Mental Health Review Board* [2000] WASC 203 (SC WA)).

Community Care

[5.178] Where a person is suffering from a mental illness the relevant court or tribunal in all jurisdictions except the Northern Territory and Queensland can make an order for community care of those who are considered a danger to themselves or to others, but can continue to function in the community with the assistance of medication or care. Where they breach an order, by, for example not turning up for depot medication or at other required appointments or fail to take medication, action can be taken to carry out the treatment, or the person may be brought into hospital for review. Whilst there is reluctance to visit the heavy hand of force on these people, the order does make them the subject of accountability to the court or tribunal. Such orders generally have a maximum time limit of six months, and the person may be discharged earlier if it is considered appropriate to do so. As with orders involving detention, the court or tribunal can set a time within the life of the order for review of the person's condition.

[5.179] Community care orders are often used for someone who is either suffering from a psychiatric illness or mental disorder which responds well to medication, but who lacks insight into the illness and/or is likely not to comply with medication requirements, with the danger of consequently becoming ill. This can lead to the "revolving door syndrome" with its cycles of well-being and illness, and resulting frequent crises and admissions to hospital. In such cases all the person may need is the regular medication to remain well enough to function satisfactorily in the community, and a community order may facilitate this by ensuring medication is administered regularly (see *Harry v The Mental Health Review Tribunal & Anor* (1994) 33 NSWLR 315).

Rights of those with a Mental Illness

Period of Involuntary Treatment or Detention is Set

[5.180] An involuntary treatment order must set limits on the period for which it operates, as noted, the maximum periods vary between jurisdictions. It is most important that this period is clearly noted and followed, as it becomes unlawful to continue the treatment after an order has expired. Sometimes the court or tribunal will require that an order be

[5.180] reviewed before it expires, so that there is adequate provision to extend it if this is warranted, and there is not a gap in treatment. The terms of an order should also be made clear in a client's notes and followed carefully. Thus those caring for someone who is subject to an involuntary treatment order are especially required to keep very clear and accurate records, and adhere to any conditions set out in the treatment order.

Care Should be Neither Unnecessary or Excessive

[5.181] Whilst courts and tribunals can order detention and care, and overall restrictions of movement or residence, the specific nature of that care (for example, the nature and dosage of medication, day-to-day physical and behavioural restrictions) cannot be determined by a court or tribunal: it can only authorise health carers to determine and administer appropriate care. Some States specifically provide that treatment is to be neither unnecessary nor excessive (for example New South Wales and Victoria) or that it must be the least restrictive practicable, and the most appropriate under the circumstances (for example, the Australian Capital Territory). However, it can be seen that the day-to-day decisions as to the nature of treatment and other aspects of the person's life come to be dependent on those who are caring for the person.

[5.182] This is particularly critical for all health carers. The hospital or other facility for those who are mentally ill is their home for the duration. They are deprived of privacy, and must live in a communal environment with limited scope for individual and sexual expression. Carers have an inordinate amount of power and control over every aspect of their lives. This can include what they eat, wear and do, how their possessions are dealt with, what movement they have, who they can communicate with and whether they will be isolated from others or not. Staff can decide whether to meet their needs, big or small, to "punish" inappropriate behaviour, to confiscate possessions, to search persons and rooms. Issues of consent permeate all these activities, and the principles cited at the beginning of this section must be applied.

[5.183] Health consumers' rights are dealt with generally in Chapter 18, but it is worth emphasising that according to common law principles health carers should afford those with a mental illness, including involuntary patients, their rights to their property, privacy and autonomy to the extent that this does not interfere with their specifically ordered treatment. Unless restricted by legislation or a treatment order, they should thus be allowed to exercise their autonomy in matters other than specifically ordered treatment, to the full extent of their abilities, with the onus of proof on those who propose to restrict that autonomy to show that they are unable to do so. Proper accounting for money and other patient property is required. It may be considered administratively convenient to cut corners when dealing with "difficult" people, due to such factors as lack of time, resources or patience. Punitive or patriarchal attitudes, stereotyping and the imposition of cultural or social values may be used to counteract "inappropriate" behaviour. There is some concern that detention and involuntary treatment and care can be authorised without due process of law in some jurisdictions, making this a medical

rather than a legal act. In all cases, but particularly where involuntary [5.186]
detention, treatment and care is authorised by a psychiatrist, precise limits
on the coercive and unconsented-to activities of staff are neither
independently set nor monitored. There have been findings of abuse and
exploitation of patients in several psychiatric institutions, the best known
ones being:

- .....the Royal Commission into events at Chelmsford Hospital New South Wales in 1990 (negligence in deep-sleep treatment, lack of consent to treatment, ignoring of drug and electroconvulsive therapy regulations);
- .....the Commission of Inquiry into events at Ward 10B, Townsville Hospital in 1991 (negligent and non-autonomous so-called group therapy, lack of confidentiality, chemical restraint); and
- .....the task force into allegations of abuse and neglect of residents of Aradale Psychiatric Hospital, Victoria (ill-treatment, stealing of food and misappropriation of patients' money).

[5.184] A National inquiry carried out by Mr Brian Burdekin (*Human Rights and Mental Illness* Canberra AGPS 1993—the "Burdekin Report") found that there was widespread lack of information given to consumers about processes and medication, discrimination against those with a mental illness, assaults and abuse and lack of privacy.

[5.185] As mental health treatment orders are very general in their nature, rarely if ever drawing limits to what constitutes the compulsory care. This is left to the understanding and good will of the carers of those subject to them. Readers may wish to consider whether compulsory treatment orders should be more specific, setting more precise limits to compulsory activities and care.

Electroconvulsive Therapy and Psychiatric Surgery

[5.186] Special provisions are made for consent where electroconvulsive therapy and psychiatric surgery are concerned in all jurisdictions except Queensland and Western Australia. The former jurisdictions set out a definition of "informed consent" for the purposes of these procedures. This includes information about the nature of the proposed treatment, its risks and alternatives, and why this treatment is recommended (the New South Wales description of informed consent is set out in section 183 of the *Mental Health Act* 1990 (NSW) and reproduced at Figure 4.1 at [4.191]). The requirements aim at ensuring the person is able to understand these matters, and weigh the benefits and risks of the treatment, and are similar to those contained in the guidelines set out for informed consent by the National Health and Medical Research Council (see Checklist at [4.122]). One could question why it has not been considered necessary to stipulate these requirements for consent to other health care procedures, whether for mental illness or otherwise.

Electroconvulsive Therapy

[5.187] Jurisdictions impose limitations on electroconvulsive therapy as follows.

[5.188] In the Australian Capital Territory (Part 7, Divisions 1 and 2 of the *Mental Health (Treatment and Care) Act* 1994 (ACT)) "informed consent" as defined in the legislation is required before ECT can be given. Where informed consent is not possible, application must be made to the Mental Health Tribunal by the Chief Psychiatrist of the mental health facility, and supported by another psychiatrist. The Tribunal can only make an order for ECT if it is likely to benefit the patient, all other reasonably available treatments have been tried unsuccessfully, and it is the most appropriate form of treatment reasonably available.

[5.189] New South Wales (in Chapter 7 Part 2 of the *Mental Health Act* 1900 (NSW)) limits the use of ECT to specific hospitals or facilities. A patient other than an involuntary patient must give "informed consent" as prescribed by the Act, two doctors must be present and anaesthesia must be administered. The treatment must be considered necessary in the face of no adequate alternative. The Mental Health Review Tribunal must agree to treatment for involuntary patients, after being satisfied the person is unable to consent, notify the person's nearest relative, guardian (if any) and up to two personal friends (unless the person objects). The treatment must be considered reasonable and proper, and necessary for the safety or welfare of the person.

[5.190] South Australia (s 22 of the *Mental Health Act* 1993 (SA)) also provides that informed consent (not defined) must be a central concern in the administration of ECT, except where the person is unable to give this, in which case an application must be made to the Guardianship Board.

[5.191] The law in Victoria (Part 5 Divisions 1AA and 2 of the *Mental Health Act* 1986 (Vic)) also requires informed consent similar to New South Wales. Exceptions to this occur where the patient is incapable of this, in which case it must be authorised by a psychiatrist who is satisfied that:

- .....it is necessary to prevent deterioration in the person's condition;
- .....alternatives have been unsuccessful;
- .....the treatment has clinical merit;
- .....is appropriate; and
- .....consented to by the primary caregiver or guardian where practicable.

Premises must be licensed for the purpose.

[5.192] In Western Australia (Part 5, Division 5 of the *Mental Health Act* 1996 (WA)) ECT cannot be given without a patient's "informed consent" where this is possible. Otherwise it must be recommended by the treating psychiatrist and approved by a second psychiatrist. Approval must not be given unless the treatment is considered to have clinical merit and is appropriate in the circumstances. If no approval is given, the treating psychiatrist may apply to the Mental Health Review Board which cannot substitute the second psychiatrist's withholding of approval, but can recommend an alternative treatment, transfer the person to another psychiatrist, or order that the person is no longer an involuntary patient. [5.198]

Psychiatric Surgery

[5.193] While Queensland, Tasmania and the Northern Territory place no special restrictions on psychiatric surgery, even stronger safeguards are placed on the carrying out of psychiatric surgery in other jurisdictions.

[5.194] The Australian Capital Territory (Part 7, Divisions 1 and 3 of the *Mental Health (Treatment and Care) Act* 1994 (ACT)) requires that before a person can receive psychiatric surgery, the doctor proposing the treatment must apply to the Chief Psychiatrist. The application must be accompanied by a copy of the consent form showing that the patient consented, or an order from the Supreme Court permitting the surgery to be carried out. The Chief Psychiatrist then forwards the application to a Ministerially appointed committee which determines whether to approve the surgery. It must be satisfied that the surgery will provide a substantial benefit to the person and that all reasonable alternatives have been tried and failed. Conditions may be applied to any approval. Where the patient has neither granted nor refused consent, an application may be made to the Supreme Court for authorisation of the surgery.

[5.195] In New South Wales (Chapter 7, Part 1 of the *Mental Health Act* 1900 (NSW)) a person must give "informed consent" as defined by the Act, and a Psychiatric Surgery Review Board must hear the matter at a public hearing at which the person may be represented. The Board must be satisfied that the surgery has clinical merit. Where the person does not consent but the surgery is still considered necessary, the matter must be taken to the Supreme Court for a decision as to whether the person can consent, and if not, whether the surgery should be given.

[5.196] South Australia (s 22 of the *Mental Health Act* 1993 (SA)) has informed consent requirements for psychiatric surgery for those who are capable of giving effective written consent. It must be authorised by two independent psychiatrists as well as the surgeon. It is unclear whether the protection provisions of the legislation allow treatment to be given in the absence of such consent.

[5.197] Victoria (Part 5, Division 1 of the *Mental Health Act* 1986 (Vic)) has a Psychiatric Surgery Review Board, to which applications are to be made by the surgeon intending to operate. The Board may give permission for the surgery, requiring the capacity of the person to consent, expected effectiveness of the treatment and failure of alternative treatments. The Board may authorise the treatment where the person is not able to consent, where that is considered by the Board to be in his or her best interests.

[5.198] Western Australia (Part 5 Division 4 of the *Mental Health Act* 1996 (WA)) requires an application for authorisation of psychiatric surgery to be made by the patient's psychiatrist and neurosurgeon to the Mental Health Review Board. The Board must be satisfied that the person has given informed consent the treatment has clinical merit, is appropriate in the circumstances and is likely to be of lasting benefit to the patient.

Consent to Non-Psychiatric Care by Psychiatric Patient

[5.199] According to common law, those with a mental illness can exercise their capacity to determine general health care in the same way as anybody else (*Secretary, Department of Health and Community Services v JWB and SMB* (*Marion's Case*) (1992) 175 CLR 218; see [5.17]). However some jurisdictions provide for substituted decision making for "medical treatment" for those with a mental disability in some circumstances. This limits the person's autonomy on the basis of his or her diagnosis rather than capacity to decide, and again causes confusion as to just what health carers can do without consent. The restriction of legal principles to "medical treatment" leaves in limbo other aspects of health care, and in the case of the mentally ill and involuntary care, their daily living activities. The source of guidance is thus the statement of rights at [5.140].

[5.200] Legislation addressing consent to non-psychiatric care is set out below. As with the previous outlines of State and Territory legislation, the following should be considered a rough guide only, and those caring for people with a mental disability should familiarise themselves with the detail of the law in their jurisdiction.

[5.201] In New South Wales (Chapter 7, Part 2 of the *Mental Health Act* 1900 (NSW)) there are a number of complicated provisions:

- *Urgent treatment*: a prescribed person may consent to urgent surgery on an involuntary patient whether or not they are capable of consenting. This is in contrast to the basic principle of common law which allows a competent person to refuse such care.
- *Non-urgent treatment*: "Special medical treatment" (resulting in permanent infertility) must not be given without the consent of the Mental Health Review Tribunal, but such consent cannot be given for someone under 16 years. Presumably, such consent is required by the Supreme Court or the Family Court. A medical superintendent must notify a patient's "nearest relative" that he or she proposes surgical treatment for either an involuntary or voluntary patient. If after 14 days the nearest relative gives written consent, the medical superintendent may apply to an authorised officer for consent to the operation. If no consent is forthcoming from the nearest relative, the superintendent may apply to the Mental Health Review Tribunal. The authorisation of treatment by a nearest relative (a spouse, parent or carer) is, where the person is competent, in contrast to the principle of autonomy, and, where the person is incompetent, to the common law principle that relatives *per se* cannot consent (see [5.71]). It differs from the concept of "person responsible" in relation to guardianship (see [5.75]ff).

[5.202] In Victoria (Part 5, Division 4 of the *Mental Health Act* 1986 (Vic)) consent of the patient or his or her guardian is required for non-urgent treatment.

[5.203] In Western Australia (Part 5, Division 6 of the *Mental Health Act* 1996 (WA)) the Chief Psychiatrist can consent to non-psychiatric treatment for an involuntary patient. Presumably common law would apply to other patients.

Seclusion or Restraint of Mentally Ill Patients

[5.204] Restraint of clients generally has been dealt with above. It is of concern that only two jurisdictions regulate restraint and seclusion, and that regulation only applies to mental health clients. Restraint in particular is a means of dealing with others, such as the elderly and those with an intellectual disability. Chemical restraint (that is, sedation for the sole purpose of management) is given even less consideration, but has been considered a significant means of control of those who are in a health care facility whether they are ill or not. See [4.174].

[5.205] Victoria (ss 82-82 of the *Mental Health Act* 1986 (Vic)) has the most extensive provisions for restraint and seclusion. Restraint must only be used for the purpose of treatment of the person, or to prevent injury to the person, others, or to property. It must be approved by an authorised psychiatrist or, in an emergency the senior nurse on duty and notified to a medical practitioner without delay. The person must be under continuous observation by a registered nurse or doctor, reviewed at least every 15 minutes by a registered nurse, and provided with adequate basic facilities such as food, clothing and toilet arrangements. The person must be examined at least every four hours or when determined by the psychiatrist. Regular reports must be sent to the chief psychiatrist (s 82). Seclusion must be used only for the protection of a client from absconding (where he or she is an involuntary patient) or to protect the client or others from an immediate or imminent risk to health or safety. Again seclusion is subject to similar requirements in relation to observation, monitoring, examination and report to those governing restraint (s 83).

[5.206] Western Australia (Part 5, Divisions 8 and 9 of the *Mental Health Act* 1996 (WA)) provides specifically for seclusion and physical restraint. Seclusion or physical restraint must only be carried out at a legally recognised facility, and authorised by a medical practitioner, or, in an emergency, a senior mental health practitioner (nurse or other person appointed as such), in which case a medical practitioner should be notified as soon as practicable. The authorisation must have a set time limit, and seclusion is subject to conditions such as proper facilities being available for basic physical needs, regular monitoring, and reporting to the Mental Health Review Board.

Guardianship and Protection of Mentally Ill Persons

[5.207] All jurisdictions have established special bodies or agents which can be a further means of protection of mental health patients. These may be, for example:

- guardianship boards or courts with the power to appoint guardians and managers of property, which may give orders regarding the general upbringing, education and training and care of the mentally ill, as well as their day-to-day affairs;
- visitors (New South Wales), who regularly inspect mental health institutions and act on behalf of patients;
- welfare officers (New South Wales), who visit patients on leave;

[5.207]
▌.....a mental health advocate (Victoria), who acts on behalf of patients when complaints have been received, or the need arises; and
▌.....the Community Advocate (Australian Capital Territory), who has a watching brief over cases brought before the Mental Health Tribunal.

Health Carers and the Mentally Ill

[5.208] Health carers should be aware of the status of admission of any psychiatric patient, what orders, if any, have been made, and of the need to inform the client of what treatment he or she is receiving, and to encourage his or her co-operation and informed decision-making whenever they can. The attitude that "because someone is an involuntary patient staff can do what they like" can lead to legal problems.

[5.209] Health carers should thus be aware of:

▌.....the rights of the patient, including rights to privacy, the facility's resources, communication with outsiders, and access to, and use of, money and possessions;
▌.....the rights of the relatives to communicate and visit;
▌.....the right to complain, and access to facilities for complaint; and
▌.....the rights and obligations of the institution and its staff in the care of the person.

[5.210] This includes an understanding of:

▌.....powers of detention and treatment in their State or Territory generally;
▌.....the specific powers and permissible treatment for any particular client in their care;
▌.....the requirements for review of detention and treatment;
▌.....rights and procedures of appeal by those involved; and
▌.....the rights of clients generally.

Special Medical Treatment—Sterilisation

Adults and Children

[5.211] All jurisdictions except Queensland and Tasmania have provisions covering specifically designated medical treatment, such as drugs of addiction, experimental treatment, and sterilisation for those who are unable to exercise the ability to make decisions. Involuntary sterilisation of those with a mental disability has caused the most controversy. This issue has been considered extensively by the courts. There have been differing approaches by judges, with the right to reproduce being recognised, but with differences over the limits to such a right. In the Australian Capital Territory, New South Wales, South Australia, Victoria and Western Australia, legislation provides that guardians for adults cannot consent to "special procedures". These are considered by the Guardianship Board or Tribunal. The treatment must be for the promotion or maintenance of the health or well-being of the person, and not the administrative convenience of carers. In the Northern Territory the local court has initial jurisdiction over the matter. The matter may be taken to the Supreme Court for a ruling in all jurisdictions. For children both the state Supreme Courts and the Family Court have jurisdiction, with the Family Court taking precedence where there is a conflict of decisions (see *P and P* at [5.22]).

[5.212] In the case of *Re a Teenager* [1989] FLC ¶92-006 (see also *Secretary, Department of Health and Community Services v JWB and SMB (Marion's Case)* (1992) 175 CLR 218, [5.17]) the Australian High Court held that a decision to authorise the sterilisation of an intellectually disabled child should not come within the ordinary scope of parental power to consent to medical treatment. The Court's authorisation is necessary because:

- ..... this surgery affects the fundamental right to a person's inviolability;
- ..... there is a significant risk of making a wrong decision, which is complicated by the potentially conflicting interests of the child (to reproductive integrity) and the carers (to the improved facility and effectiveness of caring for the child); and
- ..... the gravity of the consequences of wrongly authorising a sterilisation, flowing from the permanency of the effects of the surgery, and the effect of surgery against one's wishes.

[5.213] The Court concluded that the Family Court has the jurisdiction to hear cases involving sterilisation of mentally impaired children. Its welfare jurisdiction is very wide, subject only to constitutional limitations, and overrides State and Territory laws to the contrary. Two States, South Australia and Victoria, allow for guardianship orders for those aged between 16 and 18 years (technically "children"). Section 35(1) of the *Guardianship Act* 1987 (NSW) also provides that treatment involving sterilisation can only be carried out to save someone's life or prevent serious damage to their health ("therapeutic sterilisation"). However Part VII of the *Family Law Act* 1975 (Cth) gives power to the Family Court to make orders in relation to the health care of a child where it is necessary in the child's interests.

[5.214] The reasons for rejecting authorisation of sterilisation of a male are set out in the following case:

[5.214] ■■■ CASE
R-B (A Patient) v Official Solicitor [2000] Lloyd's Law Reports (Medical) 87 (CA UK)

A was a 28-year old with Down's Syndrome, lacking capacity to give or withhold consent to treatment. His mother applied to the High Court, under its inherent *parens patriae* jurisdiction for a declaration that sterilisation was in his best interests, despite A not wanting it. She was concerned that should he need to enter residential care in the future, he could form a relationship with another resident. One consultant psychiatrist testified that the sterilisation would give A more freedom and would result in the need for less supervision. Another disagreed, stating that A was unlikely to engage in sexual intercourse and that the operation was not in his best interests. Whilst A was not likely to engage in frequent sexual intercourse, the operation would not free him from the possibility of disease, or the problems that might arise from a close relationship with another person. The Official Solicitor argued also that the fact that A did not want the operation should be taken into account, as should the right, conferred by the *European Convention on Human Rights* (to which England is a party) to privacy and to found a family (a right also enshrined in the *Declaration of Human Rights*, to which Australia is a signatory).

[5.215] The court refused to authorise the sterilisation. It held that the best interests of the patient included medical, emotional, and all other welfare issues. Doctors not only have to act according to responsible and competent professional opinion, but also in the interests of a mentally incapacitated person. The judge, not the doctor decides what is in the person's best interests. In A's case he would not be any more free from supervision, as he could still be subject to exploitation, emotional implications of a close relationship. If A were to be later in a situation, such as residential care, where he was in danger of the disadvantages mentioned, a fresh consideration of the situation could be undertaken.

[5.216] The basis for authorising surgery that will result in the sterilisation of a child was set out in the following case.

■■■ CASE
JLS v JES (unreported, SC NSW Equity Division, No 1871/1996)

JES was severely intellectually disabled. Her mother applied to the New South Wales Supreme Court for the Court's consent to an abdominal hysterectomy which would render her permanently infertile. Under section 20B of the *Children (Care and Protection) Act* 1987 (NSW) a court can only authorise such an operation if satisfied that it is necessary to prevent serious injury to the child's health. The court had previously authorised the administration of DepoProvera for the purposes of contraception. However, JES suffered from the side-effects of the drug, and still had intermittent bleeding at the sight of which she was terrified. Doctors decided that surgical intervention was necessary to control her symptoms. They argued that hysterectomy would prevent serious damage to her health by eliminating haemorrhage and preventing psychological distress. It would enhance the quality of life and prevent pregnancy.

[5.217] The Court gave its consent pursuant to section 20B of the Act that a hysterectomy be carried out on the child. It held that:

- ..... the effects of menstruation constituted serious damage to the health of JES;
- ..... it was necessary to carry out the operation because alternative therapy was ineffective;
- ..... JES's intellectual disability and neurological disorders were such that she could never exercise a right to have children with any understanding of what was happening; and
- ..... the proposed surgery would improve her mother's ability to continue to care for her.

[5.218] Given the courts' reasoning in other cases, it appears that the last criteria should only be applied when the former ones are present.

[5.219] Sandor (1999) argues that sterilisation should be a procedure of last resort, but that "Even government estimates suggest that medical assaults through sterilisation procedures on children are undetected and undeterred" (p 21). The figures are stark: whilst courts and tribunals had authorised 17 sterilisations of girls between 1992 and 1997, data collected by the Health Insurance Commission showed that "at least" 1045 girls had been sterilised during that period (p 17, quoting Brady & Grover (1997)). He concludes that "informed adherence to the law" is required of those involved in a special medical procedure on a child:

> If neither money nor morality is an incentive to the redress of medical assaults by sterilisation, and the representative body for medical practitioners wants past violations shielded from scrutiny, then people with disabilities and those who care for their integrity have every right to wonder which period in history they are living in (Sandor, p 21).

[5.220] Medical practitioners are not the only ones involved in sterilisations. Other health carers, particularly nurses, take part in this allegedly massive denial of human rights. It is yet another area where autonomy is ignored by the health care profession.

Important Reminder for Health Carers

This Chapter sets out the law in a general fashion. Health carers should become familiar with the law in their jurisdiction, and be clear as to the distinction between legal requirements and guidelines. Whatever guidelines and recommendations are established, health carers run the risk of legal action if they do not act according to the law.

REFERENCES AND FURTHER READING

See also Further Reading list for Chapter 4.

Australian Health and Medical Law Reporter (CCH, Sydney, 1991)

Carney, T, *Law at the Margins* (OUP, Melbourne, 1991)

Dickey, A, *Family Law* (2nd ed, Law Book Co, Sydney, 1990)

Eades, J, "Parens Patriae Jurisdiction of the Supreme Court is Alive and Kicking" *Law Society Journal* (February 2000), p 53

Foukas, T, "Psychiatric Advance Directives—Part 1" 8 *Australian Health Law Bulletin* 1; "Part II", 8 *Australian Health Law Bulletin* 13

Freckelton, I and Petersen, K, *Controversies in Health Law* (The Federation Press, Sydney, 1999)

Gutman, J, "Comment, R v M" 7 *Journal of Law and Medicine* 113

Hayes, S and Hayes, R, *Mental Retardation: Law Policy and Administration* (Law Book Co, Sydney, 1982)

Human Rights and Equal Opportunity Commission, *Human Rights and Mental Illness: Report of the National Inquiry into the Human Rights of People with Mental Illness* (Australian Government Publishing Service, Canberra, 1993)

Hundert, E, "Competing Medical and Legal Ethical Values" in Rosner and Weinstock (see below) (1990), p 53

Kennedy, I, "Commentary Re H (mental patient) [1993] 1 FLR 28 (1993)" 1 Med Law Rev (1993), p 237

Kerridge, I, et al, "Advance Directives" in Freckelton, I and Petersen, K, *Controversies in Health Law* (The Federation Press, Sydney, 1999), p 302

McFarlane, P, *Health Law: Commentary and Materials* (The Federation Press, Sydney, 2000)

Mason, A, "The Year 2000: Psychiatric Lecture" presented at the Hyatt Hotel, Canberra, ACT, on 15 November 2000

Morgan, J, "Minors and Consent to Medical Treatment: Reflecting on Gillick", Law Reform Commission of Victoria, Symposia 1986 (Globe Press, Melbourne, 1987)

O'Sullivan, J, *Law for Nurses* (Law Book Co, Sydney, 1983)

Rosner, R and Weinstock, R, *Ethical Practice in Psychiatry and the Law* (Plenum Press, New York, 1990)

Roth, M and Bluglass, R, *Psychiatry, Human Rights and the Law* (Cambridge University Press, Cambridge, 1985)

Sandor, D, "Sterilisation and Special Medical Procedures on Children and Young People: Blunt Instrument? Bad Medicine?" in Freckelton, I and Petersen, K, *Controversies in Health Law* (The Federation Press, Sydney, 1999)

Stewart, C, "Qumsieh's Case, Civil Liability and the Right to Refuse Medical Treatment" 8 *Journal of Law and Medicine* Vol 7 (August 2000), p 56

Skene, L, *Law and Medical Practice* (Butterworths, Sydney, 1998)

Chapter Six

NEGLIGENCE

INTRODUCTION

[6.1] Once clients have given consent to their care, health carers have an especially recognised legal relationship with a client, which requires proper professional care for that client. Failure to provide this leaves them open to being sued by an aggrieved client for negligence, and/or for breach of contract, through which the client seeks damages for harm suffered as a result. The law of contract is dealt with in Chapter 10.

Professional Negligence or Malpractice

[6.2] Professional negligence, sometimes called malpractice, is perhaps the area of greatest legal importance for health care workers, as it provides the most common reason for legal action against them. It is the way of seeking compensation for harm wrongfully suffered at the hands of the health care profession, whereas there is not such a compelling reason for action where assault or battery may have occurred, but no harm suffered as a result of it. Negligence is called a "tort" (French for "wrong") at law. As its name implies, the action can only be taken for harm that should not have occurred in the normal course of events, so a health carer is not liable for harm that occurs despite care which is reasonable in the circumstances. Thus the fact of harm or injury does not of itself necessarily mean that someone was negligent (see, for example *Roe v Minister of Health* at [6.80]). This chapter outlines the factors that will make a health carer liable for negligence.

[6.3] A finding that a health carer is liable for an isolated act of negligence is different from a finding that he or she is incompetent (*Professional Indemnity Review* (1995), p 169; Nisselle (1999), p 135). Even the best of practitioners may make an error of judgment leading to a finding of technical legal negligence. In contrast, the medical Registration Boards investigate allegations of incompetence (see Ch 13).

Preventable Adverse Events

[6.4] A nationwide study, the *Australian Hospital Care Study*, commissioned by the then Minister for Human Services and Health,

[6.4] found that in the year 1992, 230,000 public and private hospital admissions involved an adverse event which was preventable. Of these, between 25,000 and 30,000 people were estimated as suffering some degree of permanent disability, and between 10,000 and 14,000 people to have died. Those aged over 60 were found to have a greater chance of experiencing an adverse event while in hospital. There was no variation according to sex, marital status, insurance status or racial background. The total hospital bed days as a result of the adverse effects in 1992 was estimated at about 3.2 million, with half of these relating to preventable adverse events. The cost of these bed-days was estimated at about 650 million dollars.

[6.5] A task force on Quality in Australian Health Care (QAHC) was established as a result of this study. This has become known as the Quality in Australian Health Care Study, or QAHCS. The QAHCS has issued an interim report of its analysis of adverse events in hospital patients. Here are some of the findings:

- .....Falls are among the most frequent incidents reported in hospitals. Sometimes these are unpreventable, but the task force did find that matters such as lack of identification of those at risk, lack of control of external factors such as poor lighting, slippery floors and inappropriate footwear often contribute to falls. The task force recommended that the National Health and Medical Research Council (NHMRC) commission the Royal College of Nursing to develop national best practice principles for the prevention of falls in hospitals and nursing homes.
- .....Another problem was the treatment of children with respiratory disease in emergency centres at night. Early discharge was a frequent cause of later complications. The treating doctor was often a very junior medical officer. There was inadequate planning of ongoing medical treatment, or continuity of care. The Task Force recommended that the NHMRC commission the Australian College of Paediatrics to develop best practice guidelines for the management of acute respiratory problems of children in hospital emergency departments. It also recommended that protocols be developed for the management of these children where appropriate.
- .....Deep vein thrombosis and pulmonary embolism occur in 30 of every 100 patients who have major surgical operations. There is a moderate risk following an operation of 45 minutes duration in those patients who have cardiovascular conditions. There is a greater risk for longer operations, especially those involving the pelvis, legs or brain. There is a need for quality assurance activities to be reviewed and improved in this area.
- .....The role doctors, nurses and other health carers have in assuring quality care is not only developing good care practices, but also in thorough incident monitoring. It involves not only identifying and improving areas of clinical practice but also establishing ways of preventing adverse incidents which might lead to legal action (see *Professional Indemnity Review* (1995), p 20).

[6.6] This Review was a wide-ranging one, but it too endorsed both a comprehensive incident monitoring scheme which could preferably be national in its scope under the National Health Outcomes Program, and other quality initiatives with the goal of improving patient safety across all disciplines. The Review also endorsed pro-active risk management in terms of identifying and anticipating those situations which might lead to [6.9] adverse incidents. One area of potential error identified by the Review was long hours of work which lead to fatigue. The established practice of requiring doctors to work long hours, and increasing pressure on nursing and other staff to double up on shifts or work extended hours, increases the likelihood of negligence occurring in health care facilities. Maximum safe working hours should be set and minimum rest periods allowed for all health professionals and institutions. Requiring health carers to work long hours as a tradition rather than a necessity could constitute negligence in the author's view. The Australian Medical Association, by pointing out that fatigue from working long hours is similar to working with an "over the limit" blood alcohol level, has shown that this practice is potentially unlawful.

Incidence of Medical Litigation

[6.7] Although claims of medical negligence have increased by 50 per cent between 1992 and 1996, only a small percentage of patients who suffer from an adverse incident actually sue in negligence (Nisselle (1999), p 130).

Communication and Adverse Incidents

[6.8] Not only is good communication essential for adequate consent to treatment, it has important roles to play in risk management, according to commentators, including Nisselle (1999) and the *Professional Indemnity Review* (1995). According to a survey nearly one-third of those taking legal action in 1994 were doing so to obtain more and better information. This, according to Nisselle, indicates "the perception of a 'conspiracy of silence' within the medical profession". He points out (at p 133) that the giving of full and frank information has the valuable effect of preventing legal action in the long run, while it may involve some short-term costs:

> The scientific "Find it—Fix it" model of medicine ignores the other half of medicine, namely, the humanist skills by which rapport is established and maintained and the patient motivated to accept the doctor's advice. More effective communication is not just a risk management tool.

He quotes Meryn (1988) who states that studies have found significant positive association between doctors' communication skills and patient satisfaction.

[6.9] Legal advice is generally to admit nothing when an adverse incident has occurred, with a view to defending any legal claim that may arise from it. However commentators such as those above argue that it is important also that clients are advised promptly and fully when something has gone wrong. Attempts to "cover up" whether real or perceived, are both fruitless and likely to inflame an already difficult situation and result in strengthening the resolve of a client for compensation. In some circumstances it may be wiser to admit fault and

[6.9] pay reasonable compensation than to create a situation where litigation is protracted, costly and hostile.

[6.10] As shall be seen, like the principles underlying the law on consent to health care, those underlying the law of negligence permeate every possible activity a carer may engage in, either on or off-duty.

What is Negligence?

[6.11] There are three main elements that constitute what is called a "negligence action" in law. A person, A, to succeed in proving negligence on the part of another, B, must show that B:

- ..... owed a duty of care to A;
- ..... has breached that duty of care, through some act or omission by B;
- ..... has, by this act or omission caused A physical or financial harm.

[6.12] All three elements must be proved to the satisfaction of the court before negligence is made out, and it is up to the injured person (the plaintiff) to prove these elements, not the other party to disprove them. This means that:

A	the plaintiff, must prove all the elements of the action (in law this is called having the "burden of proof"); and
B	the defendant, need only throw enough doubt on A's argument to convince the decision-maker (either a judge or, more rarely, a jury) that B was not guilty of any one of the elements above (see *Barnett v Chelsea Hospital* below [6.159]).

Duty of Care

[6.13] Because of the dependence upon the health carer for physical and mental care and wellbeing of the patient, the law has established that he or she owes what it calls a "duty of care" to the patient. This is based on the principle that a person must take reasonable care to avoid acts or omissions which would be likely to harm any person they ought reasonably foresee as being so harmed (their legal "neighbour"). If they fail to do this, they may be subject to the civil action of negligence. Where the health carer's act has been so grossly negligent as to have been deliberately reckless of life and limb it may be prosecuted by the criminal courts as criminal negligence or manslaughter. This chapter deals with the civil action for negligence. Criminal negligence is dealt with in Chapter 14.

[6.14] To understand duty of care, let us consider a little history.

■■■ CASE
Donoghue v Stevenson (The "snail in the ginger beer bottle" case) [1932] AC 562 (House of Lords England)

A woman's companion bought her a bottle of ginger beer and poured it out for her. The ginger beer contained what appeared to be the decomposing remains of a snail, which caused the woman both physical and mental harm, severe enough for her to sue the manufacturer of the drink.

[6.15] This was a landmark case in establishing the modern definition of duty of care. The woman issued a writ alleging negligence against the manufacturers, but they responded with a demurrer (a claim that the facts did not give rise to any action in law). This was because, at the time, one only had a legal duty of care in certain specific relationships, such as master and servant, parent and child, carrier of goods or people. A manufacturer had no personal obligation to someone who bought its goods unless there was one of these special relationships, or a contract between the manufacturer and the purchaser: here no such relationship existed, and there was no such contract—any contract had been between the manufacturer and the retailer in the first instance, and the retailer and the companion who bought the drink in the second. So many people had been harmed by faulty goods that they had purchased and had no redress at law that it was widely believed within the legal profession that it was time to change the law. The *Donoghue* case was in fact very important in this respect.

[6.16] The trial judge ruled that there was no case to answer, so the woman (described as a "pauper", but no doubt generously supported by lawyers who saw the need for change) appealed to a higher court, and the case was taken, after further appeal, to the House of Lords, who, in their ruling made a strong legal statement which changed the course of the law, and is influential even today. This ruling set out a new principle of negligence. The Law Lords established that the manufacturer of ginger beer had a duty of care to all foreseeable users of its goods, whether they personally bought the goods from the manufacturer or not. But the case had much more far-reaching consequences than that. One of the judges, Lord Atkin, in his judgment at 580, stated what has become known as the "neighbour test":

> The rule that you are to love your neighbour becomes in law, you must not injure your neighbour; and the lawyer's question, Who is my neighbour? receives a restricted reply. You must take reasonable care to avoid acts or omissions which you can reasonably foresee would be likely to injure your neighbour. Who, then, in law is my neighbour? The answer seems to be—persons who are so closely and directly affected by my act that I ought reasonably to have them in contemplation as being so affected when I am directing my mind to the acts or omissions which are called in question.

[6.17] [6.17] This test was not the ratio of the case, so the case stood for a much narrower principle. However, judges adopted it formally in the English courts in the ratio of a later decision.

CASE
Dorset Yacht Co v Home Office [1970] AC 1004 (House of Lords England)

> Some young Borstal inmates who escaped from a camp damaged vessels from a nearby Yacht Club in their attempt to get away. The yacht club sued the Home Office, which was responsible for the Borstal. The Home Office argued that, among other things, one cannot be held responsible for the acts of another who is of full age and capacity, and who is not one's servant or acting on one's behalf.

[6.18] The court (again the House of Lords) rejected this. It held that it was not the action of the boys which was the negligence in question, but the failure of the officers to supervise them adequately. The issue was not the foreseeability of the harm resulting from a third person's acts, but the foreseeability of the consequences of one's own acts or omissions. The Home Office was found negligent. Lord Reid (at 1026-1027), expressed the court's view of the "neighbour test" thus:

> [Lately] . . . there has been a steady trend towards regarding the law of negligence as depending on principle so that, when a new point emerges, one should ask not whether it is covered by authority but whether recognised principles apply to it. *Donoghue v Stevenson* may be regarded as a milestone, and the well-known passage in Lord Atkin's speech should I think be regarded as a statement of principle. It is not to be treated as if it were a statutory definition. It will require qualification in new circumstances. But I think that the time has come when we can and should say that it ought to apply unless there is some justification or valid explanation for its exclusion.

This has been endorsed by the Australian High Court.

[6.19] A "qualification" has been made by the courts, that there must be a relationship of "proximity" between the plaintiff and defendant. This was elaborated in the case of *Jaensch v Coffey* (see below [6.52]). There it was held that the relationship of proximity is to be determined by considering the existence of:

- *physical proximity* (that is, closeness in space and time between the plaintiff and the defendant);
- *circumstantial proximity* (for example the relationship between the plaintiff and the defendant); and
- *causal proximity* (for example, the closeness or directness of the relationship between the particular act or omission and the injury sustained).

[6.20] In conclusion, says Katter ((1999), p 5):

> in testing for a duty of care in Australia the integral constituents to be satisfied in any type of case are, reasonable foreseeability and proximity of relationship, with the qualification that in physical damage cases

Chapter 6—Negligence | 191

reasonable foreseeability may itself indicate the existence of a sufficiently [6.24] proximate relationship.

That is, the very fact that you can foresee probable harm may indicate that you have a duty of care to prevent it.

[6.21] The ramification of both of these developments in law is important for health care workers. Not only may they have a duty of care to another who is directly in their care, leading to responsibility for their actions towards that person, but they may also be deemed to have a duty of care to people of whose specific existence they may not even be aware, but whose existence they ought to foresee as probable. Thus they may be responsible for the harm caused to third persons by someone in their care (see [6.177]ff).

Reasonable Foreseeability

[6.22] It is important to note that the harm foreseen must be probable, not merely possible. No doubt one can imagine no end of cataclysmic possibilities bedevilling the simplest procedures. There is a recorded case of a person who regularly took a short-cut through a graveyard being killed by a tombstone which, after many, many, years, happened to fall on him just as he was passing beneath it. But, as mere mortals, we are expected by law only to anticipate the probable—something which has a significant probability factor. One should not try to put a figure on this, however, as the courts are not, at this stage, in favour of approaching such mathematical specificity as the *Wagon Mound* case (discussed below) indicates. Some courts have looked with favour on a formula of "more probable than not" or, "more than 50 per cent probability", or that the occurrence of the event is "not far-fetched or fanciful" (the latter being the currently accepted test).

▌▌ CASE
Overseas Tankship (UK) Ltd v The Miller Steamship Co Pty Ltd ("The Wagon Mound") (No 2) [1967] 1 AC 617 (Privy Council England)

A ship spilled bunkering oil into Sydney Harbour. Workmen at a nearby dock were carrying out welding, which caused sparks to fall into the water. The ship's engineer believed (correctly) that bunkering oil is very hard to ignite when spread on water. However, a nearby dock and ships berthed there were destroyed by fire when cotton waste in the water, saturated with oil, caught fire from molten metal from the dockside welding activities. The owners of the damaged ships sued the owner of the engineer's ship.

[6.23] One of the questions which the Privy Council (which at that time heard appeals from Australian courts, [2.29]), had to consider was the reasonability of the ship's engineer failing to act on the fact that the oil could burn, albeit in rare circumstances. A little more history may help the reader to follow its reasoning.

[6.24] Until the 1950s the law recognised two types of situation:

[6.24]
- ..... A situation which, if contemplated, would be considered either impossible, or, so fantastic or far-fetched that no reasonable person would have paid attention to it; or
- ..... A situation where there was a real and substantial risk of the harm occurring, and which a reasonable person would take necessary steps to prevent.

[6.25] A third type of situation, however, had been first recognised in a case involving a cricket ball which, as the result of a terrific hit, soared over the 17-foot high fence of a cricket pitch in a little town, and hit a passerby, injuring her (*Bolton v Stone* [1951] AC 850). Such a hit had occurred, it was revealed, about six times in 28 years, no one having been hit before. It was also established that the cost of building a suitable fence to prevent its occurrence would be difficult for the cricket club to meet. This sort of situation was identified as one where the harm is plainly foreseeable and possible, but the probability is very remote. The House of Lords held in the cricket ball case that the risk was so small, that a reasonable person would be justified in disregarding it. The court held, however, that in such a situation a reasonable person would not always disregard the risk. He or she would only disregard it if it were reasonably justifiable to do so, for example, the benefits outweigh the risk, or the cost of averting the risk is disproportionately high.

[6.26] The judges believed that both those factors were present in the cricket case, but those sitting on the *Wagon Mound* case decided there was no justification for ignoring the risk of fire, despite its low level of probability. The horrendous damage that can (and did) result from fire, and the easy means of preventing the spread of oil which were available, made the failure to prevent the risk, even though considered unlikely, negligence at law. One must balance the various factors, the court said: on the one hand how serious and immediate the foreseeable harm might be, and on the other hand the likely benefits of the planned activity.

> It is not enough that the event should be such as can reasonably be foreseen; the further result that injury is likely to follow must also be such as a reasonable man would contemplate, before he can be convicted of actionable negligence. Nor is the remote possibility of injury occurring enough; there must be sufficient probability to lead a reasonable man to anticipate it.

CASE
Goode v Nash (1979) 21 SASR 419

> A doctor was participating in a program for screening people for glaucoma. This involved placing a tonometer on the eye. To prevent cross infection, the tonometer was sterilised over an open flame. The plaintiff suffered serious and permanent injury to his eye when the tonometer was placed on the eye before it had properly cooled down.

[6.27] The court held that the doctor was liable even though this had never happened to him before. The activity was so potentially dangerous and the consequences of negligence so grave, he ought to have taken precautions to prevent its happening.

[6.28] All the approaches mentioned above have been accepted at one time or another, and all one can say as a generalisation is that the reasonable health carer should use cautious common sense when considering whether a risk is worth avoiding under the particular circumstances that exist at the time. It must be remembered that health carers are recognised by law as being involved in busy schedules, emotionally and physically tiring work, and should, both because of that and despite it, act in the most effective, efficient and harmless way that they reasonably can under the circumstances.

[6.29] With this in mind, and as far as they can reasonably foresee, health carers should guard against probable harm that could occur as a result of their actions. They do not have to take precautions against every remotely possible danger.

Precise Nature or Amount of Harm Need Not be Foreseen

■ ■ ■ CASE

Vacwell Engineering Co v BDH Chemicals [1971] 1 QB 111 (note) (CA England)

Chemical manufacturers were aware that one of their products had explosive qualities, but were unaware that it was highly explosive on contact with water. A scientist, using the chemical, but improperly warned of its volatility, was killed when it exploded on contact with water. His employers sued the manufacturers in negligence for not properly warning them.

[6.30] The court held that the manufacturers had been negligent in not properly warning users of the chemical's nature, for although they knew it provided a risk of violent reaction and possibly explosion they had not been adequately warned of this. The fact that they did not know the likely magnitude of the explosion and the extent of the danger was no excuse. See also *Richards v State of Victoria* [1969] VR 136 where a blow to the temple in a classroom fight led to a ruptured cerebral artery, resulting in spastic paralysis. The court held that it was foreseeable that such a blow might cause injury to the brain, and the defendant could not complain if the injury was greater than expected.

Duty of Care is a Question of Law

[6.31] As indicated, the difference between the tort of negligence and other nominate torts, such as assault, nuisance or defamation, is that the types of action for which a negligence action can be brought are limitless and undefined: they cover the full spectrum of human behaviour. By allowing compensation for anyone who suffers harm from another's

[6.31] actions, we would certainly stifle initiative and suppress our avowed social policy of individualistic private enterprise. People would be either too frightened to do anything, or required to pay compensation for any and every harm they caused. Life would not be worthwhile! So the primary concern with negligence actions has actually been to limit claims; containing them within reasonable levels.

[6.32] So, despite the fact that both duty of care and breach of that duty rely on the establishment of what is "reasonable", it is the judge, who decides whether an activity in question is within the bounds of the defendant's duty of care or not, the power to remove the matter altogether from the jury's consideration (if there is one), and abort the whole issue. Thus, even where the defendant's behaviour has been below a reasonable standard, and the activity has caused great harm to the plaintiff, the matter can be a non-issue if the judge finds that a duty of care did not exist. Of course, if there is no jury, as is the case in most jurisdictions for negligence actions, the judge decides both whether there was a duty of care between the parties, and whether the defendant breached that duty of care, thus combining both issues. Establishing whether or not a duty of care exists is all-important, it is the threshold test for establishing negligence. If no duty of care between the parties to an action can be established, there is no case to answer (as seen in *Donoghue v Stevenson* at [6.14]).

"Reasonable Foreseeability" as Policy

[6.33] If the test of reasonable foresight were simply applied in determining whether a duty of care existed in a given situation, it would be no more than the test applied in determining whether the defendant breached her or his duty of care by acting unreasonably in the situation being considered. In fact it has been established that there is a need for the judge also to consider public policy (see [3.63]ff), an approach which was acknowledged by Lord Diplock as the basis for deciding when to exclude the "neighbour test" (see [6.16]), and has been elaborated in later cases. Katter ((1999), pp 14 ff) notes that the very word "reasonable" is value-laden, and that determining what is "reasonably foreseeable" involves injecting a subjective value judgment into objective factual issues of duty and standard of care. Policy considerations are often used to determine proximity, writes Katter ((1999), p 93), and thus may be disguised as legal principle. At p 58 he quotes Fleming ((1953), p 486) who describes the use of proximity as:

> an ingenious exploitation of the inherent indeterminacy of the foreseeability concept in the interest of furthering a specific policy demanded by contemporary social opinion.

[6.34] Katter is critical of the use of policy, however the concept of negligence does involve socially accepted standards and values, and it could be argued that this is the most fair and just way to deal with compensation for "medical misadventure", as it can include those considered worthy of compensation from those considered to have acted unreasonably. Other approaches have been used—for example [6.37] conciliation and mediation through the health care complaints agencies which have been established in some jurisdictions in Australia (see [2.53]ff), and "no-fault" compensation schemes, where State compensation is paid to those who suffer injury, regardless of cause or culpability. These approaches are useful in certain circumstances, (health care complaints systems are dealt with in some detail in Chapter 18, however litigation under the current law of negligence is very much a part of the law for health carers.

[6.35] It would seem, then, that policy considerations involving many factors, such as history, morals, justice, convenience and social practice have influenced judicial decisions with regard to the presence of duty of care (see, for example, Katter (1999), Ch 2). Examples of policy can be found in the cases below, particularly those establishing a duty of care (see especially *Chapman v Hearse* at [6.49]). One might be confused when reading the judgment of a case, for, while it may seem that the reasonable person could have foreseen harm occurring as a result of his or her actions, he or she may be found to have had a duty of care (or vice-versa). It is thus useful to consider whether the judge has resorted to public policy to come to what is considered a just decision in the case. Katter suggests that a policy-based approach is identified where the judge does not direct his or her mind to whether the sequence of events leading to the ultimate outcome was something the reasonable person would have had in contemplation, and ought to have foreseen. Readers may question whether the inability to escape from the concept of "reasonable" makes pure objectivity impossible.

[6.36] There is no absolutely sure way, then, that we can know what activities are covered by duty of care and what activities are not. As Katter points out, use of value charged precepts such as reasonable foreseeability means that there is more than one possible result for each individual case since they are not verifiable by objective empirical observation (p 14). However there is adequate case law to give some strong indications as to when one assumes a duty of care.

When Does one Assume a Duty of Care?

[6.37] Given the above, it can be said that a duty of care will probably arise either when the reasonable person becomes aware (or ought to be aware) of potential harm to another from her or his activities or omissions, or when one accepts the care of another, whichever applies to the situation at hand. However, there is no question that a duty of care arises between a health carer and a person who has been accepted as his or her client. There may be an issue as to whether that actually happens in some circumstances.

[6.37] ▌▌▌ CASE
Albrighton v Royal Prince Alfred Hospital [1980] 2 NSWLR 542 (CA NSW)

The patient suffered from kypho-scoliosis and spina bifida from birth, and had a large hairy naevus on her lower back. She was admitted to hospital at age 15 for corrective surgery on her spine, and for possible halo-pelvic traction for straightening and lengthening it. Because of the hairy naevus, there was a recognised danger of "tethering" of the spinal cord (adherence to surrounding tissue) and consequent damage to the cord resulting in paraplegia from the traction. In fact traction was applied and paraplegia resulted. She sued in negligence, but the question was, who was liable? Involved in the case was a neurosurgeon, who had been asked to see the patient to advise on traction, but who had not done so by the time the damage occurred.

[6.38] There was not much evidence of what had happened to cause this unfortunate result, but the medical records showed that the orthopaedic surgeon had written a consultation request to the neurosurgeon, who had received it and written in the patient's medical notes: "As she has had (just) [sic] traction I will see her next week." (In fact traction did not occur until two days later). The court held that the neurosurgeon both knew of the potential danger, and had accepted the patient into his care, although he had not seen her, and thus a duty of care existed. One does not have to be in direct contact with someone to owe them a duty of care, and as *Donoghue v Stevenson* indicates (see [6.14]), one need not even be aware of a specific individual at all. This means that where a reasonable health carer would be aware of potential harm from her or his actions to foreseeable but unknown people in general, there is a duty of care (for example, a duty of care to visitors to a hospital; see [12.62]ff).

Duty of Care to Third Persons

[6.39] The above principle means that a duty of care is owed not only to patients and clients but to any others whose personal wellbeing and property may be harmed by failure to take reasonable care of a client.

[6.40] Thus, for example, potentially dangerous individuals must be properly supervised and cared for to prevent them from harming others, and not carelessly allowed to leave an institution if they show a tendency to violence (*Holgate v Lancashire Mental Hospital Board* [1937] 4 All ER 19). In this case the hospital made no proper inquiry as to the circumstances obtained after discharge of the patient.

[6.41] Care should also be taken with an individual who shows a tendency to harm herself or himself.

CASE
Pallister v Waikato Hospital Board [1975] 2 NZLR 725 (CA New Zealand)

A patient being treated for suicidal tendencies was confined in a room. The door was left open for ventilation and in the hope the patient would learn to cope with freedom of movement. He left the room and jumped from a window, killing himself. His widow sued the hospital in negligence.

[6.42] The court held that the hospital had breached its duty of care. Staff were on notice that the patient would be likely to harm himself, and so the duty to act accordingly was clear. This raises the question of what should happen when a person threatens, or talks about, suicide. Where the person is a client, then particular consideration should be given to appropriate action. This advice may also be recommended in other situations.

Is There a Duty to Rescue a Stranger from Harm?

[6.43] It has been stated that at common law there is no duty to assist a person who is in danger, where no relationship of care has been established. Thus there is no legal obligation to stop at the scene of an accident to provide care, or go to the aid of a stranger in trouble. The *Medical Practitioners Act* 1958 (NSW) provides that a doctor who does not respond to an urgent call for assistance may be guilty of professional misconduct. However that is a different matter to being sued in a court of law and being held negligent for not assisting. An exception to the common law principle was made in the following case.

CASE
Lowns v Woods [1996] Aust Torts Reports ¶81-376 (CA NSW)

A 10-year-old boy, Patrick, who had a history of epilepsy was on holiday on the northern New South Wales coast. One day his mother found him suffering a serious and prolonged epileptic fit. She immediately sent her son to a nearby ambulance station, and her daughter to a nearby doctor's surgery, knowing that Patrick required intravenous valium. The daughter gave evidence that she arrived at the doctor's surgery and told Dr Lowns that her brother was having the fit. He told her to bring him to the surgery, and she replied that this was impossible. He then said to get an ambulance, which she said had been done, and insisted that the doctor was needed. He refused to go. The ambulance officers had to take Patrick to a local medical centre before he could receive the IV valium, however it was not successful in stopping the fit, and he had to be taken to Gosford Hospital for treatment. As a result Patrick was seriously brain-damaged. Patrick, through his parents, sued Dr Lowns in negligence for failing to attend to, and treat him. The trial judge found, for the first time in an Australian court, that Dr Lowns' refusal to treat Patrick when asked to do so was negligent. Dr Lowns appealed against this finding to the Court of Appeal.

[6.44] The Court of Appeal upheld the trial judge's ruling. The three judges acknowledged that the decision was at odds with the general common law position that there is no duty to rescue or assist someone who is in danger, even where it can be foreseen that such a failure might cause harm. However two of the judges held that in this case a duty of care did arise, as proximity existed between Dr Lowns and Patrick. One of the judges, Cole JA, expressed the reasoning by stating that proximity existed in all four possible ways:

- ..... there was *proximity of relationship* because Dr Lowns foresaw that his refusal could cause harm to Patrick;
- ..... there was *physical proximity* because he was not far away;
- ..... there was *circumstantial proximity* as there were no barriers to his attending and assisting Patrick; and
- ..... there was *causal proximity* because the administration of IV valium could have prevented the brain damage.

[6.45] This was the basis for establishing a duty of care. Kirby P was also swayed by the special duty of the "noble" medical profession, which is subject to higher standards than is the ordinary citizen. He also determined that s 27(2) of the *Medical Practitioner's Act* 1958 (NSW) is relevant. This section makes failure to assist a person in an emergency unprofessional conduct. While it does not create a duty of care for the purposes of tort law, it sets a standard of conduct expected as appropriate and proper by medical practitioners.

[6.46] The Court thus applied the proximity test of *Jaensch v Coffey* (see [6.51]), but Cole JA based the test of relational proximity on the foreseeability of harm, tying together the tests for both the presence of a duty of care and the standard of care to be applied. By doing this they were able to establish a duty of care to go to the aid of a "stranger" (one to whom a relationship of care has not been otherwise established), at least where the test of proximity has been met. Whilst one might agree that the approach taken was a just and fair one, it is, in the author's view, a clear example of policy influencing the judges' rulings (raising the question of whether such an approach is to be commended). Whilst it is a New South Wales Court of Appeal case, and thus of limited binding precedent, it could open the way for a general requirement for doctors, and also other health carers, to aid such people in need. In his minority judgment, Mahoney J, questioned where the limits to the duty would be set, and stated that he believed the obligation to assist strangers in an emergency should not be imposed through tort law.

[6.47] It should be noted that health carers are *encouraged* by the law to assist those in urgent need. No health carer has been held liable in Australia for acting as a "good Samaritan", and cases overseas have approached such people with sympathy, understanding the difficulties under which they operate, and holding them not liable for actions done in good faith and without gross (wanton) negligence. Queensland has enacted protection for medical practitioners and nurses who "render medical care, aid or assistance to an injured person in circumstances of emergency", both at the scene and during transport to a place for medical [6.50] treatment, where that act or omission is done in good faith without gross negligence and performed without fee or reward (*Law Reform Act* 1995 (Qld), s 16).

[6.48] Whilst health care providers may not have a duty of care to go to the aid of those injured in an accident, if they do, by their actions they *establish* a duty of care towards those they assist. The courts have shown a tendency to be very understanding when dealing with rescuers, as there is a stated recognition that rescuers are to be encouraged. Thus, although the duty of care exists, courts will give every consideration to factors such as shock to all concerned at the accident, the speed with which decisions have to be made, and the difficult circumstances in which aid has to be rendered. They have adopted the requirement that one would have to show *gross* negligence before being liable at law. Legislation along the lines of Queensland, although codifying what is already the law, would encourage health professionals to assist those in need in emergencies.

Duty of Care Owed to Rescuers

[6.49] The courts have considered the situation where person A negligently causes harm to another, person B, and person C is harmed in trying to rescue person B, A may be liable for the harm caused to the rescuer.

CASE
Chapman v Hearse (1961) 106 CLR 112 (High Court of Australia)

Chapman, driving in bad weather conditions, negligently negotiated a right-hand turn at an intersection. This resulted in a pile-up of cars on the road, with Chapman being thrown onto the road, unconscious. A passerby, Dr Cherry, went to his aid, and was kneeling on the road administering assistance to Chapman. They were on the right side of the road. An oncoming car, also driven negligently, hit and killed Dr Cherry. His widow sued the driver of that car, a Mr Hearse, and Mr Hearse claimed contribution to the damages from Chapman, arguing that his negligence in the first place also contributed to Dr Cherry's death, as he would not have been hit if it weren't for Chapman's need of care, to which Dr Cherry was responding. Chapman argued that, negligent as he was, he did not have a duty of care to his rescuer, Dr Cherry, as he could not have foreseen that he would come to his aid.

[6.50] The High Court of Australia disagreed with this argument. The judges held that Chapman should have foreseen that if he drove negligently he might not only harm another, or himself, but be the author of harm to a third person who came to his aid. The Court approved of a United States case, *Wagner v International Railway Co*, 232 NY Rep 176 (1921) at 180, where Cardozo J said of this sort of situation:

> The risk of rescue, if only it be not wanton, is born of the occasion. The emergency begets the man. The wrongdoer may not have foreseen the coming of a deliverer. He is accountable as if he had.

Duty of Care to the Emotionally Involved

[6.51] There is also a duty of care to those who might be psychologically harmed by the horror of the damage one may have caused.

▌▌▌ CASE
Jaensch v Coffey (1984) 155 CLR 549 (High Court of Australia)

A policeman was seriously injured by the negligent driving of the appellant, Mr Jaensch. The policeman's wife was witness to the events at the hospital to which she was called. These involved several critical returns to theatre to repair internal injuries, and seeing her husband in considerable pain. She was told he was pretty bad and was urgently recalled later to intensive care as his condition had deteriorated. At this time she was told he had damaged kidneys and liver. She saw him with "all these tubes coming out of him". She feared her husband would die, and continued to do so for three to four weeks. As a result she suffered severe anxiety and depression, which led to gynaecological problems and hysterectomy.

[6.52] In the lower court the judge held that the defendant could foresee that his causing of harm to another could result in a wife having to go to the hospital, having to wait anxiously for her husband's recovery, and suffering mental harm as a result. The appeal by Mrs Jaensch was disallowed in the Court of Appeal of South Australia, so she appealed to the High Court of Australia. There the original decision was upheld. The implications of such a finding are clear: where one can reasonably foresee harm to another, one will be held by the courts to also foresee psychological harm that close relatives may suffer as a result of such harm. It has also been held that those who witness a horrific accident, and rescue workers at the site of an accident, are also in the class of people to whom a duty of care is owed. A more recent case held that where a daughter died three years after a car accident, the mother could not claim for her resultant psychiatric illness because there was no sudden sensory perception which caused the illness. Rather the court believed that it was more likely the stress which resulted from caring for the child, and the loss when she died (*Spence v Percy* [1991] Aust Torts Reports ¶81-116). This result can be contrasted with those cases where the courts have recognised psychiatric illness following the sudden death of a child as the result of negligence (for example, *Petrie v Dowling* [1989] Aust Torts Reports ¶80-263; *McCabe v Auburn District Hospital* (unreported, 31 May 1989, SC NSW); *Streelec v Nelson & Ors* (13 December 1996, SC NSW, No 012401/90); *Harrington & Anor v Macquarie Pathology Services & Ors* [1998] Aust Torts Reports ¶81-489; *Lamphud Marchlewski, Roman Marchlewski and Dolores Marchlewski v Hunter Area Health Service* (14 August 1998, SC NSW, No 20937/95).

[6.53] Legislation in some jurisdictions has sought to restrict recovery of damages for nervous shock to parents or spouses of the harmed person, with other members of the family being able to recover damages only if they were within sight or hearing of the accident (for example, *Law Reform (Miscellaneous Provisions) Act* 1955 (ACT); *Law Reform (Miscellaneous*

Provisions) Act 1944 (NSW); *Law Reform (Miscellaneous Provisions) Act* 1956 (NT)).

Duty of Care to the Unborn

[6.54] It has been held by the courts that a duty of care is owed to a foetus, although it is not a person at law, and therefore cannot bring an action in law until it is born. Thus, although the harm has been caused before the foetus is a person at law, the right to sue for harm caused before birth becomes exercisable once the foetus does become a person. When one cares for a pregnant woman, one owes a duty of care to her and to the foetus.

▎▎▎ CASE
Watt v Rama [1972] VR 353 (SC Vic)

A pregnant woman was involved in a car accident in which the other driver was at fault. The child, when born, had obviously suffered some harm from the accident. The child sued the driver in negligence through a "next best friend" (that is, a representative).

[6.55] The issue was whether the negligent driver owed a duty of care to the foetus. The court held that as there are a significant number of pregnant women in the community, and pregnancy can be reasonably foreseen in others in the general community, not only do drivers have a duty of care to other drivers and passengers, but also to a potential child who may be harmed. This approach was approved in a later English case.

▎▎▎ CASE
B v Islington Health Authority [1991] 1 All ER 825 (Queen's Bench Division England)

The plaintiff's mother had undergone a dilatation and curettage. At the time, unknown to her, she was pregnant. She later gave birth to the plaintiff, a baby girl, who suffered numerous physical abnormalities, which impaired her relationship with men and her earning capacity.

She sued the health authority in negligence alleging that her injuries had been caused by the surgery on her mother, and that the staff should have ascertained whether her mother had been pregnant at the time of the operation. The hospital argued that they had no duty of care to the plaintiff, as she was at the time the injuries were caused an embryo, which under English law lacks legal personality.

[6.56] The issue was that at the time of the operation the plaintiff, by reason of being in utero according to English law did not have an independent legal personality and thus no duty of care could be owed to her, nor could it be said that she suffered injuries. By some tortuous reasoning the court held that the three elements of negligence crystallise

[6.56]　　at the time of birth, and thus the three requirements of negligence were fulfilled. This could be called a legal fiction, as the event causing the harm actually occurred before the duty of care would have arisen. The decision thus appears to be based on public policy, rather than established legal principle, for the purpose of providing a means by which a child can be compensated for harm caused by another's fault.

▌▌ CASE
Lynch v Lynch and the GIO [1991] Aust Torts Reports ¶81-117

A child born with cerebral palsy suffered prenatal injury as the result of an accident in a car driven by her mother. The child sued the mother and mother's insurer. The defendant argued that the child was not a person when the accident happened, and indeed there was unity of personality with the mother, and so the child could not sue her, as the mother could not have a duty of care to herself.

[6.57]　The court followed *Watt v Rama* holding that once the child was born alive the right to sue crystallised. It also rejected the unity of personality argument, and stated that parents have a duty of care to their "unborn children", and should be liable for any injuries they negligently cause to them.

[6.58]　In the case of *R v F* (CA NSW, No 60773/95 1996) it was also held that where a foetus was born, lived independently and then died as a result of injuries sustained before birth by culpable driving (an offence under section 52A of the *Crimes Act* 1900 (NSW)), the foetus was a person for the purposes of the *Crimes Act*.

▌▌ CASE
McKay v Essex Area Health Authority [1982] 2 All ER 771 (CA England)

A pregnant woman had contracted rubella in the early months of pregnancy. However, this was not diagnosed, and the child was born severely disabled. The mother and the child sued the doctor, who failed to diagnose the illness, in negligence. The issue was whether the doctor owed a duty of care to the child to have advised abortion.

[6.59]　The court considered the issue thus: first, the doctor had not caused the harm; the disease had. The duty of care involved preventing the effects of the disease as much as was reasonable, which involved advising the mother on the possibility of abortion. However, the duty of care did not extend to entitlement of the child to prevention from life itself (such an action has been called a "wrongful life" action) as this is a principle repugnant to public policy. Therefore, compensation could be claimed by the mother for the cost and burden of providing care for the child. As the child's disability existed independently and prior to the doctor's action, she could not claim damages for the disability. The only other claim could be compensation for wrongful life, and the law does not recognise that non-life is of more value than life.

[6.60] A duty of care may be owed to someone, even before they are conceived, where a health care worker would be reasonably able to foresee harm occurring to a foetus through negligent care of the potential parent. The most common situations that would come under this category of events are the negligent cross-matching of blood leading to disorders of a child later conceived, the negligent giving of X-rays, and negligent genetic counselling.

▮▮▮ CASE
Kosky v Trustees of The Sisters of Charity [1982] VR 961 (SC Vic)

The plaintiff, who was Rh-negative, had been negligently given Rh-positive blood after a car accident by the defendant hospital. There were no immediate effects, but eight years later she gave birth to a child suffering from complications due to Rh iso-immunisation and prematurely induced birth which it required.

[6.61] The court said there was a duty of care to the future child, even though it was not conceived for many years after the initial action, which later caused the harm, had occurred.

Occupier's Duty of Care to those on Property

[6.62] A duty of care is owed to those who come on to property for which one is responsible. This is discussed in Chapter 12.

Standard of Care

[6.63] The tort of negligence extends over the whole range of human activity and is not confined to particular types of conduct or activity, as are most other torts. It is concerned with how activities are carried out, rather than with the activities themselves. It is difficult to separate the notions of duty of care and breach of that duty, as both depend on reasonable foreseeability. In considering whether one has breached a duty of care, the courts look at the standard of care which would reasonably be expected from a person acting in the defendant's circumstances, in the capacity in which the defendant was acting (as for example, a physiotherapist, doctor, nurse). The discussion of duty of care and its breach thus necessarily revolves around the notion of reasonable care, notwithstanding that commentators may differ in attributing matters to the category of "duty", "breach" or "standard" of care.

[6.64] One could say that the tort of negligence is the method by which our law lays down a standard of social behaviour. Just as the criminal law upholds, for example, the notion of private property, and the crime and tort of assault and battery enforce the idea of the right to personal autonomy, the action of negligence endorses the principle that a person cannot behave in a way that reason should warn is likely to harm those people he or she should consider.

[6.65] **[6.65]** Tort law differs from contract law in that tort law covers all people, whether they have had prior association with each other or not, and it sets a broad standard that is common to all. Contract, on the other hand, requires that the parties involved have already set their own standard of behaviour by agreement.

[6.66] Lord Atkins' "neighbour principle" in *Donoghue v Stevenson* (see [6.14]) also sets out the standard of care owed by health carers: that is, one of reasonable care. Health carers do not have to be perfect, but have only to exercise the skill that a reasonable health carer professing the skills in question would be expected to exercise in the circumstances. This is what is called the "objective" test. The court does not look at, for example, the *actual* intelligence, experience or personality of the particular health carer on the particular day in question, but rather at a hypothetical "reasonable" carer in similar circumstances, and consider what he or she would do. To help them do this, other carers who are experienced in the field (called "expert witnesses") are called to give their opinion as to whether the actions in question were in fact reasonable under the circumstances.

[6.67] The best way to understand is to consider past cases and examples. In the case of *Bolam v Friern Hospital Management Committee* [1957] 1 WLR 582 McNair J, in his address to the jury (at 586-587), described the test of the reasonable health carer in the following terms:

> [Where one is considering the standard of care of a skilled person] the test is the standard of the ordinary skilled man [sic] exercising and professing to have that special skill. A man need not possess the highest expert skill; it is well established law that it is sufficient if he exercises the ordinary skill of an ordinary competent man exercising that particular art.

Standard of Care Depends on the Circumstances

[6.68] It is impossible to set out a comprehensive explanation of what is a reasonable standard of care that covers every possible health care situation in one statement. No two situations are exactly the same, and individual cases must be considered on their merits. Some examples will be given in this chapter, but as the duty to practice a reasonable standard of care covers all health care activities, be it sponging patients, giving medication, writing reports or anything else, further chapters of the book will, where relevant, cover the standard of care for the particular health care activity dealt with there.

▮▮▮ CHECKLIST [6.70]
SUGGESTED CONSIDERATIONS IN IDENTIFYING A REASONABLE STANDARD OF CARE

- ▮.....Is this the way I've been taught to proceed in these circumstances?
- ▮.....Is this situation covered by official Hospital Procedure or instructions?
- ▮.....Is this the way freely available textbooks or journals tell me to proceed?
- ▮.....Is advice and/or assistance reasonably available and should I seek it?
- ▮.....What do my colleagues and superiors say should be done in this sort of situation?

Factors determining "reasonable" care include:

- ▮.....the circumstances (for example, urgency, resources);
- ▮.....practice established by the profession;
- ▮.....the condition of the client (for example, see *Mahon v Osborne* at [6.90]); and
- ▮.....the magnitude of any probable harm (for example, see *Bolton v Stone* at [6.25]).

[6.69] A list of negligence cases dealing with health care situations is set out in Appendix 2, however some important examples of the courts' approach to the standard of care for health carers follow.

▮▮▮ CASE
Spivey v St Thomas' Hospital, 31 Tenn App 12 at 211; SW 2d 450 (1947) (CA Tennessee United States)

Jesse Spivey was admitted to St Thomas' Hospital suffering pneumonia. He was febrile. His bed was on the first floor near a window. During the night, while he was delirious and unaware of his actions, he got out of the window, fell to the ground and as a result of head injuries caused by the fall, died the next day. The court was presented with the following facts:

6 pm	On admission Spivey was delirious, and trying to get out of bed; the window was two or three feet from his bed, and there was conflicting evidence as to whether it was locked or not.
8.30-9.30 pm	Spivey's brother and friend had been sitting with him and they were told to leave several times between 8.30 and 9.30 pm, despite their request to stay and prevent him getting out of bed.
1 am	He was restless and tossing. Siderails put on bed, sodium luminal imi given.
2.30 am	He was more restless, temp 105.8F, irrational. Ankle and wrist restraints and canvas sheet to prevent his getting out of bed. This required two "strong" orderlies and took half an hour. Ten minute visual checks through glass door panel.
3.20 am	He was apparently sleeping.
3.45 am	He was out of bed, "sitting there looking out in the hall". Assistance called, but by the time it arrived he had fallen out the window.

[6.70] When his relatives sued the hospital for negligently causing his death, the court looked at whether the staff had been unreasonable in not

[6.70] taking more precautions against harm which they could foresee (at least in general terms). It concluded that the failure to secure the window and to keep a closer watch on the patient in view of his earlier violence was a breach of the nurses' duty of care to the patient. Their care fell below the standard of care which a reasonable nurse would give.

What is reasonable will depend on the circumstances: however, it has been held that the use by staff of hot water bottles on a patient who was anaesthetised, which resulted in burns, was not a dereliction of duty, because, under the circumstances (a very real danger of massive haemorrhage and no other means of heating available) the actions taken were reasonable (*McDermott v St Mary's Hospital*, 133 A 2d 608 (1957)).

One must weigh the harm which may result against the benefits one may confer, and the court will look at both what harm could have been reasonably foreseeable by the reasonable health carer, and what safeguards a reasonable carer would take to prevent harm. Where it is considered that a risk should be taken and the benefits warrant the risk, the question becomes what measures ought to be taken to minimise any potential harm.

[6.71] Although they consider evidence from experts as to what is considered reasonable care, courts do not blindly follow what is the current practice. In *Albrighton v Royal Prince Alfred Hospital* [1979] 2 NSWLR 165 Reynolds J said that this would be:

> plainly wrong, because it is not the law that, if all or most of the medical practitioners in Sydney habitually fail to take an available precaution . . . then none can be found guilty of negligence.

[6.72] Courts thus reserve to themselves the right to determine that although the actions of a defendant might have been consistent with current practice within the profession, current practice may be unreasonable. This would include such practice as never questioning the instructions of a senior professional, or doing things the way he or she prefers, when probable harm is clearly foreseeable. Courts will, however, accept that some degree of experimentation is desirable in medicine (see discussion of *Roe v Minister of Health* below at [6.79]). Also, where there is a difference of professional opinion:

> a judge's 'preference' for one body of distinguished professional opinion to another also professionally distinguished is not sufficient to establish negligence in a practitioner whose actions have received the seal of approval of those whose opinions, truthfully expressed, honestly held, were not preferred [*Maynard v West Midlands Regional Health Authority* [1984] 1 WLR 634].

[6.73] In the case of *Bolam v Friern Hospital Management Committee* [1957] 1 WLR 582 McNair J said at 586: "there may be one or more perfectly proper standards [of care] and if [a doctor] conforms with one of those proper standards, then he is not negligent". There thus may be several acceptable standards of care, based on the views of experienced practitioners. As long as a method of care is accepted as reasonable by health carers who are experienced and recognised as well qualified in the profession, although some (even a majority) might personally prefer another method, it could be acceptable at law.

[6.74] What is good health care is, then, often open to debate. One of the reasons for drawn-out and expensive court cases is the scope for argument as to whether a particular activity is reasonable or not. When considering the reasonableness of an action, the court will take into account, among other things, the following factors.

Circumstances Surrounding an Event

[6.75] Those attending an emergency which occurs on a road or in a rehabilitation centre or small regional health care centre, for example, where experience, equipment and preparation are not geared for this, would not be expected to react with the same efficiency as those, say, in an accident and emergency or intensive care ward. Where staff are trained and prepared for emergencies, a higher standard of care is required. Where this is not the case, carers should at least be able to identify an emergency, and know how to get help in the area where they work. Industrial nurses, for example, should be prepared for reasonably foreseeable accidents, and have a plan of action prepared.

[6.76] Health carers may in some cases be justified in carrying out procedures for which they are not trained, or which are normally only carried out by those with different or more specialised education in emergencies, but if they do, they must act reasonably under the circumstances: they must not be wanton in their rescue attempts (see *Wagner's* case at [6.50]).

[6.77] It would seem, from the case law, that four main principles should be followed in relation to emergency treatment:

- .....health carers should be able to identify potential emergency situations and symptoms indicating the need for emergency care, and be familiar with appropriate procedures for dealing with them (such as services or people to contact). That is, they should continually ask themselves "what if. . .?" and know when to call for help;
- .....health carers should be familiar with appropriate procedures to be followed in reasonably foreseeable emergencies. Equipment should be checked and in readiness, and procedures rehearsed;
- .....records should be kept as carefully as is possible under the circumstances. This may involve some unorthodox measures (for example, recording the administration of drugs or application of tourniquet, pressure bandage is left on a client's forehead when patients are evacuated to the hospital grounds during an earthquake);
- .....management have a responsibility to ensure that proper procedures for emergencies are developed and in place, that equipment is in readiness and staff are properly advised and trained. Health workers in industry and other non-hospital settings may need to educate management on the need to do this.

Statutory Law

[6.78] Breach of statutory provisions is a prima facie (but not absolute), indication of unreasonable (and therefore negligent) practice. The most obvious example here would be the statutory provisions for the administration of drugs (see Ch 8). These are intended, among other things, to protect patients from harm (for example, provisions for the checking of, and signing for, those drugs which are given). In these provisions the legislation is setting out a general standard of reasonable practice. It is conceivable that breach of legislative provisions may not be negligent behaviour (for example, in an emergency or extraordinary situation) (see [6.114]ff), so other factors listed here may also be taken into account.

Procedure Manuals, Departmental Directives, Health and Safety Policies, Protocols etc

[6.79] Courts will also consider these as evidence of recognised reasonable practice for those in the health care profession. Staff are expected to be aware of hospital procedure manuals, etc, and employers should make them available. In dispensing reasonable care, it is expected that staff would follow such advice, although there may be exceptional circumstances. The health carer would have the burden of proving that in such circumstances the actions taken were reasonable. Evidence that a carer acted contrary to the hospital procedure manual in carrying out post-operative care, for example, would be prima facie evidence of negligence, and would place a heavy burden on her or him to convince a court that the circumstances justified the deviation from established procedure.

General Knowledge and Practice of the Profession

■■■ CASE
Roe v Minister of Health [1954] 2 QB 66 (CA England)
An anaesthetist adopted a practice, recently developed at that time (1947), which was to prevent the danger of infection when administering spinal anaesthesia. This practice was to soak ampoules of the anaesthesia in phenol, thereby rendering them sterile for use. On the day in question, he used two of these ampoules to provide two patients with spinal anaesthesia for knee surgery. Both men subsequently became paraplegic as a result of corrosion of the spinal cord from leaking of minute amounts of the antiseptic into the apparently intact ampoules which contaminated the drug (no one had been aware of the possibility of this happening).

[6.80] The court found that no one in the doctor's position could have known of the possibility of the seepage, although of course at the time of the trial it was well and truly known. The court held that the state of knowledge of those involved at the time of the event, not hindsight, is what is considered by law and therefore the anaesthetist had not been negligent.

▮▮▮ CASE
Lowns & Anor v Woods & Anor [1996] Aust Torts Reports ¶81-376 (CA NSW)

Some of the facts of this case are outlined above (see [6.43]). A second action in negligence relating to the unfortunate outcome of Patrick's fit was brought on his behalf against the specialist (Dr Procopis), who was his treating doctor at the time. The action against Dr Procopis was based on his failure to advise Patrick's parents about the administration of rectal valium to stop or ameliorate the effect of his fitting. Dr Procopis gave evidence that there were questions about the safety and effectiveness of administering rectal valium at the time, and that only in a limited number of cases would he advise family to use it, one of these being where there was poor control of seizures by medication and the child was more than an hour away from medical care. Expert evidence overwhelmingly supported his decision not to advise its use for Patrick. The trial judge, however, determined that it was reasonable to foresee that Patrick could suffer status epilepticus, and that this could occur when he was more than an hour away from medical assistance. Given the relative risks of brain damage without the administration of valium and the effect on the respiratory system of administering it, the reasonable response would have been to have advised the parents in its administration. Dr Procopis was thus found negligent. He appealed to the New South Wales Court of Appeal, which heard the case along with the action against Dr Lowns.

[6.81] The New South Wales Court of Appeal upheld Dr Procopis' appeal. The Court reviewed the evidence before the trial judge and determined that he had not taken enough notice of some of the reasons for the practice of not advising parents about rectal valium in cases such as Patrick's. These included the absence anywhere in the world of such a practice, the risks of respiratory depression involved, the absence of such a practice in authoritative textbooks and publications, and the fact that valium was not licensed or produced in a form for rectal use in Australia.

[6.82] On the issue of accepting the evidence of medical practice, Mahoney JA said that judges can substitute their own view of what a medical risk involves for that of a treating doctor, as set out in *Rogers v Whitaker* (see [4.98]). But he went on to say that

> the courts should be slow to intervene where what is involved is the weighing up of advantages and disadvantages, medical necessities and the like by the profession.

[6.82] ■■■ CASE

John Edwin Caley v Northern Regional Health Board [1997] Aust Torts Reports ¶81-429 (SC Tas)

Mrs Caley died two weeks after giving birth to her third child, suffering from a pulmonary embolism by a clot of blood formed elsewhere in the body. It was argued that an embolus had developed post-partum and that the respondent hospital was in breach of the duty of care it owed her in failing to take appropriate steps to avoid the risk that in fact eventuated.

The particulars of that breach were that the hospital:

1)......Failed to examine Mrs Caley sufficiently, competently or at all.
2)......Failed to take heed of the swelling in her right foot.
3)......Discharged her without any or any adequate discharge plan.
4)......Discharged her without advice as to what she should do if the swelling in the right foot persisted.
5)......Failed to warn her that a blood clot could develop which could be fatal.

The jury found for the respondent. The plaintiff appealed this finding. It was not disputed that the respondent owed Mrs Caley a duty of care, but that the trial judge erred in law in failing to put adequate directions to the jury in relation to determining whether the hospital breached that duty of care.

[6.83] The Appeal Court decided that, in relation to deciding whether the hospital's duty of care had been breached, that they had to be satisfied on the balance of probabilities:

1)......that a reasonable hospital authority in the position of the respondent would have foreseen the risk of an embolism developing in the sense that such an "injury" or condition was not far fetched or fanciful; and
2)......that the respondent failed to do that which a reasonable hospital authority would have done in the circumstances to avoid that injury; and
3)......that failure caused death.

[6.84] The Court held that Step 1 was not an issue, as it was accepted by both parties that the risk of embolism was not "far-fetched or fanciful". However, in relation to Step 2, the Court said that the jury must be told that they should consider from the point of view of the reasonable hospital, "the magnitude of the risk and the degree of the probability of its occurrence, along with the expense, difficulty and inconvenience of taking alleviating action and any other conflicting responsibilities which the defendant may have" (*Wyong Shire Council v Shirt* (1980) 146 CLR 40 per Mason J at 47-48).

[6.85] In short, the jury had to consider not only whether the likelihood of risk was reasonably foreseeable, but also whether those responsible reasonably weighed:

■......the likelihood of the risk becoming a reality;
■......its probable effects; and
■......other responsibilities they might have,

with the practicality of measures to avoid that foreseeable risk.

Anticipating a Patient's Actions [6.88]

■■■ CASE
Wendover v State, 313 NYS 2d 287 (1970) (CA New York United States)
An obese, mentally deficient epileptic patient was admitted for her second stay as a result of a suicide attempt. She was in a private room, but under close supervision. Despite this, and the fact that she was extremely restless, repeatedly letting down the siderails, she managed to move the bed next to a radiator without staff's knowledge. As a result she was badly burned when she had an epileptic fit.

[6.86] In this case the court was satisfied that the nurses could not have foreseen the patient moving her bed, and that there was no way the hospital could have prevented the accident. The court would have considered the patient's past behaviour, her mental state, her medical condition, and the general nursing experience in this area, to evaluate the reasonableness of the nurses not keeping an even closer watch on her. Readers might like to compare this case with that of *Spivey* (see [6.48]). Part of legal reasoning is to analyse two similar cases, as these are, and attempt to come to some principle which will reconcile the different outcomes.

Different Practices Accepted within the Profession

[6.87] Where there are different accepted practices within the profession, it is recognised by law that a reasonable practitioner may follow any one of them without attracting liability in negligence. As long as there is a responsible body of practitioners subscribing to the method used by the defendant in a case, and the method is applied according to that body of thought, then, despite the fact that some practitioners would not act in that way, it is open to the court to find the defendant not liable (*Bolam's* case; see [6.73]).

[6.88] Departure from recognised practice may, as already stated, be indicative of negligence, although not necessarily so. In the case of *Hunter v Hanley* [1955] SC 200 it was expressed by Lord Clyde (at 206) that three things must be established to show negligence when the defendant has departed from recognised practice:

■......there must be an established and usual practice;
■......the defendant departed from that practice; and
■......no reasonable practitioner would have departed from the practice if he or she had been acting with ordinary care.

[6.88] ||| **CASE**
Chasney v Anderson [1950] 4 DLR 223 (SC Canada)
A surgeon carrying out a tonsillectomy followed common practice in that hospital by not using sponges with tapes attached to them nor having nursing staff carry out a sponge count. Sponges with tapes attached were available, as were nursing staff to carry out the count. The child suffocated to death because a sponge was left in situ. The issue was whether the hospital was negligent, and whether the doctor, by following the usual practice there, was also negligent.

[6.89] The court held that the hospital was not negligent because it provided the means for reasonable precautions, while the surgeon was (but the employer is liable for knowingly allowing employees to act dangerously: see vicarious liability, [6.188]). He had departed from a recognised and available practice for no good reason, despite expert evidence that the practice he adopted was a general and approved one at the time. Where the defendant practitioner pleads common practice, the court will take evidence of this into account as prima facie pointing to reasonable practice, but maintains the right to rule that such practice was, at least in the situation being considered, negligent (see also *Sidaway v Governors of the Bethlem Royal Hospital* [1985] 1 All ER 643, discussed at [4.50]).

Other Limiting Factors

[6.90] The condition of the patient may cause one to act in ways which might otherwise be hazardous.

||| **CASE**
Mahon v Osborne [1939] 2 KB 14 (CA England)
A surgeon operated on a young man with a burst appendix under difficult circumstances: the patient was having respiratory difficulty, it was 4 am, and there was not the usual number of staff available. After carrying out the surgery, it was revealed that respiratory difficulty was increasing, and the surgeon decided to "close up" as quickly as possible. Before doing so he did, however ask the nurses whether the swab count was correct, they checked and told him it was. The patient was returned to the ward in a satisfactory condition but some days later became very ill as the result of a pack which had been left inside him. After emergency surgery to remove it he died. His family sued the surgeon and nurses in negligence (in those days a hospital was held to be not responsible for the actions of staff during surgery).

[6.91] The plaintiffs argued that, among other things, the nurses were negligent in their counting of the packs and swabs, and that the doctor was also negligent in this, as well as being the person responsible for the overall conduct of the surgery. The trial court found the doctor negligent (there is no explanation as to why the nurses were not tried) and he appealed, arguing, among other things, that the circumstances of the surgery as explained should have been taken into account in the trial, and

that they had not. The appeal court agreed, stating that the difficult [6.94]
circumstances of the surgery may well have prevented the surgeon acting
in what otherwise would have been a reasonable fashion, and remitted the
case for retrial.

Probability of Harm

[6.92] The same statements apply here as were made regarding the
foreseeability of the probability of harm. Here we are talking about harm
that is foreseeable as likely to happen, but are now looking at the question
of how likely it is to happen (see *Bolton v Stone* at [6.25]). A 70 per cent
chance of side effects may warrant more drastic precautions than a 10 per
cent or 15 per cent chance. This consideration is closely bound up with
the following factors.

Person Suffering from Specific Disability

[6.93] A person will be held liable for harm which occurred because the
victim had a specific disability, of which the person was, or ought to have
been, aware. The standard of care will depend on the facts of the situation.
The following two cases may assist in explaining this.

❚❚❚ CASE
Haley v London Electricity Board [1965] AC 778 (House of Lords England)

The plaintiff had been blind for many years. He conquered his disability to such an extent that he was employed by the London County Council. He routinely walked a short distance along the footpath, using a white stick to avoid obstacles, to a spot where he asked someone to assist him to cross the road to where he caught a bus to work. On the morning of the accident Electricity Board workmen had dug a trench in the footpath. To prevent harm to pedestrians they placed a punner, which was a stick attached to a weight, across the footpath. The punner was attached to a railing on the inside of the footpath, so it sloped across the footpath from ground level to a height of about two feet. This was not the normal type of barricade used by the Board. The walking stick used by the plaintiff to guide him did not detect the punner, and he tripped over it. As a result of his injuries he became deaf. He sued the Electricity Board in negligence.

[6.94] The House of Lords held that the Board should have foreseen that
some people using the footpath could be blind. The Board gave evidence
that it did cater for blind people in the type of barricade normally used.
The court said that it could accept that the Board would not have to take
extra precautions if it could not foresee that blind people would be using
the footpath at that time, or that the probability was so remote the Board
would be justified in not taking extra precautions. In this case, however,
these considerations did not exist, and the Board should have foreseen the
possibility, and so was liable. Consideration of the inability or disability of

[6.94] those who are immature or feeble in mind or body is owed by those who know of, or ought to anticipate, the presence of such persons within the scope and hazard of their own operations.

[6.95] Those who deal with a section of the population which has a higher than average number of those with a disability need to be particularly conscious of anticipating their special needs. Where there is no clear indication of a person's disability, however, one is not expected to foresee it.

Magnitude of Harm

[6.96] If a danger is remote but potentially catastrophic if it occurs, more care should be taken than if it were just as remote but not so serious (see *Bolton v Stone* at [6.25], *The Wagon Mound*, above at [6.22]). An example given by the courts is that of a car approaching a hill on a little used country road. If the car behind it overtakes while approaching the crest of the hill (the driver being unable to see any approaching car), it may have only a remote chance of meeting another car, but if it does the results could be disastrous. The driver's decision not to overtake in this situation, would depend more on the magnitude of the harm that would occur if he or she met an oncoming car than on the (remote) likelihood of doing so. This has been expressed in the maxim that the greater the magnitude of the foreseeable harm, the less the probability of its occurring is required before preventative measures are taken. This is an important consideration in medicine, which is not often articulated clearly.

Social Utility of the Activity

[6.97] A dangerous action but one necessary to bring about more good than foreseeable harm may be accepted by the court. This is based on a similar principle to that of necessity.

■■■ CASE
Daborn v Bath Tramways Motor Co Ltd [1946] 2 All ER 333 (CA England)

During the Second World War, when London was being bombed, all ambulances which could be found were pressed into service as they were needed to attend to the injured. Several old left-hand-drive vehicles were used, and because of difficulties in seeing the signalling driver, a bus collided with one of them, causing injury.

[6.98] The court held that the plaintiff, the ambulance driver, was not guilty of contributory negligence as the special need for ambulances outweighed the need to have better equipped vehicles on the road. This defence would most likely only arise where there is some disaster or catastrophe (for example, the landslide at Thredbo, where people were submerged in the rubble, where rescue operations and emergency care may pose some risks to third parties).

Some Special Situations

Learners and the Inexperienced

[6.99] Generally, the law will give no special consideration to beginners and learners. The beginner who takes on a particular health care role is just as responsible for providing a reasonable standard of care as are those who are more experienced in that role. Thus, a person taking on the role of a senior health professional should act as a reasonable senior health professional, a junior as a reasonable junior one, and so on. Health care facilities, or those supervising students, are expected to provide an adequate standard of care to clients to prevent harm from negligence, and this involves adequate supervision and training of students for this purpose. The student is also responsible for ensuring that he or she does not undertake care for which he or she is not prepared.

▌▌▌ CASE
Collins v Hertfordshire County Council [1947] KB 598 (High Court England)

A final year medical student was employed as a resident junior house surgeon despite not being so qualified, because of the demands of wartime. She was asked by the surgeon in charge by telephone to obtain procaine 1 per cent from the hospital pharmacy. She mistook the order to be for *cocaine* 1 per cent and ordered cocaine orally from the pharmacy. It was given to the patient, who died.

[6.100] The court's finding in this case was in contrast to that of *Daborn* (above) in two apparent respects. In this case, it was held that the junior had opportunities to consider and correct her mistake, and that she should be held to the standard of a junior house surgeon, as that was the position the institution placed her in (although she was not so qualified). This is in accord with the legal principle that if one holds oneself out to have a certain level of skill, or holds a particular position requiring it, or claims that staff are adequately trained to provide that level of skill, one must operate as a reasonable person of the class of practitioners at that level. A medical officer would have known (and in fact the student did) what a lethal dose of cocaine was, and should have followed more stringent measures in executing the surgeon's orders.

[6.100] ■■■ **CASE**
Wilsher v Essex Area Health Authority [1988] 1 All ER 871 (House of Lords England)

> A neonate suffered almost total blindness after intensive care. He had been born prematurely, and suffered from several serious illnesses, one of which was oxygen deficiency. There was a low probability that he would survive. During his treatment in the neonatal intensive care ward, a catheter was inserted into a vein rather than an artery by an inexperienced junior doctor. A registrar was asked to check this, failed to notice the mistake and made the same mistake himself several hours later. In both cases the neonate was given excess amounts of oxygen and suffered from near blindness, and, through his representatives, sued the hospital in negligence. There were two issues involved in this case, one was the standard of care owed to the child, the other was whether the doctor's actions actually caused the harm. The latter issue is discussed below (see [6.159]). The lower court found that the standard of care owed by the doctors was only that reasonably required of doctors having the same formal qualifications and experience as those involved, and so there had been no breach of the standard of care. The plaintiff appealed and the case finally went to the House of Lords.

[6.101]   The House of Lords considered three possible standards of care:

1)......a "team" standard, that is, that each of the members of a unit held themselves out to be able to offer the specialised procedures the unit set out to perform;
2)......a standard of care that can actually be offered by an individual, based on his or her personal experience and qualifications; and
3)......a standard of care based not on the individual, but the *post* that he or she occupies.

[6.102]   The "team" standard was rejected, as it would mean that, for example an intern or student nurse would be required to possess the skill and experience of a consultant medical specialist. The standard of care based on the individual was rejected as being tailored to the actor, and not the action, and to tie the client's right to complain to the chance skill of the person who happens at the time to be caring for him or her, rather than the standard of care given by the hospital. It was held to have no place in tort law.

[6.103]   The third standard was accepted as the correct standard. It rejected the view that the standard of care to meet is what a reasonable person of the carer's qualifications and experience would do. Rather, the *Bolam* test, that of the ordinary person exercising and professing a special skill, is the correct test, and thus, as Lord Glidewell put it:

> the law requires the trainee or learner to be judged by the same standard as his more experienced colleagues. If it did not, inexperience would frequently be urged as a defence to an action for professional negligence.

[6.104]   It thus may be that a hospital will be found negligent for requiring or allowing a person to practice at a level at which he or she is manifestly not adequately trained or competent. Where the desired level of skill cannot be offered, this should be made quite clear to clients, so that they can determine if they want to assume some of the risk of harm.

Otherwise, clients can expect a reasonable standard of professional care, [6.106] with adequately trained staff, proper allocation of responsibilities and supervision of care. This is a part of the function of an employer offering services to the public. This issue is considered more fully below at [6.177].

[6.105] Failure to provide proper and adequate information can be the basis of a negligence action at law. This is dealt with in Chapter 4 as part of the consideration of consent. What is said there also applies to advice in the form of treatment.

What if a Person Disagrees with Instructions?

[6.106] The duty of care owed to clients by health carers includes the obligation to question the directions of those superior to them which they reasonably believe are likely to result in harm to a client. The unusual medication order, for example, should be checked with the medical officer concerned (see Ch 8). This also applies to the failure of carers to act where medical direction is believed to be necessary. Health carers should not adopt the attitude that they are "only carrying out orders", but should use their knowledge and experience in rendering reasonable care to those who depend on them. This requires that they discuss any direction about which they are concerned with the person giving it. If they are not comfortable with the result, the matter should be taken further.

■■■ CASE

Darling v Charlston Community Memorial Hospital, 211 NE 2d 253 (1965) (SC Illinois United States)

The plaintiff was a young man who broke his leg while playing football. He had a comminuted fracture of the right tibia and fibula. The attendant surgeon at the well-equipped and staffed hospital brought the bones into proper alignment and applied a plaster cast without underlying stockinette or padding. The patient was admitted to a ward of the hospital, where, over a two week period, the leg deteriorated, until his family moved him to another hospital where the leg had to be amputated due to infection. The family sued the hospital and treating surgeon in negligence.

Nurses' notes contained repeated notations of increasingly oedematous, darkening and insensitive toes, and of increasing pain and ineffectiveness of the analgesia which was ordered. The surgeon visited the patient frequently at the request of the nurses, but did not call an orthopaedic specialist because, in his opinion, the situation was satisfactory. He cut back the plaster cast and removed a section of it to relieve pressure, but inadvertently cut the patient's skin exacerbating the development of infection.

The doctor admitted liability and settled out of court, so the case proceeded against the hospital. The jury found the hospital liable, because of the lack of action on the part of the nurses. The hospital appealed, stating that it was not liable for the nurses' conduct because they were under the instructions of the doctor.

[6.107] The appeal court dismissed the appeal. It held that the duty of care of nurses extends further than bringing to the attention of the responsible doctor the deteriorating condition of a patient, and so broke new ground. The duty of care of nurses, the court held, includes informing the hospital administration of any departure from normal or proper care that puts a patient's life or health in danger. The nurses could not say simply: "Well, we told the doctor and reported all unusual developments, we could not do any more." The court disagreed. As well as some neglect in their observations and reporting, it held, they were negligent in not taking the matter further, until they got satisfaction on behalf of the patient by reporting it to the next appropriate person on the hospital staff who could take action, and so on up the line of authority. When the nurses were aware that there was a dangerous impairment to the circulation in the patient's leg, which would become irreversible in a matter of hours,

> it became the nurses' duty to inform the attending physician, and if he failed to act, to advise the hospital authorities so that appropriate action might be taken (at 258).

[6.108] Unfortunately, nurses have often been considered the servants of the medical profession by the law, and where they have questioned it they have been considered to have stepped outside of their role and warranted dismissal, or subjection to harassment and even assault. Johnstone ((1994), Ch 6) gives a detailed study of cases in which nurses have questioned the medical treatment of their patients. This is dealt with further in Chapter 11.

[6.109] Below is a Checklist of recommended steps, according to legal and ethical principles, for questioning either instructions that have been given, or a particular situation, such as a problem with staffing or resources. It is recognised that health carers may be unwilling to follow them because of the possibility of reprisals by those who could make their working life difficult (or non-existent!). Crispin Hull points out, for example, that in relation to the activities at Sydney's Chelmsford Hospital in the 1960s and 1970s, where deep-sleep therapy was used and many patients died, resulting in a Royal Commission:

> Chelmsford nurses complained to authorities in the early 1970s. They and relatives of victims were threatened with defamation proceedings if they spoke out. [Hull, C, "Justice hides behind the law", *Canberra Times*, 2 April 1994, p C3.]

[6.110] It is recognised that the Checklist provides a guide as to what is the conventional approach to questioning instructions. The law is likely to become more demanding of health carers, especially nurses, who are increasingly being recognised as professionals, but are still subject to the stereotype of "handmaids" to the medical profession. This developing recognition will hopefully lead, conversely, to more mutual support of management and staff in asserting the right to question orders which cause concern, and recognition of that right by both the medical profession and the law.

▮▮▮ CHECKLIST [6.111]
PRINCIPLES FOR ACTION WHEN A SITUATION CAUSES CONCERN

(This applies to such matters as a treatment order, short staffing, inadequate resources, faulty equipment etc. It may also involve a client demanding care under circumstances which would prevent reasonable care.)

▮ ..... Discussion of the matter is most important in resolving such situations. Firstly, attempts should be made to discuss it with those directly involved, or responsible for the situation. Only then, and if the matter is serious enough, should one take it further, to management or, if not in a health facility, a relevant authority. This is an important procedure legally: it establishes concern at the standard of care on the part of the health carer, preserves confidentiality, and demonstrates his or her intention to remedy the situation.

▮ ..... Care to the client is a central concern (for example, emergency, surgery, dependent client), and he or she should not be abandoned. Carers should consider continuing necessary care, with action to remedy the situation (or prevent an adverse situation arising) at the first opportunity.

▮ ..... As an employee, whilst health carers are required to follow reasonable and lawful instructions of the employer (see Ch 11), they are also required to:
— exercise a duty of care towards their clients; and
— further the employer's operation, including its activities as a health care facility, or if in another area of enterprise, its legitimate activities (including employment and welfare of workers).

Thus if health carers feel that failure to act will endanger the health or wellbeing of a client or colleagues, or is contrary to the good operation of the employer's activities, this is a matter for management, as it is ultimately responsible for the standard of care given to clients, and/or the proper operation of its activities.

▮ ..... A record should be kept of the event, and action taken, for example, in the client's notes, an incident report to management (see Ch 7), or, whoever is responsible for the situation or instruction (this could even be the client, for example his or her behaviour, failure to co-operate, or demand for particular treatment, requiring the health carer to refuse to continue the relationship under those circumstances). Good contemporaneous notes may counteract a claim of negligence against the health carer, especially where he or she has continued to work under the circumstances complained of in the interests of the client's welfare. Records can become lost or destroyed: it may be that independent records should be made and kept in secure circumstances. If a signature to this is witnessed at the time (the contents don't have to be disclosed to the witness) this document can become valuable independent evidence in the future (see Ch 7).

[6.111] One example of dealing with an unsatisfactory situation is where, in a busy ward, more nurses are considered necessary to give adequate care to patients. Request by the charge nurse for more staff is met by the response that this is not possible. The charge nurse is advised to make a note of this through an incident report, as well as in patients' notes. He or she should also make a statement to this effect, for safekeeping in case any allegation of negligence is made in the future (a statutory declaration is the strongest form of legal evidence). The author is aware of a case where on the second telephone request for staff and being

[6.111] told there were none to provide, the charge nurse of a cardiac ward told the supervising nurse she was noting the refusal in writing. Several extra staff arrived to help a short time later!

[6.112] A recent case involved a surgeon who did not consider himself competent in a particular specialty.

CASE
Luck v Blamey & Associates [2000] VSC 77, 3 March 2000

A woman was referred to a general surgeon for treatment. After biopsies were performed, she was diagnosed as suffering from scleroderma. The surgeon wrote to the woman stating that, as he was not a specialist dermatologist, from whom she would require treatment, he did not wish to continue treating her. She sought an interlocutory injunction from the court compelling the surgeon to treat her, which was denied.

[6.113] The court held that the doctor was entitled to refuse to carry out treatment which he considered was beyond his specialty. This case also involved the issue of specific performance of a contract for personal services (see Ch 10).

Emergency Care

[6.114] There is no specific law which sets out the role and duties of health carers or hospitals in relation to emergency treatment. This is subject to the common law principles set down by the courts, and is based on the general principles of negligence: that is, reasonable action is required to prevent reasonably foreseeable harm. There are some specific laws about drugs (see Ch 8).

Emergency Workers: Ambulance, Rescue etc

[6.115] Emergency workers are under the same duty of care as other health carers. A duty of care could be said to arise wherever it becomes known to emergency workers that there is a need for services. There is no specific Australian case law on the matter, however there is English and American precedent:

▌▌▌ CASE
Kent v Griffiths and Ors [2000] EWCA 16 (3 February 2000)

The plaintiff, an asthmatic, suffered an attack and was attended by her doctor. At 4.25 pm the doctor telephoned the London Ambulance Service (LAS) and asked for an ambulance to take her to casualty "immediately". Despite several further calls, the ambulance did not arrive for 35 minutes which was held not to have been a reasonable time to travel the necessary 6.5 miles. In the process the plaintiff suffered respiratory arrest. The plaintiff sued several parties, one of the issues being breach of duty of care by the LAS. The trial judge found the LAS liable, but gave them permission to appeal the question as to whether there was a duty of care owed to the plaintiff by the LAS as it was a novel one. Earlier cases had held that the fire brigade and the police do not have a duty of care to individuals who seek their assistance, as their duty is to the community as a whole, and specific activity is discretionary, based on the wider duty (see, for example, *Capital & Counties Plc v Hampshire County Council* [1997] QB 1004 which held that a fire brigade did not have a duty of care to answer calls to fires or take reasonable care to do so; *Alexandrou v Oxford* [1993] 2 All ER 328 as to police when responding to an emergency call, and *OLL Ltd v Secretary of State for Transport* [1997] 3 All ER 897 in relation to coastguards when making a rescue at sea). The LAS thus argued that they did not have a duty of care to the plaintiff, and were therefore not liable.

[6.116] The Court of Appeal, in a case that drew heavily on public policy, held that the acceptance of the emergency call created the duty of care. It found a distinction between the services provided by the abovementioned services and the ambulance service. They owe a duty to the public at large, and responses to individual cases are subject to discretion in the operation of that overall responsibility. By contrast, once a call to the ambulance service has been accepted, the service is dealing with a named individual upon whom the duty becomes focused. Furthermore, once the call has been made and the ambulance service agrees to transport the patient, those caring for him or her are likely to refrain from further attempts to get the person to hospital. This was not a general reliance but a specific one, and it is foreseeable that a specific person would suffer if there was a delay. The court stated ambulance transport was really an extension of the services offered by doctors and nurses at the hospital. The ambulance was an extension of the means provided by the public purse by which the plaintiff was to be treated by the hospital.

[6.117] The court went on to say that the requirements of proximity were fulfilled. Further, there were no circumstances which made it unfair or unreasonable or unjust that liability should exist. It finally pointed to its belief that the public would be greatly disturbed if they held that there was not a duty of care in this case.

[6.117] ▮▮▮ CASE
American National Bank & Trust Company, Special Administrator of the Estate of Renee Kazmierowski, v City of Chicago (Cook County Circuit Court) (10 August 2000)

The administrator of the estate of a deceased person brought an action in negligence against the City of Chicago and two paramedics. After a call had been received from the deceased, who stated she was suffering an asthma attack and gave her address, the paramedics went to her apartment. There was no response to their knocking on the door, nor could a firefighter (also called), get a response at the back door. There was no sign of anyone being at the apartment, and after checking that they had the right address, the paramedics decided they were not needed and left. Later, in a response to another call, they returned and were let into the apartment where they found the person lying dead on the floor. The action cited negligence and wilful misconduct on the part of the paramedics in failing to enter the apartment (it was claimed the door was unlocked), and the operator in failing to keep the decedent on the phone while the paramedics responded. The question arose as to whether there was a duty of care. Legislation covering paramedics was held to provide that they were immune from action in negligence if they acted within the scope of their training, so long as their activity was not "wilful or wanton".

[6.118] The court agreed that the defendants could not be held liable in negligence, unless their actions were "wilful and wanton". The court considered the definition of "wilful and wanton" adopted by the court in a previous case *Schneiderman v Interstate Transit Lines Inc* (1946) 394 Ill 569 at 583:

> A wilful or wanton injury must have been intentional or the act must have been committed under circumstances exhibiting a reckless disregard for the safety of others, such as failure, after knowledge of impending danger, to exercise ordinary care to prevent it or a failure to discover the danger through recklessness or carelessness when it could have been discovered by the exercise of ordinary care.

[6.119] The operator had been told by the deceased "I think I'm going to die. Hurry". The operator did not attempt to keep her on the phone despite standards adopted by the service requiring dispatchers to do so. This, the court held, fulfilled the test set out for wilful and wanton misconduct, which also applied to the actions of the paramedics. The policy of "Try Before You Pry" which dictates that emergency workers try doors before using destructive measures to enter premises was also part of the training of paramedics. The fact that they confirmed the address, did not try the door or other means to determine if someone was inside amounted also to wanton and wilful misconduct.

[6.120] These cases are not binding precedent in Australian law, and so the principles they establish may not be adopted here. They raise the question of just what, if any, duty of care is owed by emergency workers, and to whom it might be owed if it does exist. These cases pose an interesting public policy issue: should a duty of care exist because the public would be concerned if it didn't? Should legislation be enacted to exonerate emergency workers from any actions, even grossly negligent ones ("wilful and wanton")?

[6.121] Alleged errors in locating scenes of emergency and time lapses in response to emergency arose in Victoria recently. An ambulance in the Australian Capital Territory recently allegedly diverted on its way to an emergency to drop a person off at his home, and then got lost. At the time of writing an inquiry is being held into the New South Wales Ambulance Service, which is allegedly performing very poorly. These highlight some of the issues relating to duty of care that are the subject of potential legal liability, and the various bodies, including government, ambulance services and individual ambulance officers, that may be jointly responsible in this regard. The lack of case law means there is no precedent on this issue.

[6.122] Given there is no law to the contrary, it would seem that the standard of care emergency workers owe is dependent upon those set as being reasonable for them. In establishing what is reasonable action, courts will consider training programs, plans and protocols to deal with emergencies. Emergency carers should consider the Checklist above at [6.68] (reasonable standard of care).

Hospitals

[6.123] Where a hospital operates an emergency ward, it has a duty of care to all who pass through its doors, for, unless the contrary is made clear to the public, all comers are offered at least initial assessment there. Once a person's presence is made known to any of the medical staff, there is a duty to provide diagnosis and first aid of a reasonable nature, and to then take reasonable care in either referring the person on for further care (for example to a ward, or to another doctor) or of discharging the person with adequate information to protect her or him from danger.

[6.124] The following cases could be held to set out principles that should apply to all those who hold themselves ready to provide emergency care.

Proper Assessment and Diagnosis

[6.125] Firstly, one could point to *Barnett v Chelsea and Kensington Hospital Management Committee* (see [6.159]), where the court held that "the duty of a casualty officer is in general to see and examine all patients who come to casualty". A doctor should not rely on the nurse's assessment although he or she may rely on the triage nurse as to the priority which patients should receive.

Triage Nurses

[6.126] Triage nurses are specialist nurses in that they are required to exercise special skill. They must have the necessary knowledge and experience to adequately carry out the functions required, and share with the hospital the obligation to ensure that those coming to the accident and emergency ward are properly assessed for their need of treatment, and

[6.126] that any doubt is referred to a medical officer. The nurse should know what signs and symptoms to look for, how to establish them and the various categories in which to place patients. For example, one hospital adopted the following categories (which may have been amended since then):

CATEGORY	PRIORITY	SYMPTOMS
Category 1	immediate	includes anaphylaxis, massive or uncontrolled bleeding, major burns, cardiac chest pain, acute heart failure with pulmonary oedema, stroke, disruptive behaviour, chemical eye burns
Category 2	urgent	includes acute abdominal pain with severe distress, bleeding lacerations, venous bleeding, alcohol withdrawal, eye injury with visual disturbance, head trauma with loss of consciousness
Category 3	semi-urgent	non-acute abdominal pain with mild distress, minor burns, eye infection, controlled nose bleed, suspected closed fractures or dislocations, migraine headache
Category 4	non-urgent	includes chronic back pain, cold or flu symptoms, earache or sore throat, mild gastrointestinal upset, chronic or mild headache, joint pain without trauma, superficial lacerations, abrasions, bruises, minor puncture wounds, rash
Category 5	seen by nurse	

These categories were reported in the *Canberra Times*, 2 April 1994, p 1.

Hospitals should have a clear set of categories, and a process for training staff and assessing their competence.

[6.127] Where clients do not fit an established category, assistance should be sought in determining what care to give, and where a person is referred elsewhere, the patient should be given a clear indication of where to go, and assured that they can and should do this. They should also be assured of what to do if their condition worsens. Often communication, particularly in the emergency ward, can allay peoples' belief that they are being ignored and neglected. Assurances that staff are sympathetic, [6.131] explanations as to why decisions are being made, and clear advice as to how appropriate treatment can be obtained can often mean the difference between whether patients feel aggrieved or empowered to deal with the situation. They may need to be encouraged to wait to see their doctor in the morning, for example, but also be made to understand that the doctor's receptionist should be informed that the matter needs prompt attention.

[6.128] The consumption of alcohol or drugs may make diagnosis difficult.

■ ■ ■ CASE
Methodist Hospital v Ball, 362 SW 2d 475 (1961) (CA Tennessee United States)

A 16-year-old boy was admitted to casualty but was unattended for 45 minutes. He was then sent, without examination, to another hospital. The doctor did not examine him because he accepted the opinion of several laymen that the boy was drunk. The boy later died of a ruptured liver, and expert evidence was heard by the court to the effect that he would have lived if he had been diagnosed promptly.

Reasonable Care

[6.129] Secondly, after diagnosis, courts have held, the patient should be offered reasonable first aid care.

■ ■ ■ CASE
New Biloxi Hospital v Frazier, 146 So 2d 882 (1962) (CA Mississippi United States)

The patient was admitted, bleeding heavily from gunshot wounds. Two nurses took his observations and called a doctor, but made no attempt to stop the bleeding. The doctor attended the man and at that time there was a large pool of blood on the floor and his vital signs were poor. He was transferred to another hospital and died there soon after.

[6.130] The court found the hospital liable in negligence for the failure of its staff, including the nurses, to keep the patient there and to offer the care necessary for his wellbeing.

Adequate Follow-up on Discharge

[6.131] There is a difference between a person leaving a health care facility of their own volition and the formal discharge of a person from the facility. The former is done at the person's own behest, whether or not they are considered fit to leave, and the latter is done with the warrant of the facility that the person is in a suitable condition to leave. Once the patient has been stabilised, and treated in the emergency department, staff must provide for proper reference to, or information about, after-care.

[6.131] ▌▌▌ CASE
Niles v City of San Rafael, 42 Cal App 3d 230 (1974) (CA California United States)

A child who had suffered a blow to the head was examined, and after a time allowed to leave. The hospital failed to admit the child, or to give the father a card they had listing symptoms which would indicate that he should return. The child already had five of the seven symptoms listed on the card.

[6.132] The hospital was found negligent. The staff had not properly considered the next step in the treatment programme. The Checklist at [6.134] could really apply to all clients who leave a health care facility, but is particularly crucial for casualty patients.

[6.133] A recent case in Sydney dealt with the care of a person who left the emergency ward of his own volition, and other aspects of care in the emergency ward.

▌▌▌ CASE
Wang v Central Sydney Area Health Service [2000] NSWSC 515

The plaintiff was a young man who was assaulted walking home from the suburban train station, possibly unconscious for a short period. He managed to walk home and two friends took him to Royal Prince Alfred Hospital at Camperdown. There they told the receptionist he needed to see a doctor urgently. The receptionist responded that they would have to wait. A triage nurse (the "first triage nurse") examined the plaintiff, and noted his pupils were even and responding, his grip strong, and that he appeared conscious and alert (although pale and in some distress). She put the plaintiff second on the list, to be seen after a complex abdominal case. Meantime she had the plaintiff sit in the waiting room, where she could keep her eye on him. They waited for attention for some time after being seen by the triage nurse, who went off duty and was replaced by a second triage nurse (the "second triage nurse") while they were there. A further group of concerned friends arrived to accompany the plaintiff.

After some time (about one and a half to two hours after arriving), and before the plaintiff had been treated, the plaintiff and friends left the Emergency Department. The court accepted evidence that one of the group approached the second triage nurse and requested that a doctor see the plaintiff. They were told that this was not possible, and they should wait. One of the group later asked her if they could go elsewhere for treatment, such as a private hospital. She told him they could do whatever they wanted to do. The group left and went to the city Superclinic, there the plaintiff was treated by a doctor, who obtained a history of the event and noted the possibility of loss of consciousness. He debrided a deep, eight centimetre cut on the plaintiff's head, and examined him carefully for brain injury. As he concluded the plaintiff had no abnormal neurological signs, the doctor told the plaintiff and friends he should really return to hospital for further investigation and treatment, but in the face of their rejection of that idea decided to advise them of what action to take if there was any deterioration in his condition. He told them the plaintiff should not be left alone, and advised them to take him to a Chinese-speaking doctor in the morning to arrange for an x-ray and any necessary on-going care. It appeared from evidence in the court that details of the doctor's advice, being passed through an interpreter, may not have been fully comprehended by those who were directly caring for the plaintiff. One fact that the Chinese witnesses mentioned was that the plaintiff's (Chinese) speech was very slow. The court recognised that the triage nurse and the doctor at the clinic may not have noticed this, being unfamiliar with the language.

Some hours later the plaintiff suffered from nausea, vomiting and then a convulsion. His flatmates, new to the country, telephoned friends and some time later the plaintiff was taken back to the hospital by ambulance. On examination it was found that his skull had been fractured and he was suffering from an extra-dural haemorrhage. Surgical intervention was unable to prevent irreversible brain damage.

The plaintiff sued the Health Service, the hospital, the clinic doctor and the clinic. It was alleged that the triage nurse's examination of the plaintiff was inadequate and alternatively that she should have consulted a doctor. Also the second triage nurse should have consulted a doctor before the plaintiff left the hospital. Further it was alleged that the clinic doctor should have insisted the plaintiff return to any hospital at all, or have kept the plaintiff at the clinic for observation and necessary emergency action.

[6.134] The court heard that the plaintiff would most likely have made a full recovery if treatment had been given at the hospital. It made the following ruling.

Treatment by the hospital

- ..... The primary duty of the hospital was to assign the plaintiff his appropriate priority through the triage system and to observe him in the waiting area in case his condition deteriorated. No duty to provide him with medical services arose until he could be accommodated in the treatment area. Under the circumstances, he was allotted the appropriate priority.
- ..... Examination by the first triage nurse is not expected to have been the same as that which would have been carried out if the plaintiff had gone to the treatment area. The examination by the first triage nurse was adequate under the circumstances.
- ..... Given the limited resources and demands on them, a triage nurse would need to notify a doctor of a patient's attendance only if the symptoms indicated the need for urgent treatment. The department was very busy at the time, and the patient did not appear to have such symptoms. The first triage nurse was not negligent in not notifying a doctor of the patient's presence.

Leaving the hospital

- ..... The hospital also had a duty to furnish the plaintiff with appropriate advice when it was intimated that he might leave the hospital. They did not do that. The judge was impressed by the practice of one hospital when patients indicated an intention to leave:
  — attempts are made to persuade them to stay, explaining why it is in their interests to do so;
  — if that fails, they are given the names of medical clinics in the area (they would be unlikely to want to go to another hospital and wait again);

[6.134] — staff consider such factors as the patient's condition, where they intend to go, the availability of resources both at the hospital and elsewhere, and the patient's capacity to deal with the situation.

Liability of the Clinic doctor and the Clinic

▌..... The doctor at the clinic had a duty to insist the plaintiff go back to a hospital, observe the capacity of his friends to care for him, enquire as to his domestic circumstances (such advice and enquiries are "embraced within the broad duty of care which a doctor owes to a patient under the *Rogers and Whitaker* ruling"). The doctor did see a return to the hospital as the best course of action, and offered to write a letter for them, but he could not persuade the group to accept this advice. The clinic did not have the resources to keep the plaintiff there for observation, and he took what he considered to be the best option under the circumstances. As to determining the domestic arrangement and ability of friends to care for him, he had not made an adequate inquiry as to their relationship to him, who actually lived with him, and whether any of them would be sufficiently able to deal with his care if he deteriorated. However, it was clear from their concern and outrage at events that they were very good friends and really cared for him, and the doctor's failure to make these enquiries was not unreasonable under the circumstances. He, and consequently the clinic, were not liable in negligence.

▌▌▌ CHECKLIST
CONSIDERATIONS WHEN CLIENTS LEAVE CARE
(whether or not they are formally discharged)

▌..... Where are they going?
▌..... What support or care will they need?
▌..... Can this be given where they are going?
▌..... Do they (or those they will be with) know how to care for them(selves)?
▌..... Do they know what symptoms indicate the need for further medical attention?
▌..... Do they know how to seek further attention?
▌..... Do they know what other complications can occur?
▌..... Do they know how to deal with any that do?
▌..... Are they physically and mentally able to deal with any complications?

Accidents and Other Incidents Surrounding an Emergency

[6.135] Sometimes the person at the scene of an accident or coming into the casualty ward with the most apparent harm (for example, bleeding) may not be the most seriously injured. Where parents have been involved in the incident which injured their child but appear unharmed, they may nevertheless be ignoring their own injuries or weakness in their concern for their child. Those accompanying a casualty at an emergency or in the emergency ward might suffer harm, faint or collapse as a result of their own minor injuries, shock, stress, or what they witness in casualty. Staff should be aware of this possibility and take as many precautions as they reasonably can. This might take the form of, for example, ensuring that if parents are with children receiving treatment such as stitches, they are seated, invited to leave for the duration, or encouraged to speak up if they feel faint. Although the possible incidents are infinite, the point must be kept in mind that:

1).....health carers are only human, cannot be expected to anticipate everything, and need only act reasonably at the time; and
2).....attention is given to those who appear to need the most urgent care, and staff would thus be expected to be concentrating on them.

Expanded Health Care Practice

[6.136] Recently several Governments have been considering provision for nurses in nominated circumstances to be given primary care tasks for which doctors are traditionally responsible, including suturing wounds, plastering fractured limbs, pathology requests, prescribing drugs such as contraceptives, managing medication and conditions such as asthma, and urinary tract infection (see Ch 13). Different State-based approaches are being considered, and the lack of uniform approach, as well as the different views of the bodies involved, makes it impossible to set out standards of care with finality.

[6.137] However, expanded nursing practice will require the establishment of new standards of nursing knowledge and skill, and those involved will need to ensure that they are able to give reasonable care in the new settings. This development may result in acknowledgement by both the nursing profession and health administrators the need to more clearly establish those areas which are to be considered the province of nursing practice.

[6.138] Overall, the expansion of nursing practice is not different in kind to the expansion of health care technologies. Both are served by the principles underlying the law of negligence, and will require consideration by those involved of what is reasonable care under the particular circumstances facing the health carer at the time.

[6.139] Those who adopt new technologies and practices before their probable consequences are properly understood are risking liability at law unless they follow protocols and guidelines that have been approved for the undertaking of research. Deliberate blindness (failure to exercise reasonable foreseeability) is a form of negligence.

Damages

[6.140] A plaintiff must show that he or she suffered from harm, and that the harm was caused by the defendant's act or omission. Just as one can cause harm to another, but will not be liable at law if he or she was

[6.140] not negligent, a person can be negligent, but will not be liable at law if no damage has been caused. You can give the wrong drug, fail to record crucial medical information about a patient, or leave that person unattended when care is required, for example, causing them distress, worry, and discomfort. But if no harm in legal terms has been caused, they can do nothing to obtain compensation through suing in negligence for this (although disciplinary action for professional misconduct can be taken; see Ch 13). Similarly, of course, you cannot bring an action if you have suffered harm but cannot show that it was caused by another's negligence.

[6.141] In law, the amount of compensation granted as the result of a successful negligence action is referred to as "damages". The harm caused may vary from being very minimal to death. In the former case the law will not award damages where harm has been so slight or vague ("de minimus") that it is considered a waste of the court's time to pursue the matter. Previously, no damages were awarded for the death of a person either, as only the person harmed could bring suit (the action dies with the plaintiff). The obvious hardship to a bereaved dependent family was mitigated in the last century in most States of Australia by legislation allowing particular close relatives to receive compensation where they can prove negligence, and that they have suffered pecuniary loss from the death of the victim.[1] Payment incurred for medical treatment, funeral expenses, etc, may also be recovered by a third person. A widow or child may sue where the deceased provided them with maintenance, but death itself, and the grief it causes, has no value in the eyes of the law, except where it results in long-term and serious psychological harm (see [6.103]). There are exceptions in South Australia and the Northern Territory, where a sum of money can be awarded for the grief and suffering caused by the death of a loved one ("solatium").

[6.142] When claiming damages, one lists financial losses as either "specific" or "general". They may also be for losses which are past, or anticipated in the future.

Types of Damages

Specific Damages

[6.143] Specific damages are those which can be accurately listed, item by item, with receipts for the amount paid. They include such things as medical expenses, cost of appliances or housing alterations for someone with a physical disability, or specific loss of income through illness. They are generally expenses already incurred, or future expenses for which a specific quote can be produced.

---

[1] *Compensation (Fatal Injuries) Act* 1968 (ACT); *Compensation to Relatives Act* 1897 (NSW); *Compensation (Fatal Injuries) Act* 1974 (NT); *Supreme Court Act* 1995 (Qld); *Wrongs Act* 1936 (SA); *Fatal Accidents Act* 1934 (Tas); *Wrongs Act* 1958 (Vic); *Fatal Accidents Act* 1959 (WA).

General Damages

[6.144] General damages are those which are not amenable to accurate assessment, such as pain and suffering, anticipated loss of income and medical expenses. They are necessarily estimates, based on such things as:

- .....actuarial calculations;
- .....opinions as to future inflation rates;
- .....likelihood of the lifespan of the plaintiff if he or she had not suffered the injury;
- .....her or his ability to earn in future years; and
- .....the probable long-term progression of the plaintiff's condition.

[6.145] The court, then, in assessing damages, will consider:

- .....payment, past and predicted, for medical care and rehabilitation;
- .....cost of amenities which may be required for both welfare and general living;
- .....loss of earnings which have been incurred, up to the normally predicted retiring age;
- .....any financial obligations, such as the maintenance of family, that one may have; and,
- .....where it is considered that pain and suffering are inordinate, a sum of money may be awarded for that as well.

Most States in Australia have a system where a "once and for all" sum is calculated and awarded at the time of the trial. No change can be made in that sum, despite either the unexpected improvement, or the unexpected deterioration, of the plaintiff. Some States are working with what is believed to be a more realistic approach—that of periodic payment, where the needs of the plaintiff are monitored and any improvement or deterioration can be catered for. "Structured settlements" may be entered into by agreement of the parties, whereby compensation is paid in increments and in a way that is more useful to the plaintiff than a lump sum.

Types of Harm

[6.146] There are three types of harm recognised at law. They are physical, economic and psychological harm.

Physical Harm

[6.147] This is self-explanatory. Harm to the body which can be objectively measured in terms of physical change to the body or to the use of it, as well as harm to mental faculties caused by physical injury, would come under this category. It is of interest that physical harm of the same magnitude may be of more serious consequence to one person than to another, for example, minor damage to the nerves of the left hand may not be of much importance to a right-handed academic, but may be a handicap of momentous proportions to a concert pianist, or even quite

[6.147] significant to a person who plays the piano for pleasure. It can be seen that these two people could be harmed, economically in the first case, and emotionally in both. It is hard sometimes to separate these different categories.

Economic Harm

[6.148] The concert pianist could certainly suffer such harm in the example given above. Loss of income, both past and future, is considered by the courts, as well as such things as expenses for medical treatment and replacement and acquisition of property which may be required due to the harm. Expenses such as those incurred in giving the plaintiff holidays away from permanent hospitalisation to maintain morale have been awarded by the courts (see for example, *Sharman v Evans* (1977) 138 CLR 563).

[6.149] Dependents of a person who has been physically harmed by negligence may sue where the injured person is no longer able to support them at all, or to the same degree, because of the harm. These may be, for example, a spouse, parents or children. The important thing is that the damages are quantified. Thus, as stated, the death of a person in itself is not recognised in compensation: it is only when those left behind can show that the death has resulted in an economic loss. As expressed by one judge:

> Sorrow does not sound in damages. A plaintiff in an action for negligence cannot recover damages for a 'shock', however grievous, which was no more than an immediate emotional response to a distressing experience, sudden, severe and saddening [*Mt Isa Mines v Pusey* (1970) 125 CLR 383 per Windeyer J at 395].

Psychological Harm

[6.150] This is called in law "nervous shock". In restricted circumstances it is compensation for medically recognised, permanent and significant psychological harm which results from someone's negligence. Generally, the only people eligible are those who directly experience or witness the harmful event, or relatives who suffer nervous shock as a result of learning of the harm. Also, the person claiming must be able to show that they were a person of normal fortitude in the first place, or if not, that the defendant knew or ought to have known that they were not, and failed to act accordingly (see *Miller's* case, below, and *Jaensch v Coffey* at [6.51] for a more detailed discussion of this issue). Most cases involving nervous shock flow from the plaintiff being present at the scene of a horrendous accident, or being a rescuer at such a scene (*Mt Isa Mines v Pusey*, above, plaintiff was present at work accident where two colleagues died, one of whom he assisted), or being a spouse or parent of someone who suffers a sudden fatal accident (*Jaensch v Coffey, Petrie v Dowling* [1989] Aust Torts Reports ¶80-263, *McCabe v Auburn District Hospital*, SC NSW, May 1999). For an outline of the gradual acknowledgement of nervous shock by the courts and an assessment of the current state of the law see Dunford and Pickford (1999).

[6.151] Two cases which involved different approaches to nurses and nervous shock suffered as the result of their actions are worth considering.

CASE
Miller v Royal Derwent Hospital Board of Management [1992] Aust Torts Reports ¶81-175 (SC Tas)

A nurse on night duty placed a six-year-old boy in a chair and secured him with a velcro strap for his protection. Unfortunately, after she went off duty, the boy slipped down in the chair and strangled on the strap. The issue in this case was not the negligence or otherwise of the boy's treatment, but rather the effect of the news of his death on the nurse, who was rung and told of the incident. She received no counselling after the incident, and her somewhat irresolute early attempts to talk about the matter to friends were unsuccessful. She suffered so extensively from the incident (including psychiatric illness) that she sued the hospital for damages.

[6.152] The court held that the hospital had a duty of care to the nurse to provide her with emotional support consequent upon her being informed of the death of the boy. The provision of such support was commonly provided in other similar circumstances. Support was offered the day staff, whilst "surprisingly" in the judge's view, no such support was offered to the plaintiff. "A moment's reflection" the court held, would have made it clear that the plaintiff would suffer emotionally more than the other staff. However what was required did not amount to offering or providing formal counselling. Evidence was accepted that in 1987 the provision of such counselling in like situations was not recognised as appropriate or suitable. Further, given the plaintiff's past history, her predisposition to such an outcome meant that the counselling would have been of doubtful assistance. The defendants exhibited "thoughtless indifference" to the plaintiff's wellbeing in not taking interventionist steps which would have prevented the nervous shock, or at least would have minimised its injurious effect. However, she had not established that the injury was foreseeable in the circumstances, or that causation had been established. This result makes it difficult to determine when counselling should be made available to nurses in the event of patients' deaths or other distressing situations. It also raises further issues which readers might like to consider:

- ..... As a lawyer, could one argue that the fact that some hospitals have more recently instituted staff counselling programs for such situations indicate that such an effect would be foreseeable today?
- ..... Should it be dependent upon health carers themselves to recognise that they need support in coping with the emotional and stressful situations that arise from their work? Health carers, particularly the medical profession, have been recognised as having an extraordinarily high level of stress-related illness, including suicide. Does this indicate foreseeability, and a duty of care, to be less dismissive of the problem? Who, if anyone, has the duty of care?

[6.152] ▌.....How does one reconcile this finding with the "egg shell skull" rule (see [6.158] below)?

[6.153] The second case was quite different.

▌▌ CASE
Millicent and District Hospital Inc v Kelly (10 September 1996, SC SA, No SCGRG 2486 of 1995 S5798)

This case involved a woman of 19 years who was 10 to 12 weeks pregnant. She was admitted to hospital after abdominal pain and bleeding, and became distressed that she may have suffered a miscarriage. After undergoing dilation and curettage, she awoke and saw a clear plastic specimen bottle containing what she took to be a part of a limb. She turned away and asked a nurse to remove the container. A group of nurses who were in the room failed to remove the container, and one of them said that sometimes doctors do that to help the patient accept that they have had a miscarriage. The patient subsequently developed a mild post-traumatic stress disorder. She sued in negligence, and was awarded $20,000 in damages, and the hospital appealed, arguing that the cause of the patient's harm was seeing the specimen in an "emotionally charged, vulnerable and prescribed drug-induced state affecting her faculties", and not the failure of the nurses to remove it when it was obviously distressing her.

[6.154] The court held that the respondent was "splitting hairs" and its argument was not relevant, and that cause was proved. It held that there was foreseeability of harm in that the defendant could and should have foreseen that the sight of the container with its contents would augment the distress of the miscarriage, and that it could, and should, have foreseen that that distress would descend into illness. By leaving the container in place, and in effect stating that this was to make her realise she had lost the child, the defendant was in breach of the duty it owed the plaintiff.

[6.155] While the second case found the nurses negligent, it is suggested that it is based on more sound reasoning, given the principles established above regarding duty of care and the standard of care to be applied, and that the purpose of the law of negligence is to ensure that care is taken not to harm those who one "ought to have in contemplation" as being reasonably likely to be harmed by one's actions. It also shows how careful health carers should be that their actions are not inconsiderate—for people can be very vulnerable, especially when ill, suffering mishaps in pregnancy, or under the influence of medication.

Legislative Provisions

[6.156] In the Australian Capital Territory, New South Wales and the Northern Territory a parent or spouse of a person harmed by another may recover damages for nervous shock regardless of whether they were present at the scene of the harm. Other family members may recover damages if they were in sight or hearing of the harmful incident. This is regardless of whether the person harmed has an action in negligence or not.[2]

Wrongful Life

[6.157] Cases have arisen where a child is born with disabilities when, had the mother known of this likelihood, she would have had an abortion. Other cases have involved failed sterilisation or contraception due to negligence. In those cases, the mother or parents can sue for the effects of bearing and rearing the child, including the economic, emotional and physical burden. Can the child sue for having been born to a life of difficulty, pain and suffering? Such an action is known as a "wrongful life" action. Courts have refused to recognise, on policy grounds, that no life is better than life itself (based on the "sanctity of life principle": see further Chapter 14). Earlier cases in this chapter have dealt with children born with disabilities due to negligence. In the case of *Rand v East Dorset Health Authority* [2000] Ll Law Rep (Medical) 181 a baby was born with Down Syndrome as the result of negligent failure to identify the condition in time for the mother to have an abortion. The court held that to pay the full cost of maintenance of the child (as opposed to that in excess of the normal cost of raising a child, would entail comparison of existence to non-existence. Only the losses related to the disability were recoverable, such as losses to a business from having to give up work to care for the child.

Amount of Damage

[6.158] Once it has been established that a defendant owed a duty of care to the plaintiff, he or she will be liable for all the harm that he or she has negligently caused. It is the *type* of harm that must be foreseen, not the extent of it. This may seem a contradiction in terms, but it matters not if the plaintiff suffered from a condition which made him or her abnormally susceptible to harm. This is called the "egg-shell skull" rule, and was established as long ago as 1901:

> it is no answer to the sufferer's claim for damages that he would have suffered less injury or no injury at all, if he had not had an unusually thin skull or an unusually weak heart [*Dulieu v White & Son* [1901] 2 KB 669 at 679].

---

[2] *Law Reform (Miscellaneous Provisions) Act* 1955 (ACT); *Law Reform (Miscellaneous Provisions) Act* 1944 (NSW); *Law Reform (Miscellaneous Provisions) Act* 1956 (NT), Pt IV.

Causation

Defendant must have Actually caused the Plaintiff's Harm

[6.159] The determination of whether a particular course of action or an omission caused an event is not without problems in the law. Often the "chain of causation" is determined by what is called the "but-for" test. That is the first step in determining legal causation, and is most appropriate where the facts are relatively simple. The "but-for" test is satisfied if it can be shown that the damage would not have occurred "but-for" the defendant's negligent act. This can best be illustrated by the following case.

CASE

Barnett v Chelsea and Kensington Hospital Management Committee [1969] 1 QB 428 (High Court England)

Mr Barnett and his fellow workers were nightwatchmen. One New Year's Eve they felt very ill after drinking their tea. They went to the local hospital, where the nurse thought they were drunk, but she was pressed to call the doctor. Unfortunately he also felt sick and left instructions for them to contact their own doctor the next day. They left, but five hours later Barnett died. It seems arsenic had been put into the tea. Barnett's widow sued the hospital and the doctor, alleging that he had a duty of care to treat her husband and had failed to discharge this duty, causing his death.

[6.160] It might seem just that the doctor pay for neglecting the man, but in fact he was not held to be liable. Let us consider why. Firstly, it would seem that he had a duty of care to Mr Barnett. Indeed he did. So he had an obligation to attend to him: the first requirement for proving negligence had been fulfilled. A reasonable doctor would have foreseen that failure to see him and treat him could result in the patient suffering from further harm. In fact he did not even attempt to diagnose Barnett's illness. The second requirement for proving negligence had been met. However, the doctor escaped liability because the doctor's lawyer was able to convince the court that even if the doctor had given Barnett the best and most prompt treatment available, he still would have died. It could not be shown that "but for" the doctor's refusal to treat him, Barnett would not have died. The doctor's failure to act was thus held not to be the cause of Barnett's death. All three elements of the negligence action must be proved for it to succeed, and Mrs Barnett had not been able to prove the third element; that of causation.

[6.161] Another important fact to take from this case is that omissions, or failure to act can be just as culpable in the eyes of the law as actions.

■ ■ ■ CASE [6.164]
Wilsher v Essex Area Health Authority [1988] 1 All ER 871 (House of Lords England)

(Different aspects of this case are also considered at [6.100]).

A premature neonate suffered almost total blindness after intensive care. During that time a catheter was twice inserted into a vein rather than an artery, and in both cases he was given excess oxygen. The child (through its representatives) sued the hospital in negligence.

[6.162] Both the trial judge and the Court of Appeal ruled in favour of the plaintiff, and the defendant appealed to the House of Lords. There was no question that a duty of care had existed between the child and the Health Authority, and that the duty of care had been breached. However, the House of Lords overturned the earlier decisions on the basis that causation had not been adequately proved. The child could have developed the blindness from several conditions he had suffered, such as patent ductus arteriosus, hypercapnia, intraventricular haemorrhage, and apnoea. Expert witnesses had differed on what had caused the blindness, and the Court was not satisfied that the plaintiff had proved, on the balance of probabilities that the blindness had been caused by the excessive oxygen. The Court held that where there are a number of possible causes of harm, one of which is the defendant's breach of duty of care, the combination of the breach of duty and the harm is not enough to make them liable. It was not up to the defendant to prove they did *not* cause the harm: the plaintiff must prove that they did. On this basis the Court could not find the defendant negligent.

■ ■ ■ CASE
Hotson v East Berkshire Area Health Authority [1987] 2 All ER 909 (House of Lords England)

As the result of a fall, the plaintiff developed avascular necrosis, but the employees of the health authority did not diagnose this for five days. The plaintiff sued the Authority, stating that the failure to diagnose was the cause of the necrosis.

[6.163] The House of Lords heard expert evidence and decided that, had the diagnosis been made promptly, the plaintiff would still have developed the necrosis. The cause was not the failure to diagnose or treat the plaintiff's condition.

Remoteness of Damage

[6.164] However, the "but for" test is an inclusive one, and, if taken to its extreme, could stretch back in time indefinitely (for example, but for your good grades at school, you wouldn't have studied medicine—but for your missing out a position at another hospital, you would not have been working at this one, but for your working at this hospital, you would not be treating cancer patients, and so on). To limit those factors which should be included in the legal causation of an event, the courts have

[6.164]   again turned to foreseeability, and limit liability to those events which are reasonably foreseeable and not too remote.

Common Sense Approach

[6.165] More recently, the courts have adopted the approach of "common sense" when determining cause. This approach was adopted in *Chappel v Hart* (see [4.111]), but there is criticism of the court's approach it being alleged that, while the reasoning of some judges was based on the common sense reasoning that the higher the skill of the surgeon, the less the risk of harm, in fact the risk of harm was just the same, no matter who operated. The skill of the surgeon may have meant that statistically the harm would have been less likely, but it was not negligence on the part of the defendant who caused the harm. There was not proof that "but for" his actions the plaintiff would not have suffered harm: she may well have done even with a more skilled surgeon. What she "suffered" as a result of Dr Chappel's omission was a lost chance, not physical or mental (Clarke (1999)). Is the "common sense" approach to causation policy in another guise? For a detailed discussion of causation, especially in relation to *Chappell v Hart,* see Grunson (2000).

[6.166] However, the "common sense" approach does not include constructing a cause where this does not exist.

▌▌▌ CASE

Metropolitan Health Service v King [1999] WASCA 236 No 204 of 1998 (CA WA)

Shortly after Mr King's discharge from the hospital after the third of a series of treatments there, he was diagnosed with thoracic osteomyelitis resulting from enterobacter cloacae infection. This required intensive treatment.

The trial judge found that the infection was contracted during the third period of hospitalisation and that it was caused by an unidentified nurse's handling of his intravenous (IV) infusion. The judge awarded the respondent $30,000 in damages.

An intravenous cannula had been inserted into a peripheral vein in the left arm. Hospital procedure required that once an IV infusion is inserted by a doctor, the nursing staff monitor it and change infusion bags or patient controlled analgesia syringes as required. The court recognised that despite aseptic procedures, infection can occur without negligence.

King alleged that he was woken in the middle of the night of either 14 or 15 December 1995 and:

▌ ..... his IV infusion bag was changed by a nurse whose name is unknown;
▌ ..... whilst the nurse was attempting to unfasten the plastic tube from the cannula she dislodged the cannula and it slid partially out of Mr King's left arm causing sharp pain and bleeding from the site;
▌ ..... the nurse mopped up the blood with Kleenex tissues, changed the saline bag, mopped up some further blood and slid the cannula back into the plaintiff's arm; and

■.....the nurse did not wash her hands or swab the cannula site with antiseptic solution prior to sliding the cannula back into the plaintiff's arm.

Nursing notes showed no change of IV infusion during the night. They recorded that it was changed late the evening before, and early the next morning.

On 16 December, at about 10.30 am, records showed that the infusion was running into the surrounding tissues rather than the vein, and the cannula was removed.

Second siting of the IV infusion

Records showed that on 16 December, at about 8.45pm, a new Intravenous infusion was inserted in another site on the same arm. They also showed that on 18 December the second infusion site was found to be red, swollen and painful, and the patient hot and feverish.

The trial judge cited hospital requirements that nurses should not attempt to push back a dislodged cannula for fear of infection and/or damage. It should be removed, and a new cannula inserted elsewhere by a doctor using proper aseptic procedures. If the events described by the respondent did happen, he ruled, the nurse could be found negligent. Relying solely on King's evidence, despite the nurses' notes, he ruled that they did occur.

The next question was whether the "cannula incident" caused the respondent's infection. That required expert opinion and is where the trial seemed to come unstuck. Experts said the infection arose at the *second site.* If the "cannula incident" occurred before the drip was resited, it could not have caused the infection in question. The trial judge resolved this difficulty by simply declaring that the cannula incident must have happened later, *after* the resiting of the cannula to the second site in the left arm.

The defendant appealed, claiming that the verdict should have been in favour of the appellant because the judge was not entitled to overcome the causal difficulty for the respondent by making a finding, unsupported by any evaluation of the evidence as to when the incident occurred (King insisted the incident occurred in relation to the first site). No reason was given by the judge for the finding that he made.

[6.167] The hospital's arguments were accepted by the Court of Appeal. It found that there was no record of the presence of signs of infection at the first site, and infection was not the reason for removal of the drip from that site. The first recorded observation of a drip site infection was at the second site, two days after. There seems little doubt that this infection, the signs of which were inflammation and soreness, was at the second site. If, the "cannula incident" occurred at any time before removal from the first site, it could not have caused this infection. There was no suggestion that the infection at the second site was caused by negligent handling of the cannula at the first site, or that both sites became infected. It found that the infected site (unquestionably the second site), was the point of infection entry. Thus, there was no evidence that the "cannula incident" (if indeed it did occur) was the cause of the infection in question.

[6.168] The Appeal Court concluded that on the respondent's own evidence at trial, any mishandling of the cannula would have occurred at a time which exonerated it from blame for the subsequent infection.

[6.169] **[6.169]** The following case is instructive regarding negligence, which also gives some good advice regarding seeking assistance where there is inadequate staff (not to mention tea breaks and care of post-operative patients).

▌▌▌ CASE
Laidlaw v Lion's Gate Hospital (1969) 70 WWR 727 (SC British Columbia Canada)

Cara Laidlaw was admitted to the post-operative room of the hospital after a routine cholecystectomy. There were eight stations in the room, and two nurses on duty at the time. When Mrs Laidlaw arrived, nurse M had left for coffee, and so nurse S was alone with two patients, a third arriving in nurse M's absence before Mrs Laidlaw and yet another patient (R) arriving after her. This last patient was accompanied by an anaesthetist and a nurse who then, it seems, left. Nurse S had interrupted her attentions to each patient as the next arrived, not finishing their observations. By this time a patient had left, so nurse S was caring for four patients. She left Mrs Laidlaw's observations to administer an injection to R, and after this answered the telephone before returning to Mrs Laidlaw who was in severe respiratory distress and required resuscitation. As a result she sustained permanent, extensive brain damage.

[6.170] This case is very complex, and only some actions of the nurses will be considered here. We will look at what the nurses later said about their behaviour to the court. They acknowledged that normally it was the practice of the hospital, and their practice, for two nurses to be on duty at all times when the room was in use. However, coffee breaks are taken when things are quiet, and the remaining nurse can also call on extra help if she needs it. The nurses said they did not expect the patients to bunch up so rapidly. The court responded that when five patients are scheduled for surgery, nurses should be ready to receive them at any time, thus nurse M should not have gone for coffee; or at least the nurses should have asked for someone to relieve her. Nurse S should have called for assistance, anyway, when things got busy (she could also have called on the staff entering the room). In giving their opinion with regard to the standard of care required, medical witnesses spoke in terms of constant and total care, with observation every minute or two, considering the particular vulnerability of post-operative patients.

[6.171] These days a different situation may arise in post-operative care rooms. Modern technology provides technology which automatically monitors vital signs such as blood pressure, pulse, temperature, etc, either constantly or at intervals, and sounds an alarm if these are abnormal. This means staff do not have to be physically at the bedside of patients so frequently and can concentrate on other matters. The legal issues will change as well. What will become important from the legal point of view will be the reliance one can place on the technology, which will be translated into such questions as how reasonable it is to trust these machines, and under what conditions and for how long it is reasonable to entrust a patient to them.

When one Does Not Feel Capable of Reasonable Care [6.174]

[6.172] There may be occasions where a health carer feels that because, for example, of lack of training, experience or resources, he or she cannot offer a reasonable standard of care. It is suggested that the Checklist at [6.111] regarding unsatisfactory situation should be followed. With proper notice, this shifts to the principal (that is, the employer or facility engaging the health carer as a visiting medical officer or otherwise, to carry out its enterprise) the legal responsibility of providing reasonable care to the client.

[6.173] This advice is based on the following reasoning:

- When negotiating a position as a health carer, prospective appointees should quite clearly confirm the area or areas in which they might be required to work. They and the principal should ensure that they will not be required in an area in which they are not suitably qualified, unless the intention is to provide necessary training and experience in that area.
- Where a principal may require an applicant for a position in, for example, employing a nurse to carry out any duties (such as "relieving" on the wards) as required from time to time, and the applicant may agree to do this, health carers should not undertake health care for which they are not competent, nor should the principal expect them to do this.

[6.174] The respective responsibilities of employees and employers are set out in Figure 6.1.

FIGURE 6.1

RESPECTIVE RESPONSIBILITIES OF EMPLOYERS AND EMPLOYEES

(That is, an employer or facility engaging them as a visiting medical officer or otherwise to carry out its enterprise).

Carer's duty to client	To provide reasonable care (as outlined in this chapter).
Carer's duty to principal	To further the objectives of the principal by providing reasonably competent health care to clients. This would include discussion of her or his experience and competencies, so that he or she can be appropriately placed to provide services to clients (see Chapter 11 on the contract of employment).
Employer's duty to client	To provide reasonable services, including adequate and competent staff (see also Chapter 11).

[6.174]

| Employer's duty to carer | To provide adequate and safe facilities, staff training and support so that he or she can provide reasonable care to the client (see also Chapter 11). As shown by *Miller's case*, it has not been established whether this includes facilities for stress, grief and psychological anguish such as counselling, de-briefing or leave. |

[6.175] By informing the principal of one's lack of competence, one is invoking the principal's, as well as the health carer's, duty of care to the patient, and placing on the principal the responsibility of finding, if he or she believes it is necessary and reasonable, someone else to provide the care for patients. The carer has taken reasonable steps to ensure proper care if the principal has been adequately and initially informed of her or his qualifications or lack of them: it is then up to the principal.

[6.176] If the employer is told that an employee does not feel competent to work in a particular area and does not change the situation, the employer has taken the risk of breach of duty of care. The employee's responsibility, in obeying the direction to work under these circumstances is:

1)......to give the best care possible under the circumstances; and
2)......to make sure that there is adequate evidence of the employer having been informed. The employee should make a written report of the situation (an incident report is one effective way, witnessed if possible). Some institutions have highly structured and quite limited incident report forms. This should not deter carers from filling them in as best they can, attaching further pages if necessary. Most systems involve regular formal review of such forms by safety committees, quality assurance review committees, etc, so matters such as frequent allocation of insufficiently experienced staff or under-staffing must be addressed at a management level if they are reported as "incidents". See the Checklist "Principles for Action when a Situation Causes Concern" at [6.110].

Vicarious Liability

[6.177] Liability at law for negligence is personal: that is, it is sheeted home to the actual individual who caused the harm. There are, however, exceptions to this principle. Where a client suffers harm as the result of negligence on the part of an employee, the client may in fact sue the employer, not the individual health carer, as an employer is vicariously liable for the negligence of its employees. This can also apply to someone who is acting as the agent of another (this is not to be confused with independent contracting, such as agency nursing, where vicarious liability depends on the determination of "control"—see [6.182]).

[6.178] Vicarious liability is based on the principle that you are responsible for the actions of those you engage to do your work for you. It stems from the ancient common law principle of responsibility of a master for his servant (women generally could not contract at law until recently). This means that despite the utmost effort on the part of the employer to ensure that the best care is given to its clients, and even the lack of knowledge on the part of the employer of the negligent activity, so long as the employee is carrying out activities which are part of the employer's enterprise, the employer is responsible for the client's welfare.

[6.179] Where a patient suffers harm from the actions of health care employees, that person can sue both the health care facility (for example, a hospital) and any staff he or she believes responsible. The hospital is the first in the line of possible defendants for three reasons. First, the hospital has a duty of care to those who come under its care, and has undertaken to have the resources to do so. Secondly, a contract exists between the patient and a hospital or other health care facility which obliges it to give reasonable care. Finally, the facility is more likely to be able to compensate the patient, because of its financial resources and insurance back-up. It is no good suing someone who cannot pay. However, a patient may choose to sue either, or both, the health carer and the hospital, in which case the court may order respective damages payable by both parties, depending on their contribution to the harm caused.

[6.180] The two questions involved in establishing the existence of vicarious liability are:

- whether the person involved was an employee or agent at the time he or she caused the harm; and
- whether the harm was caused by actions carried out in the course of employment.

Who is an Employee?

[6.181] A person who works for another for pay may be either an employee or an independent contractor. This is another complex and confusing issue at law, but it is suggested that the best way to determine it is to consider the case of *Stevens v Brodribb Sawmilling Co Pty Ltd* (1986) 60 ALJR 194. In that case the High Court of Australia considered how to determine whether someone was an employee. The judges considered various tests that have been devised in the past and came to the conclusion that tests should be applied to a contract to do work for someone, to distinguish the employee whom one engages to work for one, from the independent contractor such as a plumber, whom one engages to carry out a specific job.

Tests used to Determine Employment

[6.182] With the development of complex outsourcing and other arrangements for bodies to carry out their functions, it may sometimes be hard to determine whether a person is an employee of a particular enterprise or not. The courts will approach the question of deciding who is an employee by using several tests, generally in the following order:

[6.182]   1).....**Control test**. This test is the surest guide to whether a contract of employment or some other contract exists between the parties. The test considers how much control the alleged employer has over the work of the alleged employee: does it control the place of work, the facilities, the manner in which it is carried out, the tools of trade, hours of work, and so on? The more often one can answer "yes" to these questions, the more likely it is that the person is an employee.

Where the person performing services is a professional or an artist, exercising skill, expertise or judgment beyond the capacity of the employer, the employer may not actually have much scope for controlling the employee's actions. However, there may be, in the conditions of employment, authority to command inasmuch as there is scope for it. A trapeze artist has been held to be an employee of a circus, because the circus management could direct times and places of performance, rehearsal times, pay and leave conditions, and supplementary duties. This was held to override any freedom the artist had in carrying out his art (*Zuijs v Wirth Bros Pty Ltd* (1955) 93 CLR 561).

2).....The **Organisation Test** can be used to clarify the position. This test considers the extent to which a person's work contributes to the general enterprise of the apparent employer. If the person's work is integral to the organisation's activities (for example, delivering health care) it is more likely to be a contract of employment. If the work is peripheral to the organisation's activities (for example, development of a new wing of the hospital building) it is more likely to be a contract of employment. This test is also not a complete approach, and has been met with judicial criticism, for example in *Ellis v Wallsend District Hospital* below. In that case Mason J stated that the organisation test does no more than shift the focus to whether the person was part of the organisation's enterprise or not.

3).....**Other tests.** Conditions such as the right to dismiss, to set the conditions and hours of work, the right to the exclusive services of the person and the ownership and maintenance of equipment also indicate that a person is an employee rather than an independent contractor.

[6.183] Courts have distinguished between health care professionals who have been selected by clients to treat them in a hospital or other institution or clinic, and those selected by the treating body itself. The case of *Albrighton v Royal Prince Alfred Hospital* [1980] 2 NSWLR 542 (see [6.37]) addressed this issue. There it was held that where the patient selects the treating health professional, the hospital is not responsible for the negligence of that professional; however, this principle must be qualified by the tests above, in that the court will consider the arrangements under which the professional works. If they are required to abide by hospital rules, standards and procedures, for example, thereby submitting to some extent to the hospital's control, they may become part of the organisation and the hospital may well be found liable for their negligence. In the *Albrighton* case the court considered that because the doctors accepted and complied with the hospital's forms and routines, and had abided by its by-laws they were employees. A lot depends on the nature of the action which caused the harm: whether it was solely based on the visiting doctor's professional judgment, over which the hospital may have had no control, or whether it was an action pursuant to hospital rules or standards by which the professional has agreed to be bound.

▮▮▮ CASE [6.186]
Ellis v Wallsend District Hospital [1989] Aust Torts Reports ¶80-289

E agreed to undergo an excision of certain neck vertebrae and division of nerve roots. The surgeon was a visiting surgeon at the hospital. Consent was given in the belief that the procedure would probably relieve chronic neck pain, after considerable hesitation and several requests for assurances from the surgeon concerning the safety of the procedure. Although the surgeon told her the procedure was unusual, he did not mention that there was a risk of developing paraplegia and a low prospect of relieving pain. After the procedure E developed quadriplegia. E commenced action against the surgeon in negligence against the surgeon and the hospital. The surgeon died and E settled her claim against his estate. She continued her action against the hospital. The court's finding in relation to negligence is set out at [6.190]–[6.193]. The question as to whether the hospital was vicariously liable was also considered by the court.

[6.184] The court held that the hospital was not vicariously responsible for the surgeon's negligence. The majority held that E had established a relationship with the surgeon before entering the hospital, which had in no sense chosen the surgeon for her. The majority approached the matter by asking the question, in treating E, was the surgeon acting on his own, or the hospital's behalf? He had an agreement with the hospital whereby he undertook to treat free of charge patients who came to the hospital for relief, in exchange for the use of facilities and nursing services for those of his own patients who he would book into the hospital. The patients he booked in would pay the hospital for its services. Honorary medical staff were subject to the control of the hospital in some degree, being required to adhere to directions for maintaining administrative efficiency and integrity. However, the majority held, these did not amount to such control as would render the hospital vicariously liable for their actions. Indeed they considered that the surgeon was an independent specialist working on his own account in the treatment of the hospital's patients. He was never an employee.

[6.185] Kirby P dissented, stating that the hospital benefited by having honorary doctors among their officers, and the hospital "should not be allowed to escape responsibility for injury to patients happening on their premises as a result of the activities of health professionals, including honorary surgeons". He held that the employment relationship did exist between the hospital and the surgeon. The by-laws of the hospital were for mutual benefit, tied the surgeon inextricably into the organisation of the hospital, integrating him into the discipline and direction of the hospital. He held that this was substantiated by the consent form, which stated that no assurance has been given that the operation will be carried out by any particular surgeon.

[6.186] In respect of direct duty of care to E, the court held that where private patients do not have doctors allocated by the hospital but choose their own doctor, the hospital does not owe a duty of care for the doctor's negligent actions, but does owe a duty of care for those of nursing staff and paramedical care.

[6.187] [6.187] An important case which clarifies the position and also deals with negligence in nursing care follows:

▌▌▌ CASE
John James Memorial Hospital Ltd v Keys (21 May 1999, Federal Court of Australia, AG 103 of 1998)

K was 73-years-old and had led an active social and family life up to the time of her hospitalisation. However, she required the aid of a walking frame. In 1996 she consulted a general practitioner with severe sciatic pain and was referred to a consultant physician, Dr G. The pain became so intense that Dr G arranged her admission to the John James Memorial Hospital Ltd for pain relief and observation. She was put on a regime of Tegretol in conjunction with Pethidine. Voltaren, an anti-inflammatory analgesic was also given.

Whilst in hospital she suffered two falls, the first occurring on 23 April. Five nurses were on the day shift (the normal complement), caring for 24 patients in the ward, plus a charge nurse and desk nurse. K was one of about five patients whose care was allocated to registered nurse D. K had been given 200 mg of Tegretol at 6 am. Later that morning, K had been assisted to the bathroom by D, and told to ring the buzzer when ready so that D could assist her to shower.

Meanwhile, D, who was making K's bed, was called to another patient in another room, from which she was unable to hear the buzzer. She returned to K's room after not more than five minutes and resumed making the bed. K's husband arrived and on going to the bathroom to say good morning, found it obstructed by K lying on the floor. After some time (it was "within the hour") and instructing K to move her legs, D gained entry and found K lying on the bathroom floor covered in soap. She was showered and returned to bed.

The second fall occurred in the early hours of the next night. After hearing a loud thump in K's room, registered nurse A and another nurse found K lying on the floor. K told her she had fallen while on the way to the bathroom.

K sued the doctor and the hospital in negligence, for injuries suffered, including exacerbation of her original condition.

The trial judge had found that Nurse D had not been negligent:
▌ ..... in being ignorant of the risk that K was so confused and disorientated that she needed especially close supervision; and
▌ ..... in failing to realise that K was so heavily affected by her medication that she needed constant supervision.

He stated that a patient should not be allowed out of bed if such supervision was required, and no-one had considered that her condition required this. He concluded that D should have been made aware that the drugs she was taking would have the likely effect on K of disorientation and confusion and that she should have been more closely supervised. He found that there was a failure in the chain of communication from the doctor to the nursing staff.

[6.190] The trial judge went on to consider that the hospital was vicariously liable for the acts and omissions of all those involved, including Dr G. He interpreted *Albrighton v Royal Prince Alfred Hospital* (above) as setting out the principle that a hospital is vicariously liable for the acts and omissions not only of its employed staff but "also those doctors whose patients the hospital admits for care and treatment under the doctors, whether the doctors are paid by the hospital or not". As he believed that the nursing staff on duty at the time had not been properly advised as to the probable effect of the drugs, the hospital was vicariously liable for the omission.

K was awarded $69,248 for the injuries she suffered in both falls. The matter was appealed by the defendant hospital.

Vicarious Liability

[6.188] The Appeal Court held that before the trial judge could hold the hospital liable for the effect of a failure at an unidentified point in the chain of communication between Dr G and Sister D, it was necessary to ensure that the hospital was liable for the acts and omissions of every participant in the chain.

[6.189] It found that the trial judge had misstated the effect of *Albrighton*. That case only provides that a hospital *may* be liable for the acts and omissions of a treating, non-employed doctor. A hospital is vicariously liable where it functions as a place where a person in need of treatment goes to obtain treatment, but not, as in this case, where it functions merely as the provider of medical care facilities as an adjunct to the doctor's treatment of the patient. Consideration should be given to the circumstances of K's admission, the arrangements regarding control of the hospital over the doctor's work, matters of remuneration, and the doctor's obligation to work. In this case K selected Dr G through her general practitioner, not the hospital. Dr G chose the hospital, not the reverse. K was being treated as a private patient in a private hospital and Dr G was apparently remunerated by her insurer.

Negligence

[6.190] Dr G and Nurse D had both testified that they knew Tegretol could cause drowsiness and could possibly lead to confusion. Nurse D was not aware of it causing disorientation. K at the time of her first fall was in a "confused and disorientated state" and both Nurse D and Dr G testified that confusion and disorientation was foreseeable by any trained person who had knowledge of K's medication regime. Nurse D had conceded in her evidence that it was not necessary for her to be informed by a "chain of communication" stemming from Dr G, that K was likely to be experiencing drowsiness and possible confusion as a result of the medication.

[6.191] **[6.191]** The Appeal Court concluded that Nurse D:

- ..... knew, or should have known, of the probability of confusion and disorientation as a result of the medication;
- ..... knew that if she left K's bedroom she would not be able to hear the buzzer inside the toilet; and
- ..... should have realised that, if she did not answer the buzzer, K might move without assistance and suffer a fall.

[6.192] It was thus negligent of Nurse D to leave the bedroom, without warning K or checking on her. It was foreseeable that, during Nurse D's absence from the bedroom, K would, forgetting or unable to obtain assistance, undertake the risky step of moving without it.

[6.193] The Court agreed that the nature and extent of the injuries sustained by K, and the effects of the accident upon her and her life, warranted a higher award of general damages than had been awarded by the trial judge. The Court increased the award to $30,000 for general damages. Judgment was entered for K in the sum of $82,448 plus costs.

Who is an Agent?

[6.194] An agent is someone engaged to act in the principal's interest, to carry out a service one has undertaken to offer the client. Honorary and visiting medical officers, anaesthetists, and others retained by an institution may be just as much the institution's responsibility in negligence as the employees. In the case of *Roe v Minister of Health* [1954] 2 QB 66 Lord Denning stated that a hospital is responsible for all its staff:

> whether they are permanent or temporary, resident or visiting, whole time or part time . . . even if they are not servants, they are the agents of the hospital to give the treatment. The only exception is the case of consultants or anaesthetists selected and employed by the patient himself.

[6.195] The principles above apply to other health carers as well. In most cases the carer engaged by a patient directly, or through an agency, is an independent contractor, the agency not being an employer, but rather simply a source of finding work. As well as specialists who are approached by patients (or referred to them) and treated by them at a facility, nurses engaged directly by a patient or through a nursing agency to care for them in a hospital would be subjected by the courts to the above tests to determine whether they personally are liable to the patient, or whether the hospital should be found vicariously liable. Where the hospital engages nurses through an agency, there is more scope for the hospital's liability, for it becomes more closely responsible for the standard of the nurses' work and having this control over nurses' services, the hospital also fulfils the "organisation test".

[6.196] If a health carer is not working under a contract of employment he or she is very strongly advised to acquire indemnity insurance, which provides cover for harm caused through negligence. Professional bodies can advise as to policies available.

What is Considered to be "in the Course of Employment"?

[6.197] Activities which are directed or authorised by an employer, or those which are reasonably incidental to directed or authorised activities are considered to be within the course of employment. Not everything an employee does is specifically stipulated by an employer. In general health care many of the activities a carer will undertake are implied and many are carried out subject to professional judgment and decision-making. These are all carried out within the course of the employment as they are considered to be authorised by the employer. The administration of a drug, ordered by a physician would be covered, for example, even if that drug were to be given negligently, for the administration of drugs is authorised by the employer. However, for example, the prescribing of a drug of dependence by a nurse would not be covered, as such an action, being beyond the scope of nursing activities, would not be authorised by an employer. Another example is where one is travelling in an employer's motor vehicle, so long as one is either directly on route, or diverting for refreshment, one is within the course of employment (*Chaplin v Dunstan Ltd* [1938] SASR 245). Where the employer has prohibited giving lifts, to do so may take one out of the course of employment. However, compulsory third party insurance would enable those injured to claim against the insurance policy of the owner of the car so long as the driver was authorised to drive it; the question thus becoming academic. In the writer's opinion it is crucial, however, where the employee is injured, in determining whether the employee is eligible for workers' compensation. This is discussed in Chapter 12.

[6.198] Employers can also be liable for negligent work practices and activities which they permit or tolerate.

Indemnity and Contribution

[6.199] Despite the vicarious liability of an employer, there is the corresponding right of the employer to turn to the negligent employee or agent and require them to contribute to compensation for the harm he or she may have caused.

All States and Territories have legislation providing for a defendant to claim a proportionate contribution from a third person who they can show contributed to the harm.[3]

---

[3] *Law Reform (Miscellaneous Provisions) Act* 1955 (ACT); *Law Reform (Miscellaneous Provisions) Act* 1944 (NSW); *Law Reform (Miscellaneous Provisions) Act* 1956 (NT); *Law Reform Act* 1995 (Qld); *Wrongs Act* 1936 (SA); *Tortfeasors' and Contributory Negligence Act* 1954 (Tas); *Wrongs*

[6.200] [6.200] This legislation is limited in New South Wales, South Australia, and the Northern Territory, which gives employees a certain amount of protection from liability.[4] In those jurisdictions without such legislation, action by employers against employees is very rare (perhaps because there is not much chance of the defendant being able to pay!). Certainly it can, and is, more likely to be claimed where the employee is guilty of serious and wilful misconduct.

[6.201] This depends, of course, on negligence being established on the part of the employee. Health carers are not completely immune from liability, and the belief that if you do anything wrong the hospital will stand behind you and take all responsibility should be treated with due scepticism. Certainly, where employees have no money, compensation cannot be extracted from them, but some contribution may be demanded from negligent staff, and the employer also has the options of disciplinary measures (see Chapter 13).

Defences to a Negligence Action

[6.202] When a person is the subject of a negligence action, there are several defences available.

Absolute Defences

[6.203] These are so called because if they can be successfully invoked they release the person from further action absolutely: the case goes no further. Absolute defences are as follows.

Expiration of Limitation Period

[6.204] All jurisdictions have a limitation period beyond which an action cannot be brought.[5] In some jurisdictions it is six years (the Australian Capital Territory, Victoria and Western Australia), others have reduced the length of time to three years (New South Wales, the Northern Territory, Queensland and Tasmania). Where the plaintiff was a minor when harmed, the limitation period does not start to run until the person has reached majority. In the Australian Capital Territory, New South Wales, the Northern Territory and South Australia the time limitation

---

[3] continued
  Act 1958 (Vic); *Law Reform (Contributory Negligence and Tortfeasors' Contribution) Act* 1947 (WA).

[4] *Employees' Act* 1991 (NSW), s 66; *Law Reform (Miscellaneous Provisions) Amendment Act* 1984 (NT), s 22A; *Wrongs Act* 1935 (SA), s 27.

[5] *Limitation Act* 1985 (ACT); *Limitation Act* 1969 (NSW); *Limitation Act* 1981 (NT); *Limitation of Actions Act* 1974 (Qld); *Limitation of Actions Act* 1936 (SA); *Limitation Act* 1974 (Tas); *Limitation of Actions Act* 1958 (Vic); *Limitation Act* 1935 (WA).

after the age of 18 is three years, in the other jurisdictions it is six years. No matter how much harm is suffered, if the action is not brought within the limitation period, it will not be heard. The limitation period runs not from when the accident happened, but from when the effects of the accident first manifest themselves. This may happen many years after the cause of the harm occurred, in the case of some cancers for example, 20 to 30 years after the originating event.

[6.205] Where the plaintiff had no reasonable knowledge of the harm, for example, where the efficacy of treatment was misrepresented, symptoms of the harm were misdiagnosed, or facts were not available, the courts are empowered to make exceptions to the limitation rules.

▌▌▌ CASE
Kosky v Trustees of The Sisters of Charity [1982] VR 961

A pregnant woman had a routine blood test in 1975. This showed she had Rh iso-immunisation. Her son was born prematurely and with brain damage. She happened to read a newspaper report some eight years later about similar effects occurring after the administration of incompatible blood to another woman. She contacted the hospital where she had been treated after a car accident in 1967 to see if she had been given blood. That hospital reported that the wrong blood had been prepared for her, but not given. She persisted in her inquiries and found that this advice was a mistake. The court was asked to extend the limitation period, which has expired, for bringing an action against the hospital.

[6.206] Because she did not have all the information, and could not reasonably have had it within the limitation period, she (and her son) were allowed to bring the action for an event that occurred 13 years earlier, and eight years before the son's conception (see Dix et al (1989), p 234).

No Duty of Care

[6.207] The defendant shows that the requirements for having a duty of care to the plaintiff did not exist or a reasonable person would not have foreseen the likelihood of harm.

No Breach of Duty

[6.208] The defendant admits there was a duty of care, but argues that there was no breach of that duty: all reasonable care was given under the circumstances.

[6.208] ■ ■ ■ CASE
Whitehouse v Jordan [1980] 1 All ER 650 (CA England)

An obstetrician applied forceps during a difficult delivery, and the child was born severely mentally handicapped. The plaintiff, the mother, claimed he had used undue force in delivering the child, and thus was negligent.

[6.209] The doctor was able to adduce evidence, through testimony of his colleagues, that he had not used force which was unreasonable. The court accepted this, expressing the view that there is a difference between genuine mistakes and unreasonable behaviour.

■ ■ ■ CASE
Hart v Herron [1984] Aust Torts Reports ¶80-201 (SC NSW)

The plaintiff sued a psychiatrist in negligence, assault and battery. He had been given electroconvulsive therapy without his consent. He later became gravely ill with pneumonia.

He alleged negligence for the following reasons:

1).....he did not require psychiatric treatment at all;
2).....proper care was not taken to obtain his informed and valid consent;
3).....proper precautions for deep sleep therapy were not taken; and
4).....timely diagnosis of pneumonia was not made, and proper treatment for it not given.

The defendant conceded negligence according to (3) and (4). The question of negligence in relation to (2) is mentioned earlier (see [4.27]).

[6.210] The court referred to *Whitehouse v Jordan* [1980] 1 All ER 650, and applied it to this case. It was thus held that although the defendant differed in his opinion from another medical practitioner this did not mean that he had been negligent. However it was held that so far as (3) was concerned, the fact that Hart was sedated so deeply that he could not be aroused for exercise or use of toilet facilities was backed by evidence that it was a departure from professional practice.

No Causation

[6.211] The defendant here argues that although there was a duty of care, and this was breached, the unreasonable behaviour did not cause the harm (review the case of *Barnett v Chelsea Hospital* at [6.159]).

▌▌▌ CASE [6.213]
X v Pal [1991] Aust Torts Reports ¶81-098 (CA NSW)

A child was born to a woman who had untreated syphilis with multiple abnormalities including intellectual disability, epilepsy and dysmorphia. Two obstetricians and a paediatrician who were treating the mother at the time had failed to test her for syphilis despite her symptoms. Expert medical evidence indicated that the abnormalities could not have been caused by congenital syphilis, for although it is possible for it to result in intellectual disability, this does not normally become evident until much later in the child's development.

Other conditions, such as hepatosplenomegaly, skin rash, jaundice or periositis which would have been pathognomic of syphilis were not present, and the abnormalities the child did have were more likely to be the result of intra-uterine developmental abnormality.

[6.212] The court held that although the child was born with congenital syphilis, many of the abnormalities were not caused by that condition but from another unspecified cause. Damages were limited to the fact that the child was, as a result of the defendants' negligence, born with the disease, and did not cover those abnormalities which the plaintiff could not show were caused by it. The sum awarded was $15,000. See also *Hotson v East Berkshire Area Health Authority* [1987] 2 All ER 909, where it was held that avascular necrosis suffered by a man after a fall and delay of five days for proper treatment after misdiagnosis was not caused by the delay but the original injury.

No cause Because of Intervening Factor (novus actus interveniens)

[6.213] Sometimes a defendant will concede that he or she acted negligently, and perhaps even caused some harm. However it is argued that after this negligent action someone else did something which exacerbated the damage to such an extent that the initial cause is no longer operative, and the defendant should thus not be considered liable for it. In this case, the defendant maintains, the result of her or his action would have been different if the second person had not come along and changed the course of events. Negligent medical care can be held to be an intervening factor, but it is considered that where someone has negligently caused harm which necessitates medical treatment, that treatment would have to be *grossly* negligent before a court would see it as breaking the chain of causation. A way of determining whether an action is an intervening factor, which breaks the chain of causation can be demonstrated by considering the following hypothetical situation:

> Jack drives through a red light and injures Mary, who is driving carefully. Mary is taken to hospital and is on the road to recovery. She is given prophylactic antibiotics, to which she develops a reaction which includes severe diarrhoea, resulting in mild dehydration. To counteract this Mary is given parenteral fluids, but the nurse negligently administers fluids too quickly. Mary develops emphysema and dies (see *Jordan v The Queen* (1956) 40 Cr App R 152).

[6.214] In this situation, as Mary was on the path to recovery, one can argue that the original tortfeasor should not be liable for Mary's death—the original action was too remote from the resulting harm. This can be contrasted with the situation where, say:

> after an original injury on a training exercise, a soldier is carried to the first aid centre. On the way he is dropped several times (causing further injury) and finally given the wrong treatment. He dies, and there is evidence that if he had received immediate and different treatment he would have survived. However the initial injury is still operative and a substantial cause of his death.

[6.215] In this case the chain of causation has not been broken by the actions of those treating the soldier as the original harm was still operative at the time of death (see *Smith v The Queen* [1959] 2 QB 35). Whilst there are contributing factors that may mean others are also liable in a civil action, the original tortfeasor would be held substantially responsible for the event.

[6.216] An intermediate situation can result where the court considers that the subsequent acts did not break the chain of events but were contributing factors to the final harm. Liability is shared according to the estimated degree of causation of each act.

▌▌▌ CASE
Bugden v Harbour View Hospital [1947] DLR 338 (SC Canada)

The plaintiff was treated at the defendant hospital for an injury to his thumb. The doctor decided to set it and asked nurse Bonnar, an experienced graduate nurse, for some novocaine. Nurse Bonnar asked nurse Spriggs to get the novocaine. Nurse Spriggs handed nurse Bonnar a phial which was labelled, and, without looking at the label nurse Bonnar handed it to the doctor, who, also without checking the label, injected it into Bugden. The drug injected was in fact adrenalin, and Bugden died within an hour.

[6.217] Each person involved argued that the other was in fact liable, as an intervening factor, but the court argued that the nurses should share the liability. Each nurse owed a duty of care to the patient, and the subsequent breach of duty by another will not relieve one who has contributed to the harm. The more appropriate defence in this case would have been that of joint liability (see [6.222]).

Partial Defences

[6.218] A partial defence is one where the defendant concedes some degree of liability for the harm, but argues that either the plaintiff or a third party should share the responsibility. If they are successful, they will be liable to pay a proportion of the compensation, in proportion to their degree of culpability.

Voluntary Assumption of Risk [6.223]

[6.219] This defence only applies to those cases where there has been some express or implied bargain between the parties to the effect that the plaintiff has expressly or impliedly given up his or her right to sue the defendant if he or she acts negligently. The plaintiff must have undergone the risk fully understanding the very kind of risk which has materialised. A classic example is accepting a ride from someone who is manifestly intoxicated. A person who agrees to undertake a course of action does not automatically waives his or her right to sue if an ordinary and inherent risk if that activity materialises. Such a waiver must be clearly entered into between the parties, that is, it must be shown that the plaintiff has expressly or impliedly agreed to bear the legal risk of injury and thus relieve the defendant of any liability arising from his or her duty of care. It thus does not apply to consent to medical treatment in normal circumstances.

Contributory Negligence

[6.220] The defendant argues that the plaintiff by her or his unreasonable behaviour, contributed to the harm.

▮▮▮ CASE

Brockman v Harpole, 444 P 2d (1968) (Supreme Court Oregon United States)

A registered nurse working in a doctor's surgery syringed a patient's ears. His eardrums were punctured, but the nurse was able to show that she was badgered considerably by the patient who did not want to wait.

[6.221] The court in this case held that the nurse did not have to pay full compensation, because the patient had contributed substantially to his own harm.

Joint Liability

[6.222] The defendant is able to point to another person and show that, through their negligence, they are jointly liable, and should share the cost of compensation, as in *Bugden's* case (see [6.216]).

[6.223] Further discussion on negligence is carried out where it applies in the following chapters on particular aspects of nursing care.

REFERENCES AND FURTHER READING

There is a wealth of literature on negligence, but the following books are helpful.

Australian Health and Medical Law Reporter (CCH, Sydney, 1991)

Balkin, R and Davis J, *Law of Torts* (Butterworths, Sydney, 1996)

Clarke, J, "Causation in Chappel v Hart: Common Sense or Coincidence?" 6 *Journal of Law and Medicine* 335 (May 1999)

Dix, et al, *Law for the Medical Profession* (Butterworths, Sydney, 1988)

Dunford, L and Pickford, V, "Is there a Qualitative Difference between Physical and Psychiatric Harm in English Law?" (1999) 7 *Journal of Law and Medicine* 36

Fleming, J, *The Law of Torts* (9th ed, Law Book Co, Sydney, 1998)

Fleming, J, "Remoteness and Duty: The Control Devices in Liability for Negligence" 31 *Canadian Bar Review* 471 (1953)

Gunson, J, "An opening of Floodgates? The Loss of Chance Argument in Medico-Legal Litigation" Address to BLEC Conference, Melbourne, 31 March 2000

Johnstone, M, *Nursing and the Injustices of the Law* (Saunders, Sydney, 1994)

Katter, N, *Duty of Care in Australia* (LBC Information Services, Sydney, 1999)

Langslow, A, "The Four Elements" (1981) 10 (No 9) *Australian Nurses Journal* 20 at 21

Luntz, H and Hambly, D, *Torts: Cases and Commentary* (Butterworths, Sydney, 1995)

Mann, A, *Medical Negligence Litigation: Medical Assessment of Claims* (International Business Communications, Sydney, 1989)

Mason, K, "Fault, Causation and Responsibility: Is Tort Law just an Instrument of Corrective Justice?" (2000) 19 Aust Bar Rev 20

Meryn, S, "Improving Doctor—Patient Communication" (1998) 316 BMJ 1922

Murchison, I A and Nichols, T, *Legal Foundations of Nursing Practice* (Macmillan, London, 1970)

Nisselle, P, "Managing Risk in Medical Practice" (1999) 7 *Journal of Law and Medicine* 130

Phillips, A, *Medical Negligence Law: Seeking a Balance* (Dartmouth, Dartmouth Publishing Company, 1997)

Review of Professional Indemnity Arrangements for Health Care Professionals, *Compensation and Professional Indemnity in Health Care: A Final Report* (Australian Government Publishing Service, Canberra, 1995)

Rice, S, *Some Doctors Make You Sick* (Angus & Robertson, Sydney, 1988)

Staunton, P and Whyburn, R, *Nursing and the Law* (4th ed, Saunders, Sydney, 1997)

Tito, F, *Compensation and Professional Indemnity in Health Care* (AGPS, Canberra, 1995)

Weir, M, *Complementary Medicine: Ethics and Law* (Qld, Prometheus Publications)

Whippy, W, "A Hospital's Personal and Non-Delegable Duty of Care for its Patients: A Novel Doctrine of Vicarious Liability Disguised?" (1989) 63 ALJR 182

Chapter Seven

RECORDING, COMMUNICATING AND ACCESSING CLIENT INFORMATION

INTRODUCTION

[7.1] Health carers necessarily obtain information about clients. Most of it must be recorded, much of it is confidential, and some of it can be accessed by different people at specified times, in specific circumstances.

Acquiring the Information

Who owns Medical Records?

[7.2] Medical records are owned by the maker of the records, that is, the Government Department or institution, the private hospital or practice, or the individual sole practitioner, as the case may be.

▌▌▌ CASE
Breen v Williams (1996) 186 CLR 71 (High Court of Australia)

The appellant, B, sought access to her medical records for the purpose of participating in class action against manufacturers of breast implants in the United States. It was conceded she could apply for these records through discovery or by subpoena, however this action was based on her right, through contract and/or other common law principles, to access to the records. She argued that she had a proprietary interest in the record, as an implied term of contract (see below, and Chapter 10). Alternatively, she claimed a right to the records as a consequence of the finding in *Rogers v Whitaker* (see [4.98]), on the grounds that that the principles the court upheld included the principle of autonomy and the patient's right to know about their health, a rejection of paternalism and the right of the medical profession to determine a patient's interests. The defendant argued that the handwritten notes were prepared and maintained in the belief that they were private to him, and that that such notes made by doctors could include commentary and musings that were not conclusive or what the doctor would consider appropriate for the patient to see, and could be confusing and cause

[7.2] anxiety without explanation. Such records also included administrative matters such as correspondence with lawyers and the medical defence union and thus did not relate to the patient's treatment and management.

[7.3] The High Court concluded that the doctor had a proprietary right to notes and records prepared by him or her. Where the health carer acts as an agent of the client in providing services, documents brought into existence as a result of that function may be the property of the client. The contract entered into by a client and health carer involves the proper care and treatment of the client, and does not include the ownership by the client of records made in the process of doing this. The client's "right to know" does not include the right to the documents.

[7.4] This means that there is no right of clients to access to their medical records held by a private practitioner or enterprise (the public sector is covered by Freedom of Information legislation, which requires the production of personal records, with some exceptions). The situation of X-rays, pathology and other reports is not so clear: it depends on the circumstances of their creation. Many practices adopt the approach that these can be accessed by the client, and are happy to make them available, unless they believe that access would be harmful to the client (for example, a psychiatric report.

[7.5] Legislation in the Australian Capital Territory provides the right of clients to access their medical records (see [7.115]).

Functions of Medical Records

[7.6] A patient's records serve two broad functions:

1)..... They are a means by which members of the health team can provide good care for clients, they become a historical account of a client's health care for future reference, and may, with the client's consent, be a useful tool in medical research. It is obviously part of reasonable standard of health care that records of a client's treatment are kept in most circumstances. There is no Commonwealth case law or legislation specifically requiring that medical records be kept for health care generally, however the Australian Medical Association Code of Ethics provides that every patient has a right to expect accurate records. State legislation[1] deals with the maintaining, keeping and provisions of access to records kept by State institutions, and some have released detailed guidelines on maintenance of records. Hospitals and health institutions may have drawn up guidelines, and there should also be procedure manuals available for guidance. Legally, many standards have been established to determine reasonable practice in making and dealing with records, as will be discussed below.

---

[1] For example, Private Hospitals and Day Procedures Centres Regulations 1996 (NSW); legislation covering the keeping of public records generally, such as *Archives Act* 1983 (ACT); *Libraries and Archives Act* 1988 (Qld); *Medical Act* 1939 (Qld); *Public Records Act* 1973 (Vic); *Library Board of Western Australia Act* 1951 (WA).

2)..... They are a contemporaneous record of events which have taken place. They are therefore likely to be an accurate account of those events. Records are critical in negligence cases in establishing the facts of treatment. [7.10]

[7.7] Both of these purposes have legal implications. As a means of patient care, records can be used in court either to prove or to refute a claim of negligence on the part of health carers. As a contemporaneous record of events, medical records can be used to enlighten the court on what care was or was not given, and the condition of the client at any particular time. Also, the lack of proper record-keeping can be used as evidence of a breach of the standard of care owed to the client. Carers should be aware of these uses by the law, and should adapt their report writing to these needs. It is suggested that health care can only be enhanced by keeping the above in mind.

[7.8] For the purposes mentioned above, the following principles should be applied.

Writing Reports: Notes for Health Carers' Protection

Reports should be Contemporaneous

[7.9] The sooner after the event that a report is made the more likely it is to be accurate, therefore a court is more inclined to accept it as evidence, and a true record of events. Also, prompt reporting shows efficiency and more likelihood of honesty and frankness. The following is an example of the acceptance of a contemporaneous report in preference to a witness's recollection of events.

▮▮▮ CASE

R v Adams, The Times, 5 November 1981 (Original hearing, Central Criminal Court London)

Dr John Adams was tried for the murder of his patient, Mrs Morrell, who was being nursed at home. Mrs Morrell had been given barbiturates and other drugs, including morphia and heroin (legally permissible). The prosecution argued that combinations of morphia, sedomid and heroin had been given over time in such quantities as to indicate that they had been given with the intent to kill the deceased rather than the intent to relieve pain. One of the nurses gave evidence that Dr Adams would visit Mrs Morrell in the evenings about 11 o'clock. At these times Dr Adams would be alone with Mrs Morrell, she said, and would administer drugs in addition to those given and recorded by the nurses, the nature of which they were unaware. The nurse said she could recall giving no drug other than morphia at night. This evidence was obviously damning to Dr Adams' case.

[7.10] Dr Adams' counsel procured a copy of the nurse's notes, and questioned the nurse mentioned above in great detail on her memory of the events. She did not know at that stage that the notes were available. She swore to the events she had outlined, and no one doubted her honesty or integrity. What counsel was able to show, however, was that

[7.10] her ability to recall accurately was less than perfect. She could recall giving injections, but not the actual doses. The nurse's notes showed that:

- ..... she had indeed given drugs other than morphia to the deceased;
- ..... all injections administered to Mrs Morrell, on previous evenings, including those given by Dr Adams, were recorded;
- ..... Dr Adams' visit on the night in question was recorded, as well as the drugs he had given;
- ..... these were the same drugs and dosages as administered on at least one previous occasion; and
- ..... Mrs Morrell's condition had been recorded as "very low" a month before she died.

[7.11] This evidence must have been crucial in the jury's decision to acquit Dr Adams, for as the doctor's counsel suggested, "mistakes of memory can be made", and the nurse would not have recorded the administration of the drugs, or the doctor's visits, unless these events had happened.

[7.12] For this important reason, medical reports may be used by a witness to refresh her or his memory, or, as in the case above, to challenge its accuracy. It is quite reasonable to assume that notes written at the time of the events would be more accurate than those written later, or the reliability of a witness's memory some months or years later at a trial.

[7.13] This principle has another implication. Whenever a person is conscious of possible legal action over some event, he or she is advised to make a written account of what occurred, separately from the client's medical record, which should be as accurate as possible. If this is made as a statutory declaration, it becomes a powerful source of evidence for any court hearing that might ensue. A statutory declaration is a signed statement made in writing with the signature witnessed by a justice of the peace or other designated person (see the list below). It must state that it is a statutory declaration, and this means that it has the same legal recognition as a statement in court under oath. A false declaration is perjury, and invokes a punishment at law. Copies of a pro forma statutory declaration can be obtained at some newsagents, but as long as the writer makes it clear that it is a statutory declaration, and it is properly signed, dated and witnessed, there is no set form required. After making such a statement, it should be placed in safekeeping in case of need at a later date.

Reports should be Adequate and Accurate

[7.14] While not including irrelevant material, reports should be carefully and fully made. As pointed out by one commentator: "Writing in a patient's chart should be taken as seriously as providing quality patient care" (Greenlaw (1982), p 125).

[7.15] Failure to report matters adequately may be evidence of negligence, as it goes to the heart of the first purpose of records stated above: the assistance of good care of the patient. In *Whitree v New York*,

290 NYS 2d 486 (1968), the defendant doctor did not make notes in the [7.18] hospital record. The court said: "It is this careless administrative medical procedure that, in our opinion, militates against adequate medical care." Greenlaw ((1982), p 126), points out that charting is not simply a clerical responsibility but a clinical one. Ideally, all institutions should have a set of minimal requirements for reporting, and means of ascertaining that these are maintained. Adequate time should be allowed on each shift for the making and receiving of reports, as they constitute one of the most important aspects of patient care.

Reports should be Objective

[7.16] Opinions are generally not accepted in courts, nor is hearsay. If you did not directly see, hear, feel, smell or taste something, but wish to report its occurrence, state your source of information in reporting it. An example is, "Mrs Jones claims she fell out of her bed"; "Mr Smith states he was attacked with a knife"; "James complaining of pain, says it has got worse". If you think Mrs Jones is suffering from shock, don't say this but rather report signs and symptoms such as "Mrs Jones is pale, sweating, has a feeble pulse with a blood pressure of 90/40" and add, if you wish, "Query shock" to alert others to its possibility. Obviously such reports for patients as "usual day", "good night", etc, are of little use to a court, and may in fact indicate carelessness on the part of those reporting.

[7.17] In discussing problems arising from record-keeping, health carers often state a fear that opinions and personal comments, such as stating a client is "difficult" or their symptoms "imagined", be used against them, as the basis of a claim in defamation or negligence. One should question why an opinion, other than an honest and reasonably determined diagnosis or preferred treatment, is necessary in medical records. Is it a record of what one has seen, heard, smelt or tasted? If not, is it clear that this is the writer's opinion? Is it a *clinical* opinion? Is it an opinion based on facts?

[7.18] There may be times when opinion is called for, for example, where problem-solving approaches to patient care are used. Nursing diagnoses, for example, may be involved, as well as identification of other problems which need to be addressed. These occasions will give rise to opinion, and it is valid to record this. However, the adequacy of the opinion is something which cannot be judged unless objective bases for the opinion are also expressed. Clinical data will therefore demonstrate the validity of the opinion. In these reports one should be aware of the need to record both objective data or clinical observations, as well as the opinions formed on the basis of this information. An indirect consequence of writing out the objective data first, is that the opinion is more likely to be an accurate one, as the need to justify it will ensure that it is well considered.

Reports should be Legible and Clear

[7.19] The need for clarity and legibility is obvious, but this rule is breached with such frequency one could be forgiven for believing health carers are required to write illegibly! Be careful in the use of abbreviations and popular terms. These should be widely used and known in the profession for example the terms "prn" ("when required") and "ADL's" ("activities of daily living") etc.

Errors should not be Obliterated

[7.20] Where a mistake has been made, rule neatly through it and write the correction beside or above the erroneous words clearly and legibly. Unless the correction is made immediately, appearing beside the crossed out mistake and forming part of the original signed report (for example "Mr Smith was ~~awake~~ asleep at 6 am"), the correction should be signed or initialled and dated by the person making it, who should be the original report writer. If this is not done it could be alleged that changes have been added by someone else, with less than honourable motives. The original mistake should still be legible, and should not be obliterated. It could be a note in the margin where the mistake is corrected after further writing. If more room is required for the correction, it may be written on a sheet of paper and attached. This should, of course, be signed and dated. A marginal note should be made on the original that the addition has been made (for example, cross out the mistake and note in the margin "see attached correction", the attached correction also being initialled and dated is then affixed to the original.

[7.21] The reason for this advice is to prevent alterations being made to reports after events have occurred when those events have become, or are likely to become, the subject of legal action. Obviously alterations should not be made for the purpose of falsifying a report, but any detection of an alteration which is not clearly and openly made, no matter how innocent its intention, may lead to suspicions that the writer intended to mislead. Clarity in establishing when and by whom the correction is made explains what precisely happened, and provides evidence of the standard of care given by those concerned.

Do not Rewrite Reports

[7.22] It is very important to note that reports and charts should never be rewritten at a later date. Errors could be made in the process. Where a report has been rewritten, whether changed or not, the courts could, where negligence has been alleged, consider the rewriting of a report as evidence of negligence:

> The value of a patient's medical record is that it is made contemporaneously with the events it documents; the existence of a 'rewrite' policy can call into question the accuracy of every patient record within the institution. If there is additional information which was forgotten at the time the entry was made, it should be included as an

addendum. A 'rewrite' policy reinforces the mistaken notion that charting [7.24]
is a clerical rather than a clinical responsibility [Greenlaw (1982), p 126].

Thus the practice of redoing charts to make them look neater is clearly a dangerous one from the legal point of view. A similar approach would be taken to the rewriting of reports when they are untidy, hard to read, or where one wishes to change them.

Do not Transcribe

[7.23] For the same reason, treatment orders should not be transcribed into a patient's notes from the original order. They might be erroneously transcribed, which is very possible if the order is difficult to read, and become the source of mistaken treatment. It is also possible, for example, that a doctor may verbally tell a nurse that he or she is going to order one medication, which is written in the client's notes, and change her or his mind, write down another order, which may be given by another nurse. Refer the reader to the drug chart, where a doctor has written the order. One would write, for example, "seen by Doctor X: medication (or 'sedation', 'pain relief') ordered as per chart". Staff should, at all times, refer to the original treatment order before carrying out the order, but transcribed orders may encourage failure to do this. Similarly, it is better not to rewrite a report from a note which has been scribbled on a piece of paper: write it straight into the patient's notes. However, where staff are busy, it is advisable to have a pocket notebook on hand to make notes contemporaneously with care, for reference for later inclusion in the client's medical report. One has then an accurate contemporaneous record, rather than having to rely on memory (when tired and rushed at the end of the shift) as to the time and nature of specific care. Keep the notebook in case it is needed for future reference. Remember that every record of health care treatment is potential evidence in a court of law, be it a scrap of paper or bound volume.

Never Write a Report or Sign it on Behalf of Another Health Carer

[7.24] Reports should represent the knowledge of the person in whose name they are written. The best way of ensuring this is never to write on behalf of another. The person signing a report vouches for its truth and accuracy. Evidence that this was not the case, on even one occasion, will cast doubt on the whole report. Thus:

- .....the health carer who actually carried out a procedure or administers a drug should write it in the client's record;
- .....if not, the person writing the report should check any entry of it on a drug/treatment record before stating that it was recorded as given at the particular time (or was given "according to chart");
- .....if charting is not required, the person writing the report should check with the person who administered the care, stating that it was "reported as given" at the particular time.

Medical Records as Evidence

[7.25] Generally, when asked to give evidence in court, or in a statement of facts, a person is required to give only an account of what was experienced by her or his own senses. Reports of what one was told is hearsay evidence, and not usually admissible. Thus, if a person is told by Jack that Fred shot Bob, such a person's evidence would be inadmissible as evidence that in fact Fred did shoot Bob. It could be admitted, however, as evidence, that the conversation between them took place. Carers should not use hearsay in their daily notes (this includes entries on charts and other reports), unless they identify it as such, because hearsay statements may not be accurate and nurses are protected from liability for negligence by alerting others to the possibility of inaccuracy.

[7.26] As medical records are not first-hand evidence of what occurred at a particular time, they would normally come under the hearsay rule in a court of law. The court would normally require the writer to swear to their accuracy in fact. However, legislation in every jurisdiction[2] allows the court to admit business records as evidence. This means that medical records can also be subpoenaed by one of the parties. Medical records are described as any record of information, including books, plans, drawings and photographs, made by an owner or employee as part of the business of the enterprise. As they are written at the time of the activity to which they relate, they are taken to be the most accurate of records of what happened at the time. Courts have held that medical records are business records, and that all medical records, are potentially admissible. It is up to the court to decide the usefulness of such records.

CASE

Albrighton v Royal Prince Alfred Hospital [1979] 2 NSWLR 165 (Appeal: [1980] 2 NSWLR 542)

The facts of this case are given at [6.37].

In the trial hearing the judge prevented the plaintiff from tendering all the relevant records. It was argued that at least entries by junior medical staff and nursing staff should not be admitted as evidence. In addition it was argued that entries that were illegible, unintelligible, heavily abbreviated, equivocal or ambiguous should be excluded on the grounds that their weight would be too slight to justify admission.

[7.27] On appeal it was held that all available records, no matter by whom they were made are admissible unless the trial judge should rule that they were not relevant to the issue, namely to liability or damages for pain and suffering. Records of a hospital are kept for the information of staff and treating doctors and are not therefore likely to be "repositories of

---

[2] *Evidence Act* 1971 (ACT), Pt 6; *Evidence Act* 1971 (NSW), Pt 6; *Evidence Act* 1996 (NT), s 29; *Evidence Act* 1977 (Qld), s 92; *Evidence Act* 1929 (SA), s 45; *Evidence Act* 1910 (Tas), Divn 2A; *Evidence Act* 1958 (Vic), s 55; *Evidence Act* 1906 (WA), s 79C.

the speculations of the inept". As to whether they were unintelligible etc, the court held that they could still be admitted because defects could be overcome by oral evidence ("the unintelligible may be explained, the abbreviated may be expanded" (at 568)). If, at the end of the day, some of the text is unintelligible to the jury, it is either harmless and can be disregarded, or if not, it can be corrected in the summing up or addresses of counsel. The jury (or judge in the absence of a jury) is to determine what weight to place on them.

[7.30]

Dying Declarations

[7.28] An important exception to the hearsay rule is the dying declaration. This is a statement by a person who is in expectation of imminent death. Therefore if Bob, who is dying, tells someone that Fred shot him, that remark could be admitted and considered as strong evidence that Fred did indeed commit the crime. The rationale for this exception is that it is considered that a person would not lie when facing death as there would most likely be no benefit in doing so. It has happened that a man who was expected to die from gunshot wounds made accusatory statements. In fact he survived, but his accusations were still admitted as dying declarations, as they were made when he truly anticipated death.

Incident Reports

[7.29] Most hospitals and other health care facilities have adopted the incident report as a means of securing good quality patient care. Any accidents or other incidents which are unusual (that is, which should not occur in the normal course of events), are recorded and reviewed by the administration. The subject matter of them is thus brought to the attention of the administration, and, from the legal point of view, where the reports indicate the need for it, the administration is subsequently obliged to take reasonable action, either to deal with any harm already caused, or to prevent future harm occurring. This becomes a matter of reasonable care in its administration of services to clients, and provision of a safe and effective working environment for staff.

[7.30] Incident reports have several uses:

- ..... they identify practices and work environments which give rise to an unacceptable level of risk of harm to clients or staff (for example, methods and equipment—or lack of it—for lifting patients);
- ..... they monitor the effectiveness of particular practices or equipment (for example, new staffing arrangements or procedures);
- ..... they assist in satisfactorily dealing with an unusual occurrence by the provision of information to those who need to know about it (for example, treatment of injuries, repair of faulty equipment); and

[7.30] ▌.....they are a means of recording events and conditions (including the condition of an injured person) which can be used in the establishment of, or defence to, legal action (for example, identification of the cause of an accident, and standard of care given to the injured before and after it).

They are therefore potentially very important legal documents.

[7.31] Incident reports may be used where health carers believe that their work conditions are unsafe, for example, to establish the extent and causation of back injuries in an area where it is thought that these are too frequent. Under-staffing is another area of concern where the incident report may be a means of discharging one's duty of care when one feels that on any particular occasion one was expected to work to a standard which was not possible through lack of resources, or where under-staffing is a regular occurrence (see also Checklist at [6.110]). They may also be used to demonstrate that particular practices are not being carried out, and to pressure staff to follow them. An example of this is one operating suite where incident reports were adopted as a means for recording any unusual occurrence, including failure to properly ensure the patient's consent. The report was to be signed by both nursing and medical staff. The result has been a more conscientious adoption of proper procedures.

[7.32] It can be seen that from the administration point of view the incident report is used at several levels:

▌.....identification of existing or potential problems;
▌.....provision of adequate remedies where these have occurred;
▌.....monitoring of the effect of remedies;
▌.....elimination of unsafe conditions or practices (industrial health and safety legislation requires employers to take specific measures for developing safe work environments);
▌.....prevention of workers' compensation claims;
▌.....prevention of and/or protection in law suits.

[7.33] Where there is the possibility of legal action, management should notify the insurance company covering the facility at the first practical opportunity. Where an incident involves staff, workers' compensation claim forms should be competed as soon as practicable (again to ensure that the report is contemporaneous and thus accurate).

Incident Report as Evidence

[7.34] Where an account of an unusual event is documented in an incident report it can be used, as can other medical records, to establish the facts for legal purposes. This means the report can provide protection for staff where it shows clearly that care was reasonable, and if the event was due to negligence, it can establish that reasonable steps were taken to remedy any harm caused, thus helping to lessen the damages for which anyone is liable. Honesty and accuracy are advisable, as detection of anything that could indicate attempts to cover up the facts could exacerbate the liability of those concerned.

[7.35] Because incident reports are admissible in court, it is very important to keep in mind that they should not contain opinion statements, for example, the cause of the accident, or allocation of fault: opinions may indicate a less than reasonable approach on the part of health carers, especially if they are wrong, and the allocation of blame may be taken as a confession (even where the one confessing was not in fact negligent).

[7.36] There is no limit to the uses of incident reports, despite the fact that forms may be drawn up in such a way that they limit the perceived methods for reporting, and the topics one can report. It is suggested that where an incident report form does not make allowances for a particular event, or give room for all the details to be included, carers should attach a sheet of paper and include these. Again, as with medical records, there should be a clear notation referring to the addition on the form, along the lines of "see Attachment A". The notation and the attachment should be signed and dated.

[7.37] Incident reports are used by quality assurance committees to identify unsatisfactory aspects of the organisation's activities, and to determine causes and rectify them. Reporting by quality assurance committees should follow specific guidelines. It should not contain names; attention should be given to the possibility of legal access to the report, (although this should not prevent the purposes of quality assurance, such as the improvement of services, being served); and the aim of the report, that is, the change of procedures or policy, and should be kept in mind.

▮▮ CHECKLIST
INFORMATION TO INCLUDE IN INCIDENT REPORTS

- ▮..... date and time of incident;
- ▮..... place where the incident occurred;
- ▮..... names and details of all parties concerned (written legibly);
- ▮..... brief but full and accurate account of what the writer experienced (no hearsay unless identified as such, and no allocation of blame);
- ▮..... if a person was harmed, their condition before the incident took place;
- ▮..... any harm caused and to whom or what it was caused (objective observations, with any opinion or diagnosis identified as such);
- ▮..... any action taken, and by whom it was taken (for example, doctor or relatives called, treatment given);
- ▮..... any further treatment ordered and follow-up requirements (such as observations, check-ups);
- ▮..... list of witnesses (legible); and
- ▮..... where the report concerns faulty equipment, the equipment should be clearly identified: location and identifying number or name, and details of the sign which has been attached to the equipment warning of its fault should be recorded.

Reporting a Serious Incident

[7.38] Where a serious incident has occurred it is crucial that authorities are notified immediately, not only to provide care for anyone injured, but also to enable the hospital insurer and solicitor to be contacted. This should be done within hours of the event, by phone at least. Staff involved should consider legal advice as soon as possible for the following reasons:

- ..... There is a difference between the incident report and any statement made to a lawyer. The latter may be protected by legal privilege, which means that it would be inadmissible as evidence against the carer in any hearing. Thus staff are advised to avail themselves of legal advice if they are asked to make a statement, or wish to do so, and are in any way concerned that they may be legally implicated by what they say. A free legal consultation may be available at a Legal Aid Office, through the State Law Society, or one's union.
- ..... If the carer is an independent contractor and insured, he or she can benefit by notifying the insurance company of the occurrence as soon as possible. Indemnity insurance covers negligent actions.

[7.39] Health carers should resist attempts to get them to make statements which they do not believe are a true representation of the facts, or to alter their statement. This may be done to prevent unfavourable legal action being brought against the hospital staff. Attention is drawn to the comments elsewhere on statutory declarations (see [7.13], [15.51]).

Communicating Information

Privacy

[7.40] Health carers are in the position where they may be the repository of information which, in the circumstances, should be confidential. Clients trust health professionals not to disclose all that they learn in their day-to-day caring for them. Although there is no clearly defined legally enforceable clients' right to privacy, the relationships of health carer and client gives rise to privacy obligations under various heads of law, which are set out below.

What is Confidential Information?

[7.41] Disclosures made to another with the express condition that they are confidential are, obviously, the subject of confidentiality at law. However, the health professional gains a lot of information which is not specifically given with the proviso that it is confidential and not to be disclosed to anyone. Also, through dealings with the client the health carer may have indirectly received information about other people, such as family members or a spouse. Unless there is a clear understanding to the contrary, information is by implication confidential due to the fact of [7.45] the carer–client relationship. This includes all information relating to the carer's professional relationship with the client. Gossip during the tea-break can be a breach of that confidentiality, and carers should be careful what they say on such occasions.

[7.42] It has been suggested that the purpose of the right to privacy is not merely the protection of the special nature of the relationship between health carers and their clients, nor the peace of mind and reputation of the patient, although these are certainly reasons for respecting clients' privacy. The most important reason, it is argued, is the need to ensure that a client feels able to disclose those facts which may be embarrassing, but vital for her or his proper care and treatment.

[7.43] Modern technology has created the potential for inroads into any absolute concept of confidentiality, as the use of electronic recording, transfer and access to information, and ever-growing corporatisation of large groups of health carers (such as medical centres, which can include doctors, pathologists and other ancillary services) means that many people other than the health carers themselves (such as clerical and receptionist personnel) may have access to client information in the course of their work. Health insurance and Medicare claims, drug prescriptions and referrals to rehabilitation workers and secretarial services in the processing and filing of records involve the creation of further records and files or simply the broadcasting of facts about the client. Research, which is a growing area of academic development, particularly for nurses and health care academics, means that the client's records may become the province of even more people. Policies and practices are often ineffective in protecting privacy, so continual vigilance should be maintained in practising this ethical and legal requirement of one's profession.

The Extent of Health Carers' Duty of Confidentiality

[7.44] The precise nature of any obligation of confidence is uncertain, as it has grown in a rather haphazard fashion (Brazier (1992), p 46). In the case of *Seager v Copydex* [1967] 1 WLR 923 it was established by Lord Denning (at 931) that:

> [A person who] has received information in confidence shall not take unfair advantage of it. He must not make use of it to the prejudice of him who gave it without obtaining his consent.

Just what this means in practical terms, however, is not clear.

[7.45] At law, it would seem, the duty to maintain confidentiality applies to all those who come in contact with the information as part of the health care process, including filing clerks and secretaries. The obligation does not cease when the professional relationship has ceased, nor with the death of the client. It also applies to the client of someone else. Breach of confidence which is unintended may be the subject of a negligence action by the client.

The Health Carer–Client Relationship is not "Privileged"

[7.46] The relationship between doctor and patient is definitely *not* the same as that between lawyer and client; which is privileged and which cannot be divulged in court. Where a judge directs a doctor or other health carer to disclose confidential information failure to do so would result in contempt of court proceedings, and could possibly lead to imprisonment. In the case of *Hunter v Mann* [1974] 2 WLR 742, an English court convicted a doctor of contempt for refusing to disclose information about patients of his who were wanted in connection with a criminal offence.

[7.47] New South Wales has amended its *Evidence Act* 1995 (NSW) to create a category of "professional coincidental relationship privilege" and "sexual assault communication privilege". Communications made by a person to another who is acting in a professional capacity and under an obligation to maintain confidentiality and communications in relation to sexual assault (such as counselling) may be exempt from production in legal proceedings. Victoria has amended its *Evidence Act* 1958 (Vic) to extend a similar privilege to communications made to a medical practitioner or counsellor by a person who has been sexually assaulted.

Statutory Provisions for Protection of Privacy

[7.48] The Commonwealth *Privacy Act* 1988 (Cth) deals with personal information collected by Commonwealth agencies. It sets out 11 Information Privacy Principles (IPPs), which cover the collection, maintenance and disclosure of personal information. These principles require that information must not be collected without consent of the subject, who must be told its purpose, or used for any purpose other than that for which it was collected. Circumstances under which personal information should be kept are set out, as well as those under which it may be disclosed (these being broadly based on common law principles of disclosure discussed below), as well as limitations on access to personal information by third parties.

There is a Commonwealth Privacy Commissioner whose function is to promote the privacy principles, provide guidelines on privacy and attempt to conciliate complaints of breaches of the Act. The Commissioner has issued Guidelines for the protection of privacy in the conduct of medical research, to be followed where it is considered impracticable for the purposes of the research to follow the IPPs (for example, where such large numbers of records are required for the research project that it is impracticable or impossible to obtain the consent of each and every person). The research proposal must then be considered and passed by an Institutional Ethics Committee. Breach of these requirements does not attract a penalty, but can result in loss of Commonwealth funding, and, more importantly, disciplinary action by a health profession licensing board, with possible loss or suspension of the right to practice.

Privacy Legislation for the Private Sector [7.53]

[7.49] The Commonwealth enacted amendments to the *Privacy Act* in December 2000 which are to come into force on 22 December 2001. The amendments apply privacy principles to the following information collected and kept by those in the private sector:

- ..... personal information (that is, that which identifies individuals);
- ..... health information (that is, information or opinion about a person's health, health services provided to them, disability, their wishes about their future health service or other information collected to provide a health service or in relation to the donation of body parts, organs or body substances); and
- ..... sensitive information (that is, information about a person's racial or ethnic origins, political, religious, philosophical beliefs or affiliations, membership of professional or trade association or union, sexual preferences or practices, criminal record or health information).

[7.50] Those providing health services, including assessment, recording maintaining or improving an individual's health, diagnosing and treating actual or suspected illness or disability, and dispensing prescriptions in private health care facilities and those in private practice will be subject to the provisions of the Act, which specifically deals with health care information. The Act covers more than conventional "medical treatment" and would seem to include such people as those providing alternative therapies.

Guidelines for National Privacy Principles about Health Information for the Private Sector

[7.51] The amendments allow the Commissioner to approve, for the purpose of giving effect to the National Privacy Principles, guidelines that are issued by the National Health and Medical Research Council or other prescribed authority. The National Privacy Principles are summarised in Appendix 3. The new provisions set standards for the collection, use, disclosure, data quality and security, storage, accessibility and correction of personal information, including health records. The legislation applies to the acts and practices of "organisations" including individuals, companies, unincorporated organisations, partnerships and trusts.

[7.52] To comply with the legislation these individuals and private organisations are required to review existing procedures and formulate and implement policies in relation to the collection, storage, disclosure and access to personal information. They must ensure that systems are in place, and employee training is carried out, so that those dealing with personal information are aware of, and follow, the Privacy Principles.

[7.53] A privacy Code may be drawn up by a record keeper and approved by the Privacy Commissioner if it complies with the Privacy Principles and other requirements of the legislation. It may then be registered with the Commission. The Code may require an independent adjudicator to review any complaint of a breach of the Code, otherwise complaints are made to

[7.53] the Commissioner, as are complaints of breach of the Privacy Principles. The adjudicator or Commissioner can investigate the complaint and make a determination that the individual's privacy was interfered with, the conduct is not to be repeated and a direction as to compensation (hurt feelings may be considered). This determination may be enforced through the Federal Magistrates Court or other Federal Court. A determination may be reviewable under the *Administrative Decisions (Judicial Review) Act 1977* (Cth).

State and Territory Legislation

[7.54] There are specific statutory requirements in the States and Territories for staff of government health authorities to respect the confidentiality of patients whom they treat, as well as general privacy legislation.[3] The requirements generally provide that it is unlawful for any person to disclose any information relating to patients except with their consent, when required by law, or to lessen a serious threat to the life and health of the individual. Health carers should be familiar with such provisions by finding out what legislation applies to them and the relevant provisions regarding confidentiality. These may also provide for those occasions when staff may be required to disclose certain matters to their employer.

[7.55] There is also a requirement in some States to report child abuse and in all States, infectious diseases. This legislation is outlined in Chapter 16.

Ethical Codes, Guidelines and Administrative Instructions

[7.56] Codes of ethics for most established health care professional bodies, such as the Hippocratic Oath, the Australian Medical Association Code of Ethics, nursing codes of conduct and ethical codes for allied health care professionals set out provision for health carers to maintain the confidentiality of client information.

[7.57] Some State governments have introduced guidelines for hospitals and other health care providers which give more specific principles to follow[4] (see eg [7.109]). Standards Australia, the standards association of

---

[3] For example, *Health Administration Act* 1982 (NSW); *South Australian Health Commission Act* 1976 (SA); *Tasmanian State Service Act* 1984 (Tas); *Health Services Act* 1988 (Vic). The *Privacy Act* 1988 (Cth) provides that all Commonwealth officers have an obligation to keep records confidential. This would include employees of Commonwealth and Defence Force hospitals and health facilities.

[4] Examples of guidelines are the New South Wales Department of Health, *Circular 82/369*, 5 Nov 1982; Queensland Departmental Standing Committee on Privacy in Health and Medical Records, *Privacy Guidelines for Hospitals*, April 1986; Western Australian Health Department, *Guidelines for Release/Access to Health Records* 1986, and Western Australian Public Service Board, *Administrative Instruction* 711.

Australia has published AS-4400, a document setting out the basic [7.60] principles (based on the OECD's *Guidelines for the Security of Information Systems*), and establishing standards for both the private and public sectors in the keeping of health care records. Hospitals and other health care establishments should develop their own careful policies, according to legal and ethical principles, protecting clients' privacy, which then set the standard of protection of clients' privacy for all those working for the facility. Also there are State bodies such as the Privacy Commission in New South Wales, which establish guidelines for those dealing with confidential information. In addition health care facilities may have their own guidelines, which, of course, must be in accord with the law.

Legislation

[7.58] Legislation in all jurisdictions requires those dealing with medical records to maintain confidentiality.[5] There is also legislation requiring any information acquired as part of activities in the public sector to maintain secrecy in relation to that information (see [7.48], [7.54]).

Breach of Confidence

[7.59] Both common law and equity provide relief for breach of confidence. The law is not fully developed in these areas, but four actions at common law appear to be available:

- breach of contract;
- tort ("breach of confidence")
- negligence; and
- defamation.

Breach of Contract

[7.60] Clients enter a contractual relationship with their health carer, whether it is implied or specific (Chapter 10). There may be a specific term of the agreement for treatment of a client that information received by the professional is to be the subject of confidence. This would be rare. However, it has been argued that there is an implied term of the contract that the health carer will act in the "best interests" of the client (*Sidaway's case* at [4.50]. But there is some degree of uncertainty as to whether this

---

[5] Examples of legislation requiring health providers to maintain patient confidentiality are: *Health Administration Act* 1982 (NSW), *Public Health Act* 1991 (NSW), *Private Hospital and Day Procedures Centres Act* 1988 (NSW), *Nursing Homes Act* 1988 (NSW); *Health Services Act* 1991 (Qld), *Health Act* 1937 (Qld); *South Australian Health Commission Act* 1976 (SA), *Public and Environmental Health Act* 1987 (SA); *Tasmanian State Service Act* 1984 (Tas), *HIV/AIDS Preventative Measures Act* 1993 (Tas); *Health Services Act* 1988 (Vic), *Health Act* 1958 (Vic).

[7.60] includes an implied contractual term of confidentiality. The High Court in *Breen v Williams* (see [7.2]) considered whether access to medical records by a client is included in an implied term to act in the client's interests. Gaudron J and McHugh J considered *Sidaway's case* and held that a doctor does not warrant that he or she would be liable for any act that objectively was not in the best interests of the patient. This would put too uncertain an obligation on the doctor, and thus be contrary to the principles of contract law. They questioned whether there is an implied term to act in the client's interests in Australian law. They held that even if there is, the only relevant contractual term implied by law would be to provide reasonable care and skill in advice, diagnosis and treatment.

[7.61] The client may have contracted for treatment by a health care provider who is an employer (for example, a hospital). Dissemination of confidential information about the client by the employee health carer would then raise the question of whether there was a breach of contract by the employer through its employees. Where a report involving information regarding a client is required by a third party such as a prospective employer or insurance company, carers should make sure that they have the permission of the client to release such information. The fact of the request may indicate the client's consent, but in any circumstances where it is possible or likely the request may be sent without the client's consent, those holding the information should investigate further.

[7.62] If information is lawfully passed on to a third person with the understanding that it is confidential, the relationship between the client and the third person, given the principle of privity of contract (see Chapter 10), is uncertain. Where A gives confidential information to a health carer, B, who passes it on to a third party, C, with A's knowledge and express or implied consent, for the purpose of rendering a service to A, the terms of the giving of information are subject to the same terms existing between A and B. It is thus B's responsibility to ensure C is aware of the confidential nature of the information, and for C to maintain the confidentiality. However, as indicated above, this would not be because of any contractual term, but rather because of other legal principles applying to confidentiality as outlined below.

The Tort of Breach of Confidence

[7.63] There does not have to be a contract between people for an obligation to maintain the confidentiality if information arises. An action for breach of confidence can be brought where:

- ..... the information is confidential in nature;
- ..... it has been imparted in circumstances giving rise to an obligation of confidence; and
- ..... it is used without authorisation to the detriment of the person who gave it.

[7.64] A breach of confidence thus occurs in equity where confidential information is disclosed without authorisation. Whether the information given to health carers by a client comes under the category of confidential [7.67] information has not been specifically ruled on by the courts, but it would seem to have the necessary quality of confidence, particularly as it is intimate and personal, and because professional ethics has deemed it so.

Equitable Remedy: Breach of Confidence

[7.65] There is a remedy in equity (see [1.9], [1.39]-[1.41]) for disclosure of confidential information which has been discovered through a relationship of trust such as a marital relationship.

▌▌▌ CASE
Argyll v Argyll [1967] Ch 302 (CA England)
The Duke of Argyll sought to sell information about the private life of his estranged wife, the Duchess of Argyll, to the newspapers. This information involved secrets disclosed to him during their marriage. The duchess applied to the court for an injunction preventing him from doing so.

[7.66] The court held that within marriage, there is a duty for each spouse to maintain the confidence of the other. Note that this is an equitable principle, not a common law one, so there is no allowance for damages for harm or hurt reputation or feelings. The only action one can bring is that for an injunction preventing a person from disclosing information where disclosure is anticipated, or from continuing to do so if information has already been disclosed.

Tort law: Action in Negligence

[7.67] Where confidential information is negligently disclosed, a person may claim that this has resulted in harm. He or she must show that:

▌.....the health carer failed to exercise reasonable care by disclosing the information;
▌.....it was reasonably foreseeable that disclosure could harm the client; and
▌.....the client suffered harm as a result of the disclosure.

[7.67] ■■■ **CASE**
Furniss v Fitchett [1958] NZLR 396

A husband and wife were having marital difficulties. They both attended the same doctor, Dr Fitchett. At the husband's request, the doctor wrote a report stating that in his opinion Mrs Furniss suffered from paranoia, and "An examination by a Psychiatrist would be needed to fully diagnose her case and its requirement." The doctor did not ask the purpose of the report, nor did he mark it "confidential". The document was kept secret by the husband for 12 months, then used by her husband's lawyer in proceedings for marital separation. As a result of being confronted by the document, Mrs Furniss suffered psychological harm. It is of note that the doctor argued that his intention in writing the report was to ensure that Mrs Furniss would not be committed to a psychiatric institution without further examination by a specialist. He also conceded that he knew that the disclosure to his patient of his opinion of her mental condition would be harmful to her. The jury found the doctor liable, and he appealed.

[7.68] The court held that:

■ .....while the doctor did not have to foresee the precise manner in which the contents of his report would come to the knowledge of Mrs Furniss, given the circumstances, he ought to have foreseen that the information could be expected to be used in some legal proceedings, and thus come to her knowledge;
■ .....he should have foreseen that in giving the document to the husband with no restrictions on its use it could come to the notice of the wife; and
■ .....the doctor thus had a duty of care to Mrs Furniss, that no expression of his opinion as to her mental condition should come to her knowledge.

[7.69] It is of note that the court adopted the attitude that it was the method of disclosure (unrestricted) rather the report itself (no expression of his opinion as to her mental condition should come to her knowledge). Readers might like to question whether giving a written report to the husband at all, even with the motive claimed by Dr Fitchett, was justified. Unless exceptions outlined below apply, confidential client information should only be given under the following circumstances:

■ .....the recipient is someone needs to know the information for the client's welfare;
■ .....it is limited to information necessary for that purpose; and
■ .....it is disclosed in a way that is least harmful to the client.

When Confidential Information may be Disclosed

[7.70] Courts have held that confidential information about a client should only be disclosed if:

■ .....the client agrees to the disclosure;
■ .....disclosure is compelled by law;

- .....there is a duty to the public to disclose; and
- .....the interests of one of the parties is involved (for example, the patient's, carer's or hospital's).

Agreement to Disclosure

[7.71] Health carers should consider all information they receive from, or about, a client as confidential, unless the client has specifically agreed to its disclosure or it is on the public record). However he or she is presumed to have agreed to the disclosure of confidential information only where it is necessary for his or her welfare, in the normal course of administration of the medical practice or health facility, or where the information is required to obtain insurance payments or other benefits which are known to the client to be part of the process of their care. Thus medical records can be stored, indexed or otherwise dealt with according to procedures adopted by the facility. Any unusual use of information must first receive the client's consent.

Compulsion by Law

[7.72] There is legislation which requires disclosure of certain information to the authorities, for example, infectious diseases and child abuse (more fully dealt with in Chapter 16). Health carers are also required to disclose any information which is required in the process of a court proceeding, or to produce records or other information in court proceedings. No action could be taken against a carer by the patient in these circumstances (see *Brown v Brooks*, below).

[7.73] It should be noted that there is no legally protected doctor–client relationship, except through statute in New South Wales and Victoria, as mentioned above at [7.46]-[7.47]. Lord Denning stated in *Attorney-General v Mulholland* [1963] 2 WLR 658 (at 665):

> The only profession I know of which is given a privilege from disclosing information to a court of law is the legal profession, and then it is not the privilege of the lawyer but of his client. Take the clergyman, the banker or the medical man. None of these is entitled to refuse to answer when directed to by a judge. . . . The judge will respect the confidences which each member of these honourable professions receives in the course of it, and will not direct him to answer unless not only it is relevant but also it is a proper and, indeed, necessary question in the course of justice to be put and answered. A judge is the person . . . to weigh these conflicting interests . . . on the one hand the respect due to confidence in the profession and on the other hand the ultimate interest of the community in justice being done.

Disclosure in the Public Interest

[7.74] A health carer may also disclose information if it is in the public interest to do so. An example could be where he or she is aware of a patient's likelihood to kill or harm another person or other people. This could be because of psychiatric illness or physical disability where the welfare of others is dependent on physical integrity: for example, an airline pilot's weak heart. In a Californian case, *Tarasoff v Regents of the University of California*, 551 P 2d 334 (1976), a patient told his psychologist that he intended to kill his girlfriend. The psychologist did not warn either the girlfriend or her family, and the man did indeed kill her. The court held that in failing to do this the psychologist breached a duty of care which he owed to the victim as a member of the public. In doing this, it stated that any duty the doctor owed to the patient was outweighed by the public interest in safety which placed a duty on the doctor to warn of the potential harm.

[7.75] The following case involving disclosure of confidential information and the duty of health carers to the public as well as their client sets out some important issues.

▌▌▌ CASE
W v Edgell [1990] 1 All ER 855 (CA England)

The plaintiff, W had been convicted of manslaughter after killing five people. He was diagnosed as suffering from paranoid schizophrenia, which involved delusion of persecution by his neighbours. W was detained under a mental health order in a secure psychiatric hospital, the order being for an indefinite period. Some years later a mental health review tribunal considered his case, and recommended that W be released to a less secure facility. This recommendation was based on a report by a Dr G, W's treating psychiatrist, that his condition was being controlled by medication and that he was suitable for transfer. The Home Secretary refused consent to the transfer, and W appealed to the tribunal for a review of the Home Secretary's decision. W's solicitor's sought an opinion from Dr Edgell an independent consultant. Dr Edgell's report was in fact unfavourable to W, and he sent it to the solicitors believing it would be presented to the tribunal. He was concerned, because he believed W was still dangerous, and his outstanding interest in explosives and guns had not been adequately explored in Dr G's report.

W's solicitors, not wanting Dr Edgell's report to be seen by the tribunal, withdrew W's application. Dr Edgell then sent a copy of his report to the hospital where W was detained, the Home Secretary and the Department of Health and Social Security.

W sought an injunction to retrain further communication of the report, return of copies and damages for breach of confidentiality.

[7.76] The court dismissed W's application holding that Dr Edgell's duty to W to maintain confidentiality was overridden by his duty of care to bring his concerns to the proper authorities. However, the competing interests were really the public interest, firstly in the maintenance by the health care profession of the confidence and privacy of clients, and secondly in the protection of the public from danger. Whilst the general [7.79] principle is that for disclosure in the public interest, the risk to others must be "real, immediate and serious", and W would not be released before further examination, the court considered the circumstances of the case, and held that the number of killings by W were enough to give rise to "the gravest concern for the safety of the public" (per Sir Stephen Brown P at 846).

CASE

Brown v Brooks (18 August 1988, SC NSW) (discussed in *Australian Health and Medical Law Reporter* (1991) ¶27-770)

A man was charged with sexual assault of his stepdaughter. He underwent counselling by a clinical nurse specialist at his local public hospital, and in the course of the counselling discussed his relationship with the stepdaughter. These sessions were recorded in his medical records. After learning about these sessions, the police required a statement from the nurse in relation to what was said in the sessions. The man sought an injunction to prevent the hospital or the nurse giving information to the police.

[7.77] The court refused the injunction, stating that it is contrary to public policy to give preference to the right to confidentiality when it would impede the investigation of a crime. While recognising the desirability of maintaining the confidentiality of consultations between clients and health service providers, the court said that confidence could not be maintained where information was necessary for the prosecution of a serious crime.

[7.78] Other examples of where disclosure has been held to be in the public interest are:

- ..... disclosure of information about a blood donor where blood recipient contracted HIV from a transfusion (*Australian Red Cross and Anor v BC* Supreme Court of Victoria (7 March 1991));
- ..... disclosure to the authorities of a client's proclivities for arson (CCH (1993) ¶27-770), or crime (Skene (1998), p 206). The Australian Medical Association and the Medical Board of Victoria supported a call by police to all doctors in Victoria to come forward if they have any information in relation to the perpetrator of attacks on young girls, dubbed "Mr Cruel" (see Mendelson (1994); Morrell, S, "Dob in Mr Cruel, Docs told" *Herald Sun,* 21 May 1992); and
- ..... where a client suffers from HIV/AIDS and will not tell his or her partner (Royal Australasian College of Surgeons, *Infection Control in Surgery, Management of AIDS (HIV) and Hepatitis B,* p 3 cited from Skene (1998), p 206).

[7.79] An example where disclosure was held not to be in the public interest is the following case.

[7.79] ■■■ CASE
X v Y & Ors [1988] 2 All ER 648 (Queen's Bench Division UK)

The plaintiffs, members of a health authority, sought an injunction to prevent publication by a newspaper of confidential information that two doctors in general practice suffered from AIDS. The plaintiffs had initially wanted to publish the names of the doctors, but agreed to publish non-identifying information. The question was whether disclosure was in the public interest, the defendants arguing that the public was entitled to such information. They said that no harm would be caused to the plaintiff if no names were given. The plaintiffs said that publication would be a breach of confidentiality, and produced evidence that with proper counselling, the continuing practice of general practitioners who had AIDS did not present a danger to the public.

[7.80] The court refused the injunction, holding that while there was a public interest in allowing the press to keep the public informed, that public interest was outweighed by the public interest in confidentiality and trust in relation to AIDS patients' records.

Disclosure in the Interest of Party Concerned

[7.81] Finally, one may make disclosures where the interests of a patient, the carer or the employer are involved, for example, where a patient is likely to cause undue expense to the hospital by planned action of which the carer is aware, or is likely to harm any person or property.

Disclosure to Relatives

[7.82] Because of dealings with the client, health carers come in contact with family and other relatives. The client's confidence should be respected here, and unnecessary information should not be given without permission. The fact that the patient is a child should make no difference to this principle when considering what one can tell relatives. It is important to remember that when disclosure is made to relatives without consent, it must only be those matters that are in the interest of one of the parties, and made only to those persons who are directly affected, or are directly responsible for further action. Health carers should consider the interest of the client above any other person's unless this is clearly outweighed by the possibility of harm to that person.

Sometimes relatives ask that information be kept from the client, whether it is in relation to their condition (for example that the client has cancer) or some other matter (for example that a close family member is dead). This should not be considered as a mandatory request, and on such occasions health carers should consider a person's right to such information, and whether it is in this particular client's interests to receive the information. It is appropriate to inform the relative(s) of one's view that the client should be told, and give them the chance to provide the information themselves, or by other means.

The HIV-Positive Client [7.84]

[7.83] Where the health carer knows that a person is HIV-positive but their spouse or partner does not, and the client does not wish to tell the partner, the question arises as to whether the carer should disclose this information. Some argue for the preservation of confidentiality, but others contend that the partner's welfare is too important: that the client's right to privacy is overridden by their partner's right to know. It is suggested that the latter argument is correct, although there are potential law suits for the carer either way: breach of privacy by the client if the partner is told, negligence by the partner if not told. Some have suggested that the way of resolving this dilemma is to tell the client that the partner should be told and that if the client has not done so within a certain time, the carer (or someone else) will inform them. This of course raises the question of time: while waiting the disease might be contracted. Society (quite rightly) considers AIDS such a serious threat to life that the writer is confident that if the carer did disclose this information after ensuring that the danger exists, taking the above action and informing only the partner it would not be considered a wrongful breach of privacy. Medical staff should notify the State government of those who are HIV-positive (Chapter 16). Disclosure to those other than the partner is a different matter (Chapter 18).

CASE

X v Sattler (unreported, 31 May 1989, SC WA) (*Australian Health and Medical Law Reporter* (1991) ¶27-760)

X sought an injunction against the disclosure by the defendants, broadcasters of a radio program, that he was not only HIV-positive, but that he knowingly or otherwise infected others with the virus. He argued that the allegation of infecting others was untrue, and that they would seriously damage his reputation, career, health and relationships. He admitted he had had a relationship with a woman who was also HIV-positive, who was at the time of the hearing dead, but that he had had no other relationship in the past three years, and had no intention of infecting anyone else.

[7.84] The court granted the injunction in the absence of evidence to support the allegations. The judge held that the imputations were clearly defamatory, and should not be broadcast.

[7.84] ▌▌▌ CASE
Royal Melbourne Hospital v Mathews (unreported, 9 December 1992, SC Vic) (*Australian Health and Medical Reporter* (1991) ¶27-770.42)

The Assistant Director of Medical Services at the Royal Melbourne Hospital refused to give police the medical records of a person who had attended the outpatients' department, and who was charged with knowingly infecting another person with HIV. The hospital sought an injunction restraining the police from searching the hospital and seizing medical records of the patient. The hospital also sought a declaration that the *Health Services Act* provision prohibiting disclosure of information relating to patients applied, or alternatively, a declaration to clarify whether the hospital was under any obligation to deliver up the records.

[7.85] The judge held that a staff member of a health service is bound to hand over patient records to police who have a valid warrant for them, and would not be breaching patient confidentiality. He required the hospital to hand over the records.

[7.86] Special consideration has been given to confidentiality in relation to HIV-positive clients. In September 1992 the Intergovernmental Committee on AIDS Privacy Working Party released a Report (Intergovernmental Committee on AIDS, Privacy Working Party, *HIV/AIDs and Privacy* (AGPS, Canberra, 1992)). This Report noted that the information privacy principles contained in the *Privacy Act* 1988 (Cth) do not provide adequate privacy safeguards for those with HIV/AIDS. The Report contains what are considered to be more appropriate guidelines to be followed by government departments and agencies which hold sensitive information relating to individuals.

▌▌▌ CHECKLIST
PRIVACY PRINCIPLES FOR HIV/AIDS

(Based on the Guidelines established by the Privacy Working Party of the Intergovernmental Committee on AIDS)

These guidelines should apply to those who have had an HIV test even where the result is negative, as well as those who are associated with a person who has HIV/AIDS.

▌..... Information should only be collected with the consent of the client and to serve the lawful functions of an agency. Potential benefits of collecting the information should outweigh any potential harm. Collection should be based on reasonable medical or scientific purposes.

▌..... Before collecting the information, the client should be informed of:
— why the information is sought;
— any law authorising collection;
— whether they are legally required to give the information or not, and in either case the consequences involved;
— what form it will take; and
— by whom and in what circumstances it will be used.

- .....Storage and access to files should be such that: [7.88]
  — only those who are authorised and need the information have access to it;
  — the identity of the person is not apparent on the face of the record;
  — this information should be kept separate from other information about that person; and
  — old and/or unnecessary information should be destroyed.
- .....Records should be
  — accurate;
  — relevant;
  — up-to-date; and
  — complete.
- .....Records should only be used for the purpose for which they have been obtained (for example, care of a particular illness, and not for employment purposes), unless one of the exceptions set out above applies.
- .....Records should only be used for research when this is necessary and names have been removed.

[7.87] In New South Wales the Director General of the Health Department can inform a person who could contract HIV through sexual activity or needle-sharing with an infected person of the infected person's condition under the *Public Health Act*. Also in Tasmania under the *HIV/AIDS Preventative Measures Act* 1993 (Tas) a medical practitioner who becomes aware that a client who is HIV-positive is continuing to engage in conduct which has the potential to infect others may disclose the HIV status of the person to that person. Doctors and authorised health care workers may disclose this information where requested by the client to do so. Other jurisdictions have legislation giving powers to the medical officer responsible for public health to detain persons or otherwise direct their movements where they are placing the public at risk (see below Ch 16).

[7.88] The Intergovernmental Committee on AIDS Legal Working Party also recommended that partner notification should be raised in post-test counselling and be voluntary rather than coercive. However it was suggested that a health carer should be protected from legal action where they notify the partner after:

- .....the client has refused to notify her or his partner;
- .....a real risk of HIV infection exists;
- .....counselling to achieve behaviour change has failed; and
- .....reference has been made to an appropriate professional or professionals, or to a body of professionals, for the purpose of advice.

The Report also recommended that health carers should also be protected where such information is given where:

- .....there is a needle-stick injury where the injured person is at real risk of transmission;
- .....alleged assault involving a real risk of HIV infection where the victim requests to know the HIV status of the alleged perpetrator;

[7.88]
- ..... there is a scientifically based need to know the HIV status of a client for treatment purposes (but not to avoid using universal infection control procedures);
- ..... disclosure in good faith to health authorities where behaviour is unreasonably putting the health of others at risk; and
- ..... where required by law.

Defamation

[7.89] Defamation is the publication of something which wrongfully tends to lower someone in the estimation of others. Communication may be either oral (slander), or in writing (libel), however oral defamatory remarks which have a wide audience or the potential for permanent recording (such as those made on the radio, television or from a stage—and presumably those communicated on the internet) are generally considered libel. The distinction has been abolished in all jurisdictions except South Australia, Victoria and Western Australia. A single person, a group of people, or a company may be the subject of a defamatory statement, and communication need only be between two people, for example, in conversation or the handing of a letter containing the defamatory statement to another for typing.

[7.90] Defamation is covered by legislation in most States and Territories,[6] and, in all States and Territories by common law. It is a different action to those already described in this chapter, and should not be confused with them. Different criteria apply to a defamation action from those for breach of contract or negligence, because the sole interest allegedly harmed in a defamation action is the reputation of the person. Therefore different elements will have to be proved, and different defences will apply. Defamation is generally a civil wrong, but in some circumstances, for example blasphemy, sedition or obscene libel, as well as defamation causing serious harm it is covered by criminal law.

[7.91] Examples of defamation may be an imputation that a colleague is incompetent, or gossip about a patient having venereal disease, or of someone having committed a crime. In the case of *Kitson v Playfair, The Times*, 23-28 March 1896, an obstetrician informed the "head of his patient's household" that in his opinion she had had a recent miscarriage. The result of this was that she was cut off from family inheritance. She successfully sued the doctor in defamation. One must, however, consider the circumstances of the case. The fact that what is said may be true is not always an excuse for telling everybody: on the other hand, not every

---

[6] ACT: *Defamation Act* 1901 (NSW) and *Defamation (Amendment) Act* 1909 (NSW); *Defamation Act* 1974 (NSW); *Defamation Act* 1957 (NT); *Defamation Act* 1889 (Qld), *Criminal Code* (Qld), Ch XXXV; *Wrongs Act* 1936 (SA), Pt 1; *Defamation Act* 1957 (Tas); *Wrongs Act* 1958 (Vic), Pt I; *Criminal Code* (WA), Ch XXXV, is similar to Queensland's Code, but has limited effect on defamation law.

defamatory statement is actionable, even when the statement is quite [7.95] false. The points below should be referred to.

[7.92] The law regarding defamation is not concerned with invasion of privacy or hurt feelings, other actions mentioned above may be more appropriate if harm is severe enough. It is also not possible to defame the dead, no matter what grief and distress may be caused to the relatives thereby. What is to be considered is the reputation of the person involved. The purpose of the law of defamation is to strike a balance between freedom of speech and protection of one's reputation.

Subject of a Defamatory Statement

[7.93] Any person or incorporated body may be the subject of a defamatory statement. As well as an individual, a company, hospital or government department may bring an action as a single legal individual where the body as a whole has allegedly been defamed. Where more than one person alleges defamation, the statement would need to have been such that all those bringing the action could show that by imputation their reputation is besmirched, even though no specific assertion has been made against them individually. The statement may be contained in verbal comments or advice, nurses' notes, patients' records or any other communication, whether as part of one's work or otherwise.

Elements of a Defamation Action

[7.94] The four elements of a defamation action are:

- ..... there must be a statement of fact or opinion or implied fact or opinion;
- ..... it must tend to harm a person's reputation by disparaging him or her, causing others to shun or avoid him or her, or subjecting him or her to hatred, ridicule or contempt;
- ..... it must have been published; and
- ..... it must refer to the person alleging the defamation.

[7.95] **The statement:** There is no established form prescribed for a matter to be considered defamatory. So long as a statement of fact or opinion is made, or an implied statement of fact or opinion (for example, a satirical cartoon, song or play), which expresses or suggests the author's low esteem of someone, which by implication invites the receiver to share that view, it is potentially defamatory. Circumstances surrounding the statement will be important: when, where and how it is made will be crucial factors in the effects it may have. Hurt pride is not enough. In the case of *Tolley v Fry* [1930] 1 KB 467 at 479 the English Court of Appeal held that "To write or say of a man something that will disparage him in the eyes of a particular section of the community, but will not affect his reputation in the eyes of the right thinking man, is not actionable within the law of defamation."

[7.96] **Defamatory material:** A defamatory statement must be shown to be one which the reasonable person would consider tends to bring the subject of it into contempt, ridicule, or diminished reputation. One can defame without intending to so do. For example, a newspaper article gave a fictional account of an English churchwarden's dallying with a woman of bad character in France, for whom the unusual name Artemus Jones was used, was the subject of a defamation action by a barrister from Wales, whose name happened to be Artemus Jones (*Hutton & Co v Jones* [1910] AC 20). A Victorian newspaper published details of allegations made against a certain constable of police named Lee, the paper mistakenly named the policeman as Detective Lee. There were two detectives named Lee in the police force, and they both successfully sued the newspaper (*Lee v Wilson* (1934) 51 CLR 276). Where the defamation is unintentional, an apology and retraction of the statement may satisfy the law.

[7.97] Defamation may occur through the implication that a patient has a socially unacceptable disease or lifestyle, or that one's colleague or employer is incompetent or less than reasonable in her or his standard of care.

[7.98] **Publication:** A statement must be made, or in legal parlance, "published". It does not have to be public. So long as one person has received the communication, there is potential defamation of the subject. Obviously, the more people who receive the material, the more harm is likely to occur.

[7.99] **Reference to the subject:** One does not have to refer directly to a person to defame them in a statement. It is only necessary that the reasonable person would be likely to associate the material with a particular subject.

[7.100] It is suggested, that one should only give information to those to whom it is necessary for the carrying out of the purpose of the communication. There should be, if possible, details and documents to support the communication. A person who successfully sues in defamation is entitled to compensation for damaged reputation.

Specific Defences to an Action in Defamation

[7.101] As well as the exceptions to the disclosure of information set out above, there are several other specific defences to the dissemination of allegedly defamatory material.

[7.102] **Justification:** The law of defamation presumes that defamatory material is false (that is, damages should not be awarded for injury to a character the plaintiff did not or ought not possess). In the Northern Territory, South Australia, Victoria and Western Australia, one is justified in disclosing something about a person as long as it is true. Truth must apply both in substance and in fact, that is not only are the facts disclosed true, but there is no suppression of facts which would alter the imputation. In other jurisdictions, such as the Australian Capital Territory, New South Wales, Queensland and Tasmania, truth alone is not enough. New South Wales requires that the matter be at least substantially true and in the public interest and the other States require both truth and public benefit. If the material complained of contains opinion (for example "In my opinion X is a scoundrel") the truth of the comment is established by proof, not that the writer believes X is a scoundrel, but that the opinion is a conclusion that *ought* to be drawn from the facts.

[7.103] Absolute privilege: This defence to an allegation of defamation, applies to situations requiring unrestricted liberty of expression without fear of litigation. Such situations may vary from jurisdiction to jurisdiction, but generally involve:

- official communications between senior Ministers of the State, and between them and the Crown;
- statements made in the course of parliamentary proceedings and official reports of them, including *Hansard*, and broadcasts of Parliament (indirect reports made of these events are subject to qualified privilege: see below);
- statements made, including evidence given, in judicial and quasi-judicial proceedings (Royal Commissions and disciplinary tribunals have to be covered by special legislation to make them situations of absolute privilege);
- some communications between a solicitor and client which are for the purpose of litigation; and
- communications between husband and wife.

[7.104] Qualified privilege: Qualified privilege applies to those occasions where:

> the person who makes a communication has an interest or a duty, legal, social or moral, to make it to the person to whom it is made, and the person to whom it is so made has a corresponding interest or duty to receive it. This reciprocity is essential [*Adam v Ward* [1917] AC 309 at 339 per Lord Atkinson].

[7.105] Situations where qualified privilege applies (again subject to variation in different jurisdictions), may be said to include:

- answers to police questions;
- communications between solicitor and client;
- evaluations of work performance;
- references written for job applications;
- a report required as part of one's employment;
- communication between employer and employee; and
- some newspaper reports which are made in the public interest, such as fair and accurate reports of those bodies mentioned above, or the revelation of facts where the duty described above exists.

[7.106] One cannot say anything one likes in these situations, statements are governed by the principle that the public good requires that expression can be given to one's beliefs for good and proper reason. Lord Atkinson elaborated on this point in *Adam v Ward* [1917] AC 309 (at 318):

[7.106] [The] authorities, in my view, clearly establish that a person making a communication on a privileged occasion is not restricted to the use of such language merely as is reasonably necessary to protect the interest or discharge the duty which is the foundation of his privilege; but that, on the contrary, he will be protected, even though his language should be violent or excessively strong, if, having regard to all the circumstances of the case, he might have honestly and on reasonable grounds believed that what he wrote or said was true and necessary for the purpose of his vindication, though in fact it was not so.

[7.107] **Fair Comment:** This defence is usually relied upon by journalists, and involves commentary on people and events in the public domain. An example of what is involved is contained in the *Defamation Act* 1974 (NSW) which provides that the comment must be based on proper material for comment and relate to a matter of public interest, "proper material" being such things as true facts, protected reports, books, plays, concerts, or activities of public people and institutions. Luntz et al (1985), p 812 state that fair comment must:

- ..... be based on fact;
- ..... be a matter of public interest;
- ..... be recognisable as comment, not fact; and
- ..... be a conclusion which ought to be drawn from the facts.

[7.108] It follows from the above discussion that consent to the giving of confidential information may be express or implied. Practitioners can presume that a client would consent to the giving of confidential information to others in the health care team where it is necessary in order to give the care which he or she has chosen, but not otherwise.

Health Carers and the Giving of Information

[7.109] The law in relation to confidentiality can be summarised as being based on two principles: first, a client's medical record and general information about her or him should not be disclosed, and secondly, information that is not relevant to the situation (for example a patient's history of an abortion when the matter has to do with a recent industrial injury) should not be disclosed. The following guideline is compiled with the aid of the New South Wales Department of Health, *Circular 82/369*, 5 Nov 1982, and the Queensland Department of Health *Privacy Guidelines for Hospitals* (note that these guidelines are subject to the exceptions already outlined):

Information requested by the client herself or himself: The information should be made available, but this is normally done through a responsible medical officer, who can decide whether he or she believes the patient would be adversely affected by any disclosure. Under freedom of information legislation the patient has a right to personal information kept by Commonwealth or State facilities, and may appeal any decision through State or federal bodies. The Australian Capital Territory provides for access to medical records (see [7.115]). [7.109]

Information requested by relatives: No information should be given without the competent client's consent, unless there are compelling reasons. Even the fact that a person is in the facility may be information that will be harmful to the client (for example, an abusive partner), and based on the principle of autonomy, the client has the right to decide who does or does not receive the information. Health carers should thus not presume that the patient's condition and details can be discussed with relatives, or even a spouse. Where the client is not competent, his or her dignity and confidentiality should be the overriding consideration, and information given on the basis of being necessary in the client's interests. Where the client is a child, parents and guardians may have an interest in receiving the information, but where a child is competent to consent to treatment, it would appear that his or her wishes as to the giving of information to parents should not be disregarded lightly. It is probably only where the welfare of the child requires notification of the parents that this would be justified.

Information requested by other health professionals: As long as the patient consents to care and the information is relevant to that care, it can be passed on as necessary. Staff members of a facility do not have an automatic right to access client information or pass it on. Information should thus not be given to professionals who are not legitimately involved with care to which the patient has consented. If a health carer wants advice, or just the opportunity to talk over treatment of her or his client with a colleague who is not involved with the client's care, identifying information should not be given.

Information requested by solicitors, insurance companies, compensation boards, etc: The patient's permission should be obtained before disclosure, and only information pertinent to the purpose of the request should be supplied.

Information requested by a court, Royal Commission or Commission of Enquiry: This is generally by subpoena (order for someone to attend court, or to produce documents) and, of course, must be complied with. Certified copies of the requested records (unless originals are specifically required) should be supplied in a sealed envelope. Anyone who is not a party to the case, whose records have been subpoenaed should be notified by those providing the records, with details of the hearing. Where medical records are sought as part of the process of "discovery" (preliminary examination by parties to a case), only copies of those documents relevant to the case should be released.

Information requested by the police: Generally, a police officer has no more right to confidential information than anyone else. Requests for information or to examine records should be referred to senior management of the facility where practicable. Information should only be passed on through a responsible health care official who is assured that the police officer is authorised to receive the information in the execution of his or her duty (for example the investigation of a crime or traffic accident). The health carer may be required to give information where the

[7.109] police have a valid warrant or are pursuing an investigation for a criminal offence. The information given should be limited to the information required. If a carer is asked by the police to give information as to, for example, what the patient has said or done while in hospital, whether or not the matter is a coronial or criminal one, he or she is under no legal obligation to answer such questions, and should politely decline to respond. Let police know you wish to be helpful, but would need to seek advice as to the client's rights. In that situation health carers are witnesses, and should only become involved in a case after discussion with legal advisers. One must answer questions when under oath, and cannot be sued in defamation for any information given in a court proceeding. Records of deceased clients should not be handed to police without specific authorisation.

Information requested under statutory right: The authority of the person or body requesting the information should be carefully checked, ensuring that only material relevant to the statutory demand is released.

Information requested by researchers: Information should not be given directly to a researcher but requests should go through an ethics committee which has ensured proper provision for the patient's consent has been made. Unless such a committee has agreed that it is necessary for the purposes of the particular research project, consent should be ensured, and all identifying information should be removed from records.

Information requested by other institutions/health carers: Where the information is required for emergency treatment, the information should be given, but after verification of the requesting body or person, by taking their name and phone number and ringing back. A note should be made of the information released, to whom it was released, and the reason for the request. Where the request is non-urgent, the client's consent should be obtained before release. It should be borne in mind that discharge summaries are the release of confidential information, and if in doubt as to whether the client is aware of the practice of issuing these, he or she should be informed. Also summaries or letters to agencies (for example, welfare agencies or rehabilitation agencies) should only be sent with the client's consent. One practice of a private practitioner known to the writer is the dictation of the letter in the presence of the client.

Information requested by the media: The patient's permission must be obtained before information is given. It should be remembered that information that may seem general and which does not seem to identify the patient may do so indirectly, and so health carers should be very careful in these circumstances. Management of the facility should take responsibility for the release of such information, either directly or indirectly through strict guidelines. It should be noted that filming or photographing part of the facility (which identifies where the person is) may be an infringement of his or her privacy.

Information requested by an employer: Consent of the person is required, and care should be taken to give only that information which is relevant to the employer's financial responsibility.

[7.110] Health care workers need to take care when disclosing confidential information as part of allegations against others such as: [7.111]

- .....the standards of treatment and care practised by their employer or other specific employees;
- .....reporting matters where the welfare of particular people or the public in general may be adversely influenced by the actions of someone else; and
- .....complaining about sexual harassment or other personal maltreatment by another.

It may be acceptable to make statements in some circumstances about others which could harm their reputations, such as their incompetence but this information should be restricted to those who have the authority to deal with the matter, such as management.

CHECKLIST
WHEN CONFIDENTIAL INFORMATION MAY BE DISCLOSED

The Information is true (or reasonably believed to be so) and given in good faith, and

- .....it is necessary for treatment to which the client has consented;
- .....the client has consented to the disclosure;
- .....it is a necessary part of the employer's function of health care, and in the interests of the employer;
- .....it is disclosure to a state authority under statutory requirement (for example, reporting child abuse, the reporting of an infectious disease (Ch 16));
- .....it is disclosure for the public good (for example, potential danger to the community);
- .....it is disclosure in response to legal requirement (for example, giving evidence in a trial) (see also absolute privilege [7.109]) or to a lawyer for the purposes of legal action (see also qualified privilege [7.109]);
- .....for the protection of a person or property, including the patient (see also qualified privilege); or
- .....to the police to aid their inquiries, although one is not obliged to answer police questions (see also qualified privilege).

Client Access to Records

[7.111] The High Court of Australia has held that medical records are owned by the maker of the records or their employer (*Breen v Williams* (1996) 186 ALR 259 at 264 per Brennan CJ), except possibly reports such as X-Rays and pathology reports, for which the client or their insurer pays (at 270 per Dawson and Toohey JJ). There is thus no legal right on the part of clients to medical records that are created by a health carer to assist him or her in providing care, and it is, at common law, the right of the owner of medical records to refuse access to them to a client. Where the health carer is an employee, ownership of the records vests in the employer.

[7.111] Medical staff generally resist client access to records because there may be material contained in them which they would rather the client not have. Some facts may be considered to be harmful to the client, and candid comments could be the subject of defamation.

[7.112] At common law, then, it would seem that the client has a right to X-rays and other reports for which he or she has paid (albeit through Medicare or private health insurance), but this has not been fully considered by the courts.

[7.113] The federal government has, however, provided that people may have access to their medical records belonging to Commonwealth bodies.[7] Some jurisdictions provide freedom of information to records held by State or Territory bodies through legislation or policy statements.[8] The legislation makes access to medical records a legally enforceable right on the part of a person about whom it is written, or a recognised person on their behalf, such as a guardian or solicitor. There is a vestige of paternalism in some freedom of information legislation or practices, in the provision that access may be withheld where the disclosure of information of a medical or psychiatric nature may adversely affect the physical or mental health (or wellbeing in New South Wales) of the person requesting access. However, in this case the person can nominate a medical practitioner to access the information and pass it on in an appropriate manner. The Commonwealth and New South Wales also provide exemption from the Act where access to information may harm any person. General exemptions, which are unlikely to be relevant, also apply, such as the public interest and national security.

[7.114] Information about a child may not be given to a guardian where there is a conflict of interest between the child and the guardian (for example, where a child's medical record reveals information given by the child indicating child abuse). This may also be the case where there would be unreasonable disclosure of a child's personal affairs, or the interests of the child would be prejudiced.

---

[7] *Freedom of Information Act* 1982 (Cth), ss 11, 41(3), 48.

[8] ACT: the federal legislation applies; *Freedom of Information Act* 1989 (NSW), ss 7, 16, 31(4), 39; NT: Administrative Instructions on Confidentiality of Patient Records, March 1986 (access upon confirmation of suitability by the attending physician); Departmental Standing Committee on Privacy in Health and Medical Records (Qld), April 1986 (patients should have access to records where they can understand and accept them, or they are records not damaging to health or prognosis); *Freedom of Information Act* 1982 (Vic), ss 13, 33(4), 39; Western Australian Health Department, *Guidelines for Release/Access to Health Records*, 1986 (access to through a medical practitioner nominated by the patient and acceptable to the particular health institution). This information is according to CCH *Australian Health and Medical Law Reporter* (1991) ¶27-890.

Legislative Moves towards a Right to Records in Private Facilities [7.119]

[7.115] The Australian Capital Territory has enacted the *Health Records (Privacy and Access)* Act 1997 (ACT) which covers both the public and private sector. It establishes a right of access to his or her medical records, while containing a set of privacy principles to protect the records from being accessed by unauthorised persons. Parents and guardians share a right to access medical records of children, and guardians can access the records of adults who are not competent.

[7.116] Where the record holder has reasonable grounds to believe that the provision of the records would create a significant risk to the life or health of the client or any other person, then access can be denied them, but a person can be nominated to access the records and present the information to the client.

[7.117] At the time of writing, the Commonwealth Government has tabled a Bill to amend the *Privacy Act* 1988 (Cth). The Bill provides for, among other things, privacy principles and access to personal information (including health information) by clients in the private sector, and inserting these into the *Privacy Act*. It provides that if an organisation holds personal information about an individual, it must provide the individual with access to the information on request, except for specific circumstances, such as where it is considered a serious and imminent threat to the life or health of any person, it would impact unreasonably on other individuals, would be illegal or unlawful, or would impede the criminal legal process. Where access is denied under the Act, the organisation must, if reasonable, consider whether the use of mutually agreed intermediaries would allow sufficient access to meed the needs of the parties.

[7.118] One result of the increased right of people to their records is an improvement in the care given to the quality of the notes. It would be detrimental if fear of legal action caused health carers to be less than honest and frank (inasmuch as is required for the good care of the client) in the writing of reports.

[7.119] When considering what rights their clients may have to their records, health carers should determine whether legislation applies to the employer for whom they work, and the policies of their employer regarding handling of patient requests for information. The employer will not be likely to countenance free and unfettered access, and clients should be made aware of their situation. Where freedom of information legislation applies, there will be formal procedures to be followed by the person seeking access, involving the filing of a request form. The person should be referred to the appropriate administrative officer. Where it does not apply, most likely access would be through a request to the administration, which will consult the attending medical officer. Those in private practice and private health facilities currently have total control of the records themselves, unless compelled to release them by law. This advice applies, of course, only to records (be they written or computer

[7.119] records), and not to verbal information, which is a matter of weighing rights, needs and policies.

III
REFERENCES AND FURTHER READING

Texts on tort law generally, as listed at the end of Chapter 6, deal with confidentiality and defamation.

Abadee, A, "The Medical Duty of Confidentiality and the Duty to Disclose: Can they Co-exist? (1995) 3 *Journal of Law and Medicine* 75

Australian Health and Medical Law Reporter (CCH, Sydney, 1991)

Brazier, M, *Medicine, Patients and the Law* (Penguin, London,1992)

Devereaux, J, *Medical Law: Text, Cases and Materials* (Cavendish, Australia, 1997)

Dix, et al, *Law for the Medical Profession* (Butterworths, Sydney, 1988), Ch 7

Greenlaw, J, "Documentation of Patient Care, An Often Underestimated Responsibility" (1982) 10 (No 3), *Law Medicine and Health Care*, 125

Intergovernmental Committee on AIDS, Privacy Working Party, *Report* (AGPS, Canberra, 1993)

Langslow, A, "High Drama Lay in Nurses' Notes" (1984) 13 (No 7), *Australian Nurses' Journal*, 29

Luntz, H, Hambly, A and Hayes, R, *Torts: Cases and Commentary* (Butterworths, Sydney, 1985), Ch 15

Mendelson, D, "Mr Cruel and the Medical Duty of Confidentiality" (1994) 1 *Journal of Law and Medicine* 120

Skene, L, *Law and Medical Practice* (Sydney, Butterworths 1998)

Chapter Eight

DRUGS

■■■
INTRODUCTION

[8.1] There are main areas of possible legal liability for health carers handling and giving drugs: breach of the statutory provisions (Acts, Ordinances and Regulations), and breach of the duty of care owed to the patient (negligence). There is also legislation which applies generally in relation to drugs, from testing and manufacture to possession and use.

[8.2] This area of health care practice is of particular concern, because many errors are made in the administration of drugs. O'Sullivan points out:

> a survey by the Pharmaceutical Society of New South Wales in 1981 found that one in four patients in a major Sydney hospital were there because prescribed drugs had been taken incorrectly. In October 1980 at a Canberra conference on drugs it was asserted that some 1,000,000 adverse reactions to prescribed drugs occur each year and between ten and 15 per cent of hospital admissions followed these reactions.[1]

[8.3] There is little indication of any real change over the years (see Review of Professional Indemnity Arrangements for Health Care Professionals (1992)). Health carers are also in a position to wrongfully possess, administer and use drugs, whether knowingly or inadvertently. As ignorance may be no excuse at law, it is important for carers to understand the legal aspects of the drugs that they handle.

[8.4] Drug induced injuries may occur from practices related to manufacture and sale of drugs, as well as research with drugs (for example, see Brazier (1992), Ch 8).

Statutory Law Regarding Drugs

[8.5] Federal legislation deals with such matters as the quality and testing, manufacture and labelling of drugs, as well as the licensing of manufacturers of narcotics. There are numerous State and Territory statutes and regulations on drugs,[2] covering all aspects of possession, sale,

---

[1] O'Sullivan (1983), p 187.

[2] The following, to the author's knowledge, is an up-to-date list: *Therapeutic Goods Act* 1989 (Cth), Therapeutic Goods Regulations 1990 (Cth), *Narcotic Drugs Act* 1967 (Cth); *Poisons Act* 1933 (ACT), Poisons Regulations (ACT), *Poisons and Drugs Act* 1978 (ACT), *Drugs of*

[8.5] dispensing and administration, including criminal offences relating to those drugs classed as illicit. The legislation categorises drugs into eight different Schedules according to their nature and effect. These are found either at the end of the relevant legislation, or in a separate poisons list or as Regulations. Each State or Territory lists those drugs to be included in the classifications which are set out above.

[8.6] The *Therapeutic Goods Act* 1989 (Cth) provides for the manufacture, importing, testing and registration or listing of drugs that meet the standards required for recognition of their safety. Drugs considered potentially more dangerous must pass the stringent testing required for registration. Those drugs which are less hazardous are placed on a separate listing.

Drug Schedules

[8.7] The National Drugs and Poisons Schedule Committee was established in 1999, to ensure a uniform approach to classification of drugs. The *Standard for the Uniform Scheduling of Drugs and Poisons*, has been adopted by all Australian Health Ministers as a basis for uniform classification of drugs across Australia. States and Territories have thus adopted the Schedules to this document which contains classifications for drugs according to their nature. The classifications are as follows:

Schedule 1	poisons of plant origin of such danger to health as to warrant supply by medical practitioners, pharmacists, dentists, veterinary surgeons
Schedule 2	poisons for therapeutic use which should be available to the public from pharmacies or licensed persons only
Schedule 3	poisons for therapeutic use that are dangerous or are so liable to abuse as to warrant restriction of the right of supply to medical practitioners, dentists, pharmacists and veterinary surgeons
Schedule 4	poisons which require a prescription (generally defined in the legislation as "restricted substances"), and substances intended for therapeutic use but which require further evaluation

---

2   *continued*
   Dependence Act 1989 (ACT); *Poisons and Therapeutic Goods Act* 1966 (NSW), Poisons and Therapeutic Goods Regulations 1990 (NSW), *Therapeutic Goods and Cosmetics Act* 1972 (NSW); *Poisons and Dangerous Drugs Act* 1983 (NT), Poisons and Dangerous Drugs Regulations (NT); *Health Act* 1937 (Qld), Health (Drugs and Poisons) Regulations 1996 (Qld); *Controlled Substances Act* 1984 (SA), Controlled Substances (Poisons) Regulations 1996 (SA), *Drugs Act* 1908 (SA), Drugs Regulations 1978 (SA), *Food Act* 1985 (SA); *Poisons Act* 1971 (Tas), Poisons Regulations 1975 (Tas), Poisons List Amendment Order 1990 (Tas); *Drugs, Poisons and Controlled Substances Act* 1981 (Vic), Drugs, Poisons and Controlled Substances Regulations 1985 (Vic), *Therapeutic Goods (Victoria) Act* 1994 (Vic); *Poisons Act* 1964 (WA), Poisons Regulations 1965 (WA).

Schedule 5	hazardous poisons which are available to the public, but which are potentially dangerous and require careful handling, such as domestic poisons, disinfectants and cleaning products	[8.9]
Schedule 6	poisons of a similar nature to, but more dangerous than, those in Schedule 5, such as agricultural and industrial poisons used by farmers, manufacturers and scientists	
Schedule 7	poisons requiring particular precautions in their manufacture, handling, storage or use, or requiring special individual regulations regarding labelling or availability. Drugs such as Clomiphene, Follicle-Stimulating Hormone, Cyclofenil and prostaglandins are contained in this category in NSW, and require special authority from the Health Department (Dix et al (1989), p 166)	
Schedule 8	poisons to which the restrictions recommended for drugs of dependence by the 1980 Australian Royal Commission of Inquiry into Drugs should apply. These are commonly called "drugs of addiction", "dangerous drugs" or "narcotics" and may include hydromorphone, methadone, morphine and pethidine however caution should be used in using terms as the schedule categorises drugs on other grounds, and these terms may cover drugs in different categories. There are severe restrictions on the dispensing of these drugs by pharmacists	
Schedule 9	poisons which are drugs of abuse, the manufacture, possession, sale or use of which should be prohibited by law except for amounts which may be necessary for medical or scientific research conducted with the approval of Commonwealth and/or State or Territory Authorities	

[8.8] The order of the Schedules of greatest to least restriction would appear to be 9, 7, 8, 4, 1, 3, 2, 6, 5. The most important categories for health carers are those listed as Schedule 4 drugs (restricted drugs: available only on prescription by a doctor, dentist or veterinary surgeon) and Schedule 8 drugs (drugs of addiction). They may change from time to time, at which stage those involved in administering drugs should be notified.

Regulation of Drug Prescription, Administration etc

[8.9] Every jurisdiction has detailed legislation governing the possession, prescription, administration and recording of the use of restricted drugs and drugs of addition. There is no short way around the matter: health carers should be familiar with the legislation (including regulations outlining the procedures required in administering drugs) in their State.

[8.9] Most hospitals and health care institutions have drawn up procedural directions, which are written to ensure that legal dictates are followed, and employees are both entitled to, and should, have access to them. Compliance with the legislation is the responsibility of the individual health carer, as vicarious liability may not be available for breaches. Senior administrative staff should also be particularly aware of the law regarding dispensing, storage and handling of drugs.

Prohibition and Controls over Drugs

[8.10] A comprehensive account of all legislative provisions throughout the country is not practicable here. Following is an outline of the main provisions that apply. A more detailed summary of the *Drugs of Dependence Act* 1989 (ACT) is set out in Appendix 4. This outline gives a more detailed summary of legislative provisions that are similar across jurisdictions.

[8.11] **Illegal or illicit drugs:** This term is given to scheduled drugs which are used for non-therapeutic reasons and are not legally prescribed or are otherwise illegally obtained. Additional prohibitions and controls over specific drugs, including quantities that can be prescribed and/or special registration of use, may be established under State legislation (for example, diazepam (valium), which is addictive, pentazocene (Fortral) a halucinogenic, and anabolic steroids.

[8.12] **Restricted drugs:** Drugs which are only obtainable on a doctor's prescription, for therapeutic purposes. They are generally those listed in Schedules 4 and 8. Note the difference from those drugs (Schedules 1 to 3), which may only be supplied by certain people.

Dispensing Drugs

[8.13] Dispensing a drug means making a drug available from a central supply for individual use, a process generally carried out by a pharmacist. There may, however, be provision in the legislation for other licensed persons to dispense where no pharmacist is available, such as administrators in nursing homes. Those allowed to dispense drugs are specifically designated by the legislation, and the process and recording of both storing and dispensing of drugs is set out in some detail.

Supplying Drugs

[8.14] At law, this means making a drug available to another person. Those who supply drugs must be licensed, and the conditions of supply are restricted. It is worth noting that legislation has established that where one has more than a stipulated amount of nominated drugs (mainly, those known as "illicit" drugs) in one's possession, the drug may be deemed to be intended for supply, no matter what the actual intention may be. Possession for supply is a more serious offence than mere possession for personal use of a prohibited drug.

Possession of Drugs

[8.15] In law this involves having a substance in one's physical control (not necessarily on one's person). Certain drugs may only be in the possession of specified persons, which can include doctors, veterinary surgeons, emergency services personnel, appropriate nursing staff in a health care institution, and rural community and industrial nurses under appropriate circumstances. (In most cases community nurses are not permitted to have restricted or addictive drugs in their possession.) In some cases now, health carers can apply to have restricted drugs or narcotics in their possession (for example, nurses in Tasmania and indigenous health workers in Queensland). Wrongful possession of prohibited drugs will attract penalties at law.

Prescription of Drugs

[8.16] This is the granting of the right to receive a drug to a particular person. "Restricted drugs" (a term here used to refer to drugs requiring prescription which are listed in Schedule 4 or Schedule 8) must be prescribed in writing by a medical officer, except in emergencies. In that case the drug may be ordered by word of mouth, in which case most States require that the prescription be written up and signed within a prescribed time, usually 24 hours. Provision for the form of prescriptions, those who can prescribe drugs and the drugs which require prescription are established by the legislation. Generally, a prescription must be written or printed in ink, signed, contain the name of the recipient, the drug, the dosage, the route, adequate instructions for use and the number of times the drug may be dispensed, or, for certain substances, the time between repeated administration. Not all legislation is this detailed, but in those States where it is not, practice directives and hospital protocols will establish the requirements. The legislation generally allows only doctors, dentists or veterinary surgeons to prescribe those drugs in the specially designated schedules, and lays down specific rules for the prescription of drugs of dependence. However, nurses are increasingly being permitted to prescribe some scheduled drugs (that is, to decide to administer a drug without a doctor's order) in certain circumstances. These include emergencies in remote areas where a doctor's prescription is not practicable, midwifery (for example, in Tasmania nurses can prescribe certain drugs under authorisation by a doctor, in Victoria a midwife may give a single dose of morphine or pethidine in an emergency, notifying a doctor as soon as practicable).

[8.17] It is an offence to write a prescription unless one is authorised to do so. It is also an offence to alter a prescription or obtain one by false pretences.

Administration of Drugs

[8.18] This means the actual giving of the drug, orally, by injection, per rectum or other route. Health carers are permitted to administer prohibited drugs where they are required to do so as a part of their duties. Drugs for which detailed instruction regarding administration is given in legislation are:

Schedule 8 drugs. These generally require that in health institutions a register be kept and the following be recorded:[3]

- patient's name;
- prescribed drug and dose;
- prescribing doctor's name;
- date and time of administration;
- balance of ampoules or capsules, tablets etc in supply;
- signature of two nurses (or a nurse and a doctor) who checked the preparation and administration of the drug (at least one of the nurses should be registered); and
- any error is to be ruled through in ink with the entry still legible, with the correction entered, dated and initialled on the same page.

[8.19] It is not possible to discuss all the different provisions that apply to drugs in the different States. A summary of important provisions of the *Drugs of Dependence Act* 1989 (ACT) is set out in Appendix 4. This will give an idea of the complexity and comprehensiveness of drug legislation, as well as the legal restrictions on such matters as prescribing, storing and administering drugs.

Storage and Recording of Drugs

[8.20] Schedule 8 drugs must be kept under lock and key, separate from other drugs, with especially nominated persons having control of the key. Some jurisdictions stipulate the nature of the cupboard in which they must be kept (for example, fixed to the wall or floor, and resistant to attack by hand tool for 30 minutes, power tools for 5 minutes). Where there is a pharmacist he or she is responsible for storage and recording of all restricted substances. Otherwise the medical superintendent or director of nursing of a health care facility is held responsible. Scheduled drugs other than Schedule 8 drugs must be stored in a place where the public does not have access, in varying degrees of security.[4] Storage of drugs and

---

[3] *Drugs of Dependence Act* 1989 (ACT); Poisons Regulations 1990 (NSW); *Poisons and Dangerous Drugs Act* 1983 (NT); Health (Drugs and Poisons) Regulations 1996 (Qld); Controlled Substances Regulations 1993 (SA), Drugs of Dependence (General) Regulations 1985 (SA); Poisons Regulations 1975 (Tas); Drugs, Poisons and Controlled Substances Regulations 1985 (Vic); Poisons Regulations 1965 (WA). Other requirements apply to first aid services.

[4] Victoria requires poisons to be stored in a locked cupboard. *Drugs of Dependence Act* 1989 (ACT), ss 114, 115, *Poisons Act* 1933 (ACT), s 17; Poisons Regulations 1990 (NSW), regs 7, 8, 30(1), 55, 67, 67a; *Poisons and Dangerous Drugs Act* 1983 (NT), ss 51, 52; Poisons Regulations 1973 (Qld); Controlled Substances Regulations 1993 (SA), reg 65; Poisons Regulations 1975

recording of their use in a ward is the responsibility of the charge nurse, who must maintain the prescribed security by ensuring that the drug cupboard is locked when not in use. The key is always to be in the possession of the most senior nurse on the ward at any time and must not be left where others have access to it. Regular inventory of Schedule 8 drugs must be kept. In health care facilities in most jurisdictions, drugs are to be transported in a locked container.

[8.21] A register of drugs of addiction must be kept, with details of number and usage (including patient's name, date and time of administration or destruction, prescribing physician, and signatures of the person giving the drug and the witness) recorded. The nurse in charge of a ward is responsible for the maintaining of the register of such drugs kept in the ward.

[8.22] Every ward must keep a drug register of specified drugs (usually Schedules 4, 8 and 9—"restricted" drugs). The Australian Capital Territory, the Northern Territory and South Australia provide that administration of a narcotic drug must be witnessed by another person. It is suggested that this should be the rule elsewhere. Both the nurse preparing and administering and at least one other witness (nurse or doctor) should sign the register. Any error must be corrected and witnessed, with the erroneous material carefully ruled through and not obliterated, and a marginal note with the correct details and the signatures of both parties legibly entered with the date (and preferably time) of the correction, and initialled by the witnesses. It is recommended that if it is possible to do so clearly and legibly, the names of the signatories should be printed as well.

[8.23] Most jurisdictions require that the balance of restricted drugs should be also checked regularly by two people, any unusable drugs destroyed as above. Any discrepancies should be immediately notified to the head pharmacist of a hospital and person in charge of nursing, so that an investigation can be carried out. Where drugs are lost or stolen, the police and the Health Department should be notified.

Destruction of Drugs

[8.24] Where a Schedule 8 drug is unusable it must be destroyed and accounted for by at least two people, who record such destruction in the register. Loss must be recorded, and where a drug is only part used, the remainder of the drug must be destroyed, again witnessed by two people and recorded in the register. Exact details differ: carers should be aware of the precise requirements in their State and workplace.

[8.25] Where less than a full ampoule, tablet or unit of a scheduled medication is used, the remainder should be destroyed, with the

---

4 *continued*
(Tas), regs 18, 19, 22, 31, 37; Drugs, Poisons and Controlled Substances Regulations 1985 (Vic), regs 401, 402, 404, 910, 1110, 1126; Poisons Regulations 1965 (WA), regs 35, 56.

[8.25] destruction witnessed and signed for by both the person who destroys the drug and the witness. Any unusable or out-of-date drugs should be returned to the pharmacist and duly recorded and witnessed in the record. Signatures of "witnesses" should not be sought after the drug has been destroyed, to satisfy requirements, and one should make sure that the ampoules, tablets, etc which remain are really the drug prescribed and not a substitute. Where there is no pharmacist, the director of nursing or medical superintendent is responsible for these procedures.

[8.26] Health carers in remote areas, paramedics, ambulance officers and doctors in private practice who are authorised to possess restricted drugs and drugs of addiction are also required to keep drugs secure, keep proper records, and record the use and destruction of drugs in a similar manner. The possession and conveyance of restricted drugs and narcotics has expanded (and will expand more) with the increased development of "hospital in the home" programs, home-based palliative care, community nursing and nurse practitioners in private practice. Those providing care in these areas should be aware of the detailed requirements for handling drugs in their jurisdiction. These health carers have responsibility for overseeing the proper adherence to legislative and administrative requirements, and of ensuring regular and thorough inventory of the drugs in their possession; immediately reporting any discrepancy in numbers to the appropriate authority. They should ensure they are authorised to possess, prescribe and administer drugs that they are expected to use, and the circumstances under which they can do so. The only way one can find out the detailed extent of these responsibilities is to have access to the legislative requirements and administrative procedures manuals, both of which should be made available through an employer. It is incumbent on health authorities to ensure that adequate legislative provisions, and detailed guidelines which conform with the law are available in this rapidly changing area of health care.

Prescription of Drugs of Addiction

[8.27] New South Wales, the Northern Territory, Queensland and Victoria doctors may not treat drug addicts with drugs of addiction, and there may be special requirements for the prescribing of such drugs for a period of more than several weeks in other cases. Special circumstances are recognised, and permission may be sought to extend the time limit for therapeutic reasons. Victoria restricts the prescription of some amphetamines, methadone and methylphenidate and required doctors to be licensed to prescribe them except in specified circumstances. In the Australian Capital Territory, those addicted can only be treated, with approval by the Medical Officer of Health, with methadone treatment regime. Health carers should be wary about the extended administration of Schedule 8 drugs and inquire into the authorisation of their administration, as in most cases notification and permission of the chief health officer (or equivalent) is required for prescription other than short-term therapeutic use. In Western Australia the Supreme Court found that a doctor who treated heroin-addicted patients with combinations of valium, doloxene and rohypnol as part of a harm-reduction policy to get them to desist from the use of heroin was not guilty of "infamous conduct in a professional respect" under the *Medical Act* 1894 (WA) (see [13.98]). [8.31]

Drug Order Forms

[8.28] Health carers should insist on the correct prescribing of drugs by physicians. This means they should be able to clearly read the name of the drug (not guess!), the dosage, route, frequency and any special instructions, as drugs should not be administered unless properly prescribed.

[8.29] A patient's drug order form is recognised by some as a prescription form for the purposes of drug legislation, and it is suggested that nurses and other health carers should not use this form except where hospital policy establishes the use of drug order forms for verbal orders. In that case it is suggested staff should be very careful that a verbal order is clearly marked as such (preferably in a different colour). It is suggested that a more satisfactory approach is that set out in the Checklist at [8.47]. If they wish to record a (temporary) oral order by a physician they are advised to enter the administration of the drug in the drug administration form, clearly indicating that the drug was given subject to a verbal order, thus preventing any mistake as to their record purporting to be a prescription as such, or the impression that the order was written by a doctor, and no further action required. It is also suggested that some clear and distinguishing marker (such as a sticker) be applied to the patient's notes with a clear notation on it of the fact that the order is to be written up, and the time by which this must be done.

Emergencies

[8.30] In emergencies, all jurisdictions provide that oral orders for administration of restricted drugs may be given to authorised health carers such as nurses and para-medics, with the requirement that the doctor giving the order must write the prescription up, for example, in the patient's notes, either as soon as practicable or within 24 hours. Because of legal limitations on the prescribing of drugs, oral orders should only be accepted in emergencies or where the doctor cannot reasonably attend to write the prescription, and should not be based on the convenience of those involved. In all cases the checklist on telephone orders (below, [8.47]) should be followed as closely as possible.

[8.31] Jurisdictions differ in provisions for the administration of opiates and other restricted drugs on verbal order in an emergency. The details of the patient, the drug, time and route of administration, amount given and further doses ordered, as well as the name of the prescribing doctor and signature of authorised person administering it must be noted. In Victoria a midwife working in a hospital may give a single dose of morphine or pethidine in an emergency, notifying the patient's doctor as soon as practicable (Therapeutic Goods Regulations 1994 (Vic)).

[8.32] **[8.32]** Recording and witnessing emergency oral orders and administration of drugs should follow the above rules as closely as is practicable under the circumstances. Temporary recording (for example, on the patient's skin, plaster cast) may be the only practical way of doing this, with proper records made as soon as possible afterwards. The use of witnesses is also an important consideration.

Non-Scheduled Drugs and Complementary Medicines

[8.33] Health carers have access to non-restricted drugs, such as panadol, kaomagma, laxatives and many different creams and lotions, which they may administer and apply on their own initiative. It should be remembered that although the handling and administering of these drugs may not be the subject of legislation, carers should carefully follow any hospital procedure requirements, or they may be subject to a negligence action (see [8.39]ff), disciplinary action (see [8.38]), or health care complaint (see Ch 18).

[8.34] Under the *Therapeutic Goods Act* 1989 (Cth), the Commonwealth Government has established a Complementary Medicines Evaluation Committee to evaluate and report on complementary medicines, and recommend or disapprove their registration. These can include vitamin, mineral, naturopathic, homoeopathic or herbal preparations, which become regulated medicines under the Act.

[8.35] This means that those involved in using complementary therapies should also be aware of the legislative requirements as to the use of these therapies, and any restrictions on them.

Re-Packaging Drugs

[8.36] An important point to bear in mind is that, ideally, drugs should never be changed from the container in which they are dispensed. Provision for labelling of drugs by the dispensing pharmacist, giving their category (such as "POISON" or "CAUTION"), or warnings and use (for example, "Not for internal use"), is made in the legislation, and this should not be altered.

Where drugs are left with clients for their own administration in special containers, with, for example, compartments for different days, this should be seen as administration of, rather than dispensing of, the drugs. In this case it is suggested that the containers are marked with the day and time the drugs are to be taken, and not the name of the drugs themselves. This means that they are not undertaking that the drugs are specific ones, which technically could be dispensing the drugs, but are rather providing for their administration. The patient should be well instructed (preferably in writing in addition to verbal instructions), as to taking the drugs. Information as to the name of the drug, its identification (colour, size etc), any information regarding the taking of it, side-effects and contra-indications that are relevant should be provided in writing elsewhere, as well as orally. This gives both the client and others who may need to deal with her or him in an emergency, necessary information, preventing liability for negligence.

Drugs and Criminal Law

[8.37] There are criminal sanctions in the legislation for the unauthorised possession, possession for supply, administration and self-administration of restricted drugs, with some specifically named drugs of dependence having more severe penalties than others. There are also penalties for the forging or fraudulent obtaining of, or wrongful giving of, prescriptions for restricted substances or drugs of dependence. Health carers have access to restricted and non-restricted drugs and drugs of dependence. They should be very careful that not only do they not misuse this privilege, but that they never cut corners and compromise the clear guidelines for handling of drugs. Misuse of drugs by health workers is considered such a serious matter by the community, that one should not give cause for doubt as to one's integrity in handling them.

Disciplinary Action

[8.38] Health professionals who are found guilty of a criminal offence in relation to drugs, or who misuse or are addicted to drugs may lose their practising certificate, even where the law has technically not been broken but one has been careless or negligent (see Chs 6, 13: *Cranley v Medical Board of Western Australia*, see [13.98]).

Common Law Concerning Drugs (Negligence)

[8.39] Apart from statutory law, health carers should be aware of their need to take reasonable care to prevent harm to patients from negligent handling and administration of drugs. The reader is referred to the discussion of negligence in Chapter 5, however here we will consider cases specifically dealing with the giving of drugs.

[8.40] Where patient agreement to treatment has been given health carers should give consideration to the following matters.

Consent

- ..... What is the purpose of the medication—therapeutic, research, behaviour modification? Has this been discussed with the client? Or person responsible?
- ..... Has information about the medication's effects, side-effects and risks been given to the client or person responsible?
- ..... Has a choice of treatment been offered where this is available?

Reasonable Care

- .....Are there less drastic, effective alternatives?
- .....Has the client/person responsible been checked for adverse reaction to the drug?
- .....Have appropriate precautions been taken where relevant (for example, client safety)?
- .....Is there an adequate agreed means of monitoring the effects of treatment, so that patient feedback is heard and acted upon?
- .....Is there an adequate means of long-term supervision of drugs (for example, proper history, prevention of addiction, etc)?

Unclear Order

[8.41] An order may be unclear because it is illegible, or does not fully specify requirements. An example of the former case follows.

CASE

Prendergast v Sam and Dee Ltd, Kozary and Miller, The Times, London, 14 March 1989

Dr M wrote a prescription for Mr P, who was suffering from asthma. The prescription was for ventolin inhalers, phyllocontin and amoxil. The pharmacist, Mr K, read 'amoxil' as 'daonil' which is a drug for treating diabetes, which P did not have. As a result of taking the daonil, P suffered irreversible brain damage. He sued the doctor pharmacist, and the pharmacy in negligence, on the basis that the doctor's writing was negligently illegible, and the pharmacist was negligent in providing the wrong drug. Dr M argued that, despite the illegible prescription, the chain of causation was broken because the pharmacist should have realised the drug prescribed was not daonil, because, among other things:

- .....K should have got in touch with the doctor when he found the prescription hard to read;
- .....the dosage strength ordered was not appropriate for daonil, but was for amoxil;
- .....that the other drugs ordered were for treating asthma, and daonil was not;
- .....that the prescription was for 21 tablets only—a short course appropriate for amoxil but not for daonil; and
- .....daonil is taken only once a day, whereas the prescription was provided for three tablets a day.

[8.42] The court rejected Dr M's argument, stating that the chain of causation had not been broken. It said that it was not outside the realms of reasonable foreseeablity that the doctor could have ordered daonil. It said that the doctor could not rely on the pharmacist to second-guess the doctor's order, or to get in touch with him if he had difficulty reading it.

[8.43] However, this does not let the person who has trouble reading a doctor's order from investigating further. The person prescribing a drug should be questioned if an order is not clear, or if the order seems an unreasonable one, and health carers are required to use reasonable knowledge and care in so doing.

■ ■ ■ CASE [8.47]
Norton v Argonaut Insurance Co, 144 So 2d 249 (1962) (CA Los Angeles United States)

A three-month-old baby was treated with lanoxin elixir, the original order being "2.5cc (0.125 mg) q6h x 3 then once daily". After the child was digitalised, the mother was instructed in administration and maintenance of the dose and the child was treated at home. On second admission the admitting doctor noted that the mother was giving medication, but did not specify what it was. He increased the dose, telling the mother, and wrote "Give 3.0cc lanoxin today for 1 dose only", neglecting to specify the form of the drug, the route, and the fact that the mother was giving the medication. Later that day the assistant director of nursing volunteered to assist in the ward due to its lack of staff, and began by checking the medications. On reading this order, and being unfamiliar with the fact that there was a paediatric suspension of lanoxin, she questioned other doctors and nurses about a written order for lanoxin which did not specify route, and appeared excessive. Due to their not fully understanding the nurse's lack of knowledge about the drug, and the circumstances of its proposed administration (the mother had already given the day's dose), the nurse was advised by these people to give the drug in the dosage written down. Wrongly believing that there is a presumption that unless specified, drugs are to be given intramuscularly, the nurse gave the child 3cc lanoxin intramuscularly. The child died.

[8.44] The court found the hospital, doctor and nurse jointly liable for the child's death. Firstly, the doctor did not properly record the specific drug (paediatric suspension), and omitted the route by which it was to be given. Two specific and important points regarding the administration of drugs was made by the court, as follows:
1 *Where a drug order is not clear, nurses should make absolutely certain what the doctor intended. This should be done by consulting the doctor who wrote the order, for, as this case shows, consulting others may lead to errors.*

[8.45] Only in emergencies, where the prescribing doctor is not available and the drug must be given, should another doctor be consulted. One must be very careful, as we learn from this case, to procure a freshly written and full order, clearly giving the name of the drug, the dosage, route and frequency, and ensuring the patient's name and history are clearly identified with the order. Do not make any presumptions.
2 *Although nurses may not be expected to have the same depth of knowledge about drugs as that expected of doctors, they should at least have some familiarity with any drug they administer.*

[8.46] Health carers should be familiar with the standard dosage, effects, side-effects and contra-indications of the drugs they give. One should consult the label on the drug itself, and a reference (a pharmacopoeia should be available). If there is a discrepancy in the information on the label and the drug order (such as an ordered dosage in excess of the recommended dose in the reference) this should be questioned.

[8.47] The further point could be made that the nurse in *Norton's* case helped out in an area of specialty in which she was not competent. Although this is covered to some extent in the second point made by the court, one could add that inexperienced carers should beware of

[8.47] undertaking specialist activities, even where attempting to help overworked colleagues. In this case it could be argued that the nurse should have undertaken only those basic nursing activities that did not require a knowledge of paediatric nursing. See the discussion of what one should do when asked to work in an area in which one does not feel competent (see [6.106]ff).

Telephone Orders

[8.48] Some comments have been made about telephone orders at [8.29]. Most health care institutions have established procedures for the taking of telephone drug orders. The following is suggested as advisable procedure in providing for reasonably careful taking of such orders (see also [8.26]).

■■■ CHECKLIST
HOW TO TAKE A TELEPHONE DRUG ORDER: RECOMMENDED PRACTICE

- ..... Write the order as it is being given.
- ..... Read it back to the prescribing doctor.
- ..... Get a colleague to hear the order from the doctor, write it down, and repeat it to the doctor.
- ..... Resolve any discrepancy or difficulty in hearing the order before the telephone conversation is completed.
- ..... The order should be written, preferably on the drug administration form (*not* on the drug order form), and clearly marked as an *administration of a drug pursuant to telephone order* (preventing it being considered a written order by the prescribing doctor, or the erroneous reading of the actual written doctor's order as a fresh order for repeat administration).
- ..... Ensure the drug and its administration is checked and witnessed as required when entered on the drug administration form.
- ..... Record on that client's notes that special action is required, namely the writing up of the order by the doctor. Take any further action to ensure follow up, such as flagging for action, contacting doctor to secure written order, etc, that is required.

[8.49] The reader is referred to the case of *Collins v Hertfordshire County Council* (see [6.99]) where a telephone order was misheard, with fatal results. The difficulties of identifying those situations where a telephone drug order may be misheard leads the author to recommend that this form of ordering should only be used in emergencies or where a written order would be extremely difficult to obtain, and should not be used as a tool of convenience. Some States require that telephone orders are restricted to emergencies, but do not define these. Use of telephone orders for convenience could very well be considered negligence by a court. Nurses should not be pressured into following legally risky procedures (let alone physically risky ones), and should be given support by nursing and medical administration to prohibit written drug orders in non-urgent circumstances.

Transcribing of Drug Orders

[8.50] To prevent drug errors, one should not transcribe orders and administration of drugs from the drug order or administration forms to other records. Where a drug has been ordered by a doctor, one should write in the patient's notes: "Seen by Dr Smith. Analgesia prescribed as per drug order form" not—"Seen by Dr Smith. Pethidine 75 mgm imi 4th hourly prn ordered." Mistakes can be made in the transcription, and someone may be tempted to rely on the secondary source rather than the original, and may end up giving the wrong medication. Conversely, nurses should not give medication that must be prescribed on the basis of any other written source than the original drug order on the drug order form (such as the nurses' notes or doctor's consultation form).

▌▌▌ CASE
Pillai v Messiter (No 2) (1989) 16 NSWLR 197 (CA)

A patient died from an overdose of phenytoin. The order for the drug had been transcribed from an out-of-date prescription sheet on to a new one. The patient had been ordered phenytoin 230 mg daily, and tegretol 1,400 mg daily. In transcribing, the doctor wrote the new order as phenytoin 1,400 mg to be given three times daily. A number of other doctors and nurses had also not noticed the error in transcription. The transcribing doctor was struck off the register for misconduct in a professional respect and appealed to the Supreme Court.

[8.51] Although the Supreme Court held that the doctor's error was an "unfortunate mistake", it held that it was not enough to constitute misconduct to the extent of attracting the penalty of being struck off the register. Certainly such a mistake could lead to liability in negligence on the doctor's part, possibly also on the part of the other nurses and doctors who failed to detect the mistake.

Giving the Wrong Drug

[8.52] There are several reasons, it is suggested, for a patient receiving the wrong drug, for example:
▌..... the drug order is unclear (dealt with above);
▌..... a verbal order is misheard; and
▌..... failure to check the label on the drug.

Mistake in Verbal Orders

[8.53]   There is a responsibility on the part of health care staff to carefully check at the time of receiving it, a verbal order for treatment with which they are not familiar.

▌▌▌ CASE
Henson v Board of Management of Perth Hospital (1939) 41 WALR 15 (SC)

A resident doctor instructed a student nurse to administer glycerine and carbol ear drops to a patient. The nurse understood him to have ordered undiluted acid carbol, but when she went to question the doctor he was gone. She checked with a staff nurse, who was also unsure, but poured some carbolic acid into a bottle to give to the patient, instructing him to pour some of it into his ear. When he did so damage was caused to his ear drum and he sustained some permanent hearing loss.

[8.54]   The court found both nurses and the doctor liable in negligence. It held that the student nurse, while not being expected to know as much as a staff nurse, should have exercised due care in ascertaining whether she had obtained the correct medication. The staff nurse, it seems, had even less chance of escaping liability, especially as it was shown that she burnt her fingers when pouring out the carbolic acid! The doctor was also negligent, the court said, because he failed to give adequate instructions when a student nurse was involved, and failed to record the order in writing.

Failure to Check Drugs

[8.55]   Failing to check drugs is, of course, is a serious failure in the eyes of the law.

▌▌▌ CASE
Bugden v Harbour View Hospital [1947] DLR 338 (SC Canada)
(initial hearing)

The plaintiff was treated at the defendant hospital for an injury to his thumb. The doctor decided to set it and asked nurse Bonnar, an experienced graduate nurse, for some novocaine. Nurse Bonnar asked nurse Spriggs to get the novocaine. Nurse Spriggs handed nurse Bonnar a phial which was labelled, and, without looking at the label nurse Bonnar handed it to the doctor, who, also without checking the label, injected it into Bugden. The drug injected was in fact adrenalin, and Bugden died within an hour.

[8.56]   Nurse Spriggs argued that nurse Bonnar's failure to read the label was an intervening factor and nurse Bonnar in turn pointed to the doctor's failure to read it as an intervening factor (see above, Ch 5). The court did not accept either argument, holding that the foreseeablity of harm to the patient was enough to require all involved to take care, and found the nurses liable, while exonerating the doctor. In the English case of *Collins v Hertfordshire County Council* (see [6.99]) the court stated (at 606) that:

> every surgeon takes responsibility for what he injects into a patient as local anaesthetic and that he should take some step reasonably to make sure, before he injects it, that he is injecting that which he ordered.

It is suggested that, based on the principles of negligence, this statement can be extended to cover all drugs given by all health care personnel.

Giving the Wrong Dosage

[8.57] There are cases where the wrong dosage has been given for various reasons, such as not reading or not hearing the order correctly. This may be because of illegibility or carelessness on the part of the doctor ordering it, or carelessness on the part of those receiving the order.

[8.58] This has been dealt with to some extent in this chapter. A case occurred in Victoria where a 19-month-old girl was given 500 milligrams of aminophylline for asthma instead of 50 milligrams. The doctor ordering the drug had been on duty for many hours and had failed to write the order clearly. The two registered nurses on duty had failed to question the excessive dosage (described in O'Sullivan (1983), p 192). Such unfortunate events lead to accountability at law. Nurses should check the label on the bottle or ampoule carefully, and the mode of administration should be clearly written down. Of course nurses must always check when the last dose was given.

▌▌▌ CASE

Smith v Brighton and Lewes Hospital, The Times, 2 May 1958 (England)

The patient was ordered 30 injections of streptomycin at eight-hour intervals for a severe case of boils. She received 34 doses, and as a result suffered damage to the eighth cranial nerve, causing loss of balance. On investigation of the facts it was found that there had not been an adequate record of the number of injections, and no cut-off date had been established. This was the responsibility of the ward sister.

[8.59] As a result the nurses who administered the extra injections were held not liable. An added feature of this case was that the ward sister, believing the nurses were the ones who would be held responsible, had attempted to shield the nurses by concealing from the doctor the fact that the extra doses had been given. This, the trial judge held, was an "ugly and unfortunate feature" of the case, and may have prevented the woman from receiving the benefit of the doctor's knowledge of the circumstances. The hospital was found liable for a large sum of money based on the ward sister's negligence.

Giving the Drug to the Wrong Patient

[8.60] Even where it is thought that a client's name is known, their identity should be carefully checked. Patients may say "yes" when asked "Are you Mrs So-and-So?" just to be polite or helpful, when they did not hear the question correctly. Positive identification should be made by having the client state their name and date of birth. Special care should be taken where it is known or suspected that there are two or more clients with the same surname. This care should be taken even where the health carer feels familiar with the client's name, at the expense of embarrassment at going through the procedure. It is better to face some embarrassment over the apparent over-cautiousness of such a procedure (one may even make a joke of it), than to regret later that, for the sake of saving face, one has caused heartache and loss to others.

Giving the Drug in the Wrong Site

[8.61] Special requirements for the administration of drugs must be known by, and/or communicated to, those administering drugs or patients taking them. Injections may cause harm if given subcutaneously rather than intramuscularly.

CASE
From Medical Protection Society Report 1974 (described in Langslow (1981), p 23)

A general practice doctor prescribed kenalog (triamcinolene acetonide) for a patient. The nurse administering it was not aware of the manufacturer's warning that the drug should be given by deep intramuscular injection to avoid subcutaneous fat atrophy. As the result of the subcutaneous injection of the drug and resulting fat atrophy, the woman sued the doctor. The Medical Protection Society settled on behalf of the doctor.

[8.62] The nurse was not sued in this case, but it is quite feasible that in a similar situation she could be. Nurses, in particular, may also be interested in the following case.

CASE
Cavan v Wilcox [1975] SCR 663 (SC Canada)

A nurse administered an injection of bicillin into a patient's deltoid muscle. Despite the fact that she had pulled back the plunger to check that no blood vessel had been pierced, the substance entered the circumflex artery, and as a result the patient developed gangrene of part of his hand.

[8.63] The court found the nurse not liable in negligence, as she had checked that she had not penetrated any blood vessel, which was satisfactory precaution under the circumstances. The court also decided that knowledge of the proximity of the artery to the injection site was not [8.66] part of nurse training, and therefore not part of the body of knowledge that should be possessed by the reasonable nurse. Readers may decide that today a court in Australia would come to a different conclusion. Hitting of the sciatic nerve is, of course, a danger of which nurses should be aware. This was the conclusion of the following United States case.

▌▌▌ CASE

Honeywell v Rogers, 251 F Supp 841 (1966) (District Court Pennsylvania United States)

A student nurse gave an injection of iron dextran to an 11-month-old child. The mother gave evidence that it was given towards the centre of the buttock and not the outer and upper quadrant.

[8.64] There the court took into account the training, supervision and knowledge of student nurses in the giving of injections, and determined that the injection was negligently given by the student nurse in question.

Failure to Check for Adverse Effects

[8.65] It should be evident by what has been said that health carers should be aware of the likely adverse effects of the drugs they give. This may be information:
▌.....learned from lectures or in textbooks current and relevant to the profession;
▌.....set out on the drug label or accompanying brochure;
▌.....established by a circular distributed by the employer; or
▌.....recorded in a patient's notes by the prescribing physician.

▌▌▌ CASE

Chin Keow v Government of Malaysia [1967] 1 WLR 813 (Privy Council England)

A doctor ordered penicillin for a patient, whom he knew had been given penicillin previously. The doctor was aware of the possibility of an adverse reaction to penicillin. However he had given many doses (as many as 100 per day) without any such reaction. In this case he went ahead and gave the injection. It was only after the death of the patient from an adverse reaction that his outpatient card was consulted and found to be marked "Allergic to Penicillin".

[8.66] The court found the doctor liable. It said that it would take into account the probability of adverse reactions, and what the reasonable practitioner should know about them when considering what, if any, liability to impose. The doctor should have made further inquiries, the fact that reactions are rare was not justification for his failure to do so. Drugs which require specific attention from health carers, such as digoxin and insulin, are the most obvious drugs about which they should take care, but as pointed out above, not the only ones.

[8.67] **[8.67]** Other cases involving the failure to take proper precautions to prevent adverse reactions are *Battersby v Tottman* (1985) 37 SASR 524 (see above, [5.95]), where the serious condition of the patient was held to warrant excessively large doses, despite the danger of adverse effects. *Robinson v Post Office* [1974] 1 WLR 1176 established the accepted medical precaution of giving a test dose of anti-tetanus serum as a legal requirement. The likelihood of adverse effects of a drug must be reasonably probable and reasonably part of the knowledge of the profession for it to be necessary to be taken into account.

Standing Orders

[8.68] Protocols or standing orders may establish procedures to be followed in the administration of some restricted drugs, which may allow for them to be given by health carers such as nurses and paramedics in certain situations, such as emergencies, or as routine treatment for the patients of particular practitioners (most often occurring in obstetric practice). They generally take the form of general prescriptions. The legality of these is far from certain, except in cases where they have been recognised by legislation (see [8.16] above). The fact that they are written orders to be followed in relation to particular patients (those in intensive care, or patients of a particular obstetrician, for example) in specific circumstances is generally considered acceptable as proper prescriptions. It is of concern that there is not clear legislative provision establishing their status at law, and setting out requirements if they are to be legally recognised. They have not been legally challenged at this stage, to the author's knowledge. In the meantime, there is a risk that they will be considered unlawful. Standing orders are often used as an administrative convenience rather than a way of dealing with emergencies. So long as they are used in cases of emergency, the following checklist should ameliorate any liability.

▮▮▮ CHECKLIST
PROTOCOLS AND STANDING ORDERS

- ▮..... Is the order clearly written, with name of the drug, dosage, route and frequency unambiguous?
- ▮..... Does it identify precisely which patients are to receive the medication?
- ▮..... Does it clearly state under which circumstances those patients are to be given the drug, and conditions which are to preclude its administration?
- ▮..... Does it note any special observations or care which may be required prior to, or subsequent to, administration?
- ▮..... Is the order not only signed, but the name of the prescribing doctor quite clear?
- ▮..... Is the order clearly dated?
- ▮..... Has the administration set a period for review of this type of order where there is no legal time limit?
- ▮..... Is the order current (within that date)?

[8.69] Where the standing order applies to a non-urgent situation, carers should recognise that it may be for the convenience of the practitioner involved rather than the welfare of the patient, and should question whether the standing order should be recognised. The patient's health is more important than the need to follow etiquette or accepted practices.

[8.70] It is the author's view that any standing order which does not set out the conditions under which a drug is to be given, for example, where the order is to give the drug "if you think it is warranted, indicated or needed" is too close to being a prescription to be acceptable. To prescribe drugs which are set out in the legislation as being prescribable by a medical practitioner only, is a breach of the drug legislation, and attracts penalties under it. If such an act leads to harm of the patient those involved may be liable in negligence. Standing orders should clearly state under what conditions the drug should be given: on admission, for pain, where certain complications obtain, etc, and only apply where the prescribing doctor cannot be reasonably contacted.

Outdated Drug Orders

[8.71] Drug orders should be periodically reviewed, and in any case nurses should check when orders were written. Sometimes a law or institutional practice may mean that an order is out-of-date. Other situations might arise where a certain number of administrations of a particular drug are ordered and a proper check on those given is not kept (the case of *Smith v Brighton and Lewes Hospital* [8.58] is also relevant here).

REFERENCES AND FURTHER READING

Looseleaf references such as *The Laws of Australia* (Lawbook Co.); *Halsbury's Laws of Australia* (Sydney, Butterworths) are useful as are the following:

Australian Health and Medical Law Reporter (CCH, Sydney, 1991)

Brazier, M, *Medicine, Patients and the Law* (Penguin, 1992), Ch 8

Dix, et al, *Law for the Medical Profession* (Butterworths, Sydney, 1988)

Forrester, K, "Use of Standing Orders—It depends on where you stand" (1999) 7 *Journal of Law and Medicine* 17

Langslow, A, "Drugs Draw Judicial Fire" (1981) 10 (No 10), *Australian Nurses Journal*, at 23

Murchison, I A and Nichols, T, *Legal Foundations of Nursing Practice* (Macmillan, London, 1970)

O'Sullivan, J, *Law for Nurses* (Law Book Co, Sydney, 1983)

Review of Professional Indemnity Arrangements for Health Care Professionals, *Compensation and Professional Indemnity in Health Care: A Discussion Paper* (Department of Health Housing and Community Services, 1992)

Staunton, P and Whyburn, R, *Nursing and the Law* (4th ed, Saunders, Sydney, 1997), Ch 7

Chapter Nine

CLIENTS' PROPERTY

INTRODUCTION

[9.1] A person, hospital, nursing home or other institution having custody of a client's property is legally bound to take reasonable care of it and therefore any employees will be required to deal carefully with it.

[9.2] At law, the entrusting of one's property to another, for purposes such as dry cleaning, repair, safekeeping (including giving them to a hospital or another person when one is ill), or pawning one's goods, as well as the hiring of goods, is called bailment. The person who gives the goods to another's care is called the bailor, the person to whom the goods are given is called the bailee. From this it follows that the legal right to goods is composed of two elements: ownership and possession. Bailment involves temporarily divesting oneself, as owner, of the possession of one's goods, while retaining ownership of (that is, title to) them.

[9.3] In fact a health care facility may find itself caring for a person's property as the result of:

- lodgment on, or during, admission (voluntary bailment);
- admission of a person in an emergency (involuntary bailment); or
- its being left behind by a person on leaving.

Bailment

[9.4] The law of bailment is mainly covered by common law, which has generally been applied to cases involving commercial activities, and is somewhat complex, but it does contain some important precepts for health care workers. The act of bailment involves principles of contract, but money is not always paid for bailment, and there is available to the bailor the remedy of negligence. Bailment does not require a specific agreement: it is based on the fact of agreement (or at least no disagreement) on the part of the owner that the property is in the possession of the bailee. For example, a person may find a lost chattel, and take it into his or her possession. He or she is under no obligation to do so, but having taken possession of it, has undertaken the obligations of a bailee. Reasonable efforts must be made to protect the chattel, find the owner and return it to him or her on demand (*Parker v British Airways Board* [1982] QB 1004 at 1018, per Donaldson LJ). It is thus useful to consider bailment as a special area of law.

[9.5] Before considering the rules relating to bailment, however, it may be useful to remember that as health carers come into contact with clients' property, both when it is given to them for safekeeping and when they have to handle it on other occasions, that there are two types of situations in which the law is interested:

- .....the wrongful interference with a person's goods, for example, the taking of a person's possessions or using them without permission of the owner; and
- .....the careless or negligent treatment of a person's goods when they have been given for safekeeping.

Interference with Goods

[9.6] This generally involves the wrongful handling of another's goods, and is divided in law into three kinds of activity:

- .....the wrongful taking of goods, out of the possession of another, for example, theft (called in tort law "trespass to goods");
- .....dealing with goods in a manner inconsistent with the rights of the owner, for example, buying or selling another's goods, "borrowing" another's goods without their permission, using goods in a way which is contrary to a person's wishes or instructions, or destroying them (called in law "conversion of goods");
- .....wrongfully refusing, after demand, to deliver goods to the person entitled to possession of them (whether that person is the owner or not). This would include the refusal of nursing staff to return clothes or other possessions when the client asked for them (called in law "detinue").

[9.7] It can be seen that these categories might overlap in any given situation. The common element is that someone is wrongfully deprived of their lawful exercise of ownership or possession of their goods, without their consent.

[9.8] **Ownership** and **possession** may vest in different persons according to law. If a client C gives her clothing to hospital H to be given to spouse S, **ownership** of the clothes vests in C. That means C has the right to the clothes against the whole world, and can do what she likes with them. **Possession** vests in H, who has a right to possession of the clothes against the whole world except against C, the owner, and S the spouse, who has a greater right of possession than H, as H's right of possession is conditional on delivering them to S. S in turn has a right of possession against the whole world except for C, as it is conditional on delivering them to C when demanded.

The Negligent Handling of Goods

[9.9] Once possession of goods has been granted to a bailee, the goods must be kept secure and handled in a reasonable manner (*Gilchrist Watt and Sanderson Pty Ltd v York Products Pty Ltd* [1970] 3 All ER 825). What constitutes reasonable care depends of the circumstances of the case. [9.13] Action can be brought by someone against a bailee where goods have been stolen or are returned damaged or altered because of negligent handling.

Categories of Bailment

[9.10] For the purposes of duty of care, the law classifies bailment into three kinds.

Bailment for Reward

[9.11] Here the bailee is paid for the bailment of the goods. Examples are the depositing of goods with someone for safekeeping in a bank, or in a railway station "left luggage" department; leaving clothes with a dry cleaner, or a car with a car repairer. It is accepted that the bailment undertaken when a person hands over money or valuables to a health care facility is a bailment for reward, as even where they do not pay directly for their care, they are paying indirectly for treatment through taxes or levies to the government or other body. In *Martin v London County Council* [1947] 1 All ER 783, where a patient had handed over her jewellery on admission to hospital, the court held that the hospital was liable as a bailee for reward because the patient paid for care indirectly through taxes. If this principle were to be applied in Australia, one could argue that Medicare contributors are similarly paying the facility indirectly for their care. In these circumstances, there is a special duty of care in the case of bailment for reward: special care must be taken with the goods. In the case of *Ultzen v Nichols* [1894] 1 QB 92 a waiter took a customer's coat and hung it on a hanger nearby. The coat was stolen while the customer was dining, and the restaurant owner was found liable, being required to replace the coat.

Gratuitous Bailment

[9.12] This occurs when goods are "deposited" with the bailee, and the bailee accepts them, but is not paid for this service. Once the goods are accepted the bailee becomes responsible for them, and remains so for as long as the goods remain in his or her possession. The goods must be returned on the demand of the owner.

[9.13] Goods may be deposited by mistake (for example when a person who is mentally incapacitated hands over their goods to another, mistaking that person for someone else). Here again, the person must take active steps to ensure the goods are kept safe, and returned on demand.

[9.14] **[9.14]** One may also find oneself an **involuntary bailee**. This can occur:

1) .....out of necessity (for example when one stops to help another and finds oneself in possession of his or her property). Here there is not a prior arrangement to bail the goods, nor is there any choice on the part of the bailee. The standard of care is more likely to be minimal, that is, one would not be required to have to take active steps to protect the goods; and
2) .....accidentally (for example where one finds something which has fallen out of a person's pocket). In this case, no responsibility to take charge of it lies with the bailee. However if he or she does take charge of the goods, then an implied bailment comes into effect, and reasonable care is required to find the owner, care for the safety of the goods and return them to the owner. An example is where a person who retrieves timber washed up on a river bank. He or she would be liable in conversion if it is not delivered up to the owner on demand.

[9.15] The duty of care involved here is what is called the "ordinary" duty of care, based on the reasonable person, and requiring one to take whatever steps are reasonable to secure and preserve the possessions and return them. However, one is only liable for "gross" negligence.

Involuntary Bailment

[9.16] This occurs when one finds oneself in possession of another's goods without prior notice or agreement. An example is where a passer-by stops to assist someone involved in an accident, which results in the custody of the accident victim's possessions. In this case the person is not under a duty of care to take special means to protect or preserve the goods: the only requirement at law is that no action is taken which will directly or indirectly harm the possessions.

[9.17] However, despite the above theoretical outline of the standard of care owed by different classes of bailee, the above approach has been modified by the adoption of many English judicial findings, making it "unlikely that a modern Australian court would distinguish between the duties owed by a gratuitous bailee and a bailee for reward" (*Halsbury's Laws of England* ¶40-120).

Recommended Procedure for Health Care Facilities

The Best Rule: Leave it at Home!

[9.18] Obviously, clients should be persuaded not to bring unnecessary property to a health facility, or relatives should be persuaded to take it away. However, this principle should be balanced with an appreciation of the emotional value possessions may have for clients who are staying for longer periods, such as nursing home residents and mental health patients. Reasonable accommodation should be made for those possessions which are of importance for their comfort and wellbeing.

[9.22]

Careful recording of property received

[9.19] As a health care facility is likely to be considered a bailee for reward, this means that property should be carefully recorded: both its nature and condition, as a record for both the client and the hospital and as evidence of the transaction of handing over the property. Property should be stored in such a way that it is clearly identified as belonging to the client, and will not be in unreasonable danger of damage or theft.

Care of Valuables

[9.20] Special care should be taken with valuables, which should ideally not be kept in a ward, but in a central office in a secure place such as locked cupboard or safe (as less than this would not, in most cases, be considered by the courts as reasonable care). Beware of being persuaded to take temporary custody of valuable or expensive possessions, to move them from place to place, or to hand them over to anyone, without careful documentation and witnessing.

Witnessing by a Third Person

[9.21] Personal possessions and a list of them should be checked by a third person as well as the client, when the list is compiled. This should be signed by all three people. If the client is unable to check the list, then a relative or friend should be asked to sign as witness on the client's behalf. Those taking custody of items should describe them accurately: there have been two cases reported verbally to the author, one where a ring was described as gold, and one where a coat was described as fur, where the clients refused to accept the proffered platinum ring and "faux" fur coat respectively, which were returned to them, and threatened to sue the hospitals concerned for the real things! There was no evidence that the objects received by the hospital were anything other than as described.

Handing of Property to Relatives

[9.22] Health carers should be conscious of the fact that it is unlawful to deal with another person's property as if they were the owner of that property. That is, if a carer hands it over to any person (other than, for example, hospital personnel for safekeeping), without the owner's permission, this is considered in law to be exercising a right in that property to which the carer may not be entitled. It has not specifically been established at law, but it is a general policy of hospitals, that goods may be handed over to a person who is reasonably believed to be a relative or friend, or otherwise has entitlement to receive them. Where the goods

[9.22] are not valuable this may be considered acceptable, as the consent of the person could be presumed, and probably happens every day. However, it is technically unlawful handling of the person's property. Handing valuable property over to relatives or friends (or police without a warrant) could be dealing unlawfully with the property. If in doubt, it should not be handed over to anyone other than the client. Management should deal with these matters and take steps to establish the validity of the claim. Whatever the circumstances, careful recording of the transaction should be made, with a description of the property, names of those who give and receive them, and the date and time. Both the person giving and the person receiving should sign for the goods.

Some Special Considerations

Valuable Possessions

[9.23] Where the facilities exist, valuable possessions (such as jewellery) should be transferred as soon as possible after recording to the hospital management, who should have proper means for safekeeping. If there is no such provision, or it is not available after-hours, then the valuables should be kept under lock and key until they can be transferred somewhere safer. Where valuables are given to a relative or other representative of the client, records should be carefully and fully kept of to whom they are being given, their particulars, and this record should be signed by the person handing the possessions over, the person receiving them, and a witness.

Money

[9.24] Money may be deposited by the health care facility in a trust account, the amount deposited becoming a debt to the client, payable on demand. The money is not the subject of bailment in this case, as the exact notes given to the facility are not demanded in return. Rather, the client is a creditor, the facility a debtor, and the amount owing could be the subject of a suit for payment of a debt, or, where the money is deposited with the intention of benefit to a third person or body, the law of trust. The debt would apply absolutely, and the issue of negligence would be irrelevant in this case.

Emergency Admissions

[9.25] Where, due to lack of time or facilities, a client's possessions cannot be carefully checked and listed, it is suggested that they be quickly and carefully put in a bag or envelope, and sealed (for example, stapled) and put somewhere as safe as circumstances will allow. If possible have someone witness this, and jointly sign across the seal and date the signature, noting the time.

[9.26] Subject to time permitting, where valuable property is contained in a wallet, purse or other container and this is not opened by staff, a note should be made to that effect on the bag or envelope containing the goods. Where the container has been opened, staff may be liable for anything allegedly missing from it. If it was opened before coming into the possession of the staff, but there is a witnessed document stating that it was not opened by them, there is less likelihood that they will be held responsible. If it is opened, for example, a wallet is searched for identification, then the contents should be listed and witnessed again to establish what was there. Where there is a dispute as to what happened to property in an emergency, the person alleging the misdeed must prove it to the court's satisfaction. This may be very difficult, or even impossible in such circumstances.

Possessions Kept with Client

[9.27] These are kept at the client's bedside and at the client's risk. Thus, a watch or radio which disappears from the client's bedside is not the responsibility of the nursing staff unless the client is unable to care for such goods, in which case if they are to remain there (which, ideally, should not occur), the staff must take reasonable measures to protect them (for example encouraging the owner to have them locked them away when not in use). Otherwise they should be put in safekeeping. If, for example, X, perfectly competent, is to undergo surgery, then arrangements should be made for care of valuables which have been kept at the bedside, for the duration of X's incompetence.

Transfer of Client

[9.28] Care should be taken to adequately check possessions when clients are being transferred from one place to another. The list of possessions obtained on admission to a ward should again be checked against the possessions being transferred, and duly witnessed by the client (or representative) where possible, and another staff member.

When a Client becomes Incompetent

[9.29] Where an adult client becomes incompetent, the health care facility should not hand over valuable property to anyone other than the person who has the right of management of the client's property. If there is no such person, the facility should hold the property on trust until one is appointed by the courts or Guardianship Tribunal before their property can be dealt with. The Public Trustee or Public Advocate or equivalent can be contacted, who can then make an application for an order to deal with the person's property. Where the client is a child, parents are the legal guardians (unless there is clear evidence to the contrary), and are entitled to deal with the property of the child. A person's spouse is not the automatic owner of her or his property.

When a Client Dies

[9.30] The law provides that when a person dies all that person's property becomes the possession of the executor of the estate. The executor is nominated by the person in her or his will, or, where there is no will, it is usually necessary for the Supreme Court to approve an administrator. Relatives may thus have no right to possession of the deceased's belongings (if they are entitled under the will, that is for the executor to determine, and he or she must go through certain procedures, such as paying taxes and debts, before distribution to them). Of course a relative may be nominated the executor under the will, but health carers are not required to solve this legal question. They should be wary of handing out the deceased's possessions to relatives, and refer requests for property of any value to the hospital administration, whose duty it is to hold such property in trust until they hand it to the person demonstrating that he or she is the executor of the deceased's estate (a court order to this effect).

Exemption (No Responsibility Taken) Clauses

[9.31] A health care facility may limit its liability for goods left with it by specifically providing that it will not be responsible for them. This would most likely be a clause in the contract of bailment (the form signed by the client) to the appropriate effect. It is important to note:

- ..... Such a limitation must be specifically brought to the client's notice (signs in a foyer are not enough) (*Mendelssohn v Normand* [1970] 1 QB 177), and it must be reasonable notice under the circumstances: for example, in a language the client can understand. It must form part of the actual agreement made by the client. Unless all reasonable measures to bring the limitation of liability to the client's attention are taken, he or she will not be bound by it (*Thornton v Shoe Lane Parking* [1971] 2 WLR 585).
- ..... The clause must be clear and unambiguous. General phrases such as "all care and no responsibility" will have no effect (*Paterson v Miller* [1923] VLR 36).

▌▌▌ CASE
Sydney City Council v West (1965) 114 CLR 481 (High Court)

West parked his car in a council car park. The ticket he received stated that the ticket must be presented for taking delivery of the car, and also that "the council does not accept any responsibility for the loss or damage to any vehicle or for any injury to any person however such loss, damage or injury may arise or be caused". An unauthorised person claimed the car, stating he had lost the ticket, and the attendant allowed him to take delivery of the car. West sued for the replacement value of the car.

[9.32] Despite the formidable exemption clause, the High Court held that although the council was relieved of liability for the consequences of

negligence where it carried out acts which were authorised by the [9.36]
contract, the contract had specifically required that the ticket be produced
for delivery of the car, and in this case the worker involved did not follow
the authorised procedure. Thus, they concluded, the council was not
covered by the exemption clause in this case, and was liable.

[9.33] Courts will accept exemption clauses so long as they have been
brought to the awareness of the contracting party, or are reasonably
available for that party to see, but will also construe them literally against
the party seeking exemption, as they do not hold such clauses in favour.
Therefore the person or institution holding goods under bailment must
show that they meticulously adhered to the terms of the bailment.

■■■ CASE
Thomas National Transport (Melbourne) Pty Ltd v May & Baker (Australia) Pty Ltd (1966) 115 CLR 353 (High Court)

An interstate carrier regularly held May & Baker's goods in its warehouse overnight in Melbourne when storage was required, before sending them on to Sydney. They also used a sub-contractor to transport the goods from May & Baker's premises to the warehouse. Some goods were destroyed while they were stored overnight, not while they were at TNT's warehouse, but at the premises of the sub-contractor. The contract had an exemption clause that said that TNT was not liable for harm occurring to goods while they were in transit or storage.

[9.34] The court said that TNT could rely on the exemption clause and
so escape liability only if it was acting strictly according to the contract.
The use of the sub-contractor was not stipulated in the contract, it was
found, and this was a deviation from the contract significant enough to
prevent TNT from relying on its exemption clause. From this one can
extract the principle that a hospital will be liable for loss or damage to
goods if staff do not take proper care of a client's belongings.

Unclaimed Belongings

Common Law

[9.35] At common law, if goods are not collected after bailment, the
bailee does not have the right to dispose of them, unless it is necessary to
do so to prevent harm to the bailee or in the interests of the owner, and
the bailee has made reasonable attempts to contact the owner.

Statute Law

[9.36] Most States have some legislation providing that unclaimed
belongings become the property of the person or body who holds them,
giving them the right to keep or dispose of them. Provisions are found in

[9.36] Limitation Acts and Disposal of Uncollected Goods Acts.[1] Some States also have legislation in relation to uncollected moneys, requiring advertising for the owner and other procedures.

[9.37] New South Wales also has a specific Act, the *Public Hospitals Act 1929* (NSW), which deals with unclaimed money and personal effects. If unclaimed within 12 months, the belongings become the property of the hospital. Other States have legislation dealing with the disposal of uncollected goods generally setting out conditions under which the bailee can dispose of goods unclaimed after a certain period of time, and what must be done with the proceeds of disposal. It is uncertain the extent to which this legislation can be applied to health care institutions, but it has been suggested that it is at least a guide for the institution even if the legislation does not apply literally.

▌▌▌ CHECKLIST
DEALING WITH CLIENT'S PROPERTY ON ADMISSION OR TRANSFER

Reference to client includes reference to client's representative where applicable.

Have I:

▌..... Informed the client about hospital policy?
▌..... Listed each object by type and condition?
▌..... Identified valuable property and separated it from other goods?
▌..... Clearly identified the location of, or the person with, custody of all property?
▌..... Secured the witness of at least one other health carer and the client, if possible?
▌..... Given the client a copy of the list (receipt)?
▌..... Made proper provision for the dispatch of property which is to go elsewhere in the hospital?
▌..... Made proper provision for any goods which are to remain in the ward or under my supervision?
▌..... Obtained a receipt on the handing-over of the goods to any person?

---

1. *Limitation Act* 1985 (ACT); *Uncollected Goods Act* 1996 (ACT); *Limitation Act* 1969 (NSW); *Public Hospitals Act* 1929 (NSW), s 40A(1), (2); *Uncollected Goods Act* 1995 (NSW); *Unclaimed Money Act* 1982 (NSW); *Limitation Act* 1981 (NT); *Disposal of Uncollected Goods Act* 1976 (NT); *Limitation of Actions Act* 1974 (Qld); *Disposal of Uncollected Goods Act* 1967 (Qld); *Public Trustee Act* 1978 (Qld); *Limitation of Actions Act* 1936 (SA); *Unclaimed Goods Act* 1987 (SA); *Unclaimed Moneys Act* 1891 (SA); *Limitation Act* 1981 (Tas); *Disposal of Uncollected Goods Act* 1968 (Tas); *Unclaimed Moneys Act* 1918 (Tas); *Health Act* 1997 (Tas); *Limitation of Actions Act* 1958 (Vic); *Disposal of Uncollected Goods Act* 1961 (Vic); *Unclaimed Moneys Act* 1972 (Vic); *Limitation Act* 1935 (WA); *Disposal of Uncollected Goods Act* 1970 (WA); *Unclaimed Moneys Act* 1918 (WA).

REFERENCES AND FURTHER READING

See references on tort law following Chapter 6.
Australian Health and Medical Law Reporter (CCH, Sydney, 1991), ¶52-500
O'Sullivan, J, *Law for Nurses* (Law Book Co, Sydney, 1983), Ch 2

Chapter Ten

CONTRACT

INTRODUCTION

[10.1] Where a client enters hospital, or makes an agreement for care from other health care facilities, or sees a private practitioner (for example, a nurse or doctor), then a contract has been entered into between the client and the care giver. The contract does not have to be spelt out as such: it is implied (*Breen v Williams* (1996) 186 CLR 71 at 78). The client undertakes to pay a fee, and the facility or practitioner undertakes to provide reasonable care in the agreed treatment. Where treatment is billed to Medicare or other insurance the patient is still considered as being the source of consideration as the health carer receives a benefit from the public purse (Staunton and Whyburn (1989), p 107, established in *Breen v Williams* at 123). There is also a contractual relationship between the health carer and the Health Insurance Commission covering those fees recoverable from the Commission under Medicare. In order to carry out their part of the bargain, health care facilities enter into specialised contracts of employment with staff, which are dealt with below, Ch 11). The employee carer has a contract with the employer, but not with the client. Poor health care is not only the basis of a potential negligence action, it is thus also a breach of that contract with the employer; as well as a potential breach of the employer's contract with the client if the employer is at fault in not providing competent staff. However, if a health carer is directly engaged by a client (for example, a home birth or private nurse) then there is a direct contract between the health carer and client. The pattern of possible contracts is set out in Figure 10.1. One must establish that a contract exists between parties before one can sue the other in breach of contract. The requirements for a valid contract are set out below (see [10.3]).

[10.2] It must be made clear that carers should be aware of the distinction between liability in contract and liability in negligence. The duty to act reasonably in caring for clients always applies, whether or not a contract exists. Where there is a contract between a professional and a client, principles applying to contracts operate in addition to those of tort law. Principles of contract law are different from those of negligence in some respects. Contract is basically about carrying out a bargain rather than care as such, and one only has to give what one agreed to give: the standard of service can be set by the parties involved. According to the law of negligence, on the other hand, the standard of care is set not by any agreement, but by an objective test: the "reasonable person" test. Unless otherwise specifically stated, the implied terms of any contract for health care is that it is to conform with this standard.

What is a Contract?

[10.3] A contract is an agreement between two or more people which, if it has certain features, will be legally binding. It need not be in writing—it can be verbal, or even implied from a person's actions. When, for example, people ask the local car mechanic to fix their car, or the dentist to fix their teeth, they are entering into a contractual relationship. Unless it is otherwise agreed, there is an implied condition that, in exchange for payment of the prescribed fee, the mechanic or dentist will give appropriate professional service. The law of contract is covered mainly by common law principles, therefore one must consult precedent to elucidate these. The following requirements have been established for contracts:

▌▌ CHECKLIST
REQUIREMENTS FOR A VALID CONTRACT
- intention by both parties to create a legal relationship;
- an identifiable offer and acceptance;
- adequate identification of parties involved;
- consideration (something of value) exchanged between those involved, or agreement made under seal;
- genuine agreement on the part of each person involved;
- legal capacity on the part of each person making the agreement; and
- lawfulness of the activity involved.

Intention to Create a Legal Relationship

[10.4] The parties commit themselves to certain obligations, which gives each the right to sue the other if these obligations are not carried out. There is a ready-made presumption however, that several types of agreement are of themselves not legally binding. Thus, for example, agreements made between husband and wife, such as agreements to pay money, carry out chores, arrangements over child care, etc, are generally not considered to involve an intention to create legal relations unless this is clearly expressed, or there is legislation which attaches legal obligations to agreements (for example, consumer legislation imposes certain standards and warranties on goods, and the *Family Law Act* 1975 (Cth) which attaches the obligation of mutual support to married couples).

[10.5] The intentions of the parties may be express or implied, but they must be mutual. If they are not spelt out in writing, they are determined by what a reasonable onlooker or person aware of the facts would deduce the parties' intentions to be from their actions, negotiations, and background to the agreement. This is called an "objective test", rather than a "subjective test", which is based on what one of the parties might have actually had in his or her mind, but not disclosed to the other.

[10.6] The legal approach can be ascertained by comparing two cases, and the reasoning of the courts in coming to different conclusions on somewhat similar facts.

■■■ CASE [10.9]
Balfour v Balfour [1919] 2 KB 571 (CA England)

A married couple had to part because of the wife's ill-health after a holiday in their homeland, England, and the husband returned to Ceylon to work. The husband agreed to pay £30 a month maintenance to the wife while she was in England. At some later stage, the wife decided she would not return to the husband, and when the payments stopped, sued him for breach of contract.

[10.7] The judgment is discussed below (see [10.8]).

■■■ CASE
McGregor v McGregor (1888) 20 QBD 529 (CA England)

A husband and wife, after charging each other with assault, agreed to drop charges and separate (*before the matter came to court*). The husband agreed to pay weekly maintenance, and the wife agreed to support herself and the children. The husband later refused to continue payments and the wife sued for breach of contract.

[10.8] The wife was unsuccessful in the first case, but in the second case, the wife succeeded. The reasoning of the courts is consistent. It revolves around the facts of the cases. In the first case, the court said, the couple did not wish to affect their legal relations. The agreement was part of their ongoing marriage, the better to manage it. In the second case, however, the intention was to affect the couple's legal relations. Whereas they were married and living together, now they were separated, and the money issue was part of this. The court was considering not so much what the parties said (though that may come into consideration) as what they were intending to do.

■■■ CASE
Jones v Padavatton [1969] 2 All ER 616 (CA England)

The defendant was a divorced woman living in Washington in 1962. She gave up a good job on her mother's promise that if she went to London and read for the Bar there the mother would pay her a regular allowance. After the defendant P, had been in London for two years, the mother bought a house there for her to live in. The house was big enough for tenants. The daughter did not send any rents to the mother, who was paying off a large mortgage, and in 1965 the daughter remarried. In 1967 the mother claimed possession of the house and the daughter counter-claimed for money she had spent on the house.

[10.9] The court decided that they had meant to create legal relations. It looked at the circumstances of the negotiations of both mother and daughter, and decided that they both intended that the daughter should have a legal right to receive, and the mother a legal obligation to pay, the original allowance of $200 a month for a reasonable time for completion of Bar exams. The new arrangement was neither a variation of the original, nor (because of its vagueness) a new contract entitling the

[10.9] daughter to stay on in the house. The mother could have possession of the house, as the agreement did not allow for indefinite possession of it by the daughter.

[10.10] In setting out the reasoning to be followed in such cases, Salmon LJ said (at 621):

> Did the parties intend the arrangement to be legally binding? This question has to be solved by applying what is sometimes . . . called an objective test. The court has to consider what the parties said and wrote in the light of all the surrounding circumstances, and then decide whether the true inference is that the ordinary man and woman, speaking or writing thus in such circumstances, would have intended to create a legally binding agreement.

[10.11] Where a person agrees to carry out treatment of another, particularly a friend, or makes an informal agreement, or no payment is to be made at all, it should be made clear if this is to be legally binding. However, the right to sue in negligence would remain in all cases.

Agreement to Oust Law

[10.12] It may be specified that an agreement is not to be legally binding, or subject to legal enforcement. Many raffles, pools and competitions have, as a condition of entry, that they are not subject to legal enforcement.

▌▌▌ CASE
Appleson v H Littlewood Ltd [1939] 1 All ER 464 (CA England)

A alleged he won some money (£4,335) in a football pool. The defendants showed that the conditions of entry had stated that the competition was not subject to legal enforcement, and did not give rise to any legal relationship, rights, duties or consequences. A was thus unable to claim the money, the court holding that the arrangement was one of honour only, and that the plaintiff had accepted it with his eyes open (at 468).

Offer and Acceptance

[10.13] Given that legal relations were intended, where a contract is in dispute the court will consider whether a clear offer of some benefit was made by one person, and an acceptance of that particular offer was also clearly and without qualification made on the part of someone else.

Tickets as Offers

[10.14] It is worth noting, however, that under some circumstances a person need not be aware of all the details of the offer. The best example of this is where, after paying for goods or services, one is given a ticket or docket on which are written the conditions under which the goods or services are to be provided, such as a bus ticket. So long as these conditions are reasonably available to be read, and the company giving the ticket could reasonably assume that people would know it contained conditions of the contract on it, then the purchaser is bound by the conditions even if informed of them after paying. If it is unreasonable to make that assumption, the company should notify each person receiving a ticket that the conditions are there (just printing such notice on the ticket may not be enough) and then, even if one is illiterate, one is taken to know the conditions. One example of this type of contract in health care could be an agreement for diagnostic tests where prerequisites such as fasting or taking certain drugs are required.

Withdrawal of Offers

[10.15] An offer may be withdrawn, but this must occur before it has been accepted otherwise the withdrawal is ineffective. The person making the offer must ensure that the offeree knows the offer no longer stands, or the offeree should clearly be expected to know the offer has been withdrawn. On this point the courts say the parties must be *ad idem* (of the same mind): where they are aware that they are not, then a contract cannot be entered into. Thus, for example where an offer to provide anaesthesia, or attend a client, for a certain fee is made, once accepted the fee cannot be changed. However, see the discussion of changed circumstances in the section on defences below.

The Following Principles Apply to Offers

[10.16] Contracts can be made orally, in writing, or by implication: An agreement only has to be in writing where the law requires this: for example, for contracts involving real property (land and buildings). An example of an implied contract is where someone enters a hospital for emergency treatment. There is an implied offer by a hospital to give necessary life-saving treatment by the fact that the Emergency Department is open, and acceptance of the offer and conditions pertaining to it are implied by a person's actions (if a patient is in need of emergency treatment and unconscious, then acceptance of treatment is also implied, but there is no contract). Refusing treatment can indicate withdrawal of former acceptance of it.

[10.17] The offer must be communicated to the offeree: A person cannot accept an offer about which he or she has no knowledge.

[10.17] ■■■ **CASE**
R v Clarke (1927) 40 CLR 227 (High Court)

The Western Australian government offered a reward for information leading to the arrest and conviction of the person or persons who committed the murder of two policemen, and stated the Governor would pardon any accomplice, not guilty of the murders, who first gave such information. Clarke was arrested in connection with one of the murders. He gave police information which indeed did lead to the conviction of two men for the murder of one of the policemen. Clarke gave evidence that although he was aware of the offer when giving the information, he had no intention of claiming the reward, and had not thought of it, but had given the information to prevent his own conviction. Nevertheless he later claimed the reward, and the government argued that they were not required to pay it.

[10.18] The case went to the High Court, where the government was reluctantly supported. The Court held that there cannot be assent without knowledge of the offer, and ignorance of the offer is the same thing whether it is from never having heard of the offer or of forgetting it. If Clarke had not so candidly acknowledged that he had forgotten it, he might have been successful!

[10.19] This principle would suggest that health care workers cannot demand payment for services which have been given and for which the client did not agree to pay, for example, where an appendix is removed during a cholecystectomy when the removal is neither an emergency nor agreed to.

Bilateral Contracts

[10.20] An example of a bilateral agreement is where a vendor, Anne Smith, offers to sell another person, Sue Jones, a boat for $2,000. The offer is clear: "Give me $2,000 and I'll give you the boat." Jones may take up the offer or turn it down. As soon as she says "yes" the two women have entered into a contract: Sue Jones must pay the money to get the boat, Anne Smith must give her the boat to get her money. Failure to honour the agreement, or the terms of it, may lead to an action in damages for breach of contract (see below [10.102]). There are situations where either party could validly get out of the contract. These are also described below.

[10.21] In this agreement, Anne is the offeror, Sue the offeree. This is the most common sort of contract. There is a widespread misconception that when goods are put on display in a shop, or advertised, the vendor is making an offer. In fact they are not "on offer" in the legal sense. They are "invitations to treat" and the shopkeeper is in fact made an offer by the customer when he or she asks for the goods. The shopkeeper then has the right to accept or refuse the customer's offer (with the proviso that under legislation one may be required to sell, and at the price on the goods as advertised).

Unilateral Contracts

[10.22] An example of a unilateral contract is where a person offers a reward for the return of a lost cat. The finder is under no obligation to return it, and the owner's obligation only comes into being when the cat is returned.

Gratuitous Offers

[10.23] Finally, one can make a gratuitous offer, for example, to give one's health carer a gift of $1,000. Such a promise is only enforceable if it is made under seal, that is, made in writing and with the formalities creating a deed (see [10.36]).

Conditions

[10.24] The test then, is whether the offeror took reasonable steps to ensure that the reasonable person would be aware what conditions exist as to the offer. The courts have considered cases where an offeree reasonably thought that the piece of paper handed to her or him was merely a receipt and not a written contract, such as, where a deck chair was hired (*Chapelton v Barry Urban District Council* [1940] 1 KB 532), or where clothes were left at the dry cleaners (*Causer v Browne* [1952] VLR 1). Under the circumstances it was not reasonable to expect someone to be bound by the conditions set out in that document. If a document is signed, however, those signing it are held to have read and understood the contents of the document, whether they have or not, and whether the conditions in it are reasonable or not, and no matter how small the print is.

Offers Must be Specific

[10.25] An offer must be specific, that is, both parties must be quite clear on the benefits to be exchanged. For health care workers, this means that treatment to be given must be clearly and fully explained to the client, and only the treatment agreed upon must be given, except for any emergency treatment, where consent is implied (see Ch 4).

Acceptance

[10.26] **Time limit:** Unless the time for acceptance is stipulated by the contract, it must occur within a reasonable time. The acceptance is not operative until it is conveyed to the offeror.

[10.27] **Privity of contract:** Only those to whom the offer is made can accept it: third parties cannot oblige the offeror to act by accepting. If an offer is made to the whole world, anyone may accept it. If there can only be one acceptor of such an offer, authority seems to indicate that the first

[10.27] acceptor is entitled to performance of the offer (*Robinson v McEwan* (1865) 2 WW & A'B 65) however, this is not clear.

Acceptance Must be in Full

[10.28] If the offeree wants to change the terms, he or she makes a counter offer, and the roles are reversed. In the case of *Neale v Merrett* [1930] WN 189, Merrett offered his property to Neale at £280. Neale responded by post accepting and enclosed £80 as deposit, promising to pay the balance later. The court held that there was no contract as Neale's acceptance was not unconditional. There was no obligation on the part of Merrett to honour his offer. Nothing further must be left to be negotiated between the parties; they must be satisfied with all the conditions.

[10.29] There could be other examples of situations where the client has accepted an offer of health care, but not carried out stipulated requirements on his or her part, such as fasting, or carrying out certain activities. However these have not been considered by the courts. Other examples are when an offer of health care if the client provides certain facilities is made and accepted and some of these facilities are not in fact provided, or an offer to provide home birth care if the client has certain preliminary tests could be made, and when the doctor or midwife arrives to attend the client only some of the tests have been undertaken. In these cases the contract was not fully carried out by one of the parties, and there may be no obligation to continue providing health care (although under tort law reasonable care may be required to prevent harm).

[10.30] This principle is also another basis for the need to fully inform clients. If clients can argue that the treatment they received was either not what they agreed to, something additional to what they agreed to, or not given in the way to which they agreed, they may argue that there was no proper acceptance of an offer of care as the offer was not properly conveyed to them. Indeed, the consent form may be part of the contract made between the client and the care giver.

Revocation

[10.31] One can revoke an acceptance, but the revocation must reach the offeror before the acceptance. When it has been received, the person accepting cannot change an acceptance without the consent of the offeror: acceptance brings the contract into being. This does not mean the person cannot refuse treatment. It means that payment agreed to is owed, even thought the treatment is not received. Where the health carer does not suffer any financial or other detriment (that is, through loss of time or expense in relation to equipment) there may be no liability on the part of the person revoking their consent).

Contracts by Mail [10.34]

[10.32] Health carers may be involved in agreements to live and work interstate or overseas. There are certain rules for contracts by mail, which may seem arbitrary, but have been adopted for convenience:

- .....An offer by mail is not effective until it reaches the offeree(s): the person must know of it. The same applies to the revocation of an offer. It takes effect when the offeree receives it. Those making an offer are advised to set a time limit on acceptance. Then they have a point in time beyond which any acceptance is not actionable, and they can follow up and ensure no acceptance is missed.
- .....An acceptance by mail is effective when it is posted. The offeror need not know of its existence to be bound by it. This is so even if the letter of acceptance is delayed or never reaches the offeror (*Household Fire Insurance Co v Grant* (1879) 4 Ex D 216). The offeree should keep a record of having sent the letter, so that proof of this is available if required, otherwise the acceptance may not be provable. It has been hotly debated, and not decided, whether one can rescind an acceptance one has sent in the mail. It is advisable to arrange for verification of the acceptance being received.

Identification of Parties

[10.33] It must be possible to clearly identify the offeror(s) and the offeree(s). Where treatment is to be carried out by a hospital, the contract is made between the patient and the hospital, but where the health carer involved is not employed by the hospital, there will be two contracts, one between the patient and the carer for provision of requisite individual care, and another between the patient and the hospital, for the care it provides. Where the health care worker is in private practice, whether working in a hospital setting or not, the contract is between her or him and the patient.

Consideration

[10.34] Unless the contract is under seal (see [10.36]) it is called a simple contract, and must involve some form of consideration. This means that something of value (that is, which can be qualified in monetary terms), is to be conferred from one party on another, be it money, property, services or information, etc. Most contracts involve promise of a mutual exchange of benefit, for example, one party undertakes to work for, or to provide health care of, the other for a sum of money. Consideration may be something which is capable of serving as the price of a promise, which another person is not otherwise bound to carry out. It must be specifically shown that detriment was suffered in reliance on the promise. When considering whether a valid contract exists the court is not concerned with whether the consideration is adequate or not, so long as it is sufficient to indicate the parties were serious about the deal.

Past Consideration, Privity

[10.35] There are two more points about consideration that should be made: past consideration, that is, something done or paid for in the past cannot hold someone to a promise to which the thing or money did not then relate. If a grateful patient, on leaving a dentist's care promises a gift of $600, that is not an enforceable promise, as the care was given with no expectation of the money. Secondly, only the person who has given consideration may enforce the contract: if a health carer is engaged to care for Mr Jones, that does not create an obligation to attend to grand-daughter Lisa's bunions!

Deeds

[10.36] Contracts under seal are called deeds. These are in writing, and are "signed, sealed and delivered". This procedure has been simplified by legislation and court decisions. More recently, in most cases parties' signatures need only be attested to by a witness who is not a party to the deed, and the document is expressed to be a deed. Actual sealing with wax is rarely necessary. Although they may be used to sanctify mutual promises, deeds apply to promises of gifts. They will be enforced in the absence of consideration, and they take effect on the moment of delivery (physical delivery is not necessary, intention to deliver is enough—the promisor who puts it in a desk to be given to her or his lawyer, with a letter to be written to the promisee tomorrow is also bound by it). Neither knowledge on the part of the promisee, nor acceptance of the offer (as with simple contracts) is required.

[10.37] Deeds last longer, that is, one can sue for breach of contract based on a deed for up to 15 years (Victoria), or 12 years (other States), after the deed has been made, whereas with a simple contract the limitation period is six years.

The Importance of Writing

[10.38] As already stated, simple contracts need not be in writing. There are exceptions to this principle through legislation, for example:

- ..... bills of exchange including cheques;
- ..... transfers of shares or title to land;
- ..... assignment of copyright; and
- ..... in some States, credit purchase agreements, and some details of door-to-door sales.

[10.39] Legislation may also require certain contracts to be evidenced in writing, such as:

- ..... sale of land agreements in all jurisdictions;
- ..... contracts of guarantee;

▌.....hire purchase agreements;
▌.....agreements not to be performed within one year; and
▌.....sales of over $20 in some jurisdictions, unless the buyer has accepted and actually received at least some of the goods, or has paid a deposit.

Terms of the Contract

The Benefit of Contracts in Writing

[10.40] Where terms of the contract are in writing, and there is no reason not to believe the parties meant the writing to constitute the whole of the agreement, the courts will consider what is written down to be final and complete. The words will be scrutinised for their meaning, the terms for their provisions, and no party will be able to argue that they did not mean what the reasonable reader would take them to mean. Only if a person can convince the court that the words on paper are not the complete or accurate agreement will it consider other evidence (such as oral undertakings also made at the time) as to what the parties arranged.

[10.41] Most readers will be familiar with being handed a document which has a large amount of small print, being shown a spot and told "just sign here". That small print constitutes the terms or conditions of the contract, and any warranty on the part of the offeror as to the nature and condition of any goods, or the quality of performance of the contract. For self-protection, this is where one smiles sweetly and states that one will "just read the terms, thank you" and take the time to do so. There is no obligation to hurry, pressure should not be placed on a person to sign a contract (this could make it unenforceable) and much may be at stake.

Implied Terms

[10.42] Sometimes not all the terms of a contract are contained in it. This might be for three main reasons:

▌.....the parties may not have thought of all the contingencies that would arise or for some reason it is necessary to read into the contract certain terms to make it work;
▌.....the very nature of the contract indicates that the parties would have accepted that the terms in question would apply, also perhaps in this category are terms implied by reason of custom, usage or course of dealing; and
▌.....there may be legislation that imposes on particular courses of behaviour certain terms and conditions (the classic example of this is the contract of employment, which by statute contains many conditions in relation to sick leave, holiday leave, minimum rates of pay, etc—see Ch 11).

[10.43] Conditions necessary for the courts to find implied terms in a contract were summarised in *BP Refinery (Westernport) Pty Ltd v Hastings*

[10.43] *Shire Council* (1977) 180 CLR 266 at 283 (High Court of Australia). These are that the proposed term must be:

- ..... reasonable and equitable;
- ..... necessary to give business efficacy to the contract, so that no condition will be implied if the contract can be carried out effectively without it;
- ..... so obvious that it "goes without saying";
- ..... capable of clear expression; and
- ..... able to operate without contradicting any express term of the contract.

[10.44] In a more recent case the High Court considered these criteria and accepted that they were best applied where there was a written, formal contract. Where there is no formal contract, as may be the case in most health care agreements, the actual terms of the contract must be ascertained before implied terms can be considered. In other words the intention of the parties must be identified, and what they actually agreed upon be established, before any question of what should be implied arises. The court accepted the finding of Deane J in *Hawkins v Clayton* (1988) 164 CLR 539 at 573, that the court should refer to the imputed intention of the parties, "if and only if, it can be seen that the implication of the particular term is necessary for reasonable or effective operation of a contract of that nature in the circumstances of the case" (*Byrne v Australian Airlines Ltd* (1995) 185 CLR 410 at 422).

Contracts for Health Care

[10.45] Cases establishing the law in relation to contracts with health carers deal with doctors and their patients, but are equally applicable to all those who undertake to provide health care to another.

[10.46] In *Breen v Williams* (1996) 186 CLR 71 (see facts at [7.2]) the High Court of Australia established that in the absence of a specific contract between a doctor and patient the consideration on the part of the client is "payment, promise of payment, of reward or submission by the patient, or an undertaking by the patient to submit, to the treatment proposed" (per Brennan CJ at 78). The payment need not come from the patient, but from another source, such as an insurer, or Medicare (per Gummow at 123). Most health care contracts are verbal or implied and most health care clients are unaware that they are entering a contract.

The use of an action for breach of contract as a means of compensation for unsatisfactory treatment is very rare, as it is often considered more appropriate to bring an action in negligence. However, the law will recognise the patient's right to receive what was implied or verbally agreed upon in the way of treatment, and an implied term of that agreement is that the treatment will be of a reasonable standard. Negligence may be easier to prove, as the implied terms of the contract are in doubt (as discussed below). Compensation is not granted for such things as pain and suffering, and loss of quality of life, as can be the case in negligence. On the other hand there is a longer limitation period in contract, damages are not limited to harm that is foreseeable, but rather whatever harm flows from the breach.

[10.47] As mentioned the parties to the contract depend on whether one has made an agreement with a health care facility, a health care corporation, or an individual practitioner. It is possible to have several actions, for example an action in negligence and in contract against an individual practitioner, with whom there was no contract, and an action in both negligence and breach of contract against the practitioner's employer.

[10.47] ### FIGURE 10.1

PATTERN OF POSSIBLE CONTRACTS IN THE PROVISION OF HEALTH CARE

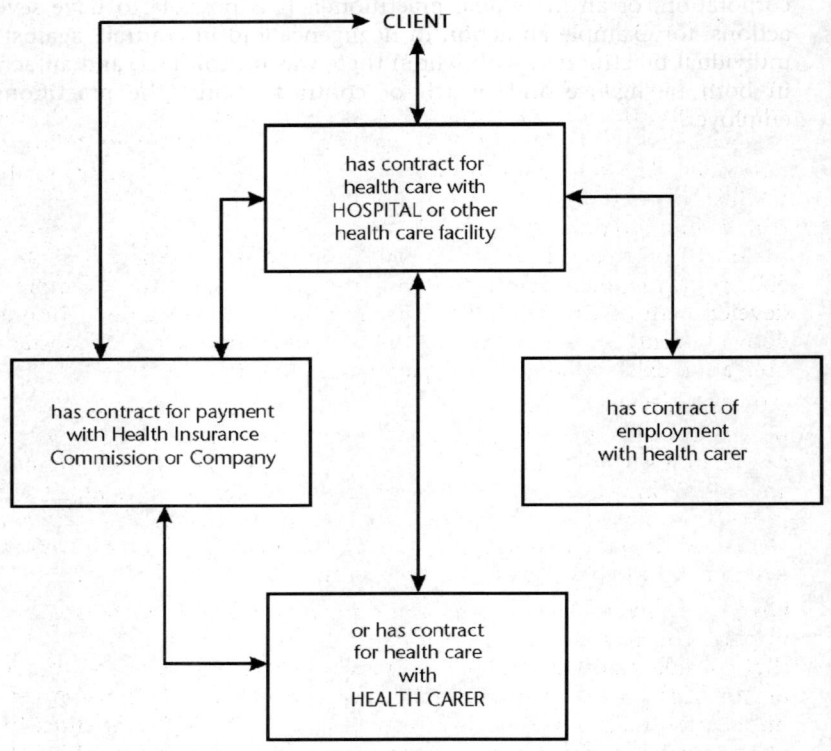

Terms of the Health Care Contract

CASE
Breen v Williams (1996) 186 CLR 71 (High Court of Australia)

The facts of this case are set out at [7.2]. The appellant argued, among other things, that she had a contract with her doctor, an implied term of which was provision of access to medical records.

[10.48] The court found that there was no formal contract between the parties. However, as indicated above, there was a contract in effect. The principles in relation to implied terms as set out above were endorsed, the provision of information being tied to the undertaking to advise and treat the patient with reasonable skill and care. This implied term for provision of health care is similar to that in tort, being based on a standard reasonable under the circumstances. Thus, Brennan CJ held (at 79), the doctor has a contractual duty to provide information or advice when [10.52] requested and:

- .....not to give it might prejudice the general health of the patient;
- .....the request is reasonable in the circumstances; and
- .....reasonable reward for the disclosure is offered or given.

[10.49] The court limited the doctor's implied duty under a contract to advising and treating the patient with reasonable skill and care. However, this may involve follow-up or contact a client after the provision of care has ended. An example of this may be the provision of information about the history or condition or treatment of the patient on an earlier occasion where failure to provide this would prejudice the patient's "future medical treatment or physical or mental wellbeing". New information about the effects of treatment given to patients in the past (for example the development of Creutzfeld-Jacob Disease from human growth hormone derived from corpses) could be such a situation where a contractual obligation exists to advise those patients (Skene (1998), p 42).

[10.50] Part of the implied terms of a contract can be said to be the provision of adequate information to provide an effective consent. This can be derived from the requirement under contract law that the parties are agreed on actions each is to undertake, and from the requirement to provide care that will not prejudice the patient's physical or mental wellbeing. Part of that wellbeing comes from being properly informed when making decisions about one's health.

[10.51] In Australian law it is uncertain as to whether there is a specific implied contractual duty to maintain patient confidentiality. It may be that confidentiality is necessary to prevent harm to health and wellbeing (again, it is necessary to show that the contract would not work if the implied term did not operate). This would make it another manifestation of the overall implied requirement of advising and treating the patient with reasonable skill and care. There is some indication in English case law that confidentiality is a term of the contract between health care provider and client (see for example *Parry-Jones v Law Society* [1969] 1 Ch 1; *Argyll v Argyll* [1967] Ch 302).

[10.52] There cannot, of course, be a guarantee of success, or that nothing will go wrong. Advertisements by plastic surgeons, for example, should be very careful in not creating false expectations as to what can be achieved. In one case, a plastic surgeon who suggested to the mother of a patient that she should undergo surgery and that he could "make her look 20 years younger" as it was his mission to make people beautiful through his specialty of face-lifting. The woman was disillusioned with the result. However she sued the doctor in negligence, not in contract. The doctor was found liable (*Senka Benkovic v Dr Eng Pen Tan* (5 February 1999, District Court NSW)).

Capacity to Contract

Who can Make a Contract?

[10.53] Someone will only be obliged to fulfil a contract if that person has the capacity to agree to it. At law this means the person must be 18 years of age and mentally able to agree. Thus infants (those under 18), those of unsound mind (including those who are drunk), may be held not to have the capacity to enter into contracts. Unincorporated associations also do not have capacity to contract. The categories of those unable to contract will be considered more fully.

Minors Generally cannot Contract

[10.54] At common law, a minor (also referred to in law as an infant), can repudiate a contract entered into by her or him before majority, or, if the minor intends to be bound by it, ratify it immediately on attaining majority. This generally involves lasting property rights (for example, as owner or lessee of land). Although this means the minor is under no obligation under the agreement until then, the adult with whom it is made may, nevertheless, still be obliged to carry it out. The law, apart from being quite clear on the point that a contract made by a minor is not absolutely void (that is, not a contract at all), but rather voidable (that is, valid from inception until whoever may be entitled to repudiate it does so), what the position of the other party is in terms of its obligation is left to the consideration of the court in the individual case.

When a Minor may be Bound by Contract

[10.55] It has generally been held that minors should be protected from unwise transactions through youthful exuberance and indiscretion. This means that if a minor purchases goods or services, he or she will not be bound to pay for them or return goods unless they were obtained by fraud. There are, however, two important exceptions to this principle.

[10.56] **A minor may be bound by a contract for necessaries:** Note the word used is not "necessities". Necessaries does not mean the necessities of life, although these are included. It means goods and services fit to maintain one in the lifestyle to which one is accustomed (the social position, means, as well as age and occupation of the minor will be considered as well as whether he or she was adequately supplied with similar goods already) and necessary for this at the time of contract. The case of *Chapple v Cooper* (1844) 153 ER 105, a nineteenth century case that is still relevant, held that "necessaries" can include food, raiment, lodging, instructions in art or trade, or intellectual, moral and religious information, attendance of others. As "class" is a part of society, the court held, the subject matter and extent of the contract may vary according the "station he is to fulfil":

But in all cases it must first be made out that the class itself is one in which [10.61] the things furnished are essential to the existence and reasonable advantage and comfort of the infant contractor. Thus, articles of mere luxury are always excluded, though luxurious articles of utility are in some cases allowed (at 107).

[10.57] The imprecise nature of what constitute "necessaries" means that there are many court cases determining the issue. Is a minor from a wealthy family who purports to purchase a stereo to be bound by the undertaking because it is necessary to her station in life? Changing social and moral values and differing circumstances may provide a variety of answers.

[10.58] **A minor may also be bound by contracts for services such as medical treatment, transportation and education:** Age, understanding and need are important considerations in determining whether to hold an infant liable, but the implications for health carers may be important.

[10.59] If a minor is seeking treatment, does an agreement to give this treatment mean a contract exists? What is the consideration involved? If parents are paying, is the contract with the parents or with the child? What if the parents agree to pay for what they believe is treatment for a sore throat and the minor is in fact receiving contraception?

[10.60] There has been little case law in relation to the contract for health care, particularly in relation to children. It can only be inferred that the following would probably be the situation: a health carer may have a contract with a minor for health care services. That would be the case if the minor is paying on his or her own behalf. Contractual duties would flow from that relationship, as well as a duty of care in giving information and provision of the care itself, a duty of confidentiality, etc. The child would be bound by the contract to pay for services, presuming the health care is considered a "necessary" (this is a different issue to consent simpliciter by the child (see Ch 5). The issue here is rather the child's obligation to pay).

However if the child's parents are paying for the health care, then the contract may well be with the parents, the other duties flowing to the child. There would have to be an agreement by the parent or parents, either specifically given or implied, that they will pay. The contract is then with the parent(s), with a duty on the part of the health carer to provide the care to the child as a service to the parents, not the child, the parents being required to pay. Other duties flowing from the health carer to the child would result from the professional relationship between them, not any contract.

[10.61] In the absence of legal guidance, it would seem that the argument could be made that parents are only obliged to pay for that treatment for which they agree to pay, subject to their obligation to provide adequate maintenance for their children. What of a 17-year-old schoolgirl who seeks contraception and parents are paying for the care? If the parents have not specifically or impliedly agreed to pay for it, does this mean neither the parents nor the child may be liable to pay under common law? Can contraception be shown to be part of "reasonable and necessary maintenance of the minor"? It may be considered necessary if,

[10.61] for example the minor insists on an active sexual lifestyle and is in danger of disease or pregnancy. On the other hand, can it be seen as simply a means of maintaining a particular lifestyle (is an active sexual activity necessary or "essential to the existence and reasonable advantage and comfort of the infant contractor" or "fit to maintain one in the lifestyle to which one is accustomed")? The reader may wish to consider these so-far unanswered questions.

Persons of "Unsound Mind"

[10.62] Who is legally of "unsound mind"? The law of contract is very old, with contract law books full of cases from past centuries. Hence the somewhat antiquated terminology of contract law. There are two categories of persons of unsound mind: those who have been certified as such under State legislation and those otherwise recognised as being of unsound mind (see above, Ch 5). Those who have been officially recognised by the law through certification as being of unsound mind have no contractual capacity as a rule. Others who are recognised as having some degree of mental deficiency are liable. If such a person wishes to escape liability under a contract on the ground of insanity, he or she must plead and prove, not merely the incapacity, but also that the other person knew of the incapacity. Unless these two things are proved the claim cannot succeed, and payment for services must be made. Thus, the contract is not void but voidable (see [10.54]).

[10.63] Intoxication does not remove contractual obligations: Those whose state of intoxication renders them unable to understand the nature of the contract they enter into are also held to contracts unless they can show that the other party to the contract knew they were intoxicated to that extent at the time.

[10.64] When the mentally incapacitated person presents for treatment: It would seem that those not certified as having no contractual capacity, but who are incapacitated to some extent could be held to be obliged by their agreement to the extent that they knew what they were doing: for example, such a person may be held to an agreement to pay for necessaries, fully understanding what is being agreed to, and the very fact that a person presents for treatment may indicate not only the knowledge that he or she is mentally ill, but also the understanding that treatment is needed, as well as the nature of such treatment. (Note, a distinction must be made between the contract and informed consent point of view (see above, Ch 5).)

Unincorporated Bodies

[10.65] What are they? Unincorporated bodies are groups of people, such as practitioners acting together as one, but who are not a registered company. Most commonly this is a partnership as these groups of people are separate entities in law and not a legal "person" as is a corporation, such a body cannot be a party to a contract. Each person separately must be a party if it is to be binding, either personally or through an agent (partners are each others' agents and so may bind each other). A group of practitioners may call themselves a "company" without being incorporated under appropriate companies incorporation legislation, and a group of people may register a business name under the business names legislation. In both cases those involved are still separate individuals under the law.

When a Contract is not an Enforceable Agreement

[10.66] Those making an agreement (contract) must, under law, be *ad idem*, that is, regarding both the terms of the agreement and their consent thereto, they must be of one mind and freely consent to all the terms of the contract. An agreement is invalid if one of the parties to it has subjected another party to it, to:

- .....misrepresentation of essential facts;
- .....mistake as to essential facts or terms in limited circumstances;
- .....duress by one of the parties to the contract;
- .....undue influence to agree exerted by one of the parties to the contract; and
- .....fraud perpetrated by one or more parties.

Misrepresentation

[10.67] A misrepresentation is an undertaking that something exists which does not accord with the true situation. It must be innocently made, as such an undertaking made deliberately is fraud.

[10.68] Misrepresentation of fact, innocently made and relied on by someone when giving her or his consent to be bound by a contract will negate any obligation under the agreement. A person's reliance on the truth of the facts given means he or she agrees subject to those facts being true. Agreement given to a contract made upon misrepresented facts is no agreement. There is deemed to be no contract from the beginning: it is void.

[10.69] It is worth mentioning here that some contracts, mainly insurance agreements, rely on the utmost good faith of the party applying for insurance to answer all questions which they are asked truthfully, and also to volunteer any other information that may be relevant to the risk being taken by the insurer. Failure to do this will render the contract inoperative.

[10.70] Fraudulent or negligent misrepresentation may lead to further action, either in criminal law or tort.

Mistake

[10.71] Courts are reluctant to hold that a contract is unenforceable because of a mistake made by one of the parties. One must distinguish mistake at law from error of judgment or mistake in personal assessment of facts. Take, for example, the person who looks at a car for sale and decides it is worth $5,000. That person cannot complain if he or she later discovers it is worth $500! There is a maxim at law "caveat emptor"—let the buyer beware. Only a few mistakes will be allowed in law. They are:

- ..... mistake as to the nature of contract;
- ..... mutual mistake as to a fact; and
- ..... mistake as to the party one is contracting with.

Mistake as to the Nature of the Contract

[10.72] This is not to be confused with mistake as to the law regarding the contract, but rather, what sort of contract you are agreeing to. An example is the elderly gentleman who signed a bill of exchange thinking it was a guarantee.

Mutual Mistake as to a Fact

[10.73] Where both parties are mistaken as to one or more facts, and they base the contract on this mistake, the contract can be held to be void only if the existence of the agreement depends on the reality of the mistaken facts. For example where a painting was sold, both parties mistakenly believing it was painted by the artist Constable, the court held that the contract was not void, as both parties were agreed on the sale of the same subject matter, the painting itself (*Leaf v International Galleries* [1950] 2 KB 86).

Mistake as to the Party one is Contracting with

[10.74] Most cases involving mistake as to the identity of the other party are about rogues passing themselves off as someone else. One of the parties must be mistaken as to the real identity of the other. As a result, he or she will not be bound by the agreement as it is void from the beginning. However, the courts have held that unless the identity of the person in question is crucial to the carrying out of the contract it is enforceable.

[10.75] Examples in health care would include the engaging of dentist Y to give care and advice to a client who believes she is a registered dentist. If she is in fact a registered dentist but her name is Z, and if she gives adequate dental care as agreed, the contract would most likely be enforceable: the client would have to pay. If dentist Y was the dentist's real name, but she is not a registered dentist, that mistaken identity could be said to go to the heart of the contract, even if the dental care is reasonable. The client would most likely have to show that he or she [10.78] would not have agreed to be cared for by Y if he or she had known the truth. However, unless that can be proved, Y is most likely entitled to be paid for services rendered.

Thus for a contract to be considered void on the ground of mistaken identity one must show that:

- .....at the time of making the contract he or she considered the identity of the other party, as a fundamental condition of the contract;
- .....he or she intended to deal with someone other than, or someone with different characteristics those of, the person dealt with; and
- .....the person dealt with knew, or ought to have known, of the mistake.

Duress

[10.76] Duress is a further ground for holding an agreement void. Common law has restricted duress to acts or threats of violence to the person, of deprivation of liberty, and the unlawful detention of goods. Recent law has extended beyond tangible property and includes the concept of economic duress, that is, the illegitimate threat of economic harm if one does not sign the contract.

Undue Influence

[10.77] If the situation falls short of the common law definition of duress, one may be able to invoke the law of equity (see [10.105]ff), which has developed remedies where one party holds an unfair advantage (moral or otherwise) over the other, through what is experienced as superior power or status. It falls short of duress, and the categories of conduct which constitute "undue influence" are not closed.

[10.78] In determining whether there has been undue influence courts may need to decide whether there was a special relationship between the two parties. Such relationships have been traditionally held to be solicitor and client, trustee (person entrusted with one's money or finances, for example, a bank) and beneficiary (person who has a claim on them, for example, account owner or person nominated to benefit), doctor and patient, parent and child, teacher and child, religious adviser and disciple (not husband and wife originally, as a wife could not contract on her own, or principal and agent). Where these relationships existed at the time consent was given, there is a presumption that there will have been undue influence unless the party with superior knowledge and resources can prove that there was no such influence, and that the consent was given freely. There is no set way of doing this, but the court will consider whether full disclosure of the facts was made to the plaintiff by the respondent, whether independent advice was given (that is, advice by a third, impartial person with relevant knowledge), and the actual circumstances of the consent. Examples are include the cases below.

[10.78] ■ ■ ■ CASE
Lloyd's Bank Ltd v Bundy [1974] 3 WLR 501

A bank secured a guarantee by a farmer of his son's overdraft. The court found that the farmer was elderly and stood to lose everything he had.

[10.79] The court found that the bank, as trustee of his money and finances stood in the role of fiduciary, it had to show it recommended independent advice. As the bank hadn't done this, it was held to have had undue influence and the contract was declared void.

■ ■ ■ CASE
Tasker v Algar [1928] NZLR 529

A mentally ill man made gifts of money to friends who cared for him. On his death. The administrator sought to have the gifts set aside, on the ground of undue influence.

[10.80] The court found that a fiduciary relationship existed between the man and his friends and that the friends therefore had to show that there was no undue influence.

[10.81] Where there is no special relationship, the person claiming undue influence will have the burden of proving that fact. The courts will vary in their approach to the claim depending on circumstances: for example, where one of the parties suffers a personal or social disability (the former could be a physical or mental handicap, the latter language or cultural differences).

[10.82] It is not hard to imagine that undue influence may affect the relationship between health carer and client in many cases. Health carers and others must be careful not to dominate clients to the point where their advice amounts to undue influence, but must allow the client to be free to decide, based on a fair and impartial disclosure of facts.

Fraud

[10.83] Fraud exists where one of the parties has intentionally misrepresented a crucial fact (not opinion or law), and:

- ......it was made knowingly, or without care as to its truth;
- ......it was made with the intention of inducing the other party to act upon it; and
- ......it must have actually misled the aggrieved party.

[10.84] In such a case the aggrieved person may rescind (cancel) the contract (the agreement was valid, so the contract has been in force until such time as fraud is discovered), and sue for any damages suffered as a result of the fraud.

Unconscionable contracts [10.88]

[10.85] A further development at law has been a willingness on the part of judges to set aside contracts which impose harsh terms on one party due to inequality of bargaining power.

▌▌▌ CASE

Commercial Bank of Australia Ltd v Amadio (1983) 151 CLR 447 (High Court)

Vincenzo Amadio was managing director of a failing company which had a very large overdraft at the plaintiff bank. To prevent closure of the account a deed of mortgage on property owned by Vincenzo's parents was executed by them. They were old and spoke little English, had been given incorrect information by Vincenzo, and although this had been corrected by the bank manager, they received no independent advice at all. When the company went into liquidation and the bank demanded $240,000 from the couple, they sued for release from the deed. They lost, but the Supreme Court (South Australia) granted an appeal. The matter went to the High Court.

[10.86] By 3-2 majority, the High Court held that the contract was unconscionable. This was not because of any dishonesty or moral obliquity on the part of the bank manager, but rather because the couple had not received proper advice as to the effect of the document they signed, or had its contents properly explained to them by their son (it was worded in very complicated legal writing). When the couple questioned the facts which (they were later to learn) had been wrongly represented to them by their son, and which the bank manager had to correct, the court said, he should have been put on notice that steps should be taken to ensure they were properly informed. Thus the couple's disability through ignorance and the inequality between them and the bank should have been evident, and it was unfair and unconscionable of the bank to proceed to procure their signature.

[10.87] Relief such as this against unconscionable dealing is a purely equitable remedy (see [10.105]ff). However, there are now statutory provisions in some jurisdictions allowing the court, where it finds a contract or a provision of a contract to be unjust, to refuse to enforce part or the whole of the contract, declare part or the whole of the contract void, or rewrite part or all of the contract (see for example, the *Contracts Review Act* 1980 (NSW)).

[10.88] This form of action has not been used widely in the medical arena, but it is considered only a matter of time before patients bring action in the courts complaining that they have been manipulated into agreeing to procedures when they did not fully understand what was going on.

Contracts which are Illegal or Against Public Policy

[10.89] An agreement may be validly made, but may be void or prohibited by statute or common law because it involves activities which are either illegal, prohibited or against public policy.

[10.90] Historically, at common law, those contracts which involve illegal or what has been considered immoral behaviour have been held to be void from the beginning. Such contracts involve subject matter such as commission of a crime (for example, an illegal abortion), a tort or a fraud on a third party; sexually immoral activity, acts which are prejudicial to public safety, the administration of justice or which lead to corruption in public life, and contracts to defraud revenue.

[10.91] While prohibited activity can be fairly easily identified, activity which is immoral and/or against public policy will depend on current opinion. As recently as 1973 in *Andrews v Parker* [1973] Qd R 93 the Queensland Supreme Court said: "The law shall not enforce an immoral promise such as a man and a woman to live together without being married." This can be compared with the 1982 case of *Seidler v Schallhofer* [1982] 2 NSWLR 80 where a contract regarding property made by a cohabiting couple was held to be enforceable (this was before legislation specifically recognising contracts between de facto couples had been passed in that State). The court stated that it had to act consistently with a law that permitted and recognised de facto relationships in other circumstances such as workers compensation. Similarly, other activities deemed immoral in the past may no longer be so considered. Carter and Harland, ((1998), p 537) note that although public policy covers everything that is *contra bonos mores*, thus touching all aspects of life, cases so far are limited to sexual morality. They ask readers if they can suggest why this is so. Could contracts involving activities relating to health care come under this category?

Contracts to Bear a Child for Another (Surrogacy Contracts)

[10.92] A controversial development in our society is the proliferation of agreements made between a woman who is willing to bear a child, and another person or couple who wish to adopt it. The federal government and most State governments have issued reports declaring that these agreements are against public policy, and thus should be discouraged at least.[1] Queensland has legislated to make the entering into a surrogacy

---

[1] Family Law Council, *Creating Children: A Uniform Approach to the Law and Practice of Reproductive Technology in Australia* (Canberra, AGPS, 1985); Australian Capital Territory, Attorney General's Department, *Discussion Paper: Surrogacy in the ACT* (Canberra, Australian Capital Territory Government Printer, 1993); New South Wales Law Reform Commission, *Artificial Conception: Surrogate Motherhood Report* (Sydney, 1988); Special Committee Appointed by the Queensland Government to Inquire into the Laws Relating to Artificial Insemination, In Vitro Fertilisation and Other Related Matters (*Report*, 1984); Select Committee of the South Australian Legislative Council, *Report on Artificial*

contract illegal, attracting a penalty (*Surrogate Parenthood Act* 1988 (Qld)). [10.94] It also makes the assistance of couples to enter into, or carry out a surrogacy contract illegal. The Australian Capital Territory, South Australia and Victoria have not gone this far,[2] they have passed legislation declaring such contracts null and void, that is, those entering a contract will not be penalised, but they cannot enforce any of the terms of the agreement: it is as if it did not exist, so the woman bearing the child cannot sue for any money promised her or force anyone to take the child, nor can she be made to give up the child as she had promised. Child welfare laws, and custody and guardianship laws would, of course, apply if they were relevant to such a situation.

▌▌▌ CASE
Matter of Baby M, 537 A 2d 1227 NJ (1988) (CA New Jersey United States)

This case involved the agreement of a woman, Mary-Beth Whitehead to bear a child, the result of artificial insemination with the sperm of a Mr Stern, and to relinquish the child to him and his wife on its birth. She was to be paid $10,000 for a live birth, and less if the child was stillborn. After the birth Ms Whitehead refused to relinquish the child, and the Sterns sued for breach of contract, demanding custody of the child (who was seized for them by the police).

[10.93] The trial judge ruled in favour of the Sterns, invoking the contract. However the Court of Appeal (at 1248) reversed this decision. It held that the contract entered into was null and void as it was against public policy. The agreement was in effect the sale of a child, and this was not sanctioned by the law: "In surrogacy, the highest bidders will presumably become the adoptive parents regardless of suitability, so long as payment of money is permitted."

[10.94] Any decision as to who should have custody of the child should be made on the basis of the child's best interest, the court continued, not on who had agreed to be the parent of the child. So although the court eventually gave custody to the Sterns, it made it clear that this was not because of the contract, but because Mr Stern was the father, and under the circumstances it was in the child's best interest to live with him and his wife. The little that there is of English precedent on this topic supports the view that surrogacy agreements (which are prohibited as commercial

---

[1] *continued*
 Insemination by Donor In Vitro Fertilisation and Embryo Transfer Procedures and Related Matters in South Australia (South Australian Government Printer, 1987); Tasmanian Committee of Inquiry to Investigate Artificial Conception and Related Matters in Tasmania (*Final Report*, 1985); Victorian Committee to Consider the Social, Ethical and Legal Issues Arising from In Vitro Fertilisation, *Report on the Disposition of Embryos Produced by In Vitro Fertilisation* (1984); Western Australian Committee of Inquiry, *Report of the Committee Appointed by the Western Australian Government to Inquire into the Social and Legal and Ethical Issues Relating to In Vitro Fertilisation and its Supervision* (1986).

[2] *Substitute Parent Agreements Act* 1994 (ACT); *Family Relationships Act Amendments Act* 1988 (SA); *Infertility Treatment Act* 1995 (Vic), Pt V.

[10.94] enterprises) will be taken into account by the court in deciding the right of any person to adopt a child, but that the court must give priority to the welfare of children (*Brooks v Blount* [1923] 1 KB 237; *Re C (A Minor) (Wardship: Surrogacy)* [1985] FLR 846).

[10.95] In Australia, the only case to deal with a surrogacy agreement is *Re Evelyn* (1988) FLC ¶92-807. That case involved a child born as a result of a surrogacy agreement, where the birth parents did not want to give her up. The Family Court of Appeal held that the agreement could not be enforced as where a case involves the custody of a child, the paramount consideration is the welfare of the child, thus considerations of immorality become irrelevant. For further discussion about the law regarding surrogacy see Chapter 17.

Discharge of Contracts

[10.96] A contract comes to the end of its life, that is, is discharged, on one of the following events:

- performance;
- agreement;
- frustration;
- election upon breach; or
- the occurrence of a specified event or condition.

Performance

[10.97] Where parties have performed their promises fully and precisely, according to the terms of their agreement, the contract is discharged. Unless a specific time for the carrying out of one's obligations is stipulated (making time of the essence), these should be carried out within a reasonable time. Where activities are to be performed for a stated period of time, the contract is discharged at the end of that time. When a party has discharged her or his obligations under a contract, that party may demand discharge (often payment) by the other(s).

Agreement

[10.98] Where a contract has not been fully discharged the parties may agree to consider it discharged. This is a further contract and all elements, including consideration, must be present. Where no one has completed her or his part of the agreement, then consideration is no problem: each party simply agrees to release their rights under the original contract in consideration for a similar release by the other. Where one party has discharged some or all obligations required under the contract but the other has not, then some further consideration is required for the agreement to be legally enforceable.

Frustration

[10.104]

[10.99] Normally contracts are based on at least a presumption that those involved will carry out their promise as long as they remain able to do so: and that only ill-health, unexpected events, accident, war, non-occurrence of a foreseen event, etc, which renders it impossible or unreasonably difficult for them to act will excuse them from their obligation. In that case each party must fulfil those obligations which fell due before the frustrating event occurred: the contract is not void from the beginning. If the frustration is self-induced the above does not apply.

Election upon Breach

[10.100] Where one party has breached a term of the contract, the other party may elect either to discharge the contract or to seek a remedy as outlined below, depending on the nature of the breach. The party may be able to claim for any damages suffered, but cannot thereafter seek specific performance of the contract (see [10.106]).

Occurrence of a Specified Event or Condition

[10.101] This is self-explanatory: where it is specified that if something happens or some stipulated condition occurs the contract will be deemed discharged.

Remedies for Breach of Contract

[10.102] There are three main actions that can be brought where the terms of an agreement have been breached.

Common Law Remedy

Damages

[10.103] The basic remedy for breach of contract is the award of an appropriate sum of money as compensation for loss of goods, business or other value that has resulted from the breach, or the cost of remedying the effects of the contract not having been fulfilled. The court considers the terms of the contract (written, oral or implied), and what could fairly be contemplated as a reasonable sum which the parties would have had in mind at the time of making the contract.

[10.104] Thus if health care has not been carried out properly, and further treatment is required to fix the effects of the bad care (for example corrective dental surgery), payment for this may be sought. As mentioned, the kind or amount of harm for which remedies are sought need not be

[10.104] foreseen, but may constitute whatever harm flows from the actions (or omissions) of the defendant.

Equitable Remedies

[10.105] These are discretionary remedies, that is, the court may make any ruling that it considers fair and just under the circumstances, although it must be applied according to principles of equity law.

Specific Performance

[10.106] Specific performance is a court order that a party perform her or his contractual obligations. The court will only do this where the award of money would not be just under the circumstances, it would not be unjust to require the specific performance by the defaulting party and the other party is still ready and willing to fulfil his or her part of the agreement. Specific performance is generally applied where it would be impossible to get a similar article, and the particular article's unique nature was relied on, such as a painting.

Injunction

[10.107] This is an order by a court forbidding, or ordering, a person to do something. It can be applied when there is a contract where someone has promised to refrain from some activity, and the other person is afraid the person will go ahead and do it, or it can be an interim measure where a further, more detailed court hearing is to be held. Whereas failure to pay damages after they have been ordered by the court can lead to seizure of property or garnishment of wages to claim the ordered amount of money, where an order for specific performance or an injunction is ignored, the person involved may be imprisoned.

[10.108] There is an implied condition in any contract for professional services that not only will the services be those agreed upon and consented to, but that they will be of a standard reasonably to be expected of the ordinary person of similar experience and skill which the practitioner here purports to have. If such service is not given, whether there is any harm suffered or not, the client can sue for breach of contract. The client can claim for any financial or physical loss suffered as a result of the breach of contract, and can also claim that no fee is payable. The client can then be restored to the financial and physical position that existed before the contract was entered into, insofar as that is practicable. Under some circumstances, where the above remedies are inappropriate, the court may make an order for specific performance, however, courts will not as a rule require any person to render personal service to another, as this smacks of slavery.

REFERENCES AND FURTHER READING

Bowden, G and Morris, A, *An Introduction to the Law of Contracts and Tort* (The Estates Gazette Ltd, London, 1978)

Carter, J, *Outline of Contract Law in Australia* (Butterworths, Sydney, 1986)

Carter, J and Harland, D, *Contract Law in Australia* (3rd ed, Butterworths, Sydney, 1998)

Dix, et al, *Law for the Medical Profession* (Butterworths, Sydney, 1988)

Graw, S, *An Introduction to the Law of Contract* (2nd ed, Law Book Co, Sydney, 1993).

Khoury, D and Yamouni, Y, *Understanding Contract Law* (3rd ed, Butterworths, Sydney, 1992)

Lindgren, K, Carter, J and Harland, D, *Cases and Materials on Contract Law in Australia* (Butterworths, Sydney, 1998)

Lindgren, K, Carter, J and Harland, D, *Contract Law in Australia* (2nd ed, Butterworths, Sydney, 1992)

Staunton, P and Whyburn, R, *Nursing and the Law* (4th ed, Saunders, Sydney, 1988)

The Laws of Australia (Law Book Co, Sydney, 1994), Vol 7, Contract

Vermeesch, R and Lindgren, K, *Business Law of Australia* (2nd ed, Butterworths, Sydney, 1992)

Vermeesch, R and Lindgren, K, *Business Law in Australia* (10th ed, Butterworths, Sydney, 2001)

Chapter Eleven
CONTRACTS TO PROVIDE HEALTH CARE SERVICES

▌▌▌
INTRODUCTION

[11.1]   The basis of a health carer's relationship with an employer is that of contract. A contract of employment is usually entered into, where wages or a salary are paid for work done. This is also called a "contract of service". However, a person may do work for another through a "contract for services". This makes one not an employee, but an independent contractor.

Employee or Independent Contractor
Determining the Difference

[11.2]   At law, there is no hard-and-fast rule to distinguish the two types of contract. Where a contract is called into question the court will consider all the facts involved. The foremost test for establishing whether a contract is one for service or services is called the "control test": the amount of control by the employer over the conditions, workplace and tools of the employee are considered. However, the courts have recognised that other factors must be considered, such as, mode of remuneration, provision and maintenance of equipment, the obligation to work, provision of holidays, deduction of income tax, and delegation of work by the putative employee (*Stevens v Brodribb Sawmilling Co Pty Ltd* (1986) 160 CLR 16). The court must consider all the facts.

[11.3]   A contract of employment generally has the following features:

- .....one person determines the work that is to be done, as they require it, and the other makes herself or himself available by the hour;
- .....the first-mentioned person also controls the premises and equipment, and how they are to be used;
- .....the first-mentioned person has the power to hire and fire at their discretion; and
- .....the person rendering the service is paid regularly, and is entitled to recreation leave and other benefits.

[11.4] **[11.4]** On the other hand, when an independent contractor is engaged:

- ..... the contractor is asked to carry out a specific task, the completion of which brings the contract to an end;
- ..... the contractor generally owns the equipment (and maybe the premises) and determines how it is to be used;
- ..... a contractor cannot be hired and fired like an employee; dissatisfaction with the work is remedied by suing for breach of contract (see above, Ch 10), or negligence (see above, Ch 6), otherwise the contractor must be paid for the whole job; and
- ..... the contractor has no claim for payment (unless special arrangements are made) until the work is completed.

[11.5] Sometimes a person may be designated in a written contract as an independent contractor, despite their position, in fact, being closely controlled by the employer. This could be a way of attempting to avoid liability for, such things as workers' compensation or holiday pay. In these circumstances one considers the facts of the situation, to determine which category most accurately describes those involved:

> in a matter of this sort the court should look at the substance of the transaction and not treat a written agreement, which was designed to disguise its real nature, as succeeding in doing so if it amounted merely to a cloud of words and, without really altering the substantial relations between the parties, described them . . . in terms appropriate to some other relation [*Cam & Sons Pty Ltd v Sargent* (1940) 14 ALJ 162 at 163 per Dixon J].

[11.6] On the other hand, a person who is ostensibly under a significant degree of control may be an independent contractor. See for example, the following case.

▮▮ CASE
Vabu v Federal Commissioner of Taxation (1996) 33 ATR 537

> Vabu Pty Ltd operated a business called Crisis Couriers, which engaged couriers using a variety of vehicles for delivering parcels and other items. Vabu paid bicycle couriers a flag-fall payment for each contract of carriage, and other motorised vehicle couriers a flag-fall and per-kilometre fee. Couriers were required to wear uniforms, appear neat and tidy, replace vehicles when required by the company, observe a starting time and work a prescribed number of hours. They were to accept work assigned to them, deliver good in the manner directed, accept re-routing and take no more leave than permitted. However, they were also required to supply their own vehicle, pay for petrol, insurance and registration of vehicles, provide their own street directories, blankets, ropes etc, received payment per delivery rather than a wage or salary independent contractors.

[11.7] The court held that the couriers were in fact independent contractors. It did not give the control test the priority it had had in the past, but considered it equally with other tests. Baragwanath ((1998), p 137) notes that now that the amount of control exercised by an employer over a worker is not so important in determining if the worker is an employee, this removes a protection workers had against employers setting up the relationship to look as if the worker was an independent contractor, when the amount of control over the worker was such that the court would declare the worker an employee.

[11.8] The tests devised by the courts are a guide only: a contract may have a mixture of features from both categories. Where there is a conflict over the nature of the relationship of the parties the court will take all these factors into account and weigh them up to decide into which category the contract falls:

> The law, as I see it, is this: if the true relationship of the parties is that of master and servant under a contract of service, the parties cannot alter the truth of that relationship by putting a different label on it. . . . On the other hand, if their relationship is ambiguous and is capable of being one or the other [that is, either service or agency], then the parties can remove that ambiguity, by the very agreement itself which they make with one another. The agreement itself then becomes the best material from which to gather the true legal relationship between them [*Massey v Crown Life Insurance Co* [1978] 2 All ER 576 at 579 per Denning MR].

[11.9] The contract itself may or may not be carefully scrutinised and relied upon according to the circumstances of the individual case. It is important to note that where there is a written contract of employment a court will be restricted to considering the terms which are expressly or impliedly contained in the written document. The court cannot go into the manner in which the parties went about putting the contract into practice, unless this can be shown to amount to an agreement which adds to, or changes the terms of, the original contract (something the parties are quite entitled to do). Such addition or change would be subject to the requirements for any contract: for example, there would have to be mutual agreement. As well as making a written document irrelevant if it is at odds with the actual agreed behaviour of the parties, there may be a change in an otherwise unambiguous document and relationship. An example would be where the original contract was for a nurse to work in the paediatric section of a hospital, but, after formal consultation with the employer, or on a regular basis when asked on specific occasions, he or she agreed to be available to work in the general intensive care unit.

When is a Health Carer an Independent Contractor?

[11.10] It follows from the above discussion that those who work in a health care establishment are most likely to be employees, except for visiting medical officers and others on contract. Those who work independently (for example, agency nurse engaged to care for a client at home, home birth nurse, general practitioner), are independent contractors. Where a hospital engages someone through an agency to fill a staffing shortage the status of the person is not so clear. There would appear to be enough control in the latter case by both the agency and the hospital to make both employers in relation to different aspects of the

[11.10] work. Matters such as pay and allocation of hours and location are areas that would be the province of the agency, maters such as the nature of the work and workers' compensation would be the that of the hospital. An aggrieved patient could argue that the hospital bears the responsibility for all whom it engages to carry out its obligations to its clients, notwithstanding that their contract may be different from others it clearly employs (for example, see *Ramsey v Larsden* (1964) 111 CLR 16 at 29 per Kitto J).

Other Relationships

[11.11] There are other relationships in which one person may do work for another. Two which may be of particular interest to health carers are:

- ..... principal and agent; and
- ..... partnership.

Principal and Agent

[11.12] An agent is one who is authorised to act for another, and has power to create and effect legal relationships between her or his principal and third parties. An agent must act with the principal's approval, and in so doing may bind the principal by contract to the third party. Examples are real estate agents and commercial travellers. However, a specific contract of agency need not exist: simply by placing another in a position where, "according to . . . law or . . . the ordinary usages of mankind [a person] is understood to represent and act for the person who has so placed him; but in every case it is only by the will of the employer that an agency can be created" (*Pole v Leask* (1863) 33 LJ (Ch) 155 at 161-162). One difficulty in establishing agency as opposed to employment is that many employees are, by the very nature of their work, agents of their employer. They may, in fact, be both.

> It is only when the surgeon is not a servant, when for instance he is brought in for the occasion as a specialist carrying on his profession *on his own account*, that the hospital is not responsible under the principle of respondeat superior. (Emphasis added)

[11.13] This, applied to other health carers, such as nurses, would mean that if they were engaged by a health care facility to carry out specific duties controlled by the hospital they would be in a situation where vicarious liability would apply.

[11.14] The court must examine the terms of employment, and consider the nature of the agreement. The difference, in effect, is that whereas a principal may direct an agent what to do, an employer can also direct her or him as to how (and sometimes when and where) to do it. Health carers may be exercising the powers of agency when they commit their employer to some service for a client, for example, community nurses signing up clients for treatment or rehabilitation services. Power of attorney is a form of agency, where a person authorises another to act on their behalf (see [4.109]ff).

Partnership

[11.15] This is where two or more people agree to combine for some object, such as providing a service. Health carers in private practice may decide to do this. A partnership is not a company. A company is a legal "person" separate from the individuals who constitute it. Those individuals are not personally liable for the debts of the company, and it can purchase goods, employ people, sue and be sued as if it was a single individual. In a partnership the members act as separate individuals, and liability for debts and negligence may be shared jointly by the individuals involved. One partner is not an employee of the partnership unless he or she specifically and separately enters such a relationship by contract. Partners are principals in their own right, and any work they do is not subject to the regime of industrial regulation which protects employees.

Implied Terms of Employment: Common Law

[11.16] Terms of a contract may be included in the employment agreement, but in some cases there are terms which are implied by the law: they exist just as if they were specifically agreed upon by the parties, and in fact no agreement can be made that contradicts some of them. This is because employment attracts common law and statutory duties and privileges for both the employer and employee. There are four other sources of implied conditions for employment contracts: common law, statutory law enterprise agreements and industrial awards. Some common law implied conditions in the employment contract, which presumably could not be ruled out, and which set out the employee's duties are as follows.

Implied Undertakings by the Employee

To Carry Out any Lawful and Reasonable Order of the Employer

> Control or the right to control is still the single most important characteristic by which the employer employee relationship is identified. And there is no better indicator of control than the existence in one party of the right to give orders as to what is to be done and how it is to be done by the other party. The right of the employer to give, and the obligation of the employee to obey orders is, in the eyes of the law, foremost among the terms of the contract of employment, even though it is often an implied term, the parties having said nothing about it [Macken et al (1990), p 96].

[11.17]   **[11.17]** A health care employee should clarify with a prospective employer just what duties are to be involved, and whether duties are limited to certain areas of care or are more general. The duty statement is a critical document in doing this, and should be carefully developed by the employer and studied by the prospective employee. If an employee is not prepared to carry out all instructions that the employer might give (for example, he or she feels inexperienced or untrained in certain areas of care), this should be the subject of discussion when the employment is being negotiated. There is a responsibility on the part of a health care provider to its clients, to provide staff who are adequately trained and experienced and employing adequately educated and experienced staff is a crucial part of carrying out this obligation.

[11.18] The requirement of obedience involves only lawful directions. Orders which endanger an employee's life or health, or which he or she reasonably believes would endanger her or his life or health are not lawful orders, and there is no obligation to obey them (*Re Dismissal of Fitters by BHP* [1969] AR (NSW) 399). Presumably this would apply to directions which it is believed would endanger the life and health of clients or others. This raises the possibility of conflicting legal duties, with possible liability for breaching either of them. The health carer must choose as to which one to follow.

Refusing to Work

[11.19] Failure to carry out the service contracted for will free the employer from the obligation to pay the employee, because service is that for which the wages are being paid. However, the duty to render service is limited to lawful commands of the employer. Some commentators claim that the command must also be reasonable, but others disagree (see Macken et al (1990), p 124).

[11.20] Refusal by staff to care for HIV-positive clients where the employer has provided adequate protection and instruction may be a breach of the contract of employment. There is still much debate on whether it is reasonable to order staff to care for such people even with the best of precautions. (Note, discrimination against those with a physical or mental handicap is prohibited in all jurisdictions (see below, Ch 18).)

[11.21] The employer is entitled to require an employee to carry out any lawful order, that is, any order reasonably related to the rendering of services contracted for. This is why it is important to let an employer know of anything one is unable or unwilling to do which could otherwise be expected of someone in the category under which one is employed. Unless otherwise stipulated, a health carer, for example, a physiotherapist, is employed to carry out any of the duties which it is reasonable to expect of someone with the training and experience he or she claims to have. A first-year doctor should not be expected to carry out the responsibilities and care expected of a specialist (or even registrar). Similarly, a general nurse should not be required to carry out the duties which only a specialist nurse would be trained to carry out.

[11.22] Under common law, absent wilful misconduct, there is no right on the part of the employer to dismiss a person unless a refusal to carry out lawful and reasonable directions is clearly an intention to repudiate the whole contract. Where the refusal occurs because the employee believes he or she cannot properly carry out a particular service, or should not carry it out under the circumstances, but expresses willingness to carry out any other orders, it seems the employer is liable for wages for any service accepted. In the face of a refusal to obey an order, the employer can determine that less than full obedience will be considered as the employee's repudiation of the contract, and the basis for non-payment, even for other work which may be of value. Therefore, where such notice is given, if one has been employed to work, for example, in intensive care, but refuses to do so and undertakes work instead in a surgical ward, the employer can refuse payment of wages, even if that work is of benefit to the employer. The amount of pay which can be withheld will be calculated according to the units of time by which pay is normally calculated. If the employer accepts the work in the surgical ward without notice, as described above, this is seen as an acceptance of the contract and wages are owed accordingly.

[11.23] The case is not the same when one does not feel competent, a matter which was discussed in Chapter 6, where the consideration was health carers' responsibility to the client, which involves providing reasonable care. Here, the issue is their responsibility to the employer, and the requirement that directions be followed. The two may not lead to the same answer. A health carer may be lawfully obliged by his or her contract of employment to care for someone (where, for example the employer insists on this, or fails to provide an adequate system of care), but feels that he or she cannot reasonably do so, lacking competence or resources. There is a conflict of duties here, and no clear legal answer, as there is no priority of legal duties: whatever choice is made, there is a potential legal sanction; threat of action in negligence, or in breach of contract (with loss of pay, or job). One may consider that the best solution under the circumstances, is to:

- consider the ethical ramifications of the issue and by taking the least morally culpable course (see Ch 19); and
- remembering to make written records of this (see Ch 7).

There is a further consideration from the employer's point of view. Given the knowledge that particular staff may not be competent in certain areas of care, the employer has a duty to consider alternative staffing to fulfil its duty of reasonable care to the client. This is where vicarious liability becomes an issue.

[11.24] However, under industrial legislation, procedures are set out where there is a difference of opinion between an employer and employee, with mechanisms for resolving conflict, which are outlined below.

To Carry out those Orders with Reasonable Care

[11.25] An employer can expect staff to carry out their duties with reasonable care. This is the same as, but separate from, the duty of reasonable care demanded by the law of torts. Here, the duty is to the employer, there it is to the client. It would seem then that harm to a client is not required for action to be taken against an employee for not carrying out duties reasonably carefully, as it is in tort law. Instead of damages, the employer can call the employment contract into question and either dismiss, discipline or refuse to pay, the employee who so acts.

[11.26] There is also a primary liability where a client has been harmed by an employee's negligence, and the employer found vicariously liable may, in some circumstances, in turn seek indemnity from the negligent employee. In New South Wales, the Northern Territory and South Australia legislation protects employees from being sued by the employer (*Employee's (Indemnification of Employer) Act* 1982 (NSW); *Law Reform (Miscellaneous Provisions) Act* 1956 (NT), s 22A(1); *Wrongs Act* 1936 (SA)). See also [6.118]ff on vicarious liability. Generally an employer is insured, and insurance policies provide that action will not be taken against a negligent employee. This does not protect the employee in New South Wales who is sued directly, or anywhere where the employer's property is damaged, or where the employee is guilty of serious and wilful misconduct.

To be Faithful to the Employer's Interests

[11.27] It is difficult to state specifically what is required in terms of being faithful to an employer's interests, as situations vary, but as a generalisation it would involve the duty to act in good faith towards the employer, and not do anything which is inconsistent with the terms of the contract, or injurious to the employer, or to the proper performance of an employee's duties under the contract. Such actions could be:

[11.28] Denigrating the standard of medical treatment given by the employer: This could be done by actions or words which undermine clients' or prospective clients' confidence in the standard of medical care offered by the employer. It may involve only one client, or be a public communication or action, or participation in debate. This duty, like the duty to carry out lawful orders, is not based on one's personal views as to the harm which may be involved in carrying it out. Where one is convinced of the poor standard of care offered by one's employer, one discloses this at the risk of action by the employer for breach of contract. The principle is based on the premise that confidential and discreet communication with the employer will resolve the issue, otherwise one moves on, to find another position elsewhere with a more satisfactory employer. This is to ignore the reality of shortage of jobs and power of employers.

[11.29] Disclosure of any information received by a health carer in furthering the employer's interest: There are two sorts of knowledge one acquires in a job: general knowledge necessarily acquired in carrying out one's duties, and knowledge gained through special access to documents, plans, procedures, and scientific knowledge which is specific to the employer. It is hard to distinguish between the two in many cases, but generally it can be said that the first is experience one can take and use elsewhere, the second is specific confidential information and trade secrets and research results which would not normally be used elsewhere. However, contractual terms may specify information which is not to be disclosed.

[11.30] Disclosure of confidential information may be made to those other than the employer, in the public interest. Such matters could be an illegal, dangerous or harmful activity other than a private wrong (that is, a particular incidence of negligence to an individual) (*Weld-Blundell v Stephens* [1919] 1 KB 520 at 525). The court will consider the motive of the employee, whether the disclosure was restricted to those with a need to know, whether it was made recklessly to too wide an audience, and whether the employee stood to gain by the disclosure.

[11.31] Disclosure also may be made where an employee is in charge of her or his employer's documents or files, and is subpoenaed to produce them in court.

To Account for the Employer's Property

[11.32] Accounting for an employer's property includes the duty to reasonably protect an employer's property from harm, to account for all money and goods received in the course of employment, and to indemnify the employer for any financial loss caused. (This includes loss caused through vicarious liability, with exceptions (see Ch 6). One cannot use one's employer's equipment or stock of goods for personal gain outside working hours, or for purposes which are not related to employment (such as helping oneself to equipment for the purpose of treating one's own or one's family's minor injuries and illnesses!). As well as being forms of larceny, such actions are breaches of one's employment contract. Inventions or patented procedures made in the course of employment belong to the employer unless otherwise stated.

Disclosure of Information to the Employer

[11.33] There is an obligation at common law to inform the employer of anything which is essential for the employer's business. Thus, incompetence or wrongdoing on the part of other staff should be disclosed, according to law, if it is in the employer's interest to know of this. Also included in this principle is the requirement to answer reasonable questions, except where to do this would incriminate (that is, expose oneself to criminal action; see [15.66]), and such protection has not been removed by statute. Where it has, an employee might be expected to answer questions, even where these may render her or him liable for criminal prosecution: however, such a situation is very rare. Where a health carer is asked to disclose information and is unsure of her or his obligation to do so, independent legal advice is advisable.

Employees' Role in Safety

[11.34] Staff should be conscious of the need to ensure that safety is maintained in the workplace. This includes the maintenance of equipment and its proper use, for instance, equipment should not be too high or too low and it should be easily accessible. Occupational health and safety legislation in some States requires staff involvement in safety matters. Employers, when defending cases where workers have been injured, may argue that the worker made an error of judgment or was tired or off-colour at the time, and therefore the employer was not to blame. However workers, being human, often do make errors of judgment, and are often tired and off-colour. Those factors should be taken into account when providing for safety in the workplace.

[11.35] Health care workers are very conscious of the need to take care with used needles, to prevent the spread of diseases such as Hepatitis B and AIDS, but there are many more sources of injury and contamination which are perhaps ignored through repetition and overwork. Workers' compensation, for which employers are insured, provides for most injuries that occur at work, but where employers are held to have been negligent, in some cases they can be sued. However, this right is limited. In the Northern Territory, workers can no longer bring an action against their employer if they are eligible for workers' compensation (*Work Health Act* 1986 (NT), s 52). In some other States they are restricted in the amount of damages they can claim (*Workers Compensation (Benefits) Amendment Act* 1989 (NSW); *Workers Rehabilitation and Compensation Act* 1986 (SA), s 54; *Accident Compensation Act* 1985 (Vic), s 135(1)) (see further Ch 12).

Implied Undertakings by the Employer

[11.36] Implied conditions of the contract which concern the employer are:

- payment of wages;
- provision of a safe place of work;
- provision of competent staff; and
- provision of a safe system of work.

Payment of Wages

[11.37] The payment of wages has been dealt with above. The employer is also required to fulfil conditions set out by common law, statutory law and industrial awards relating to holidays, sick leave etc. Standing by ready to work, and being available for emergencies will, if part of one's duties, be considered service, and the basis for pay.

> Payment of wages is conditional upon performance by the employee of the full range of work assigned, or, at least, a readiness and willingness to

do so [*Csomore v Public Service Board (NSW)* (1987) 10 NSWLR 587 [11.40] at 595].

Provision of a Safe Place of Work

[11.38] The provision of a safe place of work is a similar duty of the employer. The duty is not absolute: very little would be produced if the workplace had to be absolutely safe; the law is perhaps too ready to sympathise with the desirability of maintaining production despite some degree of risk. However, it has been held by the House of Lords that there must be a balancing of the benefits to be gained with the degree and likelihood of risk posed to employees. This duty arises at common law, and also as a result of occupational health and safety legislation (see Ch 12).

▌▌▌ CASE
Latimer v AEC [1953] AC 643 (House of Lords England)

A particularly heavy rainstorm caused oil to spread onto the floor of a factory, making it slippery. The plaintiff did slip on the floor, and sued the employer, arguing that the factory should have been closed down until it was safer.

[11.39] On appeal from a finding in favour of the plaintiff, the House of Lords argued that there was not enough evidence that the risk of harm was great enough to warrant closing down the whole operation. They reversed the original order, finding for the defendant. The court stated that provision of a safe workplace is a duty which is non-delegable and personal. That is, responsibility cannot be delegated to any other person (although performance of tasks necessary to provide the safe workplace may), and the duty is owed to each worker personally.

▌▌▌ CASE
Sroka v Ridge Park Private Hospital (1981) 28 SASR 15 (Supreme Court)

A nurse's aide injured her back when she assisted a difficult, elderly, hemiplegic patient who was attempting to move from a commode to a chair without waiting for assistance. The aide broke the patient's fall, and after the patient was on the floor attempted to move her into a chair. The aide sued the employer hospital, arguing that it had not provided adequate assistance or equipment for the lifting and care of patients which would also provide for the prevention of back injuries. The hospital responded that in her attempts to drag the patient to a chair, the aide was contributorily negligent in not seeking assistance from other staff, and thus they were not liable.

[11.40] The court held that the employer was negligent in that it could foresee that patients would provide occasional emergencies, and that nurses would be called upon to act quickly, with little time for reflection. Given this possibility, the employer should have made appropriate

[11.40] provision for a safe system for lifting patients. This may include adequate staffing and equipment, and nurses should not have to search for assistance when it is needed. The court did accept the argument that the nurse had acted carelessly in attempting to move the patient after she was on the floor, but only to the extent of 20 per cent of the damages. The hospital had to pay 80 per cent. A large proportion of nursing staff injure their backs lifting patients, and this case is a clear message that employers should consider the need to employ adequate staff, procedures and facilities for lifting patients. Health carers should also take care in lifting patients.

[11.41] The circumstances of the individual employee must be taken into account where these ought to have been known by the employer, for example, where the employee suffers from a disability (for example, only one eye). Special precautions should be taken to prevent harm to the employee. *Paris v Stepney Borough Council* [1951] AC 367, was a case involving such a situation. A maintenance worker who was known to be blind in one eye was blinded completely when he struck a rusty bolt with a steel hammer and a chip from the bolt pierced his good eye. Lord Morton of the House of Lords stated:

> I think that the more serious the damage which will happen if an accident occurs, the more thorough are the precautions which an employer must take . . . I think it follows logically that if A and B, who are engaged on the same work, run precisely the same risk of an accident happening, but if the results of an accident will be more serious to A than to B, precautions which are adequate in the case of B may not be adequate in the case of A, and it is a duty of the employer to take such additional precautions for the safety of A as may be reasonable . . .

Provision of Competent Staff

[11.42] The employer also owes a duty to employees (as well, of course to clients) to hire competent staff. Staff who carry out their duties in an unsafe or negligent manner, putting other employees at risk, can be admonished or, if they persist with unsafe practices can be dismissed. Dangerous and persistent skylarking should not be allowed. Special attention should also be given to the training of new, inexperienced employees and those from non-English speaking backgrounds, to ensure they can carry out their duties safely. However, where employees are experienced and skilled, the employer should not be expected to have to treat the worker like an "imbecile child" (*Smith v Austin Lifts* [1959] 1 All ER 81 (House of Lords)).

Provision of a Safe System of Work

[11.43] A further aspect of safety, and one which ties the others together, is the duty to provide a safe system of work. This means that the combination of workplace, staff, equipment and the method of work should all, when taken together, provide a smooth and safe system for the carrying out of work. It is much easier to do this where a routine can be established which is unlikely to be broken. The likelihood of accidents arises most frequently in unusual circumstances, such as emergencies and disasters, which are part of most health carers' work. Planning a safe system of work should take these possibilities into account, and aim at foolproof systems that withstand the frailties of the human condition. Under-staffing and cost-cutting including lack of planning, may lead to breach of this duty.

Discipline of Employees

[11.44] Employers have a common law right to discipline employees and this is qualified by legislation and awards (see below). This power was quite extensive in the past. The case of *R v Keite* (1697) 1 Ld Raym 138; 91 ER 989 held that "if a master gives correction to a servant it ought to be with a proper instrument, as a cudgel, etc. And then if by accident a blow give death, this would be but manslaughter" (quoted from Creighton et al (1983), p 116). Today, of course, corporal punishment would be a criminal activity, and discipline of employees is now much more constrained! Generally, the principles to be applied to disciplinary actions are as follows:

- .....any power to discipline is ultimately subject to the terms of the contract, which may include award conditions and statutory rules;
- .....any sanction which does not derogate from these contractual rights of the employee (and the general law of the land) may be lawfully imposed;
- .....any sanction which does derogate from the employees' contractual rights is a breach of contract;
- .....any sanction which is expressly or impliedly authorised by the contract of employment is prima facie lawful;
- .....disciplinary action may not involve payment of wages for work done which is less than the award rate. Wages above award rates may be reduced and some bonuses withdrawn. If, for example, a bonus entitlement is expressed as being the entitlement of all employees and attached to something like company profits, these could probably not be reduced as a disciplinary measure. If they were conditional on employees' work (for example, attached to good conduct, or maintenance of good work practices), they could be reduced (Macken et al (1990), p 116).

[11.45] Boland and Anderson ((1987), p 159) set out a proposed disciplinary procedure which involves clearly advising the employee of the behaviour complained of, and allowing her or him adequate opportunity to respond and explain the behaviour if they wish to. It is suggested that it is desirable to secure the employee's agreement to refrain from the conduct, but that if it is felt necessary to resort to disciplinary action, it should be appropriate, applied consistently, and conform to the employer's disciplinary code.

[11.46] Disciplinary action may involve withholding or reducing payment of wages and bonuses subject to the principles above, demotion,

[11.46] transfer to other duties or areas of work, refusal of promotion and dismissal as the ultimate sanction. There is very little law on this topic, so little further guidance can be given in a text such as this.

▌▌▌ CASE
Howden v City of Whittlesea (1990) 32 AILR 392 (6 September 1990, Industrial Relations Commission of Victoria)

A nurse who suspected that a child she was attending was the subject of abuse reported her concerns to Community Services Victoria as she felt this was a matter beyond her expertise. When the mother discovered that she was under investigation she made a formal complaint to the Manager of the Family and Children's Services Branch. The nurse was summoned to a meeting with the Manager and the Director of Human Services. She was read the letter of complaint but was not given a copy or allowed to read it for herself. She was then asked to resign, but as she did not, she was dismissed for professional misconduct for breaching confidentiality. The Australian Nurses Federation took her case to the Victorian Industrial Relations Commission, arguing that the nurse had been denied procedural and natural justice, and that her dismissal was harsh, unjust and unreasonable.

[11.47] The Commission held that the nurse's dismissal had been harsh, unjust or unreasonable because she was not guilty of misconduct. She had also been denied procedural justice as she was given no opportunity to answer the allegations and no time to consider her position when she was asked to resign, nor was she given a copy of the letter which contained the allegations about her. In relation to the allegation of misconduct for breach of confidentiality, the Commission pointed out that her actions were not misconduct, as nurses cannot be expected to keep all information confidential because if they did, they could not function well in the best interests of their clients and the community (see Ch 7). It also pointed out that the *Community Welfare Services Act* 1970 (Vic) permits notification of suspected child abuse (see Ch 16). Developments in the law relating to unfair dismissal are outlined in Chapter 11.

[11.48] As mentioned above, those who refuse to follow, or question, their employer's instructions (which may be through a doctor), are often subjected to dismissal or to some form of discipline or harassment. Johnstone ((1994), Ch 2) discusses the dilemma which results from the conflict between a nurse's right to exercise independent judgment with the obligation to restrict her or his actions to following the directions of others. On the basis that health carers are employed simply to follow orders of others and not to act independently, contracts of employment have been considered to be breached when they question, reject or act independently of those orders, or codes of ethics (which lay the basis for allegations of misconduct). The debate surrounding this issue is beyond the scope of this book, but it is hoped that health carers will be better equipped to actively pursue the interests of their particular profession as a result of reading it.

Implied Terms of Employment: Statutes, Enterprise Agreements and Industrial Awards

[11.51]

[11.49] There are State and Commonwealth statutes and awards setting out basic conditions of employment, which become just as much terms of the employment contract as those specifically agreed upon by the parties. Such provisions may deal with recreation leave, hours of employment, frequency of wage payments, etc. Government hospitals and statutory health facilities will have rather extensive legislation setting out work conditions. However an enterprise agreement or industrial award (see below) may in fact be more generous to the employee than the legislation. In this case the agreement or award takes precedence over the legislation. Health carers can find out about legislation and awards from the federal or State Departments of Industrial Relations (the title may differ), or the appropriate union or employees' association office.

Industrial Relations Generally

[11.50] There are two areas of statutory law regarding industrial relations. First, there is the mechanism for establishing and registering awards, and for conducting industrial relations in such matters as union–employer negotiation and handling disputes through conciliation and arbitration. The federal government has jurisdiction under s 51(xxxv) of the Constitution to legislate with respect to conciliation and arbitration for the prevention of industrial disputes extending beyond the limits of any one State. State facilities exist under various State Acts.[1] Other legislation, both for federal bodies and private employers, as well as State Governments themselves, are set out in different Acts, covering the particular categories of employers and employees concerned.

[11.51] Examples of important issues covered by industrial legislation are the payment of wages (such requirements as payment in cash, without deductions except specifically authorised ones, and the furnishing of full details of wages), payment of sick leave, provision of holiday leave, and the power of the appropriate tribunal or court to make void (of no effect) in whole or in part, contracts, or provisions in them that are harsh, unfair or unconscionable, against public interest, provide for less payment than allowed by law, or are designed to avoid a statute or an award.

---

[1] ACT and NT: covered by the Commonwealth Act; *Industrial Relations Act* 1996 (NSW); *Industrial Relations Act* 1990 (Qld); *Industrial and Employee Relations Act* 1994 (SA); *Industrial Relations Act* 1984 (Tas); *Commonwealth Powers (Industrial Relations) Act* 1992 (Vic); *Industrial Relations Act* 1979 (WA).

Subsequent Conduct of Parties Changes Nature of Contract

Legislation may provide that where an employment contract is a fair one, the Industrial Commission may declare it an unfair contract because of the conduct of the parties or variation of the contract (see, for example, *Industrial Relations Act* 1996 (NSW), s 106; *Reich v Client Server Professionals of Australia Pty Ltd* (2000) 49 NSWLR 551). This is consistent with the principle that the terms of a contract of employment may be considered to change according to changing conditions and behaviour, despite the original written or verbal agreement.

General Principles of Industrial Relations Law

[11.52] Whilst jurisdictions differ in the details of their industrial relations legislation, there are some generalisations that can be made about industrial relations.

Development of Industrial Relations Mechanisms

[11.53] All contracts may involve a degree of bargaining, and in recognition of the inequality that generally exists between the employer and employee, a system of industrial relations arose to give strength to the bargaining position of workers. A centralised system that established an Industrial Relations Commission was instituted. Through this system unions could bargain with employer groups to develop awards. These are sets of conditions to apply to nominated enterprises. Once an award was agreed to by the union and employer group and satisfied the Commission as to its fairness, it was certified, and became the implied terms of any contract of employment under which a person in that industry or enterprise was engaged. Awards became numerous and detailed, and any difference of opinion or claim of breach of an award was arbitrated by the Commission. An award is changed by a union lodging a log of claims in the Commission, thus starting a "dispute", which could then bring the negotiations under the auspices of the Commission.

[11.54] The situation has changed since the 1980s. There has been a move away from centralised bargaining. This is to provide for a more co-operative and flexible relationships between employers and employees. Whilst this may seem to provide for a "fair go for all" as the current Government calls it, there is the potential some employees will not be able to bargain for a "fair" deal. Particularly where unemployment figures are high, employers can operate on a "take it or leave it" basis. Unions are in a less influential position in pursuing the interests of their members.

Resolution of Disputes

Conciliation

[11.55] Industrial tribunals are based on the principle of conciliation and arbitration, that is, the attempt to settle matters by discussion and negotiation rather than by formal trial. Initially, any dispute between a [11.60] union (either on behalf of all of its members or an individual member) and an employer may be notified to the relevant tribunal. The dispute is argued under the guidance of a member of the tribunal, who is generally required to attempt peaceful resolution through informal means. Compulsory conferences may be used, but confidentiality and privacy are maintained. Agreement leads to a memorandum of agreement or a consent award being handed down.

Arbitration

[11.56] If the parties cannot resolve the dispute, it will become a matter for arbitration. This is a more formal affair. Although lawyers are generally not allowed to participate, it is similar to civil court proceedings with evidence on oath and adversarial submissions. Here the presiding officer or officers of the tribunal will make an order prescribing an award which is binding on the parties. If the parties, or one of them, refuse to accept this decision the matter becomes a full-blown legal dispute, with the tribunal able to issue orders which may attract sanctions.

Strikes and Bans

[11.57] During a dispute, if the employer is considered intransigent by the union, work bans and strikes may be used to attempt to put pressure on the employer. The employer will generally take the matter to the tribunal in an effort to have the bans or strike considered a breach of contract and to obtain an order for the workers to return to work or lift bans.

[11.58] Where the union, after unsuccessful attempts through negotiation with the employer, resorts to strikes or work bans, the matter is taken before the relevant tribunal. The general attitude of tribunals is that they will not deal with a union's claim while its members are on strike. A compulsory conference may be called by the tribunal to resolve the dispute, and orders may be made where resolution is not forthcoming. The tribunal attempts to bring about agreement, but if it fails it makes a recommendation based on what it sees as the fairest way of resolving the dispute.

[11.59] If this is not put into practice, the tribunal may order one or both of the parties to take specific action (for example, for the employees to resume work, or the employer to provide a safer workplace). Depending on the award provisions and the outcome of procedures, the employer may be legally justified in standing down, suspending or dismissing workers.

[11.60] Industrial action is not illegal as such, however it is a potential breach of the contract of employment. Employers are not required to pay employees for the time not worked, unless it is found that the loss of income was unjust under the circumstances. Action may be taken against unions and employees under tort law for loss through conspiracy to cause

[11.60] harm. Legislation in most jurisdictions now provides that no action in tort law may be taken against employees as a result of industrial action that is taken in the course of bargaining, where certain conditions apply. These involve making a genuine attempt to resolve the dispute, giving 72 hours notice, notifying the Industrial Registrar and restricting action to the recognised bargaining period. Conversely, the employer can under similar conditions lock out employees. Employees will be protected from any action to recover damages from unions arising from industrial action, except where the Commission is of the opinion that conciliation would not be effective, it would result in substantial injustice, or that the Commission's attempts at resolving the dispute are ineffective after 72 hours of notification of the intention to sue.

Termination of Employment

[11.61] A contract of employment may come to an end where:

- ......it is a fixed term contract, that is, there is agreement at the beginning that it will only last for a certain time;
- ......death or unexpected inability on the part of the employee make it impossible to continue working (frustration);
- ......closing down of the business of the employer occurs (agreements may provide that where a business changes hands the employees will be retained by the new owner);
- ......mutual consent of the parties, or notice by one or other party according to the agreement or award has been given (usually two weeks unless otherwise stipulated, but employers may be able to pay in lieu of notice, and employees may forfeit up to two weeks' pay); or
- ......summary dismissal on the grounds of misbehaviour occurs. This must be the result of serious misconduct or utter incompetence (*Harmer v Cornelius* (1858) 5 CB (NS) 236 at 246; 141 ER 94 at 98, discussed in Macken et al (1990), p 196), or refusal to work (Macken et al, p 199) which strikes at the very essence of the contract: "it must be inconsistent with the continuing relationship of master and servant".

[11.62] A union may bring an action before an industrial tribunal or court for reinstatement or compensation for a worker where they think dismissal has been unfair. The tribunal will not interfere in a dismissal where it considers that the employer's actions were fair and reasonable under the circumstances.

Federal and State Industrial Legislation

[11.63] Every jurisdiction in Australia has a "basic" industrial relations Act, and other legislation providing for specific conditions (such as long service leave, superannuation etc). The main industrial legislation of each

jurisdiction is set out below, with some detail given to the *Workplace* [11.67]
Relations Act 1996 (Cth), as it has brought about significant change in the
industrial scene.

Commonwealth Industrial Relations Legislation

[11.64] As mentioned above, the Commonwealth has the Constitutional power to legislate for the conciliation and arbitration of industrial matters covering those who are:

- employed by a constitutional corporation under a federal award, certified agreement, Australian Workplace Agreement (AWA) (see below);
- a federal waterside worker or, maritime worker or interstate or international flight crew officer;
- a Commonwealth public sector employee;
- a Territory employee; or
- a Victorian non-Government employee.

Workplace Relations Act

[11.65] The *Workplace Relations Act* re-organises the Australian Industrial Relations Commission (AIRC). Its role under the new Act includes:

- overseeing the award system as a safety net;
- facilitating the negotiation of certified agreements between employers and employees;
- registering awards and certified agreements when employers and employees have reached agreement on them; and
- conciliating disputes arising from the negotiation, or operation, of workplace agreements, and where this fails, arbitrate under certain circumstances.

[11.66] The former Industrial Relations Court, which formed part of the Commission, has been abolished, with matters that require a judicial ruling (for example where a dispute cannot be resolved before the Commission, or interpretation of the law is required), now going before the Federal Court.

Awards

[11.67] Whereas in the past, awards covered whatever matters the parties agreed would be included, the *Workplace Relations Act* has reduced the matters that they can deal with to 20 "allowable matters". This makes the award system a basic "safety net", being the minimum of conditions that can be applied to any employment situation which is covered by that award. The "allowable matters" are limited to:

- classification of employees and skill-based career paths;

[11.67]
- ordinary time hours of work and the start/finish and rest times;
- rates of pay, public holidays allowances, redundancy pay, tallies and bonuses;
- annual leave and leave loadings, long service leave and other leave, such as jury service and bereavement, parental, adoption and maternity leave;
- notice of termination and stand-down provisions;
- dispute settling procedures;
- type of employment, that is, whether full-time, permanent, part-time, casual, etc;
- superannuation benefits; and
- protection for outworkers.

[11.68] Any other matter must be negotiated between the employers and employees, and the AIRC is only empowered to arbitrate in relation to the above matters in the event of any dispute.

[11.69] Awards have the effect of law (a contract). However the *Workplace Relations Act* provides for some minimum standards where there is no award, such as rates of pay, equal pay for work of equal value without discrimination on the grounds of sex, and leave. It also prohibits discrimination on such grounds as sex, race and age. Individual employees who believe their employer is breaching the award should seek assistance from their union (if they belong to one) or from the Federal Department of Industrial Relations. As unions no longer have a right of access to workplace premises, the onus is on employees to bring breaches to their notice.

Industrial Agreements

Non-Award Agreements

[11.70] Under the federal industrial relations system, employees may enter a contract of employment under:

- a **Certified Agreement** (CA), being an agreement under either
  — s 170LJ or 170LL of the *Workplace Relations Act* (an agreement between the employer and union(s) representing the employees);
  — a certified agreement under s 170LK of the *Workplace Relations Act* (an agreement between the employer and a majority of employees in the workplace); or
- an individual **Australian Workplace Agreement** (AWA) under Part VID of the *Workplace Relations Act*.

Certified Agreements: Part VIB of the Workplace Relations Act

[11.71] The *Workplace Relations Act* provides that employees at a particular workplace may collectively negotiate with their employer to develop an agreement as to conditions and pay for that workplace. Employees may request a relevant union to participate in the negotiations, or to negotiate on their behalf, but union involvement is no longer necessary. Employees may elect representatives from among them [11.74] to participate in the negotiations. Once an agreement has been developed, it is put to the vote of the employees, and a majority of the employees who vote must approve the agreement. The agreement will thus cover all employees (no matter what their view) and new employees unless otherwise agreed. Once voted for, the agreement goes before the AIRC for certification. The AIRC checks the agreement to ensure it does not provide for wages and conditions that are overall less advantageous than the relevant award (the "no disadvantage" test). Once certified by the Commission, the agreement is in force for a maximum of three years but can be terminated at any time with the approval of the majority of employees. If the expiry date has been reached and no further certification has been sought, the agreement remains effective until changed. A certified agreement will override any inconsistent provision in the award.

[11.72] A certified agreement under s 170LK does not necessarily involve the union or employees in developing the terms of the agreement: it is put to the employees and voted on. The conditions of the voting, certification and coverage of the agreement are similar to those set out above.

Disputes and Industrial Action

[11.73] Industrial action, such as strikes "work-to-rule" and lockouts, are unlawful under the *Workplace Relations Act* and attract severe penalties, except when it is carried out in a "bargaining period" (see *National Workforce Pty Ltd v Australian Manufacturing Workers' Union* (unreported, CA 6 October 1997, SC Vic, No 7001 of 1997)). A "bargaining period" is that period from when notice is given to the AIRC that negotiations over an agreement are taking place until the agreement has been accepted by employees. Limited industrial action (strikes by employees and lockouts by employers) may be taken in that time to support the workers' claims, without attracting civil liability or dismissal. However it can only be undertaken during the protected period, and:

- those concerned must have made a genuine attempt to negotiate the action must be properly authorised (a common reason for action is where one side believes that negotiations are being protracted unnecessarily by the other);
- notification of the proposed action has been made; and
- proper procedures (for example, a vote of employees) have been followed.

[11.74] The AIRC can suspend or terminate a bargaining period (and thus the "protected period" for industrial action) on a number of grounds. These include:

- genuine bargaining is not occurring;
- a party taking industrial action is not complying with AIRC directions or recommendations;
- the industrial action is threatening to endanger the life, personal safety, health or welfare of the community;
- significant damage will be caused to the economy; or
- there is no prospect of the parties reaching agreement.

[11.75] **[11.75]** Once an agreement has been certified, any dispute as to its operation is dealt with according to the mandatory dispute settling procedures in it. If these fail, the matter can be taken to the AIRC either by the union, or an individual employee who is covered by the agreement.

Australian Workplace Agreements (AWAs): Part VI of the Workplace Relations Act

[11.76] An individual and an employer may make an exclusive employment agreement. This AWA must be approved by the Employment Advocate (a body to approve AWAs and advise and assist employers and employees in relation to AWAs). The employee or prospective employee may appoint a bargaining agent (including a union). Whilst AWAs may differ from one employee to another, they must pass the "no disadvantage" test. If the Employment Advocate requests (for example, in novel cases where interpretation of the test may be required) the AIRC may assess whether the agreement does involve some disadvantage. The test has been applied very broadly, with considerations such as undertakings by the employer, and the need to meet crises in the business, used to help the agreement to pass the test (see, for example, *AWA Test Case* (unreported, 26 September 1997, AIRC, Print P5472): Baragwanath (1998), p 93). The Employment Advocate has indicated an even more liberal interpretation of the "no disadvantage" test for AWAs, enabling employees to cash out leave entitlements (including sick leave), conditions that the AIRC has considered must be retained. Considering that in fact there is an inequality in bargaining power between individual employees and management, this indicates that those who choose AWAs (or feel obligated to choose: while coercion to agree to an AWA is an offence, the signing of an AWA can be offered as a condition of employment), are more vulnerable to adverse working conditions than those on certified agreements.

[11.77] An AWA overrides a relevant award and any certified agreement that may apply at the workplace (unless provided for in the AWA). Alleged breaches of an AWA are investigated on request by the Employment Advocate, who may assist a person free of charge to prosecute any breach. However, prosecution must be undertaken in the Federal Court. This will potentially involve incidental expenses of bringing such an action in a court.

[11.78] Short term casual employees are excluded from access to the unlawful termination provisions (see below), but determining a "casual employee" for the purposes of those provisions is not always straightforward and many employees who are employed as "casuals" may be eligible to be covered by those provisions.

Termination of Employment: Part VIA of the Workplace Relations Act

[11.79] An employee may be dismissed without notice for "serious misconduct". Otherwise, where no specific conditions in relation to termination of employment exist in an agreement, employers must give notice of termination of employment as prescribed in the legislation. Notice periods are one week for those employed less than one year, two weeks for those employed for one to three years, three weeks for those employed for three to five years, and four weeks for those employed for more than five years (s 170CM).

[11.80] There is one week extra in each category if the employee is over 45 years and was employed by the employer for at least two years. Minimum notice requirements do not apply to casual employees, employees on fixed term contracts for less than six months; contracts for specific tasks; probationers; short term casuals; trainees and non-award employees receiving remuneration of more than $64,000 per year.

[11.81] This Part of the Act applies to all employees, as it gives effect to the UN *Termination of Employment Convention,* the *Convention concerning Discrimination in respect of Employment and Occupation,* and the *Family Responsibilities Convention* and thus comes under the Foreign Affairs power.

Unlawful Termination

Under s 170CK, a person may not be dismissed for:

- temporary absence from work because of illness or injury;
- membership, non-membership of a trade union or participation in union activities;
- acting as a representative of employees;
- filing a complaint or taking proceedings against an employer for alleged breach of the law;
- race, colour, sex, sexual preference, age, physical or mental disability, marital status, family responsibilities, pregnancy, religion, political opinion, national extraction or social origin;
- refusal to negotiate an AWA; or
- absence from work during maternity leave or other parental leave.

[11.82] Agreements should provide for redundancy. Where at least 15 employees are to be made redundant, each employee's union must be notified and negotiations on alternatives must take place. Otherwise, the AIRC may make determinations in relation to the redundancies.

Unfair Dismissal

[11.83] Provision for remedies for unfair dismissal apply to those covered by the federal legislation, except for:

- employees who are on fixed term contracts for less than six months;
- employees on contracts for specific tasks;
- probationers;
- short term casuals;
- trainees; and
- non-award employees in the Federal Public Sector whose remuneration is more than $64,000 per years (subject to adjustment).

[11.84] [11.84] A form of unfair dismissal may occur when a person has been subject to "constructive termination", that is where an apparent resignation was the result of untenable working conditions. Examples are sexual harassment, threats of termination if the person does not resign, or bullying.

[11.85] The AIRC must consider whether there was a valid reason, going to the capacity or conduct of the employee, whether the employee had been told that reason and had the opportunity to respond to it, and whether there had been any warning of unsatisfactory work.

[11.86] There are restrictive provisions for applying for relief. Application must be lodged within 21 days (with discretion to extend this on the ground of unfairness). An application form provided by the AIRC registry must be filled in and returned to the registry within the time limit. Also a filing fee of $50 is required "to discourage frivolous and vexatious claims", and costs may be awarded against either party. The *Workplace Relations Act* includes a schedule of costs, including non-legal, legal and professional costs.

[11.87] Whether an employee claims unfair dismissal (that is, that the dismissal was harsh, unjust or unreasonable) or unlawful termination (that is, the employee was dismissed for a legally prohibited reason), the claim must first be dealt with the same way, by conciliation, by the Commission. That means that even where one party has allegedly breached the law, the matter is treated as one where both parties may have acted unreasonably, and attempts to come to a resolution satisfactory to both parties is made. On the positive side, this is cheaper than going to court. If conciliation fails the employee can apply for arbitration (for an unfair dismissal) by the AIRC or go the federal court (for an unlawful dismissal claim). Again, taking the matter past conciliation means the applicant may have costs awarded against him or her. A decision as to which approach tto take must be made quickly (within seven days of failure of conciliation).

[11.88] The AIRC is required to follow the principle of "a fair go all round", which allows for overlooking breaches of the law by an employer for the sake of "fairness". The standard of proof is the balance of probabilities, and the AIRC can order reinstatement, payment for lost income or compensation of not more than six months pay or $32,000 (subject to adjustment). The remedy is dependent on the employer's resources and viability, and the employee's attempts to find other work.

Anti-Discrimination Issues

[11.89] As actions for discrimination (that is, under s 170CK) that are taken to the Federal Court are costly and time-consuming, it may be worth considering action under the anti-discrimination law of one's State or Territory. However, it may be possible in some circumstances to be reinstated under the *Workplace Relations Act,* and then apply for compensation on other grounds such as pain and suffering under State/Territory legislation. It may be worth seeking advice as to the legal options.

Minimum Wages

[11.90] The AIRC can, where appropriate make a minimum rates award for specified groups or categories of employees where wages are not already set by a federal award or agreement, or where employees do not have access to a compulsory State arbitration system. In the absence of an adequate alternative remedy, the Commission can also make an order to ensure that men and women will receive equal pay for work of equal value. An application may be made by an employee, a trade union or the Sex Discrimination Commissioner. This again is based on the federal government's external affairs power.

Parental Leave, Family Leave

[11.91] The Act invokes international instruments as the basis for providing for a minimum of 52 weeks unpaid parental leave and adoption leave. This is to ensure that a mother or father can take leave to care for a new child and not jeopardise their employment position. Leave is also to be available for family reasons, such as caring for a sick family member. The Commission is also charged with holding an enquiry on the circumstances under which such leave should be granted, and to report to the Minister on this matter.

Industrial Relations in Each State and Territory

[11.92] In New South Wales the *Industrial Relations Act* 1996 (NSW), accords a more prominent role to awards than any other State. However, whilst it does not provide for AWAs, the Industrial Relations Commission of New South Wales can register an enterprise agreement which has been entered into by an employer, a union, at least 69 per cent of employees of an enterprise, or a committee representing the employees. The Industrial Court may declare an agreement void on the basis that it is unfair, harsh, unconscionable or the result of duress. The Commission has jurisdiction to deal with a broad range of matters to do with industrial matters, including:

- interpretation application, breaches, and enforcement, of conditions of an award or agreement;
- unfair contracts;
- industrial action; and
- employer and employee organisations.

[11.93] An industrial relations committee may be established with a member of the Commission presiding, and representatives from an industry or part of an industry to exercise the functions of the Commission for that industry or portion of it. Industrial magistrates may hear matters that the legislation refers to a magistrates court. The judicial members of the Commission can sit as a court, and make binding rulings on the parties. Dispute resolution includes procedures for employee and

[11.93] union consultation, and the Commission has a general jurisdiction to conciliate and arbitrate disputes. The Commission must attempt conciliation, and may require conferences between the parties. During the process it may make orders in relation to the conduct of the parties. There is limited protection for industrial action while a dispute is being dealt with by the Commission (a more extensive protection than offered by the Commonwealth).

[11.94] Minimal conditions are set out in the legislation setting hours of work and leave. Other legislation sets out enterprise-specific conditions, such as conditions for work in mines and with hazardous materials. Some of these affect health care workers who deal with, for example, radiation and X-rays.

[11.95] An employee may lodge a complaint with the Commission where there is an alleged actual or threatened harsh, unreasonable or unjust dismissal. The application must be made within 21 days. The Commission may order reinstatement, re-employment, remuneration or compensation. Discrimination against employees or prospective employees is prohibited by the *Anti-Discrimination Act* 1977 (NSW).

[11.96] In 1996 Victoria referred most of its industrial relations legislation powers to the Commonwealth. As a result:

- ..... the *Workplace Relations Act* covers matters in the Victorian private sector as industrial disputes, certified agreements and AWAs;
- ..... the Commonwealth AIRC is the sole industrial tribunal for Victorian workers, and the State Employee Relations Commission is no longer in existence;
- ..... Commonwealth Parliament now has the power to make legislation in relation to:
  — employment agreements;
  — conciliation and arbitration of industrial disputes;
  — minimum terms and conditions; and
  — termination of employment.

Excluded are such employees as public servants, Victorian parliamentarians, ministerial assistants, parliamentary officers and judicial officers, statutory office holders.

[11.97] Between 1997 and 1999, Queensland had a "clone" of the *Workplace Relations Act*, with awards reduced to 20 allowable matters, and individual agreements similar to AWAs ("Queensland Workplace Agreements" or QWAs). However, with the accession of the Beattie Labor Government the law was changed to mirror the New South Wales legislation. The *Industrial Relations Act* 1990 (Qld) establishes an Industrial Relations Commission similar in structure and function to that of New South Wales, but with some differences. A modified version of QWAs was retained (with accountability and identification of parties), and a version of certified agreements that is a hybrid of New South Wales and the Commonwealth agreements.

The Act provides for registration of both industrial agreements (negotiated and agreed upon by employer and employees) and enterprise flexibility agreements (brought to the Queensland Industrial Relations Commission by an employer and approved after consultation with, and agreement by, employees), which may be approved by the Commission, [11.102] declared to have the effect of an award, or altered or declared void. A contract of employment that is harsh or unconscionable may be declared void, or varied, by the Commission, and application may be made to the Commission where dismissal has bee considered harsh, unjust or unreasonable.

[11.98] The *Industrial and Employee Relations Act* 1994 (SA) maintains the Industrial Relations Commission and the Industrial Court of South Australia. Industrial agreements or enterprise agreements and awards must be approved by the Commission, and have in-built protection similar to those of the other States. There is an industrial Advisory Committee, that assists the Minister in relation to policy and legislative proposals, and an Employee Ombudsman —an independent body that advises employees on their rights and obligations, scrutinises awards, and agreements that are before the Commission, investigates claims of coercion in the negotiation of agreements and the conditions of outworkers, represents employees in proceedings in certain circumstances and provides advice on occupational health and safety matters.

[11.99] The *Industrial Relations Act* 1979 (WA) and the *Workplace Agreements Act* 1993 (WA) provide for industrial agreements and workplace agreements, which may be registered by the Western Australian Industrial Relations Commission. They override any relevant award, are subject to safeguards, and may be varied, rescinded, etc by the Commission.

[11.100] The *Industrial Relations Act* 1984 (Tas) provides for certification of awards and agreements by the Tasmanian Industrial Commission, under similar conditions to those in other States, may be registered by the Tasmanian Industrial Relations Commission. The Act is modelled on that of New South Wales, but requires only 60 per cent agreement by the workplace for acceptance of an enterprise agreement. There is an Enterprise Commissioner who approves enterprise agreements after determining that the process of bargaining was satisfactory, the agreement is fair, and minimum conditions have been met. This is probably the most interventionist role allowed for the scrutiny of agreements.

[11.101] The Australian Capital and Northern Territories are both subject to the Commonwealth legislation.

[11.102] It follows that employees can take questions or disagreements with their employer to the union of which they are a member, and which has the knowledge and expertise to represent them in resolving their difficulties. Some unions provide specified legal services free to members.

REFERENCES AND FURTHER READING

Anderman, S, *Labour Law: Management Decisions and Workers' Rights* (2nd ed, Butterworths, London, 1993)

Australian and New Zealand Equal Opportunity Law and Practice (CCH, Sydney, Looseleaf Service)

Australian Council of Trade Unions, *Changes in Industrial Relations: Summary of the Workplace Relations Act 1996* (Australian Council of Trade Unions, Melbourne)

Australian Employment Law Guide (CCH, Sydney, Looseleaf Service)

Australian Enterprise Bargaining Manual (CCH, Sydney, Looseleaf Service)

Australian Labour Law Reporter (CCH, Sydney, Looseleaf Service)

Baragwanath, M, *Workplace Relations Act in Practice: The Essential Cases* (NSW Newsletter Information Services, Manly, 1998)

Boland, R and Anderson, N, *Handbook on Employment Law and Practice* (Allen and Unwin, Sydney, 1997)

Creighton, B and Stewart, A, *Labour Law: An Introduction* (Federation Press, Sydney, 2000)

Cripps, Y, "Protection from Adverse Treatment by Employers: A Review of the Position of Employees who Disclose Information in the Belief the Disclosure is in the Public Interest" (1985) 101 LQR 506

Deery, S, Plowman, D, Walsh, J, *Industrial Relations: A Contemporary Analysis* (McGraw-Hill, Sydney, 2000)

Federal Industrial Law (Butterworths, Sydney, Looseleaf Service)

Industrial Law New South Wales (Butterworths, Sydney, Looseleaf Service)

Johnstone, M, *Nursing and the Injustices of the Law* (W B Saunders/Baillie Tindall, Sydney, 1994)

Leo Cusson Institute, *Employment Law and Industrial Relations* (Leo Cusson Institute, Melbourne, 1999)

Luntz, H, Hambly, A D and Hayes, R, *Torts: Cases and Commentary* (Butterworths, Sydney, 1985)

Macken, J, McCarry, G and Sappideen, C, *The Law of Employment* (3rd ed, Law Book Co, Sydney, 1990)

McKenna, D, *The Labor Council's Easy Guide to Your Rights at Work* (Pluto Press, Sydney, 1993)

Nolan, D, *The Australasian Labour Law Reforms* (Federation Press, Sydney, 2000)

NSW Department of Industrial Relations, *Enterprise Bargaining: Enhancing Productivity Innovations and Equity* (NSW Department of Industrial Relations, Sydney, 1997)

NSW Department of Industrial Relations, Sydney, *Enterprise Bargaining: Enhancing Productivity Innovations and Equity* (1997)

Recruitment and Termination Guide (CCH, Sydney, Looseleaf Service)

Chapter Twelve

ACCIDENTS AND INJURIES RELATED TO HEALTH CARE

Injuries to Clients

[12.1] Whilst accidents and injuries may be the fault of no-one, action may be taken by clients where they have suffered harm from an accident that is the result of:

- .....negligence of the management of a health facility;
- .....negligence of the staff of a health facility;
- .....negligence of a self-employed health carer; or
- .....negligence on the part of the "occupier" of the premises (see [12.62]ff).

The law in relation to negligence is covered in Chapter 6.

[12.2] Where there is an accident to a client, this should be reported as soon as possible, no matter what the cause. "Accident" here includes wrong treatment. From the legal point of view, apart from the need to avoid allegations of negligence, there is an issue of veracity in prompt reporting. Delay or lack of full and frank disclosure of events can give rise to the suspicion that facts have been hidden. Also, the sooner after the event the report is given, the more likely it is, in the court's eyes, to be an accurate account of what happened, as memories are not served well by time (see [7.9]ff). Some details may not be so important for the patient's immediate health, but may be vital, some years later, to establish what happened. Note should be made of the day, time and place of the event, the details of the accident and its cause, if known. Finally, the names of witnesses to the accident, or the whereabouts of the nearest person or people should be recorded. If one is at all concerned about the event and thinks that it may give rise to legal action, a written account, apart from any official incident report, can be made and kept for future use. See the note on statutory declarations at [7.13].

[12.3] Advising the insurer of a health facility or practice as soon as possible is also necessary, in anticipation of likely legal actions.

Injuries to Health Carers

Safe Working Environment

Common Law

[12.4] Employers and those hiring independent contractors both have a contractual duty to provide safe premises and a safe system of work. There is also a duty of care under tort law to prevent foreseeable harm from those who it could reasonably be foreseen could be harmed from their actions or omissions. Under common law, also, a worker must take reasonable care for his or her own safety and protection, and that of co-workers. Some actions under tort law are restricted by workers' compensation legislation (see below). Of course it also makes good health care sense to provide safe work environment and practices, as this is the most efficient and effective approach to good quality care of clients. Codes of practice for health care facilities establish standards for safe working environments, safe working practices and the development of suitable codes of practice for both medical and other workplace emergencies.

■■■ CASE

State of NSW v Seedsman [2000] NSWCA 119 (CA NSW) (described in *Australian Torts Reporter* ¶35-110)

A woman who served with the New South Wales Police Service was exposed to crimes against children. Her duties required her to interview 200-300 victims of physical, sexual and emotional child abuse when she was new to the Service and untrained in this work. Scenes she confronted included children with fractures, burns, brain-damage, retinal detachment, and dead and mutilated bodies of children. She developed insomnia, nightmares, tearfulness and flashbacks, and became subject to a constant fear that her own son could become a victim of abuse. After being diagnosed with post-traumatic stress disorder, she applied for discharge on medical grounds, and instituted a proceeding against the State of New South Wales claiming damages for her psychiatric injury.

The trial judge found that the New South Wales Police Service had failed to provide the woman with a safe system of work. Attempts had not been made to protect her from mental injury that could result from exposure to the type of human tragedies with which she was required to deal. It determined that the State of New South Wales had the requisite knowledge that stress in the workplace of this type could lead to psychiatric disorders. The State of New South Wales appealed to the New South Wales Court of Appeal, arguing that it was not foreseeable, at the relevant time, that a police officer could suffer recognisable psychiatric injury (as distinct from stress) as a result of the work the respondent was required to do. Specifically, it was submitted that post-traumatic stress disorder in the workplace was unknown until the 1990s.

[12.5] The Court determined that the possibility of mental disturbance was foreseeable, given the extensive exposure by a young, new recruit without special training or preparation. It could not be argued that the

foreseeability in this case had to be related to police work, for negligence is [12.7]
concerned with human beings and not specific occupations. The case was
unique in that it involved a very young police officer without adequate
training dealing with exceptional human depravity, a significant number
of occasions of death in intense suffering of young children, and the
frequent observation of dead and mutilated children. The court further
held that although the common law in Australia requires proof of a
sudden shock to the senses, before allowing a claim for pure psychiatric
injury, the fact of the employment relationship imports a non-delegable
duty to ensure the health and safety of employees. In a case like this where
a person of ordinary fortitude would be likely to have been affected
similarly, a claim for injury in the absence of physical injury is allowed
(see also *Mt Isa Mines v Pusey* (1970) 125 CLR 383).

Statute Law

[12.6] The right to a safe workplace has been underscored by both
federal and State and Territory policy and legislation. This addresses:

- .....prevention of injury and the provision of a safe working environment, which is dealt with by the development of "occupational health and safety" legislation, policy and practices;[1] and
- .....compensation when injuries, accidents and illnesses occur which arise out of, or occur in the course of, work, or activities incidental to work.[2]

Both these issues will be considered below.

Occupational Health and Safety

[12.7] Formerly, legislation subjected specific machinery or work sites
(which were recognised as being harmful) to safety regulations and
required such measures as fencing, protective shields for machinery, and
protective equipment for workers. Recently, however, industrial health

---

[1] *National Occupational Health and Safety Commission Act* 1985 (Cth), *Occupational Health and Safety (Commonwealth Employment) Act* 1991 (Cth); *Occupational Health and Safety Act* 1989 (ACT); *Occupational Health and Safety Act* 1983 (NSW), Occupational Health and Safety (Committees in Workplaces) Regulation 1984 (NSW); *Work Health Act* 1986 (NT); *Workplace Health and Safety Act* 1995 (Qld); *Occupational Safety, Health and Welfare Act* 1986 (SA); *Workplace Health and Safety Act* 1995 (Tas), Industrial Safety, Health and Welfare (Employees' Safety Representatives) Regulations 1982 (Tas); *Occupational Health and Safety Act* 1985 (Vic) (and Regulations (Vic)); *Occupational Safety and Health Act* 1984 (WA).

[2] *Safety Rehabilitation and Compensation Act* 1988 (Cth); *Workers' Compensation Act* 1951 (ACT); *Workers' Compensation Act* 1987 (NSW), *Workplace Injury Management and Workers Compensation Act* 1998 (NSW), *Compensation Court Act* 1984 (NSW); *Work Health Act* 1986 (NT); *WorkCover Queensland Act* 1996 (Qld); *Workers' Rehabilitation and Compensation Act* 1986 (SA); *Workers Rehabilitation and Compensation Act* 1988 (Tas); *Accident Compensation Act* 1985 (Vic), *Accident Compensation (WorkCover Insurance) Act* 1993 (Vic); *Workers' Compensation and Rehabilitation Act* 1981 (WA).

[12.7] and safety legislation has put more responsibility on both employers and employees to create and maintain an overall safe environment for all workers. This means that all situations and personnel may be the subject of a general consideration for optimal conditions, rather than some specific situations being subject to minimal specific standards.

[12.8] This raises the question of what constitutes a safe workplace. As well as harm from physical dangers such as faulty equipment, substandard infection control and structural dangers, health carers can be subject to physical or sexual assault or harassment, verbal abuse from clients or colleagues, and stress resulting from such events as client death, lack of communication or co-operation among team members and events affecting the provision of quality care (Michael and Jenkins (2001)). It is the author's view that these specific dangers are not given enough consideration when occupational health and safety plans are developed.

Employers

[12.9] Most responsibility for ensuring a safe workplace lies on the employer (through management). The duty is to provide, as far as is reasonably practicable, a safe working environment or to protect the health and safety of workers, independent contractors, those present at the workplace (including visitors and trespassers), and those outside the workplace but affected by operations at the workplace. Self-employed people owe a duty to those who may be affected by their operations. To the extent that they may have control over the premises, owners and others in control of premises or (in some jurisdictions) plant and machinery, must make them safe places for those who work there subject to variations across jurisdictions.

[12.10] There is some difference in approach as to what is practicable or reasonably practicable in relation to a safe working environment. This includes assessment of health and safety problems, ensuring the place is safe for workers, clients and visitors, training of staff to use equipment, provide a safe means of access to, and egress from the workplace and the implementation of measures to correct these problems, as well as arrangement of appropriate insurance cover. However others such as the manufacturers of equipment and raw materials also have the obligation to ensure these are of a satisfactory standard, and that any hazards are clearly indicated to those concerned.

[12.11] The **Commonwealth, Australian Capital Territory** and **South Australia** require all, and the **Northern Territory** requires some, employers to develop a written health and safety plan. All jurisdictions have established bodies[3] that develop codes of practice to provide

---

[3] Cth: Commission for the Safety, Rehabilitation and Compensation of Commonwealth Employees; ACT: Occupational Health and Safety Council; NSW: WorkCover Authority; NT: Work Health Authority; Qld: the Minister; SA: the Minister; Tas: the Minister; Vic: WorkCover Authority; WA: the Minister on the recommendation of the WorkSafe Western Australia Commission.

employers and the self-employed with guidance for providing safe workplaces. Failure to follow the guidelines can be used as evidence of failure to provide a safe working environment or system.

Workers

Also included among those with responsibilities are workers themselves, who should:

- take reasonable care to ensure their own safety, as well as that of the safety of other workers. What is reasonable depends not only on the totality of the circumstances that exist, but also on an assessment of difficulties to be surmounted and the available staff and resources (for example, *Inspector Callaghan v De Sandre* [1989-92] Australian Industrial Safety, Health and Welfare Cases 48,966 (¶52-864); *Inspector Callaghan v Longley* [1989-92] Australian Industrial Safety, Health and Welfare Cases 48,967 (¶52-865));
- comply, so far as is reasonable, with instructions (such as safety rules or infection control instructions) given by the employer for promoting the health and safety of employees (including the wearing of protective clothing or use of protective equipment, such as gowns, gloves, masks);
- ensure the proper use of equipment which is provided in the interests of the health and safety of employees and not recklessly or wilfully place at risk the health or safety of another at the workplace;
- report any situation that is hazardous and that they cannot, or should not, fix; and
- report any accident which has arisen in the course of, or in connection with, work.

[12.12] The National Occupational Health and Safety Commission, known as Worksafe Australia, is administered under the *National Occupational Health and Safety Commission Act* 1985 (Cth).

[12.13] Safety representatives are to be elected in workplaces with such rights as the right to:

- time away from work for training;
- access to certain categories of information;
- inspect the workplace;
- inquire into accidents;
- accompany official inspectors;
- require an employer to establish a health and safety committee in some circumstances; and
- be present at interviews between an inspector and an employee on health and safety matters.

Joint staff-management committees are required in some jurisdictions, with powers to act in an advisory, consultative and investigatory capacity, with special powers of investigation, inspection and access to information given to members in some cases. Such committees must be representative of the workforce and in larger workplaces there should be committees

[12.13] representing different sections or locations. Requirements vary between jurisdictions, but such matters as the size and composition of the workforce, the operation of different shifts, departments and sub-units, different occupations and types of hazards are features that variously determine the number and size of committees.

Their function is to review general measures taken to promote health and safety, investigate problems with these, formulate procedures, make recommendations, and otherwise become concerned with representing the health and safety issues of workers, creating and maintaining health and safety in health care institutions. Particular interest, presumably, would be given to such issues as needle-stick and splash incidents which create a risk of viral Hepatitis B, and HIV, and the much more likely occurrence of other infections from handling infectious materials, and also to back injuries. Protocols and education programmes should be drawn up by the committees to prevent all recognised potential risks, as well as to study incident reports of other accidents and unexpected occurrences. Filing of incident reports (discussed above Ch 6) to report potential accidents as well as actual mishaps should be encouraged.

Immediate Threat to Health and Safety

[12.14] Where there is an immediate threat to health and safety, it follows from the worker's duty to take reasonable steps for self protection and protection of others that he or she may take reasonable measures to render the situation safe or stop work if such a move is warranted. In some jurisdictions, in the face of an immediate threat to safety, a health and safety representative must inform the employer or person supervising the employees, or where such a person is not available, direct employees to cease work.

Default Notices

[12.15] Under **Commonwealth, Australian Capital Territory, South Australian** and **Victorian** legislation a health and safety representative can issue a Provisional Improvement Notice or Default Notice to the employer. Such a notice states that the health and safety legislation has been breached and requires action to be taken. The notice must be displayed in designated (relevant) places in the workplace, and the employer is to take reasonable steps to remedy the breach. An inspector may be summonsed and may verify or cancel the notice. Where it remains in place, failure to comply with it is an offence.

Protection of Representatives and Committee Members

[12.16] All jurisdictions except Queensland specifically protect health and safety representatives and members of health and safety committees from victimisation such as demotion or changing working conditions, or dismissal, because of their activities as a health and safety representative or member of a committee.

Inspectorate [12.19]

[12.17] All jurisdictions establish "inspectors" or "investigators" authorised to do such things as enter and inspect premises and documents, take photographs, conduct tests, take items of equipment, question people and issue notices to improve premises or cease specified activities. They are appointed by the responsible authority. Their role is to ensure that the requirements of the legislation are being observed, and to identify and make recommendations concerning the causes of accidents, illnesses or dangerous occurrences in the workplace. Inspectors may be called in where issues of health and safety cannot be resolved within the workplace.

Workers' Compensation

[12.18] It has long been recognised by governments that serious injuries suffered at work cannot generally be adequately dealt with by common law action (suing the employer or a third party in negligence, or breach of contract), sick leave conditions, or social security payments where these apply. Employers argued contributory negligence and voluntary assumption of risk, which were hard to disprove in the employment environment, where one agrees to take on tasks. Australia has a very high industrial accident rate, with an average of at least 1.7 deaths and nine serious accidents per day occurring at work. The social cost of such injury and loss of income has led to the requirement, through legislation, that employers insure their employees against "personal injury arising out of or in the course of employment". Similar in some respects to compulsory third party insurance of drivers, it provides for all employers to insure employees with an insurance company so that payment for medical treatment, loss of income and rehabilitation will not be a burden on the public purse.

[12.19] Workers' compensation is covered by federal, State and Territory legislation,[4] so there are diverse approaches, and these have been changing rapidly in recent years. Whilst the basic features (which will be outlined below) are common throughout the nation, readers are cautioned against relying on what is read here to determine just what their entitlements are, and advised to find out details of provisions in their State or Territory for details. Information can be obtained from the State Workers' Compensation Board, Commission or Court, Department of Industrial Relations, legal aid office or union. Employers should have claim forms and information for those who wish to lodge them. There are,

---

[4] *Safety, Rehabilitation and Compensation Act* 1988 (Cth); *Workers Compensation Act* 1951 (ACT); *Workers Compensation Act* 1987 (NSW), *Workplace Injury Management and Workers Compensation Act* 1988 (NSW); *Work Health Act* 1986 (NT); *WorkCover Queensland Act* 1996 (Qld); *Workers Rehabilitation and Compensation Act* 1986 (SA); *Workers Rehabilitation and Compensation Act* 1988 (Tas); *Accident Compensation Act* 1985 (Vic); *Workers Compensation and Rehabilitation Act* 1981 (WA).

[12.19] however, some general principles which are common throughout Australia.

No Fault

[12.20] The basic principle of workers' compensation schemes is that they apply regardless of fault. It cannot be argued by the employer that the worker was negligent, or the author of her or his misfortune. The fact that the harm can be classified as an injury arising out of, or in the course of, employment, and the person harmed is a worker according to the legislation, is enough to create eligibility for compensation. The only exception to this is where the worker is guilty of serious and wilful misconduct (interpreted by the courts as involving such activities as drunkenness, dangerous driving and practical jokes). There is no requirement to prove duty of care, breach of duty or direct causation, which makes it a much simpler means of getting compensation for harm at work.

[12.21] Several general aspects of workers' compensation are worth noting. One is the increasingly bureaucratic and rule-bound approach to the administration of claims, with restricted avenues of appeal and inroads into the principles of natural justice. Some jurisdictions have abolished the right of injured workers to sue their employers in negligence, and only allow them to claim under workers' compensation (the Northern Territory, South Australia). Others limit the right to sue an employer as well as make a claim under workers' compensation where the latter yields inadequate compensation (New South Wales, Victoria, Western Australia). The remainder do not limit claims under both common law and workers' compensation, however if one is successful in a negligence action, workers' compensation entitlements are lost.

[12.22] A positive aspect of workers' compensation is the emphasis that has developed on rehabilitation, so that instead of paying (and laying) off workers who are injured, employers are required to provide means for workers to either return to their previous employment, or find satisfactory employment doing other work where this is reasonably available.

Who is Covered by Workers' Compensation?

[12.23] Any employee who suffers injury through accident caused by or in the course of employment; or disease arising out of or significantly contributed to by employment, may be entitled to apply for workers' compensation. In the case of death, the employee's dependants may be able to claim. Usually, there are some exclusions and added categories to this rule, which differ from State to State. For example, all jurisdictions except Tasmania cover accidents "arising out of or in the course of employment". Tasmania covers accidents "arising out *and* in the course of employment". That is, in Tasmania the accident has to be both caused by the employment *and* occur during the course of the employment. In other jurisdictions only one of these criteria need be proved, thus the accident may be caused by the employment but occur out of work hours or even after the person is no longer employed. Entitlement to compensation for disease is generally more restrictive.

[12.24] Courts have held that interpretation of workers' compensation should be liberal, so that where two or more meanings can be given to the legislation, the meaning most favourable to the worker should be used (*Wilson v Wilson's Tile Works Pty Ltd* (1960) 104 CLR 328 at 335, per Fullagar J; *Heath v Commonwealth* (1982) 151 CLR 76 at 89 per Murphy J). As the legislation in all jurisdictions is aimed at rehabilitation of injured workers, consideration should be given to the circumstances of individuals (*Workers Rehabilitation and Compensation Corp v James* (1992) 57 SASR 365 at 393-394 per Zelling J). The interpretation should also take account of contemporary industrial practices and social attitudes (*Hatzimanolis v ANI Corp Ltd* (1992) 173 CLR 473 at 482-483 per Mason CJ, Deane, Dawson and McHugh JJ).

Who is a "Worker"?

[12.25] First one must establish that one is a "worker" according to the applicable legislation.

[12.26] There is a definition in the workers' compensation legislation as to who is considered a worker. Generally, that will be anyone who has entered into or works under a contract of service or apprenticeship (see, for example, *Workers Compensation Act* 1987 (NSW), s 3(1)). Some specific categories of workers are included where their situation may not otherwise clearly fit into the general definition, giving those in them the right to claim under the legislation. For example, casual workers, when the work they perform is part of the employer's trade or business, salespersons, canvassers, collectors, or those paid by commission in the Australian Capital Territory, New South Wales, Queensland and Western Australia. Independent contractors under some circumstances are to be included in some jurisdictions, as are police officers, public office holders (under Commonwealth legislation) and volunteer emergency workers and firefighters. Other categories of worker are specifically excluded in some jurisdictions, removing compensation rights from them (for example members of Parliament are excluded, as are outworkers and seamen in some States). There may be separate compensation schemes for some categories of excluded workers.

[12.27] Where there is doubt as to whether a person is actually a party to a contract of service, the courts consider the common law tests to establish whether the person is an employee (see Ch 10). The totality of the relationship between alleged employer and worker must be considered.

[12.28] Health carers are employees under a State or Commonwealth Act where they have entered into a contract of service with the Commonwealth (for example, in repatriation hospitals), with a State health care facility, or for a private employer. They are not covered by the legislation if they are private practitioners or independent contractors,

[12.28] that is, for example, under a contract for specific services as a visiting health care professional, or privately engaged by a client as an agency nurse or homebirth midwife. In that case they have to arrange their own insurance.

What is an "Injury"?

[12.29] The definition of "injury" varies, but in most States means physical or mental injury or the aggravation, acceleration, or recurrence of a pre-existing injury arising out of, or suffered in the course of work, and generally includes also the contraction, exacerbation or acceleration of a disease where work is a contributing factor (which may have to have been "significantly substantial", material or major, according to jurisdiction). An autogenous disease (for example, subarachnoid haemorrhage), was held not to fall within the definition of "injury" under New South Wales and Queensland law in *Hockey v Yelland and Ors* (1984) AWCCD ¶73-555. The courts have established that the word "injury" should be given its ordinary meaning, which has generally meant the adverse impact of any external agent on the body.

■ CASE
Favelle Mort Ltd v Murray (1976) 8 ALR 649 (High Court)
A worker contracted viral meningeal encephalitis and claimed workers' compensation. The court had to decide if the worker had suffered an "injury" within the ordinary meaning of the word.

[12.30] The court decided that the disease was an injury because it was caused by an external factor. Sir Garfield Barwick CJ decided that the meningeal encephalitis was neither idiopathic nor autogenous: it was the result of the introduction into the employee's body of a foreign body, the virus. The morbid condition was not itself the relevant injury but merely the consequence of introduction of the virus into the body from without. The attack by, or reception of, the virus was the injury. He went on to say (at 655) that a disease was a morbid condition of the body which may be initiated by either an outside cause or be idiopathic or autogenic: "Quite clearly when such a condition is idiopathic or autogenous, it will not qualify as an injury in the normal use of language."

[12.31] Injury by accident can presumably include the effects of chemical agents or other substances on the skin (for example, warm water coming into contact with a worker's boots, leading to perspiration of the feet and exacerbation of tinea; *Pasminco Australia Ltd v Fairchild* [1990] Tas R (NC 18) 262), inhalation of gases, fibres and invasion by bacteria and viruses (for example, inhalation of asbestos fibres; *American Home Assurance v Saunders* (1987) 11 NSWLR 363). "Injury by disease", for the purposes of workers' compensation legislation, is specifically defined in some jurisdictions. It may include diseases which can occur generally in society, such as heart disease, peptic ulcers and cancer, in which case the employee has to prove that the disease was caused, exacerbated, aggravated or accelerated by her or his work. There are, however, [12.34] particular diseases already proven to be associated with particular work. These are labelled "industrial diseases", and include such illnesses as silicosis in miners, or anthrax in those in the meat industry. The benefit of associating these diseases with an industry which tends to cause them is that when a worker in that industry contracts an industrial disease designated to that industry, the burden of proof is on the employer to prove that the disease was *not* caused by the person's work, rather than being on the employee to prove the causal connection. Thus, it is important to determine whether the harm is by accident or disease, and if by disease whether it is an industrial disease or not, as the burden of proof will differ. As legislation varies over the different jurisdictions, one has to find out exactly what the particular legislation in one's own jurisdiction says on this issue.

[12.32] "Injury" could also be considered to include the "injuries" health carers may be more likely to suffer than most workers, such as back and needle-stick injuries, attacks, infections and psychological trauma.

What Events are Covered?

[12.33] One must establish the connection between the harm and employment. The central wording of the legislation describing the type of injury it covers is the same for Commonwealth employees and those in all jurisdictions other than Tasmania. This wording covers all injury "arising out of or in the course of" employment. It has been interpreted very widely, to include any activity ancillary to one's work.

❚❚❚ CASE
Kavanagh v Commonwealth (1960) 103 CLR 549 (High Court)

K was employed packing stationery. During work he stopped and went to the washroom. He returned, telling his workmates he felt ill and had diarrhoea. He subsequently began vomiting, and was taken to hospital where he died. The cause of death was apparently a ruptured oesophagus resulting from the violent vomiting. The question before the High Court was whether he had died from an injury "arising out of or in the course of" his work, as it was argued that because the injury was not caused by K's work, he should not be eligible for workers' compensation.

[12.34] The court decided that the ruptured oesophagus was an injury, so the issue was the meaning of the phrase "arising out of or in the course of employment". In so doing, it considered the fact that legislation had been changed. Originally the phrase had been "arising out of, and in the course of employment". The first three words require a causal connection with work, and so the phrase overall required that the connection be made. However, the change of the preposition "and" to "or" indicated a purpose,

[12.34] to eliminate the necessity of finding such a causal connection. If there was such a causal connection, the injury was to be compensable even though it did not occur while the worker was engaged in his employment or anything incidental to his employment. [The meaning of "arising out of" employment.] If, on the other hand, the injury occurred in the course of the employment, it was to be compensable even though no causal connection could be found between it and the employment . . . I think, that the words "arising in the course of his employment" ought not to be regarded as meaning anything more or less than "arising while the worker is engaged in his employment" [at 558-559 per Fullagar J].

[12.35] Dixon J (at 555) held that it included the situation where the worker was "momentarily standing by considering his capacity to resume his duties". The distinction between the two elements in the words "arising of or in the course of" employment is now well established.

Activities Incidental to Employment

The requirement that the accident or injury must arise in the course of employment is not limited to the required service, but extends to all activity incidental to that service. Thus cleaning or procuring equipment for use in employment may be incidental to it, including journeys to and from places for this to be done.

Activities During Breaks

[12.36] Workers may be covered by workers' compensation for injury occasioned through activities during normal breaks whilst at work or in circumstances considered incidental to the particular employment situation. One is covered during morning tea, lunch and other normal breaks, if on the employer's premises, whatever one is doing. Sport and other activities engaged in during breaks are accepted as being part of work. In one case the playing of sport during the lunch hour was the subject of a workers' compensation claim. The employer had prohibited the playing of sport but had never bothered to enforce the ban. The Australian High Court said an employee may do that which may be required, expected or authorised, which it held could include "taking a walk, dozing in the sun, or playing a game of table tennis or cricket" (*Commonwealth v Oliver* (1962) 107 CLR 353).

[12.37] It would seem that one may also leave the employer's premises during a break (for example, to buy lunch, or collect clothes from the dry cleaner's), as long as one's activities are incidental to work, and one does not subject oneself to abnormal risk of injury. However not all excursions for lunch will qualify. The Australian High Court in *Humphrey Earl Ltd v Speechley* (1951) 84 CLR 126 rejected the claim of an employee who was injured returning from a lunch consumed some distance away from the workplace. Dixon J made the following point:

> The eating of lunch is not in itself a thing which is done for the purpose of (the employee's) duties. It is the satisfaction of a recurrent human want.

But the conditions of the employment may be such as to make the [12.39] obtaining and consumption of a meal something reasonably incidental to the performance of the actual duties. The point in such a case as this is not whether it is reasonable to eat lunch or reasonable to want fish for lunch. The question is whether the course adopted by the employee was reasonably incidental to the performance on that occasion of his duties. This cannot be stretched to make everything he chooses to do during the interval he takes for lunch incidental to his employment . . . There is a great difference between, on the one hand, the worker's taking advantage of an allowable interval for lunch in order to make it the occasion for an excursion for his own purposes and on the other hand his acting in a way which is reasonably calculated to fulfil the purposes of his employment and at the same time provide for his own reasonable wants.

[12.38] The test, then is one of degree, based on the reasonableness of travelling the distance travelled to be able to secure the kind of meal that was obtained. It would also seem that a festive lunch with friends may not be considered to be in the course of employment, but a management-organised festive lunch with the staff of a community health centre could well be so considered (see [12.46]ff).

CASE
Thompson v Lewisham Hospital [1978] WCR 113 (Workers' Compensation Commission NSW)

A worker in the ward had a mechanical problem with her car, rang the National Roads and Motorists Association and asked them to send a representative to the hospital at about 3 pm that day. The representative arrived, and the car was towed, with the worker in attendance, to a nearby garage from which she began walking back to the hospital, stopping off for a few minutes at her home. On the way from her home to the hospital she was injured by a truck. She would have been absent from her workplace about 26 minutes if she had not been injured. The period of her absence was between 3 pm and 4 pm, a time, she argued, which was a "normal break" for those assisting in the ward. She gave evidence that instead of only spending the nominated time of 15 minutes from 3.45 pm until 4 pm for afternoon tea, non-nursing staff regularly spent the visiting hour from 3 pm to 4 pm in the day-room, because the "sister on duty doesn't like the girls to be going into the room and collecting flowers, or interrupting because we are not nurses".

[12.39] The Commission decided that the evidence could support a finding that the normal break allowed at the hospital was one of no less than 15 minutes but could be up to one hour: the break ordinarily began at 3 pm and concluded at 4 pm. Absence from work taken with the permission of the employer, and incidental to work, may not remove one from the course of employment.

[12.39] ■■■ **CASE**

Kyriakidas v Rondo Building Services Pty Ltd [1974] WCR 62 (Workers' Compensation Commission NSW)

A worker used to drive home each day for lunch as the employer did not provide facilities and his home was nearby. On the day in question he detoured from his route home to give his brother and friends a lift to a hotel. He was exceeding the speed limit, and collided with a telegraph pole, resulting in his injury. The Commission accepted that he was absent during a normal break, but had to determine whether he had subjected himself to an abnormal risk of injury.

[12.40] The Commission accepted earlier case law which defined "abnormal risk" as meaning one which is no more than unusual, and that a risk is abnormal when, in the particular circumstances, an act is accompanied by an unusual degree of risk, or is incidental to an act which in itself is inherently dangerous. It found that the employee had subjected himself to an abnormal risk of injury by speeding. Lack of qualifications, and inexperience, may be considered in determining whether one subjects oneself to an abnormal risk; so something done by a learner may be considered more risky than the same thing done by an experienced person. The legislation generally requires that the abnormal risk be voluntarily undertaken, thus requiring that the person undertakes it by freely exercised choice. Note also that the burden is on the employer to prove that there was an increased risk undertaken by the employee.

[12.41] An employee who is injured while remaining at home or elsewhere for the purpose of being on call would be eligible for compensation if injured while carrying out all activities incidental thereto (for example, rushing to answer the telephone, preparing a snack, walking to or from a car to respond to a call to work) (*Australian Workers Compensation Guide* (CCH, Sydney, 1987), ¶4-310).

Journeys

[12.42] Travel to or from home and work is generally included in the activities covered, as is travel for the purposes of work, however some jurisdictions restrict the type of injury they will consider on such journeys (especially Tasmania, Victoria and Western Australia). Wording of the statutes differs, and a guide to the different approaches of the jurisdictions is set out in Figure 12.1. Generally travel must be by the most reasonably direct route. In the Australian Capital Territory (possibly the most liberal approach) one may deviate from a direct route for refreshment or other activities which are reasonably ancillary to one's work, or for any reason which does not result in a substantial deviation, and/or increase in the risk of harm, or wilful and serious misconduct.

FIGURE 12.1 [12.42]

JOURNEYS CONSIDERED PART OF WORK FOR WORKERS' COMPENSATION

Note that these categories are generalisations, and subject to jurisdictional conditions and qualifications. They should not be relied on without checking the precise terms of the legislation.

PURPOSE OF TRAVEL	Cth	ACT	NSW	NT	QLD	SA	TAS	VIC	WA##
Home to/from work	✓	✓	✓	✓	✓	✓	✓**		
Home to place of pickup*			✓						
Home to/from work residence			✓						
Between places of work	✓				✓	✓			
For purpose of employment	✓	✓	✓	✓	✓	✓		✓#	
To obtain medical certificate for compensation claim	✓	✓	✓	✓	✓	✓			
To receive medical treatment for injury	✓	✓	✓	✓	✓*	✓			
For rehabilitation for workers' comp.	✓	✓	✓	✓	✓*	✓			
To receive payment for workers' comp.	✓	✓	✓	✓	✓	✓			
For assessment for workers' comp	✓	✓	✓	✓	✓	✓			
To collect pay	✓		✓						
To place for work-related/approved education/training	✓		✓	✓	✓	✓			
As trade union or workers' representative			✓						
Temporary absence during ordinary recess and injury not due to voluntary abnormal risk	✓	✓	✓	✓	✓			✓	

Safety Rehabilitation and Compensation Act 1988 (Cth), s 6; Workers' Compensation Act 1951 (ACT), s 8; Workers' Compensation Act 1987 (NSW), s 10; Work Health Act 1986 (NT), s 4; WorkCover Queensland Act 1996 (Qld), s 37; Workers' Rehabilitation and Compensation Act 1986 (SA), s 30; Workers Rehabilitation and Compensation Act 1988 (Tas), s 25; Accident Compensation (WorkCover Insurance) Act 1993 (Vic), s 83; Workers' Compensation and Rehabilitation Act 1981 (WA), s 19.

*   It would seem logical that travelling to a place of pick-up would be considered to be travelling to or from work in other jurisdictions. Travel must be by the shortest convenient

[12.42]
      route, without substantial deviations or voluntary interruptions. One is generally considered on one's journey when one leaves the boundary of one's residential property.
** Only where on the specific request of employer or if journey is work-related.
# Victoria specifically excludes journeys to and from the place of employment, places at which the worker receives training, medical certificate, medical advice or treatment, personal and household services, rehabilitation or payment of compensation.
Western Australia specifically **excludes** journeys between home and work, journeys between home and education, places for treatment or to receive compensation, and journeys between places of residence.

[12.43] A worker is also covered whilst at the places to which he or she has made a work-related journey (for example, undergoing education or training, receiving medical care etc).

CASE
Buckman v Electricity Commission of New South Wales [1975] WCR 128 (Workers' Compensation Commission NSW)

A worker travelling home in Sydney stopped for two and a half hours at a nightclub where he consumed a substantial amount of alcohol. After falling asleep on a suburban train he awoke just as the train was about to leave a station and wished to alight. He tried to jump from the train as it began to move and as a result fell between the train and the platform which resulted in injury.

[12.44] The Workers' Compensation Commission had to determine whether the time spent at the nightclub was a substantial deviation from his journey home, and if it was, whether he had materially increased the risk of injury to himself. It found that the two and a half hours spent at the club was a substantial interruption, and the amount of alcohol drunk materially affected his judgment to the extent of materially increasing the risk of him suffering harm on the way home. The judgment carries the implication that the circumstances of the particular case (for example, the fact that he did not get a taxi but travelled by train, and that the train journey was at night), was crucial in judging the presence or absence of risk of harm. If, after a substantial deviation, one resumes the journey whether one is again on the course of employment depends on the facts and the particular provisions of the relevant legislation.

Statutory Extensions of the Course of Employment

[12.45] Legislation in some jurisdictions has extended the activities that are covered by workers' compensation. They are set out in Figure 12.2.

▌▌▌ FIGURE 12.2   [12.46]

STATUTORY EXTENSIONS OF THE COURSE OF EMPLOYMENT

(Adapted from *Halsbury's Law of Australia*, [450-210]-[450-300].) Note that these categories are generalisations, and should not be relied on without checking the precise terms of the legislation.

ACTIVITY	Cth	ACT	NSW	NT	QLD	SA	TAS	VIC	WA
Violence arising as a result of employment	✓								
Attendance at educational facility for work-related/approved activity	✓	✓		✓	✓	✓		✓	✓
Attendance at place for workers' compensation purposes	✓			✓	✓			✓	✓
Activity as accredited trade union or employee organisation with employer's consent or authorised by an agreement or award			✓						

Safety Rehabilitation and Compensation Act 1988 (Cth), s 6; *Workers' Compensation Act* 1951 (ACT), s 7; *Workers' Compensation Act* 1987 (NSW), s 10; *Work Health Act* 1986 (NT), s 4; *WorkCover Queensland Act* 1996 (Qld), s 37; *Workers' Rehabilitation and Compensation Act* 1986 (SA), s 30; *Workers Rehabilitation and Compensation Act* 1988 (Tas), s 25; *Accident Compensation (WorkCover Insurance) Act* 1993 (Vic), s 83; *Workers' Compensation and Rehabilitation Act* 1981 (WA), s 19.

Sporting and Other Activities

[12.46] Under some circumstances, participation in sports as part of a workplace team, or in work-generated leisure activities which are authorised by the employer are covered. See the discussion on lunchtime and break activities at [12.36]. Where more formal organised sporting matches are undertaken by workers in off-duty time or on weekends, even where they are authorised, encouraged or otherwise supported by the employer, it is doubtful whether workers' compensation would apply to any accidents occurring either on journeys to or from the event, or at the event itself. However, where attendance is expected by the employer, or where payment or promotion is dependent upon attendance, it probably would apply.

[12.46] **CASE**

Wolmar v Travelodge Australia Ltd (1975) 8 ACTR 11 (Supreme Court)

A worker was injured at a Christmas party on the employer's premises, held by the management, to which workers were invited and expected to attend.

[12.47] In this case the court adopted the following test when asked if attendance at a particular event was part of one's job:

> Here we have the situation where, on the one hand, the employer, for the purposes of improving relationships all round, offers hospitality to an employee and her spouse in the form of a gathering on the employer's premises attended solely by the manager and his wife and by other employees and their spouses. On the other hand the employee co-operates by bringing along herself, her spouse and her plate and thereby helps to make the occasion a success. It seems to me that this whole enterprise is so closely associated with the employment as to be incidental to it. I think the average office worker in Australia . . . if asked about the matter, would express what I have said . . . by saying that, these days, attendance at the annual Christmas staff party is part of the job [at 16 per Dixon J].

Other cases have since established that the party need not be at work and the employee need not be obliged to attend.

[12.48] It would seem, by the reference to contemporary expectations, that the approach taken above was meant to provide for flexibility over time, and that events other than Christmas parties, such as farewells to staff, celebrations and "team building" events could be included where these are considered part of the job. It is also arguable that events that are organised for the wellbeing of the hospitalised or institutionalised, which involve staff, such as trips away or to sporting events, even on a voluntary basis, could be considered incidental to work.

Accommodation

[12.49] Workers may be compensated for injuries which occur while off duty if they are required to live in certain premises; or while on call.

CASE

Regan v Gladesville Hospital [1977] WCR 107 (Workers' Compensation Commission NSW)

A nurse was injured when he fell on the stairwell in the nurses' residence of his place of employment while engaged in his own private affairs. He was not required by his employer to reside in the quarters, and was living there to benefit from the cheap and convenient accommodation it provided.

[12.50] If the nurse could show that his residence in the nurses' home was required as a condition of his employment, he could be eligible for workers' compensation. The Workers' Compensation Commission considered earlier cases which dealt with employees living on or near their place of employment rather than at their permanent home. It decided [12.54] that in these cases there were two kinds of accommodation according to the facts: those situations where employees have no real choice of where they live, and those where they choose to live in premises purely for the sake of convenience, after exercising a real choice. In deciding this case the following questions were considered:

- ..... Does the applicant's job require frequent movement from place to place, with or without short periods in any one place, making accommodation difficult thus requiring workplace accommodation?
- ..... Is the applicant on call, or in any other way does he or she have restrictions on their activities at the time?
- ..... Is it somehow disadvantageous or unreasonably impractical for the worker, in discharging her or his responsibilities, to live elsewhere?

[12.51] If any of the above questions could have been answered in the affirmative, the Commission may have held that living in the nurses' home was incidental to the employment of the nurse in this case. However, the questions were answered in the negative by the Commission, therefore compensation was not available. It is useful for nurses to note that even "working" at home may be covered by workers' compensation, so one may be able to claim for accidents occurring when one is at home on call.

[12.52] Given that residence in a particular place may be required for the purposes of work, as long as one's activities in that residence are directly or indirectly ancillary to one's work, or one is "subsisting in conventional manner" (presumably washing, dressing, eating, relaxing, etc), one's activities would seem to be in the course of employment. Extraordinary and unrelated activities would be excluded.

Travel

[12.53] Travel to, and attendance at, classes, conferences or for other purposes approved by the employer and considered part of one's development as an employee are generally considered to be part of one's employment for the purposes of workers' compensation law (see Figure 12.1).

Assault at Work

[12.54] It is not unknown for health carers to be the subject of attack from clients, and under most circumstances, these situations are covered by workers' compensation legislation. Where the assault is the result of a private quarrel (which is not part of one's work) it would most likely not be accepted. Compare the case of *McCleod v Cockatoo Docks* [1971] WCR 313 where an assault after a jocular remark made while workers were waiting for a union meeting (which was being held during a lunchtime break) was held to be in the course of employment, with the case of *Bill Williams Pty Ltd v Williams* (1972) 126 CLR 146, where Williams, having

[12.54] punched another man, O'Neill, over an argument about his alleged affair with O'Neill's wife, was threatened with a gun by O'Neill. Williams ran out of the premises and was shot in the back. The court held that the argument was unrelated to the employment and interrupted the "course of employment".

Application for Workers' Compensation

[12.55] As noted above, workers' compensation is bound by rules and procedures. There are time-limits for making claims, and it should also be remembered that the longer after an accident before a claim is made, the less likely that it is to be accepted as accurate. A worker wishing to make a claim does so by first notifying the employer, and is advised to do so as soon as possible after the injury. Then a claim must be made. Larger employers have specially designated personnel for dealing with compensation claims. All jurisdictions, except Western Australia (where the time limit is 12 months), the Northern Territory (which does not set a time limit) and Victoria (where different time limits apply for different types of claims) require that the claim be made within six months of the injury. Most States allow special leave for the court to grant an extension, but this may be difficult to obtain. The claim is to be made in writing and is lodged by the employer with the insurer. To challenge the claim the insurer must go to the appropriate board or tribunal.

[12.56] The usual way to initiate a claim is to obtain a form from the employer when reporting the accident or illness. The report is then lodged with the Workers Compensation Commission.

Importance of Claiming all Injuries

[12.57] It is important that workers recognise the need to report injuries, even minor ones for which they do not need treatment or time off. This particularly relates to back injuries that are considered minor and not deserving of any attention. After a series of these, an injury may occur which is exacerbated by the already existing weakness caused by the earlier minor injuries and requires more treatment or leave than it would, in isolation, require. Unless there is a record of the previous injuries, there may be no way of proving that the full extent of the harm is work-related. It is also important:

- ......not to treat minor injuries oneself, for if anything goes wrong or one has not realised the full extent of the harm, one's interference in the course of treatment will adversely affect one's claim to compensation;
- ......to consider whether sick leave should more appropriately be claimed under workers' compensation where the reason for leave is work-related "injury" or disease;
- ......that employers have provisions for recording incidents of injury, illness or pain even if there is doubt as to whether they are work-related or not. Workers should ensure that such incidents are recorded; and

.....to produce to the employer any certificate stating that the worker is able to [12.61] undertake light duties, even where there is no work of such nature available. Where light duties are not available, the worker may be deemed under the law to be totally incapacitated, and entitled to appropriate compensation. However the opportunity to offer such work must be made available to the employer.

Compensation

Death

[12.58] Where a worker dies as a result of an industrial injury, payment of compensation may be made to dependants, under all legislation. The definition of "dependant" varies, but spouses, legal or de facto, children, step-children, children in the care of the worker or those in a close family relationship who can show dependency on the worker at the time of death may apply. Compensation may be apportioned between dependants. There is generally control of the moneys payable by a designated body.

Incapacity

[12.59] Where a worker is rendered unable to work, compensation for medical treatment and loss of wages is awarded according to amounts established in the legislation. Where the worker is fully incapacitated the amount payable for loss of wages is generally based on the previous pay rate of the worker, with either the full amount or a percentage thereof applying for an initial period (for example, unlimited in the Australian Capital Territory, 26 weeks in New South Wales and Queensland, one year in South Australia and 13 weeks in Victoria). Thereafter the States differ markedly in their provision of compensation. Some States continue to compute the amount payable on the average weekly wages of the particular worker, and no special provision is made for dependants. Others compute the amount on different permutations of the average weekly wage and add an amount for each dependent person. If incapacity is partial, as well as medical and rehabilitation expenses, the amount payable will generally be the difference between the amount the worker can now earn and the amount which would have been earned if the injury had not occurred. In some States the employer is obliged to provide alternative work for an employee partially incapacitated by injury or disease.

[12.60] Normally, compensation payments are in the form of regular payments, but under some circumstances a lump sum may be paid.

Common Law Claim for Compensation

[12.61] As noted above, eligibility for workers' compensation does not rule out the right of the worker to sue the employer if negligence can be proved, however, one's right to sue in negligence is severely limited under

[12.61] workers' compensation legislation. Generally, a successful negligence action will provide substantially more compensation, although it is, of course, much harder to prove. A worker who has been receiving workers' compensation and who later brings a successful action against the employer in negligence will have the amount of workers' compensation already received taken into account in the amount of damages awarded. The time limit for such an action is, in most jurisdictions, six years.

Liability of Occupiers for Accidents on their Property

[12.62] There is a body of common law that establishes a separate area of liability of an occupier of premises for harm to those who come onto those premises. There is also legislation in some jurisdictions covering occupiers' liability.[5]

Who is an Occupier?

[12.63] Occupiers are those who have the control of premises: they may or may not be the owner.

> Wherever a person has a sufficient degree of control over premises that he ought to realise that any failure on his part to use care may result in injury to a person coming lawfully there, then he is an 'occupier' and the person coming lawfully there is his 'visitor': and the 'occupier' is under a duty to his 'visitor' to use reasonable care . . . [an occupier need not] have entire control over the premises. He need not have exclusive occupation. Suffice it that he has some degree of control [*Wheat v E Lacon & Co Ltd* [1966] AC 552 at 578 per Lord Denning].

[12.64] Management of health care facilities would normally be the occupiers of the premises. However, this quote could lead to the argument, for example, that a nurse or pathologist is in control of premises in which he or she works to the extent that he or she has knowledge of, and can affect, the safety of those premises (for example, charge nurse in a ward). The duty of care normally owed to one's "neighbour" (see [6.5]) would apply as well, the two duties merging into the test of foreseeability of harm. However health carers would not be liable as occupiers simply because they are employees working on the premises (*Stone v Taffe* [1974] 1 WLR 1575). However, employees have a duty of care to the employer (as occupier) to take reasonable steps to further the employer's interests, including the interest in maintaining safe premises. Thus the employee should do what is reasonable to remove

---

[5] *Law Reform (Miscellaneous Provisions) Act* 1955 (ACT); *Wrongs Act* 1936 (SA); *Wrongs Act* 1958 (Vic); *Occupiers Liability Act* 1985 (WA).

hazards and remedy any unsafe conditions (for example, wet, slippery [12.67] floors or exposed dangerous equipment) either themselves, or through notifying the appropriate responsible person.

[12.65] An occupier does not have to be in physical occupation of the premises, but may be an absent landlord or owner (*Thompson v Commonwealth* (1969) 70 SR (NSW) 398). Several people may be liable, to a different extent (depending on, for example, contractual agreements).

Standard of Care of an Occupier

[12.66] Until recently the standard of care an occupier owed to those entering premises depended on the category of the entrant. An entrant may be:

- An **invitee** or one with whom the occupier has a special relationship based on pecuniary, material or business interests. It would include patients, messengers, florists, chaplains, those delivering goods. It would also include patients' visitors although there is some difference of opinion about this. It would *exclude* those entering purely for social reasons, or reasons unrelated to the enterprise of the occupier, who are licensees (see below).

■■■ CASE
Western Suburbs Hospital v Currie (1987) 9 NSWLR 511

An elderly woman visiting her husband, fell down a flight of stairs in the hospital grounds. The trial judge decided that she was an invitee, and that the stairs were an unusual danger, requiring a warning or protective measures. The hospital appealed saying that she was not an invitee, and so had to take the premises as she found them.

[12.67] The New South Wales Court of Appeal dismissed the appeal, holding the hospital bound by the ordinary duty of care, and that this care is determined by the nature of the hospital's business, encouraging the old and disabled (and the worried) to use the route in question.

- A **licensee**, who enters with the permission, express or implied, of the occupier, including visitors for social reasons or reasons unrelated to the occupier's business, and reasons other than those mentioned above. This would include the continual crossing of an owner's premises as a short-cut on their journey, or travelling salespeople seeking to become invitees by creating a business relationship. Where occupiers know (or ought to know) of the use of their premises in this way and do nothing to prevent it, those doing so become licensees.
- An **entrant under contract**, such as a visiting medical officer or maintenance worker, who is engaged to enter the premises for certain specified purposes. The liability of the occupier may be limited by specified conditions.

[12.67]
- .....An **entrant as of right**, or one who enters under some statutory power, not requiring the occupier's permission to do so. Such people may be health inspectors, meter readers, police under warrant or other powers of entry, and the general public where the premises (or part of them) are open to the public. Only designated areas of a health facility are available to all-comers.
- .....**Trespassers**, or those who enter premises without the consent, express or implied, of the occupier. Where there is no forewarning that people are forbidden entry, and there is access to the premises for example, a gate or path they may enter. They are at that stage a licensee (implied permission) until told clearly they are not welcome. They then become a trespasser and should exit with reasonable speed. If they don't, the occupier can use reasonable force to eject them. There is an implied consent for members of the public to enter business premises such as hospitals, nursing homes and clinics, and be in areas reasonably understood to be accessible by the public.

[12.68] An occupier does not have to make premises totally safe, but must prevent harm to those entering, or warn of dangers which a person entering would not be expected to know about. The categories above carried different duties of care in the past; however, it can be seen that this leads to difficulty and even absurdity in the attempt to determine the status of an entrant. As suggested above, an entrant may change categories at any moment, when told that he or she is welcome or unwelcome, when friendly discussions become more seriously businesslike, etc. Divisions between the categories are also hard to draw: for example, does a dinner party for a friend who happens to be a more senior colleague (which may lead to favourable references or promotion) make them an invitee or a licensee?

[12.69] The High Court recently stated categorically that *all* entrants, regardless of their purpose, are owed a similar duty of care according to the rules of the law of negligence. *Australian Safeway Stores Pty Ltd v Zaluzna Pty Ltd* (1987) 61 ALJR 180, quoting from *Hackshaw v Shaw* (1984) 155 CLR 614 adopted the principle that all that is necessary for a duty of care for an occupier is a reasonable foreseeability of a real risk of injury to a visitor, and the standard of care is "What a reasonable person would do by way of response to the foreseeable risk?"

[12.70] The categories described above are thus no longer relevant to the fact that a duty of care may exist to the entrant upon premises, but they will remain important in determining the foreseeability of harm and the reasonability of prevention from harm. Trespassers, for example, are not likely to be foreseeable or easily planned for in prevention of harm, so one would not be expected to take the same care to prevent harm to them as one would in the case of invitees, who one knows will be entering. If an occupier is aware of the likelihood of trespassers (for example, children who play in the grounds of a hospital), the occupier is held to foresee that they may be harmed by dangerous structures or other hidden dangers. The occupier is also obliged to make sure the trespassers know of a specific danger: that is, provide adequate warning or make the premises inaccessible.

[12.71] The categories also help to determine who is an occupier for the purposes of the law (for example, if one invites a person on to premises for one's benefit, it would seem one becomes an occupier for the purposes of that person's visit).

[12.72] An occupier has a duty to warn a licensee of any hidden danger in the property (for example, faulty steps) which he or she knows about, and which is likely to cause harm if no warning is given. Invitees (and it would seem independent contractors, such as a plumber and visitors of right), are entitled to more than just warnings of hidden danger: the premises must be made safe for them by measures to protect them from dangers not only known to the occupier, but those which ought to be known. Thus, slippery floors, be they in a home or a hospital, can result in liability to a patient, visitor or community nurse (all invitees). Of course a health carer who is aware that a client being visited is not well enough to keep the premises in good order would be foolish to trust in this legal principle and not keep a reasonable lookout for danger: he or she could be considered contributorily negligent and partially responsible for any harm he or she suffers. As all premises are different, one does enter them, to some extent, at one's own risk.

Community Health Carers and Occupiers' Rights

[12.73] The legal principles described above affect everyone, but are most relevant to community workers. The owner or anyone in legal occupation of premises (for example, a tenant or a friend using someone's home), has the right to control who is allowed on those premises. This means that anyone may be excluded from premises for any reason, unless they have a statutory right to enter, such as a police officer with a warrant.

[12.74] The owner or occupier of property is entitled to enjoyment of that property to the exclusion of all others, unless permission is granted to others to enjoy its use as well.

[12.75] Where premises have an unlocked gate or door, or a path which is not obstructed, and there is no sign to indicate that a person is not welcome, a health carer may enter the premises and take reasonable steps to determine whether he or she is welcome, and remain unless or until permission to stay is revoked. Where there is no indication as to whether he or she is welcome or not, he or she is there on sufferance, a licensee. If welcomed, the carer remains a licensee unless it is established that there is a benefit to be gained by the occupier, the carer then becomes an invitee. If unwelcome, the carer becomes a trespasser, and the occupier has the right to either remove her or him with reasonable force, or sue. Health carers may be confronted by refusal of entry by an occupier where someone on the premises (for example a sick or abused child) needs care.

[12.76] If the carer were asked to leave a premises by the occupier, then even though someone, be they the occupier or another person, needs care, he or she should consider doing so. Where there is concern that people may suffer as a result of such a request, and the health carer has no statutory right to remain, he or she should leave, seeking appropriate legal

[12.76] assistance for the provision of care for the person needing it. The exceptions to this are where there are statutory powers (for example under child protection legislation). Whilst there is no legal authority on the point, it is considered likely that a court would entertain a defense of necessity where a health carer remains on property to give assistance to someone requiring it, considering the "trespass" resulted in more benefit to the occupier or another person than detriment. In either case care should be taken for the safety of all concerned.

Injuries by Dogs and Other Animals

[12.77] There is State legislation that makes the owner of a dog liable for harm it causes without proof of viciousness or negligence, outside of the owner's premises. Animals must be kept in such a way that people may enter their premises without being harmed, or are warned by a sign of the animal's presence on the premises. It may be a defence that the plaintiff is a trespasser (with adequate warning) or has provoked the dog under the principles relating to contributory negligence or voluntarily undertaking the risk. Occupiers Liability principles may apply.

[12.78] Animals are generally not allowed to be outside those premises unless adequately restrained. Legislative provisions covering dogs (which are not at law deemed to be dangerous unless they have shown this propensity), makes the owner of a dog liable for any harm (or fright in some States) it causes whilst not on its owners' premises. When the dog is on its owners' premises the principle outlined above for harmful animals applies: that is, if there is no indication of a harmful dog being on premises, the visitor should not be confronted by one. If there is a "Beware of the Dog" sign or other warning then the visitor enters at her or his own risk. Of course where someone is asked onto premises to render services he or she is an invitee (independent contractor) and can expect that the owners will adequately curb any animals they have. Health carers arranging to attend premises would be wise to ask the occupier if there is a dog on the premises, and, if so, what precautions may be required.

[12.79] Generally, the owner is liable not only for harm caused directly by physical contact with the dog, but also harm caused indirectly, for example, when avoiding the dog or running from it (*Twentieth Century Blinds Pty Ltd v Howes* [1974] 1 NSWLR 244), or a traffic accident caused by a dog (*Martignoni v Harris* [1971] 2 NSWLR 102). It could also be harm as a result of fright or fear.

REFERENCES AND FURTHER READING

General references on tort law listed at the end of Chapter 6 may have a section on liability for harm caused by animals.

Australian Health and Medical Law Reporter (CCH, Sydney, 1991, Looseleaf Service)

Castile, P, "Alternative Dispute Resolution in Workers' Compensation and People of Non-English Speaking Background in New South Wales" 1 *Torts Law Journal* (2) July 1993, pp 184-193

Comment, "Changes to Workers' Compensation" *Queensland Police Union Journal* March 1997, p 27

Halsbury's Laws of Australia (Butterworths, Sydney, Looseleaf Service)

Ison, T, "Promoting Excellence: National Consistency in Australian Workers' Compensation, 1996, Interim Report of the Heads of Workers' Compensation Authorities to the Labour Minister's Council" 4 *Torts Law Journal* (3) December 1996, pp 286-294

The Laws of Australia (Law Book Co, Sydney, 1993, Looseleaf Service)

Michael, R and Jenkins, H, "Work-Related Trauma: The Experience of Perioperative Nurses" 8 *Collegian* No 1, p 19 (January 2001)

Purse, K, "Common Law and Workers' Compensation in Australia", 13 *Australian Journal of Labour Law* (3) December 2000, pp 260-277

Staunton, P and Whyburn, R, *Nursing and the Law* (4th ed, Saunders, Sydney, 1997, Ch 6)

Trindad, F and Cane, P, *The Law of Torts in Australia* (OUP, 1999), Ch 17

Chapter Thirteen

REGISTRATION AND PRACTICE

INTRODUCTION

[13.1] As a citizen of the state, the health carer is, of course, subject to the laws of the land. However, the special occupation of health carer gives rise to legal considerations peculiar to that occupation. As with all major professions, such as law, medicine, and accountancy, the state establishes a self-regulatory system which gives health care professions respectability in the eyes of the public, autonomy in establishing the standards and procedures they recognise are necessary for such respectability, and a means of disciplining members of the profession if they fall short of that standard. The state itself will only step in and take over these functions where activities are considered to be a breach of the criminal law (see below, Ch 14) or are challenged in court by an aggrieved individual as, for example, battery (Ch 4) or negligence (Ch 6).

The Health Professional and Registration Boards

[13.2] Each jurisdiction has legislation and facilities for registration and regulation of health workers (see Figure 13.1).

[13.2] ■■■ **FIGURE 13.1**

REGISTERABLE HEALTH PROFESSIONS

HEALTH PROFESSION	GOVERNING ACTS	JURISDICTION IN WHICH REGISTRATION REQUIRED
Medical practitioners	*Medical Practitioners Act* 1930 (ACT); *Medical Practice Act* 1992 (NSW); *Medical Act* 1995 (NT); *Medical Act* 1939 (Qld); *Medical Practitioners Act* 1983 (SA); *Medical Practitioners Registration Act* 1996 (Tas); *Medical Practice Act* 1994 (Vic); *Medical Act* 1894 (WA)	All jurisdictions
Nurses	*Nurses Act* 1988 (ACT); *Nurses Act* 1991 (NSW); *Nursing Act* 1999 (NT); *Nursing Act* 1992 (Qld); *Nurses Act* 1999 (SA); *Nursing Act* 1995 (Tas); *Nurses Act* 1993 (Vic); *Nursing Act* 1992 (WA)	All jurisdictions
Chiropractors	*Chiropractors Registration Act* 1983 (ACT); *Chiropractors and Osteopaths Act* 1991 (NSW); *Health Practitioners and Allied Professionals Registration Act* 1985 (NT); *Chiropractors and Osteopaths Act* 1979 (Qld); *Chiropractors Act* 1991 (SA); *Chiropractors and Osteopaths Registration Act* 1979 (Tas); *Chiropractors Registration Act* 1996 (Vic); *Chiropractors Act* 1964 (WA)	All jurisdictions
Physiotherapists	*Physiotherapists Registration Act* 1977 (ACT); *Physiotherapists Registration Act* 1945 (NSW); *Physiotherapy Act* 1964 (Qld); *Health Practitioners and Allied Professionals Registration Act* 1985 (NT); *Physiotherapists Act* 1991 (SA); *Physiotherapists Registration Act* 1951 (Tas); *Physiotherapists Act* 1998 (Vic); *Physiotherapists Act* 1950 (WA)	All jurisdictions
Optometrists	*Optometrists Act* 1956 (ACT); *Optometrists Act* 1930 (NSW); *Optometrists Act* 1980 (NT); *Optometrists Act* 1974 (Qld); *Optometrists Act* 1920 (SA); *Optometrists Registration Act* 1994 (Tas); *Optometrists Registration Act* 1996 (Vic); *Optometrists Act* 1940 (WA)	All jurisdictions

[13.2]

HEALTH PROFESSION	GOVERNING ACTS	JURISDICTION IN WHICH REGISTRATION REQUIRED
Psychologists	*Psychologists Act* 1994 (ACT); *Psychologists Act* 1989 (NSW); *Health Practitioners and Allied Professionals Registration Act* 1985 (NT); *Psychologists Act* 1977 (Qld); *Psychological Practices Act* 1973 (SA); *Psychologists Registration Act* 1976 (Tas); *Psychologists Registration Act* 1987 (Vic); *Psychologists Registration Act* 1976 (WA)	All jurisdictions
Pharmacists	*Pharmacy Act* 1931 (ACT); *Pharmacy Act* 1964 (NSW); *Pharmacy Act* (NT); *Pharmacy Act* 1976 (Qld); *Pharmacists Act* 1991 (SA); *Pharmacy Act* 1908 (Tas); *Pharmacists Act* 1974 (Vic); *Pharmacy Act* 1964 (WA)	All jurisdictions
Dentists	*Dentists Registration Act* 1931 (ACT); *Dentists Act* 1989 (NSW); *Dental Act* 1986 (NT); *Dental Act* 1971 (Qld); *Dentists Act* 1984 (SA); *Dental Act* 1982 (Tas); *Dental Practice Act* 1999 (Vic); *Dental Act* 1939 (WA)	All jurisdictions
Aboriginal Health Workers	*Health Practitioners and Allied Professionals Registration Act* 1985 (NT)	NT
Occupational Therapists	*Health Practitioners and Allied Professionals Registration Act* 1985 (NT); *Occupational Therapists Act* 1979 (Qld); *Occupational Therapists Act* 1974 (SA); *Occupational Therapists Registration Act* 1980 (WA)	NT Qld SA WA
Opticians	*Optical Dispensers Act* 1963 (NSW); *Optometrists Act* 1920 (SA); *Optometrists Registration Act* 1994 (Tas); *Optical Dispensers Act* 1966 (WA)	NSW SA Tas WA
Osteopaths	*Chiropractors and Osteopaths Act* 1991 (NSW); *Health Practitioners and Allied Professionals Registration Act* 1985 (NT); *Chiropractors and Osteopaths Registration Act* 1997 (Tas); *Osteopaths Registration Act* 1996 (Vic); *Osteopaths Act* 1997 (WA)	NSW NT Tas Vic WA

[13.2]

HEALTH PROFESSION	GOVERNING ACTS	JURISDICTION IN WHICH REGISTRATION REQUIRED
Podiatrists	*Podiatrists Act* 1994 (ACT); *Podiatrists Act* 1989 (NSW); *Podiatrists Act* 1969 (Qld); *Chiropodists Act* 1950 (SA); *Podiatrists Registration Act* 1995 (Tas); *Podiatrists Registration Act* 1997 (Vic); *Podiatrists Registration Act* 1984 (WA)	All jurisdictions except NT
Radiographers	*Radiographers Act* (NT); *Radiographers Registration Act* 1971 (Tas); *Health Act* 1958 (Vic); *Health (Medical Radiation Technologies) Regulations* 1997 (Vic)	NT Tas Vic
Speech Therapists	*Speech Pathologists Act* 1979 (Qld)	Qld

[13.3] To regulate each profession and establish an acceptable and uniform standard of care, the legislation provides for registration of practitioners by an established statutory Registration Board or Council. Each State has its own standards, and, although they are similar, one must meet the requirements of the individual State before one is eligible for practice in it. In this chapter the term "Registration Board" or "Board" will be used to refer to the appropriate body.

Mutual Recognition

[13.4] Until 1993 any registered health care professional intending to practise in another State or Territory had to apply to the appropriate body in the second State or Territory in advance for registration. Registration was not automatic, and each case was treated on its merits, so application had to be made some time before the applicant could practise in the new jurisdiction. As the respective Governments recognised the inefficiency of this approach, it was agreed to pass legislation providing for mutual recognition of registration between jurisdictions. The Commonwealth and all States and Territories have passed legislation giving effect to this principle.[1] The *Mutual Recognition Act* in each jurisdiction allows health professionals registered in one jurisdiction to practise in another simply by giving notice, including evidence of registration, and paying the prescribed fee to the relevant authority. This, however, does not affect:

---

[1] *Mutual Recognition Act* 1992 (Cth); *Mutual Recognition Act (ACT)* 1992 (ACT); *Mutual Recognition Act (NSW)* 1992 (NSW); *Mutual Recognition Act (NT)* 1992 (NT); *Mutual Recognition Act (Queensland)* 1992 (Qld); *Mutual Recognition Act (SA)* 1993 (SA); *Mutual Recognition Act (Tasmania)* 1993 (Tas); *Mutual Recognition Act (Victoria)* 1993 (Vic); *Mutual Recognition (Western Australia) Act* 1995 (WA); *Medical Act* 1894 (WA).

▌.....the application of laws in the new jurisdiction to the health professional and her or his practice in that jurisdiction; or

▌.....the powers of the relevant Board in the new jurisdiction to regulate the conduct of the health care professional in respect of her or his practice in that jurisdiction.

[13.5] Cancellation of a practising certificate in the first jurisdiction will have the effect of cancelling the certificate in the subsequent jurisdiction.

[13.6] All jurisdictions except Tasmania and Western Australia also have legislation (called *Trans-Tasman Mutual Recognition Acts*) that provide for inter-country recognition of registration between Australia and New Zealand.

Function and Powers of Registration Boards

[13.7] Although legislation varies throughout the country, there is much similarity in the general model of registration legislation. The Registration Boards generally have the following features and powers.

Composition

[13.8] Registration Boards are composed of members appointed by government and representative bodies, as well as members elected by the profession. This is to achieve an experienced and balanced body which can adequately deal with the many interests, functions and concerns of the nursing profession. Some jurisdictions require at least one medical practitioner on the Registration Boards of some professions, such as those for nurses, which could be considered to be an unnecessarily cautious approach to self-regulation by that profession.

Education and Research

[13.9] Registration Boards set the standard of education and practice (for example, the amount of clinical practice, prescription of exams, minimum age for acceptance), for the different classes of practitioners. They may set and recognise curricula, approve teaching programmes by granting recognition to universities, hospitals, nursing homes and/or other teaching institutions offering courses in health care, and the awards and qualifications they grant. The Registration Board may grant exemptions in some cases from requirements or conditions otherwise applying to educational requirements.

[13.10] Registration Boards may have additional powers to carry out research into their particular profession and aspects of practice, to consult with bodies concerned with the use and employment of practitioners, to advise the government on matters relevant to the profession, to establish different branches of the profession, to develop a code of practice, and to authorise reports on, or disseminate information to, the profession.

Registration

[13.11] The Registration Boards maintain a register of those who have qualified for registration, with different registers for different branches of practice (for example, different specialties, such as "general", "mental health" and "enrolled" nurses. It may also register membership of specialist colleges (for example, fellows of Medical Colleges of paediatrics, psychology or gynaecology). The Boards maintain these registers, and practitioners must renew their registration regularly, mostly annually. One can only practise in a State or Territory in which one is registered or enrolled.

[13.12] In theory there is no law which specifically prohibits a person from carrying out the functions of a some health carers, for example those of a qualified nurse or enrolled nurse, without registration. The law does, however, prohibit practising as a registered nurse, or holding oneself out to be a registered nurse, without registration. The purpose of registration is to maintain an acceptable standard within the nursing profession, and clients must not be misled as to whether their health carer has met the requirements of the State.

[13.13] Each Registration Board determines the mode of application and requirements for registration, and all States require regular renewal of registration by payment of a fee. A function not required but generally carried out by the Registration Board is the gathering of information through statistical data with regard to the number and characteristics of those registered.

Applicant must be of Good Health and Character

[13.14] It should be noted that, as well as educational qualifications, one of the requirements for registration as a registered health care practitioner is that the registrant be of good health and character. This is usually established by requiring certification from appropriate persons as to the applicant's state of health or character, such as a doctor's certificate, a reference from an employer or teacher, etc. This sets an additional personal (as opposed to a professional) standard for those entrusted with the care of the sick.

Temporary and "Special Events" Registration

[13.15] Temporary or provisional registration may be available for exceptional cases, such as those from overseas jurisdictions who are visiting for purposes of research or teaching, or where the Registration Board determines that provisions should attach to registration. The details will differ from State to State.

[13.16] In all jurisdictions except the Northern Territory there are procedures for authorising visiting health professionals to provide health care services to visitors for special events, such as sporting events (for example, the Olympics and Paralympics) or conferences.² The authorisation can include issuing prescriptions and processing or supplying certain drugs and substances. The Minister responsible may make a declaration that an event or class of events is a "special event" for the purposes of the legislation and set the period for which the authorisation is to have effect. Visiting health professionals are required to notify the stipulated authorities of their intention to provide the services and to comply with the law of the visited jurisdiction, along with any conditions placed on the authorisation.

Conditional Registration

[13.17] Registration may be conditional where the applicant belongs to a particular group (for example, graduate medical practitioners who are undertaking postgraduate training approved by the Board) or where the applicant is suffering from an impairment, requiring the imposition of a condition in the interests of professional integrity.

Registration of Nurse Practitioners

[13.18] The most dramatic change to occur in relation to regulation of health care practice is the recognition of the expansion of nursing practice through registration of nurse practitioners. Most States and Territories are moving towards provision for expanded responsibilities and practices of nurses. New South Wales and Victoria have passed legislation to bring this into effect.

Nurses Amendment (Nurse Practitioners) Act 1998 (NSW)

[13.19] The *Nurses Act* 1991 (NSW) was amended by this Act to do several things, including:

1) .....**Providing for the Nurses Registration Board to authorise registered nurses to practise as nurse practitioners.** Such authorisation is to be given only if the Board is satisfied that the person has sufficient qualifications and experience to practise as a nurse practitioner (s 19A). A certificate of authorisation is to be issued to the nurse practitioner (s 17) and the particulars of the authorisation are to be entered in the Register of Nurses (s 13). Provision is also made for the issue of temporary authorisations (s 24). If an application for authorisation to practise as a nurse practitioner is refused, the applicant will be able to appeal against the determination (s 32(1)).

---

2   *Health Professionals (Special Events Exemptions) Act* 2000 (ACT); *Health Professionals (Special Events Exemptions) Act* 1997 (NSW); *Health Professionals (Special Events Exemptions) Act* 1998 (Qld); *Health Professionals (Special Events Exemptions) Act* 2000 (SA); *Health Professionals (Special Events Exemptions) Act* 1999 (Tas); *Health Professionals (Special Events Exemptions) Act* 2000 (Vic); *Health Professionals (Special Events Exemptions) Act* 2000 (WA).

[13.19] 2)..... **Authorising the Board to carry out functions in relation to nurse practitioners**, such as setting requirements or conditions relating to authorisation to practise as a nurse practitioner (s 10). These are similar to the functions of the Board in relation to authorised midwives. Section 10 of the Act now also allows the Board to recognise different areas of practice as a nurse practitioner.

3)..... **Allowing the Director-General of the Department of Health to approve guidelines relating to such functions of nurse practitioners as considered appropriate** (s 78A). These guidelines may make provision for the possession, use, supply and prescription of certain substances by nurse practitioners (note that a poison or restricted substance is a substance specified in the Poisons List under the *Poisons and Therapeutic Goods Act* 1966 (NSW), but does not include a drug of addiction). The guidelines may specify the types of substances and the circumstances in which they may be possessed, used, supplied or prescribed. Contravention of these guidelines is not an offence but may constitute professional misconduct or unsatisfactory professional conduct.

Similar provisions to those applying to nursing practice in general apply in relation to nurse practitioners regarding such matters as:

- ..... offences such as falsely claiming to be, or indicating that one is, a nurse practitioner, false statements in applying for registration as a nurse practitioner, etc; and
- ..... suspension and cancellation of authorisation to practise as a nurse practitioner.

[13.20] The amendments also change the *Poisons and Therapeutic Goods Act* 1966 (NSW) to allow the Director-General of the Department of Health to authorise a nurse practitioner, or class of nurse practitioners, to possess, use, supply or prescribe any poison or restricted substance (other than a drug of addiction) in accordance with the guidelines approved by the Director-General. A *poison* is a substance specified in Schedule 1, 2, 3, 5, 6 or 7 of the Poisons List. A *restricted substance* is a substance specified in Schedule 4 of the Poisons List.

A nurse practitioner who is authorised by the Director-General to possess, use, supply or prescribe a substance is not guilty of offences under the *Poisons and Therapeutic Goods Act* 1966 (NSW) that relate to the authorised activities. Also, those who supply or possess, a poison or restricted substance in accordance with the prescription of a nurse practitioner, are exempted from the relevant offences under the Act (ss 10, 16).

Nurses Amendment Act 2000 (Vic)

[13.21] The impetus for provision for nurse practitioners in Victoria came in July 1998, when the Victorian Nurse Practitioners Task Force issued a report on the provision for nurse practitioners. Amendments to the *Nurses Act* were passed recently, but have not yet come into force at the time of writing. The amendments:

1) .....**Give authority to the Nurses Board of Victoria to establish categories of** [13.23] **nurse practitioner for endorsement of registration certificates.** The Board can then endorse already registered nurses to practise as nurse practitioners in nominated categories where they have satisfactorily completed a course of study and clinical experience that qualifies them to use the title "nurse practitioner" (s 8B). Different categories of nurse practitioner are to be established, and the Board may impose restrictions or conditions of the licence. Refusal to endorse a licence may be appealed to the Victorian Civil and Administrative Tribunal (VCAT).

2) .....**Give authority to the Board to accredit courses of study and define clinical skills and experience required for each category of nurse practitioner.** These guidelines will relate to the clinical assessment, management, evaluation and the obtaining, possessing, using, selling or supplying of drugs applicable to the category of practice. Wynne (2001) states that as these changes are extensive, requiring the development of educational criteria and standards, as well as clinical practice guidelines "there will be a lead time of some 12 to 18 months before those practitioners will be recognised and employed in the Victorian health sector" (p 51).

3) .....**Give authority to the Board to authorise nurse practitioners to possess, use, supply and prescribe any Schedule 2, 3, 4 or 8 drug** (see [8.7]). This also involves amendments to the *Drugs, Poisons and Controlled Substances Act* 1981. The authorisation in relation to the possession, use, supply and prescription of these drugs is dependent upon the Board's approval of guidelines relating to the particular category of nurse practitioner. Those practitioners are subject to legislation prohibiting prescribing or administering Schedule 8 poison to a person who is a drug dependent person.

4) .....**Require the board to establish a nurse practitioner advisory committee.** The Board is to have regard to the advice given by this committee in relation to all the new functions the Board now possesses in relation to the role of the nurse practitioner.

5) .....**Provide the Board with the discretion to require a nurse practitioner to be covered by professional indemnity insurance.** This is to ensure that nurse practitioners are protected against actions in negligence against them, and that those who suffer from any such actions can have recourse to compensation.

[13.22] In respect of offences, cancellation and suspension, discipline etc, the provisions applying to nurses in general apply to nurse practitioners.

Appeals

[13.23] Those who are refused registration may appeal in all jurisdictions for review of the Registration Board's decision. Generally, however, the Registration Board may hold its own hearing into the matter, giving applicants an opportunity to put their case to it. If it still refuses to register the applicant or provide the type of registration sought, it must provide a written explanation of its reasons, and the applicant has the right to appeal to a court or an independent tribunal. For example, nurses may appeal as follows:

[13.23]
- **Australian Capital Territory:** Applicant may appeal to the Administrative Appeals Tribunal.
- **New South Wales:** Applicant may appeal to the District Court within 30 days of refusal.
- **Northern Territory:** Applicant may appeal to the Magistrates' Court within one month of refusal.
- **Queensland:** Applicant may appeal to the District Court within 28 days of refusal.
- **South Australia:** Applicant may appeal to the Supreme Court within 60 days of refusal.
- **Tasmania:** Applicant may appeal to the Supreme Court within 14 days of refusal.
- **Victoria:** Applicant may appeal to the Magistrates' Court within three months of refusal, or to the Victorian Civil and Administrative Tribunal (VCAT).
- **Western Australia:** Applicant may appeal to a magistrate of the Local Court within three months of refusal.

[13.24] In each case the court or tribunal may re-hear the case and, with the exception of South Australia (where it may remit the matter to the Registration Board for reconsideration), make a decision which upholds the Registration Board's decision, reverses it, or in some cases varies the Registration Board's decision. This decision is binding on the relevant Registration Board. The precise powers of the court or tribunal and the type of order it can make differs from State to State. Advice on how to appeal, such as which documents to file, should be sought from the appeal body involved, from a lawyer (or legal aid office) or one's union.

Disciplinary Action

Suspension or Cancellation of Registration

[13.25] All jurisdictions empower Registration Boards to carry out inquiries into complaints against practitioners for behaviour or practice which falls below standards generally established for professional practice. For medical practitioners and others, the Board may liaise with the Health Care Complaints Commission (or equivalent) on the best way to deal with the matter. The Board may be empowered to establish a special committee or tribunal to consider cases of alleged misconduct. The precise nature of the proceedings varies, but they are typically informal, with the Board setting its own methods of inquiry. However in some circumstances there may be a power to summon witnesses and subpoena documents. However, any investigation by the Board or its committee must not deprive the applicant of natural justice, that is, proper notice of the nature of the complaint, and the opportunity to present an adequate defence (see *Howden v City of Wittlesea* [11.46] (Howden)).

[13.26] It is important to note that the primary intention of disciplinary procedures carried out under registration legislation is neither to punish those involved (the function of criminal law), nor to compensate those harmed (the function of civil law). The primary intention of disciplinary procedures is the protection of the public, and the maintenance of standards within the profession. Disciplinary provisions apply to both registered and enrolled nurses.

Grounds for Suspension or Cancellation of Registration

[13.27] The wording of the legislation varies from State to State, but the following is a guide to those activities which will attract disciplinary action:

- .....suspected mental or physical incapacity;
- .....professional misconduct;
- .....alcohol or drug addiction;
- .....ceasing to hold or having qualifications withdrawn;
- .....conviction for a serious offence;
- .....committing an offence against the registration legislation;
- .....making a false statement for registration;
- .....failing to comply with a lawful requirement of the Board; and
- .....canvassing for the purpose of procuring patients or practice (Australian Capital Territory).

Lack of Mental or Physical Fitness

[13.28] A Board may inquire into the mental or physical fitness of a person to practice. He or she may be suffering from impaired mental or physical health which is considered to be likely to detrimentally affect his or her ability to practice competently. A case considered an applicant's level of fitness, and the requirements for natural justice follows.

CASE

R v Medical Council of Tasmania; Ex parte Blackburn (26 February 1998, SC Tas, No M66/1997) (*Australian Health and Medical Law Reporter* ¶3-920)

The applicant was a 78-year-old doctor who was denied renewal of his practising certificate on the ground of lack of mental fitness to practice. It was alleged that, among other things, he was responsible for inappropriately prescribing anorectic stimulants, benzodiazepines and drugs of abuse. The Medical Council of Tasmania interviewed the applicant, who appeared on his own, and asked him a series of questions about medical practice, providing him with the appropriate answers if he was wrong. He was then asked if he had any questions and he said he did not. The Council produced a report that was unfavourable to him. This report, as well as other documentation was not made available to the applicant, and he was denied an opportunity to make further submissions to the Council. He was sent a letter stating that he was not permitted to renew his registration due to lack of mental incapacity and skill, and told he could appeal to the Supreme Court.

[13.29] The Court held that the applicant was entitled to the exercise of the principles of natural justice. This was denied him by the Council having the documents in their possession without the contents being disclosed to him, and without his being allowed the opportunity to respond or make submissions in relation to them. This resulted in a real risk of prejudice to the applicant. The Court ordered that the Council's decision to refuse renewal of the certificate be quashed.

[13.30] Addiction to, dependence on, or overuse of drugs or alcohol can be a manifestation of lack of capacity to practice.

Unprofessional Conduct or Misconduct

[13.31] These concepts have been named and interpreted in different ways in most jurisdictions. They range from including an unsatisfactory standard of care to culpable behaviour, and are quite extensive in some jurisdictions. To give an idea of the different approaches, an outline of the main features of each jurisdiction for medical practitioners and nurses follows:

New South Wales

[13.32] For medical practitioners, "unsatisfactory professional conduct" includes:

- lack of skill, knowledge, judgment or care;
- contravention of the Act or regulations;
- conviction under specified statutory provisions;
- accepting or offering benefits in relation to referring patients or recommending products, and failing to disclose any pecuniary interests in referring a patient or recommending a product;
- overservicing (providing a service that is "unnecessary, not reasonably required, or excessive");
- being involved in practice by unregistered persons;
- the refusal or failure, without reasonable excuse, to render professional services within a reasonable time to someone requiring urgent attention, or to ensure someone else provides such services; or
- other "improper or unethical conduct" (*Medical Practice Act* 1992 (NSW), s 36).

[13.33] "Professional misconduct" is defined as unsatisfactory professional conduct which is serious enough to justify the removal of the doctor's name from the register (*Medical Practice Act* 1992 (NSW), s 37).

[13.34] For nurses, "unsatisfactory professional conduct" is defined as:

- any conduct that demonstrates a lack of knowledge, experience, skill, judgment or care, or unethical or improper conduct;
- contravention of a provision of the Act or its regulations, or a condition of registration;

- .....holding oneself out as having qualifications other than those for which one is registered;
- .....any other improper or unethical conduct relating to the practice of nursing, including contravention of guidelines approved by the Director-General of Nursing (*Nurses Act* 1991 (NSW), s 4).

[13.35] "Professional misconduct" is the same as for doctors.

Queensland

[13.36] For medical practitioners the legislation defines "misconduct in a professional respect". This includes:

- .....recent drug or alcohol addition;
- .....unauthorised use of a title or false claim to qualifications;
- .....infamous conduct in a professional respect, malpractice or unprofessional conduct or practice;
- .....promoting or allowing an unregistered person to act in a way that endangers another;
- .....advertising or canvassing for clients;
- .....failure to notify police of known criminal activity or attempted criminal activity, or bullet wound or non-accident from a cutting instrument or other weapon by "the most speedy method";
- .....negligence; or
- .....accepting or giving payment for referring patients, or having patients referred to him or her (*Medical Act* 1939 (Qld), s 35).

[13.37] For nurses, the law provides that the Queensland Nursing Council can formulate a code of conduct about nursing practice, the contravention of which may result in action being taken against the nurse (*Nursing Act* 1992 (Qld), s 102).

South Australia

[13.38] For both medical practitioners and nurses the law provides that "unprofessional conduct" includes improper or unethical conduct, incompetence or negligence in relation to practice, contravention of the registration legislation or a condition of registration, and in the case of nurses a code of conduct or professional standard endorsed by the Board. It is of note that both Acts include unprofessional conduct committed before the commencement of the Act or within or outside South Australia or the Commonwealth (*Medical Practitioners Act* 1983 (SA), s 5; *Nurses Act* 1984 (SA), s 3).

Tasmania

[13.39] For both medical practitioners and nurses there is a similar list of actions for which disciplinary action can be taken. These include:

[13.39]
- .....lack of physical or mental capacity or skill to practice, or no longer holds or is entitled to hold a qualification by reason of which he or she was registered;
- .....being guilty of professional misconduct, which includes contravening the registration legislation, a condition of registration, requirement of the Board or a foreign medical law or incompetence, fraud or dishonest behaviour in professional practice. This also includes, for nurses, contravening a provision of the *Nursing Code* (*Medical Practitioners Registration Act* (Tas), s 45; *Nursing Act* 1995 (Tas), s 56).

Victoria

[13.40] For medical practitioners "unprofessional conduct" includes:

- .....professional conduct of a lesser standard than would reasonably be expected of a doctor, or by one's peers or the public, or causing patient care to be compromised;
- .....a finding of guilt of an indictable offence, or other specified offences; or an offence which is likely to affect ability to practice;
- .....professional misconduct or infamous conduct in a professional respect; and
- .....overservicing, that is, providing a service that is "unnecessary, not reasonably required, or excessive" (*Medical Practitioners Act* 1992 (Vic)).

[13.41] For nurses, "unprofessional conduct" includes:

- .....professional conduct of a lesser standard than would reasonably be expected of a registered nurse;
- .....professional misconduct; and
- .....a finding of guilt of an indictable offence, or other specified offences; or an offence which is likely to affect ability to practice (*Nurses Act* 1993 (Vic), s 3).

Western Australia

[13.42] For medical practitioners, the grounds available for striking off or suspending a medical practitioner include:

- ....."infamous or improper conduct";
- .....alcohol dependence or addictions to deleterious drugs;
- .....gross carelessness or incompetence;
- .....contravening conditions or restrictions to practice; or
- .....suffering from physical or mental illness (*Medical Act* 1894 (WA), s 13).

[13.43] Nurses may be suspended from practice or de-registered for:

- .....fraud or misrepresentation in gaining registration;
- .....addiction to, or misuse of, a deleterious drug or alcohol to a degree that renders them unfit to practice; or
- .....suffering from any mental or physical disorder to a degree that renders them unfit to practice.

[13.44] Nurses may also be disciplined for "unethical conduct", which includes carelessness, incompetence, impropriety, misconduct, a breach of the *Nurses Act* 1992 (WA) or non-compliance with any condition or restriction imposed under the Act (*Nurses Act* 1992 (WA), s 61).

Australian Capital Territory

[13.45] For medical practitioners "unsatisfactory professional conduct" includes:

- conduct demonstrating a lack of adequate knowledge, skill, judgment or care;
- breach of the *Medical Practitioners Act* or the *Health Insurance Act* 1973 (Cth) or regulations or a condition of registration;
- permitting an unregistered person to carry out medical procedures requiring professional discretion or skill, holding him or her self out as registered when not;
- advertising or canvassing for clients; or
- improper or unethical conduct relating to the practice of medicine, or conduct that adversely affects the practice of medicine or brings it into disrepute.

[13.46] Like New South Wales, the Australian Capital Territory also lists as unsatisfactory professional conduct the refusal or failure, without reasonable excuse, to render professional services within a reasonable time to someone requiring urgent attention, or to ensure someone else provides such services.

[13.47] It also defines "professional misconduct" as "unsatisfactory professional conduct of a sufficiently serious nature to justify suspension of the practitioner from practising medicine or for the removal of the practitioner's name from the register" (*Medical Practitioner Act* 1930 (ACT), s 35(3)).

[13.48] For nurses, the legislation provides a list of matters which can lead to cancellation or suspension of registration or enrolment. These include:

- contravention of the Act or its regulations, or a condition of registration;
- conviction of an offence punishable for more than one year, or that renders the nurse unfit for practice;
- canvassing for clients;
- habitual drunkenness or addiction to a deleterious drug that renders the nurse unfit to practice;
- engaging in improper or unethical conduct or conduct that adversely affects practising nursing by the person; or
- failure to exercise adequate judgment or care, or being incompetent to practice nursing.

It does not use the concept of "professional misconduct" or an equivalent concept at all. It refers instead to being "unfit to practice nursing" (*Nurses Act* 1988 (ACT), s 61).

Northern Territory

[13.49] The grounds for complaint against medical practitioners include:

- .....fraud or misrepresentation in relation to registration;
- .....conviction of an offence that renders him or her unfit to practice medicine;
- .....mental or physical disability, or addition to liquor or drugs that render him or her unfit to practice (including having been taken into custody under the *Mental Health Act*);
- .....other lack of adequate knowledge, skill, care or judgment in the practice of medicine; or
- ....."any other unprofessional conduct", which includes advertising or procuring clients *(Medical Act* 1995 (NT), s 38).

[13.50] For nurses the law sets out similar grounds on which the Nurses Board may cancel or suspend registration or enrolments of a nurse, and then goes on, interestingly, to provide that "unprofessional conduct" does not include conduct which, "either from its trivial nature or from the surrounding circumstances, should not in the public interest disqualify a person from practising her (sic) profession" (*Nursing Act* 1999 (NT), s 21).

Other Health Care Professions

[13.51] Due to complexity and lack of space, specific provisions of legislation covering other health care professions are not considered in detail here. They are similar in principle and effect to the above, but these health carers are encouraged to review the legislation that covers their profession in their jurisdiction.

Unprofessional Conduct or Misconduct in a Professional Sense

[13.52] As to what constitutes conduct that is considered grave enough for disciplinary action depends so heavily on circumstances and perceived standards of professional conduct, it is considered that the most useful way of determining such conduct is to review some of the cases that have dealt with questionable professional conduct.

Provision of Drugs to Addicts for Cash and other Services

[13.53] A medical practitioner who supplied drugs for cash, Medicare payments and on one occasion for sexual favours was found guilty of misconduct in a professional respect, and had his name removed from the register by the New South Wales Medical Tribunal. The Tribunal found that he was suffering from a bipolar disorder but not to the extent that it affected his judgment. The doctor appealed to the Court of Appeal claiming, among other things, that his psychiatric condition affected his behaviour and it thus did not amount to professional misconduct. The Court held that his psychiatric condition and its effect on his behaviour was a matter for the Medical Tribunal to determine and not subject to review (*Kirumba v Walton* (4 October 1990, CA NSW) (see *Australian Health and Medical Law Reporter* ¶4-005.40)).

Surgery Carried out in Non-Orthodox Fashion

[13.54] Surgery carried out in non-orthodox fashion has had different reactions according to its acceptance by the medical profession.

▌▌▌ CASE
Ex parte Meehan; Re Medical Practitioners Act [1965] NSWR 30 (SC)

A doctor carried out major elective surgery without the presence of another practitioner to assist with surgical procedures or to administer anaesthetics. No harm occurred to the patients, but his behaviour was found to be misconduct and he was suspended for 12 months. He appealed to the New South Wales Court of Appeal.

[13.55] The Court of Appeal decided that the doctor had been ill-advised but neither reckless or indifferent to the patient's welfare. The Court reduced the suspension to a reprimand, because it was convinced the doctor would not repeat the conduct. It agreed that this behaviour was, however, misconduct:

> the only generalisation as to the meaning . . . of 'infamous conduct in any professional respect' [the wording of the relevant legislation] which can be attempted as capable of application to the varying situations which may arise, is that it refers to conduct which, being sufficiently related to the pursuit of the profession, is such as would reasonably incur the strong reprobation of professional brethren of good repute and competence [at 35, per Sugarman J].

[13.56] However, it was held more recently that a doctor who carried out a non-urgent appendicectomy in a day surgery where there was no proper operating table, no operating theatre lights or recovery room was not guilty of professional misconduct, as there was a small but respectable minority view that such operations are acceptable (*Qidwai v Brown* [1984] 1 NSWLR 100).

[13.57] In *Medical Board of Queensland v Bayliss* (6 & 8 February 1995, Queensland Medical Assessment Tribunal, No 10 of 1995), a doctor was found guilty of misconduct in a professional respect for failing to provide oxygen and a pulse oximeter and proper monitoring (including no recovery staff) in a clinic where general anaesthetics were administered. It was found that a patient fell into a coma and subsequent persistent vegetative state as a result of this.

Intimate Relations with Clients or Past Clients

[13.58] The following cases deal with intimate relations between practitioners and patients or ex-patients.

CASE
Childs v Walton (13 November 1990, CA NSW)

A psychiatrist engaged in sexual relationships with two former patients. She also disclosed confidential information to one of them. Her name was removed from the register by the New South Wales Medical Board and she appealed to the Court of Appeal, arguing that as the men were former patients, there was no misconduct "in the practice of medicine" as required by the legislation.

[13.59] The Court of Appeal held that the words "in the practice of medicine" does not describe the time at which the conduct occurs, but rather the nature of the conduct.

CASE
Jacobsen v Nurses Tribunal and Anor (3 October 1997, SC NSW, No BC9705032)

J, a registered mental health nurse and member of the Hunter Area Health Service's Rehabilitation Scheme, became the case manager of ZD, a woman variously diagnosed as schizophrenic, and manic depressive, and a client of the Residential Rehabilitation Team with which he worked. ZD's marriage had broken down and her five children were living with their father. She was anxious to have them move back with her, and, as J had space in his house, it was decided that ZD and two of her children would move into it as boarders, and he would cease to be her case manager. At this time it was found that J had no intention of having a personal relationship with her, but rather that he had a financial interest in her moving in and paying reasonable rent. It was also considered of benefit to her to have her children with her. ZD moved in about three weeks after another person was appointed case manager. J arranged for a new case manager without explanation and no reference was made to the fact that ZD's address was to be the same as J's. Some time afterwards, J's superiors in the Area Health Service expressed their opinion that it was inappropriate that ZD remain in the premises, and several months after moving in ZD, who was no longer a client of the Residential Rehabilitation Team, left the house. Three months later, after frequent contact, J and ZD commenced a sexual relationship which lasted seven months.

The Tribunal found the plaintiff guilty of unsatisfactory professional conduct because:
- .....he invited or permitted ZD to reside in his home and subsequently engaged in an intimate relationship with her without adequate termination of the professional relationship between them; and
- .....he ended a formal professional relationship with a patient when about to be engaged in a personal relationship, demonstrating a lack of adequate knowledge in the practice of nursing.

The Tribunal held that forming a close personal, emotional and later sexual relationship with a patient against the advice of his colleagues and superiors was of a particularly serious nature, offended against the foundations of the nurse/patient relationship and amounted to professional misconduct.

J appealed to the Supreme Court on procedural matters, on the basis that no, or inadequate, reasons were given for the finding and that the penalty was excessive.

[13.60] The Court found J was aware that ZD was suffering various mental disorders which rendered her vulnerable and troubled and liable to be exploited and hurt. J fostered the relationship, and the transfer of her case to another case manager did not effectively terminate his power and influence over her. He still had all the confidential information he had gained about her case, and it was implicit that he would still assist in, and be at least partly involved in, her care and rehabilitation. The Court found it immaterial that ZD was no longer a client of the Health Service: if she became ill again, she could again become a client. The Court concluded that the conduct was of a particularly serious nature and "offended against the foundations of the nurse/patient relationship". This was of itself enough to take it out of the category of "unsatisfactory professional conduct" into that of "professional misconduct". However, given J's excellent record, his lack of intent to do harm, and lack of adequate advice and supervision, the Court reduced the period of removal of his name from the Register for six rather than 12 months.

[13.61] The Court several times emphasised the point that the Tribunal's role is primarily protection of the public, not one of punishment. It also confirmed the principle that, whilst the practitioner is entitled to have allegations against him or her specifically identified in dealing with professional conduct, individual charges do not have to be made out specifically in the same way as they do in criminal law: a person may be charged with a course of conduct in the carrying out of a course of practice, so long as the separate allegations on which the charge against him or her is based are specifically identified.

Failure to Properly Assess and Treat Injuries to Child

▌▌▌ CASE
Medical Board of South Australia v Christpoulos (2000) SADC 47
(*Australian Health and Medical Law Reporter* ¶4-020.41)

A mother called the locum doctor when she noticed her child had red and bruised penis when changing his nappy, thinking he may have been bitten by a spider or some other creature. The defendant attended at her residence, and the mother alleged he looked at the naked child, said that his penis was bruised, said it looked as if the child had been hit, pinched or punched, prescribed panadol and left a few minutes later. Several days later the child was admitted to hospital unconscious, with bruises to the head, bilateral corneal abrasions and bruises around and to the penis. He died of cerebral anoxia. A man was later convicted of manslaughter in relation to the death.

In later investigations, the doctor told police the child was naked at the time of examination, and had a small bruise of one centimetre to the thigh only. He also stated that he could not find his consultation notes, which were normally stored in the boot of his car, or removed to his parents' garage.

When the Board was dealing with his matter 12 months later, the doctor "corrected" his initial statement, saying that the child was wearing a nappy at the time of examination and he did not remove it, or examine the child's groin or testicles, and that nothing would have warranted suspecting child abuse (however he later admitted he could not dispute the mother's account of events).

The doctor was charged with:

1)......knowingly making inconsistent, false and misleading statements;
2)......failing to carry out a proper examination of the child;
3)......failing to keep proper notes;
4)......failing to consider non-accidental injury and make further enquiries; and
5)......failing to report suspected child abuse to authorities, as required by South Australian legislation (see Ch 16).

[13.62] The Medical Practitioners Professional Conduct Tribunal found that, in respect of (1), the practitioner did not intentionally mislead the Tribunal in his revised statement. As he did not have his notes when he gave his statement to the police or later when he revised it, he rationalised the situation when he found out about the severity of the later injuries, and constructed a reason as to why he missed seeing the gross injuries to the child's penile area. However, his approach to presenting as unqualified fact what was in reality supposition was careless, and he should have been more sure of the accuracy of what he was reporting. His actions were improper and unethical.

As to the charges (2) to (5), the doctor was also guilty of unprofessional conduct. His examination of the child was perfunctory and below the standard expected of a medical practitioner. Given that, according to the mother, he recognised that the child had been assaulted, he should have made further enquiries and considered reporting the matter to authorities as required by law.

All Circumstances must be Taken into Account

[13.63] In determining whether conduct warrants disciplinary action, all the circumstances of the case must be taken into account.

▌▌▌ CASE   [13.63]
Heathcote v New South Wales Nurses Board (unreported, 12 April 1991, Dist Ct NSW)

On the night of 24 June 1987, at 2.10 am, a patient was brought to Wilcannia Hospital by his relatives. He was described as being "in the dings", a colloquial term meaning suffering from alcohol withdrawal. He was hallucinating, but as he had no signs of tremor, vomiting, or sweating, or feeling hot or cold, nor was he complaining of any head or chest pain, the charge nurse, Nurse Heathcote decided he was not seriously ill. She checked his history and found he had previously been admitted for alcohol withdrawal.

The patient, confused and vague, wandered around the premises and disappeared temporarily, returning with wood to boil the billy for tea. Nurse Heathcote had rung the police because she feared for the patient's well-being when he disappeared. He disappeared a second time, and so Nurse Heathcote rang the Director of Nursing at her home and told her about her concerns for the patient's safety. The Director of Nursing agreed with her contacting the police.

The police arrived soon after with the patient in their "paddy wagon", and in their presence Nurse Heathcote rang the medical officer of the Royal Flying Doctor Service at Broken Hill and discussed the situation with him. She stated her concern that she could not ensure the safety of the patient in his present condition, as she had no adequate means of restraining him. She explained his condition and suggested he remain in police custody overnight. The doctor agreed, saying that the only other thing she should do "before he heads off to the police station is just do his sugar . . . And wish him well as he goes away".

After a blood sugar test, which was normal, was carried out, Nurse Heathcote arranged with the police that they should let her know how the patient settled at the Police Station. She undertook to call in at 8.30 am to take his blood pressure. At 3 am the police reported that the patient was "sleeping", but at 8.30 am when she called at the Station, they informed her that he was dead, having hung himself.

Subsequently, a complaint was made to the New South Wales Nurses Registration Board under section 19 of the *Nurses Registration Act* 1953 (NSW) which was then in force. Nurse Heathcote was found guilty of misconduct by the Board, which suspended her registration for one year. Specifically, it alleged that she had:

1)..... failed to follow the Hospital Manual, which required staff to "obtain all relevant facts about a patient before calling the doctor";
2)..... failed to take and record basic observations;
3)..... failed to consult the patient's history and inform the doctor of it;
4)..... failed to obtain a proper history from the patient and his friends;
5)..... failed to tell the doctor her diagnosis or the results of her observations;
6)..... gave the patient over to police, and failed to consider alternative action;
7)..... failed to consider the suitability of police custody and to advise them of necessary precautions and observations; and
8)..... failed to ask police to stay at the hospital for carrying out of (1), (2) and (3).

She appealed to the District Court as provided by the former Act, arguing that under the circumstances she had acted ethically and with all due care.

[13.64] **[13.64]** The District Court overturned the finding of the Board, thus exonerating the nurse's care of the patient. Ward J in his judgment stated that conduct cannot always be assessed in abstract terms and by consideration of text book or teaching utterances. It must be considered in the light of the circumstances existing at the time, including available facilities, misunderstandings, and "aberrant human behaviour". He went on to say that the question to which the Board must address itself is, "does the conduct of the nurse incur the strong reprobation of professional peers of good repute and competence?"

[13.65] The Court held that Nurse Heathcote did make a proper systematic assessment within the limits of what was available to her in terms of co-operation by the patient, the amount of time available to her, and within the scale of priorities she faced at the time. She was trying, by observation to find the cause of the patient's condition and was faced with some difficulty as he was "wandering uncontrollably". She did make and record adequate observations under the circumstances. She was faced with a novel situation, did not know what to do, and sought assistance from the Director of Nursing and the doctor.

[13.66] The Court further held that Nurse Heathcote did read the history and inform the doctor of it. No further information had been sought by the doctor. Also there was strong argument before the Court that medical diagnosis is not part of a nurses' practice. Nurse Heathcote did state her opinion that the patient was "in the dings", and the doctor did not indicate that he did not understand that expression. However the doctor was not entitled to rely on her diagnosis. One witness did suggest that Nurse Heathcote should have insisted on either the doctor coming to see the patient or his being sent to another hospital with better facilities. The Court nevertheless decided that "It is not sufficient for some peers merely to express criticisms of judgments when other judgments are properly open in the circumstances" and relied on the fact that "there was a strong body of opinion that none of her conduct was such as to incur the strong reprobation of her professional peers of good repute and competence".

[13.67] Ward J went on to say Nurse Heathcote did not have a duty to determine the suitability of the police custody and noted that she did ask the police to report to her, and arranged to check on the patient in the morning. Finally, he held that there was no obligation to consider alternative treatment, as the doctor had directed she "only" test the patient's blood and "wish him well as he goes away".

[13.68] It would appear that there can be problems when disciplinary provisions are very general and quite vague. They depend on past court decisions, and therefore do not give clear directions to health carers. They may not consider the particular nature of the health carer's role, and the fact that they, unlike other professionals, may be employees of hospitals, working under the direction of others, as well as exercising their own judgment in some matters, and thus may face a conflict of responsibilities. However, Ward J pointed out (at 21) of the decision, it is also necessary to take into account the fact that:

> conduct cannot be always assessed in the abstract. It must be evaluated in the light of the exigencies existing due to factors which so often include

aberrant human behaviour, insufficient facilities and misunderstandings [13.70] due to language use. It is important the Board directs its attention in relation to consideration of professional misconduct to the question—does the conduct of the nurse incur the strong reprobation of professional peers of good repute and competence?—and that it recognises that what may appear initially to be misconduct will not necessarily be deemed so, if it is considered to be acceptable by a reputable minority view. The test is not met by merely finding contentious areas of criticism, often founded on abstract conceptions without consideration of existing unusual circumstances.

Meaning of "in the Practice of Medicine, Nursing", etc

[13.69] Sometimes the question arises as to whether actions complained of took place in the practice of the professional's practice.

CASE
Kahler v Nurses Registration Board and Anor (21 February 1995, SC NSW, BC9504318)

K was a registered nurse administrator and supervisor of a hostel complex for ex-service personnel. A resident of the hostel, Mr G, who suffered from dementia, had been authorised for transferral from the hostel to a nursing home in the complex after his condition deteriorated and he was recognised as requiring the more specialised and intensive nursing care available at the nursing home. K failed to arrange for the transferral for several months. As a result Mr G did not receive necessary care, and on admission to the home was found to be in a serious condition, suffering from dehydration and multiple bedsores and lesions resulting from lack of proper care and treatment. The Nurses Tribunal directed that K's name be removed from the Register, finding that she failed to arrange for Mr G to be transferred to the nursing home after approval had been granted, and when Mr G's condition deteriorated over a period of over two months, she failed to ensure that he receive proper nursing care. These failures, the Tribunal said were serious and fundamental in nature and deprived Mr G of a reasonable quality of life during the last months of his life. K appealed from this finding to the Supreme Court, arguing, among other things, that her actions were not part of the practice of nursing, but rather as an administrator of the hostel.

[13.70] The Court considered the phrase "in the practice of nursing" as it appears in the legislation. It considered, and approved, of the ruling in the case of *Childs v Walton* (see [13.58]), which determined the meaning of "in the practice of medicine" and held that the phrase does not have a temporal meaning but rather a qualitative or descriptive character. It does not limit the period during which the questionable conduct must occur if it is to be capable of satisfying the description, but rather describes its nature. Thus it need not occur while the relationship of health care practitioner and client exists. It may occur at any time, and need not be conduct which occurs in the course of treating a patient. Further, the court held, the actions of a registered nurse performing only the narrow

[13.70] functions of an administrator of a combined hostel and nursing home complex could fall within the meaning of the term. However, in this case such considerations were not necessary, as K was directly involved in the day-to-day nursing care of Mr G, which removed her from the category of being only an administrator at the relevant times.

[13.71] The following case is dealt with in some detail, because it deals with the nexus between activities that are related to professional practice and those that are not. It is also relevant to all professional health carers subject to similar legislative provisions, which apply in the majority of jurisdictions.

CASE
Yelds v Nurses Tribunal & Ors [2000] NSWSC 755 (2 August 2000) (SC NSW)

The Health Care Complaints Commission lodged a complaint with the Nurses Tribunal that over a period of about six months a male nurse engaged in conduct that demonstrated a lack of adequate judgment and care in the practice of nursing and/or engaged in improper or unethical conduct relating to the practice of nursing. The nurse was employed as a counsellor at a drug and alcohol counselling centre, having no nursing duties to perform there the relevant complaints were that:

1).....He falsely informed a client, Ms MF, that he was a psychologist during a professional consultation.
2).....He conducted counselling sessions at the centre with Ms MF in an inappropriate intimate manner and inappropriately suggested that she engage in conduct of a sexual nature with him.
3).....He engaged in social contact with Ms MF outside of formal counselling such as conversing on personal and sexual matters, providing her with personal contact details and attending her home.
4).....He maintained a sexual relationship with Ms MF for a period of approximately three months.
5).....He invited Ms MF to Network 21 meetings and encouraged and permitted her to purchase an Amway's business pack with himself and his wife as her sponsor.

The Tribunal found that the complaint was established to its "comfortable satisfaction" (see *Briginshaw v Briginshaw* (1938) 60 CLR 336 at 361). The Tribunal made findings adversely to the appellant to the effect of complaints 1, 4 and 5 and the general opening words of paragraphs 2 and 3 of the complaints. It held that whilst the behaviour of the appellant did not occur "in the course of nursing" itself, but that it demonstrated inadequate knowledge and judgment that reflected on the nurse's ability to practice nursing, and involved conduct related to the practice of nursing. It held that the nurse was guilty of unsatisfactory professional practice in relation to counts 1 to 4, and of professional misconduct in relation to count 5. The nurse appealed, arguing that even if the alleged behaviour was proven and reprehensible, it did not reflect or reveal a specified defect so far as the appellant's ability to practice as a nurse is concerned, for the simple reason that he had not been employed and was not working as a nurse, but as a counsellor with very limited functions.

[13.72] The court found that the nurse "certainly was not acting as a nurse, let alone a mental health nurse" (at 498). It upheld the appeal, not on the basis that the behaviour was not unethical or unprofessional, but because the Tribunal did not adequately consider whether the nurse's actions fulfilled the requirements of the *Nurses Act* 1991 (NSW) to constitute professional misconduct or unsatisfactory professional conduct. Under section 4(2)(a) this includes conduct demonstrating a lack of adequate knowledge, experience, skill, judgment or care *in the practice of nursing*, and under section 4(2)(e) of the Act, "any other improper or unethical conduct *relating to the practice of nursing*" (emphasis added).

[13.76]

Section 4(2)(a): Conduct Demonstrating Inadequate Knowledge, etc

[13.73] Adams J, the judge in the case, held that under the Act, "professional misconduct" necessarily adopts as its starting point a finding of "unsatisfactory professional conduct". It is essential to a finding of professional misconduct or unsatisfactory conduct that the conduct occur in, or be related to, nursing. It must demonstrate a lack or insufficiency of the specified qualities of the kind necessary for the practice of nursing in a real and significant way. However the conduct need not occur in the *course* of nursing to satisfy the requirements of section 4(2)(a): it is both necessary and sufficient if it demonstrates a lack or insufficiency of the specified qualities of a kind necessary for the practice of nursing.

[13.74] The judge referred to *Childs v Walton* (above, see [13.58]) in holding that the phrase "in the practice of medicine" does not have a temporal meaning, but rather a qualitative or descriptive character, and *Jacobsen v Nurses Tribunal & Anor* (above, see [13.59]), in deciding that the nurse's position, was one of power and influence that promoted his personal, private and economic interests.

[13.75] Conduct, for the purposes of section 4(2)(a) need not be conduct as a nurse: the provision refers to "*any* conduct" (emphasis added). The issue is whether it demonstrates any of the specified defects relevant to his being a nurse. The fact that impugned conduct occurs when a nurse is undertaking nursing care of a patient strengthens the link between the conduct and the practice of nursing.

[13.76] The judge found that the alleged exploitation of the centre's client in this case might reasonably have been regarded by the Tribunal as betraying such an attitude to appropriate professional responsibilities and was itself so inappropriate as to demonstrate, at least, a lack of adequate judgment or care within the meaning of section 4(2)(a)(iv) or (v) of the Act.

> It was the fact that the appellant's alleged conduct concerned a relationship with a client or patient of his, rather than the particular responsibilities of a counsellor compared with those of a nurse . . . allowing "power and influence" over her, which was capable of providing a sufficient nexus between what he did at the Centre and the practice of nursing to satisfy the requirements of s 4(2)(a) of the Act. However, this

[13.76] line of reasoning, which required an analysis of both the requirements of general nursing and the duties actually performed by the appellant to demonstrate this nexus, was not adopted by the Tribunal [at 500].

Section 4(2)(e): Improper or Unethical Conduct

[13.77] The alleged sexual conduct was improper or unethical only because of the relationship between the appellant and the client through his employment at the centre as a counsellor. It was, therefore, capable of falling within section 4(2)(e) of the Act, providing the character of the employment and his professional relationship with the client showed that this sort of conduct, in the circumstances, was related to his ability as a nurse.

[13.78] The alleged pretence by the appellant that he was a psychologist was found to be both unethical and improper in the circumstances could relate to nursing. This also was, a question of fact.

[13.79] The basis of the alleged misconduct in respect of the client's involvement with Amway was that the nurse would benefit financially from it. Such activity is on the face of it quite legal, and the Tribunal did not explain why this conduct amounted to professional misconduct. This was simply assumed. However, the judge found that taking financial advantage of the client which involved no deceit or dishonesty, does not, necessarily demonstrate any of the specified defects in section 4(2)(a), nor would it, considered in isolation and provided there was no abuse of trust, constitute improper or unethical conduct relating to the practice of nursing. The necessary relationship between the alleged misconduct and the practice of nursing for the purposes of section 4(2)(e) is demonstrated "where the misconduct shows attitudes or characteristics inconsistent with the moral qualities fairly required of a person undertaking the responsibilities of nursing" (at 501).

[13.80] The judge concluded that the conduct taken as a whole, was unethical and reflected on the appellant's suitability to be entrusted with the work of a nurse. If it amounted to unsatisfactory professional conduct depended on the "aptness of the analogy between the responsibilities of a counsellor and those of a nurse". This essential link was not discussed at all in the Tribunal's reasons, though it referred extensively to the incidents of mental health nursing. Instead, the case was conducted on the basis that the questioned behaviour, if established of itself amounted to unsatisfactory professional conduct.

Meaning of "Infamous Conduct in a Professional Respect"

[13.81] The meaning of "infamous conduct in a professional respect" was considered in the following case.

▮▮▮ CASE [13.83]
Jemielita v Medical Board of Western Australia (Supreme Court of Western Australia No 1106 of 1992) (*Australian Health and Medical Law Reporter* ¶77-063)

A total of 16 matters formed the basis of a complaint to the Medical Board of Western Australia in relation to a rural general practitioner. The Board found the doctor had been careless, incompetent or guilty of misconduct on six occasions, and removed his name from the register. On these occasions the doctor had:

1) ..... severed the left lateral popliteal nerve during an operation to strip and ligate varicose veins. This resulted in the patient suffering foot drop. The appellant had carried out an inadequate neurological examination of the patient, noting the foot drop, but failing to associate it with nerve damage;
2) ..... inappropriately applied a vacuum extractor to a baby's left buttock during its delivery;
3) ..... applied sponge-holding forceps to the scalp of another baby during its delivery, causing abrasions and injury;
4) ..... failed to use sufficient anaesthetic when suturing cervical lacerations following delivery of a child and in so doing exhibited indifference to the patient's pain and suffering; and
5) & 6) ..... falsely claimed medical benefits for carrying out a modified radical mastectomy on two patients (which would have major surgery under general anaesthetic) when he had in fact carried out a modified simple mastectomy in both cases (which required local anaesthetic), thus making him eligible for a lower rate of payment than that for which he claimed.

The doctor appealed to the Supreme Court of Western Australia. He claimed that the Board's decision to remove his name from the register was a grossly excessive penalty not warranted on the evidence. He argued that as he was a rural general practitioner, the Medical Board had erred in requiring a standard to be expected of a specialist and/or highly skilled medical practitioner who practised in the city. He claimed that as he had in fact provided a service to the mastectomy patients, and the difference in the fee for the service was small, he should not be held to be guilty of professional misconduct in respect of those cases.

[13.82] The Court considered the case of *Bolam v Friern Hospital Management Committee* [1957] 1 WLR 582 (see [6.67]) in coming to its decision that:

▮ ..... urban and rural medical practitioners owe the same standard of care to their patients;
▮ ..... a general practitioner does not owe the same standard care as a specialist, as a general practitioner is not required to possess the same level of skill as a specialist; and
▮ ..... thus the doctor, as a rural general practitioner who at times carries out surgical and obstetric procedures, is required to have the same level of skill required of all general practitioners who also occasionally carry out surgical procedures and obstetrics.

[13.83] The Court agreed that the actions of the doctor did not warrant the removal of his name from the register, but ordered that he be

[13.83] suspended from practice or reprimanded, according to the nature of each incident. It found, in relation to (1), that the severance of the nerve was grossly careless and demonstrated incompetence, but that the failure to diagnose the patient's permanent nerve damage could not be said to amount to serious neglect of the patient's welfare. The failure of the appellant to acknowledge that the nerve had been severed despite the evidence of three surgeons who identified the divided nerves during a later operation, caused the Court concern. It ordered suspension for nine months for this incident. In relation to incidents (2) and (3)—the use of the vacuum extractor and the forceps on the babies—the Court found that the former action was inappropriate and the latter unwise. No one had suffered serious or permanent harm, but the incidents showed impatience and poor judgment in the doctor's management of labour, and thus brought his competency in this area of practice into doubt. He was suspended for nine months for these incidents. In relation to incident (4), the Court acknowledged that the situation was a medical emergency, and the appellant was motivated by the need to stop the cervical bleeding. Whilst not ignoring the patient's pain and suffering, the Court held that a reprimand was an adequate response to this incident. The Court held that the false claims of incidents (5) and (6) amounted to infamous conduct in a professional respect, despite the fact that the sums involved were small. It suspended his registration for 12 months for each of these incidents.

[13.84] Once the period of suspension expired, the doctor would be required to adhere to conditions of practice set down by the Board.

Meaning of "Incompetence" and "Recklessness"

[13.85] Whilst the different jurisdictions use terms differently, a helpful approach to determining what constitutes incompetence and recklessness was offered in the following case.

CASE
Boerema v Medical Board of Western Australia (10, 19 June 1998, SC WA, BC9802646)

Mr B was struck from the register for his treatment (or lack of it) of two patients.

Mr D: The first incident was his post-operative care of a Mr D, who had a reversal of a colostomy, after complications. Shortly after surgery, poor fluid output was noted, and considered of concern. The next morning nursing notes showed that Dr B was paged because Mr D's abdomen was "grossly distended from pubis to sternum". Mr B withdrew the naso-gastric tube six inches, ordered physiotherapy and for the distension to be observed. Meantime, fluid flowed freely into the Yates inter-peritoneal drain. On the evening of the second post-surgery day Mr B was contacted by nursing staff and informed that Mr D had a hard and distended abdomen, fluid sounds in the abdomen and dark green fluid and air passing into the Yates drain bag. Mr B said he would visit the following day. The Board was told in a specialist report that these facts, plus eight recorded incidents of vomiting, a nasogastric drainage of 3,439 mls during the day, a raised white blood cell count and albuminuria presented an indication of intestinal fistula and a life-threatening

condition within 48 hours of surgery. At this stage he required urgent corrective [13.87]
surgery. Instead no management plan was put in place for Mr D. On the fifth day
after surgery, Dr B saw Mr D and noted that he was "better". He order free fluids by
mouth and removal of the Yates drain (considered at the coroner's inquest to be
the two worst procedures that could have been taken). Seven days after surgery, a
nurse questioned Dr B on the possibility of septic shock and the need for more
active treatment, and was told that if operated on, Mr D would not survive.
A second opinion was sought on Mr D's treatment on the eighth day post surgery.
Removal to Royal Perth Hospital for observation and possible laparotomy was
recommended by a consulting surgeon who provided the opinion. This was
agreed to and Mr D arrived at Perth Hospital in a state of shock. He underwent an
emergency laparotomy, at which copious faecal stained peritoneal fluid was found
throughout the abdominal cavity, leaking from a portion of the bowel
re-anastomosis. Mr D's condition deteriorated and he died five days later from
multi-organ failure and peritonitis following a carcinoma of the colon.

Mrs W: Mrs W underwent surgery for the removal of varicose veins in her leg.
Instead of removing the long saphenous vein, as intended, the femoral artery was
removed, resulting in serious injury to the leg, with the prospect of amputation.
Expert evidence to the Board was that recognition of the femoral artery is an
integral step in the performance of such surgery and there is a clear difference
between the pulsating artery and a saphenous vein. The error was not noticed
either during or at the end of the operation. It concluded that a competent surgeon
exercising reasonable skill and diligence would not have made this mistake.

The Board's finding: The Board considered Mr B's long and distinguished surgical
practice. It also took into account the fact that he conceded that his actions
demonstrated incompetent and negligent professional conduct, and that he had
elected to cease practising surgery. He did wish to continue limited non-surgical
practice and consultancy. He demonstrated that circumstances at the time placed
him under extraordinary stress and that this may have been the cause of his less
than acceptable care. However, the Board held that its primary consideration is the
public interest, and not to punish those before it (see *Jemielita v Medical Board of
Western Australia* at [13.81]). It found Mr B guilty of both gross carelessness or
incompetence. Instead of deregistration, it ordered that he be of good behaviour
for five years, refrain from surgical, procedural or medicolegal practice, and only
carry out professional activities permitted by the Board. Mr B appealed to the
Supreme Court, arguing that the restrictions were excessive.

[13.86] The Supreme Court upheld the Board's ruling. It considered
Jemielita's case and confirmed that incompetence involves unfitness to
practise the particular field of medicine which is under examination, or an
ability to perform the techniques or reach the judgments required for
proper practice in that field. On the other hand, gross carelessness
involves unacceptable conduct without any intentional wrongdoing on
the part of the practitioner, suggesting also that the practitioner is unable
to give the care required or is indifferent to the need for such care despite
having the intellectual and technical ability to supply the care required
(which may not be present in relation to incompetence).

[13.87] The Court concluded that although there was no lack of care
towards Mr D, there were elements of gross carelessness or incompetence

[13.87] on the part of Mr B. In respect of Mrs W, there was no doubt that his conduct was grossly careless or incompetent. Merely ceasing to operate would not protect the public from any error of judgment he might make in some subsequent mode of practice if he were to be again subject to stress. If such practice were to be limited to such an extent that it is of minimal financial benefit to Mr B, that is a "necessary incident of his name remaining on the Register of medical practitioners".

Unsatisfactory Behaviour must be Related to Professional Practice

[13.88] One must also distinguish between conduct which may be improper and reprehensible in a general sense, and that which is improper and reprehensible in a professional sense.

[13.89] Readers might like to consider the situation of nurses in this case. There was evidence that on several occasions concern was expressed in relation to Mr D's treatment. Should they have taken further action to have his treatment reviewed? In what circumstances could they be held liable for not doing so?

CASE
Hoile v Medical Board of South Australia (1960) 104 CLR 157 (High Court of Australia)

A doctor had formed and pursued a sexual relationship with a nurse in the hospital. He was the medical superintendent of the hospital, and sexual activity occurred on hospital premises while the woman was on duty and on at least one occasion she was the only nurse on duty. This was held by the Medical Board to be misconduct. The doctor appealed to the High Court.

[13.90] The Court held:

> [not all] departures on the part of a medical practitioner from the standards of moral conduct amount to misconduct in a professional respect. But if his professional relationships are the occasion or source of the misconduct and it is sufficiently serious it may be deemed by the Medical Board to be infamous conduct in a professional respect [at 163].

[13.91] In this case the activity was held to be professional misconduct for:

> However much the general moral aspect of the matter may be emphasised as going to the relationship between man and woman, it remains true that the place was the hospital, the woman was a nurse, the man a doctor and moreover superintendent of the hospital [at 163].

[13.92] A recent case which set out some general guidelines regarding the nature of misconduct is *Pillai v Messiter (No 2)* (1989) 16 NSWLR 197, the facts of which are set out in [8.24], [8.51]. In that case the court (per Kirby P) made the following points:

▌..... The purpose of discipline is protection of the public from not only "delinquents [13.94] and wrong-doers within professions" but also "seriously incompetent professional people" who are "ignorant of basic rules or indifferent as to rudimentary professional requirements" (at 201).

▌..... Something more than professional incompetence or deficiencies in practice is required:
It includes a deliberate departure from accepted standards or such serious negligence as, although not deliberate, to portray indifference and an abuse of the privileges which accompany registration as a medical practitioner [at 200].

[13.93] The court also considered the effect of removal of the appellant from the register, considering whether this would achieve the objective of protecting the public. It decided it would not where, as in that case, the event was an isolated, unintended error, which could not have been prevented by removal of the doctor from registration. Also, in that case, others had failed to notice the mistake, making the punishment of one person inappropriate.

▌▌▌ CASE
Versteegh v Nurses Board of South Australia (4 December 1992, SC SA) (*Australian Health and Medical Law Reporter* ¶77-064)

The nurse who worked at a nursing home faced charges in relation to:

1) ..... *drugs* (failing to give residents drugs as prescribed, failing to check, count and record as required by law, discarding a bottle that contained methadone tablets, and failing to record administration of drugs);
2) ..... *breach of confidentiality* (requesting a medical practitioner other than the resident's own practitioner to review the resident's leg ulcer without seeking the resident's consent or authority from her doctor); and
3) ..... *unsatisfactory nursing care* (not permitting a patient with multiple sclerosis to be seated when being washed, causing pain and suffering).

The nurse was found guilty of professional misconduct under section 41 of the *Nurses Act* 1984 (SA). She was reprimanded by the Registration Board, and certain conditions placed on her right to provide nursing care. The Board had referred to its own guidelines, the policy of the nursing home where she worked, legislation on drugs and the International Council of Nursing Code of Ethics.

The nurse appealed to the Supreme Court arguing, among other things, that she had not fallen short of the required standard. She argued that in respect of (1), she had rather made a simple mistake in some circumstances, and in others had failed to make necessary entries because she had been very busy. In respect of (2), she argued that she had only been trying to act in the patient's best interests, and in respect of (3), she had acted in the most suitable way in the circumstances.

[13.94] The Court held that the failure to give drugs when they were prescribed and to make accurate records of drug administration was likely to compromise the care of the residents significantly. It noted the importance of checking drugs to ensure none are missing (see above, Chapter 8 on legislative provisions relating to the administration of drugs). It also found that the nurse had breached confidentiality by calling

[13.94] in another doctor. She could not say she was acting in the resident's interest, it concluded, for if she was, she would have discussed the matter with the resident's practitioner (and one might add the resident) first. Finally, her conduct with the resident suffering from multiple sclerosis could not be excused on the basis that she had acted according to her own judgment (as presumably her judgment should have led her to treat the resident differently). The Court held that "unprofessional conduct" has a broader meaning than common law negligence and is not limited to "disgraceful or dishonourable" conduct. Rather it is conduct which falls short of that followed and approved of by other members of the nursing profession.

Intention of Practitioner

[13.95] Two cases which involved what was considered serious misconduct, but which attracted different responses by the respective Medical Boards give insight into the legal approach to the intention of the practitioner involved.

CASE
Ex parte Fitzgerald; Re New South Wales Medical Board (1945) 46 SR (NSW) 111 (SC)

A practitioner issued a certificate under the *Lunacy Act* 1898 (NSW) in circumstances the Board found to be "gravely and inexcusably wrong". He had not examined the person for whom the certificate was written. The doctor was suspended for 12 months. He appealed to the Supreme Court.

[13.96] The Court, while accepting the gravity of the behaviour, nevertheless allowed the doctor to retain his practising certificate. Jordan CJ said that this case was exceptional, and indicated that the Court would consider:

- ..... the general depravity or lack of scruple on the part of the doctor; or
- ..... the likelihood of repetition of the behaviour.

CASE
Stevenson v Medical Board of Victoria (unreported, 27 June 1986, SC Vic) (cited in Dix et al (1988), p 40)

A doctor dealing with home births diagnosed pre-eclampsia but "deliberately prescribed a course of treatment which he knew was unorthodox and contrary to long-accepted medical opinion and practice, and he thereby, and knowingly, put at serious risk both the mother and the foetus".

[13.97] The court found against the doctor because he acted on beliefs which had no reasonable scientific foundation, which had been given no scientific credence, and which, the court held, he must have known were likely to endanger the mother and child irrespective of the correctness of his beliefs. One should not act on beliefs that: [13.100]

■.....have no established scientific foundation;
■.....are not accepted by one's profession; *and*
■.....would put another person in danger,

even if one believes one is right.

[13.98] Readers may wish to note the different dates of these cases, and to consider whether:

1).....the facts in the case of *Fitzgerald* fit into the criteria mentioned above; and
2)..... *Fitzgerald* would be decided differently today.

■ ■ ■ **CASE**

Cranley v Medical Board of Western Australia (21 December 1990, SC WA) (*Australian Health and Medical Law Reporter* (1991) ¶77.036)

A doctor had been charged with infamous behaviour in a professional respect under the *Medical Act* 1984 (WA). He had adopted the "harm reduction" approach to drug addiction. This involved prescribing for known drug addicts doses of intravenous Valium for self-administration, oral Doloxene and Valium, and oral Rohypnol and Valium. The doctor prescribed these drugs because, under the circumstances the physical and social harm resulting from this approach to treatment of the patients justified the risk of abuse. He argued that the addicts were "needle-fixated", that Schedule 4 drugs were less harmful than Schedule 8 drugs, and that the substitution of these drugs could lead to a cure. The Board rejected this approach and opted instead to rule that on the basis that:

1).....the treatment was not orthodox treatment; and
2).....by regulation the prescription of the drugs should have been authorised by the Health Department, the doctor was guilty of the charge. The doctor appealed to the Supreme Court.

[13.99] The Supreme Court, in relation to (1), accepted evidence that although the doctor's treatment was unorthodox, there was a "respectable" body of medical opinion which recognised the potential therapeutic value of the "harm reduction" approach. It would not be appropriate to find someone who did not follow the orthodox approach guilty of misconduct on that basis alone. There might be a fine line between harm reduction strategy and misconduct, but it would be unsafe to find misconduct on the basis of particular doctors disagreeing with his judgment. In relation to (2) the Court held that although the doctor should have notified the Health Department, his failure to do so did not in the circumstances constitute misconduct. Whilst the Court did not specifically apply the test in *Stevenson*, this finding appears consistent with it. This case is also relevant to the discussion on drugs in Chapter 8.

[13.100] In most States conviction for a serious criminal offence can render a person subject to disciplinary procedures. The seriousness of the

[13.100] offence in some cases is defined by the penalty it attracts; there being no specific definition in others. Criminal conviction itself need not lead to disqualification from practising: see the outline of legislation relating to disciplinary action above at [13.25].

■ ■ ■ CASE
Skinner v Beaumont [1974] 2 NSWLR 106 (CA NSW)

The doctor in this case had been convicted of conspiring to unlawfully procure two miscarriages. He had referred them to an unregistered practitioner. He was duly removed from the medical register. He appealed against that removal on the grounds that it was not in the public interest for disqualification for this type of offence.

[13.101] Hutley J of the Supreme Court held (at 109):

> The deliberate defiance, even with good motives, of a legal and professional responsibility, cannot in my opinion be excused, otherwise the distribution of drugs to alleviate the cravings of addicts would be an exculpatory circumstance.

[13.102] However, he considered the doctor's good reputation and the fact that the occasion would not arise again (due to change in the law which made abortion more widely available). This fact, the judge said, was critical to his decision. He also considered the welfare of the public, declaring that it would be deprived of a good practitioner.

[13.103] Contrast this case with the following one.

■ ■ ■ CASE
Basser v Medical Board of Victoria [1981] VR 953 (SC)

A doctor provided prescriptions to patients for toxic drugs improperly and unreasonably, without proper medical grounds and in greater than reasonable doses. He neither examined the patients adequately nor supervised their use of the medication. His name was removed from the register. He appealed from this decision to the Supreme Court.

[13.104] The Court treated his behaviour as very serious, here invoking such descriptions as "reckless indifference" and "gross negligence", although they did not consider the criminality or otherwise of his actions. The Court said:

> It should not be accepted that the concept of moral turpitude was an additional ingredient in every charge of infamous conduct. If a sense of reckless indifference or gross negligence were proven against a medical practitioner in any respect right-thinking colleagues of the person charged would inevitably regard such conduct as reprehensible, disgraceful, shameful or dishonourable.

[13.105] The fact that reprehensible and even illegal behaviour may not lead to disqualification was demonstrated in the case of a lawyer who was convicted of culpable homicide through negligent driving. It was held that his behaviour did not render him any less able a lawyer, and so any [13.109] disciplinary action should take account of this. He was suspended from practice only while serving his prison sentence (*Ziems v Prothonotary of Supreme Court of New South Wales* (1957) 97 CLR 279). Lawyers fiddling the trust funds, however, will find little sympathy or mercy, for such activity reflects on their ability to act competently and in the interests of the client. Similarly, abuse of drugs could be considered as going to the very heart of health care practice, while a criminal conviction for an unrelated offence may not render one unable to competently carry out health care.

[13.106] It can be seen that there are difficulties in determining exactly what professional misconduct is, but the above cases do give some general idea.

Fitness to Practice

[13.107] Registration Boards may undertake an investigation into the mental or physical fitness of a person to practice. Such matters as drug addiction or misuse may come under this heading if there is no specific provision for disciplinary action for those conditions in the legislation of a particular State. Where a person has been found unable to cope with stress, or has some other emotional, psychological or physical difficulty in providing care of a proper standard, the Board may take action. In reviewing a person's fitness to practise, the Board may require the person to undergo a medical examination before it will allow her or him to practise. One situation which would come under this heading would be a health carer contracting an infectious disease which would endanger the health of clients.

Disciplinary Action or Removal or Suspension from Registration

[13.108] On receiving notice of a potential ground for such action, the Registration Boards have various powers to carry out inquiries, and to require evidence to be brought, and witnesses to appear, before them. A health carer who is subject to an inquiry has the right to appear before the Board either in person or, in New South Wales and Queensland, by counsel, to present a defence to the charges. There is provision for appeals to the State courts (or in the Territories to the Administrative Appeals Tribunal) against a finding by any of the Boards. Health carers should be aware of the provisions of any registration Board or council that governs them. Information should be sought from the Board itself, or the relevant union. Legislation can be obtained from the State Government Printer's Office (ask for the Act and regulations made under it) or from the internet at http://bar.austlii.edu.au.

[13.109] Whatever the legal procedure of an inquiry by a Board, any health carer who is being dealt with under disciplinary provisions is advised to seek legal advice.

[13.110] **[13.110]** In the interest of maintaining a high quality profession, the Registration Boards are provided with the power to take the following measures against someone found guilty of behaviour which may attract disciplinary action:

- reprimand;
- suspension from practice for a period of time;
- cancellation of registration;
- a fine; or
- an undertaking to refrain from similar behaviour in the future.

[13.111] A Board may also remove from its register anyone who is shown to be ineligible to remain on it. This includes those whose registration has lapsed, or those who no longer fulfil the technical requirements for registration.

Appeal from the Board's decision

[13.112] A person against whom a decision has been made by a Board may appeal to a court or tribunal nominated in the legislation (for example, for nurses in New South Wales it is the District Court, in the Australian Capital Territory it is the Administrative Appeals Tribunal, see [13.23]). The appeal may be by way of rehearing (a reconsideration of the facts), and the appeal court (or Administrative Appeal Tribunal in the Australian Capital Territory) may uphold, reverse or substitute the Board's decision.

❚❚❚ CHECKLIST
TYPICAL STEPS OF DISCIPLINARY PROCEDURES FOR HEALTH CARERS

- Complaint or information brought to Board's notice, health carer notified.
- Board decides to hear matter. If Board finds sufficient evidence on initial inquiry, it will decide to hold a formal hearing.
- Health carer supplied with written complaint, required to respond.
- The Board reviews the evidence, calls witnesses, considers the person's defence.
- If the health carer is found guilty Board takes disciplinary action:
    — reprimand;
    — place on probation;
    — suspend registration;
    — refuse to renew practising certificate;
    — suspend practising certificate; or
    — cancel practising certificate and remove health carer's name from register.
- Health carer may appeal Board's decision in court or tribunal nominated by State or Territory legislation.
- Appeal will result in:
    — upholding of Board's decision;
    — reversal of Board's decision; or
    — substitution of Board's decision with another.
- Health carer or Board may appeal this decision in higher court.

REFERENCES AND FURTHER READING

Australian Health and Medical Law Reporter (CCH, Sydney, 1991, Looseleaf Service)

Chiarella, M, "Nurse Practitioner Stage 3 Report" 4 *Health Law Bulletin* (1996), p 85

Chiarella, M, "Nurse Practitioners" 3 *Collegian* 6 (October 1996), p 25

Dix, et al, *Law for the Medical Profession* (Butterworths, Sydney, 1988)

Edwards, S, "Appeal against Medical Board's Decision Upheld (*Jemielita v Medical Board of WA*)" 1 *Health Law Bulletin* 2 (1993), p 61

Halsbury's Laws of Australia (Butterworths, Sydney, Looseleaf Service)

Joint Committee on the Health Care Complaints Commission *Unregistered Health Practitioners: the Adequacy and Appropriateness of Current Mechanisms for Resolving Complaints: Discussion Paper*, Sydney, Joint Committee on the Health Care Complaints Commission, 1998

Ottley, R, "Sexual Misconduct—to what Extent are Doctors Accountable?" 4 *Health Law Bulletin* (1996), p 49

Shinn, M, "Guidelines for Misconduct Hearings", 2 *Health Law Bulletin* (1993), p 49

Staunton, P and Whyburn, R, *Nursing and the Law* (4th ed, Saunders, Sydney, 1997)

The Laws of Australia (Law Book Co, Sydney, Looseleaf Service)

Wynne, A, "Nursing Practitioner Services in Victoria" 9 *Health Law Bulletin* 13 (2001), p 47

Chapter Fourteen

CRIMINAL LAW AND HEALTH CARE

INTRODUCTION

[14.1] Criminal law deals with actions against people or property, that whether someone is harmed or not, are considered wrongs against the state rather than against individuals. This is reflected in the fact that offenders are prosecuted by the state. The interest of criminal law is in the punishment of the perpetrator, not in the fate of the victim, who must pursue remedies in civil actions. This lack of interest has been mitigated somewhat by the recent development of criminal injuries compensation law in each State and Territory (see above, Ch 3).

[14.2] The basic outline of a criminal action and the proof required for a conviction is dealt with in Chapter 3. It is important to have this in mind when considering specific actions under criminal law.

[14.3] It should be noted that in criminal law assault and battery are generally grouped together, both in statutes and in case law, and (inaccurately) called "assault". To avoid confusion, the term "assault", when used in this chapter, includes the concepts of both assault and battery.

[14.4] Apart from its general application to all people with its prohibition of interference with another person's physical integrity (for example, homicide and assault), or property (for example, forms of theft and fraud), criminal law involves some offences which are of particular interest to the health care professions. These include:

- murder (see [14.69]);
- manslaughter (see [14.70], [14.153]);
- euthanasia (see [14.74]);
- abortion (see [14.155]);
- surrogacy agreements (see [10.92]);
- dealing with victims and perpetrators of crime (see [14.189]ff);
- domestic violence and child abuse (see [16.54]ff);
- offences related to infectious diseases (see [16.1]ff); and
- drug offences (see [8.9]ff).

[14.5] Over the centuries, English common law has developed a series of principles that underlie criminal law. Before specific criminal offences are dealt with, the most important principles will be considered.

Principles of Criminal Law

Principle No 1: Criminal Offences must be Established by Law Prior to a Charge

[14.6] Each State and Territory, as well as the Commonwealth, has legislation establishing criminal offences and penalties. However, as we inherited the common law from England, we also inherited our initial set of criminal offences from there. In New South Wales, South Australia and Victoria, as well as the Australian Capital Territory, common law has continued to be the main source of criminal offences, modified over time by statute.

Technically, criminal law covers all statutory provisions that authorise the prosecution of, and set penalties for, a nominated activity. Offences are scattered throughout all legislation, but each State has a major statute covering the more serious offences.[1] The Northern Territory, Queensland, Tasmania and Western Australia have Criminal Codes,[2] which are supposed to be independent of the common law (although it may be used as an aid for interpreting the provisions; Colvin et al, (1998), p 8). Again, the Criminal Codes are not the sole source of criminal offences—other legislation, such as that on drugs, also sets out prohibitions and penalties.

[14.7] There is nothing inherent in an act that makes it criminal: crimes are defined as such by law. In fact most crimes are established by statute, as it is considered important that where one may be deprived of liberty and property, and subject to a criminal record, offences must be clearly established and available for all to identify.

[14.8] Criminal law comes from the establishment of two kinds of offences. First, there are the general catalogues of criminal offences, in the Crimes Acts or Criminal Codes. These are dealt with in this chapter. Secondly, there is a body of offences created in the multitude of Acts, regulations and by-laws, which are not part of the criminal law as such, but do attract penalties. These offences are an adjunct to the main thrust of the legislation in which they appear, and generally are not considered bad enough to classify the offender as "criminal", even though the penalties might be quite severe. They may cover anything from using a hose at prohibited times to polluting water: from misuse of computer information to parking in the wrong place.

---

[1] The main ones are: *Crimes Act* 1914 (Cth); *Crimes Act* 1900 (ACT); *Crimes Act* 1900 (NSW); *Criminal Law Consolidation Act* 1935 (SA); *Crimes Act* 1958 (Vic); *Crimes (Capital Offences) Act* 1975 (Vic), *Crimes (Theft) Act* 1973 (Vic).

[2] *Criminal Code Act* 1983 (NT); *Criminal Code Act* 1899 (Qld); *Criminal Code Act* 1924 (Tas); *Criminal Code* 1913 (WA).

[14.9] Generally, a crime must involve:

- ..... *action* which is recognised at law as being criminal, or
- ..... *intention* to carry out the action.

Principle No 2: There must be an Act

[14.10] Generally it has been held that a crime cannot be committed by omission, that is, by failing to act, stemming from the basic idea that one shouldn't be punished for something one didn't do.

Omission

[14.11] This is not always the case, however, for failure to act may make a person open to conviction for either aiding and abetting, thus as a principal in the second degree (rather than being a principal in the first degree), or failing to fulfil a duty of care (see [14.13], [14.151]ff).

> A man may be principal in an offence in two degrees. A principal in the first degree, is he that is the actor, or absolute perpetrator of the crime; and, in the second degree, he who is present, aiding and abetting the fact to be done. Which presence need not always be an actual immediate standing by, within sight or hearing of the fact; but there may also be a constructive presence, as when one commits a robbery or murder, and another keeps watch or guard at some convenient distance [Williams et al (1983), p 443].

▌▌▌ CASE
R v Coney (1882) 8 QBD 534 (Court for Crown Cases Reserved England)

Coney was in a crowd watching an illegal prize fight. He took no part in it, nor in the management or encouragement of it. He said and did nothing. He was convicted of assault as a principal in the second degree, although the jury found that he did not aid or abet the fight.

[14.12] Hawkins J stated (at 557-558):

> It is no criminal offence to stand by, a mere passive spectator of a crime, even of a murder. Non-interference to prevent a crime is not itself a crime. But the fact that a person was voluntarily and purposefully present witnessing the commission of a crime, and offered no opposition to it, though he might reasonably be expected to prevent and had the power so to do, or at least to express his dissent, might [provide prima facie evidence] . . . that he wilfully encouraged and so aided and abetted.

[14.13] In the case of *R v Russell* [1933] VLR 59 (SC Vic), Russell, who after an argument with his wife, stood by and watched her drown herself and their two young children in a swimming pool, was convicted of being

[14.13] a principal in the second degree, because the jury was entitled to find that his mere voluntary presence indicated that he assented to and was willing to abet the crime. The position with regard to homicide is special, and will be dealt with more specifically below. There was another element in the case of *Russell*: so far as the children were concerned, his failure to prevent them from drowning resulted in his being found guilty of manslaughter. If a person has a particular relationship of care to another, or has put them in danger, and intentionally refuses to give reasonable aid to them, that person may be guilty of a crime. This is similar to the duty of care and its breach, of a negligence action, which in this case it must be such as to attract criminal sanction (see the discussion of criminal negligence below [14.151]ff). This could apply to health workers who fail to resuscitate or otherwise aid a person in their care who requires life-saving attention.

Principle No 3: There must be an Intention to Commit the Act

[14.14] The accused must have intended to carry out the prohibited act. Intention may include three states of mind:

1) ..... having the *aim of doing the prohibited act or causing the prohibited event* (for example, the death of a person); or
2) ..... being *reckless* that certain consequences may result from one's act that are not the primary aim; or
3) ..... being *criminally negligent* in one's actions. This is sometimes referred to as "gross negligence". It requires a much more serious degree of negligence than the civil action, and is dealt with in more detail below. However, it is different from recklessness in that it requires advertence to the probable harm by the defendant.

[14.15] The level of culpability is less in the event of (2) or (3).

[14.16] The Code States build in the element of intention required in the legislative provision for each offence listed. Where there may be some ambiguity, the above principle will inform the court in its interpretation.

[14.17] Continuation of an act which is accidental, and to which one then applies criminal intent becomes a criminal act.

▮▮▮ CASE [14.19]
Fagan v Metropolitan Police Commissioner [1969] 1 QB 439; [1968] 3 All ER 422 (Divisional Court England)

Fagan accidentally drove his car onto the foot of a policeman who was directing him how to park it. The policeman said several times "Get off, you are on my foot". Fagan indicated that he could wait, and after the policeman repeated his order several times slowly turned on the ignition and moved the car. The court was undecided as to whether the initial driving onto the officer's foot was a deliberate act, but the accused argued that he had not intended any assault when he actually drove onto the officer's foot. Therefore, he argued, mens rea (criminal intent) was absent at this time. Later when he had mens rea, he continued, he did not carry out any act, and thus he could not be convicted of assault. He was convicted and appealed.

[14.18] The court decided that where an act was a continuing one, there did not need to be mens rea at the inception of that act, so long as at some stage while it was ongoing, the accused formed the mens rea. He was convicted. This principle was followed by the Court of Appeal in *R v Miller* [1982] 3 All ER 386. The defendant in that case fell asleep in another person's house while smoking. He awoke to find the mattress alight, and left without doing anything, allowing the house to catch fire. In determining whether actus reus (guilty act) and the mens rea concurred in time, the court said the whole course of events should be considered. The judges held that the innocent setting in train of events culminating in criminal harm imposes on the defendant a duty of invention sufficient to make them guilty in law if they have a guilty mind at the time of inactivity.

This approach was recently endorsed in principle by the High Court of Australia in the recent case of *Royall v The Queen* (1990) 172 CLR 378, although the issue was approached in different ways. In that case the defendant had engaged in a course of violent conduct towards his victim, causing her to fall (either because she was pushed or she fell or jumped in trying to escape him). The question was what was the correct time for assessing whether the accused had the relevant mens rea for murder. The court allowed the consideration of the overall sequence of events, even though it may have been difficult for the jury to be confident precisely when the defendant's mens rea crystallised.

This principle can be applied to health care, with examples such as the failure to act when a despised client has an unanticipated adverse drug reaction, so that they will die, or more trivially, the unintended removal of goods from their rightful owner (for example, equipment put in the pocket and forgotten, and discovered later on), which would become theft where the health carer decides to keep them.

[14.19] A person may be held criminally liable for unintended consequences when a planned offence "goes wrong". This can include, for example, a bank robbery where someone is hurt, contrary to initial intentions, or where a victim unreasonably attempts escape by opening a car door when it is in motion and jumping out (*R v Roberts* (1971) 56 Cr App R 95).

Principle No 4: Any Act must be Voluntary

[14.20]   One cannot be found guilty of an act over which one does not have physical control. As well as accidents, there are the defences of duress and automatism (see [14.50]ff). Where an accidental occurrence cannot be isolated from other actions which constitute an intention to commit a crime, one cannot plead that it was involuntary.

▎▎▎ CASE

Ryan v The Queen (1967) 121 CLR 205 (High Court of Australia)

Ryan took a loaded and cocked rifle into a service station and pointed it at an employee, Taylor, demanding money, which he was given. When Ryan was about to tie Taylor up, he was startled by a sudden movement by Taylor. Ryan's finger involuntarily squeezed the trigger and Taylor was killed. Ryan argued that he should not be found guilty of murder because the squeezing of the trigger was involuntary. He was found guilty by the Supreme Court of New South Wales, appealed unsuccessfully to the Court of Appeal, and applied for leave to appeal to the High Court.

[14.21]   The High Court said that the death was caused by a combination of events which were carried out with the intention to rob. All actions, including the loading and cocking of the gun were as much a part of causing death as was the actual pulling of the trigger. This final act could not be isolated from the earlier ones, and so it could not be held to have been purely accidental and unforeseen.

[14.22]   This ruling is in keeping with the felony–murder rule, which in some States provides for the treating of unintended death during the commission of some serious offences as murder. The general approach to unintended consequences during the commission of criminal offences is that people are responsible for the natural and probable effects of their actions.

Strict Liability

[14.23]   There is a general requirement that all offences require both actus reus and mens rea; however, in some cases one may be found guilty of an offence even where one did not have mens rea. Such offences require only that one has committed the act prohibited, one's state of mind being irrelevant. The removal of the requirement of mens rea must be clear from the wording of a statute, either explicitly or by necessary implication. Necessary implication occurs when the act prohibited is a grave social evil, the legislation is known to the public at large, and the activity can be reasonably easily avoided. Possession of drugs has been made an offence of strict liability in some jurisdictions, but courts in both England and Australia have tended to reject the principle on the basis that it is not in the public interest to find people guilty of offences in situations over which they have no control (see for example, *Lim Chin Aik v The Queen* [1963] 1 All ER 223; *Sweet v Parsley* [1970] AC 132).

Proudman v Dayman (1941) 67 CLR 536 established that where the imposition of strict liability would result in punishment of a class of people whose conduct could not in any way affect the observance of the law, strict liability should not be used. If one does have control then one may be held liable for not taking proper care. The courts established the defence of mistake, or reasonable ignorance of fact or reasonable care taken in the circumstances, thus tending to turn apparently strict liability offences into offences involving negligence. Strict liability usually applies to: [14.25]

- ..... traffic offences (for example, parking);
- ..... preparation and selling of food (for example, content of sausages); and
- ..... activity on licensed premises.

The person charged need not even be aware that the offence has occurred.

Status Offences

[14.24] These are offences which apply to situations rather than actions. One can be found guilty despite the absence of both mens rea and actus reus. One is convicted not because of any voluntary action one may have taken, but the situation one is in, even if it is against one's will. In some jurisdictions children may be found guilty of being neglected or in moral danger under child welfare legislation, thus rendering them subject to action by the Children's Court (not as punishment but as a welfare measure). The case below is an extreme example of a status offence.

CASE
R v Larsonneur (1933) 24 Cr App R 74 (Court of Criminal Appeal England)

Ms Larsonneur (L) was convicted under the Aliens Order 1920 (UK) which stated that "if any alien, having landed in the United Kingdom after having been prohibited from doing so . . . is at any time found within the United Kingdom, he shall be guilty of an offence". L had been prohibited, and so went to Ireland. She was not wanted there either, so she was escorted back to England by the police, where she remained in their custody, and was subsequently charged for her presence there. She argued that she could not be guilty as she was not in England voluntarily.

[14.25] The court found that the whole purpose of the legislation was whether she was found in the United Kingdom: "How she got there makes no difference at all." This case is regarded as the sole English example of a conviction where action was involuntary, and it is suggested that status offences will not be accepted by the courts as a basis for punishment.

Principle No 5: One Cannot Normally be Vicariously Guilty in Criminal Law

[14.26] Generally, guilt must be personal, as mens rea is normally required.

▮▮▮ CASE

R v Huggins (1730) 2 Ld Raym 1574; 92 ER 518 (all the judges of King's Bench, Exchequer and Common Pleas England)

In 1730 a prison superintendent, Huggins, was convicted of murder. His underling, Barnes, had placed a prisoner in a cell in conditions which eventually caused his death. Huggins was not fully aware of the conditions of the deceased's incarceration.

[14.27] On appeal the court held that Huggins could not be found guilty because only the one who immediately does the act is guilty. If it is the act of an employee, unless it is done by the command or direction of the employer or superior, or he or she is an accomplice to the crime, the latter is not guilty.

[14.28] Exceptions to this principle are:

- liability through others;
- liability through incitement;
- delegation; and
- accomplices to crime.

Liability through Others

[14.29] One may carry out a crime through another who has not the appropriate mens rea: for example the woman who, wishing with her lover to kill her husband, gives her children poison in the guise of good medicine to put in his drink, may, with the lover, be found guilty of murder. The children, who unknowingly carried out the act, would not be guilty (*Female Poisoner's Case* (1634) Kelyng 53; 84 ER 1079). This very ancient principle has been adapted into legislation regarding, for example, murder.

Liability through Incitement

[14.30] When a person incites another to commit a crime, that person will, in most circumstances, be guilty of the completed crime as an accomplice. The means for doing this are not important, rather the court is interested in determining whether the accused sought to reach and influence the mind of the other person towards commission of a crime. It is not essential that the person who incites the other is successful in so doing: where the incitor does not reach the mind of the prospective incitee (for example, a letter goes astray), the offence will be one of attempted incitement. Where the incitee's mind is reached, but not [14.33] influenced enough to commit the offence, the incitement has still occurred. The intentions and actions of the person inciting are vital to the proof of the offence, regardless of any action or otherwise of the prospective perpetrator.

Delegation

[14.31] The case of *Huggins*, above, dealt with this situation, but there the court held that delegation did not exist. However, a corporation may be criminally liable for the offences of employees where the crime can be shown to be the act of the corporation (for example, where the employee is instructed to carry it out). Corporations may be liable for certain statutory offences, such as the serving of liquor to underage drinkers, or occupational health and safety breaches. It is suggested that the reasoning of the courts is that where one delegates a function, and that function is bound by a licence, one cannot complain that one was not aware of the delegate knowingly carrying on the enterprise in contravention of the licence (it has yet to be considered by the courts whether this would apply to a health facility, especially with the handling of drugs).

Accomplices to Crime

[14.32] An accomplice to a crime assists in the event, and may be either a principal in the second degree, who is present during the act (see above), or an accessory who is not present during the act, but has been of assistance before or after the act. The distinction is of little comfort to the accomplice, however, because principals in the second degree and accomplices before the act are liable to the same punishment as a principal in the first degree.[3]

Principle No 6: The Precise Act for which one is Charged must have been Committed

[14.33] A person cannot be found guilty of an offence unless the act specified in the charge against her or him has been committed. Even where one believes one is committing a crime, and intends to do so, if the act has not been established by law to be criminal, there is no crime. The following case has also raised much discussion on the practical and philosophical aspects of when an attempt to commit a crime where the commission is factually or legally impossible should be punished (see, for example, Brett, Waller and Williams (1997), p 450ff.).

---

[3] See, for example, *Crimes Act* 1900 (ACT), ss 345, 346, 347; *Crimes Act* 1900 (NSW), ss 345, 346; *Criminal Code* (NT), ss 7, 8, 9; *Criminal Code* (Qld), ss 7, 8, 9; *Criminal Code* (Tas), ss 7, 8, 9; *Crimes Act* 1958 (Vic), s 323; *Criminal Code* (WA), ss 7, 8, 9.

[14.33] ■■■ **CASE**
Haughton v Smith [1975] AC 476; [1973] 3 All ER 1109 (House of Lords England)

> Smith was convicted of attempting to handle stolen goods. In fact the goods had been seized by the police and were in their custody in a van. Smith, ignorant of the police involvement, met the van and arranged for disposal of the goods. The Crown conceded that the goods were, while in the custody of police, no longer "stolen goods" in the strict sense of that term, when the alleged offence was committed. Smith appealed on the ground that as the goods were no longer stolen, he could not be convicted of attempting to handle stolen goods.

[14.34] The House of Lords agreed. Lord Morris said (at 1122): "the presence of a guilty mind does not transform what a man actually does into something that he has not done".

[14.35] Viscount Dilhorne added (at 1126):

> A man cannot attempt to handle goods which are not stolen. A man taking an umbrella from a club thinking it the property of someone else [when it is in fact his own] does not steal. His belief does not convert his conduct into an offence if his conduct cannot constitute a crime.

[14.36] This was a case involving *legal impossibility*, that is, the attempted act is not a crime, contrary to the accused's belief. Other cases may involve *factual impossibility* where the act would be an offence, but (unbeknownst to the accused in most cases) it is impossible to complete. An example is where the accused fires into a room believing the victim is inside, when in fact he is a long way away. There is some difference of opinion as to whether this should constitute a crime.

[14.37] This principle also includes the rule that criminal law cannot be retrospective: that is, any offence for which a person is charged must have been clearly established by legislation as an offence *before* the commission of the act.

Principle No 7: Ignorance of the Law is no Excuse

[14.38] This principle has been held as a basic rule in criminal law. The accused cannot say that he or she did not know that the conduct constituted an offence. However, a mistake as to what the law is may mean that the requirement for mens rea has not been met (simply put, one can't have a guilty mind if one doesn't know the action is wrong). This, of course, does not mean that one can remain blissfully deliberately ignorant of the law, everyone has a responsibility to take reasonable steps to know what is wrong, and it appears that the principle applies unless the accused can show that it was not reasonably possible for them to have known the law (for example, the legislation had not been published). Even then, it would most likely be a mitigating factor in determining penalty rather than culpability. Many problems have arisen in determining whether the accused's confusion stemmed from a mistake of fact (which may be an excuse) or a mistake of law (see, for example, Brett, Waller and Williams (1997), Ch 13).

Principle No 8: Presumption of Innocence [14.42]

[14.39] All readers are probably familiar with the aphorism that one is "innocent until proven guilty". This is one of the fundamental principles of criminal law, and leads to the rule that the prosecution must prove the guilt of the accused, and that the accused does not have to prove anything.

[14.40] In the courtroom the accused attempts to throw doubt on the prosecution case, in adducing evidence, but at no stage, with the exceptions below (see [14.45]ff), does the accused have to present proof of *not* having committed the offence, except in a handful of statutory exceptions. Thus if nurse Jane Doe is accused of murder, it is not her lawyer's task to prove that she did not commit the offence: it is up to the prosecution to prove that she did, the proof being strong enough to convince a jury beyond a reasonable doubt that she was the person who caused the death and that she had the intention to do so. Her lawyer's task is to produce evidence which will cause the jury to have reasonable doubt as to her guilt and, unless they are convinced beyond a reasonable doubt that she committed the murder, even where they think she probably did, they must enter a "not guilty" verdict.

▌▌▌ CASE

Woolmington v Director of Public Prosecutions [1935] AC 462 (House of Lords England)

Woolmington had an argument with his wife. He told the court that he threatened to kill himself, and produced a loaded gun. Somehow in the ensuing activity it went off, killing her. The jury convicted him of murder, the judge having told them that if they were satisfied that he killed his wife, the killing was to be considered murder unless he convinced them that it was something less, for example manslaughter or excusable homicide. Woolmington appealed, basing his argument on error in the judge's instructions. The Appeal Court upheld the conviction, but the case went to the House of Lords, where the conviction was quashed.

[14.41] The House of Lords, in one of the most quoted statements of criminal law, stated that:

> Throughout the web of English Criminal law one golden thread is always to be seen, that it is the duty of the prosecution to prove the prisoner's guilt subject to . . . the defence of insanity and subject also to any statutory exception. If, at the end of and on the whole of the case, there is a reasonable doubt . . . whether the prisoner killed the deceased with a malicious intention, the prosecution has not made out the case and the prisoner is entitled to an acquittal.

Exceptions

[14.42] Exceptions to this principle, situations where the accused has the onus of proof, are where he or she offers the defences of insanity or diminished responsibility (see below, [14.45]ff).

Defences to a Criminal Charge

[14.43] A defence to a criminal charge may be an absolute or a partial (or qualified) defence. An absolute defence is one which, if successful, leads to a finding of "not guilty" (for example, where a jury finds a person insane (see below), at the time of an alleged offence, they are to find the person "not guilty on the grounds of insanity"). A partial defence results in one being found guilty of a lesser offence than that charged (for example, if a jury finds the accused suffered from diminished responsibility, at the time of an alleged murder, they are to find the accused guilty of manslaughter instead).

[14.44] While insanity may be pleaded as a defence to any alleged crime (although it is usually reserved for more serious offences), diminished responsibility is a specific statutory defence to a charge of murder. If the jury finds the defendant did carry out the act for which he or she is being tried, but was suffering from diminished responsibility at the time, they are to return a verdict of manslaughter.

Insanity

[14.45] The defence of insanity, as stated, is always an absolute defence, in that those who successfully plead insanity are not guilty of the offence on that ground. This does not mean that they are allowed to go free. Instead of being convicted and punished for a crime, they are dealt with according to their illness. The defence has the onus of proving insanity, and must positively adduce evidence to convince the jury of this. In practice insanity is mainly used as a defence to a charge of homicide, and the general result is that the accused will be kept in a mental institution, "at the Governor's pleasure", or in another form of detention and/or treatment. However, the plea of "unfitness to plead" is often entered before the accused has pleaded (see above, Ch 3) and there is much criticism of the law because of the consequences of this, as it is claimed it leads to indefinite incarceration of those ruled unfit to plead, despite recovery from their illness (Roulston (1980), Ch 7; Williams et al (1983), Ch 11).

McNaghten Rules

[14.46] The rules relating to common law establishment of insanity were formulated in 1843 by the House of Lords, who had to decide how to establish whether one Daniel McNaghten, charged with murder, was insane according to law. He had attempted to shoot the Prime Minister, Sir John Peel, but mistakenly shot his secretary. McNaghten was allegedly suffering delusions of persecution. The Lords decided that jurors should be instructed that every person is to be presumed sane, and to possess normal responsibility for her or his crimes, unless the contrary is proved to the jury's satisfaction. To establish a ground of insanity the accused must show that, at the time of committing the act, he or she was labouring

under such a defect of reason, from disease of the mind, as not to know [14.50]
the nature and quality of the act (that is, not to know what they were
doing) or, if they did know, that they did not know that what they were
doing was wrong (for example, knowing that they were killing someone
but wrongly believing it was in self-defence, or that the person was a
wartime enemy).

[14.47] The wording of the rules, including the requirement that the
person be suffering from a "disease of the mind", has caused much
confusion and legal argument, and also liberal and loose application of
the rules. Lawyers argue that they are an incomplete formulation (for
example, see Brett, Waller and Williams (1997), p 678) and do not take
account of the diversity of situations that may arise. Psychiatrists argue
that they are based on faulty principles of psychology, omitting important
conditions from which one might suffer (Williams et al (1983), p 683;
Gillies (1993) p 257). Gillies states at p 248:

> The insanity defence has in a number of jurisdictions been supplemented
> in more recent times by the statutory defence of diminished
> responsibility. This defence may only be pleaded in relation to a charge of
> murder. In not being [as is the defence of insanity] confined to disruption
> of the cognitive process resulting from disease of the mind (it is
> formulated in terms of a mental impairment of D's mental responsibility
> for D's conduct, resulting from abnormality of mind), [diminished
> responsibility] does, however, help to suggest the terms in which a more
> broadly based statutory defence of mental illness might be cast.

Diminished Responsibility

[14.48] Available as a defence to a charge of murder in some
jurisdictions, diminished responsibility generally requires proof of an
abnormality of the mind (whether arising from a condition of arrested or
retarded development of mind, or any inherent illness, or induced by
disease or injury) which had substantially impaired the accused's mental
responsibility at the time of the offence. This defence has been formulated
as a way of resolving some of the problems posed by the McNaghten
Rules. Again, it must be proved by the accused.

Other Defences to a Criminal Charge

[14.49] Insanity and diminished responsibility are thus exceptions to the
rule that the accused does not have to prove innocence. Other defences,
which are raised to throw doubt on the prosecution's case are automatism,
duress, self-defence and provocation.

Automatism

[14.50] This defence is used where physical conduct has occurred which
was involuntary because all bodily movements were wholly uncontrolled

[14.50] and uninitiated by any function of the conscious will. It gives to someone who is relying on the fact that at the time he or she was incapable of knowing the nature of the act, but who does not fit the criteria of insanity or diminished responsibility, the chance of a "not guilty" verdict.

[14.51] Automatism is a condition of mind which is temporary, may have one of many causes, and results in a person carrying out acts of which he or she is totally unconscious.

[14.52] It may be drug-induced, or the result of disease (for example, post-epileptic automatism or hypoglycaemic episodes), or of injury (for example, concussion):

> The jury might not accept the evidence of a defect of reason from a disease of the mind, but at the same time accept the evidence that the prisoner did not know what he was doing. If the jury should take that view of the facts they should find him not guilty [*Bratty v Attorney-General (Northern Ireland)* [1963] 3 All ER 386 at 403 per Lord Kilmuir].

For a good introductory discussion of automatism, see Roulston (1980), p 99; Bennett and Hogan (1989).

[14.53] It has been held that a self-induced incapacity will not excuse a person, nor will one which could have been reasonably foreseen as the result of an action or omission.

■ ■ ■ CASE
R v Quick and Paddison [1973] 3 All ER 347 (Court of Appeal England)

> Quick was a nurse who suffered from diabetes, requiring regular doses of insulin. On the morning in question he turned up to work having taken the prescribed insulin, but no food and some alcohol, something he knew was dangerous. He later assaulted a patient and, on trial for assault, adduced evidence that at the time he was suffering from hypoglycaemia, causing him to be unconscious of his acts. He was convicted and appealed to the above court.

[14.54] The Court of Appeal held that whatever the malfunctioning of his mind, it was caused by an external factor, not a disease of the mind, so automatism could be considered by the jury. The judges also said, however, that events that could be foreseen by the accused, as arising from his act or omission, such as hypoglycaemia from failing to have regular meals while taking insulin, may not excuse him: the jury would have to consider how much he could have foreseen, and decide his responsibility.

[14.55] The response in Australia to the question of responsibility for crime committed while under the self-induced influence of alcohol or drugs has been different.

■ ■ ■ **CASE** [14.59]
R v O'Connor (1980) 54 ALJR 349 (High Court)

> O'Connor was charged with wounding with intent to resist arrest. He had consumed an hallucinogenic drug and alcohol when he stole items from a policeman's car. The policeman, happening upon the scene, arrested him for larceny. O'Connor stabbed the policeman with a knife. It was accepted by the court that at the time O'Connor "could have been rendered incapable of reasoning and of forming an intent to steal or wound". He was convicted, failed on appeal to the Court of Appeal, and went to the High Court.

[14.56] The Court held that the fact that intoxication was self-induced does not mean that the person had the intention (mens rea) for the commission of an offence which may have been done involuntarily. Barwick CJ stated (at 465) that:

> It seems to me to be completely inconsistent with the principles of the common law that a man should be conclusively presumed to have an intent which, in fact, he does not have, or to have done an act which, in truth, he did not do.

The onus of proof of intention lies upon the Crown. A later case, *R v Coleman* (1990) 19 NSWLR 467, applied this case, holding that the only question the jury has to determine in relation to the requisite states of mind was whether the accused had in fact formed them.

[14.57] In some cases, however, the prosecution may be able to argue that the accused, in voluntarily becoming intoxicated or taking drugs was in itself criminal negligence where he or she was aware of the of a risk of becoming violent or otherwise likely to act in an antisocial or criminal way as a result.

[14.58] This is obviously an area of law which has caused, and will continue to cause, much controversy and legal confusion as such offences increase, and the approach of *Quick* will be pressed by those who believe it morally wrong not to hold such persons responsible for the effects of their self-induced automatism.

Duress

[14.59] Duress as a defence to a criminal charge is very imprecise, and has not been clearly defined and articulated. However, the following principles were established in the case of *R v Dawson* [1978] VR 536, and substantially followed in *R v Lawrence* [1980] NSWLR 122:

- the accused carried out the offence under threat of death or grievous bodily harm being unlawfully inflicted on someone if the offence were not carried out;
- under the circumstances a person of ordinary strength would have capitulated;
- the threat was present at the time of offence, was continuing, was imminent and impending;
- the accused reasonably believed that the threat would be carried out;
- the crime was not murder or some other offence so heinous it should be excepted;

[14.59]
- .....the accused had not exposed herself or himself to the application of duress; or
- .....the accused had no way of safely preventing the application of the threat.

[14.60] Note that the accused has to take the first opportunity to seek help from the threatened danger, and that danger must be a serious physical one, not, for example, a threat to job or reputation. Thus, for example, it could not be argued that a threat of sacking if a health carer did not assist in an illegal abortion, provided a defence of duress.

Self-Defence

[14.61] Self-defence may be offered as a defence to a criminal charge in some circumstances. It is the commission of an offence undertaken to preserve one from threatened harm by another. It is possible that a health carer may reasonably believe a client poses a real and imminent threat to his or her physical safety, that cannot be avoided.

[14.62] Self-defence may be so well balanced that the action taken precisely prevents the harm (called here "reasonable self-defence") or it may be excessive.

CASE
Viro v The Queen (1976) 141 CLR 88 (High Court)

Viro and another man were charged with murder. They had attacked the victim with intent to rob him, but he fought back vigorously. Viro argued that by the time he killed the man he was acting in self-defence. The New South Wales Supreme Court convicted him, he appealed to the Court of Appeal which upheld the conviction. He appealed finally to the High Court.

[14.63] The High Court listed requirements for the determination of whether self-defence to a charge of murder is a valid defence. Because health carers are often be the subject of attack these have been adapted to create the following guide.

CHECKLIST
WHEN SELF-DEFENCE IS A VALID DEFENCE TO A CHARGE OF ASSAULT

- .....Did the accused have a reasonable and honest belief of actual or imminent attack likely to harm? If no, self-defence is ruled out: consider guilt, stop here. If yes, continue.
- .....Was the force used more than required for the accused's protection? If no, self-defence is established. If yes, continue before ruling it out.
- .....Did the accused realise that the force was more than required? If no, self-defence is established. If yes, consider assault or manslaughter, depending on the circumstances.

[14.64] This checklist can be applied to charges of murder, manslaughter or assault. Generally, no alternative finding to a charge of assault is

available, as there is with murder (see [14.69]ff) so the finding will either [14.67]
be "guilty" or "not guilty". However there are grades of assault, such as
"assault with intent to cause grievous bodily harm", "assault causing
actual bodily harm", and simply "assault". Each has progressively
diminishing penalties.

Provocation

[14.65] In some jurisdictions there is provision for mandatory sentences for murder (some States have a mandatory sentence of life imprisonment) or specific property or other offence (for example, Western Australia and the Northern Territory have mandatory sentences for some offences). Otherwise, the judge has a discretion in the sentence imposed, within the limits set by the legislation for the particular offence. Where there is no discretion, provocation is raised as a defence, as obviously, if the judge has no discretion in the sentence which must be imposed it is no good waiting until after conviction to raise provocation. Where there is discretion in the severity of the sentence that can be imposed, it is more likely to be raised in the plea of mitigation. (A plea of mitigation is made after conviction, and is an argument for lenient treatment by the judge in sentencing. Matters which do not excuse the defendant, but have worked unfairly to her or his disadvantage, either in regard to the actual offence or the personality of the accused, and which therefore in the name of justice should be taken into account, are raised at this point. They may include such matters as emotional or economic hardship, or abuse as a child, etc.)

[14.66] Provocation was defined in *R v Duffy* [1949] 1 All ER 932, Lord Goddard quoting Devlin J at 932:

> [It] is some act, or series of acts, done by the dead man to the accused, which would cause in any reasonable person, and actually causes in the accused, a sudden and temporary loss of self-control, rendering the accused so subject to passion as to make him or her for the moment not master of his [sic] mind.

[14.67] Some jurisdictions require that any response to provocation be sudden and in the heat of passion, as an immediate reaction to the provocation. In other States provocation can apply where murder is not necessarily immediate to the provocation, which allows a jury to consider, for example, the killing of a spouse who has been abusive or violent for a long time, but doing it when that person is not an actual threat, when the retaliation is more likely to be effective, for example, when they are asleep. A successful plea of provocation will reduce a murder charge to that of manslaughter. Where, for example, a woman has been charged with murder or assault of her spouse, medical evidence given by nurses of injuries caused by the deceased in the past may be used to argue provocation.

Substantive Offences Relevant to Health Care

The unlawful causing of death (homicide)

[14.68] Homicide is the unlawful killing of another person. It may be either murder or manslaughter.

Murder

[14.69] Murder is causing the death of a person by another who intended the death, and where the killer had no legal justification for bringing about that death. Examples of where deliberate killing is justified are war, execution as the result of a conviction where this is a prescribed punishment, or self-defence. Where the killing of another is lawful it is known as justifiable homicide. All jurisdictions in Australia prohibit unjustifiable, intentional killing.

Manslaughter

[14.70] Manslaughter is the unlawful causing of the death of another, but with lack of intention to kill, so that death results from an unlawful act, or one which is grossly negligent. It is in these circumstances called involuntary manslaughter. A verdict of voluntary manslaughter, however, may result where a person has intended to kill, but the charge is reduced because of mitigating circumstances such as provocation or diminished responsibility. Another example is an altercation between A and B. A's response to B's aggression is unduly excessive. This causes B to react with such force that A is required to defend himself, which leads to the initially unintended death of B (see *Viro's* case, [14.62]).

[14.71] The victim of homicide must be a human being, generally defined at common law as any being having been born by being completely extruded from the body of its mother and having an independent existence in the sense that it does not derive its power of living from its mother:

> legally a person is not in being until he or she is fully born in a living state. . . . It is not material that the child may still be attached to the mother by the umbilical cord. . . . [B]ut . . . the child should have an existence separate from its mother, and that occurs when the child is fully extruded from its mother's body and is living by virtue of the functioning of its own organs [*R v Hutty* [1953] VLR 338 per Barry J at p 339].

[14.72] Evidence that the child breathed, coughed or sneezed has been accepted as sufficient evidence that it was born alive. Definitions to the same effect are contained in the Codes of Queensland, Tasmania and Western Australia. Where, as the result of criminal injuries before birth, a child who is born alive subsequently dies, this will also be homicide.

[14.73] The killing of a foetus (abortion) (see [14.155]), or of a child in the process of birth (child destruction) (see [14.187]) may be subject to different considerations. There is also provision in some States (for example, New South Wales, Tasmania and Victoria) for separate consideration for the killing of a child by its mother, who is suffering from the consequences of its birth or lactation subsequent upon it, within 12 months of its birth (infanticide). This is really a form of the diminished responsibility defence, reducing the offence from murder to manslaughter.

Euthanasia

[14.74] Euthanasia (a Greek word meaning "good death") is the deliberate bringing about of the death of a person to end what is considered to be an intolerable existence. Euthanasia is defined here as either an active measure to cause death (called "active euthanasia") or the withholding of treatment which causes, or hastens death (called "passive euthanasia"). The former may be the criminal offence of homicide, the latter is more problematic. Some commentators say it cannot be homicide as there is no act to cause the harm, but it has been quite clearly established that, where there is a duty of care, an omission can amount to criminal negligence at least (see [14.151]ff). It could also, of course, constitute civil negligence.

[14.75] Technically, whether active or passive, euthanasia can amount to homicide. The courts, however, have sought relief from the harshness of such provisions by developing principles which nevertheless are vague and unable to deal satisfactorily with the advancement of modern technology. This has resulted in intense legal debate and calls by law reform bodies for change. In the meantime, every day medical decisions are being made to withhold treatment or remove life-sustaining machinery from patients—actions which are potential offences—and no prosecutions are laid. There is confusion among medical personnel as to where they stand with the law, and uncertainty as to what action they should take in these situations. A basic reason for this confusion, not only among medical personnel but in the law itself, is the fact that legal principles on this issue are in conflict.

The Principle of "Sanctity of Life"

[14.76] The sanctity of life is a principle established by law, that is, the prohibition of murder applies for all human beings (see Lipman (1986)). It states that life has an absolute value, and one cannot dispense with a life even when it is considered an inferior one, as at law there is no such thing as an "inferior" life, or a life that is not worth living. However, there is also a right to be free from unwanted or harmful actions. This right is protected by criminal sanctions against assault and battery (see, for example, Brett, Waller and Williams (1997), Ch 3) and civil actions available for assault and battery (see above Ch 4) including specific provisions relating to domestic violence and child abuse. One could note

[14.76] here also that medical treatment given to children which is not therapeutic (that is not directly for the child's benefit, but rather for ease of management or for the development of medical science) is severely curtailed, if not prohibited, in most jurisdictions (see, for example, legislation covering transplantation of tissues for the various States of Australia). Active killing is forbidden, but so are omissions which adversely affect someone whose welfare is one's responsibility. A recent departure from the sanctity of life principle was the recognition that sometimes a life may be so awful that it is recognised, at least morally, that one may be justified in not extending what amounts to a painful and unbearable existence by extraordinary means (Templeman J of the English Court of Appeal in *Re B (A Minor)* [1981] 1 WLR 1421; see [14.133]). In *Airedale NHS Trust v Bland* [1993] AC 789 (see [14.91]) Lord Keith of Kinkel spoke for the majority (at 859) when he clarified the well-established legal principle:

> The principle [of the sanctity of life] is not an absolute one. It does not compel a medical practitioner on pain of criminal sanctions to treat a patient, who will die if he does not, contrary to the express wishes of the patient. It does not compel the temporary keeping alive of patients who are terminally ill where to do so would merely prolong their suffering [see also the extensive coverage of the sanctity of life in *A (Children)* at [14.139]].

[14.77] In considering the law regarding assisting a person to a "good death" there are three categories of person to be taken into account:

- ..... those who can be restored to reasonable health who do not wish to live;
- ..... those whose death is imminent and whose final days are considered unbearable; and
- ..... those whose death is not imminent, but whose quality of life is so diminished continued existence is considered unbearable.

Suicide

[14.78] As has been stated earlier (see above, Ch 4), an adult who understands the implications of such a decision can refuse treatment necessary for the continuation of life. Where a person ends their own life, medical personnel are not implicated, unless they assist them to do so. Making available the means to suicide, such as drugs or instruments, or giving information *with the specific intention of assisting the suicide may be an offence* (*AG v Able* [1984] 1 All ER 277). Without that clear intention proved, negligence or carelessness may be alternative findings by a court.

[14.79] The withholding of life-saving treatment is less easily dealt with. It involves the distinction between a positive act which causes an unlawful killing, and the failure to act, which, unless there is an established duty to act (such as caring for one's patient), may not be a criminal offence. It can be argued, however, that an omission may be one of a series of events which could be held to constitute the active bringing about of a particular result. Modern technology has helped to blur the distinction between active and passive measures of causing a person to die [14.82] (indeed death itself has become a matter of uncertainty): the law has not been able to provide a clear delineation.

[14.80] Whether a person's refusal of treatment amounts to suicide is a matter that is the subject of conjecture and discussion among lawyers and ethicists. However, it was emphasised in *Bland's case* (see [14.91], [14.106]) that where treatment has been refused there is no question of health carers who accede to the refusal having aided or abetted suicide unless that is the health carer's clear and positive intention. It is simply that the patient has, as he or she is entitled to do, declined to consent to treatment which might otherwise have the effect of prolonging life, and the doctor has, in accordance with the law, complied with the patient's wishes. The person must be fully aware of the decision he or she is making, and of the consequences of it. It would seem that so long as staff have made reasonable attempts to ensure this understanding, and voluntary refusal on the part of the person, the provision only of care and comfort should not amount to criminal behaviour.

▐▐▐ CHECKLIST
WHEN A CLIENT REFUSES TREATMENT

- ▐ .....Is the client competent and aware of the decision?
- ▐ .....Has the client had the opportunity to discuss the decision with family (or others he or she may wish to consult) and staff?
- ▐ .....Have the consequences and effects to the client, family (and staff) been discussed?
- ▐ .....Have the reasons for rejecting the treatment and alternative action or treatment—including that offered by other doctors or facilities—been canvassed?
- ▐ .....Has the client been offered general care and comfort if the decision to refuse treatment is maintained?
- ▐ .....Have all staff who are and will be involved in the client's care been included in any staff decision-making discussions?

[14.81] This checklist will prevent those concerned in this situation feeling that they are doing something that is wrong, that they do not believe in, or about which they have not been fully informed. It cannot guarantee the legality of any decision made, so, while recognising that there are some situations where a person makes a genuine decision to refuse treatment, health carers should act on any reasonable doubt as to their ability to do so.

End-of-Life Decision-Making

[14.82] Where a person is terminally ill, and death is imminent, the law remains the same: one should not kill (and that means actively to hasten death), no matter how unbearable the person's situation and no matter how much he or she may wish to die.

[14.82] **CASE**
R v Cox, *The Age*, 15 May 1992 (Queen's Bench Division)

Dr Cox treated Mrs Boyes, an elderly patient who was terminally ill with rheumatoid arthritis complicated by internal bleeding, gangrene, anaemia, gastric ulcers and bedsores. She was in constant and unbearable pain, to the extent that she howled with pain "like a wounded animal" when her son touched her hand. Massive doses of heroin did not help her, and she decided she wanted to die. Having informed her family of this, and stating that she would refuse all treatment except analgesics, she begged Dr Cox to "cut short her agony". Dr Cox gave her two ampoules of potassium cyanide, a doubly lethal dose. The injection was given at the request of the patient and in full knowledge that it would cause her death. Charges were brought against Dr Cox after a nurse who was aware of his action reported him to the police. As Mrs Boyes had been cremated before the investigation began (thus preventing the prosecution proving the drug caused the death), Dr Cox was charged with attempted murder. Dr Cox did not deny giving the drug in the full knowledge that it would cause death, but argued that a doctor is entitled to do all that is proper and necessary to relieve pain and suffering even if the measures taken might incidentally shorten life (see *R v Adams*, [14.91]).

[14.83] Dr Cox was found guilty, the judge directing the jury that it is never lawful to use drugs for the sole purpose of hastening death (although the principle of "double effect" can apply where medication is given in doses which may incidentally hasten death; see [14.90]ff). A case against a nurse in Queensland, which was held amid a storm of publicity and controversy, had a different result.

CASE
R v Jenkin (June 1993, SC Townsville) (from the *Canberra Times* April 23-May 25, 1993).

The defendant, a nurse, was charged with the murder of one patient and attempted murder of three others at Charters Towers Hospital in north Queensland between March and December, 1989. The prosecution alleged she administered unprescribed drugs to all four patients, and then "bluffed her way" through the situations. All patients were terminally ill from cancer, and tests had discovered levels of unprescribed drugs in the bodies of at least some of them. The defendant denied administering the drugs, and the judge told the jury that to convict her they would have to find two facts were proved: that the injections of the unprescribed drugs were administered to the alleged victims, and that it was the defendant who administered them. They would also have to find from the facts that she intended to cause the death of the patients. The judge pointed to the conflicting evidence given by nurse witnesses, and said the jury would have to decide which evidence to believe.

[14.84] The jury returned a "not guilty" verdict. Their reasoning will not be known, particularly as the judge advised the jury not to discuss what went on in the jury room with the media. However it appears from media reports that the major issue in the case was lack of evidence, rather than any question of what activity is or is not permissible by law. It is notable that members of the families of most of the patients were supportive of the defendant, and stated their belief in her innocence.

Legislation Allowing Voluntary Euthanasia

[14.85] The Northern Territory made news when the Legislative Assembly there passed the *Rights of the Terminally Ill Act* 1995 (NT), which provided that where:

- .....a patient was terminally ill and subject to unbearable suffering, with no prospect of relief from alternative treatment, and persistently requested assistance to die; and
- .....a comprehensive list of requirements, such as further medical opinions including a psychiatric report, informed consent and waiting periods, and counselling had been met;

any action by a doctor in assisting that person to die through active measures would not be homicide.

[14.86] This was the first legislation of its kind in the world (the Dutch Government has, after decades of official toleration of assisted termination of life under strict guidelines, passed similar legislation in 2000). Contrary to the name of the Northern Territory Act, it did not in fact bestow an enforceable right: no one was obliged to assist the person, and assistance was dependent upon medical assessment. However it did provide a means of assisted death for those who found their suffering unbearable, with no alternative treatment. Four people were assisted to die under the Act, until the Federal Government, using its powers under s 122 of the Constitution (which permits it to make laws for the Northern Territory, the Australian Capital Territory and Norfolk Island) passed the *Euthanasia Laws Act* 1997 (Cth), prohibiting those Territories from enacting laws that would allow "the form of intentional killing of another called euthanasia, (which includes mercy killing) or the assisting of a person to terminate his or her life".

[14.87] There are conflicting views as to whether there is any difference in the eyes of the law between withholding treatment, or discontinuing it once it has been started, even at the patient's request. Dix et al argue that once life support has been started, to discontinue it may be murder, even where the patient requests this (Dix et al (1989), p 296). Presumably this view would require that the life support be maintained until the patient is pronounced dead. Brody ((1981), p 235) points out the irrationality of this approach. He points out that not wanting to cease life-preserving treatment once it has been started is an understandable emotional, but ethically inconsistent, reaction:

> If you begin administering penicillin for a patient's sore throat, and the culture turns out to be negative for strep, you are not obligated to treat the patient with a full course of penicillin just because you started it and are therefore committed.

[14.88] **[14.88]** Other commentators base their considerations on the category into which the patient fits, agreeing with the opinion of Lord Devlin (see [14.91]).

[14.89] There are two principles at law that provide guidance in dealing with this difficult issue.

Principle 1: "Double Effect"

[14.90] Despite the fact that the administration of drugs, when it is anticipated that they will hasten death, would normally be unlawful homicide, judges at common law have held that where a patient has no prospect of recovery and is in severe pain, someone may administer increasingly potent doses of a drug necessary to relieve that pain, even if it is known that the drug will, in all likelihood, hasten the patient's death. It is argued that the intention is to relieve pain, not to cause death, and therefore not wrong. This means of pain relief must be the only reasonable choice in the circumstances, and death must be imminent, that is, any shortening of life which can be anticipated must be insubstantial. What is "insubstantial" is a matter of judgment for the doctor.

[14.91] This principle was enunciated by Lord Devlin in the case of *R v Adams*, *The Times*, 9 April 1957, where he was directing the jury as to the administration of drugs to a patient who was terminally ill and in pain. He stated that no doctor has the right in the case of the dying (nor in the case of the healthy), to "cut the thread of life". If the purpose of medicine, the restoration of health, is no longer possible for someone, however, the administration of adequate pain relief should not be considered the cause of death:

> [T]here is still much for a doctor to do, and he is entitled to do all that is proper and necessary to relieve pain and suffering, even if the measures he takes may incidentally shorten life. That is not because there is any special defence for medical men. . . . The law is the same for all . . . no act is murder which does not cause death. 'Cause' means nothing philosophical or technical or scientific. . . . If, for example, because a doctor has done something or has omitted to do something death occurs . . . at 11 o'clock instead of 12 o'clock or even on Monday instead of Tuesday, no people of common sense would say: 'Oh the doctor caused her death.' They would say the cause of death was the illness or the injury which brought her into hospital.

[14.92] Of this statement one can warn that, first, how imminent death has to be was not stated by Lord Devlin, thus his words should be treated with caution. Secondly, the measures taken to relieve pain should be appropriate, necessary and not excessive.

[14.93] This case was endorsed in *Bland's case* (see [14.106]) where Lord Goff of Chieveley stated:

> The doctor who is caring for a [terminally ill patient] cannot, in my opinion, be under an absolute obligation to prolong his life by any means

available to him, regardless of the quality of the patient's life. Common [14.96] humanity, requires otherwise, as do medical ethics and good medical practice accepted in this country and overseas. As I see it, the doctor's decision whether or not to take any such step must (subject to his patient's ability to give or withhold his consent) be made in the best interest of the patient. It is this principle too which, in my opinion, underlies the established rule that a doctor may, when caring for a patient who is, for example dying of cancer, lawfully administer pain killing drugs despite the fact that he knows that an incidental effect of that application will be to abbreviate the patient's life. Such a decision may properly be made as part of the care of the living patient, in his best interests; and on this basis, the treatment will be lawful. Moreover, where the doctor's treatment of his patient is lawful, the patient's death will be regarded in law as exclusively caused by the injury or disease to which his condition is attributable.

■ ■ ■ CASE
R v Arthur, The Times, 6 October 1981, pp 1, 12

Dr Arthur, when confronted with a newborn Down's Syndrome baby, who had other complications as well, ordered (with the parents' consent) "nursing care only" and dihydrocodeine 5ml 4 hourly. After the child's death Dr Arthur was charged with murder.

[14.94] Some important points of law were made by the judge, which, although not tested on appeal, nevertheless give some guidance to health carers.

"Double effect" as Cause

[14.95] Because of the facts which indicated that the cause of death was most likely pneumonia (rather than drug overdose or starvation), the judge ruled that there was not enough evidence to show that Dr Arthur caused the child's death, and the charge against him was altered to one of attempted murder. This shifted the focus to Dr Arthur's intentions—did he have murder in his heart?—an issue that relates to the second principle, that of double effect as intention (see [14.99]).

[14.96] This highlights the fact that it is very difficult to prove that one's failure to act caused something to happen, although in many cases it is possible to argue that omissions hastened what was going to happen anyway. Strictly speaking, as everyone eventually dies, even murder as we commonly know it is simply a hastening of the inevitable. The law has had problems with this, as drawing a line between acceptable and unacceptable hastening of death proves difficult when death is imminent. The question becomes whether there is a valid difference in effect between failure to feed and failure to carry out life-sustaining surgery. It would seem that they are both life-sustaining activities, and as the court recognised in *Re B (A Minor)* (see [14.133]) failure to carry out surgery may be just as much a bringing about of death as failure to feed (or the giving

[14.96] of a lethal drug) Lord Templeman stated that a baby on whom surgery for intestinal blockage was refused would be "in effect condemned to die".

[14.97] The court will consider whether the accused's act was operative at the time of death. In *R v Hallett* [1969] SASR 141 a man was beaten unconscious by the accused and left lying on the edge of the beach, where he later drowned. The accused's act was held to have caused the death. The court held that where an act or series of acts (or omissions), were:

- ..... consciously performed by the accused;
- ..... a *substantial causal* factor in the death; and
- ..... still operative at the time of death,

they can be considered a cause of death, even if other casual factors were also present at the time of death.

[14.98] However, policy has been applied here as well, and the House of Lords has ruled that even where physical cause has not been established, the creation of a substantial risk of death can constitute manslaughter. This has also led the courts to rule that there is no proof of cause of death in cases where doctors have withheld treatment from a terminally ill patient whose death is imminent. See, for example, President's Commission (1983), p 69ff; *Bland's case* [14.91]; see also [14.106].

"Double effect" as Intention

[14.99] Intention to kill, which became the issue in *R v Arthur*, need not involve hatred or wishing someone to die, but may involve actions that it is known will, or are likely to, bring about someone's death, even though the perpetrator's motive is based on that person's best interests. The intention in *Arthur's* case would have to have been the intention to bring about an otherwise avoidable death. The jury decided that this was not the case, and acquitted the defendant. Although there seems to be plenty of scope for finding this absence of intent with regard to this particular child it is, in the writer's view, disturbing to note that the judge focused the jury's attention on what it is suggested were improper grounds for so finding. He relied on the assumption that the doctor's intention can be defined in terms of those intentions which the medical profession claims to have—that the right intentions must necessarily be held by someone simply because he or she is a doctor of good repute. This, in fact, fails to account for the actual intention of the doctor in the case under consideration: it infers her or his personal intention from the fact that doctors in general have good intentions. This makes the doctor's opinion unassailable and is not, it is submitted, correct reasoning at law, although courts may accept both it and the result. For discussion of the principle of "double effect" see McLean ((1985), p 63): "it is submitted that not all life will be allowed or helped to survive—the premise is that some babies don't have a right to live". See also the President's Commission ((1983), pp 82ff), and the discussion by Skegg ((1984), pp 135-138). Note that the Director of Public Prosecutions in England stated after this case that he had no intention of challenging the legal principle of "double effect".

[14.100] Courts have, however, approached the problem of double effect by arguing that the giving of medication, ostensibly with the intention of giving comfort and relief from pain, but in doses which it is recognised will most probably result in side effects causing death, is to give the medication devoid of any intention to cause death. According to McLean this is part of the law's approach of applying "the intellectually deceitful device of differentiating between acts and omissions and adopting a more humane practice of humane killing" (McLean (1985), p 68).

South Australia: Legislative Provision of "Double Effect"

[14.101] Section 17 of the *Consent to Medical Treatment and Palliative Care Act* 1995 (SA) has provided protection for health carers who administer drugs to those who are terminally ill for the purpose of pain relief only, despite the fact that it may shorten their life expectancy.

▋▋▋ STATUTE

Consent to Medical Treatment and Palliative Care Act (South Australia) 1995 (SA)

17. (1) A medical practitioner responsible for the treatment or care of a patient in the terminal phase of a terminal illness, or a person participating in the treatment or care of the patient under the medical practitioner's supervision, incurs no civil or criminal liability by administering medical treatment with the intention of relieving pain or distress—

(a) with the consent of the patient or the patient's representative; and
(b) in good faith and without negligence; and
(c) in accordance with proper professional standards of palliative care,

even though an incidental effect of the treatment is to hasten the death of the patient;

(2) A medical practitioner responsible for the treatment or care of a patient in the terminal phase of a terminal illness, or a person participating in the treatment or care of the patient under the medical practitioner's supervision, is, in the absence of an express direction by the patient or the patient's representative to the contrary, under no duty to use, or to continue to use, life sustaining measures in treating the patient if the effect of doing so would be merely to prolong life in a moribund state without any real prospect of recovery or in a persistent vegetative state.

(3) For the purposes of the law of the State—

(a) the administration of medical treatment for the relief of pain or distress in accordance with subsection (1) does not constitute an intervening cause of death; and
(b) the non-application or discontinuance of life sustaining measures in accordance with subsection (2) does not constitute an intervening cause of death.

Principle 2: "Extraordinary measures"

[14.102] Another means of avoiding the intransigence of the "sanctity of life" principle is the dictum that no one is required, morally or legally, to prolong life by extraordinary means under certain circumstances. Of course the question arising here is what is meant by extraordinary means, and there is uncertainty in both medical and legal circles on this point.

[14.103] This approach has been developed by moral theologians to distinguish those attempts at preserving life which are morally required of any person (for example, Pope Pius XII (1957)). But note the change of approach to that of treatment being "disproportionately burdensome" (Skegg (1984), p 146).

> In a medical context [writers] regard 'ordinary' means as 'all medicines, treatments, and operations, which offer a reasonable hope of benefit for the patient and which can be obtained and used without excessive expense, pain, or other inconvenience', whereas 'extraordinary' means are . . . medicines, treatments and operations which cannot be obtained without excessive expense, pain or other inconvenience, or which, if used, would not offer a reasonable hope of relief [Skegg (1984), p 144].

[14.104] Obviously the definition is not only vague, but covers classifications which will differ over time. This, Skegg argues, is not a reason for abandoning it, but he gives two other reasons for doing so. First, he points out that courts should not adopt the moralists' distinction because it is quite different from that used by the medical profession, which considers "extraordinary" more in the light of "heroic" or "unusual", and distinctions are blurred. Secondly, he argues that the moralists' distinction is based on Roman Catholic theology, and so based on presumptions not all would accept. Courts have adopted the ordinary/extraordinary means approach, and have accepted that some treatment, such as naso-gastric feeding and intravenous fluids are ordinary treatment, whereas intra-gastric feeding and mechanical means of respiration has been considered extraordinary treatment. (See discussion in *Bland's Case* at [14.106]). The President's Commission has suggested that the more appropriate test would be that of proportionate or disproportionate benefit ((1983), p 88).

[14.105] In South Australia, section 17 of the *Consent to Medical Treatment and Palliative Care Act* 1995 (set out at [14.101]) provides that for the purposes of the law in that State, the administration of medical treatment for the relief of pain or distress in accordance with subsection 17(1) of that Act, or non-application or discontinuance of life sustaining measures in accordance with subsection 17(2) of that Act "does not constitute an intervening cause of death", although a medical practitioner is not relieved from the consequences of negligence in deciding whether a person is terminally ill. Life sustaining measures are defined as those that "supplant or maintain the operation of vital bodily functions that are temporarily or permanently incapable of independent operation, and include assisted ventilation, artificial nutrition and hydration and cardio-pulmonary resuscitation". The Act is apparently based on the presumption that there is no need to consider nurses or other health [14.107] carers and their role in the care of the terminally ill.

Persistent Vegetative State

[14.106] A person diagnosed as being in a persistent vegetative state is in a particularly difficult legal category. The person has overwhelming damage or dysfunction of the cerebral hemispheres, which removes the capacity for self-aware mental activity, where the diencephalon and brainstem functions remain, preserving autonomic and motor reflexes such as respiration, swallowing, blinking, and spontaneous unco-ordinated movement, and sleep-awake cycles. The person thus has no cognitive functions, such as awareness or sensory perception. Whilst very much alive according to law, and with a possibly indefinite life expectancy, the question of whether the person has any "interests" in continued health care is problematic. For a discussion of the issues surrounding the decision to withdraw treatment from those in a persistent vegetative state, see Freckelton (1993).

▌▌▌ CASE
Airedale NHS Trust v Bland (Bland's Case) [1993] 1 All ER 821 (House of Lords)

Anthony Bland, a 21-year-old patient in the care of the applicant health authority had been in a persistent vegetative state for three and a half years after suffering a severe crushed chest injury which caused catastrophic and irreversible damage to the higher functions of the brain. He was being fed artificially and mechanically by a nasogastric tube. The unanimous opinion of all doctors was that there was no hope whatsoever of recovery or improvement of any kind, or expectation that Tony Bland would ever recover from his persistent vegetative state.

The consultant specialist reached the conclusion that it would be appropriate to cease treatment, including the withdrawal of the nasogastric tube and thus nutrition, as well as such treatment as antibiotic therapy. This view was supported by others, and the health authority applied to the court for declarations that it and the responsible physicians could lawfully discontinue all life-sustaining treatment and support measures designed to keep Tony Bland alive including ventilation, nutrition and other medical treatment. This was to be for the sole purpose of enabling him to end his life and die peacefully with the greatest dignity and the least pain. The plaintiff's action was supported by Bland's parents and family.

The Official Solicitor appealed to the Court of Appeals which affirmed the judge's decision. The Official Solicitor then appealed to the House of Lords. The argument was that the withdrawal of life support was both a breach of the doctor's duty to care for Tony Bland indefinitely if need be, and a criminal act.

[14.107] The House of Lords held that where a patient is incapable of deciding whether or not to consent to treatment, health carers are under no absolute obligation to prolong the patient's life regardless of the circumstances. Medical treatment, including artificial feeding and the

[14.107] administration of antibiotic drugs, could lawfully be withheld from an insensate patient who had no hope of recovery when it was known that the patient would shortly thereafter die, provided reasonable and competent medical opinion was of the view that it would be in the patient's best interests not to prolong her or his life by continuing that form of treatment and that such treatment was futile and would not confer any benefit on the patient.

[14.108] This is a landmark case in that it established that a person can have life-preserving measures removed with the sole intent that they should die. The judges' finding goes against the principle of "double intent". They also broke with common law precedents by rejecting the formerly accepted notion that only extraordinary measures can be withdrawn from a person by allowing the discontinuance of life support by removal of hydration and nutrition. In doing this they accepted the argument of expert witnesses that nutrition and hydration were treatment just like any other, as it substitutes a function that has naturally failed. The removal of the feeding tube, they said, did not amount to a criminal act because if the continuance of an intrusive life support system was not in the patient's interests the doctor was no longer under a duty to maintain the patient's life but was simply allowing the patient to die of the pre-existing condition and the death would be regarded in law as exclusively caused by the injury or disease to which the condition was attributable. Throughout the extensive consideration of the law by the Law Lords is expressed their dissatisfaction with the common law as it stands. They recognised its inappropriateness in many cases, and its inability to cope with modern medical knowledge and technology, as well as changing social attitudes.

[14.109] As a result some of the judges made the following points:

- ..... The taking of active steps to end a patient's life is unlawful;
- ..... Doctors should, from time to time seek the guidance of the court in all cases before withholding life-prolonging treatment from a patient in a persistent vegetative state. This should be by way of declaratory relief. In time a body of expertise would develop, and only those cases which are exceptional would need to be brought to court.
- ..... Lords Browne-Wilkinson and Mustill declared that it is imperative that the moral, social and legal issues raised by the withholding of treatment from an insensate patient with no hope of recovery should be considered by Parliament (that is, that legislation clarifying the law be passed).

[14.110] Diagnosis of persistent vegetative state, as opposed to other forms of brain function deficit, should be very carefully undertaken. In the case of *Northbridge v Central Sydney Area Health Service* (discussed at [5.56]), O'Keefe J pointed to evidence that the Royal College of Physicians in the UK recognises a transient vegetative state, a chronic vegetative state, which should only be made after a period in excess of four weeks of being continually in a vegetative state, and persistent vegetative state, which should only be made after a patient has been in a chronic vegetative state for more than 12 months following a head injury or more than six months following other causes of brain damage. Scans of the brain and other tests may be used to determine whether there are signs of cerebral activity in assisting diagnosis.

"Locked-in" State

▮▮▮ CASE
Auckland Hospital v Attorney General [1993] 1 NZLR 235 (High Court of New Zealand)

"L" was suffering from Guilliam-Barre syndrome. He was unable to communicate or respond in any way to his environment. He was not brain-dead but the extent of denervation meant that his brain was not connected with any part of his body, except perhaps with the visual pathways. He required ventilatory support in order to exist. The Hospital Board and L's doctor sought a declaration from the New Zealand High Court that disconnecting the ventilator would not be a criminal act.

[14.111] This case, as the *Bland* case, above, caused the judges some concern that the legal principles which have been developed are not suitable to modern medical technology and knowledge. Strict adherence to the principle that removal of so-called "life-preservation" is a crime poses problems. Thomas J expressed his concern by stating that the issues before the court could not be resolved by legal logic, but required rather the application of the common principles of humanity. The court stated that while it could make a declaration to this effect, it would have to do so very carefully. It said that the question to answer was whether the doctor had a legal duty to continue life support, or whether there was justification in removing it. Justification in ceasing treatment is its futility. The court declared that a doctor who removes life support for a patient who is effectively lifeless should not be held responsible for the person's death. In this case the ventilation was deferring death rather than preserving life. The court held that removing it would not be a criminal offence.

[14.112] This case should be treated carefully, in the author's view. It dealt with a person who was very seriously ill, to the point where the court considered him "effectively lifeless". Any similar cases should be dealt with by the courts, until the passage of legislation which clarifies the legal situation. Again, the role of nurses and other health carers are not considered in these cases, and it appears the presumption of the courts is that they are not in a position to act on their own judgment. It is important that any future legislation, guidelines or policies to deal with withdrawing or withholding treatment from those who are terminally ill address the role of others in caring for them as well as medical practitioners.

Discussion

[14.113] It is argued that the principles of double effect and extraordinary measures are in fact "intellectually deceitful devices" (to use McLean's words, see [14.99]-[14.100]), adopted to maintain the semblance of the "sanctity of life" principle, as an absolute principle, rather than to accept that both the medical profession and society in general acknowledge that in some cases there should be an exception to the "sanctity of life" principle for those whose lives are "so awful" as to be a burden too cruel for them (or their families or society) to bear. The real issue, says the President's Commission (p 82, n 13),

> is whether decision makers have considered the full range of foreseeable effects, have knowingly accepted whatever risk of death is entailed, and hold the risk to be justified in light of the paucity and undesirability of their options.

[14.114] The criminal law arrives at a similar resolution of the problem but unfortunately via a more obtuse and distorted path through the fictions of double effect and extraordinary means. Where death is imminent, one can give medication for relief of pain even if it would otherwise be contra-indicated, and can withhold treatment which is extraordinary in the circumstances.

[14.115] The logic behind the principle that omissions to act (for example, the withholding of treatment) cannot be held to be the cause of death and thus culpable, whereas actions (such as the giving of a lethal injection to end unbearable suffering) can be held to be the cause of death and thus culpable, is questioned by Skene (1998, p 229).

Legislation and Guidelines

[14.116] To clarify the law and assist both the terminally ill and their carers, the Australian Capital Territory, the Northern Territory, South Australia and Victoria have enacted legislation, and New South Wales has issued guidelines.

Victoria

[14.117] The *Medical Treatment Act* 1988 (Vic) attempts to clarify the law relating to rights of patients, when they cannot do so at the time, to ensure that they do not receive medical treatment, and to protect doctors who comply with directions to cease or withhold treatment given by a patient, or their appointed agent through an enduring power of attorney (see also [5.119]). It should be noted that the Act does not apply to nurses or health carers other than "medical practitioners", and so they are excluded from both the responsibilities and the immunities of the Act—a failure by the law to recognise their real and valuable role in the care of these patients. The Act provides that the patient can clearly express in writing, or any way in which he or she can communicate, refusal of treatment, except for palliative care. It creates the offence of medical [14.120] trespass if a medical practitioner provides treatment in spite of the refusal.

[14.118] Significant issues relating to this legislation are the fact that any person can execute the document, whether they are ill at the time or not. Critics have argued that this detracts from the use of the document, as it may be expected to be acted upon when circumstances are materially different to those obtained when it was executed, and the person may have changed their mind. The second issue is doubt created about the right of a person to refuse palliative care. At common law one can refuse all treatment or care, and thus be the instrument of one's own demise. It would seem, however, that what the Act is providing is immunity for a doctor where a person is unconscious, and he or she has to decide what treatment to give. Palliative care must be given, but if there is a document refusing other care, properly executed, on which the doctor acts, then no action can be brought at law, and indeed the doctor must honour the wishes expressed in the document.

■■■ CASE

Re Kinney (unreported, 23 December 1988, SC Vic, No M2/1989) (CCH ¶22-340)

A man who suffered from leukaemia, and was on bail facing a charge of murder, attempted suicide and was being treated in hospital. His wife sought an injunction to prevent doctors carrying out exploratory surgery to stop bleeding and/or other active measures to prolong or save her husband's life. She based her claim on the severe pain he was suffering, the fact that he had expressed a wish to die, and her belief that he would rather die than return to gaol. She argued that he could thus be considered to have refused treatment.

[14.119] The Supreme Court of Victoria held that as no refusal of treatment certificate had been signed by the patient in accordance with the *Medical Treatment Act* and there was no other documentary evidence that he did not wish to receive treatment, either for the leukaemia or the overdose, it could not issue the injunction. Compassion and sympathy alone were not enough to allow the court to issue the injunction, it said, and to do so would be to assist suicide. Very powerful consideration would be required to prevent doctors from saving a person's life. This is in accordance with the general principle that despite the fact that suicide is not an offence, the state has an interest in preventing suicide.

South Australia

[14.120] The *Consent to Medical Treatment and Palliative Care Act* 1995 (SA) allows an adult to give directions that he or she does not want extraordinary measures in the event of suffering a terminal illness or is in a persistent vegetative state (and by implication is unable to communicate these wishes at the time). Where a direction has been made in accordance with the Act, the person is in the terminal stage of a terminal illness and unable to make decisions and there is no reason to believe the direction

[14.120] has been revoked, it is taken as consent to being treated according to the direction. The Act also provides protection for medical practitioners who act in good faith according to a direction. Where a person is in the terminal phase of a terminal illness, a medical practitioner, will incur no civil or criminal liability for administering, discontinuing or withholding, care, is he or she acted in good faith and without negligence, in accordance with consent of an authorised authority and with proper professional standards of medical practice, even though an incidental effect of the treatment is to hasten the death of the patient. The practitioner faced with a direction made under the Act who in good faith and without negligence makes a decision that a person is not suffering from a terminal illness, or either revoked the direction which was made, or did not understand the nature and consequences of making it, will not be liable at law.

[14.121] Where there is no direction or authority for consent, a medical practitioner is under no duty to use, or continue to use, life sustaining measures if the effect of doing so would be merely to prolong life in a moribund state without any real prospect of recovery or in a persistent vegetative state.

Northern Territory

[14.122] The *Natural Death Act* 1988 (NT) allows terminally ill patients who are competent to refuse "extraordinary measures" (that is "measures that prolong life, or are intended to prolong life by supplanting or maintaining the operation of bodily functions that are temporarily or permanently incapable of independent operation"). Palliative care cannot be refused.

Australian Capital Territory

[14.123] The *Medical Treatment Act* 1994 (ACT) provides a legal immunity for a doctor or nurse who in good faith withholds or withdraws medical treatment from a person who has made a directive refusing that treatment for an illness from which he or she is suffering at the time of the directive. A special form is provided for this, or where the patient is unable to sign the form, procedures are set out for the patient to communicate his or her wishes. The special immunity provided does not cover palliative care (pain relief, nourishment and comfort)—health carers are covered by the common law in these circumstances (see Figure 14.1 below). Carers must not give effect to the direction unless reasonably sure the patient understands the information he or she is to be given under the Act, so that the decision is an informed one. They must also be reasonably sure that the patient is able to weigh the various options available, and to affirm their decision. The *Medical Treatment Act* also provides for the making of an enduring power of attorney which allows another, named, person to refuse treatment on behalf of the patient if he or she becomes incapable of refusing the treatment. The person refusing treatment on the patient's behalf is required to act according to the known wishes of the

patient. The Act introduces the right of patients to receive maximum pain [14.126]
relief which is reasonable under the circumstances, and goes on to say that
in determining what amount of pain relief to give, health carers are to pay
due regard to the patient's account of his or her level of suffering.

New South Wales

[14.123] New South Wales has issued guidelines on the treatment of the
terminally ill. These guidelines are aimed at generating a respect for
human life, patients' autonomy, consultation with relatives, access to
medical care and a professional approach to the issues involved. They
stress that a management plan should be developed in consultation with
the patient, establishing goals and lengths of treatment, as well as
circumstances in which it may be foregone. Where the patient cannot
participate in decision making, the family should be consulted to establish
his or her wishes and expectations in as much as they can be identified. If
death is impending and a patient (or family where he or she is
incompetent) requests removal of life-support, full assessment and
documentation of the patient's condition and the decision-making
process should be made, and where life support (except for palliative care)
is considered burdensome and futile it may be removed.
Cardio-pulmonary resuscitation should not be carried out if the patient
does not want it, or it would be "clearly futile" or "prolong suffering". In
all cases records should be made which are clear and unambiguous, which
detail discussions and set out the patient's wishes, clearly identifying what
treatment is to be given and what treatment is to be foregone.

[14.124] The New South Wales Health Department has released a
discussion document that canvasses a revision of the Guidelines to take
into account such issues as cultural differences, the development of
modern technology, and the need for formalisation of the continued
development of the Guidelines.

Queensland

[14.125] The *Powers of Attorney Act* 1988 (Qld) allows individuals to make
an "advance health directive", and the Queensland Government has
released a model form that provides for advance decisions in the case of
terminal illness. A valid directive is consent to, or refusal of, health care
for the purposes of the law.

Quality of life

[14.126] Given that there is a legal obligation on the part of doctors to
maintain life, and further, to treat those patients in their care, it has been
argued that the quality of the life they are preserving is of no concern to
the law at all. Thus, a person must be kept alive even where the quality of
their life is very poor. Indeed this was argued by Vincent J in a recent
hearing in the Supreme Court of Victoria when he ordered the Queen

[14.126] Victoria Hospital to take all necessary and reasonable measures consistent with proper medical practice to preserve the life of a baby born with spina bifida in that hospital (*Re F: F v F* (unreported, 2 July 1986, SC Vic) (quoted from *The Age*, Melbourne, 3 July 1986, p 1, see also *Re 'A' Children*, [14.139]). The judge said: "The law does not permit decisions to be made concerning the quality of life nor any assessment of the value of any human life."

[14.127] This statement highlights an unfortunate ambiguity in the terms "quality of life" which has bedevilled the law, and which, with respect, was not recognised by the learned judge in this statement. Apart from the fact that it contradicts the purpose of the "double effect" principle, it has not been followed in other jurisdictions.

■ ■ ■ CASE
Re Quinlan, 348 A 2d 807 (reversed on Appeal 355 A 2d 647 (1976)) (Court of Appeal New Jersey United States)

> In this landmark case Karen Quinlan, a 22-year-old, was in a permanent comatose state, which was diagnosed as being irreversible. Her unfortunate position was that she was not "brain dead", but was also not "sapient". In the court hearing, Dr Fred Plum described her condition as follows:
>
>> We have an internal vegetative regulation which controls breathing, which controls to a considerable degree blood pressure, which controls to some degree heart rate, which controls chewing, swallowing, and which controls sleeping and waking. We have a more highly developed brain, which is uniquely human, which controls our relation to the outside world, our capacity to talk, to see, to feel, to sing, to think. Brain death necessarily must mean the death of both of these functions of the brain, vegetative and sapient [137 NJ Sup Ct at 238; 348 A 2d 807; see also on this point Hunsaker (1984)].

[14.128] In the words of the court, she was in a "permanent vegetative state". When her father requested that all extraordinary life-sustaining treatment be discontinued, the New Jersey Superior Court disagreed, stating that the decision to discontinue the treatment would be making a decision based on giving an evaluation to the quality of a particular sort of life.

[14.129] This is what the writer would call the "bottom line" approach: if life can be substantially maintained, no matter in what condition, there is an obligation to sustain it. It is also known as the "medical feasibility model" developed by Macmillan (1978). She argues that the only grounds for withholding treatment should be that of medical unfeasibility, which must be diagnosed with a "high degree of certainty" (p 624) and only occurs in two situations:

1)......death is imminent (it will occur within six months to a year); or
2)......the person is irreversibly unconscious.

There was, in this decision, however, reliance, in the last analysis, on the opinion of the physician attending: so long as he felt compelled to maintain life, it should be maintained. This decision contains a fundamental logical flaw in its adoption of two potentially conflicting [14.131] principles: the need to maintain life if it can be maintained, but the reliance on the physician's opinion as to whether it should be maintained. The point should not be laboured, however, at this stage, because the case was taken on appeal to the New Jersey Court of Appeal which overturned the lower court's decision (*Re Quinlan*, 355 A 2d 647 (1976)).

[14.130] That Court held that there is a constitutionally guaranteed right (in the United States), of privacy, which includes a right to permit one's existence to terminate by natural forces. This right could be enforced in this case by Karen's guardian on her behalf, and could be exercised where the family and physicians were of the opinion that her condition was irreversible, and they had consulted with an ethics committee of the hospital and received the committee's concurrence (at p 671). Hunsaker (1984), points out (at p 23) that basing its decision on the prognosis of the reasonable impossibility of return to cognitive and sapient life, rather than on the fact of brain death, shifted the cessation of treatment to the prediction rather than the post-diction of brain death (the problem with this, he points out, is that the prediction can be wrong). This is quite clearly a permission by the Court to make a decision based on the predicted quality of life of the patient. The approach was followed in the following case.

▌▌▌ CASE

The Superintendent of Belchertown State; School et al v Saikewicz, Mass 370 NE 2d 417 (1977) (Court of Appeal United States)

This case involved a profoundly retarded adult, resident of the school, who contracted acute myeloblastic monocytic leukaemia. The applicant requested a guardian ad litem be appointed to decide whether chemotherapy should be given. The guardian was appointed, and recommended no treatment, on the grounds that the benefits would be outweighed by the discomfort, increased by the patient's inability to appreciate its purpose and the temporary relief it would give. The judge of the Probate Court ruled accordingly, and the matter was taken to the Appeal Court to consider, inter alia whether the decision was correct.

[14.131] That Court recognised the ambiguity in the term "quality of life". It can refer to a value placed upon a particular person's life, or the actual interests and values of the person herself or himself. The Court (at 432) preferred the latter approach:

> Rather than reading the judge's formulation in a manner that demeans the value of the life of one who is mentally retarded, the vague, and perhaps ill-chosen, term 'quality of life' should be understood as a reference to the continuing state of pain and disorientation precipitated by the chemotherapy treatment. Viewing the term in this manner, together with the other factors properly considered by the judge, we are satisfied that the decision to withhold treatment from Saikewicz was based on a regard for his actual interests and preferences, and that the facts supported this decision.

[14.132]　[14.132] It is suggested that Vincent J, in *Re F* (above), confused these two meanings. As a result of similar confusion by medical personnel patients may be subjected to painful and inhumane treatment, which is not in their actual interests, but is considered necessary because of the mistaken interpretation of the argument that "quality of life" is not a legitimate consideration. This form of reasoning is consistent with *A (Children)* (see [14.139]), where the English Court of Appeal held that it was not a matter of determining whether a person's life is worth living or not, based on what is seen as that person's quality of life, but the interests and preferences of that person in continuing life, giving the quality of experience it provides.

Withdrawing Treatment from Newborn Infants

[14.133] When a baby is born with serious handicaps or of very low birth weight, the prognosis and expected quality of life (in any meaning of the term) of the child may be a more critical issue in determining whether to institute treatment. As it is not always possible to make a rapid assessment of the baby's condition and the extent of her or his disabilities, health carers must sometimes make quick decisions relating to resuscitation and commencing or continuing treatment based on incomplete information. Different policies have been adopted to deal with this problem, some facilities insist on full care for all babies over, say, 23 weeks gestation, others withhold treatment from all babies under a nominated weight or with specified ailments, yet others adopt a case-by-case decision-making approach, in consultation with parents. The English Court of Appeal attempted to clarify the term "quality of life" where handicapped neonates are concerned.

▌▌▌ CASE
Re B (A Minor) [1981] 1 WLR 1421 (Court of Appeal England)

An infant was born with Down's Syndrome, intestinal blockage and certainly with severe mental and physical handicaps, though it was probable she would have some sapient functions in the sense used in *Quinlan*, above. The court saw the question as being whether it was in the best interests of the child to be allowed to die within the next week, or to have the operation required to correct the bowel problem. If she did have the operation it was not certain whether she would suffer any handicap or whether she would have any quality of life.

[14.134] The court ruled (at 1424):

> at the end of the day it devolves on this court to decide whether the life of the child is demonstrably going to be so awful that in effect the child must be condemned to die, or whether the life of this child is still so imponderable that it would be wrong for her to be condemned to die.

[14.135] Lord Templeman went on to say that there may be other instances where damage is so certain and the child's life bound to be so full of pain and suffering that the court might be moved to rule that treatment be withdrawn; but he found too little certainty of such a future for the child in this particular case. The court ordered that the required [14.139] treatment be given. The novel point here, for English law, is the possibility that the certainty of a very poor quality of life, in the meaning accepted as a ground for withholding treatment in the United States *Saikewicz* case, may be accepted by the English courts.

[14.136] Since then, the English courts have recognised consideration of the quality of life of moribund infants, and the lawfulness of managing some neonates "towards their deaths", giving them treatment to make them comfortable rather than to extend their lives (*Re C (a Minor) (wardship: medical treatment)* [1989] 2 All ER 782; *Re J (a Minor)* [1990] 3 All ER 930, [1992] 4 All ER 614; *Re C (a Minor) Lloyd's Law Reports (Medical)* [1998] FamD 1; and see *A (Children)* (22 September 2000, Court of Appeal, No B1/2000/2969) [14.139].

[14.137] The appropriateness of the question of whether the child's future looks grim receives judicial recognition here, but as in so many cases this language is vague, and continues to beg the question raised by this situation. How bad must the infant's future appear before it is considered that the withdrawing of treatment is warranted? It can be argued that the language does suggest a more liberal interpretation of the child's best interest in the United States than that officially accepted by English courts. This is succinctly stated in the proposition that "permanent handicaps justify a decision not to provide life-sustaining treatment only when they are so severe that continued existence would not be a benefit to the infant" (President's Commission (1983), p 218). The Commission in fact referred to this as a "very restrictive standard", so it is presumed that its definition of "benefit to the infant" does not involve consideration of, for example, the effect of the handicap on other members of the family or society. This ignores the question of reasonable expectation of adequate conditions for the care of the child in the future, which is becoming a more crucial factor as more and more handicapped children are requiring a share of scarce resources. There is widespread support in the medical profession that decisions to forego treatment should be made by parents and physicians and not the law (President's Commission (1983), p 207), including the Judicial Council of the American Medical Association (President's Commission (1983), p 207).

[14.138] It is recognised that this does not explain much. The President's Commission offers the argument that many people who appear to have a life so burdensome as to offer no benefits can be helped to "develop realistic goals and satisfactions". On the other hand, this may just as easily not be the case. Children who continue to live a handicapped life may not appreciate that life. A concern often raised is that if society requires that such children be saved, it should require that they and their families at least be given the assistance and resources required to make the most of their often very difficult life.

[14.139] The question of quality of life for infants came painfully into focus in the following case.

[14.139] ■ ■ ■ **CASE**
A (Children) (22 September 2000, Court of Appeal, No B1/2000/2969)

Two girls, Mary and Jodie, were born joined at the ischium. Each had four limbs, but the lower part of the spines were fused, and the spinal cords conjoined. Each twin had her own brain, heart lungs, liver and kidneys, with a shared bladder. Jodie's aorta fed into Mary's aorta, and the arterial circulation ran from Jodie to Mary. Jodie was alert, responsive and fed well. Evidence was that if she were to be separated from Mary she would have the opportunity of a separate good quality life and to participate in activities appropriate to her age and development. If she were not separated, it was predicted that her heart, which was supporting both twins, would fail in three to six months. She would be restricted in movement and development by the increasingly deteriorating body of Mary.

Mary was in a very poor state. Mary had a poorly developed brain not compatible with normal development, and her heart and lungs were incapable of sustaining life. She shared Jodie's circulatory system and depended on it. If not separated from Jodie, she would be dependent upon her vital organs until they gave out, and this time would be spent in pain and discomfort. She would not develop physically or mentally. Separating her from Jodie would inevitably cause her instant death.

Either both twins were condemned to a very short and poor quality of life unless surgery was carried out to save Jodie that would result in the effective intentional termination of Mary's life.

[14.140] In a long and obviously difficult and sad consideration of the circumstances, the Court of Appeal authorised the surgery. It endorsed the following principles in coming to that decision:

■.....intention;
■.....necessity and self-defence;
■.....application in Australia; and
■.....legislation.

Intention

■.....Mary had a right to life. Every human being is of equal value, and one life cannot be considered less valuable than another, however Jodie also has a right to life.
■.....All persons are entitled to bodily integrity and autonomy, and to have their bodies whole and intact. Mary and Jodie do not have this integrity and autonomy. There is thus a strong presumption that an operation would be in their interests.
■.....The object of an operation would be to provide this integrity, and Jodie would benefit accordingly. The death of Mary would not be intended, although it would be an inevitable consequence. She would gain bodily integrity as a human being, and she would die, not because she was intentionally killed, but because her body could not sustain that integrity. Continued life would hold nothing for her except pain and discomfort, if indeed she could feel anything at all.

..... The operation would therefore be in the best interests of each of the twins, and [14.144]
the court does not have to value one life over another.

Necessity and Self-Defence

[14.141] Ward LJ (with whom Brooke LJ agreed) considered that there was also an argument based on the principle of self defence. He likened the circumstances of the twins to one where the life of a person is threatened by another, and stated at paragraph 7.7:

> I can see no difference in essence between [the] resort to legitimate self defence and the doctors coming to Jodie's defence and removing the threat of fatal harm to her presented by Mary's draining of her life-blood. The availability of such a plea of quasi self-defence, modified to meet the quite exceptional circumstances nature has inflicted on the twins, makes intervention by the doctors lawful.

[14.142] The judges gave much attention to the principle of necessity in the criminal law (see also [4.68]). The judges, in discussing it, considered other situations where one is faced with the choice between two evils, both threatening loss of life: one involving the loss of more lives than the other, but both requiring an action which will end life. An example is the order by a ship's commander to seal the engine room of his warship where there was a fire and flood it with inert gas, knowing that if anyone was inside they would be killed, to save the rest of the crew. They concluded that the least harmful option must be taken, and that to do so is a defence to a charge of murder in criminal law. The act must be taken to avoid inevitable and irreparable evil, no more must be done than is reasonably necessary to avoid the evil, and the harm done must not be disproportionate to the harm inflicted. All judges urged caution in using the defence of necessity, emphasising the need to act in proportion to the harm to be avoided. They agreed that this was a case in which the surgery was justified, as it was the less harmful option.

Application in Australia

[14.143] The principles on quality of life must be recognised as not necessarily applying in Australia, as we have little legislation or case law on point. However there is little reason to believe that the case law mentioned above would not be followed here, and legislation in some States indicates a willingness by society to move in that direction.

Legislation

[14.144] The right to reject a personally unacceptable quality of life by rejection of treatment is recognised at law. Legislation in several States allows a person to make an advance directive to reject treatment if they become incompetent (see [5.109]). Judges in *Airedale* and *A (Children)* expressed regret that there is little legislative clarification of the law in

[14.144] relation to withholding or withdrawing treatment where the person is not competent. Readers might like to consider whether it is possible or feasible to develop such legislation. What situations would be covered? How would principles apply? How would "extraordinary treatment" or "quality of life" be defined? What defences would be available?

Life support

[14.145] The principles set out above also apply to the withholding or withdrawing of life support. The difficulty here is that removal of a patient from a machine is seen as a positive act. In all jurisdictions, except Queensland and Western Australia, death has been defined for all purposes as the irreversible cessation of circulation of the blood, or irreversible cessation of all function of the brain. Queensland has this definition only for the purposes of the *Transplantation and Anatomy Act 1979* (Qld). In these circumstances in those States, the patient is already dead and the life support machinery may be switched off. In other places and circumstances one would have to rely on the principle of extraordinary care, which makes the decision much more difficult. Health carers other than doctors should not be expected to make this decision, and should not be required to turn off a respirator at the direction of anybody else. However, as they are involved in the care and/or treatment of these patients, they should be consulted during the decision-making process, and given the opportunity to express their views and concerns in relation to the care given to, or withdrawn from, those in their care.

[14.146] The difference between coma, brain death, permanent vegetative state, and "locked in syndrome" must be clearly established in the minds of those who are caring for those suffering from these conditions. Before any decision to withhold or withdraw treatment is made, all staff should be clear on the distinctions, and diagnosis as to which condition is present should be made as carefully as is medically possible, all of those involved being satisfied that the diagnosis is correct.

Do not Resuscitate Orders

[14.147] Since the development of cardio-pulmonary resuscitation for patients with particular heart conditions, this procedure has been adopted in most situations of sudden cardiac failure in hospitals and elsewhere. The result may be the prolongation of life, which is of a quality so poor that the resuscitation is recognised as not being in the patient's interest.

[14.148] The legal issues for medical personnel involve those discussed throughout this chapter. Is the failure to resuscitate a criminal act? Are there some circumstances which make it a criminal act? As can be seen, the answers are not certain. Staff should take into account the patient's wishes, their prognosis, and what they can reasonably expect to be the outcome of cardio-pulmonary resuscitation on this particular person in the circumstances. The patient, treating doctor, health care team and family should be consulted where cardiac arrest is anticipated wherever possible.

[14.149] In the writer's view, considerations in anticipating cardiac arrest should include the following:

- Has the patient left instructions not to resuscitate? If so, these should be respected unless there is reason to believe that circumstances have changed since the instructions were given, or that the patient would for some reason have changed her or his mind. Legislation should ensure this right. If no, then CPR is an option.
- Can CPR be expected to work in this case? If not, or it confers no real benefit, or simply prolongs the dying process, then it is quite legitimate to consider not using it. No person is required to give futile medical treatment.
- Given we can expect life to be prolonged, are there indications that the quality of life will be substantially reduced? If yes, then in consultation with the patient, or relatives if this is not possible (who may give advice on the patient's preferred lifestyle and wishes), those responsible may determine that CPR is not in the person's interests. It is recognised that as cardiac arrest is an emergency, little time is available for consultation or deliberation.
- Where either the outcome of CPR, or the patient's wishes in relation to its administration is uncertain, it is suggested that CPR should be attempted until the outcome can reasonably be predicted.

[14.150] There should not be a policy of disguising "Do not resuscitate" orders, for example by using codes or stickers. This creates distrust, not only on the part of the patient, but also on the part of those who must consider the legal implications of such an instruction. Where a code or unspoken instruction has been issued, it may be open to a court to find that the reasons for the order may not have been properly considered, or could be malicious or reckless, whereas the full recording of reasons, with the result of consultation with the patient and/or family if this has occurred, indicates an intention to abide by ethical and legal principles. Writers consider this an important part of the medical relationship with those who are considered in danger of cardiac arrest (see, for example, Brazier (1997), p 458). Hospitals are developing policies which include increased involvement of patient and family in "Do not resuscitate" decisions, although progress is, in the writer's view, all too slow.

[14.150] ▌▌▌ FIGURE 14.1

SUMMARY OF LAW RELATING TO WITHHOLDING OR WITHDRAWING TREATMENT FROM PEOPLE IN DIFFERENT CIRCUMSTANCES

Palliative Care: Includes nursing care such as provision of comfort, prevention of pressure sores, warmth, proper hydration and nutrition, and pain relief.	Refusal to give palliative care by someone who owes a duty to care for another who has not competently refused it is neglect and can lead to conviction for homicide if the person dies as a result. See however *Bland's* case (see [14.91], [14.106]) as an example of an exception to this where the person is in a persistent vegetative state (below) and the court held that such care would not be in the person's interests. In Australia it would seen that a similar fact situation would also have to be considered by a court before palliative care could be withheld.
Extraordinary Care: Generally, care other than palliative care. Depends on the specific circumstances of the case.	Withholding extraordinary care from a patient who cannot decide on treatment is accepted at law where it is considered futile or not in the interests of the patient, when weighed with the life expectancy of the patient and pain and distress it might cause (see *Saikewicz* [14.107], [14.130]; *Bland* [14.90], [14.106]).
Those who are competent	These people may refuse all treatment. Necessary and/or reasonable treatment may not be withheld or withdrawn from them against their will as this may constitute negligence, however they cannot demand futile treatment. Active measures cannot be taken to end their lives, nor can they be assisted to take their own lives. Suicide is not an offence, but it is not assault or battery to prevent someone from committing suicide. Common law indicates that those who are terminally ill may be given adequate pain relief, even though this is expected to shorten their life (see [14.77]ff, [14.90]ff).
Coma: Coma, as distinct from vegetative state or "locked-in syndrome", is a state of unconsciousness, from which the person may be reasonably expected to recover, even if it lasts for months.	Where a person is in a coma, only critical treatment which is clinically futile can be withheld or withdrawn from them. The person may have made an advance directive, stating their wish to have treatment withheld or withdrawn under certain circumstances. The only jurisdiction where failure to obey an advance directive is an offence is Victoria, where the *Medical Treatment Act* 1988 (Vic) creates the offence of medical trespass for so doing.

		[14.151]
Vegetative-State: The cerebral cortex is no longer functioning, but the brain stem is (see description in *Quinlan*). The person has no perception or cognition, breathes spontaneously, has no hope of recovery but may live for many years. Diagnosis is currently based on CAT and PET scans to detect brain function. To be differentiated from long-term coma.	There is no case law in Australia on withdrawal of treatment from these people. In the United States courts have allowed that removal of both extraordinary care and basic nutrition (see [14.127]; *Saikewicz* [14.130]). In Australia futile treatment (ie treatment other than basic life-preservation and nursing care) can be withdrawn (see [14.90]ff). *Bland's* case (see [14.106]) is persuasive precedent that in some circumstances even that may be withdrawn but the matter would have to be decided by an Australian court.	
"Locked-in Syndrome": This condition is different from PVS: the cerebral cortex may be operative, but the brain stem is not. It may, for example result from Guillain-Barre syndrome or cerebro-vascular accident. The patient is conscious but unable to respond to their environment, and requires ventiliation and other artificial life-preserving measures.	As with the patient with coma or PVS, this patient is legally alive, and technically critical treatment cannot be withdrawn or withheld unless it is futile. As artificial life-preservation cannot be considered futile in a strict sense, it would seem that removal of this would be homicide. See, however, for an exceptional case *Auckland Hospital v Attorney-General* at [14.110].	
Brain-death: Total absence of brain activity, with artificial ventilation required to maintain circulation.	Legally the person is dead, and no further treatment of any kind need be given. Logically, "treatment" of a brain-dead person is covered by the laws relating to organ transplants from cadavers and handling of dead bodies.	

Criminal Negligence

[14.151] It is rare for a charge of criminal negligence to be laid against a health worker. It may, however occur where something has gone horribly wrong, with unintended results, and it is established that the health carer in question either intended some degree of harm to occur, or was so reckless with regard to human life or safety that a jury finds their actions serious enough to amount to a criminal act. There is no definition of "criminal negligence" in the legislation (where it involves an unintended death it may be termed involuntary manslaughter), so we must look to the case law for it. However, there are not many cases to help.

▌▌▌ CASE

R v Bateman (1925) 19 Cr App R 8 (Court of Criminal Appeal England)

A doctor unintentionally caused severe internal injury to a patient during delivery of a child, and then neglected to send her elsewhere for necessary treatment with the result that she died. The patient's bladder was ruptured, her colon crushed against the sacral promontory, the rectum ruptured and the uterus almost entirely missing. This led to charges of manslaughter as a result of criminal negligence.

[14.152] [14.152] The court said that, contrary to civil negligence, criminal negligence is based on the amount of negligence—the degree of culpability involved—rather than the amount of harm caused. The defendant has to have shown a disregard for the life and safety of another, and this has to be so reckless as to amount to a crime against the state and conduct deserving of punishment. Based on these considerations, Bateman's conviction in the lower court was quashed at its appeal hearing. Findings of criminal negligence have involved, for example, an anaesthetist addicted to anaesthetic drugs who removed the anaesthetic tube from a child during an operation and put it to his own mouth, causing the child to die from oxygen deprivation (*The Lancet*, 28 February 1959). In that case the doctor received a sentence of 12 months' imprisonment. A physician who had given prescriptions for an inordinately and irresponsibly large number and high dosage of drugs to a patient who subsequently died from the effects of drug induced depression of the gag reflex was also held to be criminally negligent (*Pennsylvania v Youngkin* 427 A 2d 1356 (1981)).

Criminal Negligence as Manslaughter

CASE
R v Larkin [1943] 1 All ER 217 (Court of Criminal Appeal England)

Larkin was convicted of manslaughter as the result of the death of his de facto wife. She died of a throat wound caused by a razor which he held. He testified that he had used the razor to frighten another man who had been intimate with the deceased, and that she had accidentally fallen against it. He appealed to this court.

[14.153] The court drew a distinction between manslaughter by an unlawful act and manslaughter by negligence. The court said that where the accused was carrying out a lawful act, and as a consequence of negligence someone died, the jury must decide whether the negligence proved against the accused amounted to manslaughter. The judge must tell them that it will not amount to manslaughter unless it is negligence of a very high degree: "the expression commonly used is unless it shows the accused to have been reckless as to the consequences of the act" (p 219). Where, as here, the act being carried out was unlawful, then it will be manslaughter simply if the act was dangerous and likely to cause harm.

[14.154] It is in fact rare for health professionals to be charged with manslaughter. The Privy Council pointed out in the case of *Akerele v The King* [1943] AC 255 where many children died as the result of too strong a solution being injected into them, that once an action has taken place, its consequences, no matter how horrible, cannot add to its criminality. Although it is the jury which decides whether the negligence of a person is criminal, the judge decides in the first place whether it has been gross enough to go to the jury. However, in the case of *R v Adomako* [1994] 2 All ER 79 the House of Lords reviewed the law of criminal negligence at length, and endorsed the principles above. In that case an anaesthetist was found guilty of criminal negligence where a patient undergoing [14.158] surgery died as the result of disconnection of a tube from the anaesthetic machine, depriving him of oxygen. Despite an alarm and the falling of the patient's heart rate and blood pressure, the anaesthetist did not check the integrity of the machine. The House of Lords said that the ordinary principles of criminal negligence apply to establish breach of duty, and causation. If these are proved, the next question for the jury is whether the breach was one of gross negligence, and therefore a crime.

Abortion

[14.155] The law regarding abortion is contained in the crime legislation of each State and Territory, as well as some case law. Despite the different wording of the various statutes, it seems to be generally accepted at law that abortion is the untimely expulsion of the foetus from the womb, either spontaneously by natural means, or by external influences (induced abortion). Generally, there are six main elements to the law:

- .....the woman need not actually be pregnant (the intention to abort is the crucial factor);
- .....the prohibition is against the *unlawful* procuring of miscarriage;
- .....a woman must not unlawfully bring about her own miscarriage;
- .....a person must not aid another in unlawfully procuring a miscarriage;
- .....an attempt by any person to procure an unlawful miscarriage is just as serious an offence as if it were successful; and
- .....a person must not supply the means for procuring an unlawful miscarriage; the means may be "any drug or noxious thing, or any instrument or thing whatsoever".

[14.156] It is important to note that each jurisdiction may have complementary legislation setting out further requirements for induced miscarriage, such as the location for the procedure, the number of practitioners certifying its necessity, etc. Some of these are set out below. Health carers should be familiar with the law in their jurisdiction, so that they are not inadvertently involved in unlawful procedures.

The Meaning of "Unlawful"

[14.157] The crucial element in the legal definition is the unlawfulness of the abortion. What is an unlawful abortion? For an answer to that one must turn to case law. Originally, the only accepted ground for inducing an abortion was imminent danger to the life of the mother.

English Precedent

[14.158] In the 1930s the courts began to clarify the term "imminent danger to the life of the mother".

[14.158] ■ ■ ■ CASE
R v Bourne [1938] 3 All ER 615 (Criminal Court England)

A specialist, Dr Bourne, when confronted with a young woman who was pregnant as a result of a particularly vicious multiple rape and likely, in his opinion to suffer severe psychological detriment from continuation of the pregnancy, carried out an abortion and then handed himself over to the police. The subsequent trial resulted in his acquittal, the judge instructing the jury that "danger to the life of the mother" included danger of psychological harm where the doctor has an honest belief that the woman would become a "physical or mental wreck".

Australian Legislation

[14.159] In Australia these jurisdictions set out the circumstances under which an abortion can be performed.

South Australia

[14.160] In South Australia, section 82a of the *Criminal Law Consolidation Act* 1935 (SA) (amended in 1969) permits a doctor to carry out an abortion in the following circumstances:

■ ..... *Non-emergency:* the operation is to be carried out in a hospital and two doctors (one of which is the operating doctor) must be of the opinion that the woman faces a greater risk to her life or mental or physical health than if the pregnancy were continued or the child would suffer such physical or mental abnormalities as to be seriously handicapped.
■ ..... *Emergency:* a medical practitioner may carry out a termination of pregnancy where it is immediately necessary to save the woman's life or prevent grave injury to her mental or physical health.

[14.161] Section 82(1) of that Act provides for a maximum sentence of life imprisonment for the termination of a pregnancy where the foetus is capable of being born alive. This is set at 28 weeks. However, this section does not apply where the termination is required to save the woman's life.

Northern Territory

[14.162] The Northern Territory has similar provisions to South Australia in its *Criminal Code Act* 1983 (NT), except that non-urgent terminations are restricted to a gynaecologist or obstetrician and the woman must have been pregnant for no more than 14 weeks (see section 174). There are three time-frames established under the Act:

- .....*Non-emergency where the pregnancy is less than 12 weeks:* a gynaecologist, with [14.168] the concurrence of another medical practitioner, may carry out a termination of pregnancy where both doctors are of the belief that the woman would suffer greater physical or mental harm than if the pregnancy were to continue, or the child would be seriously handicapped.
- .....*Emergency where such harm is immediately imminent and pregnancy not more than 23 weeks:* a medical practitioner may terminate such a pregnancy.
- .....*Emergency where the woman's life is in immediate danger:* a medical practitioner may terminate the pregnancy. There is no time restriction.

[14.163] Where the woman is under 16 years of age or otherwise unable to give consent, the consent of each person who has the right to give consent on her behalf is required (the Act fails to make any stipulation about emergencies, but presumably all the common law defences would apply; see [4.58], [5.4]).

Victoria

[14.164] The principle in the case of *R v Bourne* was expressed more practically in a Victorian case in the Supreme Court, *R v Davidson* [1969] VR 667, where it was held that the prosecution must establish that:

- .....the accused did not honestly believe on reasonable grounds that the woman would suffer serious danger to life or physical or mental health "not being the normal dangers of pregnancy or childbirth"; and
- .....the accused did not honestly believe that nothing less than abortion was required to avert the danger.

New South Wales

[14.165] A later case in the District Court of New South Wales, *R v Wald* (1971) 3 NSWDCR 25 adopted the approach of *Davidson*, but extended the considerations the person carrying out the abortion may take into account to include any

> economic, social or medical ground or reason which in their view could constitute reasonable grounds upon which an accused could honestly and reasonably believe there would result a serious danger to her physical or mental health.

[14.166] Both *Davidson* and *Wald* recognised the defence of necessity to a charge of unlawful abortion, that defence involving the above two requirements of need and proportion.

[14.167] Note also that the accused does not have to be correct in her or his belief in the necessity of abortion, only to have a reasonable and honest belief in it. This would require that some consideration of alternatives would have been considered by the accused, and rejected on reasonable and honest grounds.

[14.168] These two cases were heard at relatively low levels of the court hierarchy, where binding precedent is not really established, but they

[14.168] have been accepted as the law on abortion so far. It is suggested that the law is more likely to favour those who ensure that the operating doctor discusses the issues with the woman, and canvasses alternatives with her, recording both this and the belief (or otherwise) in the necessity of the abortion.

▮▮ CASE
CES & Anor v Superclinics Australia Pty Ltd & Ors (1995) 38 NSWLR 47 (CA NSW)

> A woman who believed she was pregnant visited the defendant's surgery on five different occasions, on all of which she was told she was not pregnant. Her purpose for seeking a determination of pregnancy was so that if she was pregnant she could have an abortion. She was in fact pregnant, but by the time this was established it was too late to have the abortion. She sued the defendant for the resulting physical and emotional harm which she endured in bearing and caring for the child.
>
> The trial judge found in favour of the defendants, on the ground that although the doctors should have recognised the plaintiff's pregnancy, she could not claim damages because for her to have had an abortion would have been illegal, as she had not established that she would have suffered serious harm to her physical or mental health. He determined that for this reason, had she found out earlier and had had an abortion, it would have been a crime. The law does not allow damages to be paid to a person who had lost the chance to perform an illegal act. Despite the doctor's negligence, she had no avenue to recover damages. The case was appealed.

[14.169] The Court of Appeal reversed this finding, ruling that the defendants had been negligent in not diagnosing the pregnancy, resulting in mental, physical and economic harm associated with carrying a child to term and giving birth when the pregnancy was unexpected and unwanted. Even if an abortion were to have been illegal, the defendants would not have been complicit in any illegal activity in giving the woman the correct results of the tests. Even so, Kirby P found that the danger to the mother's health need not be restricted to the period of the pregnancy: it could crystalise at the birth, or even after it. Given the increased recognition of such conditions as post-natal depression and serious economic and social pressures on women with children, the gravity of the dangers posed by a pregnancy have to be balanced and evaluated in each case. In this case there was sufficient evidence to suggest that a medical practitioner could form the opinion that the woman was facing a serious danger to her mental health by having to continue with the pregnancy.

[14.170] Kirby P, with general agreement of Newman J, made some further points:

> ▮.....He disagreed with precedents that held that the birth of a child is always a "blessing" and "cause for celebration" (*Uldale v Bloomsbury Area Health Authority* [1983] 2 All ER 522), and recognised that this is not always the case (hence the widespread use of contraceptives). Courts should not adopt this fiction.

❙.....From the legal point of view, it is the economic cost of raising the child that is the [14.175] damage, not the birth or existence of the child: damages are not about love, but about recoverable costs.

❙.....Also to be taken into account are lost opportunities for financial and personal development, such as university studies, that were anticipated by the woman.

Queensland

[14.171] The *Criminal Code* 1899 (Qld) makes it an offence for a person to unlawfully terminate a pregnancy, the exception for this being an abortion carried out "for the preservation of the mother's life". This has, however been interpreted to include preservation of her physical or mental health, along the lines of *Attorney-General (Qld) (Ex rel Kerr) v T* [1983] 1 Qd R 404; *R v Bayliss and Cullen* (unreported, 31 January 1986, District Court Brisbane); *Vievers & Anor v Connelly* (1994) Aust Torts Reports ¶81-309).

Western Australia

[14.172] The *Criminal Code* (WA) provides that carrying out an illegal abortion is an offence. It is not an offence to perform an abortion if it is carried out by a medical practitioner in good faith, with reasonable care and skill in circumstances where:

1).....the woman has given informed consent; or
2).....the woman will suffer serious personal, family or social consequences if the abortion is not performed; or
3).....the woman will suffer from serious physical or mental health problems if the abortion is not performed; or
4).....the pregnancy is causing serious danger to her physical or mental health.

[14.173] In all cases the woman must give informed consent unless, in the case of (3) and (4), it is impractical for her to do so. If the pregnancy is over 20 weeks, two medical practitioners who are members of a panel appointed by the Minister must agree that the termination is justified on the basis of the health of the woman or the foetus. A late abortion must be carried out in a ministerially-approved health facility.

[14.174] Informed consent is defined as freely given consent where a medical practitioner (other than the practitioner carrying out the abortion) has properly, appropriately and adequately provided counselling about medical risks of both termination and continuation of the pregnancy, and advised the woman of the availability of further counselling and advice, whatever her decision.

[14.175] A woman who is under 16 who is supported by a custodial parent or guardian cannot give informed consent unless a parent or guardian has been informed and has had the opportunity to be involved

[14.175] in the counselling process and consultation with the doctor as to whether the abortion should be performed.

Australian Capital Territory

[14.176] The Australian Capital Territory follows common law in relation to the matters for consideration to determine the mental and physical harm to the woman, therefore looking to precedent (at present that mentioned above, which is persuasive). The *Health Regulation (Maternal Health Information) Act* 1988 (ACT) requires the approval of facilities by the Minister for Health for the carrying out of terminations of pregnancy, and provides that they be carried out by medical practitioners. It requires doctors to make available to women contemplating a termination of pregnancy, specific information prepared by an expert panel. The woman and the doctor must sign a form stating that the information has been provided, and a period of 72 hours must elapse before the woman can then give her consent to the termination. Regulations under the Act require the Minister to make available brochures containing the required information and any other information (such as pictures of the foetus at different stages of growth), but it is not required that these be provided to the woman.

Who may Carry Out an Abortion?

[14.177] Any person may offer the defence that they carried out a procedure in an emergency, and it was intended to prevent a real and imminent danger of death or serious harm, so long as it is done in a responsible way, and there is no better medical help available. At common law this constitutes the defence of necessity. Section 282 of the *Criminal Code* (Qld) provides:

> A person is not criminally responsible for performing in good faith and with reasonable care and skill a surgical operation upon any person for his benefit, or upon an unborn child for the preservation of the mother's life, if the performance of the operation is reasonable, having regard to the patient's state at the time and to all the circumstances of the case.

[14.178] The person must weigh the dangers and not aggravate the existing condition. Where there is no emergency it is advised that a nurse should not carry out an abortion unless supervised by a doctor, as it is considered a medical procedure although there may be no criminal sanction against this. Note, however, the provisions in South Australia and the Northern Territory above. Also, in the Australian Capital Territory only a medical practitioner may carry out a termination of pregnancy.

[14.179] Other jurisdictions may have legislation determining who may or may not carry out a termination of pregnancy. Hospitals may have procedural requirements. For example, a hospital board may require certain procedures, such as certification of the need for the termination by two doctors, and permission by the superintendent.

[14.180] Some Nurses Registration Acts prohibit the carrying out of terminations by nurses. This means that nurses who carry out, assist, or attempt to carry out or assist, a termination by another nurse may be subject to disciplinary action, unless supervised by a doctor.

At What Stage of Pregnancy Can a Termination be Carried Out?

[14.181] Where there is no emergency, and a foetus is capable of independent life, it is possible that termination of pregnancy could be murder or child destruction. Unless there are specific requirements for late-term abortions, the law is generally unclear as to where the line is drawn. Specific guidance for emergencies, such as where the woman is in immediate danger of severe mental or physical harm, exists in some jurisdictions (see outline above), and it would seem illogical to set a time limit in such situations. The Northern Territory and South Australia specifically state that, in emergencies, one doctor is required to be of the opinion that the termination is required.

Does the Foetus have any Rights?

[14.182] The short answer to this question would appear to be: no. The foetus is not a person until it has lived independently outside the mother's body (see also [6.54]). The courts have considered the question of whether the foetus has a right to live in several cases.

▌▌▌ CASE
F v F (1989) FLC ¶92-031

A husband applied to the Family Court for an injunction to prevent his estranged and pregnant wife from terminating the pregnancy of their prospective child. He argued, among other things, that the foetus had a right to protection against abortion, and that he could enforce that right on its behalf.

[14.183] The court considered precedent, and made the following important points:

▌.....A court cannot make ethical judgments—it is concerned with legal rights. Its task is to interpret and apply the law, not particular moral or ethical precepts (readers may like to compare this approach with the use by many courts of public policy, see [3.63]).

[14.183]   ▌....."The foetus has no right of its own until it is born and has a separate existence from its mother." This was held by the English case of *Paton v British Pregnancy Advisory Service* [1979] 1 QB 276. Note also the case of *K v Minister for Youth and Community Services* (see [4.23]), where an application was sought to be brought in the name of a foetus to prevent an abortion, Street CJ (with whom the other judges agreed) said:

> "I am not, as at present advised, satisfied that the unborn child or foetus has the requisite status to participate as a party in proceedings of a character of those before the equity division or in those such as are sought to be brought before this court."

[14.184]   See also the Australian High Court case of *Attorney-General (Qld) (Ex rel Kerr) v T* (1983) 57 ALJR 285. Both of those cases involved the father of a foetus unsuccessfully attempting to prevent the mother from having an abortion.

[14.185]   Some other countries are considering offering protection to the foetus under criminal law, thus creating offences of causing harm to a foetus. Note also the law on reporting stillbirths at Chapter 15.

Do Others have any Rights?

[14.186]   In the case of *F v F*, the court also addressed the right of third parties to determine whether a termination will be undertaken. The court followed those cases mentioned in determining that a father has no right to stop the mother having a legal abortion (at 77-438):

> To grant the injunction would be to compel the wife to do something in relation to her own body which she does not wish to do. That would be an interference with her freedom to decide her own destiny.

Child Destruction

[14.187]   There is a period when a child may, for the purposes of criminal law, be neither a foetus whose destruction is abortion, nor a legal person whose destruction is murder. Some may consider this the period from when the child is capable of being born alive, others require that the child be in the process of being born. In some States a special offence of child destruction covers the intentional killing of such a being. The Northern Territory has an offence of "killing unborn child" which provides for life imprisonment for preventing a birth where a person is about to be delivered of a child (*Criminal Code Act* 1983 (NT), s 170). Procuring an abortion where a foetus is viable is a different offence, attracting a penalty of up to seven years (s 174(1)(b)). South Australia and Victoria require that a foetus not be viable for an abortion to be legal (except in emergency). The offence is more serious than unlawful abortion, but less serious than murder.

[14.188]   Midwives especially should be aware of the law relating to abortion and child destruction in their jurisdiction. This book cannot deal with the detail of particular regulations and administrative procedures in each State, which can change relatively quickly. These may establish further restrictions on the carrying out of terminations, and should be consulted.

[14.193]

Victims of Crime

[14.189] Where the patient is apparently a victim of a criminal offence (for example, assault, rape) the health carers should be aware that evidence of the offence may be required (for example, vaginal smears, samples of clothing, photographs and descriptions of wounds). Police, or other investigators appointed by them, will want to collect such evidence, so for this purpose it is important that the patient be undisturbed as much as possible, after any urgent treatment has been given. However, it must be remembered that the physical examination is subject to the consent of the person, and police have no right as such to such. Special training in forensic health care, which includes the mental, physical and emotional care of the victim, the gathering of evidence, presentation in court and principles of giving testimony is recognised as essential for proper dealing with victims of crime.

[14.190] A victim of sexual assault should ideally not have a bath or shower no matter how desirable this may be, until examination has been carried out and evidence collected. It should be borne in mind, however, that the person must not be forced against their will in this matter, but should be reminded that prosecution by the police will be virtually impossible without this evidence. Reassurance and comforting will therefore be an essential part of the health professional's caring for victims of violence, as they will be distressed and uncomfortable.

Collection of Forensic Evidence

[14.191] Those working in emergency and other receiving wards should be familiar with the hospital's procedures for dealing with such patients and should be aware of any special personnel for handling the collection of evidence or liaison with police. Where someone believes a crime has been committed there is also an obligation to inform appropriate authorities in the public interest. Failure to report serious crime may amount to complicity in it under circumstances where is assists the perpetrator.

[14.192] Where there are no specially trained personnel for gathering forensic evidence, it may help the client if health carers dealing with victims of crime consider how they might retain useful evidence (for example, descriptions of injuries and events, samples of blood, tissue, hair, clothing). However, caution is advised: they should not adopt the role of detective.

[14.193] Because of their close relationship with the victims of crime, health professionals may find that they possess information and witness

[14.193] events and facts which may make them useful witnesses in later court cases. They may have received a dying statement which can later be admitted in evidence. It is suggested that while they should not shirk their civic duty to assist in the process of justice, they should not actively involve themselves in potential criminal cases by undertaking activities for the patient (such as, getting or giving information, contacting people, discussing the case with others, or intervening in private disputes) which are not part of their normal professional duties.

[14.194] It is equally important for health workers to remember the requirements of confidentiality, no matter how much one might be tempted to discuss exciting details of criminal events with others. Potential witnesses in a case are warned by lawyers involved in the case against discussing certain matters with other witnesses or the press. Spreading allegations about the guilt of specific or identifiable persons may amount to defamation.

Patients Allegedly the Perpetrators of Crime

Care, Examination and Forensic Evidence

[14.195] Similar advice applies to those caring for people who are charged with, or accused of, crime, with several further important points. There are many rules relating to the collection of forensic evidence. In most jurisdictions these are set out in their respective *Crimes Acts* or *Criminal Codes* (see [14.6]). South Australia enacted the *Criminal Law (Forensic Procedures) Act* in 1998. Recently enacted updated provisions for forensic procedures (entitled the *Crimes (Forensic Procedures) Act* 2000) in the Commonwealth, the Australian Capital Territory and New South Wales) generally establish the following rules with some variations. Forensic procedures are divided into intimate procedures (including photography and taking of casts) which involve the external anal and genital regions and buttocks, the breasts of women, the taking of blood samples, dental impressions and pubic hair. Non-intimate procedures involve other parts of the body and the taking of fingerprints, buccal swabs and other hair. A medical practitioner or nurse may carry out forensic procedures at the request of police, who are responsible for ensuring there is proper authority to carry out the procedure. Unless it is considered that there is a reasonable chance that a procedure will produce relevant probative evidence of the commission of an offence, or the person has been convicted of a serious offence, it should not be authorised. The person must be given the opportunity to consent to a forensic procedure, and informed of the legal implications of its being carried out. If the person does not consent, a senior police officer can generally order the carrying out of a non-intimate procedure. Intimate forensic procedures can only be carried out in certain circumstances, generally requiring a magistrate's order, and the person is entitled to the presence of a medical practitioner. A child or incompetent person cannot consent to a forensic procedure—this requires an order by a magistrate. Children and those who are incompetent can have an interview friend (parent, guardian or other nominated person) and/or a lawyer to represent them. The interview friend and/or lawyer can also be present. A person of the same sex as the subject of the procedure must carry it out where this is reasonably possible, or such a person may be present. Unless the person objects or it is not practicable, the procedure is to be videorecorded.

Health carers called on to carry out a forensic procedure are responsible for informing the person of the medical aspects of the procedure (in line with the law generally) where consent is requested. They are not required to inquire into the apparent legitimacy of police or court authority to order such procedures, but might consider that in some circumstances it is appropriate to advocate for witnesses and counselling for those who are to be subjected to them.

[14.196] A person is not guilty at law until they have been convicted by a court. It is for a court to determine guilt, not health care staff. Even where the patient has been convicted of a crime, it is not for health care workers to determine and carry out their punishment. That is the task of law enforcement agencies. These principles are established by the *Human Rights and Equal Opportunity Commission Act* 1986 (Cth), which prohibits discrimination against anyone for the reasons given (Ch 18). Health carers should give the same standard of treatment to every person they care for, although the degree of friendliness they exhibit may vary. Failure to give this standard may result in a complaint to the Human Rights and Equal Opportunity Commission.

■ ■ ■

REFERENCES AND FURTHER READING

Battin, M, "Voluntary Euthanasia and the Risk of Abuse: Can we Learn anything from the Netherlands?" (1992) 20 *Law Medicine and Health Care* 133

Bennett, G and Hogan, B, "Criminal Law, Criminal Procedure and Sentencing" [1989] *All ER Annual Review* 94

Brazier, M, *Medicine, Patient and the Law* (Penguin, 1992)

Brody, H, *Ethical Decisions in Medicine* (Little Brown, Boston, 1981)

Brown, D, Farrier, D, and Wesibrot, D, *Criminal Laws: Materials and Commentary on Criminal Law and Process of NSW* (Federation Press, Sydney, 1996)

Buchanan, J, "Euthanasia: the Medical and Psychological Issues" (1995) 3 *Journal of Law and Medicine*, (November 1995), pp 136-145

Dearden, I, and Tronc, K, *Criminal Precedents* (LBC Information Services, Sydney, 1996)

Dix, et al, *Law for the Medical Profession* (Butterworths, Sydney, 1988), p 296

Freckelton, I, "Withdrawal of Life Support: The 'Persistent Vegetative State' " (1993) 1 *Journal of Law and Medicine*, p 34

Gillett, G, "Ethical aspects of the Northern Territory Euthanasia Legislation" (1995) 3 *Journal of Law and Medicine* (November 1995), pp 145-152

Gillies, P, *Criminal Law* (4th ed, Law Book Co, Sydney, 1993)

Gillon, R, Editorial (1981) 7 *Journal of Medical Ethics* 56

Halsbury's Laws of England (4th ed, Butterworths, London), Vol 30

Hunsaker, D, "Unnatural Life vs Natural Death: Some Legal and Ethical Considerations" (1978) 7 (No 1) *GMUL Review*

Kuhse, H and Singer, P, "Active Voluntary Euthanasia, Morality and the Law" (1995) 3 *Journal of Law and Medicine* 3:2 129-135 (November)

Kuhse, H, *Caring: Nurses, Women and Ethics* (Blackwell Publishers, Oxford UK, 1997)

Kuhse, H, (ed), *Willing to Listen, Wanting to Die* (Penguin, Sydney, 1994)

Kuhse, H, "Quality of Life and the Death of 'Baby M'" (1992) 6 *Bioethics*, pp 233-250

Lanham, D, *Taming Death by Law* (Longman Professional Publishing, Melbourne, 1993)

Lipman, Z, "The Criminal Liability of Medical Practitioners for Withholding Treatment from Severely Defective Newborn Infants" (1986) 60 *Australian Law Journal*, p 286

Macmillan, E, "Birth Defective Infants: a Standard for Non-Treatment Decisions" (1978) 30 *Stanford Law Review* 595

McLean, S, and Maher, G, *Medicine, Morals and the Law* ((Gower) Publishing, Hampshire, 1985)

Mendelson, D, "The Northern Territory's Euthanasia Legislation in Historical Perspective" (1995) 3 *Journal of Law and Medicine* (November 1995), pp 136-145

Meyers, D, *Medico-Legal Implications of Death and Dying* (Lawyers Co-operative Publishing, San Francisco, 1981)

Miller, F and Brody, H, "Professional Integrity and Physician-Assisted Death" (1996) 26 *Monash Bioethics Review*, p 41

O'Connor, D and Fairall, P, *Criminal Defences* (Butterworths, Sydney, 1996)

Ormrod, L J, "A Lawyer Looks at Medical Ethics" (1977) 45 (Pt 4) *Medico-Legal Journal* 104

Otlowski, M, *Active Voluntary Euthanasia—a Timely Reappraisal* (University of Tasmania Law School Occasional Paper, University of Tasmania Hobart, 1992)

Paris, J and Reardon, F, "Court Responses to Withholding or Withdrawing Artificial Nutrition and Fluids" (1988) 253 (No 15) *Journal of the American Medical Association* 2243

Pope Pius XII, "Address of 24 November 1957 to Doctors" (1957) 49 *Acta Apostolicae Sedis* 1027-33

President's Commission for the Study of Ethical Problems in Medical, Biological and Behavioural Research, *Deciding to Forego Life-Sustaining Treatment* (Government Printer, Washington, 1983)

Robertson, J, "Organ Donations by Incompetents and the Substituted Judgment Doctrine" (1976) 76 *Columbia Law Review* 48

Roulston, R, *Introduction to Criminal Law in New South Wales* (2nd ed, Butterworths, Sydney, 1980)

Royal College of Nursing 1994, Memorandum, *House of Lords Select Committee on Medical Ethics, Volume II- Oral Evidence* (HMSO, London), p 70

Schurr, B, *Criminal Procedure NSW* (LBC Information Services, Sydney, 1996)

Skegg, P, *Law Ethics and Medicine* (Clarendon Press, London, 1984)

Starke, J, "Current Topics: The Problem of the Legal Status of the Foetus in Utero" (1990) 63 *Australian Law Journal* 719

Thompson, P, "The Law and Active Euthanasia: Whose Life is it Anyway?" 1995 2 *Journal of Law and Medicine*, 233-246

United Kingdom Central Council for Nursing, Midwifery and Health Visiting ("UKCC") 1994, Memorandum, *House of Lords Select Committee on Medical Ethics, Volume II- Oral Evidence* (HMSO, London), p 139

Waller, L and Williams C R, *Brett, Waller and Williams Criminal Law* (8th ed, Butterworths, Australia, 1997)

Wallace, M, "Euthanasia and the Law: Some Implications for Nurses" *The Politics of Euthanasia* (Royal College of Nursing Australia, Sydney, 1995)

Williams, C R, *Brett and Waller's Criminal Law* (Butterworths, Australia, 1983)

Williams, G, "Euthanasia" (1973) 41 *Medico-Legal Journal* 14

Chapter Fifteen

STATE INVOLVEMENT IN BIRTH AND DEATH: REGISTRATION AND CORONIAL INQUIRIES

INTRODUCTION

[15.1] There are times when matters concerning individuals must be reported to the state. These include births, deaths, child abuse and neglect, and the knowledge that someone has an infectious or sexually transmitted disease. There are also deaths which, because of their unusual or unexplained nature, or other circumstances defined by statute, should come to the notice of the coroner (usually via the police). Health carers may believe that they will probably not be concerned with reporting these events very often, if at all. However, child abuse and domestic violence in particular are matters of growing public concern. Also, those nursing in remote regions, or practising in homebirths or other aspects of health care which have become increasingly concerned with matters of life and death, may be involved in reporting to the authorities concerned. The notification of births and deaths, as well as coroner's inquests, will be dealt with in this chapter, the reporting of infectious diseases and child abuse in Chapter 16.

Notification of Births

[15.2] In each State and Territory there is legislation that establishes a register of births deaths and marriages, maintained by a body known as the "Registrar of Births Deaths and Marriages".[1] All births, including stillbirths (defined below [15.9]) must be recorded in the register, along with the parentage of the child (parentage of artificially conceived children is determined by statute, see [17.44]). The furnishing of details of

---

[1] *Births, Deaths and Marriages Registration Act* 1997 (ACT); *Births, Deaths and Marriages Registration Act* 1995 (NSW); *Births, Deaths and Marriages Registration Act* 1996 (NT); *Registration of Births, Deaths and Marriages Act* 1962 (Qld); *Births, Deaths and Marriages Registration Act* 1996 (SA); *Registration of Births and Deaths Act* 1895 (Tas); *Births Deaths and Marriages Registration Act* 1996 (Vic); *Births, Deaths and Marriages Registration Act* 1998 (WA).

[15.2] a birth to the Registrar is generally the responsibility of the parents of that child, but health care personnel who have knowledge of, or who were present at, a birth, may have this responsibility in some circumstances.

Who is Responsible for Notification to Registrar-General

[15.3] In all States the occupier of premises or chief executive officer where a child is born is required to ensure that the birth is registered. A doctor or midwife who is present at the birth also has responsibility for ensuring registration. Queensland, Tasmania, Victoria and Western Australia also require a person present at the birth to ensure registration. This does not mean that parents, occupiers and nurses must all register the birth. Failure to notify is an offence unless there are reasonable grounds for believing that notice has already been given.

Time Limit for Notice

The time limits for registering are—Australian Capital Territory: seven days; New South Wales: 21 days; Northern Territory: 10 days; South Australia: seven days; Queensland and Tasmania: 60 days; Victoria: 24 hours; and Western Australia: one month.

[15.4] Generally, the father of the child is only to be recorded if both parents consent to this, or a court order or declaration has been issued, establishing paternity. Unless this is the case, the father's name should be left blank on any form.

Additional Requirements

Victoria

[15.5] In addition to making persons present at a birth responsible for registration, Victoria requires notification of a birth within 48 hours to the clerk of the municipal district in which the mother of the child usually resides, or if unknown the municipal district where the birth takes place. Notification is made:

- ..... where the birth is in a hospital or other institution, by the matron or person in charge of the institution;
- ..... where the birth occurs elsewhere, by the midwife or other attendant at the birth, within 24 hours;
- ..... where there is no attendant, by the father, or if he is not resident in the house where the birth occurs, the occupier of the house (*Health Act* 1958 (Vic), s 160). The form of notification is contained in the Schedule of the Act, and it must be accompanied by a pre-paid letter, letter-card or post card.

This is to ensure that the local infant welfare centre or the Director-General of Community Services can be notified.

Chapter 15—State Involvement in Birth and Death: Registration and Coronial Inquiries ▌517

[15.6] Victoria also requires that the birth be reported to the consultative body which has been set up to study obstetric and paediatric conditions under the *Health Act* 1958 (Vic). Persons responsible for reporting to this body are:

- .....where the birth is in a hospital, the proprietor of the hospital;
- .....where the birth occurs elsewhere, the midwife or other attendant at the birth;
- .....in other cases, the proprietor of a hospital to which mother and child are admitted as a result of the birth, or any other medical practitioner who undertakes care and treatment of the mother and child.

New South Wales

[15.7] New South Wales also requires that homebirths be reported to the Health Commission within 36 hours of the birth. This is to be given by:

- .....the father of the child if he resides in the house where the birth took place at the time of its occurrence; or
- .....any person in attendance upon the mother at the birth or within six hours of the birth (*Notification of Births Act* 1915 (NSW), s 3).

[15.8] There is a penalty in both cases for failure to report to the appropriate body, but there is also the defence that the person reasonably believed the birth had already been reported by some other person.

Stillbirths (Child not Born Alive)

[15.9] In all States and Territories except the Australian Capital Territory a stillbirth, or child not born alive, is defined as a child of at least 20 weeks' duration or at least 400 grams in weight who has not breathed (New South Wales and Victoria), or whose heart has not beaten (Queensland, South Australia and Tasmania) after delivery. No mention of heartbeat or breathing is made in the Australian Capital Territory, Northern Territory or Western Australia. In the Australian Capital Territory the foetus must be 22 weeks or at least 500 grams in weight.

[15.10] Stillbirths must be registered in the same way as births, with the same people being responsible; however, in Tasmania a stillbirth is registered as a death rather than a birth. Note the different definitions of what is a "child" according to the requirements for registration of stillbirth, and the definition of "person" for the purposes of criminal law (see [14.71]) and civil law (see [6.54]ff).

[15.11] All jurisdictions make it an offence to fail to give notice of a birth or stillbirth, or to give false information.

[15.11] ▌▌▌ **CHECKLIST**
WHEN HEALTH CARERS HAVE A RESPONSIBILITY TO REGISTER THE BIRTH OF A CHILD

To determine a birth for the purposes of registration:

▌.....Is the foetus of at least 20 weeks' gestation (22 weeks in the Australian Capital Territory)?

▌.....Does it weigh 400 grams (500 grams in the Australian Capital Territory)?

If yes to either then it is a "child" for the purposes of registration, and is a live birth or stillbirth.

Determination of live or stillbirth:

▌.....Has the foetus breathed after delivery (New South Wales, Northern Territory, Victoria)?

▌.....Has its heart beaten after delivery (Queensland, South Australia, Tasmania)?

If yes it is a live birth.

Otherwise: momentary breathing or heartbeat will not rule out the child being classified as stillborn.

Notification of Death

[15.12] All deaths must be notified to the relevant Registrar in each State and Territory. Still-births may be dealt with differently (see below). New South Wales has a Child Death Review Team, which records details of the deaths of children for review. All sudden, suspicious or unexpected deaths should be reported to the police and the coroner (see below [15.38]). There are, under more normal circumstances, other reporting obligations on members of the public.

Who is to Report the Death?

[15.13] In all jurisdictions except Queensland, Tasmania and Western Australia the medical practitioner attending the person must be the notifier of the death. In Queensland and Tasmania any person present at the death, and in Western Australia the funeral director or other person who arranges for the disposal of the remains must report it to the Registrar.

[15.14] In Victoria any person in attendance during the last illness of the deceased or present at the death must report the death to the funeral director or undertaker who is to bury the person, or a local registrar. All States require the occupier of the premises in which the death occurs to notify the appropriate person. In all jurisdictions except New South Wales the appropriate person is the Registrar. In New South Wales the appropriate person is the person disposing of the body. Time limits are as follows: New South Wales, one month; Queensland, 30 days; Victoria, 21 days; South Australia and Western Australia, 14 days; Northern Territory and Australian Capital Territory, 14 days (forthwith upon finding the body or being present at death); Tasmania, seven days. Certification by a doctor, and/or a coroner's certificate, if an inquest has been held, must accompany registration.

[15.15] There is a penalty in both cases for failure to report to the appropriate body, but there is also the defence that the person reasonably believed the death had already been reported by some other person.

Perinatal Deaths

[15.16] Perinatal death occurs in all jurisdictions when a child dies within 28 days of birth. Except for New South Wales, Queensland and Victoria, notification of the death is the same as for all other deaths. A stillborn child is thus registered on both birth and death registers, except in Tasmania (see [15.10]). In Tasmania special provision is made for notification of perinatal deaths of the Council of Obstetric and Paediatric Mortality and Morbidity under the *Perinatal Registry Act* 1994 (Tas).

Coroners' Inquests

[15.17] Coroners have a long history. The role of coroner was created as a means of accounting for suspicious deaths and disappearances in the days when there was not the same efficiency in keeping track of persons through central records that we have today. However, the role has continued, to ensure that sudden or unexpected deaths are accounted for, and foul play ruled out. It is a way of contributing to an orderly means of accounting for the death of every person in our society, unearthing criminal and negligent activity, and identifying otherwise unrecognised harmful practices.

[15.18] The Coroner's Court investigates a sudden, suspicious or unusual death, or one which occurs when a person at the time of death was undergoing surgery, or is a mental patient or in prison or other detention. The coroner is a magistrate appointed for the purpose of a particular inquiry, or as a permanent coroner. The Coroner's Court is at the level of the Magistrates' or Local Court. Health carers, especially doctors and nurses, stand a good chance of being witnesses in such an inquiry, which is also called an inquest. Coroners are also given jurisdiction to inquire into the cause of fires. The legal terminology used is "inquest" for a determination of the cause of death, and "inquiry" for a determination into the cause of a fire.

[15.19] All States and Territories in Australia have legislation providing for a coroner and Coroner's Court.[2]

---

[2] *Coroners Act* 1956 (ACT); *Coroners Act* 1980 (NSW); *Coroners Act* 1974 (NT); *Coroners Act* 1958 (Qld); *Coroners Act* 1975 (SA); *Coroners Act* 1957 (Tas); *Coroners Act* 1985 (Vic); *Coroners Act* 1920 (WA).

Role of the Coroner

[15.20] The purpose of a coroner's inquest is to determine the cause of a person's death where that has occurred suddenly, unexpectedly or without explanation, specifically to detect such matters as homicide or negligence, or to identify the deceased where identity has not been established. Additionally, the coroner investigates the cause of fires. It is important to note that the coroner does not make a finding as to guilt or innocence. If, however, the coroner decides that there is a prima facie case of homicide (see [14.68]ff), in some jurisdictions he or she can commit the person concerned to a higher court for trial. The inquest, therefore, is an inquiry rather than a trial (see for example Queensland, South Australia and Western Australia). In New South Wales and Victoria, where a coroner makes a prima facie finding (that is, there is enough evidence to suspect) that the death has resulted from an indictable offence, he or she refers the matter over to the Director of Public Prosecutions. It is up to the Director to decide whether to lay charges. Where the coroner's finding indicates that there could have been negligence on the part of any person, it is up to relatives who may be entitled to sue to take any appropriate action.

[15.21] The coroner may go further than a simple finding of cause. Based on evidence presented, he or she may make findings on the law relating to matters relevant to the death, and the practices of people and bodies who were involved in the circumstances under inquiry. The coroner may also make recommendations as to future safe practices to prevent accidents occurring.

[15.22] A further function of the coroner's office is the publicity which may be given to unsafe practices or products, and resultant educative effect on the public. Waller ((1982), pp 6-7) points out, for example, the publicity and agitation for protective laws and education of the public as a result of the deaths of infants in backyard pools in Sydney in the 1970s. Not only were the coronial inquiries a source of information and education, but the coroner's office lent support to the moves to reduce the number of deaths. Staunton and Whyburn ((1997), p 224) mention also the fact that hospitals in New South Wales have adopted thermostatically controlled hot water systems to prevent patient burns after a coroner recommended this preventative measure after investigating a death by burning from hot water in a shower.

[15.23] Some jurisdictions require that when a coroner's report is presented to a government department with recommendations, the department is required to respond within a certain time, stating what action it is taking in respect of the recommendations. Where the death occurred in custody there are generally strict requirements as to investigation and accountability.

[15.24] The coroner may find that the standard of health care was not the cause of the death, and exonerate, and even praise, health carers involved in the deceased's treatment. Where he or she finds a health professional's actions were the cause of death and there appears to be a breach of provisions of the relevant registration legislation, the matter may be referred to the relevant Registration Board for investigation and possible disciplinary action. [15.26]

When is a Coroner's Inquest Held?

[15.25] Coroners' inquests are subject to State legislation, varying from State to State, but generally coroners have a discretion to initiate an inquest, except where the legislation requires an inquest to be held. An inquest is mandatory where a person dies

- .....under, or as a result of, anaesthesia; or
- .....when receiving, or as a result of, health care, where the death is not from natural causes.

An inquest also may be mandatory where relatives request one within a certain time.

[15.26] More specifically, an inquest is mandatory or discretionary under the circumstances listed in Figure 15.1.

FIGURE 15.1

GROUNDS FOR HOLDING AN INQUEST

('M' = MANDATORY, 'D' = DISCRETIONARY)
Because of the vagueness and/or differences in wording of the categories, the wording is approximate in some cases, for the sake of generalisation, and it should be noted that literal reliance on them could lead to error. Legislation should be checked if a more precise listing for a particular jurisdiction is required.

	ACT	NSW	NT	Qld	SA	Tas	Vic	WA
Suspected homicide/suspicious circumstances	D	M	M	D		M	M	
Identity of deceased not known		M	M			M	M	D
Sudden death of unknown cause				M		D^8	D	
Fact, time or place of death not known		M			D^5			
Violent, sudden or unnatural death of unknown cause, or person killed	D	D	D	M	D^6	D		D
Person found drowned	D			D				
Death occurred in the process of detaining a person or person escaping from custody						M		
Death occurred while person in custody	M	M^2	M	M	D	M	M	

[15.26]

	ACT	NSW	NT	Qld	SA	Tas	Vic	WA
Death caused as a result of custody			M		D			
Place or circumstances of death require inquest				M		M		
Deceased was in care or psychiatric institution		M		D[4]	D	M	M	
Death while held in care							M	
Death while under, or as a result of, or within 24 hours of receiving an anaesthetic	M	M[1]	D[3]			D[7]	M	
Death during, or within 72 hours of, or as a result of, an operation or a medical, surgical, dental, diagnostic or like nature	D	D		D			M	D
Death within 366 days of cause		D						
Inquest prescribed by regulation							M	D
The Minister, Attorney-General, Coroner or Chief Magistrate requires investigation		M		M		M	M	M
Inquest requested by relative				M			D	
Requested by police				M				
Death may have been caused or contributed to by police, or care	M		D		D			M
No certificate as to cause	D	D		D			D	D
Not seen by a medical practitioner within 3 months before death	D	D		D				
Death is attributable to accident	D		D				D	

1. Inquest must be requested by a relative or any person with a sufficient interest in the circumstances of death.
2. Also where deceased was absent from care.
3. Includes death while under an anaesthetic or as a result of it, and not due to natural causes.
4. Limited to psychiatric institutions.
5. Includes the disappearance of a person ordinarily resident in the State.
6. Includes the death of a person in an aircraft during a flight, or on a vessel during a voyage, to a place in the State.
7. Death occurs during, or due to, an anaesthetic or sedation and not as a result of natural causes.
8. Includes the sudden and unexpected death of a child under 1 year old.

[15.27] Where a coroner is of the understanding that another inquiry is being undertaken into a death (for example, a trial or royal commission) he or she may dispense with an inquest.

[15.28] In cases described above the death should be reported to the coroner.

[15.29] All jurisdictions, except South Australia have some sort of provision for the request by designated relatives under specific circumstances, and within a specific time, that the coroner carry out an inquiry.

[15.30] In the Australian Capital Territory, a coroner may hold a hearing into whether an inquest, or review of the findings of prior findings in relation to a death, should be carried out where requested to do so by immediate family over 18 years or a person with sufficient interest in the death (*Coroners Act* 1997 (ACT)).

[15.31] In New South Wales, the *Coroners Act* 1980 (NSW) provides that a spouse, parent, child or sibling, or person having a sufficient interest, may request an inquest within 28 days of the death of a person within 24 hours of receiving an anaesthetic. The coroner must hold an inquest or provide reasons for declining to do so. An appeal against the coroner's decision not to hold an inquest may be made to the Supreme Court, and that court may order the coroner to conduct an inquest.

[15.32] In the Northern Territory, there is no specific provision for relatives to apply for an inquest, but the legislation required that the coroner notify the "senior next of kin" or "any person" if he or she decides not to carry out an inquest where one is authorised under the Act. This means that where the coroner is authorised to carry out an inquest and declines to do so after being asked to by a person, the coroner, if they are the senior next of kin they must be notified of the reasons for this. If they are any other person the coroner may notify them. Any person receiving notification of the coroner's decision can appeal that decision to the Supreme Court (*Coroners Act* 1993 (NT)).

[15.33] In Queensland, immediate family or guardian, or an interested person or the Commissioner or an Inspector of police may request an authorised inquest; no time limit is imposed, and reasons must be given for refusal (*Coroners Act* 1958 (Qld)).

[15.34] In Tasmania a person with a "sufficient interest" may seek an authorised inquest. The coroner has a discretion to determine if a person has a sufficient interest, and whether the inquest is warranted. A refusal must be accompanied by reasons, and may be appealed against to the Tasmanian Supreme Court (*Coroners Act* 1995 (Tas)).

[15.35] In Victoria, any person may request an inquest that is authorised under the legislation. There is no limit on the circumstances of the death, and no time limit is given. The coroner must give reasons for refusal, and appeal against the coroner's decision not to hold an inquest may be made to the Supreme Court, and that court may order the coroner to conduct an inquest (*Coroners Act* 1985 (Vic)).

[15.36] In Western Australia, any person may ask a coroner to hold an inquest into a death where such an inquest is authorised by the legislation. Again, written reasons for a refusal must be given, and an appeal against the refusal may be made to the Supreme Court (*Coroners Act* 1996 (WA)).

[15.37] Health carers should ascertain the precise circumstances which apply in their jurisdiction: there will probably be established practices and

[15.37] procedures which they need to know. Also it should be noted that the catch-all categories for reporting used in some jurisdictions, such as "sudden death from unknown cause" or "circumstances requiring investigation", would most probably include many of the more detailed circumstances listed by other jurisdictions. It is safe to say that a death under, or as the result of, an anaesthetic, or any sudden, unexplained or unexpected death where a person is receiving health care or in a health care or welfare institution, would be one which could be considered to require investigation. This could include the involvement in an inquest of the health carer(s) of such person, even if the death had no apparent connection with the health care. In these cases, health carers should be prepared for possible appearance at an inquest.

Reporting of Deaths

[15.38] As set out above, there is legislation in all States for the reporting of deaths and signing and lodging of death certificates with the government. Where a death may be the subject of a coronial inquiry the coroner or police must be notified (generally the police are the first to be notified). Where the person was in a health care facility, notification would normally be the responsibility of the administration[3] (notification by the occupier of the building or place in which the death occurred) and procedures have presumably been established for such an event.

[15.39] In all jurisdictions a person who has knowledge of a death that he or she reasonably believes is reportable (that is, examinable by a coroner) and has not already been reported, must report that death to a police officer or coroner. In practice this would in most cases cover unexpected deaths occurring in health care facilities or in custody, as well as other sudden, unnatural suspicious or unexpected deaths. It would also mean that the chief medical officer or other designated person in a health care facility, and the superintendent of a prison, would be responsible for reporting the death, whether or not they are specifically required to do this under legislation. If the administration, or whoever else is in charge of reporting the death does not do so, a health carer who knows of the death is required to report it. The general requirement for reporting has been added to in different jurisdictions.

[15.40] Queensland also specifically requires that if a person finds a body or has knowledge of a death that is listed in the Act (see Figure 15.1) and does not believe that it has been reported to the police, he or she must do so. In such circumstances, a doctor is not permitted to issue a death certificate.

---

[3] *Registration of Births Deaths and Marriages Act* 1963 (ACT), s 27; *Registration of Births, Deaths and Marriages Act* 1973 (NSW), s 23; *Registration of Births, Deaths and Marriages Act* 1962 (NT), s 26; *Registration of Births Deaths and Marriages Act* 1962 (Qld), s 30(1); *Births, Deaths and Marriages Registration Act* 1966 (SA), s 29; *Registration of Births and Deaths Act* 1895 (Tas), s 23; *Registration of Births Deaths and Marriages Act* 1959 (Vic), s 18(1); *Registration of Births, Deaths and Marriages Act* 1961 (WA), s 33.

Chapter 15—State Involvement in Birth and Death: Registration and Coronial Inquiries | 525

[15.41] South Australia also specifically requires that all deaths of persons accommodated in institutions for the mentally ill, those with an intellectual disability or those who are drug dependent must be reported.

[15.42] Victoria also specifically requires that a doctor present at or after a death is responsible for it being reported to the coroner if it is reportable, or the doctor has not seen the body or is unable to determine the cause of death.

[15.43] Western Australia places a specific obligation on medical practitioners to notify the State Coroner where they were present at the time of a reportable death or shortly after, or the cause of death is unknown. It also specifically provides that the person under whose care the deceased person was at the time of death is responsible for reporting the death.

[15.44] Health carers should be aware of the reporting requirements they are expected to fulfil by the State and their employer, and the allocation of responsibility for preparation of requisite forms.

Postmortem and other Examination of the Body

[15.45] Although not obliged to view the body, under some circumstances the coroner may do so. As an inquest is an inquisitorial process rather than an adversarial one, the coroner can undertake a more active role to inform him or herself as to the facts of the case than can a magistrate or judge at a judicial hearing.

Postmortem

[15.46] A coroner can order a postmortem examination of the deceased, either as part of a preliminary investigation to determine if an inquest is required, or as part of the inquest itself. In the Northern Territory, Tasmania, Victoria and Western Australia, any person can request the carrying out of a postmortem, and if the coroner declines to order one, he or she must furnish reasons for so doing. These can be appealed to the Supreme Court. Generally, where the coroner is of the opinion that some suspicion of having wrongfully caused death falls on a particular medical practitioner, the practitioner must be advised of this by the coroner, and shall not take part in the postmortem examination, although he or she may be present at the examination.

[15.47] In recognition of sensitivities and cultural beliefs that may cause serious distress to relatives and family of the deceased, all jurisdictions except Queensland and South Australia provide for coroners to allow for an objection to the holding of a postmortem by next of kin. Whilst not obliged to accede to the objection, coroners must give reasons for not doing so, and time must be given for an application to the Supreme Court appealing the decision may be made. In the Australian Capital Territory, whilst there is no provision for appeal, the coroner is required to consider cultural beliefs and religious beliefs before directing that a postmortem be carried out.

[15.47] ■■■ CASE
Abernethy v Deitz (1996) 39 NSWLR
A man died after a road traffic accident. The coroner ordered a postmortem, which was objected to by his widow, as his family were strong adherents to the Jewish faith, and believed that a postmortem was a desecration of the deceased. The coroner refused to accede to the objection. This decision was appealed.

[15.48] The court held that the causes of death, including septicaemia, pneumonia renal failure and multiple trauma, were not questioned, and there was no indication of any other cause. Medical evidence was accepted that a postmortem would reveal nothing in relation to the cause of death that was not already known. The cause of death was clearly known, and there was no evidence that the interests of society would be served if there was a postmortem. In these circumstances, the wishes of the deceased legal personal representative and family should be the determining factor in deciding whether to carry out a postmortem.

■■■ CASE
Simon Unchango (Jnr), Ex Parte Simon Unchango (Snr) (19 August 1997, Supreme Court of Western Australia in Chambers, CIV 1891 of 1997) (from *Australian Health and Medical Law Reporter* ¶34-220.41)
A 12-day-old Aboriginal baby died suddenly. The most likely cause of death was considered to be Sudden Infant Death Syndrome (SIDS), however the coroner held that without a postmortem other causes could not be ruled out, and that it was in the interests of the health of the Aboriginal community to determine more accurately the cause of death. Concern was expressed that the age of the child was low for SIDS, that SIDS is related to respiratory disease and this may have a public health significance. It was also suggested that, as the baby had been in shared accommodation, there was the possibility that intoxication in co-sleepers could have led to "overlay" of the baby, a matter that should be inquired into by police. Finally, concern at the high Aboriginal mortality rate and a consequent desirability to make proper medical inquiries into deaths was cited as a reason for the postmortem. The child's father testified to the traditional belief of his people that if subjected to a postmortem, the child's spirit would roam and not be able to enter dreamtime, affecting both the child's spirit and the community.

[15.49] The court overruled the coroner's order for a postmortem for the following reasons:

- ..... the evidence indicated that death occurred as a result natural causes, and intervening factors such as "overlay" were excluded by police;
- ..... the court's intervention would not prevent the coroner from definitively establishing the cause of death;
- ..... the finding that there was a cause of death other than SIDS would not advance the situation; and
- ..... it is necessary to consider the strong cultural beliefs of relatives and the community, and the traumatic effect of a postmortem.

Chapter 15—State Involvement in Birth and Death: Registration and Coronial Inquiries | 527

Exhumation [15.53]

A coroner may issue a warrant for the exhumation of a body where this is necessary to investigate a death and this may include the exhumation of the body and other orders for the removal of a body to a designated place. The Northern Territory, Tasmania, Victoria and Western Australia provide that a short period is allowed for next of kin to object and appeal the matter to the Supreme Court if the objection is not acceded to.

Preparation for Inquest

Disposition of the Body

[15.50] Inquiries into death are made by the police on behalf of the coroner. They need to gather information and interview those concerned. If an inquest is likely and this is known at the time of death, the body should be left as it was at that time. Drainage and naso-gastric tubes, and catheters, should remain in or on the body, disconnected and capped where required. Again, staff should be aware of the procedures established by their employer in this regard.

Keeping an Account of the Events

[15.51] As soon as health carers are aware that an inquest may be held, it is in their interest to write personal statements as to what happened, date them and keep them. These may later be used to aid their memories, when they give evidence later (sometimes much later).

Preparation of Statement

[15.52] If their evidence is considered of interest, health carers may be asked questions, and to make a formal statement, by police. They should assist police in their inquiries, although they are not obliged to do so. Legal advice may be sought if there is concern about what to say. One may decline to answer questions but provide a short written statement. Even if not approached by police, a person may decide to consult a lawyer if they are in any way concerned that they may be implicated in the death of a person, and in this case should consider legal advice before making any statement to police. If they feel there is likely to be a contradiction between their statement and that of any other person, and they are absolutely certain of their facts, they should consider making a statutory declaration as soon as practicable after the event (see [7.13]).

The Inquest

[15.53] The Australian Capital Territory, Queensland, South Australia and Tasmania specifically provide that a coroner sits without a jury. The Northern Territory and Western Australia do not make any provision for having a jury. An inquest may be held by a coroner with a jury in New

[15.53] South Wales and Victoria if this is considered appropriate, and must be so held if directed by the Minister.

Giving of Evidence to the Coroner

[15.54] Coroners have wide powers for the directing of evidence to be placed before them. This includes the testimony of witnesses, records and exhibits. As an inquest is an inquisitorial process, there are no actual parties. Those who appear before the coroner do so at his or her discretion, as witnesses. Anyone considered to have a sufficient interest may appear in person, or be represented by a lawyer. They may examine and cross-examine other witnesses. Western Australia includes specific people in the list of those interested, such as a person whose act or omission may have contributed to the death, and a union member where the death arose from the course of employment. In some jurisdictions the Director of Public Prosecutions may assist the coroner, and the Attorney-General may appear or be represented, call and examine witnesses and make submissions.

[15.55] The coroner is not bound by the rules of evidence except in Queensland, and has a broad discretion to conduct the proceedings as he or she sees fit and appropriate for the particular case. However, he or she is bound by the rules of natural justice (see [1.59]). In practice there is therefore a degree of formality, inasmuch as it assists the provision of fairness to all concerned. Thus witnesses may be examined and cross-examined, opinion evidence will often be restricted to specialists, and hearsay excluded when it is considered irrelevant.

[15.56] An example of the use of hearsay evidence occurred in an inquest that was held in Canberra into the death of a baby who died after undergoing an operation to correct a skull abnormality (*Canberra Times*, 27 February 1993). A nurse who assisted anaesthetists during the operation gave evidence that she had thought there had been an emergency during the surgery, and gave details of anaesthetists asking the surgeons to stop the operation because of concern for the baby's condition. She had herself accompanied the baby to the intensive care unit and stayed there for half an hour because of her own concern. Despite this and other evidence of things going wrong, the coroner found that there was not enough evidence of negligence, although he criticised the care the baby received.

Summons to Appear

[15.57] Health carers may agree to give evidence at an inquest, in which case they answer questions under oath if so required. They will usually be approached by the police and asked for information regarding the incident, and if their evidence is considered of potential use, asked to give testimony.

[15.58] Health carers should be aware that if relatives of a deceased person believe that staff or the hospital are at fault regarding the death, they may insist on an inquest as a means of testing the case, to decide whether there is enough evidence to proceed with a negligence action. They can have lawyers cross-examine those involved.

[15.59] Where it seems a person who is required to give evidence will not appear voluntarily, the coroner may compel that person's appearance by summons. A notice of summons is served personally on the required witness, or, if they cannot be reasonably found, left at their last or usual place of residence. If a summons is not obeyed, a warrant for the arrest of the person may be issued. The person can be forcibly brought before the coroner by the police, and kept in custody or released on recognisance (a promise with or without a monetary surety) to ensure their presence at the hearing. Failure to turn up or refusal to give evidence when required to is an offence, with severe penalties. These powers can also apply to the production of documents in the witness's possession or over which he or she has power.

[15.60] Any person or body with a sufficient interest is also to be granted the right to appear or be represented by legal counsel at an inquest. The coroner has the discretion to decide who has sufficient interest. Where, for example, a hospital's practices may be in question, or a union or other body believes its reputation has been damaged or legal liability may result from the findings, or a party has some financial interest in the outcome, for example an insurer, they will most likely be allowed to have their counsel appear, produce documents or witnesses, and examine and cross-examine other witnesses at the inquest.

[15.61] Health care records, or any other documents may be required by the coroner, usually with the person who wrote them being present to testify to their having written the documents, and to explain them where this is required. However it is no longer the case in all jurisdictions that records cannot be admitted without the writer being there to testify to them. Poorly written and illegible medical records may well speak against the standard of health care given to the deceased (see [7.6]ff).

[15.62] Depositions (statement on oath) of witnesses, and medical reports are made available to those who can demonstrate a sufficient interest. These will be the other witnesses in the case, and may be the relatives of the deceased and those who were involved in his or her care.

Procedure During an Inquest

[15.63] The coroner is required to examine witnesses on oath or affirmation. This means that any false testimony is perjury and subject to punitive action. Evidence of witnesses is generally given by way of an affidavit (sworn written statement) which the person is asked to read out in court, and given the opportunity to amend or expand if they wish.

Answering Questions

[15.64] When giving evidence in any hearing, witnesses should keep in mind that questioning is often designed to test the accuracy and truth of their answers. Some general rules to follow are:

- Speak slowly and clearly.
- Consider answers carefully. It is better to pause and collect one's thoughts than to rush into answers. Back-tracking, correcting oneself (or worse, being corrected by others), and stumbling through the answer give a bad impression. However don't pause for too long, you may appear to be concocting an answer. If it is difficult to remember precisely how something happened, or to express things clearly, say so.
- It is no disgrace to forget. The best approach is to be honest and say that one can't remember something, or cannot recall precisely how it happened than to answer untruthfully or to fabricate an answer. One is not in the witness box to please the person asking the questions, nor to appear efficient and helpful, but to answer questions to the best of one's ability.
- Remain calm, despite attempts to test one's self control.

[15.65] Witnesses may be required to answer all questions (except those where the answer might incriminate them, see [15.71]). It is an offence to refuse to answer other questions, even on the ground of breach of confidence. It is also an offence to refuse to take the oath or affirmation, to refuse to produce documents, or to impede or disrupt the proceedings. Such actions may be contempt of court, attracting fines or even imprisonment. It is also an offence to disrupt proceedings or to misbehave during them.

[15.66] Coroners' inquiries are generally held in open court. However the coroner may order that:

- the court be closed to the public;
- witnesses be excluded from the court until they have given their evidence; and
- reporting of evidence given, or of the proceedings, be prohibited.

[15.67] The law is different across jurisdictions, but grounds for carrying out the above include the belief that witnesses may be exposed to retaliation, that juveniles require protection, that publication would prevent the fair trial of a person or that it is in the public interest to suppress reporting of the hearing.

Rules of Evidence

[15.68] As stated, although the coroner is not bound by the rules of evidence and procedure (as this is not a trial, but a fact-finding inquiry), the general practice has resembled fairly closely the adversarial procedure of trials. Thus, after reading out her or his statement, the witness, if necessary, is led through the statement by her or his counsel to clarify it and emphasise important points. Counsel for other parties then cross-examine and the witness's counsel may re-examine the witness to [15.71] clarify matters that may have become confused in the cross-examination.

[15.69] Because the coroner is aware of the need for fairness he or she will generally keep the rules of evidence in mind, and therefore will disallow irrelevant evidence and opinion. Hearsay evidence may however be admitted. It is within the coroner's jurisdiction to allow evidence according to the perceived justice of so doing.

Must Witnesses give Incriminating Evidence?

[15.70] When under oath or affirmation, one is obliged to tell the truth. This puts one in an awkward position where to answer a question one is admitting that one has committed, or was otherwise party to, a criminal act (incriminating oneself). Witnesses are not compelled to answer a question that may incriminate them in New South Wales, the Northern Territory, Queensland (except an inquiry in respect of missing persons) and South Australia (if the coroner is satisfied the answer would tend to incriminate). In the Australian Capital Territory a person is not excused from producing a document or thing on the grounds of self-incrimination, but such evidence cannot be used against them in other proceedings against them (with the exception of proceedings for an offence against the *Coroners Act* itself) (*Coroners Act* 1997 (ACT), ss 48, 79, 80, 86). In Western Australia a person need not answer a question that may incriminate him or her unless the coroner rules that the answer is necessary for the ends of justice, but if the question is answered to the satisfaction of the coroner, a certificate must be given to the witness, which makes the evidence inadmissible against the person in any criminal proceedings (*Coroners Act* 1996 (WA), s 47).

When may a Statement be Incriminating?

[15.71] This may occur in two ways:

- .....a person may be asked a question, such as "Did you give the wrong information to the doctor?", the answer to which may directly indicate that he or she committed a crime by concealing information and thus deliberately risking the patient's death. In these circumstances, to answer yes to this question would incriminate the person;
- .....a question may be asked that the witness perceives is part of a pattern of questioning which, if continued, might lead to the inference that he or she committed a crime. For example the person may be asked a question when, if the answer is yes, it is anticipated that this will invite further questioning that will show that the person deliberately and recklessly jeopardised the deceased's life, determining a course of action which resulted in the person's death. This perceived trend may only be a suspicion, but the witness may, nevertheless, claim the privilege. It may be that the coroner requires an investigation into why the question is not being answered: a reasonable apprehension of the danger of incrimination is grounds for not answering.

[15.71] ▌▌▌ CASE
Ex parte P; Re Hamilton (1957) 74 WN (NSW) 397 (Supreme Court)

This involved a criminal case, not a coroner's inquest. In a criminal case the accused has no immunity from answering incriminating questions, but any other person has. In this case a woman, P, was called as a witness in the prosecution of R for illegally procuring abortions. P had turned up at the door when police were arresting and questioning R. When asked at the committal, "On 29 March, did you go somewhere at about 9 am?" P refused to answer this question on the ground that her answer might incriminate her. The magistrate ruled that she was in contempt of court. P appealed to the Supreme Court.

[15.72] The Supreme Court held that to ask P where she went on 29 March was, in the light of the evidence of the police, to seek to forge a link in a chain of evidence which, if completed, would support a finding that P had conspired to procure the commission of a crime, that is, unlawful abortion, and that as long as she was neither acting in bad faith nor attempting to obstruct the course of justice, her refusal to answer was not contempt.

[15.73] This case is extracted from the *Australian Digest* (2nd ed), Vol 12, col 289. A full account of the privilege is given in the more recent case of *R v Coroner; Ex parte Alexander* [1982] VR 731. There the court held that the privilege does not automatically operate upon the witness making the objection. The court should form a view whether a claim to privilege is bona fide and has substance. But it must also ensure that a person claiming the privilege is not unfairly deprived of it. A person should not be required to answer the question to which he or she objects so that the court can judge whether it would be incriminating or not.

Finding of Coroner

[15.74] The coroner (or jury in a Coroner's Court) cannot make a finding of guilt, or otherwise, regarding the death of a person. The result of the inquest will be the establishment of:

▌..... whether, where a person has disappeared, there is enough evidence of the person's death;
▌..... the identity of the deceased;
▌..... the time and place of death; or
▌..... the manner and cause of death.

[15.75] In all jurisdictions except New South Wales, Queensland and South Australia the coroner may make observations on other matters, such as public health or safety, the administration of justice, or that a person caused the death of another in self-defence), or that a particular government agency acted too slowly or inappropriately to a crisis situation. It has been held that the findings (limited to those facts mentioned above) can be challenged, but that insofar as the coroner may consider it appropriate to make additional observations with respect to such findings, it is not appropriate for a court to overturn those observations (*Kahn v West* [1999] VSC 530 paragraph 37, per Warren J). [15.79] The coroner cannot find that a person is guilty of an offence, and in most jurisdictions this extends to his or her comments on those findings. If the coroner is satisfied that there is sufficient evidence against a person to put them on trial for an indictable offence, the Director of Public Prosecutions, Commissioner of Police or Attorney-General as nominated must be notified, and the coronial inquiry may be discontinued, for the disposition of the criminal proceedings. There may also be limits on findings and comments on civil liability. The coroner may also have the power to commit a person for trial in the Supreme Court if there is enough evidence for a prima facie case of homicide.

[15.76] Examples of recent findings of coroners include the following cases.

CASE
Melbourne, 1991: Death of woman after giving birth: "Doctor 'contributed' to woman patient's death" *Canberra Times*, **9 October 1991**

- Ms Cox died after suffering shock from post-natal haemorrhage.

The coroner concluded that the doctor attending her contributed to her death, and:

- ..... the doctor, (Dr Barnett) had failed to take sufficient steps to stop her condition deteriorating and so caused her death, in that he left the hospital having given her drugs to minimise bleeding after the birth, believing staff were monitoring her condition, and that he made "no enquiries of her condition during the morning and did not know of her condition until he was paged";
- ..... there was uncertainty as to who had clear responsibility for the patient's condition, as her regular obstetrician, Dr Lucas, was replaced by Dr Barnett during his absence, and he also failed to appreciate her condition, failing to consult fully with Dr Barnett;
- ..... both doctors and an anaesthetist did not act properly in agreeing that her condition was stable after a blood transfusion, even though she was unwell;
- ..... Ms Cox should have been transferred to a hospital with an intensive care unit, or at least had a doctor remain with her; and
- ..... the hospital staff did not act properly in not informing the doctors that they had an emergency supply of blood for transfusion.

[15.77] In this case it would be open to those concerned to consider bringing a civil action in negligence, but the coroner's criticism does not mean that they would succeed.

[15.78] Two cases were reported in 1992 involving the deaths of patients that were investigated by the coroner ("Deaths of elderly patients after surgery 'from natural causes': 'No negligence: coroner' " *Canberra Times*, 27 May 1992).

[15.79] One patient had died after an operation to remove a tumour from her colon. The tumour had been much bigger than anticipated, and

[15.79] more tissue than expected had had to be removed. The coroner found that:

- .....the tumour had been malignant and the surgery necessary;
- .....the cause of death was loss of blood; and
- .....the evidence indicated that the doctors involved "performed the procedure properly and nothing could be done".

[15.80] The second case involved a man who died after elective surgery to remove his prostate gland and had probably contracted septicaemia as a result. The coroner was satisfied on the evidence that the patient suffered from complications that could be expected in a man of the patient's age (71 years) and that there was no negligence on the part of the doctors who treated him or advised on his condition.

[15.81] In another case, *Death of baby after surgery*: "Baby death: no evidence of negligence" *Canberra Times*, 5 February 1994, the coroner found that:

- .....there were deficiencies in the preparations for the operation, although the evidence did not establish that these caused the death;
- .....there was lack of communication between the surgeons and the anaesthetists;
- .....there was an irretrievable absence of records;
- .....despite the evidence of the above problems, testimony by a nurse that she and doctors had been concerned at the condition of the patient during and after the operation, and by a specialist that he believed the surgery inappropriate, there was not enough evidence to indicate negligence on the part of any person;
- .....a system should be implemented whereby records of patients who die after surgery are quarantined until the coroner takes possession of them; and
- .....where no specialist facilities for particular care exist at a particular hospital, health consumers should be made aware of the existence of specialist services elsewhere.

[15.82] In this case, again, an action could be brought despite the coroner's finding, as this is based on the evidence to hand at the time of the coronial hearing, and could be challenged.

A case where the coroner's findings were challenged follows.

▌▌▌ CASE [15.84]
In the matter of an application pursuant to sec 28a of the Coroner's Act 1975: Ex parte Crowe (20 February 1992, SC SA, No 2223 of 1989)

A woman died three days after minor gynaecological surgery. She developed pleural effusion requiring an underwater-sealed drain of the plural cavity. The forensic pathologist produced a report that in his opinion the patient was in renal failure in the days before her death. However he repeatedly stressed that it would be advisable to obtain the opinion of specialists in the area. Indeed there was evidence put to the deputy coroner by experts in renal medicine and intensive care.

An expert in renal medicine testified that the deceased was not suffering from renal failure, but from a physiological response to hypovolaemia induced by low serum albumin caused by loss of albumin into the pleural cavity. However the renal expert did express the view that more careful monitoring of fluid balance should have taken place in view of the deceased's condition at the time.

One expert in intensive care opined that the deceased suffered from pulmonary embolus resulting in pulmonary infarction, and the deceased had developed a disorder of "capillary leakage", with the intravenous fluids leaking into the pleural cavity. He did not believe the cause of death was excessive intravenous fluid, but also stated that central venous monitoring more a regular fluid balance should have been undertaken. Another intensive care expert could not determine the cause of the deceased's illness but believed she had pneumonia and septicaemia. He was also critical of the non-availability of fluid balance charts.

The deputy coroner nevertheless relied on this evidence and made adverse comments on the treating doctor's care of the patient, finding that she died of cardiac failure consequent on acute pulmonary oedema caused by too much intravenous fluid.

The applicant doctor appealed to the Supreme Court, arguing that the Deputy Coroner's findings were against the evidence, and inadequate.

[15.83] The Court concluded that excessive amounts of fluid were not given, but rather the deceased had developed escape of fluid due to endotoxic shock. There was pulmonary oedema, but its cause had not been demonstrated.

Disappearances

[15.84] Where the coroner investigates the disappearance of a person he or she can determine:

▌..... the circumstances of the disappearance;
▌..... whether the person is alive or dead; and
▌..... if alive, where the person is believed to be.

REFERENCES AND FURTHER READING

Australian Health and Medical Law Reporter (CCH, Sydney, 1991)

Chivell, W, "Coronial Investigation" (1996) 165 *Medical Journal of Australia* 396

Freckelton, I, "Causation in Coronial Law" (1997) 4 *Journal of Law and Medicine* 289

Lynch, M, "Forensic Pathology: Redefining Medico-Legal Death Investigation" 7 *Journal of Law and Medicine* 67 (1999)

Lynch, M, "The Coroner, the Forensic Pathologist and the Unborn Child" 7 *Journal of Law and Medicine* 415 (1999)

O'Sullivan, J, *Law for Nurses* (Law Book Co, Sydney, 1983), Ch 18

Selby, H, *The Aftermath of Death* (Federation Press, Sydney, 1992)

Selby, H, *The Inquest Handbook* (Federation Press, Sydney, 1998)

Staunton, P and Whyburn, R, *Nursing and the Law* (4th ed, Saunders, Sydney, 1997), Ch 9

Waller, K M, *Coronial Law and Practice in New South Wales* (2nd ed, Law Book Co, Sydney, 1982)

Chapter Sixteen

STATE INVOLVEMENT IN THREATS TO HEALTH OR WELFARE

INTRODUCTION

[16.1] The state has an interest in the affairs of its citizens when their illness or activities pose a threat to the health of others in society. This may require the reporting of those who have a notifiable disease or who engage in child abuse.

Notifiable Disease

[16.2] A person may have a contagious disease which requires isolation and special treatment, or be engaged in activity which is potentially or actually dangerous to the health of others. The state role, therefore, involves prevention as well as cure.

[16.3] There are many ways in which the state acts to maintain public health. This is mainly by activities such as:

- .....regulating standards such as care of public baths;
- .....licensing and regulating the preparation and serving of food;
- .....developing community public education programmes; and
- .....encouraging regular health checkups and providing specialised clinics and information centres.

[16.4] The state goes further, however, when dealing with notifiable infectious and sexually transmitted diseases. It reserves the right to intervene in the private lives of the citizens involved, and where necessary quarantine them and subject them to compulsory treatment.

[16.5] This raises the issue of the relative weight to be given to the freedom of the individual. As with mental health there may be conflict between the "medical" centred approach and the "rights" centred approach. However, there is much less conflict regarding the nature, cause and treatment of diseases in the public health area. The appearance of the HIV virus has raised a lot of basic questions, and brought into the public arena many issues which were given little attention before. The case of a New South Wales woman who was detained involuntarily because she was HIV-positive and had announced that she would continue to act as a

[16.5] prostitute, raised questions as to the manner in which the state regulates public health, and under what circumstances, if at all, a person should be detained and treated against their will on the basis of a doctor's diagnosis.

[16.6] There is legislation in each jurisdiction[1] that lists those diseases that must be reported to the state, and the powers given to relevant authorities to ensure the containment of any threat to public health. In some circumstance this may involve detention and treatment of individuals, seizure of goods and property for de-contamination and the closure of premises and enterprises. The diseases involved are described variously by such terms as "infectious", "dangerous", and "notifiable" in the different State and Territory legislation dealing with public health. In this chapter, all diseases that must be reported are called "reportable diseases".

[16.7] Jurisdictions differ in their classification of reportable diseases and the consequent obligations and powers applying to each classification. The list of diseases that must be reported also changes over time. The list is published in the Government Gazette (the official publication of Government notices in each jurisdiction) when changes are made.

[16.8] Some jurisdictions retain a distinction between sexually transmitted, infections and notifiable diseases. Those suffering from infectious diseases may be subject to more stringent controls than those with diseases categorised as notifiable; those with sexually transmitted diseases coming under powers more specifically related to the nature of such disease. Different jurisdictions list AIDS as either a notifiable or sexually transmitted disease. (In this chapter the term "notifiable disease" will be used to refer to all three categories.)

Examples of Notifiable Diseases

Infectious and Transmissible Diseases

[16.9] Diseases which are notifiable across jurisdictions are:

AIDS: considered in some jurisdictions to be a sexually transmitted disease (see below);
Anthrax (except New South Wales and South Australia);
Arbovirus infection (including dengue fever);
Brucellosis;
Campylobacter infections (except New South Wales);

---

[1] *Public Health Act* 1997 (ACT); *Public Health Act* 1991 (NSW), Public Health Regulations 1991 (NSW); *Cancer (Registration) Act* 1988 (NT), and Regulations, *Notifiable Diseases Act* 1981 (NT); *Health Act* 1937 (Qld); *Public and Environmental Health Act* 1987 (SA), South Australian Health Commission (Cancer) Regulations 1991 (SA); *Public Health Act* 1997 (Tas), Public Health (Notifiable Diseases) Regulations 1989 (Tas); *Health Act* 1958 (Vic), Health (Infectious Diseases) Regulations 1990 (Vic), *Cancer Act* 1958 (Vic), Cancer (Reporting) Regulations 1992 (Vic); *Health Act* 1911 (WA), *Health (Infectious Diseases) Order* 1993 (WA), Health (Notification of Cancer) Regulations 1981 (WA), Health (Cervical Cytology Register) Regulations 1991 (WA), Health (Notification of Adverse Event after Immunisation) Regulations 1995 (WA).

Chlamydia infections; [16.11]
Cholera;
Diphtheria;
Haemophilus influenzae (except Victoria, the Northern Territory);
Hepatitis (mostly all forms) (except the Northern Territory);
Human immunodeficiency virus;
Hydatid disease (except New South Wales, Queensland);
Legionellosis or Legionnaire's Disease;
Leptospirosis;
Listeriosis (except the Northern Territory);
Malaria;
Measles;
Meningococcal infections;
Mumps;
Pertussis (whooping cough);
Plague (except Tasmania);
Poliomyelitis;
Q Fever;
Rabies;
Rubella;
Salmonella infections;
Shigella infections (except New South Wales);
Syphilis (except Western Australia and the Australian Capital Territory);
Tetanus (except New South Wales);
Tuberculosis (except New South Wales and South Australia);
Typhus or Typhoid Fever (except South Australia);
Viral haemorrhagic fever (except the Northern Territory);
Yellow Fever (except Queensland);
Yersinia infection (except New South Wales).

Cancer

[16.10] All jurisdictions require the reporting and registering of cancer, with some States having special legislation for this purpose. Cancer is generally defined as:

> a malignant growth of human tissue which if unchecked is likely to spread to adjacent tissue or beyond its place of origin and which has the propensity to recur.

[16.11] Most jurisdictions go on to include carcinoma, sarcoma, any mixed tumour, leukaemia, any type of lymphoma, melanoma and non-invasive *in situ* carcinoma. Western Australia adds all neoplasms of the brain, spinal cord and cranial nerves, and any other intracranial neoplasms, whether benign or malignant. Most jurisdictions now have special cervical cytology registers and breast screening services that register instances of cancer. Legislation requires reporting of cases of

[16.11] cancer in similar terms to the reporting of other notifiable diseases.[2] Registers have been established for epidemiological purposes as well as for the early detection and prevention of cancer.[3] Identifying information on the registers is confidential except with the consent of the person involved.

[16.12] There are many more diseases listed as notifiable diseases, and procedures for reporting them, in different jurisdictions. The account which follows is general only.

Who must Report Notifiable Diseases?

[16.13] In New South Wales notifiable diseases are listed and categorised in Sch 1 of the *Public Health Act* 1991 (NSW). Section 14 requires that:

- ..... any medical practitioner who has attended the person and has reason to believe that person is suffering from the disease, or who attends a deceased person (that is, a postmortem) who was suffering from the disease; or
- ..... in some cases a pathologist who certifies that a person is suffering from the disease,

notify the Director-General of the Health Department.

[16.14] A person who provides care for someone in a hospital or other health care facility who becomes aware that a person is suffering from a notifiable disease must notify the chief executive officer of the facility, who in turn must notify the Director-General. Whilst identities of those who are HIV-positive are to be strictly confidential, the Director-General can inform a person who could contact HIV through sexual contact or needle-sharing with a person that the latter is HIV positive.

[16.15] In Queensland, Schs 2 and 3 of the Health Regulations 1996 (Qld) list notifiable diseases. The *Health Act* 1937 (Qld) requires anyone who suffers from a notifiable disease to undertake treatment for the disease. It is an offence to knowingly infect another with a notifiable disease. A medical practitioner who examines or treats such a patient must

---

[2] Public Health (Cancer Reporting) Regulations 1994 (ACT), reg 4; Public Health Regulation 1991 (NSW), cl 81(a) (requires notification), *Public Health Act* 1991 (NSW), ss 42E-42P (establishes the New South Wales Pap Test Register); *Cancer (Registration) Act* 1988 (NT), s 5, Cancer (Registration) Regulations 1990 (NT), reg 3; *Health Act* 1937 (Qld), ss 100C, 100D, Health Regulation 1996 (Qld), ss 16-21; South Australian Health Commission (Cancer) Regulations 1991 (SA), Public and Environmental Health (Cervical Cancer Screening) Regulations 1993 (SA); Public Health (Notifiable Diseases) Regulations 1995 (Tas), reg 4(3)(b), *Public Health Amendment (Cervical Cytology) Act* 1993 (Tas), s 53A; *Cancer Act* 1958 (Vic), ss 59-62, Cancer (BreastScreen Register) Regulations 1994 (Vic), Cancer (Reporting) Regulations 1992 (Vic); *Health Act* 1911 (WA), ss 289B, 289C, Health (Notification of Cancer) Regulations 1981 (WA), Health (Cervical Cytology Register) Regulations 1991 (WA).

[3] For example see, Public Health (Cervical Cytology Register) Regulations 1996 (NT); Public and Environmental Health (Cervical Cancer Screening) Regulations 1993 (SA); *Cancer (BreastScreen Register) Regulations* 1994 (Vic); *Health (Cervical Cytology Register) Regulations* 1991 (WA).

notify the chief health officer unless working at a health facility, in which case the medical superintendent (who must then notify the chief health officer). [16.20]

[16.16] In South Australia, notifiable diseases are listed under the *Public and Environmental Health Act* 1987 (SA). Notification is to the South Australian Health Commission, and is required where a medical practitioner suspects that a person suffers from an infectious disease (rather than waiting for positive results). The Commission has obligations to report the instance of infectious diseases to local councils. South Australia also provides that local councils must be notified by the Health Department of any occurrence of notifiable disease in their jurisdiction, as a result of which the councils may have delegated powers of containment and control (*Public and Environmental Health Act* 1987 (SA), ss 33, 36).

[16.17] In Victoria, a list of notifiable diseases is in Sch 2 of the Health (Infectious Diseases) Regulation 1990 (Vic). Medical practitioners must notify the Chief General Manager of the Health Department of any person suffering from a notifiable disease (s 7). Pathologists are required to report certification of specified diseases, both in relation to individuals certified and overall statistical reports. There are instances where the relevant municipal council must be notified by the Health Department. There may be legal requirements to notify those who are in immediate attendance upon the person, and the head of the household or institution where they reside, and detain people and property (*Health Act* 1958 (Vic), ss 124-128).

[16.18] In Western Australia the occupier of premises (including a hospital or other health facility) in which a person is found to be suffering from an infectious disease must report it. The parent or guardian of a child, or head teacher at a school attended by a child is similarly obliged (*Health Act* 1911 (WA), s 276).

[16.19] In Tasmania (Part 3 of the *Public Health Act* 1997 (Tas)), the Northern Territory (section 8, Part II of the *Notifiable Diseases Act* 1981 (NT)) and the Australian Capital Territory (Part 6 of the *Public Health Act* 1997 (ACT)) the relevant legislation has similar requirements to other jurisdictions regarding notification by medical practitioners, chief executives of health care facilities and pathologists.

The Role of Health Carers

[16.20] Health carers should all be aware in general of the legal requirements regarding notifiable diseases. Notification by medical practitioners is required, and in some cases the health facility involved, but employees should make sure that suspected notifiable disease is brought to the notice of the management. They may also act as diplomats, explaining the requirements of the law and its purpose to a client who is probably distressed and confused and feeling like an outcast.

What Information must be Given?

[16.21] Personal information, as well as the details of any contacts must be supplied in circumstances where there is a danger to public health (for example, caused by a person's actions). Facts such as the school attended, in the case of a child, and details of contacts there if the disease is very infectious. However, the general principle is that the notification of identifying information is strictly limited, and privacy preserved wherever possible.

What can Authorities do?

[16.22] There are powers provided by legislation that the designated person (usually the chief medical officer or other similarly designated medical officer within the Health Department), may cause the inspection of premises where the person is residing or elsewhere. In some cases property may be seized and/or dealt with (for example, disposed of, fumigated) according to the orders of that officer, and the nominated person and any other person may be required to undergo tests, and/or be removed, by force if necessary, to a specified institution to undergo specified treatment. There may be distinctions drawn between powers available where different diseases are concerned.

Sexually Transmitted Diseases (Other Than AIDS)

[16.23] Such diseases include gonorrhoea, syphilis, chancroid, lymphogranuloma venereum and granuloma inguinale. However, as these diseases are no longer the threat to community health that they once were, in some jurisdictions they are no longer reportable, or if they are, they are categorised along with other notifiable diseases. Thus the above provisions, as well as powers to examine and detain the person apply generally to sexually transmitted diseases, but there are some specific requirements which apply to this type of disease.

[16.24] In New South Wales, a medical practitioner must provide the person with information including ways of preventing transmission of the disease to others. Prescribed treatment must be followed until the person is certified free of the disease and notification must be given of change of address or medical practitioner. The spouse or partner may be notified of risks associated with sexual activity with the person by the Director-General of Health (*Public Health Act* 1991 (NSW), ss 11-16; Public Health Regulations 1991 (NSW), regs 4, 5, 9, 10).

Victoria requires that a person with an infectious disease must take all necessary precautions to prevent others unknowingly being placed at risk.

In Queensland the *Health Act* 1937 (Qld), and in South Australia the *Public and Environmental Health Act* 1987 (SA), make it an offence to fail to take reasonable measures to prevent others from contracting either [16.28] syphilis or gonorrhoea. It is also an offence in most jurisdictions to knowingly or recklessly place others at risk through sexual relationships with them. It is an offence in all jurisdictions not to comply with an order by an authorised officer.

Confidentiality must be Maintained

[16.25] In some jurisdictions the name of the client and contacts need not be disclosed if he or she is following a treatment programme as required. Identity may only be required if the person refuses treatment and then may be subject to other requirements of confidentiality; for example, names must be kept confidential by authorities.

[16.26] A parent or guardian or other person in charge of a child may be required to notify the authorities in some jurisdictions, for example, New South Wales and Victoria.

Acquired Immunodeficiency Syndrome (AIDS)

[16.27] This is the most serious infectious disease because of its predicted increase in the population. It is also of concern because of the social and psychological ramifications of its connection with intravenous drug use, homosexuality and blood transfusions. See also [7.40]ff.

Legal Requirements

[16.28] Legislation regarding the reporting of AIDS is similar to other notifiable diseases with some differences and exceptions. There are several systems of categorisation by which stages of the illness have been divided by the medical profession. Confusion sometimes exists as to which categories must be reported by law as these are not always defined with accuracy. In its National HIV/AIDS strategy of 1989 the Federal Government has divided the stages of the disease into four groups:

Group I	acute infection stage, involving lymphadenopathy, myalgia, fever and rash, with serum antibodies appearing one to two weeks after infection
Group II	an asymptomatic stage with positive evidence of antibodies to the HIV
Group III	where there is persistent generalised lymphadenopathy
Group IV	where other diseases are present, whether symptoms are minimal or more serious (this form of classification of AIDS was first adopted by the report *AIDS—a time to care, a time to act*, 1988 AGPS Canberra)

[16.29] **[16.29]** The wording of some legislation has caused differences of opinion as to whether all categories of the disease are notifiable, however the author is of the opinion that the lack of specific definition of the term "AIDS" in legislation where it appears, and other legislation requiring general public health measures, can be interpreted to mean that the occurrence of HIV positive serum tests is notifiable in all States and Territories, and unless specifically provided otherwise, reference to AIDS is a reference to infection by the HIV at any stage.

[16.30] Any medical practitioner who is aware, or has reasonable grounds to believe, that a person is suffering from, or died of AIDS, must report this to the prescribed authority. Also, those carrying out pathology tests are generally required to notify the Health Department of the results if they show that a person is suffering from AIDS. In most jurisdictions the identifying information is not disclosed on notification forms, and this information remains confidential unless specific circumstances require such information to be supplied, such as the need to trace contacts, or notify partners, where the behaviour of the person involved necessitates this (as recommended by the Intergovernmental Committee on AIDS Legal Working Party, which produced its Final Report at the end of 1992). It is only where the behaviour of a person becomes a public health issue that such information would be disclosed to a state authority.

[16.31] New South Wales, the Northern Territory and Western Australia require that the medical practitioner provide the client with information on safe sexual practice, the medical treatment available, the progress of the disease and the availability of counselling.

Testing

[16.32] Testing for HIV is generally not compulsory, however jurisdictions may provide that testing is required for some purposes (for example, all jurisdictions require testing of blood for transfusion), or immunity from legal action if precautions have been taken by testing of tissue (for example, where donor sperm is to be used). Tasmania has introduced the *HIV/AIDS Preventative Measures Act* 1993 (Tas) which provides that confidential testing is available for those who request it, or for those required by statute to undergo testing. Also, a magistrate can order that the person be detained for up to six months to prevent the spread of infection, and the Supreme Court a further period of detention (*Public Health Act* 1997 (Tas), ss 40-60). Legislation in most jurisdictions requires that counselling and information be given to those who are to be tested for HIV.

Blood Transfusion, Tissue Donation and Blood-Borne Disease

[16.33] Legislation in all States requires that a declaration may be required by blood donors to the effect that they are not, to their knowledge, infected with the HIV virus, and have not been involved in activities which place them at risk of being so infected.[4] This prevents [16.35] action against those collecting blood, unless they lacked reasonable care in so doing. Falsification of this form is an offence, either specifically established, or under provisions in the crimes legislation regarding false representations.[5]

[16.34] Most States require a similar declaration from donors of semen, and in its recent White Paper *National HIV Strategy*, the federal government recommended compulsory testing for semen donors.

Sexual Relations, Prohibited Behaviour and Disease

[16.35] In New South Wales, Queensland, South Australia and Victoria it is an offence to have sexual relations with another person knowing one has a sexually transmissible condition, where the other person has not knowingly consented. In South Australia the Health Commission may give directions to a person as to their conduct (which presumably includes sexual conduct).[6] Whether having sexual relations under such conditions could also be considered homicide, attempted homicide, or civil or criminal negligence, has been mooted but not decided by the courts (see also [16.41]). The spreading of disease has not been considered to be a criminal offence in the past (*R v Clarence* (1888) 22 QBD 23). However, this was before AIDS appeared. Webb and Howie (1985) argue that it is possible that a person who infected another intentionally or recklessly could be guilty of murder or attempted murder if the illness is fatal. They, nevertheless, point to problems of proving causation and the effects of time limits where the disease takes a long time to develop. Factors such as the degree of risk involved, the likelihood of contracting the disease, and the intention to infect the other person must be established (*R v Nuri* [1990] VR 641). Where a single act of intercourse held a one in 200 chance of HIV transmission, a court held that the defendant was not guilty of placing another in danger of death or serious injury as it did not amount to the necessary "appreciable danger" of death or injury required to make out the criminal offence (it could nevertheless amount to an offence under public health legislation) (*R v B* (unreported SC Vic 1995)).

---

[4] *Blood Donation (Transmittable Diseases) Act* 1985 (ACT), ss 4, 5; *Human Tissue Act* 1983 (NSW), Pt 3A (applies to blood and semen); *Notifiable Diseases Act* 1981 (NT), s 26A(2)(a), Sch 6; *Transplantation and Anatomy Act* 1979 (Qld), s 48A; *Blood Contaminants Act* 1985 (SA), ss 4, 5; *Blood Transfusion (Limitation of Liability) Act* 1986 (Tas), ss 4, 5, *HIV/AIDS Preventative Measures Act* 1993 (Tas), s 8(3); Health (Infectious Diseases) Regulations 1990 (Vic), Sch 6, 7; Blood and Tissue (Transmissible Disease) Regulations 1985 (WA), regs 5(1), 6(1), 9(1), 10(1), 11.

[5] For example, it is specifically prohibited under the following legislation: *Human Tissue Amendment Act* 1983 (NSW), s 21D; *Transplantation and Anatomy Act* 1979 (Qld), s 48A; *Human Tissue Act* 1985 (Tas), s 30; *Health (Blood Donations) Act* 1985 (Vic), s 133.

[6] Examples of specific legislation are: *Public Health Act* 1991 (NSW), s 13, *Crimes Act* 1900 (NSW), s 36 (causing grievous bodily disease); *Health Act* 1937 (Qld), s 48(2); *Public and Environmental Health Act* 1987 (SA), ss 33, 37; *Health Act* 1958 (Vic), s 120(2), *Crimes Act* 1958 (Vic), s 19A.

[16.36] Concern about the use, or threat of the use, of syringes filled with HIV-infected blood to intentionally infect others, either out of malice or during the commission of offences, has led some States to make specific provision and heavy penalties for such offences. For example New South Wales (*Crimes Act* 1900 (NSW), s 36) and Victoria (*Crimes Act* 1958 (Vic), s 19A) provide that the intentional infliction of a very serious disease is an offence carrying a penalty of up to 25 years' imprisonment. In other jurisdictions such offences would be covered by more general provisions related to actions ranging from reckless endangerment and attempted murder to assault and threatening harm to another. As a person may be potentially liable for the death, many years later, of someone from a disease with which they have been maliciously infected, the offence could possibly amount to murder. This would also apply to the malicious actual or threatened injection of a person with HIV-positive blood, or other attempts to infect a person.

[16.37] It is more likely that public health legislation would be invoked where a person has knowingly placed another at risk of disease by their actions. All jurisdictions have established offences for such behaviour.[7] Victoria has created the offence of knowingly or recklessly infecting another.

Disclosure of the Identity of a Person with a Notifiable Disease

[16.38] Whilst legislation is generally framed to avoid the recording of identifying information where possible, particular attention has been paid to the protection of identities in the reporting of HIV-positive status, coded information being sufficient.[8] In most jurisdictions it is an offence to disclose the identity of a person with a notifiable disease, subject of course to reporting requirements. See [7.70]ff on disclosure to third persons.

Discrimination Against those with AIDS

[16.39] Discrimination against those with AIDS has taken many forms, from refusal to treat them, special categorisation of patients, unwarranted isolation and special methods of handling food and equipment. It also

---

[7] See, for example Public Health (Infectious and Notifiable Diseases) Regulations 1930 (ACT), regs 13, 14; *Public Health Act* 1991 (NSW), ss 11, 13; *Notifiable Diseases Act* 1981 (NT), s 7; *Health Act* 1937 (Qld), s 48; *Public and Environmental Health Act* 1987 (SA), s 37; *Public Health Act* 1962 (Tas), s 30; Health (Infectious Diseases) Regulations 1990 (Vic), reg 7; *Health Act* 1911 (WA), ss 264, 310.

[8] See, for example Public Health (Infectious and Notifiable Diseases) Regulations 1930 (ACT), reg 4; *Public Health Act* 1991 (NSW), s 16; *Cancer (Registration) Act* 1988 (NT) and Regulations (NT), *Notifiable Diseases Act* 1981 (NT); *Health Act* 1937 (Qld), s 32; Public Health (Notifiable Diseases) Regulations 1995 (Tas), reg 5; Health (Infectious Diseases) Regulations 1990 (Vic), Sch 3.

extends to many day-to-day matters which are incidental to the lifestyle of those concerned, for example, where the sufferer is living in a homosexual relationship. Laws and rules which give benefits to married couples may exclude such a person from the comfort of visits from her or his partner, from information, access to property, or the courtesies normally granted to a spouse or de facto spouse.

[16.40] There is federal legislation and legislation in all jurisdictions prohibiting discrimination against those with mental or physical handicap or impairment. Most jurisdictions include as handicap or impairment the "presence in the body of organisms capable of causing disease". Commonwealth legislation also provides that some international human rights instruments are to be followed in Australia. New South Wales has also prohibited discrimination on the ground of a person's sexual preference, and this ground has also been included in the grounds covered by the *Human Rights and Equal Opportunity Commission Act* 1986 (Cth). The law needs clarification and strengthening, but it appears to be directed at providing for treatment for those who are HIV-positive or have AIDS (see below, Ch 18).

[16.41] Anti-discrimination legislation would thus appear to establish that health carers cannot refuse a client treatment, or give inferior treatment simply because a person is HIV-positive or has AIDS, and that a patient can attempt to obtain redress for discrimination on the grounds of their sexual preference. This poses a problem for those who have objections to caring for these clients. Also involved in the issue is the rule that an employee should obey the reasonable and lawful directions of the employer (see [6.106], [11.21]ff). A health carer could be in breach of anti-discrimination legislation if he or she gives a client less favourable care or treatment than would be given another client who does not have the illness, simply because of the illness and not because of the reasonably anticipated consequences of giving them the same treatment. Matters that would have to be considered are:

- .....the chances of the health carer contracting the disease;
- .....whether the risk of infection can be reasonably reduced if care is given;
- .....the consequences of non-treatment for the patient (and others, if relevant);
- .....the balance between harm to the health carer and others by giving care and to the patient by not giving it;
- .....any less drastic solution to the problem than not giving care; and
- .....the course of action indicated by authorities on the issue (see Flaskerud (1989), p 224).

[16.42] Discrimination can best be dealt with by educating medical staff and their clients, and by carefully considered programmes where special treatment is required for the safety, comfort, convenience and wellbeing of those concerned. Where there are genuine fears for their safety, or it is believed that conditions are not such that proper care can be given, nurses should discuss the matter with their supervisor or the management.

State Control of those who are HIV-Positive

Compulsory Examination

[16.43] Like all those who have a notifiable disease, a person with HIV/AIDS must undergo medical examination if required by the chief medical officer. In Victoria a person may be removed to a hospital or other place (for example, quarantine centre), and detained if their behaviour poses a danger to the community. This is covered by specific provisions, or general public health legislation.

Compulsory Blood Testing on Admission to Facilities

[16.44] No jurisdiction has legislation providing for compulsory blood testing of clients on admission to hospital or other health facilities, although there have recently been calls to pass such legislation. A person may however be required by a health services provider to undergo HIV testing before elective medical or dental procedures are carried out. If he or she refuses, the health provider can either carry out the procedure according to the Infection Control Guidelines of the National Health and Medical Research Council, or refer the person to someone else. Advice may be sought from the Secretary of the Health Department (for example, *HIV/AIDS Preventive Measures Act* 1993 (Tas)). There are many arguments for and against such measures, some of the major considerations being the cost, doubtful value and emotional disadvantages on the one hand and protection of staff and other clients on the other. Health care providers should very carefully consider the legal implications of whatever policy they adopt:

- what is reasonable care for all clients should be established;
- compulsory testing should not make clients careless where tests are negative (considering that seroconversion can take some months);
- treating every client as potentially positive could be cumbersome, expensive and cause some distress to the client, but could be the only reasonable way of preventing the spread of the disease;
- consent to the taking of blood is not a blanket consent to carry out unspecified tests;
- special provision for proper counselling could be essential, as, not only would those who are HIV-positive be confronted with an unexpected disaster with which to cope, in addition to the illness for which they have been admitted, but the very fact of being tested could cause undue anxiety and distress to clients in general; and
- there are privacy issues as well. Use of identifying records must be strictly limited to protect the privacy of clients. Storage and disposal of records should also be carefully controlled. An instance of discarded laboratory reports from a major city hospital which included the results of HIV testing is an indication of possible situations to be anticipated and prevented.

State Control of those with Infectious Diseases [16.48]

Powers to Detain and Treat

[16.45] Under public health legislation, all jurisdictions provide the power to health authorities to require those with a notifiable disease to undergo compulsory medical tests and treatment, and, if necessary (usually meaning if the person refuses to undergo treatment or behaves in a way that poses a danger to others) to be removed to a hospital or other health facility and be detained there until they are no longer infectious. Restrictions may be imposed on a person, or they may be isolated. A situation which arose recently in New South Wales involved a prostitute who was HIV-positive and who refused to refrain from plying her trade. She was detained under the order of the chief medical officer of health under section 500A(1) of the *Public Health Act* 1991 (NSW).

[16.46] The *HIV/AIDS Preventive Measures Act* 1993 (Tas) provides that those who are infected with the HIV virus will be required to take all reasonable steps to prevent transmission of the disease to others. A magistrate can impose restrictions for a period of 28 days on the movements of a person who behaves recklessly. The person may also be required to undergo medical and psychological assessment. Partners must be told of a person's positive HIV status, and the infected person will be able to request a medical practitioner or counsellor to inform and counsel their partner.

[16.47] There is concern that these provisions allow for detention of citizens without proper legal process. In New South Wales, South Australia and Victoria there are specific provisions for periodic review of the orders, and appeals to the court against them. The Australian Capital Territory, the Northern Territory, Tasmania and Western Australia do not have specific provision for time limits on detention, or appeal to the courts. In these jurisdictions one would have to rely on common law and/or administrative law rights to appeal a decision to detain. Victoria provides emergency powers which may be proclaimed by the Governor in Council. These powers permit the Chief General Manager of the Health Department to specify areas of quarantine, prevent entering or leaving these areas by any person, cause the arrest without warrant and detention of persons within the area, and the seizing, disinfecting or destroying of property (*Health (General Amendments) Act* 1988 (Vic), Div 4).

Needle Exchange

[16.48] This is a positive measure for infection control. There are laws specifying the method and facilities for disposing of needles and syringes. As the possession or supply of equipment for administering illicit drugs is a criminal offence, development of needle exchange programs/supply programs has required provision exempting workers in the programs from criminal liability for their activities. The following is generally the rule:

[16.48]
- ▪ .....it is illegal to possess specific ("illicit") drugs except for trace amounts such as that left in syringes and needles (thus allowing for needle-exchange programmes)
- ▪ .....it is illegal to possess equipment for the administration of illicit drugs, except for the possession of needles and syringes;
- ▪ .....it is an offence to self-administer illicit drugs.[9]

[16.49] The Australian Capital Territory *Drugs of Dependence Act* 1989 (ACT) provides that medical practitioners, nurses, pharmacists and needle exchange workers can apply to the Chief Medical Officer for authorisation to distribute syringes and needles, and protects them from prosecution under the *Crimes Act* 1900 (ACT).

[16.50] In New South Wales the *Drugs Misuse and Trafficking Act* 1985 (NSW), section 11(1A), (B) and the Drugs Misuse and Trafficking Regulations (NSW), regulations 5, 6 provide that possession of implements for the administration of drugs except syringes and needles is an offence, however possession of needles and syringes may be evidence of drug use. Pharmacists and needle exchange users may be in possession of equipment for use of illicit drugs if this is for harm minimisation purposes. They are also exempt from prosecution for aiding and abetting illicit drug use or supply of equipment for administration of a prohibited drug if they are participating in a needle exchange program.

[16.51] The Northern Territory *Misuse of Drugs Act* 1987 (NT) provides that authorised people are exempt from the offence of supplying needles and syringes.

[16.52] In Queensland, medical practitioners, pharmacists and authorised needle exchange workers may supply syringes and needles (*Drugs Misuse Act* 1986 (Qld), s 10(2), (3)). The Drugs Misuse Regulations 1986 (Qld), regs 9 and 10 set out requirements for safe disposal of needles, syringes and dangerous drugs.

[16.53] In South Australia, the South Australian Health Commission issues licences for needle exchange workers rather than agencies. The Drug and Alcohol Services Council advises the Government and trains workers. It is not an offence to distribute syringes and needles and to give advice in relation to their safe use by medical practitioners, nurses and pharmacists. See the Controlled Substances Act (Exemptions) Regulations 1989 (SA), s 2a.

[16.54] In Tasmania permits are issued for a specified period to medical practitioners, chemists and needle exchange officers to supply needles and syringes, who may authorise their employees to supply them (*HIV Preventive Measures Act* 1993 (Tas), Pt 3).

---

[9] *Drugs of Dependence Act* 1989 (ACT), *Crimes Act* 1900 (ACT); *Drugs Misuse and Trafficking Act* 1985 (NSW); *Misuse of Drugs Act* 1990 (NT); *Drugs Misuse Act* 1986 (Qld); Poisons Regulations 1974 (Qld); *Controlled Substances Act* 1984 (SA); *Poisons Act* 1971 (Tas); *Drugs Poisons and Controlled Substances Act* 1981 (Vic); *Poisons Act* 1964 (WA).

[16.55] In Victoria, those who sell or supply needles and syringes as part of a needle exchange program are also exempt from criminal liability. No provision is made for those who are involved in other activities related to needle exchange, such as education of IV users. A list of those authorised to sell or supply needles and syringes is kept by the Secretary of the Health Department, and places authorised to act as needle exchange centres are specified in regulations (*Drugs Poisons and Controlled Substances Act* 1981 (Vic), s 80(5), Drugs Poisons and Controlled Substance Regulations 1985 (Vic)).

[16.56] In Western Australia, the possession of needles and syringes is not an offence, whilst the possession of other utensils for smoking or manufacturing illicit drugs is (*Misuse of Drugs Act* 1981 (WA), ss 5-9). Pharmacists and needle exchange workers are exempt from criminal sanctions for aiding and abetting offences (*Poisons Act* 1964 (WA), s 36A).

Other Infection Control Measures

Immunisation

[16.57] The Commonwealth provides vaccines for such diseases as polio, mumps, measles, rubella, diphtheria, influenza, hepatitis B, pertussis and tetanus. It requires children to be vaccinated under certain circumstances, for example, for eligibility for the child care benefit. The National Health and Medical Research Council has recommended that school entry be dependent on children being immunised according to its schedule of child immunisation. At the time of writing, it appears that only the Australian Capital Territory, New South Wales and Victoria have legislated this requirement.[10]

Other Measures

[16.57A] Public health legislation provides wide powers to health authorities to search quarantine and sanitise premises, seize property, detain and treat people and order them to undergo examination and treatment where there is an actual or suspected danger to another person or the community. Control of hazardous materials and practices, as well as prosecution of offences, including intentionally or recklessly placing others at risk are other authorised means of infection control. Authorised inspectors can enter premises and inspect them for compliance with health standards (for example, inspection of air-conditioning units, food preparation areas). Health care facilities such as hospitals, hostels and nursing homes may carry out other activities that are covered by public health legislation and are also subject to infection control standards required for licensing and accreditation (for example under Hospitals,

---

[10] Public Health (Infectious and Notifiable Diseases) Regulations 2000 (ACT), regs 4, 5, 8, 9, 11-14, 17, 19; *Public Health Act* 1991 (NSW), ss 42A-42D, Public Health Regulations 1991 (NSW), reg 10C; *Health Act* 1958 (Vic), ss 144, 145, Health (Immunisation) Regulations 1999 (Vic), regs 5-9, Schs 1, 2.

[16.57A] Private Hospitals, Nursing Homes and Supported Accommodation legislation, that provide for sanitary conditions, clean and dirty utility rooms, sterilising and autoclaving equipment, and infection-control procedures).

Disclosure by Health Carers with a "Notifiable Disease"

[16.58] There is much controversy about whether employers or clients should be informed when a health care worker is suffering from a notifiable disease, especially if he or she is HIV-positive or has AIDS. There has been no definitive legal pronouncement, as yet, on this point, but the general thrust of legislation and government policy is that confidentiality should be given priority, and disclosure of the fact should not be mandatory. The Legal Working Party of the Intergovernmental Committee on AIDS ((1992), p 59) recommended that there should be no positive duty to disclose their HIV status to employers. General, not specific, public health transmission and exposure offences should apply to workers (for example intentionally or recklessly exposing another to an infectious disease).

[16.59] The law relating to negligence requires that health professionals ensure they are not posing an unreasonable risk to clients (for example, not being involved in invasive procedures and surgery, sealing of lesions, wearing of gloves for direct patient care). However, there is no *legal* requirement to tell them or the employer. Special care would have to be taken, as carers could be sued in negligence if a client or colleague contracted AIDS from their care. Any lesions would have to be properly sealed, and other precautions taken to prevent infection.

[16.60] A health carer is protected by legislation against unlawful discrimination on the basis of impairment (including suffering from an infectious disease). This is dealt with in Chapter 18.

Domestic Violence: Child Abuse

[16.61] The basic legal principle applying to the welfare of children is that parents have the responsibility of the care, protection and upbringing of their children. The parenting of a child is a private matter, with any disputes or disagreements within the family being dealt with under the *Family Law Act* 1975 (Cth). Parties are encouraged to work out differences through mediation and conciliation, or, failing that, through a parenting order of the Family Court. However where a child is charged with an offence, abused or in need of care, State child welfare authorities are authorised to act, and the Family Court is precluded from jurisdiction. All States and Territories provide for the reporting of suspected child abuse except Western Australia, and this is outlined below. Other manifestations of domestic violence are being reported more frequently than in the past. Although they are not required to report domestic violence that does not involve children to the state, health carers are often the first to learn of it in many cases, and can assist the victims in preventing it from happening again.

Child in Need of Care or Maltreated

[16.62] Jurisdictions differ widely in their definitions of maltreatment of children or children in need of care.[11] Similar patterns occur, however, in the multiple descriptions of those children. They include:

- neglect—lack of care;
- maltreatment and abuse;
- adverse environment; and
- child's behaviour.

Neglect—Lack of Care

Under the category of "neglect—lack of care" children are included:

- who have no parents or guardian, or are neglected or abandoned by them, or whose parents or guardians are unwilling or unable to care for them;
- who are homeless, have no fixed address, have no visible means of support, begging or loitering, sleeping in public places, missing school without reason; and
- where there is an irretrievable breakdown between the child and parents.

Maltreatment and Abuse

Children who have been maltreated and abused include those:

- who are, have been or are in danger of being, physically, mentally or emotionally harmed;
- who have been sexually abused or exploited, or are involved in prostitution; and
- engaged in dangerous work, entertainment (including activity dangerous to the health and welfare of the child or the community).

---

[11] *Children And Young People Act* 1999 (ACT); *Children (Care and Protection) Act* 1987 (NSW), s 10; *Community Welfare Act* 1983 (NT), s 4; *Children's Services Act* 1965 (Qld), s 46; *Children's Protection Act* 1993 (SA), s 6; *Child Welfare Act* 1960 (Tas), ss 2, 31, *Child Protection Act* 1974 (Tas), s 2; *Children and Young Persons Act* 1989 (Vic), s 63; *Child Welfare Act* 1947 (WA), s 4.

Adverse Environment

Children falling under the category of "adverse environment" include:

▌.....children exposed to moral danger, in "bad" company, whose physical, mental or emotional development is in danger because of the company they are in.

Child's Behaviour

Those falling under this category may include:

▌.....children who commit an offence while under the age of criminal responsibility, are involved in illegal activity, likely to fall into a life of crime, or are uncontrollable.

Reporting of Child Abuse

Voluntary Reporting

[16.63] Six jurisdictions provide for the voluntary reporting to the authorities that a child is maltreated or in need of care. In other jurisdictions one could, of course also report it, but in those jurisdictions there is not the same protection from legal action such as defamation.

[16.64] In the Australian Capital Territory a person who believes or suspects that a child or young person (between 12 and 18 years) is in need of care and protection may report the circumstances to the chief executive of the Department of Health, Housing and Community Care (*Children and Young People Act* 1999 (ACT), ss 158-163).

[16.65] In New South Wales sections 24, 103 of the *Children and Young Persons Act* 1998 (NSW) provide that any person believing on reasonable grounds that a child is at risk of harm may notify the Director-General of the Department of Community Services either orally or in writing.

[16.66] In Queensland a person can notify the Children's Commissioner about an alleged offence, or make a complaint about delivery of service, in relation to a child (*Children's Commissioner and Children's Services Appeals Tribunals Act* 1996 (Qld), s 19). A parent, guardian, relative or "person of good repute" can apply to the child welfare authorities to have a child taken into care and protection (*Children's Services Act* 1965 (Qld), s 47, Children's Services Regulations 1965 (Qld)).

[16.67] In South Australia a person may notify the Department where he or she suspects a child is being abused or neglected (*Children's Protection Act* 1993 (SA), s 12).

[16.68] In Tasmania a person may notify an authorised officer if he or she believes that a child has, or is likely to, suffer maltreatment (*Child Protection Act* 1974 (Tas), s 8).

[16.69] In Victoria where a child is believed to be in need of protection a person may notify a protective intervener (Director-General of Community Services or police officer) (*Children and Young Persons Act* 1989 (Vic), s 64).

[16.70] In these jurisdictions, where a person acts in good faith in reporting suspected child abuse this is considered not to breach privacy laws, and the person cannot be sued in defamation.

Mandatory Reporting

[16.71] All jurisdictions except Western Australia make it an offence for nominated professionals to fail to report suspected child abuse to the authorities. Again, reporting in good faith and to the right authorities is not a breach of confidentiality, and the professional cannot be sued for this, or for defamation.

[16.72] In the Australian Capital Territory, section 159 of the *Children and Young People Act* 1999 (ACT) contains a list of people including doctors, registered dentists, enrolled or registered nurses, teachers, police officers, public servants providing children's services, school counsellors and child-care centre workers who must report suspected abuse in certain circumstances. These people must report the name or description of a child or young person when, in the course of their work, they suspect that he or she has suffered, or is suffering, sexual abuse of non-accidental physical injury (note the different criteria in the Australian Capital Territory for voluntary and mandatory reporting).

[16.73] In New South Wales, section 27 of the *Children and Young Persons Act* 1998 (NSW) imposes a duty on those who, in the course of their professional work deliver health care, welfare, education, children's services residential services or law enforcement wholly or partly to children, or hold a management position in an organisation that carry out these activities. The duty is to inform the Director General of Community Services, as soon as practicable, if they have reasonable grounds to suspect a child is at risk of harm. Others, including health carers, are not required to report, but may do so. Under the *Ombudsman Act* 1974 (NSW) the head of a government agency must notify the Ombudsman of details of child abuse allegations of convictions against any employee, and must arrange for employees to notify him or her of such matters that come to their attention. Disclosure under these Acts does not breach obligations of confidentiality.

[16.74] In the Northern Territory, section 14 of the *Community Welfare Act* 1983 (NT) provides that *any person* who suspects maltreatment to report this to the police or Minister for Community Welfare. Where a report has been made to the police, it may be investigated by them and action taken for the protection of the child.

[16.75] In Queensland sections 76K, 76L of the *Health Act* 1937 (Qld) provide that a medical practitioner must report suspected maltreatment or neglect of a child causing unnecessary injury, suffering or danger within 24 hours. A child who is believed to be maltreated or neglected may be

[16.75] detained by a hospital for treatment for up to 96 hours before further action is required to keep the child in care. The person to be notified is an officer authorised by the chief health officer.

[16.76] In South Australia, sections 10-18, 26 of the *Children's Protection Act* 1993 (SA) provide for mandatory reporting of suspected maltreatment or neglect by doctors, pharmacists, dentists, registered or enrolled nurses, psychologists and social workers. Others who come into contact with children in the course of their work, such as teachers, police, day care workers and employees or volunteers in a government agency providing services for children are also obliged to report maltreatment or neglect. Notification is to be made to the Department for Community and Family Services.

[16.77] In Tasmania, sections 2, 8 of the *Child Protection Act* 1974 (Tas) require a wide category of professionals, including medical practitioners, registered nurses employed in child health services, psychologists, social workers, school principals and kindergarten teachers, probation officers, welfare officers, who suspect maltreatment of a child must report this to an officer of the Child Protection Board.

[16.78] In Victoria section 64 of the *Children and Young Persons Act* 1989 (Vic) targets doctors, registered or enrolled nurses, teachers, or police officers. These people must report their belief on reasonable grounds that a child is in need of protection because he or she has suffered or is likely to suffer significant harm as a result of either physical injury or sexual abuse and parents are unlikely to protect the child from this harm. The report must be made to the Secretary to the Department of Health and Community Services.

Accompanying Evidence of Abuse

[16.79] Those reporting should be as objective as possible in the reasons for their conclusion that a child has been abused. The criteria for reporting in some states, especially Queensland and Tasmania, which list such factors as being exposed to moral danger or in bad company, are subjective, making it difficult for health carers to determine whether the state should intervene. One of the difficulties with reporting child abuse is that the response by the authorities may result in the child being in a worse situation than if the matter were not reported. This should not lead to toleration of child abuse but to attempts to deal more appropriately with it.

Care of an Abused Child

[16.80] All jurisdictions provide for the appropriate authority to remove children from danger and provide for their protection and welfare. Generally, authorised officers or police officers can enter premises and take children to a place where they can be assessed and treated. All jurisdictions provide that either welfare officers police officers or a medical officer may if necessary direct that a child be detained in a hospital or elsewhere for examination and immediate treatment. The [16.83] child may only be detained for a specified period before an application must be made for an order for further care if required.[12] This may be done by a medical practitioner against the parents' will. Depending on the situation, the child may be made a ward of the court, or alternative action may be taken to ensure the child's welfare. Magistrates' Courts and Supreme Courts of the States and Territories also have jurisdiction to deal with children who are in need of care, as have community advocates and guardianship tribunals (see Chapter 5).

Domestic Violence: Spouse Abuse

Domestic Violence as Criminal Activity

[16.81] Abuse of an adult family member is, like child abuse, a crime. There is no excuse for violence against or maltreatment of, another, except self-defence, even though one may feel some sympathy for a person's condition (for example exasperation from caring for a "difficult" relative). Provocation will not exonerate a person from being answerable to the law for their actions (although it may mitigate the punishment they may face) (see [14.65]ff). As well as being the subject of general assault and violence provisions in each jurisdiction's Crimes Acts, there are special laws relating to domestic violence.[13]

[16.82] Health carers may be confronted by cases of domestic violence. This is a growing phenomenon. Unfortunately, the law has been party to the social acceptance of this form of domestic violence, only recently condemning any sort of physical or mental abuse of wives (Scutt (1990), Ch 9, *R v Jackson* [1891] 1 QB 671, *R v Reid* [1973] QB 299). There is no legal obligation, however, for health carers to report suspected domestic violence that does not involve children.

[16.83] Domestic violence includes spouse abuse (including de facto partners) and increasing recognition of violence by any person against another in their domestic environment (for example, relatives who assault and abuse, abuse of elderly parents). Despite common conceptions, spouse and child abuse occur across the social spectrum (Scutt (1985)). As

---

[12] *Children's Services Act* 1986 (ACT) (may be kept up to 72 hours); *Children (Care and Protection) Act* 1987 (NSW), s 23(1) (a medical practitioner nominated by the Director-General of the Department of Youth and Community Services may keep a child for up to 72 hours); *Community Welfare Act* 1983 (NT), s 15 (may be kept up to 48 hours); *Health Act* 1937 (Qld), s 76L (may be kept up to 96 hours); *Community Welfare Act* 1972 (SA) (may be kept up to 96 hours); *Child Welfare Act* 1960 (Tas) (may be kept up to 120 hours); *Community Welfare Services Act* 1970 (Vic) (no specific time limit); *Child Welfare Act* 1972 (WA) (may be kept up to 48 hours).

[13] *Domestic Violence Act* 1986 (ACT); *Crimes Act* 1900 (NSW), *De Facto Relationships Act* 1984 (NSW); *Domestic Violence Act* 1992 (NT); *Domestic Violence (Family Protection) Act* 1989 (Qld); *Summary Procedures Act* 1921 (SA); *Justices Act* 1959 (Tas); *Crimes (Family Violence) Act* 1987 (Vic); *Justices Act* 1902 (WA).

[16.83] the problem has been increasingly recognised, governments have attempted to give the victims of domestic violence more appropriate protection through the law. However, there is still reluctance to face the problem fully, especially where the violence is perpetrated against a woman, and as a result many women (who make up the vast majority of victims) find they are not believed when they complain of being abused, or the attitude is that they "deserved it", and so feel isolated and helpless. Very often this causes them to drop any charges they may have initially made, or where police lay the charges (rather than the woman herself), refuses to give evidence against the abuser. Health carers who come across such situations can help by being aware of the possibility of obtaining legal and other assistance, and by pointing this out, helping victims to take control of the situation, whilst themselves remaining objective. General practice surgeries and hospital emergency rooms should have information available about victims' assistance programs and services, as well as legal aid offices. Often domestic violence may involve sexual assault: clients may not be aware that unwanted sexual activity may constitute an assault, even where the parties are married or living in a de facto relationship.

Dealing with Domestic Violence

Immediate Assistance

[16.84] In New South Wales, the Northern Territory, Queensland, Tasmania and Victoria police now have varying enhanced powers of entry into homes, search, seizure of weapons and detention without a warrant where they believe domestic violence has taken place, is taking place or is threatened. There are also units of specially trained police officers to deal with domestic violence and child abuse. Victims and those fearing domestic violence should consider making use of domestic violence services existing in the larger cities (whether run by the police or not) to assist them in deciding the best course to take for their protection and that of their children. The Legal Aid Office or Magistrates Court Registry can also give advice. Emergency accommodation can be arranged in some circumstances.

Prosecution

[16.85] Assault is a crime which invokes the possibility of prosecution. In the past, the practice has been that the alleged victim is the prosecutor, not the State (similar to the requirement that the victim has been considered the prosecutor for rape). Thus, despite the amount of evidence the police might have, if the alleged victim decided not to go ahead with the case, it would be dropped. The victim of spouse abuse may understandably not wish to pursue criminal action, as this often makes matters worse.

[16.86] Now, however, in all jurisdictions if police believe, and have evidence to show, that there has been domestic violence, they can apply for a protection order (see below) for a person, or arrest them and take [16.90] them to the police station to be charged. Any person who has committed, or is in the process of committing, an offence, may be arrested by the police and charged, and a court can release such a person on bail. Strict conditions can be imposed to ensure violence is not undertaken or repeated. If the conditions are breached the person can be arrested and detained.

[16.87] Police often claim they cannot prosecute unless they have proof of the event. It is often one person's word against another's. Even where the victim is obviously wounded, this evidence is often considered insufficient. Police argue that:

- there is difficulty in obtaining proof;
- the victim often drops the claim;
- prosecution does not solve anything; and
- there may have been provocation (this approach can lead to stereotyping of the nature of domestic violence and raises a false defence for it).

[16.88] The power to arrest and prosecute independently of the alleged victim's wish to do so can relieve him or her from this task, and may prevent exacerbation of the actual or potential offender's wrath against the victim (as they can be seen to have no choice in the matter). Once a protection order is in existence, a breach of the order allows police to arrest and charge the person: they are not required to prove an assault or likely assault. This makes it much easier for the police to arrest a person who creates a potential threat to another. Police can generally only arrest in response to:

- offences already committed;
- complaints of threatened violence (in some jurisdictions); or
- an order or injunction issued by a court.

Protection from Future Domestic Violence

Commonwealth Legislation

[16.89] Under section 114 of the *Family Law Act* 1975 (Cth) the Family Court may issue an "injunction" restraining the movements and actions of a person who it is believed poses a threat to the welfare of their spouse or children. The injunction may prohibit the person at whom it is directed from contacting the applicant or person on whose behalf the injunction is issued, or from entering premises or areas where that person lives, works, or goes to school. The legislation does not cover de facto relationships.

State and Territory Legislation

[16.90] In all States and Territories, where a person fears violence from another, either towards themselves or a child, that person can apply to a

[16.90] magistrate's court for an injunction to restrain the person (variously called a "domestic violence", "non-molestation", "intervention" or "protection" order). Under crimes or justice legislation the magistrates' courts can hear an application where someone alleges a potential breach of the peace. An injunction restraining the potential offender may be issued. Some jurisdictions have enacted legislation to cover domestic violence specifically, with special procedures and orders available.[14]

[16.91] In New South Wales police are obliged to apply for a protection order where domestic violence has occurred or is threatened, unless the victim/intended victim does so, or there is good reason not to apply. The term "molestation" has been defined very broadly, so the threat involved can be a lot wider than physical violence. The Full Court of the Family Court considered the term in *English v English* (1986) FLC ¶91-729. The Court held that the term "molest" was broad, however it involves an element of objective, discernible conduct. The Court did not reach a firm conclusion as to what behaviour it did include. It is clear that it believed that the term "annoy" was too broad a meaning for "molest". This approach to the problem is different to that of criminal law, because:

- ..... the burden of proof for establishing abuse or potential abuse is the balance of probabilities, not beyond a reasonable doubt, thus making proof easier;
- ..... action can be taken before an offence is committed;
- ..... the offence or apprehended offence is molestation, which is wider than criminal law offences of assault and battery; and
- ..... the effect may be more restrictive than that offered by criminal law.

[16.92] Legislation differs across jurisdictions, but the following chart gives a general list of those who can apply for protection orders and those who may be protected by them.

---

[14] *Domestic Violence Act* 1986 (ACT); *Crimes Act* 1900 (NSW), ss 562A-562R (inserted 1987), *De Facto Relationships Act* 1984 (NSW), ss 53-55; *Justices Act* 1928 (NT); *Domestic Violence (Family Protection) Act* 1989 (Qld); *Justices Act* 1921 (SA), s 99 (inserted 1982); *Justices Act* 1902 (WA), ss 172-174; *Justices Act* 1959 (Tas), ss 106A-106F (inserted 1985); *Crimes (Family Violence) Act* 1987 (Vic).

▌▌▌ FIGURE 16.1 [16.95]

PROTECTION ORDERS UNDER DOMESTIC VIOLENCE LEGISLATION*

THOSE WHO MAY SEEK A PROTECTION ORDER	THOSE WHO MAY BE PROTECTED BY A PROTECTION ORDER
Person for whom protection is sought. Police officer. For a child: parent, guardian, person acting on behalf of child. For an adult: someone given authority to do so by the person, court or legislation.	Spouse/ex-spouse of alleged perpetrator. Person living/has lived in same household as alleged perpetrator. Relative/ex-relative of alleged perpetrator. Person having intimate personal relationship, present or past, with alleged perpetrator. Biological parent of alleged perpetrator. Child who regularly resides with target of violence. Child of whom the target is or has been a guardian. Child of whom the target is or has had custody.

"Spouse" includes de facto spouse.

[16.93] A lawyer is not required, and the police, the court, or a domestic crisis centre may assist in the application. In some jurisdictions the respondent may be remanded in custody pending the hearing where this is considered necessary.[15]

[16.94] In granting an injunction the court must be satisfied that:

▌..... the respondent has used violence against the applicant or her or his children and is likely to do so again;
▌..... the applicant or the children have been threatened and the respondent is likely to carry out the threat; or
▌..... harassment by the respondent leads the applicant to fear for her or his own or the children's wellbeing.

[16.95] When considering an application, courts will also take into account the need for protection of those threatened, the nature of the threat, hardship caused by the situation to the applicant, and hardship that would be caused to the respondent by an injunction. Normally a court will not impose restrictions on someone unless they have been heard in their own defence, but where the matter is serious and urgent enough, an order may be made ex parte, that is, in the absence of representation by the respondent.[16] In some jurisdictions a member of the police force may apply to a magistrate for an order by telephone. This is available only where it would not be practicable to apply more formal means (for example, *Crimes Act* 1900 (NSW), s 357G; *Justices Act* 1928

---

[15] *Justices Act* 1928 (NT), s 100; *Domestic Violence (Family Protection) Act* 1989 (Qld), s 69(1); *Justices Act* 1959 (Tas), s 106 (1).
[16] *Justices Act* 1928 (NT), s 100; *Domestic Violence (Family Protection) Act* 1989 (Qld), s 32; *Justices Act* 1921 (SA), s 99(4) (inserted 1982); *Crimes (Family Violence) Act* 1987 (Vic), s 16.

[16.95] (NT), s 100). Such orders may be interim, that is, pending a full hearing where both parties put their case.[17] A full hearing is the ideal legal model, but the circumstances may be such that the magistrate or judge decides such an order may be a final one.

Effect of a Domestic Violence Order

[16.96] Where an order has been made whether the respondent was present at the time, or not, if after receiving a copy of the order the respondent contravenes the order in any respect, he or she is guilty of an offence and liable for punishment.[18]

[16.97] If an order is made, it must be served on the respondent, and has effect from the time he or she receives it. Breach of the order will lead to arrest and detention. The applicant should keep their copy of the order and show it to the police.

Caring for Those with an Order

[16.98] If a client has a non-molestation order restricting access to them by another person, those attending the client may lawfully refuse to assist that person in access. Hospital authorities may deny such a person entry on to premises, on the ground that they have a duty of care to the client involved, which involves protecting the client from those who may cause them harm. However, health carers are advised that the law is not theirs to administer, and, if the person insists on access, they should contact the police (through administrative channels where appropriate) on the client's behalf. While not getting directly involved in others' domestic concerns, health carers should assist in the lawful protection of their clients.

Gun Laws

[16.99] A person who is subject to an injunction under the domestic violence law, who also holds a gun licence, may be deprived of that licence unless the court decides otherwise, and the court may order seizure and detention of any gun or pistol possessed by the person.

---

[17] *Domestic Violence Act* 1986 (ACT), s 14(1); *Crimes Act* 1900 (NSW), s 562(1); *Domestic Violence (Family Protection) Act* 1989 (Qld), s 31(1); *Justices Act* 1959 (Tas), s 100; *Crimes (Family Violence) Act* 1987 (Vic), s 8.

[18] *Domestic Violence Act* 1986 (ACT), s 27; *Crimes Act* 1900 (NSW), s 562; *Justices Act* 1928 (NT), s 100(1); *Domestic Violence (Family Protection) Act* 1989 (Qld), s 80; *Justices Act* 1921 (SA), s 99(6) (inserted 1982); *Justices Act* 1959 (Tas), s 106(1); *Crimes (Family Violence) Act* 1987 (Vic), s 22; *Justices Act* 1902 (WA), s 173(1).

REFERENCES AND FURTHER READING

Australian Health and Medical Law Reporter (CCH, Sydney, 1991) ¶39-210ff

Breckenridge, B and Laing, L, *Challenging Silence: Innovative Responses to Sexual and Domestic Violence* (Allen & Unwin, Sydney, 1999)

Byard, R, Donald, I and Chivell, W, "Non-lethal and Subtle Injury and Unexpected Infant Death" (1999) 7 *Journal of Law and Medicine* 47

Department of Human Services, South Australia, *Reporting Child Abuse and Neglect: Mandated Notification* (Department of Human Services Adelaide)

Flaskerud, J, *AIDS/HIV Infection: a Reference Guide for Nursing Professionals* (WB Saunders Co, Philadelphia, 1989)

Intergovernmental Committee on AIDS Legal Working Party, *Final Report* (Department of Health, Housing and Community Services, Canberra, 1992)

Kelsall, H, Robinson, P, and Howse, G, "Public Health Law and Quarantine in a Federal System" (1999) 7 *Journal of Law and Medicine* 87

Reeson, L, "The NSW Pap Test Register and its significance to GPs" (1997) 6 *Health Law Bulletin* 15

Reynolds, C, *Public Health Law in Australia* (Federation Press, Sydney, 1995)

Scutt, J, *Women and the Law* (Law Book Co, Sydney, 1990), Ch 9 (this book has an extensive bibliography)

Scutt, J, *Even in the Best of Homes* (Penguin, 1985)

Scutt, J, "Nursing, Law and AIDS" (1989) 18 (No 9) *Australian Nurses Journal*

The Community Law Reform Committee of the Australian Capital Territory, *Research Paper No 1, Domestic Violence* (Australian Institute of Criminology, Canberra, 1993)

Chapter Seventeen

HUMAN TISSUE TRANSPLANTS AND REPRODUCTIVE TECHNOLOGY

Human Tissue Transplant

[17.1] Legislation exists in all States and Territories regarding the transplantation of human tissue from both live and dead donors.[1] All jurisdictions prohibit "trading in tissue", that is, an arrangement whereby tissue is supplied in exchange for money. This does not include necessary expense in the removal of tissue, or sale of tissue that has been treated or processed for therapeutic, medical or scientific purposes.

What is "tissue"?

"Tissue" is broadly defined in transplantation legislation as an organ or part of a human body, as well as part of an organ or a substance extracted from an organ or from part of a human body. It does not include embryos, semen or ova, the transfer of which is covered in some jurisdictions by separate legislation (see [17.39]ff). Tissue may be:

- ..... regenerative, that which is replaced in the body by natural process after it is removed (for example blood or bone marrow); or
- ..... non-regenerative, that is all other tissue.

Transplantation legislation is mainly concerned with establishing the requirements for valid consent to removal of the tissue: who may consent and under what circumstances they may do so. It also prescribes some of the conditions which apply to the removal of the tissue. Legislation dealing with donations from live donors usually covers:

- ..... blood transfusions;
- ..... other regenerative tissue;

---

[1] *Transplantation and Anatomy Act* 1978 (ACT); *Human Tissue Act* 1983 (NSW); *Human Tissue Transplant Act* 1979 (NT); *Transplantation and Anatomy Act* 1979 (Qld); *Transplantation and Anatomy Act* 1983 (SA); *Human Tissue Act* 1985 (Tas); *Human Tissue Act* 1982 (Vic); *Human Tissue and Transplant Act* 1982 (WA).

■.....non-regenerative tissue; and
■.....conditions under which consent must be given.

[17.2] In dealing with donations from dead donors, the legislation usually covers:

■.....a definition of death;
■.....postmortems; and
■.....determining those who may give permission for removal of tissue.

Non-Therapeutic Nature of Tissue Removal

[17.3] The first point to note regarding tissue transplantation is that under the common law it has never been lawful to remove a body part where that removal was not therapeutic for the donor. It constituted the criminal offence of maiming, and as one cannot consent to the commission of a crime against oneself, there was no legal way one could donate parts of one's body (Devlin, *Samples of Lawmaking* (Oxford University Press, London, 1962), pp 83-103; Lord Justice Edmund Davies "A Legal Look at Transplants" (1969), 62 *Proceedings of the Royal Society of Medicine* 633; Australian Law Reform Commission 1977, pp 22ff).

[17.4] Since tissue donation became acceptable in Australia there has been strict control over the conditions under which it is done, and prohibition of any profit making from donation of tissue, by the donor or anyone else. Australia has adopted the approach of "opting in", that is, requiring a person to positively indicate when competent that he or she is willing to donate tissue after death. Thus a person is presumed not to consent unless positive consent has been given. The alternative approach, adopted by some other countries is a system of "opting out", that is, a person is presumed to consent to donation unless there is a clear indication that he or she does not wish to do so. Western Australian legislation provides that the Minister can issue codes of practice in relation to tissue donation.

Blood Donations and Transfusions

Giving of Blood

Adults

[17.5] Any adult of sound mind may donate blood for therapeutic medical or scientific purposes. There is no requirement that the consent be written, nor special procedures or requirements regarding what information is given for consent, so the law follows the general law of consent.

[17.6] Some jurisdictions require that blood is donated in a particular place, such as a Red Cross Centre (Australian Capital Territory, New South

Wales, Northern Territory and Tasmania) or hospital (Australian Capital Territory, New South Wales, Northern Territory and Tasmania), and all have special requirements to be observed to protect public health.

[17.7] Special requirements are set out in legislation for the protection of the community. New South Wales requires that those carrying out the transplant of blood, blood products or semen must have an authorisation to do so. All jurisdictions require donors to provide a statutory declaration regarding sexual practices and intravenous drug use. Blood suppliers are indemnified against liability for the contraction of blood-borne diseases such as hepatitis and HIV where proper practices are followed.

Children

[17.8] Parents or guardians may give consent to the donation of blood by children, but most jurisdictions require not only that it be for therapeutic or scientific purposes, but that there be medical assurance that the child will not be harmed by the donation, and that the child has also consented.[2] Because of the scarcity of blood in some circumstances, some jurisdictions are considering removing the requirement for parental consent to older children, so that more "recruits" can be signed up in schools.

Blood and Tissue Testing

[17.9] Statutory provisions in all jurisdictions permit the taking of blood for testing in certain circumstances, such as:

- ..... where a person has been involved in a motor accident and is suspected of having a blood alcohol or drug level in excess of that permitted;
- ..... where a breathalyser test is positive;[3]
- ..... where it is part of general powers of diagnosis or treatment, for example of children the subject of suspected abuse (see [5.44]ff), those subject to mental health legislation (see [5.139]ff), for public health purposes (see [16.43]ff);
- ..... when ordered by a court for determination of paternity,[4] or for any other reason; and
- ..... in relation to driving under the influence of drugs, or the use of illicit drugs.

---

[2] *Transplantation and Anatomy Act* 1978 (ACT), ss 20, 21; *Human Tissue Act* 1983 (NSW), ss 19, 20; *Transplantation and Anatomy Act* 1979 (Qld), ss 17, 18; *Transplantation and Anatomy Act* 1983 (SA), ss 18, 19; *Human Tissue Act* 1985 (Tas), ss 18, 19; *Human Tissue Act* 1982 (Vic), ss 21, 22; *Human Tissue and Transplant Act* 1982 (WA), ss 18, 19. There is no provision for the donation of blood from a child in the Northern Territory, so the general law in relation to consent applies.

[3] These two categories of situations are covered in: *Motor Traffic (Alcohol and Drugs) Act* 1977 (ACT); *Traffic Act* 1909 (NSW); *Traffic Act* 1987 (NT); *Traffic Act* 1949 (Qld); *Road Traffic Act* 1961 (SA); *Road Safety (Alcohol and Drugs) Act* 1970 (Tas); *Road Safety Act* 1986 (Vic); *Road Traffic Act* 1974 (WA).

[4] The Family Court can order such a test under section 69W of the *Family Law Act* 1975 (Cth). Other States providing for compulsory blood testing for paternity are: *Status of Children Act*

[17.10] **[17.10]** In most jurisdictions the same legislation which permits the obtaining of blood samples, allows the taking of both blood and urine samples without the consent of the person except in the Australian Capital Territory and Tasmania, where unreasonable refusal is an offence. Detailed provisions surround the obtaining, labelling and processing of samples. Medical practitioners and nurses may take samples, and health carers are immune from legal action where they obtain blood or urine for testing if they have reason to believe a police officer has directed that the specimens be obtained. In fact it may be an offence for a medical practitioner to fail to obtain a sample after a motor traffic accident unless there is a reasonable belief that to obtain the specimen would jeopardise the health of the person. It is also an offence to hinder the taking of a specimen.

[17.11] Time limits for the taking of mandatory specimens apply, varying across jurisdictions from two hours to four hours.

[17.12] Specimens such as blood, semen, hair and saliva left behind at the scene of a crime can be tested, and under some circumstances similar tissue can be taken from a suspect. The Australian Capital Territory, New South Wales, Tasmania and Victoria permit police to require a blood test from people charged with specified criminal acts, and in the Northern Territory, Queensland, South Australia and Western Australia they can require suspects to submit to medical examinations. Moves are being made in some jurisdictions and federally to routinely obtain tissue (normally saliva) for DNA testing of those charged or convicted of a criminal offence. Health carers involved in collecting or testing such specimens should familiarise themselves with their legal rights and obligations as well as those of the person being tested.

Blood Transfusions

Adults

[17.13] Adults may, of course, agree to the administration of a blood transfusion to themselves. The law in this respect is the same as that applying to all medical treatment to adults (see above, Ch 4).

Refusal of Blood Transfusions

[17.14] An adult may refuse a blood transfusion, even if that refusal puts her or his life (or the life of a foetus but see *Qumsieh* [5.108]) in jeopardy. The person refusing, and their estate, have a legal action in battery if the person is given a transfusion against her or his will. On the other hand, however, the person or relatives might take action against staff for not

---

[4] *continued*
1996 (NSW), ss 26-31; *Status of Children Act* 1979 (NT), ss 13-15; *Status of Children Act* 1978 (Qld), s 11; *Community Welfare Act* 1972 (SA), s 112; *Status of Children Act* 1974 (Tas), s 10.

treating someone when they needed the treatment, arguing that refusal [17.17]
was either not voluntary or not properly informed. The ethical, and
possibly legal, duty to treat someone should also be considered.

[17.15] As pointed out in Chapter 4, emergency or necessity could be used as a defence by medical staff. Such an approach, it is suggested, should not be used simply to impose medical values on clients: the issue is whether one respects individual autonomy or is prepared to substitute paternalism. The question is not legal-the legal issues are clear: staff who have to decide whether to give treatment against the client's will choose between the possibilities of being sued in battery if they act, or negligence if they do not-it is ethical, and not an easy problem to solve. Community discussion as well as discussion among health care staff is essential for establishing an accepted approach to deciding one's values. Giving a transfusion to an adult of "sound mind" against that person's will is a breach of their legal right to refuse it, and so should be carefully considered (see *Shulman's* case [4.32]).

Children

[17.16] Normally parents, as guardians, can give or refuse consent for medical treatment of their children. However, where parents refuse to allow for emergency or life-saving treatment medical staff can act against their wishes (see above, Ch 5). Specific legislation in each State and Territory provides for the giving of a blood transfusion to a child where its life is in danger and parents either cannot be reasonably contacted or refuse the transfusion.[5] This is either through provisions permitting blood transfusions themselves, or permitting emergency treatment generally. Most States provide that a practitioner can only proceed with giving the transfusion when consent is not reasonably obtainable; that corroboration of the need is supplied by another doctor; and the transfusion is necessary for the saving of the life of the child and is both necessary and proper.

Blood Transfusions and HIV

[17.17] Due to the danger of transmitting HIV through blood donations, some States require that blood donors sign declarations as to their suitability as donors. Legislation exempting medical bodies, health workers and donors from liability if someone becomes HIV-positive as a result of a blood transfusion where statutory requirements have been carried out has proliferated. This immunity applies if the donor signed the

---

[5] *Transplantation and Anatomy Act* 1978 (ACT), s 23; *Children (Care and Protection) Act* 1987 (NSW), s 20A, *Medical Practitioners (Emergency Medical Treatment) Amendment Act* 1983 (NSW); *Emergency Medical Operations Act* 1973 (NT), ss 2, 3; *Transplantation and Anatomy Act* 1979 (Qld), s 20; *Consent to Medical Treatment and Palliative Care Act* 1985 (SA), s 13(5); *Human Tissue Act* 1985 (Tas), s 21; *Human Tissue Act* 1982 (Vic), s 24; *Human Tissue and Transplant Act* 1982 (WA), s 21.

[17.17] requisite declaration of suitability, and the blood was tested and certified as HIV-negative. It is lost if those collecting and/or handling the blood have reason to believe that the blood may be contaminated, and have not taken adequate steps to prevent its administration. All jurisdictions have legislation to this effect except Queensland (where the government has undertaken to indemnify the transfusion service for inadvertent transmission of HIV).[6]

[17.18] Testing blood for the purpose of diagnosis involves more than just simply testing blood. Where it is likely that the results may indicate serious disease, especially one like HIV, those who are giving the blood should be counselled as to this possibility, and even more care should be taken in informing them if the results are positive. Of course those donating blood who have testified to being suitable donors are indicating that they are extremely unlikely to be HIV-positive, however one would expect that such considerations would have as much priority as, for example, in an AIDS clinic. However, the fact that a positive result is not expected may make a blood donor even more susceptible to shock at the result. Reasonable care should be taken, as negligent communication to a person resulting in nervous shock or other harm could lead to legal action. Staff in blood donation centres should be aware of this issue.

Donation of Tissue by a Living Person

[17.19] At the time of writing only South Australia, Victoria and Western Australia have legislation covering storage and use of ova, spermatozoa, or foetal tissue. Other jurisdictions follow ethical guidelines. The law relating to the donation of these tissues is discussed below at [17.39]ff.

Regenerative Tissue

Adults

[17.20] Any adult of "sound mind" may give consent to the removal of tissue from their body. There are, however, provisions in the legislation for all States except South Australia and Western Australia for a further certificate, signed by a medical practitioner other than the surgeon who is to carry out the transplant, stating:

- ..... the terms of consent;

---

[6] *Blood Donation (Transmissible Diseases) Act* 1985 (ACT); *Human Tissue Act* 1983 (NSW) and Regulations (NSW); *Notifiable Diseases Act* 1981 (NT); *Blood Contaminants Act* 1985 (SA); *Blood Transfusion (Limitation of Liability) Act* 1986 (Tas); *Health Act* 1958 (Vic), Health (Infectious Diseases) Regulations 1990 (Vic); *Blood Donation (Limitation of Liability) Act* 1985 (WA).

- .....that the consent was freely given in the presence of the doctor who is signing; [17.23]
- .....that proper medical advice and information was given; and
- .....that the person consenting is an adult of "sound mind".

[17.21] Where this certificate is provided, the legislation states that it is sufficient authority for a medical practitioner (other than the doctor signing the certificate) to carry out the transplant, as long as he or she is not aware of any revocation of the consent.[7] South Australia and Western Australia require that family members and friends must be absent when the consent is signed.

Children

[17.22] All jurisdictions except the Northern Territory provide for donation of regenerative tissue from children. This invokes more restrictions than apply to adults. Parents (and in some jurisdictions guardians) may give consent for a child to donate regenerative tissue but this usually must be in writing with further restrictions:

- .....The recipient may be restricted to other members of the family.[8]
- .....There are special requirements regarding consent. This must be accompanied by a certificate stating that information was given, consent was obtained from the child as well as the parents and the child both understood and agreed to the removal of the tissue. This latter requirement does not apply in Queensland and Victoria, where a child who is incapable, by reason of age, of understanding the procedure may nevertheless be a donor of tissue where the recipient family member is in danger of death. A cooling-off period is allowed in some jurisdictions (see [17.24]).[9]

Testing of Transplant Tissue for HIV/AIDS

[17.23] All jurisdictions require that donors of tissue for transplantation sign a form stating that to their knowledge they are not HIV positive, and all tissue for donation is tested for the presence of HIV antibodies.

---

[7] *Transplantation and Anatomy Act* 1978 (ACT), ss 8, 10; *Human Tissue Act* 1983 (NSW), ss 7, 9, 12; *Human Tissue Transplant Act* 1979 (NT), ss 10, 12; *Transplantation and Anatomy Act* 1979 (Qld), ss 10, 12, 13; *Transplantation and Anatomy Act* 1983 (SA), s 9; *Human Tissue Act* 1985 (Tas), ss 7, 9, 14; *Human Tissue Act* 1982 (Vic), ss 7, 9; *Human Tissue and Transplant Act* 1982 (WA), ss 8, 16, 17.

[8] *Transplantation and Anatomy Act* 1978 (ACT), s 6; *Human Tissue Act* 1983 (NSW), s 6; *Transplantation and Anatomy Act* 1979 (Qld), ss 12A-12E; *Transplantation and Anatomy Act* 1983 (SA), s 7; *Human Tissue Act* 1985 (Tas), s 6; *Human Tissue Act* 1982 (Vic), s 5; *Human Tissue and Transplant Act* 1982 (WA), s 6.

[9] *Transplantation and Anatomy Act* 1978 (ACT), ss 12, 13; *Human Tissue Act* 1983 (NSW), ss 10, 11; *Transplantation and Anatomy Act* 1983 (SA), s 13 (this section requires reference to a committee for approval); *Human Tissue Act* 1985 (Tas), ss 11, 12, 13; *Human Tissue Act* 1982 (Vic), s 15; *Human Tissue and Transplant Act* 1982 (WA), ss 11, 13.

[17.23] ■■■ **FIGURE 17.1**

SUMMARY OF PROVISIONS FOR CONSENT AND USE OF REGENERATIVE TISSUE FROM CHILDREN

JURISDICTION AND ACT	PARENT MAY CONSENT	GUARDIAN MAY CONSENT	TISSUE FOR SIBLING	TISSUE FOR RELATIVE
Transplantation and Anatomy Act 1978 (ACT)	Yes	No	Yes	Yes
Human Tissue Act 1983 (NSW)	Yes	No	Yes	No
Human Tissue Transplant Act 1979 (NT)	No	No	No	No
Transplantation and Anatomy Act 1979 (Qld)	Yes	No	Yes	No
Transplantation and Anatomy Act 1983 (SA)	Yes	Yes	Yes	Yes
Human Tissue Act 1985 (Tas)	Yes	Yes	Yes	Yes
Human Tissue and Transplant Act 1982 (WA)	Yes	No	Yes	Yes

Non-Regenerative Tissue

Adults

[17.24] Non-regenerative tissue can be taken from an adult under the same conditions as for regenerative tissue, with the added requirement that the removal occur no less than 24 hours after consent is given, to provide a cooling-off period. The tissue may be removed only for transplantation into another living person.

Children

[17.25] Donation of non-regenerative tissue by children is specifically banned in South Australia, Victoria and Western Australia.[10] In other jurisdictions it is impliedly prohibited. In the Australian Capital Territory similar certification to that prescribed for removal of regenerative tissue from children is required, along with the additional statement that it is for a family member recipient who will die without the transplant, and that

---

[10] *Transplantation and Anatomy Act* 1983 (SA), s 12; *Human Tissue Act* 1982 (Vic), s 14; *Human Tissue and Transplant Act* 1982 (WA), s 1.

along with the consent of the child, both parents of the child consent [17.28]
where that is possible. The matter is then referred to a Ministerial
Committee for decision comprising a judge, medical practitioner and
social worker or psychologist (*Transplantation and Anatomy Act* 1978
(ACT), ss 8, 10).

Person other than Operating Surgeon must take Consent

[17.26] To prevent vested interests in securing consent, the person who
gives information about transplantation of tissue must not be the person
or persons who removes the tissue. Consent permits a third party to carry
out the operation, and gives that party immunity from an action in
battery.[11]

Revocation of Consent

[17.27] All donors may revoke their consent at any time, according to
legislation, and this revocation is absolute in its effect. In some
jurisdictions[12] the law specifically requires that health care workers to
whom the donor indicated her or his revocation must inform the
designated officer or equivalent, who is authorised under the legislation,
for example, a senior administrative medical practitioner in a hospital,
who must then inform the operating surgeon. It has already been stated at
[4.32], that revocation of consent to any treatment may take place at any
time, and is absolute, so it would seem a legally sound argument that a
carer who is aware of a patient revoking consent to any treatment should
promptly inform those who propose to carry it out. Except in South
Australia and Western Australia, where a designated officer becomes aware
of a revocation of consent, he or she must determine if any person is
intending to rely on the consent, and inform them of the revocation. He
or she must also return the certificate of consent to the person who made
it. Those who are caring for donors should know who the designated
officer is.

[17.28] The requirements for consent do not apply to the removal of
tissue where this is part of therapeutic treatment and with consent, or in
an emergency to preserve the person's life.

---

[11] *Transplantation and Anatomy Act* 1978 (ACT), ss 15-18; *Human Tissue Act* 1983 (NSW), s 12; *Human Tissue Transplant Act* 1979 (NT), ss 11, 12; *Transplantation and Anatomy Act* 1979 (Qld), s 13; *Transplantation and Anatomy Act* 1983 (SA), ss 15-17; *Human Tissue Act* 1985 (Tas), s 14; *Human Tissue Act* 1982 (Vic), ss 10, 11, 16; *Human Tissue and Transplant Act* 1982 (WA), ss 15-17.

[12] *Human Tissue Act* 1983 (NSW), s 16(2)(a)(iii); *Human Tissue Transplant Act* 1979 (NT), s 16(2)(a)(iii); *Human Tissue Act* 1982 (Vic), s 18(2)(a)(iii).

Donation of Tissue after Death

[17.29] Perhaps one of the most challenging situations for medical staff is to deal with the family of those who have died suddenly and violently and who are on artificial respiration to preserve tissues for donation. To their family, these people may seem to be alive. The important thing for all to remember is that a person must be legally dead before any action can be taken to remove tissue from that person. The family may be consulted, and consent gained prior to death, and they should be assured that this will not affect the treatment of the patient.

Definition of "Death"

[17.30] All jurisdictions except Western Australia have a statutory definition of "death", which states that it involves irreversible cessation of all brain function, or irreversible cessation of blood circulation. Western Australia provides that human tissue which is to be removed from a dead person shall not be removed unless two doctors have certified to irreversible cessation of brain function. In all jurisdictions except Queensland and Western Australia the definition of "death" applies for all purposes. Queensland's definition is restricted to removal of tissue for purposes of the *Transplantation and Anatomy Act* 1979 (Qld).

[17.31] Most jurisdictions require that where a prospective donor is on life support there are certain requirements regarding both the number and seniority of the medical personnel who declare the person dead, and the specific certification that is required of them as to the cessation of circulation or brain function.

Consent for Donation of Tissue

[17.32] Where the deceased died at a hospital, or where the person is on life support, the medical officer authorised under the legislation may inquire whether the person has specifically expressed their consent to the use of any organ after death, and there has been no change of mind. Some jurisdictions require that consent be in writing, others that, if oral, it be before witnesses. Such consent is considered to be conclusive at law. Where the person has expressed unwillingness to donate, that too is conclusive. The difficult situation is where no opinion either way has been expressed. The next of kin may be asked for their consent or otherwise to the removal of tissue.

[17.33] For the purposes of the legislation, with minor variations, next of kin are defined in a list in hierarchical order, so that where permission is required from next of kin, those in the category closest to the patient should be sought. The categories are generally in the following order:

For a deceased child: [17.37]

- .....parent;
- .....brother or sister 18 years of age or older;
- .....person who was a guardian of a deceased child immediately before death.

For a deceased adult:

- .....current spouse;
- .....son or daughter 18 or over;
- .....parent;
- .....brother or sister 18 or over.

[17.34] The law requires that permission be sought at all times from the senior available next of kin where practicable, seniority being established according to the above list. Withdrawal of consent by the relevant relative must of course be honoured, and the law may also provide that objection by two or more senior next of kin to permission given by the appropriate relative shall be effective. This places the duty on staff to report withdrawal of consent by the next of kin, and in this situation such report would obviously have to be rapid and unequivocal.

[17.35] Where there is no indication of the person's wishes and there is no available eligible next of kin, the designated office may give permission for the transplant, except for Tasmania and Western Australia which are silent on this point.

Postmortems and Anatomical Examinations

[17.36] At the time of writing there is controversy surrounding the use of bodies and body parts obtained in postmortems for research and teaching purposes. Before considering removal of tissue from a deceased person, one must first rule out any situation where the coroner will have jurisdiction over the body (as established in Ch 15). Even where this is the case, the coroner may, if satisfied it will not prejudice the coronial inquiry, permit removal of tissue from the body, and may stipulate conditions under which the removal is to take place.

[17.37] Consent for the postmortem examination of a body, or its use for scientific or teaching purposes, is subject to similar requirements to those outlined above for the donation of tissue after death. This means that a postmortem may be carried out, other than at the direction of a coroner:

- .....where the deceased expressed a wish or consent;
- .....where no wish or consent was expressed and senior next of kin consents; or

[17.37]   ▌.....where no wish or consent has been expressed and senior next of kin have not disagreed.[13]

[17.38] It is the responsibility of the designated officer of the health facility involved to establish the situation in each case.

Assisted Conception and Reproductive Technology

[17.39] Despite the fact that assisted conception and reproductive technology raise many very difficult social and legal questions which touch the nature of the body as property, motherhood, parenthood and less fundamental questions of succession and inheritance (for example, Bates and Turner (1985), especially pp 451ff, 465ff, 468ff) there is very little law affecting assisted conception and reproductive technology, except in South Australia, Victoria and Western Australia as outlined below at [17.48]. There are, however, many Commonwealth and State reports which make ethical and legal recommendations.[14] Where there is no law, various ethical guidelines form the basis of medical practice. The main ethical statement is that of the Australian Health and Medical Research Council (see [17.59]).

[17.40] Terminology by different jurisdictions makes the law somewhat confusing in the area of infertility treatment. In the following paragraphs an attempt is made to establish a common language to clarify the ever-increasing complexity of this rapidly growing area of science.

---

[13] *Transplantation and Anatomy Act* 1978 (ACT), s 30; *Human Tissue Act* 1983 (NSW), s 28; *Transplantation and Anatomy Act* 1979 (Qld), s 26; *Transplantation and Anatomy Act* 1983 (SA), s 25; *Human Tissue Act* 1982 (Vic), s 28; *Human Tissue and Transplant Act* 1982 (WA), s 25.

[14] For example, Family Law Council of Australia, *Creating Children: A Uniform Approach to the Law and Practice of Reproductive Technology of Australia* (AGPS, Canberra, 1985); Senate Select Committee on the Human Embryo Experimentation Bill 1985, *Human Embryo Experimentation in Australia* (AGPS, Canberra, 1986); Senate Standing Committee on Constitutional and Legal Affairs, *In Vitro Fertilisation and the Status of Children* (AGPS, Canberra, 1985); NSW: Department of Health, *In-Vitro Fertilisation* (Sydney, 1985), Law Reform Commission, *Human Artificial Insemination*, Report No 49 (NSW Government Printer, Sydney, 1986), Law Reform Commission, *Report on Artificial Conception-In Vitro Fertilisation*, Report No 49 (NSW Government Printer, Sydney, 1988); Qld: Special Committee Appointed by the Queensland Government, *Report to Inquire into the Laws Relating to Artificial Insemination, In Vitro Fertilisation and Other Related Matters* (Brisbane, 1984); SA: Select Committee of the Legislative Council, *Report on Artificial Insemination by Donor, In-Vitro Fertilisation and Embryo Transfer Procedures and Related Matters in South Australia* (Adelaide, 1987); Vic: Committee to Consider the Social Ethical and Legal Issues Arising from In Vitro Fertilisation: 1 *Interim Report* (Melbourne, 1982); 2 *Report on Donor Gametes in In Vitro Fertilisation* (Melbourne, 1983); 3 *Report on the Disposition of Embryos Produced by In Vitro Fertilisation* (Vic Government Printer, 1984); WA: Western Australian Department of Health, *Report of the Committee Appointed by the Western Australian Government to Enquire into the Social, Legal and Ethical Issues Relating to In Vitro Fertilisation and its Supervision* (Perth, 1984).

[17.41] The term "assisted conception" is here used to include the various means of transplanting material from one person to another for the purposes of bearing a child. It is included in this chapter because it is a form of transplantation. However only three jurisdictions, South Australia, Victoria and Western Australia have enacted legislation on reproductive technology, and that is in stand-alone Acts (see [17.48]ff and [17.57]ff).

[17.42] For the purposes of this discussion the approach to classification of procedures is that used by the New South Wales Law Reform Commission, *Report on Artificial Conception-In Vitro Fertilisation*, Report No 58 (NSW Government Printer, 1988). This report describes conception as the fertilisation of an ovum by a sperm. This would differentiate some procedures to which modern technology is applied and strictly speaking bring about fertilisation itself (including artificial insemination and in vitro fertilisation) from those through which an already fertilised egg is transferred into another woman for the duration of the pregnancy. Procedures such as ZIFT (zygote intra fallopian transfer), PROST (pro-nuclear stage ovum transfer), TEST (fallopian embryo transfer), are included in the report's definition of in vitro fertilisation. Other procedures which have been developed, including the direct fertilisation of an egg by injection of sperm, would also be covered by the legislation.

[17.43] Reproductive technology also involves such procedures as GIFT (gamete intra-fallopian transplant), hyperovulation treatments and research on both adults, gametes and embryos.

Who are the Parents?

[17.44] All jurisdictions, as well as the Commonwealth, have established quite clearly that where a woman gives birth to a child as the result of assisted conception the child is the child of that woman and her spouse (including de facto husband), if he has given his consent to the procedure. Conversely the law states that a person donating sperm (and eggs in most States), has no legal connection whatsoever with any resulting child.[15] This means that where the spouse does not consent to the procedure, or there is no spouse, the genetic father does not become the legal father of the child: there is, it seems, a gap created in the parental relationships of the child.

[17.45] The result of the legislation is that a donor of gametes has no legal claim whatsoever on a child born as the result of an assisted conception procedure, and the child also has no right to the parentage of that person. This applies even where donors are known.

---

[15] *Family Law Act* 1975 (Cth), s 60B; *Artificial Conception Act* 1985 (ACT); *Artificial Conception Act* 1984 (NSW); *Status of Children Act* 1979 (NT); *Status of Children Act* 1978 (Qld); *Family Relationships Act* 1975 (SA); *Status of Children Act* 1974 (Tas); *Status of Children Act* 1974 (Vic); *Artificial Conception Act* 1985 (WA).

Artificial Insemination

[17.46] Artificial insemination, or implantation of seminal fluid into the vagina or uterus through means other than natural physical copulation has been used for many years as a means of promoting conception where the sexual act is not desired. This is not illegal when carried out by a medical practitioner, although some States require licensing of those carrying out the procedure. One growing concern of the state is for more accurate recording of genetic origins of children, as a result of the recognition of:

- ..... the psychological need for such information on the part of those born as a result of assisted conception procedures; and
- ..... the need for proper medical histories where these may have significant effects on children.

Common Law

[17.47] Artificial insemination can be legally carried out by any person, and has become an accepted way of dealing with infertility. At common law there is a presumption that a woman giving birth to a child is its mother, because no other possibility was considered. There is also a presumption that if that woman was married at the time of conception, her husband is the father. This presumption is rebuttable, however, where paternity is known to be otherwise. This common law presumption has been supplanted by legislation (see [17.44]).

Legislation

[17.48] The only jurisdictions to have legislated regarding artificial insemination are Victoria, South Australia and Western Australia.[16]

[17.49] In South Australia under the *Reproductive Technology Act* 1988 (SA), a licence is not required in respect of artificial insemination if it is carried out by a medical practitioner who has specially registered with the Health Commission, or it is carried out as a personal act and not for profit or as part of one's medical practice. The procedure must also be in accordance with ethical practice formulated by the South Australian Council on Reproductive Technology.

[17.50] In Victoria, section 7 of the *Infertility Treatment Act* 1995 (Vic) specifically identifies the process of donor insemination, that is, artificial insemination of a woman using sperm from a man who is not her husband or de facto husband. Such a procedure must be carried out only:

---

[16] *Family Relationships Act* 1975 (SA); *Infertility (Medical Procedures) Act* 1984 (Vic); *Human Reproductive Technology Act* 1991 (WA).

- .....at a hospital or licensed centre by, or under the supervision of, a doctor approved by the Infertility Treatment Authority, and the requirements of the *Infertility Treatment Act* have been followed; or
- .....elsewhere, by a doctor approved by the Infertility Treatment Authority, and the requirements of the *Infertility Treatment Act* have been followed.

The Act does not impose conditions on artificial insemination by husband.

[17.51] In Western Australia the *Human Reproductive Technology Act* 1991 (WA) provides that a licence from the Commissioner of Health on the advice of the Reproductive Technology Council is required to carry out artificial insemination, unless the person is a medical practitioner to whom an exemption has been granted, and who has agreed in writing to comply with the Code of Practice which has been established by the Council.

[17.52] Elsewhere, it seems that the practice is self-regulated. This is of some concern with regard to:

- .....records of genetic origin;
- .....maintenance of medical history;
- .....control of the spread of disease, especially AIDS, and lack of screening for congenital defects;
- .....liability for negligent practice; and
- .....issues of consent.

[17.53] Consequently there have been recommendations from some States that artificial insemination should be regulated, at least when it is not a private act, and not a regular part of one's practice. The New South Wales Law Reform Commission, for example, draws a distinction between artificial insemination as a practice and as an act (New South Wales Law Reform Commission, *Human Artificial Insemination*, Report No 49 (NSW Government Printer, Sydney, 1986)). It recommends that the former, defined as carrying out the procedure for fee or reward, or advertising or holding oneself out as being prepared to carry out the procedure, should be performed by or under the supervision of a medical practitioner. The latter, according to the Commission (p 26), is a private act, and one which should not be regulated:

> neither the law nor parliament should presume to regulate the private sexual behaviour of mature, competent persons . . . the principles of personal freedom and autonomy should apply so far as possible, and that if a woman chooses or a man and woman choose, to achieve pregnancy by AI that is no concern of the State.

[17.54] In those jurisdictions where there is no legislation regarding artificial insemination, it is generally carried out as a practice in fertility clinics where sperm is screened and ethical codes of practice followed. However no qualifications or specific conditions are legally required. Health professionals carrying out the procedure elsewhere should consider the potential legal implications of doing so. As with any other medical procedure, a duty of care is owed to the woman who is the subject of

[17.54] artificial insemination. As well as the responsibility not to harm her through general medical procedures, there is a duty to her to ensure all reasonable measures are taken to prevent infection by sexually transmitted disease and AIDS; and to prevent harm to the future child.

Other Reproductive Technology Procedures

[17.55] Clinics carrying out reproductive technology procedures in jurisdictions other than South Australia, Victoria and Western Australia are subject to the general law. There are also requirements for accreditation by the federal government (see [17.59]).

[17.56] Despite the inference in legislation and ethical guidelines that only some reproductive technology consists of experimentation or research, some commentators argue that the proceedings involved are all experimental in the sense that they have a relatively low chance of resulting in a viable pregnancy, and the effects of such treatments as super-ovulation therapy are recognised as being neither entirely predictable nor safe (Scutt (1990), p 189). For this reason health carers should take particular care to ensure that clients are adequately informed of the nature and risks, and the low success rate of the technology. Indeed Victoria provides an extensive list of matters to be discussed with clients of infertility clinics by counsellors, such as the risks involved, the role and responsibility of the doctor, side effects and alternative treatments.

"The possibility of exploitation is even greater where experimental treatment is involved. A physician's concern for advancing medical knowledge can blind the doctor to the patient's best interests" (Simpson (1981), quoted in Scutt, *Women and the Law* (Law Book Co, Sydney, 1990), p 191).

Regulating Bodies

[17.57] In Victoria, the *Infertility Treatment Act* 1995 (Vic) creates the Infertility Treatment Authority, a body that administers the Act by such means as issuing licences, approving facilities, administering the keeping of records and access to them, monitoring compliance with licences, administering the storage of gametes and embryos and promoting research. Licensing decisions may be reviewed by the Administrative Appeals Tribunal.

[17.58] In South Australia, the *Reproductive Technology Act* 1988 (SA) establishes the South Australian Council on Reproductive Technology, and in Western Australia, the *Human Reproductive Technology Act* 1991 (WA) establishes the Western Australian Reproductive Technology Council. These have such functions as advising the Minister on matters relating to reproductive technology, including conditions for licences, developing a code of practice, promoting research on the causes of infertility, and the social implications of reproductive technology. They also promote debate on reproductive technology and collaborate with similar bodies. The Western Australian Council also has a monitoring role.

[17.59] In other States and Territories fertility clinics are governed by the *Ethical Guidelines on Assisted Reproductive Technology*, issued by the National Health and Medical Research Council of Australia (NHMRC). The guidelines require that facilities offering reproductive technology be accredited under a recognised accreditation body. This is the Reproductive Technology Accreditation Council. Research must be approved by a Human Research Ethics Committee (HREC) established by the facility (or the Committee of another facility) in conformance with NHMRC requirements (*Statement on Human Experimentation and Supplementary Notes*). Innovations and major changes in treatment procedures require approval of a HREC.

[17.60] Other requirements under the NHMRC Guidelines are:

- registers should be confidential;
- special restrictions should apply to ovum donation;
- there should be no element of commerce;
- married couples only should be recipients of IVF treatment;
- research with sperm, ova or fertilised ova are inseparable from the development of safe and effective IVF: however embryos should not be developed in vitro beyond the stage at which implantation would occur;
- sperm and ova belong to the donors, and their wishes as to use, storage and disposition should be respected. Where there is a difference of opinion between joint donors the institution should decide the course of action;
- storage of human embryos may carry biological and social risks, and so should be subject to restrictions. It should be for no more than 10 years, and not beyond the time of conventional reproductive need or competence of the female donor; and
- cloning of humans, and the use of gametes from deceased persons is unacceptable.

Regulation of Procedures

[17.61] In Victoria, a fertilisation procedure storage of reproductive material or research, must not be carried out except in accordance with the *Infertility Treatment Act*.

[17.62] Certain procedures are prohibited. These include:

- alteration of the constitution of a gamete, zygote or embryo;
- implantation of gametes, zygotes or embryos that have been used for research;
- cloning of human beings;
- fertilisation of the gametes of a man or a woman with the gametes of an animal;
- experimental procedures not approved by the Standing Review and Advisory Committee;
- procedure involving the gametes of people known to be dead;
- use of zygotes or embryos removed from the body; and
- research on an embryo where:
    — the embryo would be damaged;
    — the ova donor is not married;

[17.62]
- the woman and her husband are not undergoing a fertilisation or relevant procedure or have not given specific written consent for the research;
- the couple have not received counselling, including counselling as required by the legislation; or
- the practitioner is not of the opinion that the research is likely to establish knowledge indicating procedures (including fertilisation procedures) that might be carried out to enable a woman who has undergone examination or IVF treatment to become pregnant.

[17.63] Doctors, scientists and counsellors, as well as hospitals and research institutions must be approved by the Infertility Treatment Authority. There is a detailed list of matters to be discussed by counsellors in the Regulations.

[17.64] The Act defines the various in vitro fertilisation procedures setting out provisions for procedures involving no donor, a sperm donor, an egg donor or both, and limits their practice to specific situations, where the above requirements are also satisfied. Detailed requirements as to by whom and how consent must be given are set out (for example, both the donor and the donor's spouse must provide consent to the donation of gametes and to the particular purpose of the donation).

[17.65] There are further conditions placed on the use of more than one egg, and the control and disposition of gametes and embryos.

[17.66] In South Australia section 13 of the *Reproductive Technology Act 1988* (SA) is similar in many ways to that of Victoria, but relies more on a licensing procedure of facilities, research projects and personnel, the licence being dependent upon the adherence to a code of ethics, established by regulation. The South Australian Health Commission can authorise officers to inspect and monitor compliance with the Act. Procedures must be carried out in accordance with licence conditions, and the codes of practice established under the Act. These codes form Regulations numbers 188 and 189 to the Act. Practices prohibited by Part 2 of the *Reproductive Technology Code of Ethical Clinical Practice 1988* (SA) and the *Reproductive Technology Code of Ethical Clinical Practice 1988* (SA) include:

- embryo flushing;
- culturing or maintaining an embryo outside a body;
- transfer of more than three embryos per cycle;
- mixing gametes or embryos from different sources;
- use of gametes in certain cases, for example, where they are of close family members, or for use of couples already benefiting from same donor's material;
- implantation of embryos that have been used for research unless there is reasonable expectation of normal development;
- payment for gamete donation; and
- mixing of reproductive material from different sources, mixing animal and human reproductive material, or placing human embryo in animal or vice-versa.

[17.67] In Western Australia, the *Human Reproductive Technology Act 1991* (WA) provides two types of licence can been issued by the Commissioner for Health: a practice licence and a storage licence. There are penalties for carrying out procedures in breach of a licence. Section 7 of the Act prohibits:

- .....unapproved research or diagnostic procedure;
- .....human cloning;
- .....embryo flushing or the production of a chimera;
- .....the replacement of the nucleus of a cell of an embryo;
- .....placement of a human embryo in the body of an animal, or animal embryo in the body of a woman; and
- .....payment for supplying reproductive material.

Eligibility for Treatment

[17.68] The issue of access to fertility treatment is being challenged at the time of writing. Legislation in South Australia, Victoria and Western Australia requires that to be eligible for treatment, a woman must be married or living in a de facto relationship (the latter of five years duration in South Australia and Western Australia) and they must be certified after the fulfilment of specified requirement as being unable, as a couple, to become pregnant. Additionally, they may be eligible where there is a likelihood of transmission of a genetic abnormality or disease (*Reproductive Technology Code of Ethical Clinical Practice* 1988 (SA); *Infertility Treatment Act* 1995 (Vic), s 8; *Human Reproductive Technology Act* 1991 (WA), s 23). The legislation has been challenged in South Australia as discriminating on the grounds of marital status under the *Sex Discrimination Act* 1984 (Cth). Section 109 of the Australian Constitution provides that a provision of a Commonwealth Act overrides a conflicting State provision. The court held that the requirement that the woman be married is indeed contrary to the *Sex Discrimination Act*, and is thus invalid (*Pearce v South Australian Health Commission* (1996) 66 SASR 486; see also Stuhmcke (1996)).

[17.69] In Victoria, the *Infertility Treatment Act* 1995 (Vic) provides, in section 8, that eligibility for infertility treatment is to be limited to women who are married or living in a de facto relationship. In a recent challenge to this provision the Federal Court ruled that it is inconsistent with the *Sex Discrimination Act* 1984 (Cth), as it is discriminatory on the basis of marital status. The provisions of section 8(1) of the Act thus appear to be inoperative to the extent that it restricts the application of any treatment procedure to a woman who satisfies the marriage requirement. This has thrown some uncertainty on the law, as there are provisions in the Act that apply to the woman's husband. It would seem, however, that an unmarried woman who fulfils the requirement of infertility set out in the Act is not barred from treatment, the section now requiring that it be determined that she would be unlikely to become pregnant from an oocyte produced by her, or that if she became pregnant from an oocyte produced by her, a genetic abnormality or disease might be transmitted to a person born as the result of the pregnancy. However, this decision is being appealed to the High Court of Australia, raising uncertainty as to

[17.69] the final verdict on whether a woman has to be legally or de facto married and involve her husband in the procedure.

[17.70] Access to infertility treatment to a woman who was living in a stable lesbian relationship was denied by a Queensland infertility clinic (*QFG & Anor v VJM* (1997) EOC ¶92-902). In that case it was held that the clinic (which specialised in infertility) had not unlawfully discriminated against her, because the reason for refusing the treatment was that she did not fulfil the requirements of infertility applied to all applicants: that is, the inability, after 12 months of heterosexual intercourse, to fail to become pregnant.

[17.71] This raises the issue of what should be considered infertility in Australia. Legislation providing for assisted reproductive technology in South Australia, Victoria, and Western Australia, and accrediting bodies in some other jurisdictions (except, for example New South Wales) envisage it as meaning that between them, a couple cannot, through heterosexual activity, produce a child. If one is considering a woman alone, whether she engages in heterosexual activity or not, the "cause" of not being able to produce a child may be social rather than physical: she does not wish to engage in heterosexual activity for the purpose. This has been called "social infertility" making the question of infertility more than a simple question of physical condition.

Storage and use of Gametes, Zygotes and Embryos

[17.72] In South Australia, there is no set time limit for storage. A person licensed to store reproductive material must destroy an embryo stored for the use of a married couple if either dies or they divorce. A person on whose behalf an embryo is stored has the right to review the storage every 12 months. Reproductive material is to be destroyed if consent for storage or use is revoked (*Reproductive Technology Code of Ethical Clinical Practice* 1995 (SA), cll 17-19; *Reproductive Technology Code of Ethical Research Practice* 1995 (SA), cl 20).

[17.73] In Victoria, reproductive material must not be stored without the consent of the donor. Gametes may be stored for 10 years and zygotes and embryos for five years, or longer if the Authority approves. The material must not be removed unless for implantation or approved research, or a donor has died, consent to store the material has been withdrawn, or under authority of the Act (*Infertility Treatment Act* 1995 (Vic), ss 51-55; Infertility Treatment Regulations 1997 (Vic), reg 12).

[17.74] In Western Australia, the time limit for storage is set by the Western Australian Reproductive Technology Council, and is generally three years. The consent of those donating the material is essential, and gametes donors have the right to deal with them as though they were personal property (and lawfully according to the Act). If the donor or donors of reproductive material have died, or their consent or intentions are not known, the right to deal with the material vests in the Commissioner of Health, who may direct its use for a specific recipient. The right to decide on disposition of an embryo vest jointly in the couple producing it, and if one of them dies, in the remaining donor. In the case of a dispute between them, if one of them applies to the Commissioner of Health, he or she may direct the licensee to maintain storage (*Human Reproductive Technology Act* 1991 (WA), ss 24-26). [17.77]

Records

[17.75] Another important issue dealt with by the Act is the keeping of records and giving (or confidentiality) of records. In Victoria, the principles underlying this part of the legislation are:

▌.....full records are to be kept of:
— all parties involved in IVF procedures;
— donors of gametes and origins of embryos;
— destruction of gametes, zygotes and embryos;
— all acts of in vitro fertilisation;
— any treatment of a woman and her partner if relevant, and the outcome of treatment; and
— collection, storage and use of material in research and transfer of material to or from a centre.

[17.76] The Act has detailed requirements in relation to the giving of information to donors (including who will receive the material and whether a pregnancy has resulted from the donation) and recipients of reproductive material (in relation to the donor). Identifying information may only be given with the consent of a person who stands to be identified. Information may be given to a person born as a result of a fertilisation procedure about his or her parents under certain circumstances, with identifying information requiring the consent of anyone who stands to be identified. Extensive provision is made for counselling and confidentiality in relation to the strictly regulated giving of identifying information. See *Infertility Treatment Act* 1995 (Vic), ss 62-70; Infertility Treatment Regulations 1997 (Vic), regs 13-18, Schs 1, 2.

[17.77] In South Australia, Part 5 of both the *Reproductive Technology Code of Ethical Clinical Practice* 1988 (SA) and *Reproductive Technology Code of Ethical Clinical Practice* 1988 (SA), cll 22-30 deals with record keeping and access to information. Similar detailed records to those required in Victoria are to be kept, including:

▌.....records relating to the assessment of a donor's personality;
▌.....collection storage use and disposal of reproductive material;
▌.....clinical standards and procedures used by the licensee;
▌.....criteria for determining the suitability of use of research embryos in treatment; and
▌.....payment of expenses to donor for research purposes.

Donors and those receiving treatment may have access to records, and a person over 16 years of age, born as the result of a treatment, may have access to non-identifying information.

[17.78] **[17.78]** Research cannot be carried out without a licence from the South Australian Council on Reproductive Technology. Interestingly, the period for experimentation on embryos in South Australia (14 days) is longer than that in Victoria (until syngamy only).

[17.79] In Western Australia, details of records to be kept are set out in sections 44-50 of the *Human Reproductive Technology Act* 1991 (WA). Details similar to those in other jurisdictions are to be kept, including the reasons why each participant was considered eligible for treatment. Records are to be available to the Commissioner for Health. Access to personal information is available to the person him or herself, and identifying information is protected, and only to be made available with the consent of the person to be identified. Further directions may be made under the Act by the Commissioner in relation to records.

Surrogacy Agreements

[17.80] Whilst surrogacy agreements do not require medical technology to be carried out, they are included here because they are a form of assisted reproduction, and often do involve medical technology, either in the form of artificial insemination or in vitro fertilisation. In fact, the critical legal aspects of surrogacy agreements are:

- .....the agreement itself, which in some circumstances may be an offence; and
- .....the changing of the legal parentage of the child.

Policy

[17.81] A general policy on surrogacy has been adopted across all Australian jurisdictions, by Health and Welfare Ministers (see discussion paper, Australian Capital Territory Attorney-General's Department (1993)). The policy holds that:

- .....surrogacy should be discouraged;
- .....that any surrogacy agreement should be unenforceable, thus totally ineffective, in law (although it need not be an offence);
- .....commercial surrogacy (that is, surrogacy involving payment except for necessary expenses) should be an offence; and
- .....that advertising, procuring and paying for surrogacy should be illegal.

Legislation

[17.82] In Victoria the *Infertility Treatment Act* 1995 (Vic) renders all surrogacy agreements void, makes commercial surrogacy (that is, surrogacy involving payment except for necessary expenses) illegal, and prohibits any publication that:

- .....seeks or induces a woman to act as what it terms a surrogate mother; [17.87]
- .....advertises for someone to act as a surrogate mother;
- .....facilitates a surrogacy agreement for money; and
- .....acts or agrees to act as a surrogate mother for money (s 30).

[17.83] In South Australia the *Family Relationships Act Amendment Act* 1988 (SA) declares that all surrogacy agreements are illegal and void. Facilitating or entering surrogacy agreements for money is an offence, as is any publication that:

- .....advertises a person's willingness to enter into a surrogacy agreement;
- .....seeks such a person; and
- .....advertises a person's willingness to facilitate a surrogacy agreement.

[17.84] Queensland passed the *Surrogate Parenthood Act* in 1988 (Qld). It is similar to those described above. However, it also simply prohibits entering into any surrogacy agreement, commercial or otherwise. It is thus the only State that makes a surrogacy agreement illegal per se.

[17.85] In Tasmania the *Surrogacy Contracts Act* 1993 (Tas) makes surrogacy contracts void and unenforceable, and commercial surrogacy is an offence. Those:

- .....attempting to arrange surrogacy contracts (whether commercial or non-commercial) on behalf of others;
- .....offering or giving technical or professional services to achieve a pregnancy for the purposes of surrogacy; or
- .....advertising in relation to surrogacy,

are guilty of an offence.

[17.86] Western Australia has produced four reports which deal with surrogacy. They all endorse the approach of the Health and Welfare Ministers' resolutions. The current government is reviewing the resolutions and determining its position on surrogacy.

[17.87] In the Australian Capital Territory, the more accurately named *Substitute Parent Agreements Act* 1994 (ACT) makes substitute parent agreements (otherwise known as surrogacy agreements) void and unenforceable. The Act creates offences in relation to substitute parent agreements. Making a commercial agreement is an offence, as is advertising in relation to any sort of agreement and procuring a person to make an agreement with a third person, whether the agreement is commercial or not. The *Substitute Parent Agreements (Consequential Amendments) Act* 1994 (ACT) gives the Minister power to suspend or cancel the license of a hospital which is involved in facilitating commercial substitute parent agreements. The Act also provides that the child's interests are paramount in any legal action that involves a substitute parent agreement. The *Artificial Conception Act* 1986 (ACT) was amended in 1999 to provide for the Supreme Court to make an order for re-registration of the birth of a child born as the result of a surrogacy agreement in certain circumstances. Those circumstances are:

[17.87]
- .....the child is conceived before 31 June 2002, has been born in the Australian Capital Territory and the applicant parents are resident in the Australian Capital Territory;
- .....the applicant (proposed) parents are (or at least one of them is) the genetic parents of the child and the birth parents are not genetically related to the child; or
- .....both the birth parents and the applicant parents are in agreement, the application being made no earlier than six weeks, and no later than six months after the birth.

[17.88] Based on the premise of the paramountcy of the welfare of the child, the legislation seeks to record the factual situation and allow a child the benefit of having its genetic parents legally recognised where this is agreed to by the birth parents. This also provides an accurate record for medical and epidemiological purposes when required. The order is similar to an adoption order, making the child the child of the applicant parents rather than the birth parents, whilst maintaining an accurate record of the child's birth. Access to information is similar to that provided to those involved in adoption. The court must make the order only if it is in the best interests of the child. In so doing it is to consider whether the birth and applicant parents underwent assessment and counselling by someone independent of the person or body who is to carry out any medical procedure (the act by implication requires surrogacy to involve assisted reproductive technology).

Other Jurisdictions

[17.89] There are no prohibitions on surrogacy in other jurisdictions. However where there is a dispute between birth and substitute parents (for example where the birth parents refuse to hand over the child) agreements are likely to be considered unenforceable as being against public policy. The birth parents would remain the legal parents for the purposes of the law, with the birth certificate in their name. A dispute as to who should have the child would be a matter for the Family Court, which would make a parenting order under the *Family Law Act* 1975 (Cth), based on the welfare of the child being the paramount consideration.

REFERENCES AND FURTHER READING

ACT Attorney-General's Department, *Surrogacy: Discussion Paper* (Canberra, ACT Government, 1993)

Australian Health and Medical Law Reporter (CCH, Sydney, 1991)

On reproductive technology see references in footnote 14.

Australian and New Zealand Intensive Care Society Working Party on Brain Death and Organ Donation, *Recommendations Concerning Brain Death and Organ Donation* (Melbourne, Australian and New Zealand Intensive Care Society, 1998)

Australian Department of Community Services and Health National HIV/AIDS Strategy (AGPS, Canberra, 1989)

Bates, F and Turner, J, *The Family Law Casebook* (Law Book Co, Sydney, 1985), Ch 13

Dawson, K, *Reproductive Technology: the Science, the Ethics, the Law and the Social Issues* (Melbourne, VCTA Publishing, 1994)

Douglas, G, *Fertility and Reproduction* (Sweet and Maxwell, London, 1991)

Finlay, et al, *Family Law: Cases and Commentary* (Butterworths, Sydney, 1986), pp 259ff

Freedman, W, *Legal Issues in Biotechnology and Human Reproduction* (Quorum Books, New York, 1991)

Health Department of Western Australia, *Directions given by the Commissioner of Health to Set the Standards of Practice under the Human Reproductive Technology Act 1991 on the Advice of the WA Reproductive Technology Council* (Health Dept of WA, Perth, 1993)

Lang, A, "What is the Body? Exploring the Law, Philosophy and Ethics of Commerce in Human Tissue" (1999) 7 *Journal of Law and Medicine* 53

Liu, A, *Artificial Reproduction and Reproductive Rights* (Gower Press, UK, 1991)

McLean, S (ed), *Legal Issues in Human Reproduction* (Gower Press, UK, 1989)

Magnusson, R, "The Use of Human Tissue Samples in Medical Research: Legal Issues for Human Research Ethics Committees" (1999) 7 *Journal of Law and Medicine* 390

National Health and Medical Research Council (Australia), *An Australian Code of Practice for Transplantation of Cadaveric Organs and Tissues* (AGPS, Canberra, 1990)

National Bioethics Consultative Committee (Australia), *Reproductive Technology: Record Keeping and Access to Information, Birth Certificates and Birth Records of Offspring Born as a Result of Gamete Donation* (Adelaide National Bioethics Consultative Committee, 1989)

New South Wales Health, *Review of the Human Tissue Act: Discussion Paper Assisted Reproductive Technologies NSW* (Health Department, October, 1997)

New South Wales Law Reform Commission, *Human Artificial Insemination*, Report No 49 (NSW Government Printer, Sydney, 1986)

Rodin, J, et al (eds), *Women and New Reproductive Technologies: Medical Psychosocial and Ethical Dilemmas* (L Erlbaum, New Jersey, 1991)

Rowland, R, *Living Laboratories Women and Reproductive Technologies* (Sun Books, Australia, 1992)

Scutt, J, *Women and the Law* (Law Book Co, Sydney, 1990)

Stuhmcke, A, "Access to Reproductive Technology: *Pearce v SA Health Commission*" (1996) 5 AHLB 39

Sutherland, E and McCall Smith, A, *Family Law and Medical Advance* (Edinburgh University Press, Edinburgh, 1990)

Chapter Eighteen

EXPANDING RECOGNITION OF HUMAN RIGHTS

Human Rights—Health Consumers' Rights

[18.1] The law as outlined in the chapters so far has described what can be said to be clients' rights: the right to refuse treatment, to reasonable and prompt treatment, to confidentiality and privacy, to access to records, to legal advice (if clients can afford it), and so on. Health carers' rights, such as those relating to natural justice employment are also described. Every duty or requirement at law applying to health carers gives rise to a subsequent right on the part of those to whom the duty is owed. Some hospitals have developed a "Bill of Rights", which points out to clients their legal rights, sometimes adding further rights which are not legally enforceable, and which could more accurately be described as moral rights or aspirations than as legal rights. The problem, perhaps, is an individual's understanding of what a "right" is.

What is a "Right"?

[18.2] For the purposes of this discussion, it is presumed that a right which is recognised by society is access to some entitlement to a benefit which is acknowledged as belonging to a particular person, and which that person can demand of others. Those of whom the demand is made in turn have an obligation to provide that access. Rights are either legally enforceable, when the person can call on the state to enforce them, or simply a recognised acceptable form of behaviour. The former attribute is obviously more valuable than the latter. The main rights of health consumers can be summarised as follows:

Common Law Rights

- .....to reasonable care (Ch 6);
- .....to informed consent (Chs 4 and 5);
- .....to refuse treatment (Ch 4);
- .....to confidentiality (Ch 7); and
- .....to correct information in relation to services (Ch 4).

Statute-Based Rights

- .....to refuse treatment (in the Australian Capital Territory, the Northern Territory, Queensland, South Australia and Victoria) (Ch 4);
- .....to special consideration if they are suffering from a disability or are aged (see below and Ch 5);
- .....to privacy in specified situations (Ch 7); and
- .....to equal consideration and freedom from discrimination in the availability and quality of services.

Administratively Established Rights

These are "rights" set out in guidelines, protocols and administrative directives developed by a government department or health facility. These "rights" may vary between service providers, but examples are:

- .....confidentiality in all cases (except where disclosure authorised under legislation);
- .....access to records;
- .....the assistance of interpreters;
- .....know costs involved in treatment; and
- .....know of available services.

[18.3] Administratively established rights generally do not have the force of law. However, breach of them could provide the basis for a civil action (for example, in negligence, breach of contract or breach of confidentiality), or for disciplinary action for unprofessional conduct. This would depend on the circumstances of the case, and whether there was a clearly established obligation on the part of the health care provider. Some State governments have drawn up charters of health rights. Perhaps the most comprehensive list of clients' rights has been drawn up by the Queensland Health Complaints Commissioner, and is outlined in Appendix 5. The Australian Hospitals Association has issued a circular called "Your Hospital Stay" which gives advice and enumerates those rights given either by law or the hospitals themselves. These documents vary in their content, and may contain rights which, as explained, are neither legally guaranteed nor morally imperative, but are a statement of the ideal. The main value of such documents is the recognition that special rights do exist, even if there is some difference of opinion about to what extent they can be enforced, or even what they are.

[18.4] Some rights which have been outlined in this book apply to a person because he or she is the recipient of health care as a client of health professionals. They are based on the emerging recognition in our society of the equality of all people and their claim to health care, and the upholding of the principle that the dignity, autonomy and integrity of all should be acknowledged and preserved. Other rights apply to those who are employees, based on the recognised need for equal access to work and a basic standard of conditions. Finally, some rights apply to all human beings regardless of personal circumstances. The specifics are based on the international development and articulation of human rights. It is this last group which is dealt with in this chapter.

Human Rights in International Law

[18.5] Alongside domestic (or national and state) law, there has grown a body of international law based on the recognition of human rights. Human rights apply to any person and are based purely on their membership of the human race. They are said to be universal (applying to everyone) and immutable (they cannot be limited or qualified). The recognition of human rights at an international level takes the form of international Declarations, Conventions, and Treaties. The documents are drawn up, and nations subscribe to the principles contained in them.

[18.6] The document initiating this recognition of human rights is the Universal Declaration of Human Rights, the founding document drawn up by the United Nations of what was to develop into a steady and growing commitment of nations, through further conventions and agreements to the recognition of the rights of all people to dignity, physical security, self-fulfilment, and equal access to justice. Australia was involved in the formulation of the declaration and is a signatory to many of the subsequent more detailed conventions and agreements. The effect of this on Australian citizens is the subject of this chapter.

[18.7] International law is complex, and in many ways different from domestic law. In the following discussion it will be outlined in very simple form only, with a view to giving an understanding of the obligations of health carers which have resulted from our federal government's involvement in the area of international human rights law.

[18.8] The first and most important point to make about law between nations is that it does not consist of a set of rules which can be enforced by a court. Nations are all sovereign entities, able to do whatever they like within their own territory. Thus a head of state or government of a particular country cannot be forced to change their ways, however disagreeable others may consider them. One can negotiate, attempt to persuade, apply economic or political sanctions, as was the case of South Africa, and is currently the case with Iraq, and only under certain closely defined situations take up arms against another nation. The United Nations General Assembly can condemn a country's activities, causing widespread international moral and political disapprobation. There is also the International Court of Justice to which nations can take their grievances, for a ruling on the legality of a nation's activities. Such opinions, however, cannot be the subject of forceful action, but rather of condemnation and political action. The United Nations may call on member nations to contribute to a peace-keeping armed force in its name, which generally only occurs to ensure that nations which have already reached the settlement of a dispute carry out their agreed undertakings peacefully (for example, the withdrawing of an army).

International Conventions

[18.9] A Declaration or Convention establishing human rights is thus not enforceable. Nations may sign a Convention, signifying their agreement in principle with it. They may then ratify the Convention (thus becoming a party to it) which means they accept its provisions, and undertake to enact laws consistent with them within their own borders ("domestic law"). They may make reservations to specific clauses of the Convention if they are not prepared or equipped to put these into effect. A Convention may also set up an international committee to which parties to it undertake to make regular reports on measures taken to give effect to the Convention within their territory. They may be asked by the Committee to explain apparent failure to act, or unsatisfactory progress in the recognition of the rights involved. Such failure can result in an adverse report to the United Nations General Assembly, and possible action by the member states as outlined above.

[18.10] The International Covenant on Civil and Political Rights has an optional Protocol, ratified by Australia, which provides that an individual can take a complaint to the United Nations Human Rights Committee. The complaint must relate to government action denying a human right to that person, and complainants must have exhausted the avenues of complaint in their own country. Several Tasmanians lodged a complaint with the Committee in relation to the provision in the *Criminal Code* (Tas) that prohibits homosexual acts between consenting adults. The Committee handed down its finding that the provision is a breach of human rights. When the Tasmanian government refused to repeal the provision the federal government passed legislation based on the foreign affairs power in the Australian Constitution (see below), and its status as signatory to the International Covenant, which provided a defence against a prosecution under the Tasmanian law.

Foreign Affairs Power

[18.11] The Australian Constitution limits the Commonwealth Parliament's powers to legislate for the States, but s 51(xxix), (the "foreign affairs power"), provides some power to legislate where the federal government has signed an international agreement (see [1.30]). As a result of this power the federal government has legislated for human rights. In fact some States have also done this (see [18.81]ff).

[18.12] The following are the main international instruments that establish rights which are relevant to health care workers:

- *International Covenant on Civil and Political Rights* (Article 7): prohibits cruel and inhumane treatment and medical or scientific experimentation without consent.
- *International Covenant on Social, Economic and Cultural Rights* (Article 12): establishes the right to the highest attainable standard of physical and mental health, to be attained by, among other measures, methods to reduce stillbirth, epidemics, endemic and occupational diseases.

■..... *Declaration of the Rights of the Child* (Article 4) and United Nations *Convention on*   [18.14]
     the Rights of the Child (Article 24): bestows on children the right to special protection of, and access to, medical care.
■..... *Declaration on the Rights of Mentally Retarded Persons* (Article 2): bestows the right of proper medical care and physical therapy.
■..... *Declaration on the Rights of Disabled Persons* (Article 6): includes the right to medical, psychological and functional care, rehabilitation, counselling and vocational training.
■..... *Principles for the Protection of Persons with Mental Illness and for the Improvement of Mental Health Care*, is devoted to setting out the rights of those with a mental illness.

Human Rights in Domestic Law

[18.13] Australia is a signatory to all the instruments nominated above, and is therefore obliged to promote legislation in Australia that promote these rights. All except the last one mentioned are attached to the *Human Rights and Equal Opportunity Commission Act* 1986 (Cth) as Schedules to that Act, and a complaint can be made to the Human Rights and Equal Opportunity Commission that an alleged breach of a Convention has occurred. The Commission has no judicial power in such cases but this is certainly a way of establishing that one has been denied one's rights, and of putting pressure on an offender to desist from such activity and to compensate for harm that has been caused. States and Territories also have anti-discrimination law to give effect to the major human rights Conventions. These matters are dealt with below.

Human Rights and Equal Opportunity Commission

[18.14] In 1981, the federal government inaugurated the Human Rights Commission. It consisted of seven part-time Commissioners, and one full-time Commissioner. That Commission became the Human Rights and Equal Opportunity Commission (the Commission) in 1986. The *Human Rights and Equal Opportunity Commission Act* 1986 (Cth) empowers the Commission to inquire into, and deal with complaints about, alleged breaches of human rights listed in the Schedules attached. The Schedules contain the *International Convention Concerning Discrimination in Respect of Employment and Occupation*; the *International Covenant on Civil and Political Rights* (establishing rights of citizenship, political freedom, rights to hold public office, to vote, etc); the *Declaration of the Rights of the Child*, *Declaration on the Rights of Mentally Retarded Persons*, and *Declaration on the Rights of Disabled Persons*. The rights contained in these documents can be summarised as follows:

■..... The rights of all people to:
    — privacy;
    — marriage and family;

[18.14]
- their own language, culture and religion;
- participation in public affairs;
- freedom of expression, movement, association and assembly;
- protection of their inherent right to life;
- liberty and security of person;
- freedom from degrading treatment or punishment; and
- equal treatment with others under the law.

▌.....The rights of children to:
- a name and nationality;
- opportunities to develop fully in conditions of freedom and dignity;
- adequate care, affection and security, including prenatal and postnatal care;
- education;
- special treatment and care of handicapped; and
- protection against cruelty and neglect.

▌.....The rights of mentally retarded or intellectually disadvantaged persons to:
- proper medical care and therapy;
- economic security;
- education, training and work and trade union membership; and
- a qualified guardian and a review of procedures which may deny them their rights.

▌.....The rights of disabled persons to:
- respect;
- family and social life;
- economic security;
- protection from discriminatory treatment (Human Rights Commission, *Annual Report, 1981-82*, Vol 1, p 1, also set out in Tay (1986), p 26).

[18.15] Section 3 of the *Human Rights and Equal Opportunity Act* 1986 (Cth) defined "human rights" as the rights and freedoms recognised in these documents, as well as "any relevant international instrument". This would include such documents as the *Convention on the Rights of the Child*.

[18.16] The Human Rights and Equal Opportunity Commission's powers include:

▌.....Scrutiny of Commonwealth legislation referred to it for breaches or potential breaches of the above rights. An example of this function was its review of the *Mental Health Ordinance* 1983 (ACT), and its *Adoption Ordinance* 1965 (ACT), before the Australian Capital Territory was self-governing; the *Electricity (Continuity of Supply) Act* 1985 (Qld), and the *Migration Act* 1958 (Cth).

▌.....the carrying out of inquiries into Commonwealth government acts and practices. An example of this function is its report on Toolemah, a mainly Aboriginal town near the New South Wales–Queensland border after riots in nearby Goondiwindi (Human Rights and Equal Opportunity Commission, *Toolemah Report* (Sydney, 1988));

▌.....the development of educational programmes for the public;

▌.....the hearing of complaints of breaches of rights as set out in the Schedules by individuals or groups who allege such breaches, within the Commission's area of responsibility (for example it does not have jurisdiction over State governments or instrumentalities, or some individuals); and

■.....hearing of complaints under the Commonwealth Racial, Sex and Disability Discrimination Acts (see below). [18.21]

[18.17] However the rights listed in the Schedule are not enforceable and are not made unlawful under the Act. The Commission's powers relating to all such rights except employment matters (see [18.41]ff) extend only to Commonwealth government authorities, or matters referred to it by the Commonwealth Attorney-General (this would include health facilities run by the Commonwealth government).

[18.18] The Act also establishes the Aboriginal and Torres Strait Islander Social Justice Commissioner, whose functions, in relation to Aboriginal and Torres Strait Islanders, include reporting to the Minister on human rights, promoting discussion and awareness of human rights, undertaking research and educational programmes and examining Commonwealth legislation.

Other Approaches to Health Consumers' Rights

[18.19] The Consumers Health Forum of Australia ((1990) Pt 3, esp pp 34-38) points out ways of determining and enforcing the rights of health consumers which it considers more effective than legislation are:

■.....licensing of facilities, manufacturers and health care personnel;
■.....establishing codes of practice, adherence to which is necessary to gain a licence; and
■.....establishment of outcome standards for facilities.

[18.20] The Forum recommends that where a practitioner breaches the code of practice, tribunals with quasi-judicial power similar to the State equal opportunity tribunals (see below) could deal with complaints. It also points out (p 38) that not only are there many problems surrounding legal redress itself but that access to the law is often hindered by barriers such as lack of information about legal mechanisms, lack of financial resources, emotional, physical and intellectual cost, and the law's delay.

Trade Practices Legislation

[18.21] The Commonwealth and the States and Territories all have trade practices legislation.[1] This legislation provides that it is an offence for a

---

[1] *Trade Practices Act* 1974 (Cth); *Fair Trading Act* 1992 (ACT); *Fair Trading Act* 1987 (NSW); *Consumer Affairs and Fair Trading Act* 1990 (NT); *Fair Trading Act* 1989 (Qld); *Fair Trading Act* 1987 (SA); *Fair Trading Act* 1990 (Tas); *Fair Trading Act* 1999 (Vic); *Fair Trading Act* 1987 (WA).

[18.21] service provider to engage in conduct which does, or is likely to, mislead or deceive in relation to the service provided. The Commonwealth legislation, constrained as it is by the Constitution, applies to corporations only, however legislation in the States and Territories applies to individuals as well. This legislation also applies to the provision of health care, providing that false and misleading representations cannot be made about such matters as the need for the medical service, its nature, quality and efficacy, the quantity, nature, characteristics or suitability of the service. In considering whether someone has breached the provision, the court can take into account any undue influence, coercion or overzealous persuasion on the part of the health carer. The legislative provisions also apply to those offering complementary health care.

Health Care Complaints

[18.22] All States and Territories except South Australia have established some form of statutory mechanism for dealing specifically with health care complaints. In the past complaints about health care which were not the subject of legal action were received by Health Departments, which acted upon them where it was thought appropriate to do so. More recently, there has been an increased recognition of patients' rights, the need for a mechanism for dealing with complaints about services and health providers independent of Health Departments. The trend has thus been to provide independent statutory units or Commissions to deal with complaints. Legislation sets up independent complaints units with power to receive and deal with complaints in relation to a very broad range of health services. These units are independent of the Health Departments, and facilitate voluntary conciliation of those complaints which are amenable to this process. Where conciliation is not appropriate, or serious allegations involving misconduct or negligence are involved, powers of investigation or referral to an appropriate disciplinary board or investigatory body are provided.

[18.23] The legislation establishing these complaints generally provides for the following functions and powers:

- investigation of complaints, including those that are not amenable to conciliation, are serious, or are referred by the Minister;
- publication of information and education concerning the operation of the legislation;
- inquiries into issues in relation to provision of health services and the causes of complaints;
- provision of advice to the Minister responsible on matters relating to health services;
- powers to examine witnesses; and
- powers to obtain warrants for search and seizure, for the production of information and documents and to impose penalties for non-compliance with directions relating to providing information, or for providing false information.

[18.24] They also provide for:

- ..... protection from reprisals against those involved in a complaint (for example, threats, bribery, refusal to provide services); and
- ..... immunity from legal action for making a complaint, statement, or report or for the performance of a function under the Act.

[18.25] In the Australian Capital Territory the *Health and Community Care Complaints Act* 1998 (ACT) establishes the Health and Community Complaints Commission and Commissioner, along similar lines to those outlined for other jurisdictions.

[18.26] In New South Wales the Health Complaints Commission is established by the *Health Care Complaints Act* 1993 (NSW). If more serious matters are investigated, and substantiated, the Commission can prosecute the matter before the relevant tribunal or professional disciplinary body. A Health Conciliation Registry deals with matters that can be conciliated. If conciliation fails, the complainant can institute legal proceedings. A Parliamentary Committee on the Health Care Complaints Commission has been established to advise the Government. Those receiving community services can lodge a complaint with the Community Services Commission, which can investigate and conciliate complaints, and monitor services (*Community Services (Complaints, Appeals and Monitoring) Act* 1997 (NSW)). Appeals are to the Administrative Appeals Tribunal.

[18.27] In the Northern Territory the *Health and Community Services Complaints Act* 1998 (NT) establishes the Health and Community Complaints Commission and Commissioner, who is to develop a Code of Health and Community Rights and Responsibilities. Consultation is to take place between the Commissioner and the relevant registration board if a registered health carer is involved. Complaints that cannot be conciliated are investigated by the Commissioner, who can require attendance and examine witnesses and documents. Review of the conduct of a complaint can be carried out by the Health and Community Services Complaints Review Committee.

[18.28] In Queensland the *Health Rights Commission Act* 1991 (Qld) establishes the Health Rights Commission. The Commissioner must investigate complaints, and may refer a matter to the health carer's registration board for disciplinary action. Conciliation is to be attempted. As mentioned above, the Code of Health Rights developed by the Commissioner is at Appendix 5.

[18.29] In Tasmania the *Health Complaints Act* 1995 (Tas) established the Health Complaints Commission. It provides for the Commissioner to establish and regularly review a Charter of Health Rights. Serious complaints can be investigated (with powers vested in the Commissioner to subpoena people and documents) and may result in criminal or disciplinary action in the appropriate forum. Conciliation is encouraged where appropriate.

[18.30] In Victoria the *Health Services (Conciliation and Review) Act* 1987 (Vic) establishes the Health Services Commissioner. More serious

[18.30] complaints are investigated, and disciplinary procedures may be brought against the respondent if these are substantiated. Conciliation of complaints is encouraged, including all possible attempts to resolve the issue between the parties before the matter is brought to the Commission.

[18.31] In Western Australia, the *Health Services (Conciliation and Review) Act* 1995 (WA) established the Office of Health Review, to which complaints may be made by consumer, representatives of consumer and health providers. Serious complaints may be investigated, and may be referred to the relevant registration board.

[18.32] The complaints bodies are not intended to actively seek or obtain damages for negligent treatment or assault or battery:

> The service is largely free of cost to consumers with complaints. While in years past the potential cost of legal advice and court action has been a major factor in discouraging users with serious claims from seeking redress, conciliation enables their claims to be negotiated with little or no cost to the parties. It combines equity of access with limitation of cost, and leads to agreement in the great majority of cases [Health Rights Commissioner, *Annual Report 1992/3* (Queensland Government Printer, Brisbane, 1993), p 9].

[18.33] The first priority of these bodies is to provide a means whereby conciliation is possible. This means encouragement of the parties themselves to come to an agreement, which may result in some compensation. Where conciliation is not a viable option, their function is to determine the facts of the situation complained about, and to bring about a more satisfactory standard of health care through influencing the establishment of more effective procedures and practices by the health provider involved. They are also a means for referral of matters to disciplinary bodies, the Ombudsman, the Director of Public Prosecutions or other appropriate body for further action where referral is indicated. Also, they may develop charters of patients' rights as in Queensland, to establish standards of practice generally. In this process, they are a means of:

- empowering complainants;
- providing them with the opportunity of acquiring necessary information which they may be otherwise unable to obtain;
- the opportunity to resolve the matter with the health provider; and
- the satisfaction of seeing that the practice complained of will cease in the future.

Discrimination and the Law

What is "Discrimination"?

[18.34] For legal purposes, discrimination is an act which makes distinctions between individuals or groups with the result of disadvantaging some and advantaging others. The act does not have to be done with the conscious intent of harm. This is why legislation is not punitive—it is aimed at conciliation, compensation and education.

[18.35] We discriminate all the time: some people we like and call our friends, with others we have more distant relationships. Seriously ill patients are given more care and attention than those whose illness is minor. Some discrimination, then, is good or at least acceptable by the standards of our society. Other discrimination—that denying recognised basic human rights—is the subject of moral approbation and, in recent times, legal prohibition.

Direct Discrimination

[18.36] All Australian anti-discrimination law prohibits direct discrimination—that is, discrimination which treats one person less favourably than another on the ground of a characteristic appertaining to the prescribed status (for example, colour) or a characteristic thought to appertain to that characteristic (for example, that all people of a particular race are lazy). The result is that on this ground, the person is treated less favourably than a person who is not of that status. They are discriminated against precisely because of their status. An example is the case of *Wardley v Ansett Transport Industries Pty Ltd* (1984) EOC ¶92-002. This case involved a complaint by Ms Wardley, a pilot, who was denied a position with an airline because of its policy of not hiring women. She claimed that she was the victim of unlawful discrimination because of her sex. In evidence there was a letter from the general manager of the airline to the Women's Electoral Lobby stating that the policy of not hiring women does not mean that women cannot be good pilots, but "we feel that an all male pilot crew is safer than one in which the sexes are mixed". Ms Wardley demonstrated her clear ability for the position, and the Anti-Discrimination Board ruled that she was the victim of unlawful discrimination.

Indirect Discrimination

[18.37] Indirect discrimination is more subtle, and hence harder to detect and to remedy. It is often the result of "policies and practices which form the structures and patterns of an organisation in particular, and society as a whole" (Ronalds (1987), p 199).

[18.38] Indirect discrimination is prohibited in all legislation and the elements necessary for it are basically the same. Indirect discrimination

[18.38] concentrates on the results of an act rather than the reasons for it. It occurs in the following way:

- ..... A, a woman, wants a service or a job (for example, to be a police officer), but is told that a certain condition is required (for example, being a certain height);
- ..... the requirement or condition is unreasonable and unnecessary (that is, a person could do the job just as well whether or not they fulfil this condition);
- ..... A cannot fulfil this condition; and
- ..... a substantially higher proportion of persons of a different status to A (for example, men, who are, on average, taller), can comply with the condition.

[18.39] The unnecessary and seemingly neutral condition, although innocently and without consideration applied, indirectly discriminates against A and many women. It is the result of an erroneous belief that only people of a certain height can do a particular job, and no conscious discrimination against women is intended, but the effect is to discriminate. Another basis of indirect discrimination, called "homosocial reproduction", is the employment of people who have similar backgrounds, education, or social status to those doing the employing, even though such attributes are irrelevant to the ability to carry out the work (recruitment in one's image) (see Wallace (1985), p 21).

Federal Legislation

[18.40] As stated above, the federal government has attempted to ensure the recognition of human rights generally in Australia under the *Human Rights and Equal Opportunity Commission Act* 1986 (Cth). This Act established the Human Rights and Equal Opportunity Commission. The Commission also hears specific complaints of discrimination in employment under the *Human Rights and Equal Opportunity Commission Act* 1986 (Cth), as well as under the *Sex Discrimination Act* 1984 (Cth) and the *Racial Discrimination Act* 1975 (Cth).

Employment Discrimination

Human Rights and Equal Opportunity Commission Act 1986

[18.41] Because the Federal Government can legislate on complaints about breaches of the human rights Conventions under its foreign affairs power, it can legislate on discrimination in employment, as it is a party to the International Labour Organisation Conventions. Thus the Act sets out provisions covering employers throughout Australia. The Human Rights Commissioner can inquire into any act by an employer that is alleged to discriminate on the grounds of race, colour, sex, religion, political opinion, national extraction or social origin, age, medical record, criminal record, impairment, marital status, mental, intellectual or psychiatric disability, nationality, physical disability, sexual preference or trade union activity. "Impairment" includes malfunction or total or partial loss of a part of the body, and the presence in the body of an organism causing disease, which includes HIV seropositivity. Discrimination means any [18.43] distinction, exclusion, or preference made on the basis of one of the listed grounds that has the effect of nullifying or impairing the equality of opportunity or treatment in employment or occupation (s 3).

[18.41A] Discrimination on these grounds is not unlawful, but enables the Commissioner to attempt to effect a settlement of the matter through conciliation. Whereas in the past, the Commission could conduct a hearing and make a finding that could be enforced by the Federal Court, amendments to the Act which commenced in April 2000 meant that this is no longer to be the case, and an unconciliated matter will have to be taken to the Federal Court for further legal action. The Commission may, among other things, inquire into any practice that may constitute discrimination, examine legislation for discriminatory employment provisions, promote equal employment opportunity and undertake research and educational programmes on the issue.

[18.42] Exceptions to wrongful discrimination apply where the discrimination is in respect the inherent requirements of the job, or where the employment is conducted in accordance with the tenets of a religion or creed and is made in good faith to avoid injury to the religious susceptibilities of adherents to that religion or creed.

[18.43] The following is an example of discrimination on the basis of disability.

■■■ CASE

Melvin v Northside Community Service Incorporated [1996] HREOCA 20 (19 July 1996) (Human Rights & Equal Opportunity Commission No H 95/93, Hearing under previous provisions of the Act)

The complainant lodged a complaint with the Human Rights & Equal Opportunity Commission against Northside Community Services Inc ("NCS") alleging discrimination pursuant to the *Disability Discrimination Act* 1992 (Cth).

After 10 years of service as a registered nurse with permanent part-time status in charge of the nursery in the employ of NCS, at its the Civic Occasional Care Centre, ("the COCC"), the complainant was dismissed from that employment. The reason given for her dismissal was that that she was unable to perform some of the inherent requirements of her employment. It was claimed that because of her defective eyesight, she would pose an unacceptable risk to the safety of the children she was employed to care for, and to herself.

The complainant maintained that there was insufficient evidence to support these claims and that her dismissal amounted to direct discrimination within the meaning of Act. In the alternative, she claimed her employer's failure to provide her with necessary facilities to enable her to carry out her responsibilities, was indirect discrimination under the Act.

The complainant's duties included:
- ..... first aid, programming and basic care of the babies;
- ..... checking the nursery and playground equipment for broken toys and food scraps and to ensure cleanliness and safety;
- ..... greeting parents and making notes in relation to the children;

[18.43]
- ..... coping with children that were unwell and who had medical problems such as diabetes, epilepsy, and physical deformity;
- ..... checking children for rashes, feeding them, observing their colour and their general health, look for "sticky eyes", runny noses or coughs and other indications of illness; and
- ..... observing the babies while they slept to make sure their breathing was normal and their colour good, and that they were neither over- nor under-dressed.

The complainant claimed that she never had difficulty performing such tasks and it was accepted that she had done so satisfactorily, having been employed at the COCC as a child carer for some 10 years. There was no evidence of her creating occasions of danger to herself or the children during all her years of employment and no evidence that her visual incapacity became critical by reason of changes occurring in the nature of child care professional services.

However, the complainant was embarrassed doing desk work because of her myopia. In order to read documents, she had to hold them very close to her face. The complainant thought that she would appear unprofessional doing this. She asked to be relieved of such work. However, at no time did she refuse, or indicate that she was unable, to do such work.

The Executive Director of NCS consulted the COCC's insurer who advised her that she would be negligent not to address the question of the complainant's eyesight, having been put on notice that it was defective. The Director of Children's Day Care Services within the Australian Capital Territory government, advised that she request the complainant to obtain documentation from her doctor or specialist indicating whether she was physically fit to perform her specified duties. A report was obtained from an optometrist who the Commissioner found was an inappropriate source of advice, and which did not adequately address the question of the complainant's ability to carry out her employment.

[18.44] The Commissioner found that pressure for the complainant to do clerical work came from other employees, and that the ostensible reason for her dismissal included other employees unhappy at having to take on more clerical work. He dismissed the evidence of the optometrist and those expressing "concerns" about the complainant's capacities, relying rather on the combined effect of the fact of the complainant having done such work through many years during which there was little change in her eye condition, of her own testimony that she was able to do the work, of that of the eyewitnesses, and of both a specialist ophthalmologist and the Royal Blind Society who gave evidence to the Commission.

[18.45] The Commissioner held that to establish discrimination, the complainant would have to show that she was employed by NCS, she had a disability as defined by the Act, she was dismissed from her employment, and this dismissal resulted in her being treated less favourably than the employer treated employees without the disability referred to. These factors were proved in this case. However, even if discrimination has been proved by reference to those elements, she would also have to show that NCS was not justified in doing what it did in virtue of the provisions of subsection 15(4) of the Act. That subsection effectively requires that, given the above elements are proved, the complainant, because of her disability, was unable to carry out the inherent requirements of the employment. This would involve taking into account her training, qualifications and experience relevant to the employment, her performance as an employee, and all other relevant factors that it is reasonable to take into account.

[18.46] The complainant had performed the work for 10 years, her eyesight had not significantly changed in that time, and there was no acceptable evidence that she was or had become unable to perform the inherent requirements of her particular employment. She was discriminated against by reason of her visual impairment. As to the issue of whether the discrimination was not justified (ie, unlawful) by virtue of subsection 15(4) of the Act, the evidence showed that the complainant was able to carry out the inherent requirements of her particular employment. At the very least her employer had not obtained evidence from a suitably qualified specialist that she was unable to adequately carry out her employment. She was in fact dismissed from her employment by reason of her disability and her complaint was substantiated.

[18.47] In awarding damages, the judge took into account the age of the complainant, which militated against her finding further work, and her retraining in order to make herself more employable. Her compensation included past and anticipated future loss of capacity to earn. In addition, embarrassment and other psychological stresses since her dismissal were taken into account. The complainant was awarded a total of $56,692.80 in compensation.

[18.48] The Federal Court considered what constitutes an inherent requirement of a job in the following case.

■■■ CASE

Commonwealth v Human Rights and Equal Opportunity Commission (1998) EOC ¶92-909

A soldier was discharged from the army when his HIV-positive status was established. He was in excellent health and symptom-free. He complained to the Human Rights and Equal Opportunity Commission that he had been unlawfully discriminated against because of his condition, as he could carry out his duties adequately. The Defence Force said that as he might suffer injury when he was deployed on training, and that this might result in the spillage of blood, he was a health risk to other soldiers. The Commission did not accept this argument, stating that the risk of exchange of bodily fluids was not confined to the army, and thus being able to "bleed safely" was not an inherent requirement of being a soldier, which it interpreted narrowly as meaning whether the complainant could perform the tasks of a soldier. The case was appealed to the Federal Court.

[18.49] The Federal Court reversed the decision of the Commission. The inherent requirements of a job include those relevant to all foreseeable activities that the job might require, and the physical and social environment in which the person must work. A soldier's life is not the same as most others—no one is seeking to kill other workers, nor do they

[18.49] train with lethal weapons in intrinsically dangerous situations. The Court also pointed out that any interpretation of the term "inherent requirements of a job" must be restricted by the duty of care owed by the employer to other workers to ensure a safe workplace within the nature of the enterprise. There is also a duty of care to fellow employees. The soldier's HIV status was thus relevant to the inherent requirements of the job and thus the need to "bleed safely".

Workplace Relations Act 1996 (Cth)

[18.50] This Act requires that the Industrial Relations Commission must refuse to certify any agreement that discriminates against an employee on similar grounds to those listed in the *Human Rights and Equal Opportunity Commission Act* 1986 (Cth). Australian Workplace Agreements are deemed to contain anti-discrimination provisions if they are not specified in the agreement. However, these do not include youth wages, inherent requirement of a job, and employment by religious institutions in accordance with the doctrines of that religion.

Exceptions in Federal Laws

[18.51] There are some exceptions to the employment provisions of the federal anti-discrimination law. Such exceptions are where:

- ..... the characteristic in question is a genuine occupational qualification (for example, a male actor for a male part in a play, or a wet-nurse);
- ..... services offered are validly applicable to only one sex (for example, counselling for women victims of sexual assault);
- ..... services are of an intimate nature, such as attendants at toilets, or where people are required or may wish to undress (for example, dressing rooms in clothing shops or for medical examination).

Religious bodies, sporting bodies, charities and voluntary bodies are excepted in some circumstances. Despite the fact that health carers provide services of an intimate nature, it is not generally considered a genuine occupational qualification that a carer be of a particular gender. Sensitive areas such as rape units in hospitals would be considered as exceptions.

Racial Discrimination

[18.52] Having ratified the *International Convention on the Elimination of all Forms of Racial Discrimination* ("Racial Discrimination Convention"), the federal government enacted the *Racial Discrimination Act* 1975 (Cth), prohibiting the discrimination, in certain areas of activity, against any person on the basis of race, national or ethnic origin or colour. Discrimination is defined by section 9 of the *Racial Discrimination Act* as the doing of any act:

> involving a distinction, exclusion, restriction or preference based on race, colour, descent or national or ethnic origin which has the purpose or effect of nullifying or impairing the recognition, enjoyment or exercise, on

an equal footing, of any human right or fundamental freedom in the political, economic, social, cultural or any other field of public life. [18.54]

[18.53] The areas of activity covered by the Act include employment, accommodation, delivery of goods, facilities and services, education, the disposal of land, and the administration of Commonwealth laws and programmes. The Racial Discrimination Convention is attached to the Act in the form of a Schedule, outlining rights and freedoms relating to people based on race. A case that shows how not only staff but management of health care facilities can be liable for racist discrimination:

▌▌▌ CASE
Daniels v Queensland Nursing Homes Pty Ltd [1995] HREOCA 2 (24 January 1995)

The complainant, of Burmese origin, was trained as a registered nurse in her home country, but as her qualifications were not recognised in Australia, was employed as an assistant nurse by the respondent company. She complained of racist comments by another staff member, Nurse D (who was the senior nurse there, and a long-term acquaintance of the Director of Nursing) and that she was dismissed from her job because of her race. She was dismissed after a third alleged incident concerning a patient. Two earlier incidents had occurred, one in which she had swung the chair of a difficult patient (Patient "R") around "with all her strength". The second incident involved lifting the leg of a patient (Patient "G") contrary to established procedures. As Patient G had severe osteoporosis (unbeknownst to the complainant or other assistant nurses), the leg fractured. Evidence was given by the Director of Nursing that she warned the complainant on both occasions that this behaviour was unsatisfactory, and told her a third incident would result in her dismissal. A "Reprimand Book" was kept by the Director, with a record of the incidents and a notation that the complainant had received a warning beside each. A third incident did occur. Nurse D claimed that he witnessed the complainant lifting a patient (Patient "F") from a chair into bed, and that while another nurse (Nurse "G") lifted the top half of the patient, the complainant had lifted the patient by one foot, causing the patient distress.

The Director of Nursing, dismissed the complainant testifying that she relied on the information about the third incident from Nurse D, as well as the incident with Patient G, and did not think the complainant should be given an opportunity to explain the incident because of the seriousness of the former incident. Whatever the complainant said would not change her mind. She also did not bother speaking to the nurse with whom the complainant was lifting Patient F (Nurse G), nor did the chief executive officer, whom she notified of her intention to dismiss the complainant. She also refused to allow the complainant to resign.

[18.54] The Commission held that having regard to the gravity of the matters alleged, the complainant must prove on the balance of probabilities, that she was a victim of unlawful racial discrimination or that her race, colour or national or ethnic origin was at least a reason for her dismissal or that there was conduct that discriminated against her. To do this, she would have to show that, dismissal of non-Australian staff was carried out in a way that was less favourable than dismissal of Australian

[18.54] staff. Non-white, non Anglo-Australian staff who contravened instructions or nursing standards, were not for that reason dealt with more harshly than white-Australian staff, in not being afforded the opportunity to resign.

[18.55] The Commission also concluded that some of the staff at the nursing home were subjected to racist comments and abuse by Nurse D, that neither the Director of Nursing nor the officers of the respondent company gave directions not to engage in racist abuse or racist jokes, and that the former had condoned Nurse D's behaviour, which was grounded in race. This had created a hostile working environment for the complainant and others of Asian origin and in this environment Nurse D was critical of the complainant. It held that the race or ethnic origin of the complainant was a reason for his report about Patient F, and he had been looking for an opportunity to report ill of her. He could not have seen what occurred when Patient F was being lifted into bed. His report was false.

[18.56] Whilst no reports were made by staff about the racist abuse to the Director of Nursing, the Commission was critical of the fact that there was no system in place whereby non-white non Anglo-Australian staff were assured that such complaints would be taken seriously nor that a complainant would not be viewed adversely for so complaining. Neither the Director of Nursing nor any other officer of the respondent could have expected anybody to make such complaint to her about Nurse D, taking into account the regard in which she held him and the length of time she had known him.

[18.57] The Commission determined that the turnover in staff of Asian origin was not the result of a racist policy, and the percentage of non Anglo-Australian staff employed at the nursing home had not decreased to such a significant respect since the current Director of Nursing had been appointed, that a racist attitude could be inferred from that. However, although there was a personality clash between the Director of Nursing and the complainant, that, or poor communication, were not the only reasons for the Director of Nursing deciding to act upon Nurse D's report of the Patient F incident. The Patient G incident caused her grave concern, but she did not in fact give the complainant a warning in respect of Patient R, and that the incidents concerning Patient R were written as they appeared in the Reprimand Book after the occurrence of the Patient G incident. The Director of Nursing, knowing of, and tolerating, Nurse D's attitude, and in reliance on his report, summarily dismissed the complainant without giving her or Nurse G an opportunity to deny that false report.

[18.58] It was also determined that the chief executive officer of the respondent company acted on the advice of the Director of Nursing, and was not himself motivated by racist attitudes in agreeing to the termination. But the respondent company did not take all reasonable steps to prevent Nurse D's ill-will towards the complainant. Its decision to terminate her employment was thus in part actuated by the race or ethnic origin of the complainant, and unlawful conduct for which the respondent should be held liable.

Sex Discrimination

[18.59] As a consequence of having signed the *International Convention on the Elimination of all Forms of Discrimination against Women* ("CEDAW"), the federal government passed the *Sex Discrimination Act* 1984 (Cth). As with the *Racial Discrimination Act* 1975 (Cth), CEDAW is attached as a Schedule to the *Sex Discrimination Act*. This Act prohibits discrimination on the ground of sex, marital status or pregnancy, in the same areas as those provided for in the *Racial Discrimination Act*. The definition of discrimination in sections 5, 6 and 9 of this Act is, however, different. It involves the discriminator treating:

> the aggrieved person less favourably than, in circumstances that are the same or are not materially different, the discriminator treats or would treat a person [of different sex, marital status or who is not pregnant].

[18.60] The Act goes on to say that the grounds of discrimination include not only a characteristic that appertains generally to persons on the grounds of their sex, marital status, or those who are not pregnant, but also characteristics which are "imputed to them" (for example, "all women complain too much"; "pregnant women are irrational").

▌▌▌ CASE
Bear v Norwood Private Nursing Home (1984) EOC ¶92-019 (Sex Discrimination Board SA)

The complainant worked as a nurse assistant at the hospital. She became pregnant. She was temporarily absent with a threatened miscarriage, but returned to work. She was dismissed, and complained that the dismissal was because of the pregnancy, and thus unlawful.

[18.61] The Board held that she was not unfairly dismissed. The basis for the action was not her pregnancy or temporary disability following the threatened miscarriage or tiredness. Rather it was because she was not doing her work satisfactorily. It would have been discrimination if:

- ▌..... there had been a policy of dismissing pregnant nurses;
- ▌..... her dismissal was the result of a belief that pregnant women in general should not be employed as nurses;
- ▌..... her appearance had been considered undesirable; or
- ▌..... the dismissal was to prevent a risk to herself or foetus.

[18.62] A case where a veterinary surgeon was dismissed on the ground of pregnancy is *Kimler v Lort Smith Animal Hospital* [1995] HREOCA 20. In that case the complainant was held to be unlawfully dismissed, as the basis of the dismissal was a belief that as a pregnant woman she should not be working. She was told that one of the nurses was bitten on the breast by a dog a few weeks previously, and the employer was concerned that something like that could happen to her.

Sexual Preference, Marital Status

[18.63] Cases where women have been denied access to reproductive technology on the basis of their marital status (or lack of it), and sexual preference have been mentioned in Chapter 17.

Sexual Harassment

[18.64] Health carers and clients should be free from sexual harassment in the workplace. The *Sex Discrimination Act*, as well as the legislation in the Australian Capital Territory, Queensland, South Australia, Tasmania, Victoria and Western Australia (outlined below), prohibits sexual harassment in the workplace and in educational facilities. Sexual harassment is defined in the *Sex Discrimination Act* as an unwelcome sexual advance, or "an unwelcome request for sexual favours . . . or . . . other unwelcome conduct of a sexual nature". Where the person being harassed has reasonable grounds for believing that rejecting the advance, refusing the request or objecting to the conduct disadvantaged or would disadvantage them in connection with their employment or their studies (*Sex Discrimination Act* 1984 (Cth), s 28). Ronalds ((1987), p 119) points out:

> The concept of 'disadvantage' could incorporate factors such as a hostile work environment, mental anguish, lack of job opportunities or other matters which had a negative result on the person. . . . In educational institutions it could involve a threat to fail a student or a failure or a deferment or a denial of access to a particular course or class, or the use of specialist equipment.

[18.65] Where management does not take proper action to prevent or remedy sexual harassment in the workplace it may be found vicariously liable, as it is also for other acts of sexual discrimination. The Act provides, however, that if management has taken all reasonable steps to prevent the employee from offending it will not be found liable.

▌▌▌ CASE

Boyle v Ishan Ozden (1986) EOC ¶92-165 (Human Rights Commission (as it was then called))

The complainant worked at a take-away shop. She brought a complaint against the manager of the shop who had allegedly unlawfully sexually harassed her. Because she rejected his advances he dismissed her the next day. The complaint also named the owners of the shop, who were overseas at the time, and who argued that they could not be responsible for actions which were taken in their absence.

[18.66] The Commission found (p 76,614) that the owners were vicariously responsible for the manager's sexual harassment, even though they did not know of it, for the purposes of this case:

> there was no evidence that any steps had been taken to prevent commission of the acts . . . complained of . . . In saying that I do not criticise them. It would be difficult to envisage a situation in which they

would have given such instructions. But the fact is that s 106 attaches vicarious liability to them unless they have done something active to prevent the acts complained of. [18.70]

[18.67] Harassment may not have a sexual content, but may nevertheless occur, motivated by the sex of the person who is victimised (that is, "sexist" harassment).

▌▌▌ CASE
Hill v Water Resources Commission (1985) EOC ¶92-127 (Equal Opportunity Commission NSW)

The complainant became the first female clerical officer to enter an almost completely male-dominated area. It was made quite clear to her that she was unwelcome, with many acts of harassment including withholding of mail she was expecting, goods being unloaded from a truck being thrown with unnecessary force to her, failure by employees to recognise her authority and carry out instructions, false information that the goldfish she kept in her office had been killed, and the fouling of toilets she had had re-allocated from males to females.

[18.68] The Tribunal held that this was discrimination, as a man would not have been harassed in this way. It accepted the complainant's argument that the harassment produced a hostile work environment and that it was sufficiently pervasive to affect adversely the terms and conditions of employment. Conditions of employment include the psychological and emotional work environment. The Water Resources Commission was found liable for acts of sexual harassment by its employees against the complainant, and damages of $34,827.34 were awarded for distress, loss of wages and promotion opportunities, and long-term psychological effects. This was because "either no action or very limited action was taken and often there was a lengthy delay before any action was taken" as a result of her complaints to management.

[18.69] There is legal argument that the federal legislation against sexual discrimination cannot cover male employees who are discriminated against, as it is based on the convention which deals with discrimination against women. There is no question, however, that prohibition against sexual discrimination goes both ways under State legislation.

▌▌▌ CASE
Ahern v Burra Burra Hospital (unreported, 22 March 1982, Sex Discrimination Board SA)

A male student nurse was refused accommodation in the nurses home attached to the hospital. This accommodation was available to female nurses and was better than alternatives. The hospital claimed that it was not obliged to provide accommodation to student nurses: that this was a benefit it could bestow at will. Ahern complained of sexual discrimination to the Board.

[18.70] The Board held that although the hospital was not obliged to provide accommodation it did so for female nurses as a matter of course. It

[18.70] was held that accommodation was a benefit applying to employment. The male nurse was thus denied a benefit enjoyed by other nurses, and this was a breach of the legislation.

[18.71] Clients and staff who are victims of discrimination or sexual harassment should complain firstly to the employing authority where it occurs. If this is neither feasible (it may be the discriminator) nor successful, one may go to:

- .....the appropriate body where there is anti-discrimination legislation in their State;
- .....the police where the act amounts to sexual or other assault;
- .....the appropriate professional disciplinary body governing the alleged offender; or
- .....(for clients), under the general complaints procedures regarding medical treatment (see [18.17]) and (for clients and employees) to the Human Rights and Equal Opportunity Commission.

Discrimination and Disability

[18.72] The *Disability Discrimination Act* 1992 (Cth) provides for complaints by those with a disability to complain of discrimination. They can also complain under complementary State legislation where it occurs. The definition of disability is broad, including physical, sensory, intellectual or psychiatric impairment, as well as the presence in the body of organisms causing or capable of causing disease (thereby including HIV and AIDS). The legislation also prohibits discrimination because a person uses a wheelchair, cane, hearing or guide dog, permitting the presence of the dogs in places where they would be otherwise prohibited. The areas of activity covered are similar to those covered by the *Racial Discrimination Act* thus including the delivery of health care services.

Discrimination and Special Consideration for the Aged

[18.73] The *Aged Care Act* 1997 (Cth) and the *National Health Act* 1953 (Cth) to establish rights for those in government nursing homes and hostels, and the *Aged Care Act* 1997 (Cth) authorises the Minister to make "quality care principles", dealing with the lifestyle and personal care of residents, and those receiving community care. "User rights principles" are also established, which require those providing residential care to ensure security of tenure, and a complaints mechanism.

[18.74] The Department of Community Services and Health, as well as community visitors and patient advocates recognised by the Department can inspect nursing homes. Government funding will not be given to hostels unless there is general compliance with the legislation, and where there is doubt about the standard of care, a Hostel Standards Review Panel can be directed to review the matter to ensure standards are upheld.

Measures to Achieve Equality

[18.75] The most important and controversial exception to discrimination in anti-discrimination legislation is the provision that measures intended to achieve equality are exempted from prohibition. It allows acts and special programmes to meet specific needs of a group, which are designed to result in furthering equality of that group with the rest of society. This provision for affirmative action gives recognition to the fact that socialisation, fewer educational opportunities and social attitudes which have been the result of, for example, racial or sexist discrimination in the past, have put some people at a disadvantage that no strictly equal treatment will remedy.

[18.76] It is thus not unlawful to discriminate in favour of one of the mentioned classes of people if that discrimination is a means of bringing about equality of access to employment or conditions of employment, or access to goods and services, where those measures are to bring about the same degree of access as that enjoyed by others. Measures such as training programmes for particular groups of people, such as English classes or nursing orientation classes for migrant employees are lawful. Exemption is also provided for discriminating where the service offered is such that it will not work effectively without it, for example, female nurses for treating rape victims, or gender-specific counselling, however, in most cases the employer or provider of services must apply for the exemption from the Human Rights and Equal Opportunity Commission.

▌▌▌ CASE
Proudfoot v ACT Board of Health (1992) EOC ¶92-417

The complainant alleged that the provision of health services for women by the Australian Capital Territory Women's Health Service and the Canberra Women's Health Service, both funded by the Commonwealth and the Australian Capital Territory governments, were discriminatory, in that they provided services for medical problems not exclusive to women. This was despite the fact that men, on average, die several years earlier than women, and men also have specific health problems. The complaint was brought under the federal *Sex Discrimination Act*, was not resolved by conciliation, and went to the Human Rights Commission. It was argued there that the health services offered were based on a holistic approach to health care, and in the recognition that many health problems faced by women, although common to both sexes, cannot be dealt with in isolation to their social and psychological environment, and their discriminatory treatment in the mainstream of the medical system.

[18.77] The Human Rights Commission (as it then was) held that the services were prima facie discriminatory, however it accepted the argument that a person's health includes indivisible physical and mental elements, and that in addressing the health needs of women some problems which are faced by both sexes may be included in ancillary services. The Commission also recognised the disadvantages in gaining access to optimal health care which women in general may face because they have less financial resources, less influence in gaining services, and

[18.77] are more burdened by their child-bearing and child-rearing role in society, and in the widespread occurrence of domestic violence. On this basis, the Commission held that the provision of the health services was justifiable under section 33 of the *Sex Discrimination Act*, which provides an exemption if the purpose of the discrimination is to ensure that a person of a particular sex may have equal opportunities with the other sex.

Remedies under Federal Legislation
Conciliation

[18.78] The *Racial*, *Sex* and *Disability Discrimination Acts* provide a mechanism for dealing with complaints of discrimination where the legislation applies. There is a Race Discrimination Commissioner, a Sex Discrimination Commissioner and a Disability Discrimination Commissioner attached to the Human Rights and Equal Opportunity Commission (the Commission) to administer the respective Acts and who refer appropriate matters to the Commission. Complaints are directed to the Commission, which, after accepting that the complaint is actionable under the law, must attempt to resolve it through conciliation. This approach, which is very different from the usual legal adversarial method of seeking satisfaction for a wrong, has been adopted because it is believed to be a more satisfactory way of handling discrimination than making it a criminal offence, which may be difficult to prove and which may make the situation worse. It is also considered better than making the sole avenue of redress a civil action, with the need for the aggrieved person (complainant) to bring protracted and expensive legal action.

[18.79] In order to bring about resolution by conciliation, a conference of the parties is to be called. The Commission may provide written notice to a person believed to be capable of doing so, to provide it with relevant information or documents, and it may require any person who can provide relevant information to attend a conference. A compulsory conference is confidential and must not disadvantage either the complainant or respondent. Failure to comply can result in a fine or result in adverse findings in the next possible step. Giving false or misleading information can lead to imprisonment for six months.

Litigation

[18.80] Where a complaint is "terminated" (for example, rejected as unfounded, or cannot be conciliated) the person may make an application to the Federal Court (within 28 days). That Court, if it is satisfied that the discrimination has occurred, can make any order it thinks fit, such as re-instatement of employment, restitution, declarations, and compensation. In doing so it can take a report of the Commissioner into account.

State and Territory Legislation [18.83]

[18.81] All jurisdictions have legislation prohibiting defined acts of discrimination on specified grounds. They have similar exceptions and exemption provisions to the federal legislation. Each has adopted an agency for dealing with complaints, which respond in a similar way to the Commission. The powers of the agency and the enforceability of its findings differ according to jurisdiction, however, unlike the Human Rights and Equal Opportunity Commission, those bodies do have some powers of enforcement of decisions.

Australian Capital Territory

[18.82] The *Discrimination Act* 1991 (ACT) prohibits discrimination on the grounds of:

- sex, sexuality, transsexuality, marital status, pregnancy, sexual harassment, status as parent or carer, breastfeeding;
- age;
- race;
- impairment;
- religious or political conviction;
- profession, trade, occupation or calling; and
- association with a person with any of the above characteristics,

in the areas of employment, provision of goods and services, and accommodation, among others. The Act also prohibits sexual harassment and racial vilification unlawful advertising and victimisation of complainants. The agency involved is the Discrimination Commissioner, who investigates and conciliates complaints, and the Discrimination Tribunal.

New South Wales

[18.83] The *Anti-Discrimination Act* 1977 (NSW) prohibits discrimination on the grounds of:

- race, colour, nationality, descent and ethnic, ethno-religious or national origin;
- sex, pregnancy, marital status; sexual preference, transgender;
- physical and intellectual impairment; and
- age,

in the areas of employment, education, provision of goods and services, and accommodation, industrial organisations, registered clubs, among others. The Act also prohibits racial homosexual HIV/AIDS and transgender vilification, sexual harassment and victimisation of complainants. The agencies involved are the Anti-Discrimination Board which investigates and conciliates complaints, and the Administrative

[18.83] Decisions Tribunal which hears and determines unconciliated matters. There is an appeal to the Supreme Court.

Northern Territory

[18.84] The *Anti-Discrimination Act* 1992 (NT) prohibits discrimination on the grounds of:

- sex, sexuality, marital status, pregnancy;
- parenthood, breastfeeding;
- age;
- race;
- impairment;
- religious belief, political opinion;
- irrelevant medical or criminal record;
- trade union or employer association activity; and
- association with a person with any of the above characteristics,

in the areas of education, work, facilities, clubs, provision of goods and services, and accommodation, among others. The agency involved is the Anti-Discrimination Commissioner, who investigates and conciliates complaints.

Queensland

[18.85] The *Anti-Discrimination Act* 1991 (Qld) prohibits discrimination on the grounds of:

- sex, marital status, lawful sexual activity, pregnancy, parental status, breastfeeding;
- age;
- race;
- impairment;
- religion, political belief or activity;
- trade union activity; and
- association with a person with any of the above characteristics,

in the areas of employment, provision of goods and services, and accommodation, among others. The Act also prohibits sexual harassment, incitement to racial or religious hatred and victimisation of complainants. The agency involved is the Anti-Discrimination Commissioner, who investigates and conciliates complaints and where it is unsuccessful, the Anti-Discrimination Tribunal which hears and determines the matter.

The *Industrial Relations Act* 1999 (Qld) also makes discrimination on a wide number of grounds unlawful. Matters are taken to the Queensland Industrial Relations Commission.

South Australia

[18.86] The *Equal Opportunity Act* 1984 (SA) prohibits discrimination on the grounds of:

- race, nationality, colour, ancestry, or origin (either of the person or their associate(s));
- sex, sexuality, marital status, pregnancy;
- physical and intellectual impairment; and
- age,

in the areas of employment, provision of goods and services, and accommodation, amongst others. The Act also prohibits sexual harassment and victimisation of complainants. The agencies involved are the Commissioner for Equal Opportunity who investigates and conciliates complaints, and where it is unsuccessful, the Equal Opportunity Tribunal which hears and determines the matter. There is an appeal to the Supreme Court. The *Racial Vilification Act* 1996 (SA) prohibits racial vilification.

Tasmania

[18.87] The *Anti-Discrimination Act* 1998 (Tas) makes discrimination unlawful on the following grounds:

- race;
- age;
- sex, sexual orientation, lawful sexual activity, marital status, pregnancy, breastfeeding, parental status, family responsibilities;
- disability;
- industrial activity;
- political or religious belief or non-belief, affiliation or activity;
- irrelevant medical or criminal record; and
- association with a person with, or believed to have any of the above characteristics,

in most areas of public life. The Act also makes unlawful conduct that offends, humiliates, intimidates, insults or ridicules another person on the basis of one of the above grounds. It also renders unlawful publicly inciting hatred of a person because of their race, disability, sexual orientation or religious belief or non-belief. Complaints are made to the Anti-Discrimination Commissioner, who attempts conciliation. Unconciliated matters and appeals from the Commissioner's findings go to the Anti-Discrimination Tribunal.

Victoria

[18.88] Section 17 of the *Equal Opportunity Act* 1995 (Vic) prohibits discrimination on the grounds of:

- race, colour, ethnic or national origin;

HEALTH CARE AND THE LAW

[18.88]
- ..... sex, marital status, pregnancy, breastfeeding;
- ..... lawful sexual activity, sexual orientation, gender identity;
- ..... age, physical features;
- ..... the state of being a parent, childless or de facto spouse;
- ..... lawful political or religious belief or activity;
- ..... physical impairment (including presence of organisms causing disease), mental illness or mental disability; and
- ..... industrial activity,

in the areas of employment, education, provision of goods and services, and accommodation, disposal of land, community service organisations, municipal or shire councils, sport among others. The Act also prohibits sexual harassment and victimisation of complainants. The agencies involved are the Equal Opportunity Commission which investigates and conciliates complaints, and the Civil and Administrative Tribunal which hears and determines unconciliated matters.

Western Australia

[18.89] The *Equal Opportunity Act* 1984 (WA) prohibits discrimination on the grounds of:

- ..... race;
- ..... sex, marital status, pregnancy, family responsibilities, and family status;
- ..... religious or political conviction;
- ..... physical or mental impairment; and
- ..... age,

in most areas of public life. The agencies involved are the Commissioner for Equal Opportunity which investigates and conciliates complaints, and where it is unsuccessful, the Equal Opportunity Tribunal which hears and determines the matter.

Which Act should one Use?

[18.90] In States and Territories which have anti-discrimination legislation, two pieces of legislation, federal and State, may cover a particular situation. The federal government has entered into an arrangement with some of those jurisdictions to enable them to act as its delegate. This means that it is possible to obtain advice on which jurisdiction is most appropriate when lodging the complaint with most State or Territory administrative bodies, and the complaint can be processed under both federal or State or Territory legislation.

[18.91] The *Racial Discrimination Act*, the *Sex Discrimination Act*, the *Disability Discrimination Act* and the *Human Rights and Equal Opportunity Commission Act* are based on international instruments (documents creating legal rights and duties), are valid enactments, and apply throughout the country. Other areas of discrimination are covered by State or Territory legislation, but not specifically prohibited by federal legislation (for example, homosexuality, status of being a parent etc). Different powers and functions held by the Human Rights and Equal Opportunity Commission and State or Territory anti-discrimination bodies may determine which Act to choose. [18.94]

Exemptions

[18.92] Exemptions which apply in the State or Territory legislation are similar to those which apply in the federal legislation.

Measures to Achieve Equality

[18.93] All State and Territory legislation (except the *Anti-Discrimination Act* 1977 (NSW)) has an exception to the prohibition of discrimination, where that discrimination is part of measures to achieve equality for a particular group of people: to put them on an equal footing with others. This allows for the taking of positive steps to overcome the effects of past discrimination. Examples are the provision of special medical services for particular groups of people such as rural Aborigines, or the provision of special education facilities so that those who may have missed out in the past because of their race or their gender can catch up and have equal access to work. The Commonwealth government has also established the Equal Opportunity for Women in the Workplace Agency under the *Equal Opportunity for Women in the Workplace Act* 1999 (Cth). Employers with more than 100 employees, education institutions, trade unions and community organisations are required to develop and implement workplace programs for women and to submit annual reports on the progress of these programs. The Act sets out steps in implementing an equal opportunity program, and the Agency provides guidelines to assist compliance with the Act reporting. Failure to implement a program or submit a report can result in naming in Parliament and ineligibility for government contracts or specified forms of financial assistance.

Implications for Health Care Workers

[18.94] The connection of international documents on human rights with domestic law means that health carers in the relevant jurisdictions should not be discriminated against on the grounds discussed above, and also that they should not discriminate in their work against others on those grounds. They should not refuse to treat, or give any less than accepted treatment to, clients because of their age, marital status (or lack of it), sexual preference, or because they are mentally ill or suffering from a contagious disease, or a socially stigmatised one such as AIDS, or because they are suffering from a drug-related illness such as alcoholism or drug dependency. Health carers should maintain confidentiality and privacy, and provide clients with full access to all available medical care.

[18.95] [18.95] Where the giving of treatment places the health carer in danger of harm, then reasonable discriminatory activity may be acceptable, for example, in nuclear medicine where special conditions may apply to pregnant women. Where carers find that the practice is to treat someone differently, they need to examine why this is so: it should be purely on the grounds of need (the client's or their own). Common examples of discrimination in the health care area are the refusal to treat HIV-positive clients, discriminatory treatment of alcoholics or the mentally ill, or the often substandard treatment of the elderly.

Discrimination and the HIV-Positive Client

[18.96] No legislation refers specifically to HIV infection or AIDS as a ground for discrimination, however complaints may be made, according to circumstances and the legislation in the particular jurisdiction, of discrimination on the ground of impairment, sexuality, sexual preference, or homosexuality. The basis for discrimination may be that the complainant is assumed to fit the category, does fit the category, is a member of a high-risk group, or associates with such a person. Complaints of discrimination by HIV-positive clients under specific legislation can thus now be made in all jurisdictions.

[18.97] Two complaints of discrimination against clients on the basis of HIV/AIDS with different outcomes can be compared.

▌▌▌ CASE
Ferguson v Central Sydney Area Health Service & Anor (1990) EOC ¶92-272

> A patient who was homosexual and whose lifestyle was considered to be at "high risk" of being exposed to HIV complained to the New South Wales Equal Opportunity Tribunal that he was discriminated against on the grounds of his homosexuality by being refused elective surgery until his antibody status was obtained.

[18.98] The Tribunal found that it was the man's medical status and high-risk category that was the causal factor in his being treated as he was, and not the fact that he was homosexual. Any person in the high-risk category, male or female, homosexual or heterosexual, whose high-risk status was discovered would be treated in the same way at that time. Readers are referred to *Commonwealth of Australia v Human Rights and Equal Opportunity Commission* above (see [18.48]).

▌▌▌ CASE
G v L (1995) EOC ¶92-712

A client, a nurse, was told by his doctor he required surgery and would be referred to a specialist surgeon. The doctor then asked him if he was gay and when the client confirmed this the doctor stated a test would be required to determine his HIV status before he could have the surgery. The complainant said he had had a test some months previously and had not participated in unsafe sex since then. He reminded the doctor he was a nurse, understood the nature of HIV/AIDS infection, and that every patient should be treated with due precautions. The doctor then reiterated his refusal to treat the complainant unless he had a test, and terminated future appointments.

[18.99] The doctor admitted that he had unlawfully discriminated against the complainant and settled with the complainant for $5,000 and $17,000 legal costs (indicating the cost of legal representation).

[18.100] Those subjected to discrimination may have a remedy in tort action for negligence where the failure to treat them resulted in foreseeable harm, and there is no defence of self-protection by the defendant available. Hospitals should provide proper training and information regarding the treatment of HIV infections, and reasonable safeguards should be taken. See also [16.35]ff.

A Client's Bill of Rights is Important

[18.101] Clients' bills of rights are not to be ignored. They are statements of the standards of social behaviour accepted by the society we live in, and by professional health care bodies. Most of the provisions may be the subject of complaint on the basis of discrimination. They can also be considered as a statement of the standard of care the institution offers the client and which the employer expects to be carried out by the nurse. Failure to meet this standard may render those concerned subject to disciplinary action by the employer or appropriate registration board and liable in negligence if harm results.

REFERENCES AND FURTHER READING

Anti-Discrimination Board of New South Wales, *Anti-Discrimination and Equal Employment Opportunity (EEO) Guidelines for Managers, Team Leaders and Supervisors* (Anti-Discrimination Board of New South Wales, Sydney, 1997)

Australian and New Zealand Equal Opportunity Law and Practice (CCH, Sydney, 1985)

Bunney, L, "Discrimination and Assisted Reproductive Technology" 5 *Health Law Bulletin* 57

CCH industrial law editors, *Countering Sexual Harassment: A Manual For Managers And Supervisors* (CCH, Sydney, 1992)

Department of Health and Family Services, *Standards and Guidelines for Residential Aged Care Services Manual*, Aged and Community Care Division, Commonwealth Department of Health (Department of Health and Family Services, Canberra ACT, 1998)

Jenkins, K and Lawrie, C, *Women in the Workplace: Sexual Harassment and Discrimination* (Prospect Media, Sydney, 2000)

Kinley, D, *Human Rights in Australian Law: Principles, Practice and Potential* (Federation Press, Sydney, 1998)

Larbalestier, J and Russell, D (ed), proceedings *Women and Law Conference: Working for Women?: Anti-Discrimination, Affirmative Action, and Equal Opportunity*, 22nd September 1995 (Women's Studies Centre, University of Sydney, 1996)

McCullough, S (ed), *Older Residents Legal Rights* (Federation Press, Sydney, 1992)

National Conference of Legal and Policy Officers from Human Rights/Equal Opportunity/Anti Discrimination Organisations, (1st) Darwin, 10-11 August 1995 (Anti-Discrimination Commission, Darwin, 1995)

Pettman, R, *Incitement to Racial Hatred: Issues and Analysis* (AGPS, Human Rights Commission Canberra, 1982)

Phillips, R and Merrilyn, J, *Older Residents and the Law* (Residential Care Rights, Melbourne, 1996)

Quinn, G, McDonagh, M and Kimber, C, *Disability Discrimination Law in the United States, Australia, and Canada* (Oak Tree Press, Dublin, 1993)

Redfern Legal Centre, *Questions of Rights: a Guide to the Law and Rights of People with an Intellectual Disability* (Redfern Legal Centre, Sydney, 1992)

Ronalds, C, *Residents' Rights in Nursing Homes and Hostels: Final Report* (AGPS, Canberra, 1989)

Ronalds, C, *Discrimination: Law and Practice* (Federation Press, Leichhardt, 1998)

Stuhmcke, A, "Access to Reproductive Technology: *Pearce v SA Health Commission*" 5 *Health Law Bulletin* 39 (1995)

Tay, Alice Erh-Soon, *Human Rights for Australia*, Human Rights Commission Monograph Series No 1 (AGPS, Canberra, 1986)

Thornton, M, *The Liberal Promise: Anti-discrimination Legislation in Australia* (Oxford University Press, Melbourne, 1991)

Wallace, M, "The Legal Approach to Sex Discrimination", in Sawer, M, *Program for Change* (Allen & Unwin, Sydney, 1985)

West, D, *Older Residents and the Law: Training Manual* (Residential Care Rights, Older Persons Action Centre, Office of the Public Advocate, Melbourne, 1996)

Williams, G, *Human Rights under the Australian Constitution* (Oxford University Press, Melbourne, 1999)

The various State and Territory anti-discrimination bodies mentioned in this chapter have produced reports on discrimination on various grounds, as well as annual reports.

On AIDS specifically there are reports by the different bodies established to deal with it, such as NACAIDS. See also References and Further Reading for Chapter 16 for other references on AIDS.

Chapter Nineteen

DECISION MAKING, LAW AND ETHICS: A DISCUSSION*

INTRODUCTION

[19.1] The purpose of this chapter is to apply the information given in previous chapters to decision-making, and to develop a model for resolving the many dilemmas which may confront the health carer in everyday experience. Examples of the kinds of questions that arise are: what to do when a client asks if they have cancer when other carers and/or family do not wish them to be told; whether to report a colleague who has acted negligently; and whether a patient should be informed that treatment under anaesthesia was negligent.

[19.2] The previous chapters in this book have been concerned with legal aspects of decision making in health care. This chapter will address ethical principles and their place in the decision-making process. The aim is to outline a proposed pattern of thinking: not to give a final answer as to how to act in any situation. A model for clarifying values will be offered, together with suggestions for reasoning so that one may reach an acceptable decision on how to proceed. As this is a book about law, it is not intended that this analysis be other than an outline of some of the main ethical issues, an indication of their relationship to the law, and a brief guide to ethical decision making developed from the author's experience.

The Ethical Decision-Making Process: One Approach

What is the Issue?

[19.3] A health carer who is confronted with a difficult situation, and is unsure how to act, needs to answer certain questions. The first step,

---

* This chapter has been revised but not updated. Some titles have been added to the References and Further Reading List.

[19.3] however, is to identify what kind of question to ask. This can be done in a logical fashion by determining what sort of issue one is dealing with:

Is it A Factual Issue?

The question of what to do may be resolved by becoming better informed on the facts of the case, for example, what the diagnosis and prognosis are, and the likely medical and social outcome of proposed action. Establishing whether a patient is temporarily comatose, in a persistent vegetative state, or brain dead, for example, is crucial in deciding what care to give. Anguish to both health carers and relatives over whether, and how, to treat such a patient may be relieved by simply establishing the facts.

Is it a Legal Issue?

Having clarified the facts, decisions as to how to act may become quite clear after determining what the law is in a particular situation, and being satisfied that fulfilling any legal requirements or obligations poses no ethical dilemma, that is, does not cause a conflict between one's moral values. One may not need to go any further.

Is it an Ethical Issue?

Here one has determined the answers to the above questions, but is uncertain how to act, because any perceived solution poses some degree of conflict with one's sense of right and wrong. The law governing a particular activity may be contrary to what the health carer considers to be the right thing to do (for example, prohibiting disclosure of facts, such as a client's likelihood to harm another person). It could permit alternative courses of action, each of which could in some way potentially conflict with an ethical principle to some degree (for example, the advantages and disadvantages of withholding of non-therapeutic but life-preserving treatment compared with those of the administering of such treatment). Health carers need to go further in this situation, and determine how they *ought* to act, either because of, or despite, the answers to the above questions. The issue here is most likely an ethical one, because it requires the health carer to rank the values involved in each alternative in some order of merit.

What is Ethics?

[19.4] First it may be instructive to consider what ethics is *not*.

[19.5] Ethics is not simply the study of "right" conduct. It is not a set of guidelines that, if followed, will always lead to correct behaviour. It is not law or etiquette, although these matters may be considerations in determining ethical issues. Ethics is not merely the study of how people act in the face of difficult choices. It is not the following of orders, or doing what everyone else does. It is not a study of policy or public [19.8] opinion, although, again, these may be relevant considerations. Ethics is definitely not a matter of "gut feelings", although these may be a starting point for canvassing the alternatives, and deciding what one ought to do.

[19.6] Ethics, it is suggested, is the study of rational processes for determining the course of action, in the face of conflicting choices. This study, of necessity, involves the identification, weighing and choice of values. This process must result in the development by a person of an initial moral (value) statement about a particular issue.

[19.7] Such a statement may be, for example, that under no circumstance should one make an untrue statement. It is a basis for clarity in reasoning out the common problems that carers face, such as being asked by a patient whether they are suffering from cancer.

[19.8] The reason for considering the issue of ethics is the author's concern as to what has prevented action in the face of clearly immoral and therefore ethically questionable activities carried out by, or condoned by, members of the health care profession in past and current practice. Examples are the frequent failure to object to lack of proper consent on the part of clients when participating in a medical procedure, and being party to the signing of consent forms which are clearly not understood; tolerating the use of anaesthetised women as anatomical exhibits (and in some cases vehicles for practising inserting and removing IUDs); of failing to tell the truth to clients when such actions are considered, under the circumstances, to be unjust. More serious examples are the activities that occurred over extended periods of time in Chelmsford Hospital in Sydney[1] and in Ward 10B of Townsville Hospital, Queensland.[2] Inquiries carried out into the treatment of psychiatric patients at both places considered the treatment not only to be grossly negligent but serious enough to raise the question of criminal charges. Many of the health carers involved, including nurses, were not the key health workers investigated by the inquiries, and no legal action could be taken against them, however they were an important part in the suspect activities and often unquestioning, either as participants or witnesses to the events. Is the failure to act in circumstances like those outlined above because these health carers see law and ethics as a matter of etiquette, or doing what they are told, or what everyone else does, or something else which points to the acceptability of failure to act? It seems the concept of ethics is in need of clarification, for these events ought never to have happened.

---

[1] Royal Commission into Deep Sleep Therapy, *Report* (NSW Government Printer, Sydney, 1991). However it must be noted that some nurses did act upon their concerns, and a key person in bringing the whole deep sleep issue to public notice and exposing the activities there was a nurse who had to persist in her efforts and take extraordinary steps to do this (Bromberger et al (1991), pp 110ff).

[2] See, for example, reports in the *Courier Mail*, 27 February 1991. Two points of interest to nurses are made in the reports: one is that nurses rated very little comment in the official report by Mr Bill Carter QC; the second is that the Queensland Nurses Union secretary announced that the union will review the question of what nurses write in medical records after the Inquiry (p 12). No elaboration was made on this comment.

[19.9]   **[19.9]** Indeed there are some major questions where the law may well be involved. Chelmsford and Ward 10B are extreme examples, and it is hoped that health carers will never again fail to question such situations. In such extreme cases of course, health carers may not only have an ethical duty to prevent them, but a legal one as well.

[19.10] In practice health carers other than doctors have rarely been the subject of legal proceedings, even where their actions (or omissions) are legally culpable under criminal law (see Ch 14) or civil law (see Ch 6). The emerging recognition of patients' rights, and increasing understanding of the legal system by clients means that this may change (see, for example, *Darling's* case at [6.106]).

[19.11] As to the connection between law and ethics, this was outlined in the case of *Furniss v Fitchett* [1958] NZLR 396. In that case a doctor disclosed details of a woman's mental condition for evidence in matrimonial proceedings in court, in circumstances in which he ought to have known she would be harmed. The court had to consider whether the ethical code was a relevant reference for determining a duty of care. The Chief Justice said (at 405):

> The British Medical Association's Code of Ethics is evidence of the general professional standards to which a reasonably careful, skilled and informed practitioner would conform. I think, it was admissible for that purpose, and it, therefore, became necessary to decide whether the law, as distinct from the ethical code of the British Medical Association, permitted any departure from those standards.

Codes of ethics thus become not only ethical guides, but, for the purposes of the law, standards by which "reasonably careful, skilled and informed" practice will be judged by the courts, disciplinary bodies and complaints units.

Codes of Ethics

[19.12] There are many codes of ethics for the different health care professions. Examples are the Hippocratic Oath for the medical profession, which has been replaced by the Declaration of Geneva and the International Code of Medical Ethics (prepared by the World Medical Association); codes of ethics of the Australian Dental Association and the Australian Physiotherapy Association. Sometimes these include etiquette and policy as well as ethical principles. The International Council for Nurses has issued a statement "A Code for Nurses: Ethical Concepts Applied to Nurses", which is considered here as an example of an ethical code. It includes the following ethical statements:

- ..... the fundamental responsibility of the nurse is to promote health, prevent illness, restore health, and alleviate suffering;
- ..... inherent in nursing is respect for life, dignity and rights of citizens, unrestricted by considerations of race, creed, colour, age, sex, politics or social status;
- ..... nurses promote an environment in which the values, customs and spiritual beliefs of the individual are recognised;

- ..... nurses carry personal responsibility for nursing practice and maintaining competence by continual learning;
- ..... nurses maintain the highest standard of practice and personal conduct, and use judgment in relating to individual competence when accepting and delegating responsibility;
- ..... nurses take an active role in promoting nursing practice, as well as health and social needs of the public; and
- ..... nurses co-operate with co-workers and protect patients from danger from co-workers or others.

[19.13] Other principles which codes of ethics have in common are those which require carers to:

- ..... maintain confidentiality;
- ..... preserve the dignity of the patient;
- ..... not abandon a patient;
- ..... maintain accurate records;
- ..... consult others where they lack competence;
- ..... restrict advertising and refrain from touting for "business"; and
- ..... maintain a high moral standard of living which does not bring the profession into disrepute.

[19.14] While the codes provide a list of principles to be followed, the very length and variety of values and principles expressed can be bewildering. Codes of ethics may guide a person in establishing values, but moral dilemmas involve choosing between more than one value, or principle. What is more important — telling the truth or protecting someone from harm? This chapter is not concerned with establishing priorities among values: there are many books that will provide guidance for that. This chapter is about establishing a rational and consistent approach to weighing values that are accepted by the individual health carer.

[19.15] As mentioned in Chapter 13, most jurisdictions provide (directly or indirectly) for disciplinary action for unethical conduct. Most registration boards have drawn (or are in the process of drawing) up codes of ethics, as have, for example, the State nurses unions and many hospitals. Health carers are thus put on notice that they should be familiar with these.

Dealing with a Decision-Making Dilemma

[19.16] Ethical principles are not absolute rules: they guide one's actions rather than dictate them. They prescribe behaviour, setting out what one "ought" to do, and thus create duties. Ethical dilemmas arise from a conflict of duties (for example, where a patient discloses to his or her psychiatrist that he or she intends to harm a third person—the duty to

[19.16] maintain a client's confidence and not disclose that information, and the duty to warn someone when we know they are in danger). This requires the weighing of values and determining to which one priority will be given. The following is a suggested guide only.

Step 1: Investigate and Communicate Facts and Reasons for Action

[19.17] The first step in resolving ethical dilemmas such as those posed in [19.1] is to make sure one has a firm grasp of all the facts. The nature of the diagnosis, the prognosis, and just what the client has been told must be known. An example is where a patient is diagnosed as having cancer and the prognosis is poor, doctor and family do not want the patient to be told, and a health carer caring for the patient believes both that this is wrong and that the patient should be informed. The health carer should be aware that there may be considerations of which he or she is ignorant, and which others have taken into account. Talking to doctor and family should establish the reasons for not telling the patient. Given that the client's attitudes and likely reaction to the news, as well as the attitudes of her or his family have been investigated, the reasons for not telling the client can be addressed. They may convince the carer that in fact not telling the patient is more in accord with their hierarchy of values than not, or, conversely, help the family to realise that is not in the patient's interest not to know, and that it is their own need to come to grips with the situation that is the barrier to telling the patient. Realising this and discussing it may help them to deal with it. The situation should thus be discussed, and all who take care of the client should be given the opportunity to air their concerns and opinions. This process may shape the nature of the final outcome of the decision making and minimise stress, ill-feeling and anger, adversely affecting both client and carers.

[19.18] The importance of this initial step cannot be underestimated: very often in the author's experience what appears to be a serious ethical problem in the care of a client turns out to be a matter of lack of understanding of the facts, or of communication between those involved in the client's care. Communication in this context not only informs, it can be a source of support, education and clarification of one's values and emotions.

Step 2: Ascertain Legal Obligations

[19.19] If, after considering the facts (and reasons for the course others are taking if this is relevant) the health carer is still unsure of the right course of action, the next thing to do is to consider the law. Are there any legal requirements attached to the situation in question? The answer may make the course of action clear cut. Good health care goes beyond considering whether one is covered by law, and in some cases, as described at [19.3], the issue becomes an ethical one. Where the law clearly establishes a course of action it should be followed but health carers might consider agitating for change in the law where it is contrary to moral statements. [19.25]

An Example—Disclosing Information

[19.20] An example of a dilemma is the situation outlined above where the nurse is asked by a client, "Do I have cancer?", when the doctor and family do not wish the person to know. The health carer has been instructed not to tell the client, but feels that he or she should know, particularly as the person suspects something serious is wrong, and is anxious.

Is there a Legal Obligation to Tell the Truth?

[19.21] There is no legal obligation to tell someone the truth. However, one can be sued for failing to give information to a person to their detriment, and deliberate lack of full and frank disclosure can amount to this. Presumably no one is trying to harm the client, and it has been decided not to tell because:

- ..... telling the client is too difficult for those involved; or
- ..... of their conviction that it is in the client's interest to act in this way.

[19.22] There is a third possible reason—to hide the facts from the client and so prevent legal action. This is considered below at [19.55]ff.

Telling the Truth is Too Difficult

[19.23] In this case the way to resolve the problem may be to engage someone else to tell the person, perhaps a counsellor or friend, or a colleague who is more experienced, or to seek assistance or support in facing this difficult task. In this case the problem is not an ethical one, but a practical one. Calling on the resources of others is a legitimate way of easing a difficult burden.

Conviction that not Telling the Truth is in Client's Interest

[19.24] Where the concern is for the client's wellbeing, it is a matter of considering whether withholding the truth is indeed in her or his interest. This involves firstly establishing facts. Would the client be likely to suffer harm if not told the truth? Does not telling the truth amount to deception (and does that matter?) It could be that the relationship between client and health carer(s) (or indeed the client–hospital relationship) could be destroyed if he or she also feels that health professionals cannot be trusted.

Legal Obligations to the Client

[19.25] From the legal point of view the probability of harm is also an important consideration where it results in detriment to the patient in terms of health or quality of life. Clients could not sue the doctor or

[19.25] hospital simply because they were not told the truth: they would have to show that:

1).....withholding the information was unreasonable; and
2).....he or she actually suffered some physical or economic harm as the result of this.

If it is foreseeable that failure to disclose the truth would cause such harm, and there is no reasonable justification for so doing, then the person should be told, according to law. On the other hand, the health carer may be concerned that telling the client may cause severe depression, or lead to other harm. In weighing up the relative potential for harm, the answer to the dilemma may be resolved by considering legal obligations to the client.

Legal Obligations to Employer and Colleagues

[19.26] Legal obligations are owed to the employer. Does the law require one to carry out the orders of a superior without question (see Ch 6)?

[19.27] One obligation owed to the employer, and indeed also to one's colleagues, is to maintain the client's confidence in them. This is an ethical duty, and in some cases also a legal one (see Ch 11).

[19.28] A consideration of the legal issues arising from this dilemma may determine what action should be taken, and resolve the issue, that is, the decision is a legal one. However, on balancing the harm that may result from either course of action, and the legal ramifications of that action (that is, looking at the *consequences* of either telling the client or not doing so), it may be difficult to determine which is the best course to take. This leads to the need to weigh the relative *values* the health carer puts on the different outcomes that would result from either action. It is time to consider the third type of issue: the ethical decision.

Step 3: Determine the Best Ethical Option

[19.29] Where there is no legal imperative to act in a particular way (that is the options are all legally acceptable, the question becomes what option to adopt based on moral principles (see for example, Johnstone (1989), p 76—she would add care and compassion to these (Ch 4)). These are:

- .....*beneficence*: the aim of health care should be to benefit the client, and the benefit should be greater than any burdens placed on her or him by medical treatment;
- .....*autonomy*: medical care should promote the self-determination of clients, which means that all decision making should ultimately be theirs;
- .....*non-maleficence*: the avoidance of harm to the client. Some writers argue that it is important to distinguish the stricture not to harm others, from that of aiming to benefit, as the latter may require active measures to prevent them from foreseeable harm, and may mean taking risks to do this; and

▌.....*justice*: can mean either giving a person their due, or ensuring equal access to the benefits available. Both of these meanings can apply to health care. In our society it is recognised that a person's due is reasonable, dignified medical care, based on their need for it, and equal access to medical care means that no one is the subject of unreasonable discrimination.

[19.33]

[19.30] There are other values which have been adopted, those above being considered "first order" principles, others, such as truth telling, loyalty to employer and colleagues, serving as "lower order" principles or rules, providing the means for "first order" principles to be assembled in rank according to one's values. This terminology is the author's. Writers distinguish between principles and rules (for example, Johnstone (1989), p 83). The model given in this chapter is based on a "rational" approach to ethics, relying as it does on a set of abstract rules and eschewing emotion. Even utilitarians, who recognise that people have desires and interests, work at rules of rational choice for maximising the satisfaction of these, concentrate on which emotions to cultivate and which desires to change, determining this by rational calculation rather than feelings. However in formulating the model set out here, an attempt has been made to take into account the feminist-generated "ethic of care". Held ((1994), pp 169-170) says of this approach:

> Some think it should supersede 'the ethic of justice' of traditional or standard moral theory. Others think it should be integrated with the theory of justice and rules . . . Achieving and maintaining trusting, caring relationships is quite different from acting in accord with rational principles, or satisfying the individual desires of either self or other. Caring, empathy, feeling with others . . . all may be better guides to what morality requires in actual contexts than abstract rules of reason, or rational calculation.

The author takes an integrative approach.

[19.31] Given that these principles are adopted, they underlie an imperative:

▌.....*If X is a desirable or necessary result of medical care, more than any other result, one ought to do those things which will achieve X.*

[19.32] For example, if one believes that autonomy is a desirable or necessary value to exercise, one would be impelled to carry out acts which foster it, and be constrained from those which inhibit it.

▌.....*If, however, in bringing about X one also causes Y, which is not desirable, and one wants to avoid Y, one is impelled to act in a way which maximises X and minimises Y to the best of one's abilities.*

[19.33] That is, for example, if to promote a person's autonomy will involve giving that person information which will cause them severe emotional harm one may be impelled to modify the amount or type of information always considering support and counselling to allow for as

[19.33] much autonomy that is compatible with achieving the desired or necessary outcome.

This imperative also applies where an undesirable outcome, is the result of any available option.

[19.34] In practice, where a problem is an ethical one, the task is generally a choice between conflicting duties. These may be legal duties (for example a duty to provide reasonable care for a client, and a duty to carry out the directions of another). They may be duties dictated by moral values (for example, the duty to uphold the client's autonomy, and the duty to prevent him or her from suffering harm from disclosure of information). It is most likely that the health carer will have to choose between favouring one accepted moral principle (such as always telling the truth) over another (such as never causing the client harm or distress). The question becomes, which principle goes? In the case of the hypothetical client with cancer described above the conflict is between beneficence (causing as little pain as possible by not telling her or him) and autonomy and justice (telling the truth). One could argue that the other values mentioned above are also involved. The answer produced should be capable of being expressed as a moral statement, which is consistent with any other moral statement the health carer may develop, and applicable to all situations. Moral statements are explained further below.

Towards Ethical (Duty) Statements[3]

[19.35] Moral values are expressed in the formula: *"In situation X, person P ought to do Y."* This involves determining:

- ..... the conditions under which the statement is applicable;
- ..... what is to be done; and
- ..... who is to do it.

[19.36] Such statements should be clearly differentiated from other statements, such as:

- ..... statements of fact: *"In situation X person P does Y"*;
- ..... aesthetic statements: *"Person P likes to do Y"*; and
- ..... commands: *"Person P is to do Y"*.

---

[3] This analysis is developed from Brody (1981), pp 18ff.

Expressive Statement

[19.37] Often people consider they are making a moral statement, when in fact they are expressing a personal reaction to a particular situation. This is rather an *expressive statement* (or "gut reaction"), for example:

A. **Expressive statement: "I feel that people should know if they have cancer."**

This is a "should/ought" statement, but does it apply all the time?

Value Statement

[19.38] To give validity to a moral statement one should be able to establish the reason which underlies it. This becomes a *value statement*:

B. **Value statement: "People should know if they have cancer (because . . .)."**

A value statement sets out what is "good" or "bad", "right or wrong". In determining whether there is justification for the expressive statement, it may become apparent that there should be some qualifications to it. One should not be able to think of any situation which negates a proposed justification. For example if the reason given in statement B was "because people always benefit from the truth", one should not be able to think of any circumstances where someone would not benefit from being told the truth. Philosophers commonly describe a hypothetical situation: A Jewish family is hiding in your house. The Gestapo knock on the door and ask if you are harbouring any Jews. It is questionable whether telling the truth in this case would benefit the Jews. This, they argue, throws doubt on the proposed justification, and the value statement must be qualified accordingly.

Prescriptive Statement

[19.39] One can then turn the value statement into a *prescriptive statement*—one which qualifies the value statement (there are arguably few or perhaps even no value statements which can be applied absolutely):

C. **Prescriptive statement: "In situation X (or every) situation, person P (or every person) ought to tell someone if they have cancer."**

Duty Statement

[19.40] A prescriptive statement turns the principle into an "ought" (duty) statement, relating the duty to a particular person or people.

D. **Duty statement: "The duty to tell a person if they have cancer is more (or less) important than any other duty (or X duty) to them or others."**

[19.40] A duty statement also stipulates situations and conditions under which action ought to be carried out. Can you think of a situation in which a health carer may not have a duty to tell someone if they have cancer? Some have argued that there are different cultural approaches to telling a person they are going to die, which would place exceptions on medical staff directly giving this news to them. Should we be influenced by the belief that such information would make a person depressed? Is it more important to tell them anyway, so that they can prepare themselves and their affairs, and not find out in a way that makes them feel the truth has wrongly been withheld from them? (It may be instructive to consider other expressive statements such as "I feel that health carers should never disclose to a third person the fact that a person is HIV-positive".) In considering exceptions to the original statement, one can identify duties arising from prescriptive statements, and rank them in order of importance.

[19.41] Another way of determining whether one can advance from an expressive statement to a prescriptive statement is by asking the question: What would happen if the proposed prescriptive statement were to be applied? Would all the consequences (for example, those suggested [19.44]) be acceptable, given *other* moral values which one holds, and which also form the basis of prescriptive statements (such as "you should never harm another by your actions" or "you should treat all people equally")? One might modify the statement about telling a person they have cancer to take into consideration different situations so that it is compatible with other statements (or change the other statements, if the duty to tell the person they have cancer is considered to apply at all times in all situations).

One Approach: Consider Consequences

[19.42] One approach to deciding which is the best course of action to take, in line with one's values (expressed as either a prescriptive or duty statement), is to list the consequences of each possible course of action in a given situation, and consider whether they are consistent with those values. Figure 19.1 represents this process. This approach can, to some extent, incorporate principles from two different ethical theories, the "deontological" theories (based on keeping to binding moral rules) and "teleological" theories (based on the results of one's actions). Brody (1981) outlines a "consequentialist" model (at p 354), on which this outline is based. He describes the different ethical philosophies, as do Johnstone ((1989), Ch 3) and Singer (1994).

[19.43] It is not a matter of acting intuitively and justifying the actions later: we ought to make our values explicit so that we can judge the consequences of acts by:

- .....stating values and consequences in plain language; and
- .....listing value statements and consequences in close juxtaposition, to make direct comparisons and decide the outcome most in line with those values.

[19.44] Some inconsistencies in one's thinking may become apparent. For example, one may start with the ethical statement that abortion is wrong because all surgery for non-illness is wrong. This leads to a prescriptive statement, for example that "Where a person is not physically ill he or she should not have surgery". The consequence of this statement would lead to the rejection of plastic surgery where the client is not "physically ill". If one believes that plastic surgery in some situations (for example, to restructure facial bone after injury which has resulted in disfigurement) is acceptable, it is necessary to revise the original statement: not all surgery for non-illness is wrong. It also means that one cannot reject abortion for this reason. Further reasons must be considered, and unless they can be applied to all possible situations must also be discarded as a ground for rejecting abortion. The process is thus repeated with each proposed ethical statement, considering all possible consequences of applying it, until consistency has been achieved.

Figure 19.1 sets out three possible outcomes of considering the consequences of a proposed action. The action will result in either:

1)......one consequence, which is consistent with all one's value statements;
2)......several consequences which are consistent with all one's value statements; or
3)......any consequence which is consistent with one value statement conflicting with another value statement.

HEALTH CARE AND THE LAW

[19.44] These are explained further:

▮▮▮ FIGURE 19.1

STEPS IN ETHICAL DECISION MAKING

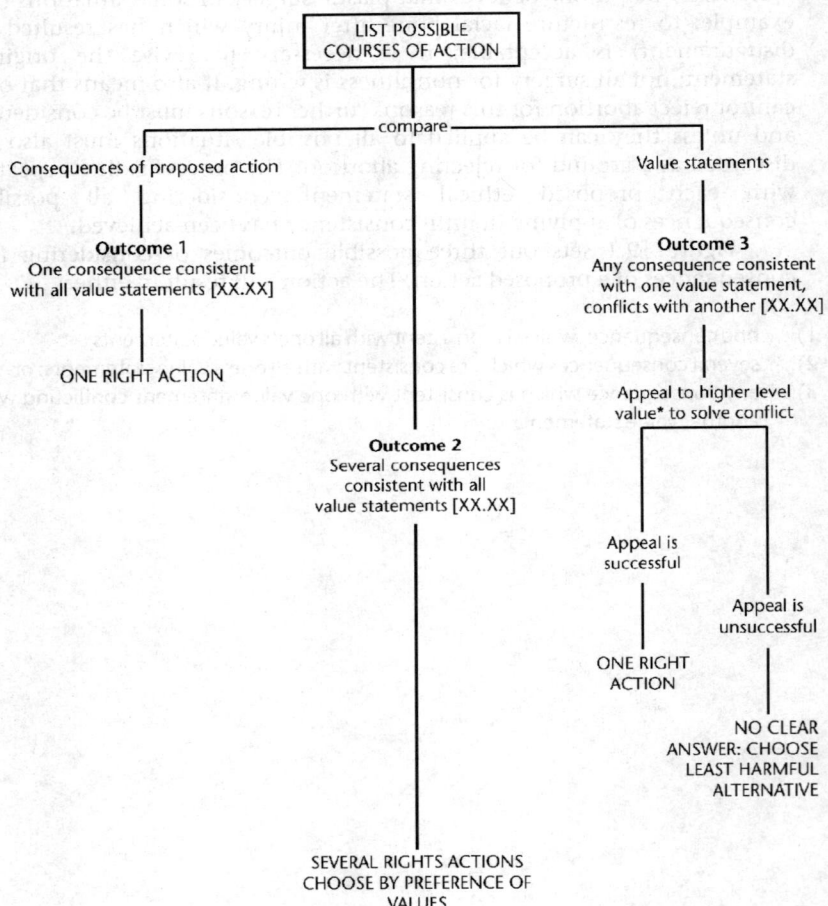

* A higher level value is one which is considered more important. For example, one might consider that all being equal, non-maleficence is more important than support of colleagues. For example, where a nurse is confronted by a conflict between protecting clients (such as reporting incompetent practices) and support of colleagues, he or she may invoke the higher value of non-maleficence to clients (consideration of the law might help to underscore this decision).

One Consequence Consistent with all Value Statements

[19.45] Here there is no real ethical problem. It is a situation where there is only one right way to act, and thus no question as to what one ought to do. Readers may be surprised, on attempting to list situations where this is the case, how few they can come up with.

Several Consequences Consistent with all Value Statements

[19.46] There may be several ways of dealing with a situation which may be consistent with one's moral values. In this case one is dealing with two "right" outcomes rather than two evils. Where this occurs it is necessary for health carers to weigh the relative preference of the different outcomes, according to their values (for example, whether it is preferable to preserve the life of a terminally ill person or allow the person to die more quickly and humanely—where both are morally acceptable outcomes. If one accepts that beneficence and non-maleficence are "higher order" principles, and preservation of life is a lesser order one, serving to bring about the higher order principles, one could argue that the dilemma is answered by choosing the "higher order" principle, beneficence, over the lower order one, preservation of life.

A Consequence which is Consistent with One Value Statement and Conflicts with Another

[19.47] Here one has to rank one's values, determining which have priorities over others. Where this leads to one consequence being consistent with the higher level value outlined above, there is a preferred action. As the other values are also desirable, one would consider action which gives as much scope to recognition of those values as possible under the circumstances. Where one cannot identify a clear preference for at least one value over others, all values being considered of equal importance, there is no clear answer.

Examples of Ethical Dilemmas

[19.48] Some examples of real life situations follow, to provide practical suggestions for dealing with different decision-making problems.

▮▮▮ EXAMPLE 1
LIGHT GETS IN THEIR EYES

> X is concerned that the bright fluorescent lights in the intensive care ward, which are never turned off, are distressing to the patients there. However, they are considered necessary for proper care of the patients. X identifies a possible conflict between values: that of the comfort of the patients, and their proper medical treatment.

[19.49] **[19.49]** However, following the steps outlined above, he or she realises that several fallacies might be involved here: first the belief that the constant light is necessary all the time for the recovery of all the patients (a presumed scientific fact), and secondly, that it has to be so bright (limited, either-or solution). X determines to do some research and clarify the facts, and, if he or she determines that the accepted amount of light is not necessary, to investigate alternative lighting with the supervisor. The facts may indicate that constant bright lights are necessary for reasonable treatment.

[19.50] Having determined just what the situation is with regard to that particular ward and the patients cared for there, X considers the consequences of different approaches to the problem according to Figure 19.1 and thus reaches a conclusion with regard to the legal and ethical obligations to her or his clients. Whatever the outcome X will at least have the satisfaction of knowing that he or she has attempted to maximise a very important value principle: beneficence (benefiting each patient), while giving all reasonable consideration to other values, such as non-maleficence (not causing undue harm or distress to any of them).

EXAMPLE 2
THE ERRANT ANAESTHETIST

An anaesthetist leaves a patient under anaesthesia in the care of a nurse while he watches a sporting event on television. The nurse reports the incident, and the anaesthetist is admonished. He later begins to ask colleagues who it was who "dobbed him in", implying she will suffer for her actions. The nurse wonders if she did the right thing.

[19.51] In this case the nurse, after considering the facts and referring to Figure 19.1, decides she has to weigh the consequences of patient care, responsibility to her employer and loyalty to a colleague. She can then review her expressive, value, prescriptive and duty statements to arrive at a decision that is consistent with these. Given that she concludes that the consequences of reporting the event are more acceptable than those of not doing so in this case, she can refine her duty statement to include such situations among those imposing a duty to report to the administration. The opposite result would occur if she decides the consequences of *not* reporting are acceptable.

[19.52] In a similar incident related to the author the nurse's colleagues refused to disclose who had reported the doctor when he sought this information. This action was consistent with the values they held in relation to both beneficence (patient care) and justice (loyalty to a colleague).

▌▌▌ EXAMPLE 3   [19.55]
THE CARDIAC ARREST

A young woman has a cardiac arrest while under anaesthesia. Y (an intern) writing up her notes is told: "Do not put this in the report". After considering the facts involved and consulting Figure 19.1 Y concludes that significant harmful consequences to A (the patient) (through lack of information) if it is not recorded in the patient's notes, and significant harm to others (through repeated similar action in the future) could result if the adverse reaction to anaesthesia is not reported, but that she may be victimised if the arrest is recorded. Y wants to do the right thing. Should the matter be recorded in the client's notes? Should it be reported to the appropriate authority?

[19.53] This problem is not only an ethical one, it also involves legal issues. There are strong legal reasons for recording the cardiac arrest. Y is not only protecting those concerned who are neglecting their responsibility for reasonable care through responsible recording, she is also acting negligently in not recording the event (see Chs 6 and 7). There is also a duty to the employing hospital to take reasonable measure to ensure patient care and safety (see Ch 11).

[19.54] Ways of dealing with this sort of situation are to take the matter to the supervisor or the next uninvolved administrator (see [19.57]) from whom one should receive support, or, as a general measure, to relieve staff of the responsibility of having to deal with this sort of pressure, to institute the use of incident reports (see [19.61]).

▌▌▌ EXAMPLES 4 AND 5
THE UNFORTUNATE REMOVALS

A woman who has a lump in her breast undergoes surgery to determine if it is malignant. While she is anaesthetised a section is sent to pathology for testing, while the surgeon waits for a result, ready to remove the breast if it is malignant. The surgeon does not want to wait for the result of tests, and, convinced they would be positive anyhow, removes the breast. In fact the results are negative. Staff are concerned that if the woman is not told of the mistake she will believe she has cancer, and if she is told they are revealing information which is damaging to the hospital and surgeon.

A woman is having a caesarean haemorrhage and instead of giving her a drug to arrest the bleeding, the anaesthetist mistakenly injects her with a drug which has the opposite effect and she bleeds even more. As a result she has to have a hysterectomy. Those who witness the event are concerned as to whether they should inform her of the reason for the hysterectomy.

[19.55] In this type of case, where health carers believe it is in the patient's interest to know, the issue involves legal considerations as well as ethical ones. Given the analysis of the law regarding disclosure, health carers are reminded that documents are the property of the hospital, subject to freedom of information where it is a public hospital.

[19.56] **[19.56]** Nurses may have a specific perspective in such a case. It is not the province of the nurse to discuss the doctor's treatment with her or his patient. The nurse could risk adverse action from the employer if the patient were told and there is thus a disincentive to disclose information. The nurse may thus find there is a difference between her or his value statements and the law.

[19.57] In this type of case some may argue that the harm done to the principles of loyalty to employer and colleagues would be serious, undermining trust in medical care in general, and resulting in defamation of innocent people. This may or may not be a valid argument. It is considered valuable, however, to look for possible alternatives to either/or solutions to dilemmas, and to minimise erosion of any ethical principle. This approach could be used here. The advisable action in the first instance may be to approach the nursing administration and agitate for some action to be taken, particularly where it is crucial to the patient's interests to be informed of the situation. The patient in example 4 perhaps has a more urgent interest in the information than the patient in example 5. One could argue however, that they both have an equal interest in knowing the truth.

[19.58] If hospital administration does not provide assistance, health carers may decide to go higher up the chain of control, until satisfaction is achieved. These matters are of such a serious nature that they are also candidates for consideration by the relevant disciplinary tribunal.

[19.59] What action is taken would depend on the result of comparison of the consequences of different alternatives with the nurse's personal value statements and priorities. It can be seen, however, that most serious ethical matters are also likely to be legal ones.

[19.60] One result of not disclosing facts to clients is that health carers might be expected to live a lie, for example, where a client wrongly believes he or she either does or does not have cancer. In this case they could, in the author's view, be justified in expressing their concern at being asked to act contrary to their values, and attempt to change the situation.

[19.61] A way of making health workers more accountable was adopted by the administrator of a theatre unit in a large hospital. This was the mandatory use of incident reports for every unusual or unanticipated occurrence which happened during surgery and was to include irregular consent procedures. The incident reports were to be signed by both the surgeon and the assisting nurse. There was no discretion in the matter. The result of doing this was twofold:

- ..... the reporting of the event was required, so no personal blame could be placed for making a report and there could be no recriminations; and
- ..... the number of unusual and unanticipated events was reduced considerably, as staff sought to avoid the need to resort to these forms.

[19.62] It is suggested that administration of hospitals should provide an avenue for reporting and discussing difficult situations, and health carers should not only be made to feel that this is encouraged, but that they will be supported when dealing with more senior staff.

Conclusion

[19.63] There are no perfect answers to these problems, and from the examples given above it can be seen that practicalities and politics may play a distorting role in decision making and should be taken into account. Consequently one cannot have an ethical program that will solve all of the problems all of the time. The purpose of this book, however, has been to argue that, as those involved hold the status of being professional health carers, they should carry the increasing responsibilities as well as the privileges which are accorded a fully-fledged profession. Accordingly, this will increase expertise and technological sophistication, as well as a heightened awareness of their own dignity and integrity. All health carers will then more consciously and effectively advocate the ethical and legal principles they adopt, and seek, in their own right, to ensure these are given effect and promoted by legislation and health care practice. Carers may sometimes need to support one another, and it is anticipated that there will be a growing recognition of the need for mutual assistance within the various health care professions and a perception by all health carers of themselves as principled professionals who can be trusted to understand the legal, ethical and social context in which they work.

■ ■ ■

REFERENCES AND FURTHER READING

There are many books that outline ethical principles and their use in medicine. This list includes some titles added for the third edition.

Annas, G, *Judging Medicine* (Humana Press, New Jersey, 1988)

Brody, H, *Ethical Decisions in Medicine* (Little Brown, Boston, 1981)

Bromberger, B and Fife-Yeomans, J, *Deep Sleep* (Simon & Schuster, Sydney, 1991)

Campbell, A, et al, *Practical Medical Ethics* (Oxford University Press, Auckland, 1992)

Held, V, "Reason, Gender and Moral Theory" in Singer, P, *Ethics* (Oxford University Press, Oxford, 1994)

Johnstone, M, *Bioethics: A Nursing Perspective* (WB Saunders/Bailliere Tindall, Sydney, 1989) (third edition (1999))

Kuhse, H, *Caring: Nurses, Women and Ethics* (Blackwell, Oxford, 1997)

Kuhse, H and Singer, P, *Bioethics: an Anthology* (Blackwell Publishers, Oxford, 1999)

McLean, S (ed), *Death, Dying and the Law* (Dartmouth Publishing Co, Aldershot, 1996)

Mason, J and McCall-Smith, R, *Law and Medical Ethics* (Butterworths, London, 1983)

McConnell, T, *Moral Issues in Health Care: An Introduction to Medical Ethics* (Wandsworth, California, 1982)

Melden, A, *Ethical Theories: A Book of Readings* (2nd ed, Prentice-Hall, NJ, 1967)

Purtill, R, *Thinking about Ethics* (Prentice-Hall, NJ, 1976)

Reamer, F, *Ethical Dilemmas in Social Service* (Columbia University Press, New York, 1982)

Singer, P, *Practical Ethics* (Cambridge University Press, London, 1979)

Appendix One

A GUIDE TO ABBREVIATIONS USED IN LAW REPORT CITATIONS*

Where a date and/or number is given for a case (for example, "27 June 1980, SC NSW, No 226/80") this means the case is "unreported" and not published in the volumes of reports for that court. It is kept in a volume of "Unreported Cases" for the court, held by some Law Libraries, or available through them. Some of the most recent cases may be published by the time this book is read. Most unreported cases on health care referred to in this book are summarised in the *Australian Health and Medical Law Reporter*.

A	Atlantic Reporter, first series: US commercial reporting service which covers State Supreme Court reports from the north-eastern States, 1885-1938
A 2d	Atlantic Reporter, second series (from 1938)
AC	Law Reports, Appeal Cases (England) 1891-present
A Crim R	Australian Criminal Reports
ACL	Australian Current Law (commercial service which provides monthly information and case digests)
ACTR	Australian Capital Territory Reports (bound with ALR)
ACTSC	ACT Supreme Court
ALD	Administrative Law Decisions, Australia (reports of the Administrative Appeals Tribunal)
ALR	Australian Law Reports
ALJR	Australian Law Journal Reports
All ER	All England Law Reports from 1936
All ER Rep	All England Law Reports Reprints 1558-1935

---

* For a fuller list, consult a Law Dictionary.

ALMD	Australian Legal Monthly Digest (commercial service which provides monthly information and case digests)
ALR	Australian Law Reports
Aust Torts Rep	Australian Torts Reports: Commercial reporting service
AWCCD	Australian Workers Compensation Case Digests
CA	Court of Appeal
Cal App 3d	Californian Appeal Cases, third series
Cal Reptr	Californian Reporter
CB(NS)	Common Bench Reports, New Series
Ch	English Reports, Chancery Division
CLR	Commonwealth Law Reports (Australia)
Cr App R	Criminal Appeal Reports
DCR(NSW)	District Court Reports (New South Wales)
DLR	Dominion Law Reports (Canada)
ER	English Reports
EOC	Equal Opportunity Cases (commercial reporting service, Australia)
ExD	Law Reports, Exchequer Division, UK (1875-1880)
F	Federal Reports, US (1880-1924)
F 2d	Federal Reports, US, second series (from 1924)
FCR	Federal Court Reports
FLC	Family Law Cases (commercial reporting service, Australia)
FLR	Federal Law Reports 1956-present (Australia); Family Law Reports (UK)
F Supp	Federal Supplement US (federal District Court cases)
Fam LR	Family Law Reports (commercial reporting service, Australia)
HCA	High Court of Australia
HL	House of Lords
KB	Kings Bench Division (England)
LR (NSW)	New South Wales Law Reports 1880-1900

Appendix 1—A GUIDE TO ABBREVIATIONS USED IN LAW REPORT CITATIONS ■ 647

LT	Law Times Reports (England)
Lloyd's Rep Med	Lloyd's Reports (Medical) Medical Case Reports (UK) from 1998
NE	North Eastern Reporter (US commercial reporting service which covers State Supreme Court reports from the north eastern region, 1881-1936)
NE 2d	North Eastern Reporter, 2nd Series (from 1936)
NJ	New Jersey Supreme Court Reports (US)
NSWDCR	New South Wales District Court Reports
NSWLR	New South Wales Law Reports
NTR	Northern Territory Reports (bound with ALR)
NW	North Western Reporter (US commercial reporting service which covers State Supreme Court reports from the north western region, 1879-1941)
NW 2d	North Western Reporter, 2nd Series (from 1941) New York Supplement, Second Series (US)
NZLR	New Zealand Law Reports
Med LR	Medical Law Reports (UK)
P	Law Reports, Probate, Divorce and Admiralty Division (England) 1891-1971 or Pacific Reporter (US commercial reporting service which covers US Supreme Court reports from the western seaboard, 1883-1931)
P 2d	Pacific Reporter, Second Series (from 1931)
PD	Law Reports, Probate, Divorce and Admiralty Division (England) 1876-1890
QB	Law Reports Queen's Bench, Division 1891-present
QBD	Law Reports, Queen's Bench Division 1875-1890
QdR	Queensland Reports 1958-present
QSCR	Supreme Court Reports (Queensland) 1860-1881
QSR	Queensland State Reports 1902-1957
SASR	South Australian State Reports from 1971
SCR	Supreme Court Reports (NSW) 1862-1876
SCR (Canada)	Supreme Court Reports, Canada

SE	South-Eastern Reporter (US commercial reporting service which covers State Supreme Court reports from the south-eastern region 1887-1939)
SW 2d	South-Eastern Reporter, Second Series (from 1939)
SR (NSW)	State Reports (NSW) to 1970
SR (WA)	State Reports, Western Australia, 1980-present
SW	South-Western Reporter (US commercial reporting service which covers State Supreme Court reports from the south-western region, 1886-1929)
SW 2d	South-Western Reporter, Second Series (from 1928)
So 2d	Solicitors' Reports, Second Series (US)—covering all States
Tas LR	Tasmanian Law Reports 1904-1940
Tas R	Tasmanian Reports
Tas SR	Tasmanian State Reports
TLR	Tasmanian Law Reports 1905-1940, or The Times Law Reports (UK) 1884-1952
VLR	Victorian Law Reports to 1956
VR	Victorian Reports from 1956
WALR	Western Australian Law Reports to 1959
WAR	Western Australian Law Reports from 1959
WCBD (Vic)	Workers Compensation Board Decisions (Vic)
WCBD (WA)	Workers Compensation Board Decisions (WA)
WCR (NSW)	Workers Compensation Reports (NSW)
WCR (Q)	Workers Compensation Reports (Queensland)
WLR	Weekly Law Reports (England)
WN (NSW)	Weekly Notes (New South Wales)
WWR	Western Weekly Reports (Canada)

Appendix Two

MORE CASES ON NEGLIGENCE*

Doctors

Abortion: incomplete, infant permanently injured (*Greco v Ors v Arvind & Ors* (13 December 1994, SC NSW, Nos 14379/87, 14595/90)).

Back injury, orthopaedic surgeon liable (*Andrew Thackray v Phillip Hardcastle* (28 April 1999, District Court WA, CIV 2096 of 1997)).

Blindness, mismanaged post-operative care (*The Canterbury Hospital v Cappelletto* (17 May 1991, CA NSW)).

Blindness, negligently caused (*Cavanagh v Bristol & Weston Health Authority* (1992) 3 Med LR 49).

Blood transfusion, HIV infection (held not negligent) (*E v Australian Red Cross Society and Ors* (1991) ATPR ¶41-085).

Breast biopsy: resulting complications (held not negligent) (*Perceval v Mater Misericordiae Hospital* (7 March 2000, NSWSC 40404/98)).

Caesarean section, inadequate anaesthetisation (*Tucker v Hospital Corporation Australia Pty Ltd & Ors* (18 February 1998, SC NSW, No 12575/92)).

Cancer, (breast) failure to diagnose (*Talbot & Anor v Lusby* (14 July 1995, SC Qld, No 1899 of 1992)).

Cancer, (cervical) failure to diagnose (*O'Shea v Sullivan & Macquarie Pathology Services Pty Ltd* [1994] Aust Torts Reports ¶81-273).

Cancer, failure to diagnose (held not negligent) (*Sonja Harp v Andrew Campbell* (16 March 1998, District Court WA, No CIV 2107)).

Deep sleep therapy, mental illness, brain damage, foot drop (*Crawford v Bailey & Ors* (28 February 1992, SC NSW, No 17289/80)).

Defective equipment or drug or other substance (held not negligent) (*Roe v Minister of Health* [1954] 2 QB 66).

Diagnosis and treatment, abdominal and gynaecological surgery (*Darley v Shale* (CA NSW, 4 Med L R 161)).

---

* Further examples can be found in CCH (ed), *Australian Professional Liability (Medical)*, looseleaf service (CCH, Sydney, 1998) especially under tab heading "Damages". Examples of English cases can be found in Maddison, D, et al, *Bingham's Negligence Cases* (Sweet and Maxwell, London, 1996). Note, most of these cases are unreported. However summaries may be available in the *Australian Health and Medical Law Reporter*.

Diagnosis of inevitable abortion (held not negligent) (*Sellers v Cook & Ors* (1990) 2 Med LR 16).

Drug, Aminophylline negligently prescribed for infant (*Lipovac v Hamilton Holdings Pty Ltd*, 13 September 1996, SC ACT, No SC501 of 1993).

Drugs, negligent prescription (*B v Marinovich* [1999] NTSC 127 (22 November 1999)).

Ear nose & throat surgery, gross negligence (*Rajagopalan v Medical Board of South Australia* (11 September 1997, SC SA)).

Fabry's disease, failure to diagnose (held not negligent) (*Christopher Payne v Dr Jane Antony and Dr Simon Clarke* (District Court NSW, No 8083 of 1995)).

Failed vasectomy (*Macfarlane & Anor v Tayside Health Board* [1994] 4 All ER 961).

Failure to advise further consultation (*Tai v Hatzistavrou* [1999] NSWCA 306 (25 August 1999)).

Failure to refer (*Burnett v Kalokerinos* (22 March 1995, SC NSW, No 11138 of 1993)).

Financial constraints no excuse (*Bull v Devon Area Health Authority* [1993] 4 Med LR 22).

Fracture treatment (and damages where effect of harm does not hinder lifestyle) (*Simon Patrick Ward and Aspi Sahukar and Anor* (3 May 1999, District Court NSW)).

Meningitis—result of surgery (*Jackson v Vercoe* (29 May 1990, SC SA)).

Negligence not established by preferring one respectable body of opinion over another: failure to exercise skill required (*Maynard v West Midlands Regional Health Authority* [1984] 1 WLR 634).

Nervous shock, death of infant (*Strelee v Nelson & Ors* (13 December 1996, SC NSW, No 012401/90)).

Placenta negligent manual removal (*Lunn v Giblin* (30 July 1998, SC NT, GRA98008)).

Plastic surgery, removal of tatoos (*Dunning v Scheibher* (15 February 1998, SC NSW, No 13776 of 1998)).

Radiology treatment, insufficient protection causing injury to the patient (although defendant not a nurse) (*Gold v Essex County Council* [1942] 2 KB 293).

Spina Bifida: failure to diagnose (*Gilbert v Castagna* (2000) NSWSC NR600048/97 (25 March 2000)).

Stroke following vascular surgery (*Andrzej Domeradski by his tutor Robert Domeradski v Royal Prince Alfred Hospital* (11 May 1994, SC NSW, No 017496/87)).

Tubal ligation, failed (held not negligent) (*Stewart v Ng* [1999] NSWCA 387 21 (October 1999)).

Nurses

Bath scalding (ordered by the doctor) too hot (*Periowsky v Freeman* (1866) 176 ER 873).

Burns, hot water bottle allowed to come into contact with the patient causing severe burns (*Hall v Lees* [1904] 2 KB 602).

Caesarean section, failure to carry out proper monitoring (*Martin v East Yorkshire Health Authority, The Times*, 12 January 1993).

Catheter, rigid, forced into the patient and perforated an internal organ (*Powell v Streatham Manor Nursing Home* [1935] AC 243).

Drug, excessive quantity (decicaine) given to a patient led to the patient's death (*Fussell v Beddard* (1942) 2 BMJ 411).

Drug, extra (34 instead of 30) unauthorised injections of streptomycin administered (*Smith v Brighton and Lewes Hospital Management Committee, The Times*, 2 May 1958).

Drug, wrong dose administered by a nurse with fatal consequence (*Strangways-Lesmere v Clayton* [1936] 2 KB 11).

Failure of nurse to turn to a senior colleague, or a doctor in the event of difficulty (*Bull v Devon Health Authority* (unreported, 1989, CA UK 235)).

Injection given too close to acromion process (*Stepanovic, Denis v ACT* (3 November 1995, ACTSC 115)).

Instruments, failure to ensure correct and sterilised (*Crotch v Miles* (1930) BMJ 620). See also *The Times*, 15 July 1955.

Operating equipment, infected (*Voller v Portsmouth Corp* (1947) 203 LT 264).

Puerperal fever, failure to take proper action (*Lindsey County Council v Marshall* [1937] 1 AC 97).

Scalding (*Hillyer v St Bartholomews Hospital* [1909] 2 KB 821).

Sponge left in patient (*Langley and Anor v Glandore Pty Ltd and Anor* (3 October 1997, CA Qld, No 10784 of 1996)).

Swab left in patient (*Fox v Glasgow South Western Hospitals* [1955] SLT 337 (many older cases turned on swabs left in the body): *Dryden v Surrey County Council* (no negligence) [1936] 2 All ER 535).

Swabs: not checked (*Crotch v Miles* (1930) BMJ 620; *Van Wyck v Lewis* [1924] ADSA 438 (South Africa), *Urry v Bierer, The Times*, 15 July 1955).

Tube left in the body (*Morris v Winsbury-White* [1937] 4 All ER 494).

Ultraviolet ray treatment, unskilful (*Lavelle v Glasgow Infirmary* (1930) SC 123, (1931) SC(HL)34, (1932) SC 247).

Hospital

Trachostomy Tube blocked (*Blackburn-Newcastle Health Authority, The Times*, 2 August 1988).

Dentists

Failure of proper skill and attention (*Doughty v General Dental Council* [1987] 3 All ER 843).

Lack of information, negligent treatment (*Campbell v Dental Board of Vic* [1999] VSC 113 (23 April 1999)).

Appendix Three

SUMMARY OF THE NATIONAL PRIVACY PRINCIPLES

(See section 6 of the *Privacy Act* 1988 (Cth))

"Organisation" means an individual, body corporate, partnership, any other unincorporated association, or trust that is not a small business (making less than $3 million), registered political party, agency, State or Territory authority or prescribed instrumentality of a State or Territory. These are covered by other legislation or common law.

Collection

An organisation must not collect information unless it is necessary for one or more of its functions or activities and is collected lawfully, by fair means and without being intrusive.
Reasonable steps must be taken to ensure the individual is aware of all of the following:

- ..... the identity of the collecting organisation, its contact details and the individual's right to gain access to the information;
- ..... the purposes for which the information is collected and to whom the information is likely to be disclosed; and
- ..... (if applicable) any laws requiring the information to be collected and the main consequences to the individual if he or she fails to provide all or part of the information required.

If it is reasonable and practicable to do so, personal information must be collected only from the individual. Unless a serious threat to a person's life or health would result, reasonable steps must be taken to inform him or her of the matters listed above that are obtained from someone else.
Sensitive information can be collected by an organisation if:

- ..... the individual has consented;
- ..... the collection is required by law;
- ..... the collection is necessary to prevent or lessen an imminent threat to life or health of any individual and the individual is physically or mentally unable to consent to its collection; or
- ..... the information is required to establish, exercise or defend a legal claim.

Exceptions to the above, where health information is concerned are where:

- ......it is necessary to provide a health service to the individual and is collected as required by law or in accordance with rules developed by competent health or medical bodies that deal with binding obligations of confidentiality; or
- ......it is impractical to obtain the individual's consent and the collection of the information:
    - necessary for purposes of public health and safety or the monitoring of a health service;
    - identifying information that is necessary for that purpose; or
    - is required by law, in accordance with rules developed by competent health or medical bodies that deal with binding obligations of confidentiality or guidelines approved by the Privacy Commissioner.

Use

Personal information must generally only be used for the purpose for which the individual consented (the "primary purpose" for which it was collected). However it may be used for a purpose other than the primary purpose (the "secondary purpose") where the two purposes are related (in the case of sensitive information, *directly* related) and where the individual would reasonably expect the organisation to use the information for that secondary purpose. Other, "secondary" purposes may be:

- ......disclosure to the person responsible, or the carer, of a person who is not competent, for the purpose of their care, and the disclosure is not contrary to any wish of the individual, and disclosure is limited to the extent necessary for the care. A person responsible is a parent, adult child or sibling, spouse, related adult, household member, guardian, medical attorney, intimate personal friend or nominated person (note the order);
- ......the fulfilment of requirements in relation to public health or safety set out above;
- ......the reporting of unlawful activity or in other circumstances where disclosure is required or authorised by law;
- ......the prevention of threats to life, health or public safety; and
- ......the lawful purpose of law enforcement bodies.

Quality and Security

Reasonable steps must be taken to ensure that personal information collected, used or disclosed by an organisation is accurate, complete up-to-date and secure. It must also be protected from misuse, loss and unauthorised access, modification or disclosure.

Personal information must be destroyed, or identifying information removed, where data is no longer needed for any authorised purpose.

Openness

An organisation must set out policies on the management of personal information and this must be clearly set out in a document available to anyone who requests it. When asked, an organisation must explain, in general terms, what sort of information is held, as well as why and how the organisation collects, holds, uses and discloses that information.

Access and Correction

An organisation must provide an individual with access to his/her own personal information on request. Exceptions apply in circumstances where, for example:

- ..... to do so would pose a serious and imminent threat to the life or health of any person;
- ..... the request is frivolous or vexatious or would compromise the privacy of another;
- ..... the information relates to legal proceedings, through which the information would be accessible, or other preparation for, conduct of, or proceedings before a court or tribunal.
- ..... access is prohibited by law; or
- ..... access would compromise an investigation of suspected unlawful activity, criminal justice procedures, the public revenue, the enforcement of laws.

Reasons must be given for refusing to give an individual access to their records. Organisations may charge a small fee for providing access to the information.
Organisations must take reasonable steps to correct the records of individuals who can show that they are not accurate, complete and up-to-date.

Anonymity

Wherever lawful and practicable, individuals must have the option of protecting their anonymity.

Appendix Four

SUMMARY OF SELECTED PROVISIONS OF THE DRUGS OF DEPENDENCE ACT 1989 (ACT)

This is a summary of some of the provisions of the *Drugs of Dependence Act* 1989 (ACT). The Act is comprehensive, and is one of three Acts covering drugs in the Australian Capital Territory. The other Acts are the *Poisons Act* 1933 (ACT), which deals with marketing, sale and supply of poisons, and the *Poisons and Drugs Act* 1978 (ACT), which deals with the supply, packaging storage of scheduled poisons and drugs, and the prescription of specifically designated poisons or drugs. Each Act has Regulations. Of these the most relevant to health carers is the *Drugs of Dependence Act,* and the summary below gives an indication of the many regulations applying to the handling of drugs by health carers. The provisions of these Acts and Regulations are similar to those in other jurisdictions.

For the purposes of this summary,

"Class I institution" means a hospital, nursing home or other institution that has a dispensary and is used for the accommodation, treatment and care of persons suffering from mental or physical conditions;

"Class II institution" means a nursing home or other institution that does not have a dispensary and is used for the accommodation, treatment and care of persons suffering from mental or physical conditions;

"Drugs of dependence" are listed in the Schedules to the Drugs of Dependence Regulations and include methadone;

"Intern" means a person approved under the *Medical Practitioners Registration Act* 1930 (ACT).

Supply and Administration

Issue of Prescriptions: s 57

A person who is not a doctor or veterinary surgeon shall not prescribe a drug of dependence. An intern shall not prescribe a drug of dependence except in the course of treatment conducted at an institution where he or she is working as an intern (penalty: $2,000 or imprisonment for 12 months, or both).

Drugs of Dependence Generally: s 58

A doctor shall not prescribe a drug of dependence except methadone for drug dependence or in any case for therapeutic reasons. If he or she believes on reasonable grounds that a person is drug dependent or has used a drug of dependence continuously for a period exceeding two months, the doctor must obtain the written approval of the Chief Health Officer before prescribing any drug of dependence for them. An exception is where the person requires the drug as a hospital inpatient for not more than 14 days. Unless a doctor believes on reasonable grounds that a person is suffering from narcolepsy, or is under the age of 19 years and suffering from hyperkinetic syndrome, he or she must obtain the written approval of the Chief Health Officer before prescribing an amphetamine for the treatment of that person (penalty: $2,000 or imprisonment for 12 months, or both).

Methadone: s 59

Where a doctor believes on reasonable grounds that a person is drug dependent he or she may, with the written approval of the Chief Health Officer, prescribe methadone for the treatment of the person's drug dependence if he or she believes on reasonable grounds that methadone would be suitable for such treatment, and the treatment is to be provided at a methadone programme treatment centre.

Written Prescriptions: s 60

Except for oral prescriptions, provided for below, a prescription for the supply of a drug of dependence shall, in addition to the requirements of any law in force in the Territory:

- ..... be in legible handwriting and written in terms and symbols used in ordinary professional practice;
- ..... specify the name, address and qualification of the person writing the prescription;
- ..... specify the date on which the prescription is issued;
- ..... specify the name and address of the person for whose treatment the drug is prescribed;
- ..... specify the drug, and the quantity, form and strength of the drug, to be supplied;
- ..... specify the number of times the drug is to be dispensed and, if it is to be dispensed more than once, the interval or intervals that are to elapse between the dispensations;
- ..... *if the prescription is for an unusual or dangerous dose—bear the initials of the person writing the prescription beside an underlined reference to the dose* (Italics added);
- ..... if the prescription is for an amphetamine:
  — if the Chief Health Officer has approved the prescription, be endorsed APPROVED BY CHO and have attached to it a copy of the approval; or
  — if the approval of the Chief Health Officer was not required under section 58—be endorsed "CHO APPROVAL NOT REQUIRED";

Appendix 4—SELECTED PROVISIONS OF THE DRUGS OF DEPENDENCE ACT 1989 (ACT) ■ 659

■ .....be signed by the person writing the prescription.

A doctor shall not issue a written prescription for a drug of dependence that fails to comply with these requirements (penalty: $2,000 or imprisonment for 12 months, or both).

Prescriptions Issued Orally: s 61

A doctor may only issue an oral prescription for a drug of dependence if the doctor believes on reasonable grounds that the quantity of the drug to be supplied is necessary for the emergency treatment of the person. It may only be issued to a pharmacist, or in a Class I Institution, if no pharmacist is available at the time at which the drug is required—a nurse in that institution.

The doctor must:

1) .....inform the pharmacist or nurse to whom the prescription is issued of:
   ■ her or his name, address and qualification;
   ■ the name and address of the person for whose treatment the drug is prescribed;
   ■ the drug, and the quantity, form and strength of the drug, to be supplied;
   ■ the number of times the drug is to be dispensed and, if it is to be dispensed more than once, the interval or intervals that are to elapse between the dispensations;
2) .....*if the prescription is for an unusual or dangerous dose—inform that pharmacist or nurse accordingly* (Italics added);
3) .....within 24 hours, furnish the pharmacist or nurse to whom it was issued with a written prescription corresponding to the orally issued prescription and complying with the requirements set out above for written prescriptions.

Where a pharmacist or nurse has supplied a drug of dependence in accordance with an orally issued prescription, and he or she does not, within 72 hours, receive a written prescription from the doctor who issued it, corresponding to the orally issued prescription and in the required form, the pharmacist or nurse must notify a drug inspector in writing accordingly (penalty: $2,000 or imprisonment for 12 months, or both).

Supply on Prescription: s 80

A person must not supply a drug of dependence upon a prescription unless the person is a pharmacist, doctor, person under their personal supervision or, where the drug is methadone, a nurse employed at a methadone programme treatment centre conducted by the Territory.

A doctor, or a person under the personal supervision of a doctor, shall not supply a drug of dependence upon a prescription otherwise than for the treatment of a patient under the doctor's professional care.

A person shall not supply a drug of dependence upon a prescription otherwise than to a person the supplier believes on reasonable grounds to be the person for whom the drug has been supplied, their guardian or parent, or the duly authorised agent of the person.

Where an intern prescribes a drug of dependence, a pharmacist in control of a dispensary in a community pharmacy (pharmacy with a dispensary other than a Class I Institution), or a person under the personal supervision of such a pharmacist, shall not supply that drug to any person upon that prescription (penalty: $2,000 or imprisonment for 12 months, or both).

Restrictions on Supply: s 81

A person must not supply a drug of dependence upon an order, written requisition or written prescription if that document:

1)..... appears to have been forged, or altered by someone other than the person who signed it;
2)..... bears the word "cancelled" or any other indication that it is cancelled; or
3)..... was written more than six months before it is presented for supply (penalty: $2,000 or imprisonment for 12 months, or both).

Forged Prescriptions, Requisitions and Orders: s 82

Where a person believes on reasonable grounds that an order, requisition or prescription for the supply of a drug of dependence has been forged or unlawfully altered they must immediately notify a police officer and a drug inspector, and forward a written report to the Chief Health Officer setting out the grounds on which he or she believes it to have been forged or altered (penalty: $2,000 or imprisonment for 12 months, or both).

Supplying Dextromoramide and Hydromorphone: s 83

A person shall not, upon a written prescription, supply dextromoramide or hydromorphone unless the person either is familiar with the handwriting of the person issuing the prescription, verifies with the person who apparently issued the prescription that they did indeed issue it, or knows the person for whom the drug was prescribed (penalty: $5,000 or imprisonment for two years, or both).

Administration—Witnesses: s 84

A person must not administer a drug of dependence to a patient in a methadone programme treatment centre conducted by the Territory (other than a specially licensed treatment centre) except, if they are an intern, in the presence of a medical practitioner, dentist or nurse, and in any other case, in the presence of a doctor, intern, dentist, pharmacist or nurse, or an enrolled nurse who has completed a course on the use of drugs of dependence approved for the purpose of this section by the Minister (penalty: $2,000 or imprisonment for 12 months, or both).

Distribution of Syringes—Approval: s 86 et seq

A doctor, pharmacist, nurse or health worker may apply in prescribed form to the Chief Health Officer for, and be granted, approval to supply syringes. An approval granted to a health worker is renewable yearly, and may be made subject to the condition that the health worker attend a further course of instruction. An approved person shall not, without reasonable excuse, fail to produce the approval for inspection by the police officer (penalty: $1,000).

Offences under Crimes Act, in Relation to Syringes: s 93

An approved person who supplies a syringe to another person shall not, by reason only of that supply, be taken to commit any offence under the *Crimes Act* 1900 (ACT) relating to supply, if they do so in the course of their professional practice or occupational duties, and have reasonable grounds for believing that it is to be used for the administration of a drug of dependence or prohibited substance. They must also believe that the supply of the syringe might assist in preventing the spread of disease. A person who prints or publishes a notice, announcement or advertisement in any form about the supply by approved persons of syringes in the circumstances referred to above shall not, by reason only of that printing or publishing, be taken to have committed any offence under the *Crimes Act* 1900 (ACT).

Records, Safe-Keeping and Disposal

Drug Registers: s 99 (see attached Form 1)

A "prescribed person" (including a pharmacist, doctor or a person in charge of a methadone programme treatment centre) shall keep, or cause to be kept, at the place where any drugs of dependence are kept by that person, a register of drugs of dependence in prescribed form (penalty: $2,000 or imprisonment for 12 months, or both).

Entries in Drug Registers: s 100

A prescribed person must, within 24 hours of manufacturing or receiving a drug of dependence, enter specified details of the drug in the relevant drug register. Where a prescribed person sells, supplies or administers a drug of dependence he or she shall, within 24 hours, enter specified details of the drug in the relevant drug register. All entries in a drug register must be signed (penalty for breach: $2,000).

Ward Registers: s 101 (see attached Forms 2 and 3)

A person who, for the time being, is in charge of a ward, shall keep in the ward a ward drugs of dependence register in the prescribed form. They must also keep in respect of methadone administered at a methadone programme treatment centre for the purpose of treating drug dependency—a ward methadone register in the prescribed form. This section does not apply to a specially designated methadone programme treatment centre, as they are covered by section 99 (penalty for breach: $5,000 or imprisonment for six months, or both).

Entries in Ward Drugs of Dependence Registers: s 102

A person who keeps, or causes to be kept, a ward drugs of dependence register shall enter, or cause to be entered, in that register, specified details in respect of each drug, of dependence that is supplied for use in the ward, within 24 hours after the drug is supplied:

- the date on which the drug was supplied;
- the name, quantity, form and strength of the drug; and
- in the case of a Class II Institution which is used for the accommodation, treatment and care of persons suffering from mental or physical conditions—the name and business address of the person who supplied the drug.

A person who is to administer a drug of dependence to a patient in a ward shall enter in the relevant ward drugs of dependence register when the drug is removed from a drug cabinet for that purpose:

- the anticipated date and time of the administration;
- the name, quantity, form, strength and dose of the drug;
- the number accorded to the relevant prescription pursuant to section 97 (which requires prescriptions to be numbered);
- the name of the doctor who prescribed the drug;
- the name of the patient to whom the drug is to be administered; and
- the quantity of the drug remaining in the ward.

The entry must be signed, and a person who supplies a drug of dependence to a ward, or witnesses the administration of a drug of dependence to a patient in the ward must countersign the relevant entry in the ward drugs of dependence register (penalty: $1,000).

Entries in Ward Methadone Registers: s 102A

A person who administers methadone during a shift at a methadone programme treatment centre for the purpose of treating drug dependency shall enter in the ward methadone register:

1)......*at the beginning of the shift*:
- the name of the centre and its location;
- the strength and form in which the methadone is to be administered; and
- the amount of methadone removed from the dispensary or other place where the methadone is stored;

2)......*immediately after each dose of methadone is administered*:
- the date and time of administration;
- the name of the patient to whom the methadone was administered;
- the quantity of methadone administered;
- the name of the person who administered the methadone;
- the name of the person who witnessed the administration; and
- the name of the doctor who prescribed the methadone; and

3)......*at the end of the shift*:
- the quantity of methadone allowed for wastage in preparing each dose (in Form 2A called the reconciliation amount); and
- the quantity of methadone returned to the dispensary or other place where the methadone is stored.

The person who administered the methadone and the person who witnessed that administration during the shift shall, at the end of the shift, sign the ward methadone register.

First-Aid Registers: s 103 (see attached Form 4)

A person authorised to have control of a first-aid kit containing a drug of dependence shall keep or cause to be kept, in a locked receptacle or room to which that person has exclusive access, a first-aid drugs of dependence register in prescribed form (penalty: $2,000 or imprisonment for 12 months, or both).

Entries in First-Aid Registers: s 104

A person who keeps a first-aid register shall enter, or cause to be entered, in the register information specified in this section in respect of each drug of dependence contained in the kit, and sign each entry (penalty: $1,000).

Record of Disposal: s 105

Where a drug of dependence in relation to which an entry has been made in a register has been disposed of or surrendered, the person who is required to keep the register shall enter in it details of the drug and date of disposal, or if surrendered, details of to whom it was surrendered, details of the drug and date of surrender or disposal, and that person shall sign the entry. The person who disposed of the drug and the person who supervised that disposal must also sign the register (penalty: $1,000).

Registers—General Provisions: s 106

Alterations: A person shall not alter, or cause or permit to be altered, an entry made in a register (this would include "whiting-out" or obliteration).

Corrections: A correction is to be made by the addition of a notation signed by the person making the notation and by a witness.

Availability of Register: Subject to section 109, a person responsible for a register shall retain possession of it for two years after the date of the last entry made in the register, and make it available for inspection on request by a drug inspector or a police officer authorised in writing for the purpose by the Minister.

Loss: A person responsible for a register shall, immediately upon discovering the loss or destruction of the register or part of the register:

1) ..... advise the Chief Health Officer in writing;
2) ..... make an inventory in the prescribed form of each drug of dependence kept by her or him for the purpose of compiling a new register; and
3) ..... from records, reconstruct, as far as possible, that part of the old register which was lost or destroyed.

(Penalty: $2,000 or imprisonment for 12 months, or both.)

False Entries in Registers: s 107

A person responsible for a register shall not make, or cause or permit to be made, in the register an entry that is, to the knowledge of that person, false or misleading in any particular (penalty: $2,000 or imprisonment for 12 months, or both).

Patients' Records: s 108

A person who administers a drug of dependence to a patient at an institution, or a methadone programme treatment centre that does not form part of an institution, shall enter a record of the date, time and mode of administration on the prescription for that drug which forms part of the patient's clinical records and that person shall initial the entry (penalty: $1,000).

Transfer of Pharmacy: s 109 (see attached Form 5)

Where a pharmacist takes control of a pharmacy other than one in a Class I Institution for more than 14 days, he or she must check the inventory with the outgong pharmacist in accord with Form 5 (attached), and if there are any discrepancies notify authorities within 24 hours.

Storage of Drugs

The Act prescribes specifications for drug cupboards, key safes, strong rooms and vaults. The specifications for drug cupboards include such matters as the material (black mild steel plate of not less than 10 millimetres thickness), the type of welding, door, and locking system (fixed locking bar, welded to the inside face of the door plus a five-lever key lock or locking mechanism). There must be a clearance around the door of not more than 1.5 millimetres. It must be securely attached to a wall or a floor (with requirements depending on the type of wall or floor).

A key safe must be designed to be opened by means of a combination lock, and is used for the purpose of keeping the key to a vault, strong room, safe or drug cabinet. A safe is to be constructed in such a manner as to prevent ready access to its contents by cutting, sawing or unbolting, and weigh not less than 350 kilograms or be securely affixed or anchored to, or embedded in, a concrete floor or a concrete or brick wall.

Strong rooms must be of brick or concrete while vaults are to be made of reinforced concrete, with both reasonably expected to resist attempts to gain entry by tools, torch or explosives for a period of not less than one hour.

Safekeeping of Drugs: s 113

A doctor, dentist, or person authorised to carry drugs of dependence as part of a first aid kit must keep the drugs locked in a receptacle fixed to the premises or a locked room, unless the drug is being carried, in which case it must be carried in a locked bag or container.

Safe-Keeping of Drugs: s 114

Where a drug of dependence is kept by:

1)......a pharmacist in control of a dispensary, not being the central store of an institution;
2)......a person in charge, for the time being, of a ward at an institution;
3)......a person in charge, for the time being, of a methadone programme treatment centre which is not a ward; or
4)......a person in charge of a Class II Institution;

that person shall keep the drug, or cause it to be kept, in a drug cabinet, or in a safe securely embedded in a concrete floor (penalty: $5,000).

Where a drug of dependence is kept in a drug cabinet or safe at a Class II Institution, methadone programme treatment centre which is not a ward, or community pharmacy, the person in charge for the time being shall ensure that the drug cabinet or safe and the key safe, if any, is fitted with such warning devices and detectors as are, or as are of a type, approved in writing by the Chief Health Officer (penalty: $5,000).

Safe-Keeping at Institutions: s 115

A person in charge of a Class II Institution shall not keep a quantity of a drug of dependence exceeding that prescribed by a doctor for the treatment of a patient at the institution. A person shall not remove any quantity of a drug of dependence that is to be administered to a patient in the institution from the receptacle or place in which the drug is stored, until that quantity of the drug is required for that purpose (penalty: $5,000).

Loss or Theft of a Drug of Dependence: s 116

Where a person keeping a drug of dependence becomes aware of the loss or theft of a quantity of the drug:

- .....where he or she believes on reasonable grounds that the drug was stolen, must notify a drug inspector and a police officer orally immediately, and in writing within 24 hours;
- .....in the case of a loss—give a written report of the circumstances of the loss to a drug inspector; and
- .....record the loss or theft accordingly in the relevant register (penalty: $2,000).

On recovery of a drug of dependence which was lost or stolen, the person who originally held that quantity or part shall record its recovery accordingly in the relevant register (penalty: $2,000).

Access to Combinations and Keys of Drug Receptacles: s 117

Where a person responsible keeps a drug of dependence in a drug receptacle designed to be opened by means of a combination lock, that person shall maintain personal access to, and keep confidential, the combination of the lock. "Person responsible" includes a pharmacist in control of a dispensary; a doctor, a nurse in charge, for the time being, of a ward at an institution and a person in charge of a Class II Institution (penalty: $2,000 or imprisonment for 12 months, or both).

Where a person responsible keeps a drug of dependence in a drug receptacle designed to be opened with a key, that person shall retain personal custody of the key; or if the key is kept in a key safe—maintain personal access to, and keep confidential, the combination of the lock of the key safe (penalty: $2,000 or imprisonment for 12 months, or both).

Safe-Keeping—General: s 118

A person keeping a drug of dependence must keep it in conditions which preserve the stability and quality of the drug and except where he or she is a doctor, veterinary surgeon or a dentist, or a pharmacist in control of the dispensary at a community pharmacy, ensure that only drugs of dependence are kept in the receptacle where the drug is kept. The drug receptacle, and the key safe, if any, used for keeping the key to it, must be kept locked at all times except when it is necessary to carry out essential operations in connection with the drugs of dependence, or to gain access to any other items kept in that receptacle (penalty: $2,000 or imprisonment for 12 months, or both).

Procedure for Disposal: s 120

A drug of dependence shall be taken to be unfit for use if it is contaminated, kept later than the "use-by" date, or otherwise unfit for use.

Where a health carer holds a quantity of a drug of dependence that the person wishes to dispose of, or which has become unfit for use, that person shall keep the quantity stored as for all drugs of dependence until it is disposed of or surrendered and ensure that that quantity is disposed of or surrendered in accordance with this section (penalty: $2,000 or imprisonment for 12 months, or both).

Disposal: The drug must be disposed of under the supervision of, and in accordance with the direction of, a drug inspector, or surrendered to a drug inspector to be disposed of as the Chief Health Officer directs. Where it is held at a Class I Institution, it shall be disposed of in the presence of a doctor, intern, dentist, pharmacist or nurse or an enrolled nurse who has completed an approved course on the use of drugs of dependence, the Chief Pharmacist of the institution.

Surrender to a drug inspector: This must be by personal delivery, registered mail or courier service. Disposal must be carried out in the presence of a Chief Pharmacist of an institution or a doctor, intern, dentist, pharmacist or nurse or an enrolled nurse who has completed an approved course on the use of drugs of dependence.

A chief pharmacist of an institution shall not be taken to hold a drug of dependence unless it is kept in the central control of the chief pharmacist.

FORM 1 (FOR SECTION 99)

DRUG REGISTER

Location ....

Drug[1] ....Strength[1] ....Form[1]

| Date[2] | Name and address/location[3] | Dealing[4] | Name and Address of prescriber | No.[5] | In[6] | Out[6] | Balance[7] | Remarks[8] | Signature[9] |

1. One drug, 1 strength, 1 form only per page of register.
2. Date of dealing.
3. Name and address of other party to the dealing (and that party's agent, where applicable), or location of ward or dispensary to which or from which the drug is supplied.
4. Nature of dealing—whether manufacture, receipt, supply, administration, disposal, surrender, loss or theft.
5. No. of prescription or requisition.
6. Quantity of the drug coming in or going out.
7. Quantity of the drug still held.
8. Including—
   - if the drug is supplied by a veterinary surgeon—species and identification details of the relevant animal; or
   - if the drug is disposed of—signature of the drug inspector or Chief Pharmacist who authorised the disposal.
9. Signature of the person making the entry in the register.

FORM 2 (FOR SECTION 101)

WARD REGISTER

Institution and location ....

Drug[1] .... Strength[1] .... Form[1] ....

Date[2]	Source of supply[3]/ Patient's name	Dealing[4]	Name of prescriber	No.[5]	In[6]	Out[6]	Balance[7]	Dose	Time of administration	Disposal[7A]	Remarks	Counter signature[8]	Signature[9]

1. One drug, 1 strength, 1 form only per page of register.
2. Date of dealing.
3. Name and address of supplier, or location of dispensary in Class I Institution from which the drug is supplied.
4. Nature of dealing—whether receipt, supply, administration, disposal, surrender, loss or theft.
5. No. of prescription or requisition.
6. Quantity of the drug coming in or going out.
7. Quantity of the drug still held.
7A. Quantity (if any) disposed of.
8. • If the drug is received—countersignature of supplier;
   • If the drug is administered—countersignature of witness;
   • If the drug is disposed of—countersignature of the person who authorised or witnessed the disposal.
9. Signature of the person making the entry in the register.

FORM 3 (FOR SECTION 101)

METHADONE REGISTER

Institution and location[1] ....

Strength[2] .... Form[2] .... Reconciliation amount[3] ....

Quantity of methadone removed from dispensary[1] .... Quantity of methadone returned to dispensary[3] ....

Signature of administrator[3] .... Signature of witness[3] ....

Date[4]	Patient's name	Time of administration	Name of prescriber	Dose	Balance[5]	Name of administrator	Ns

1. Complete at beginning of shift.
2. One strength, 1 form only per page of register.
3. Complete at end of shift.
4. Date of administration.
5. Quantity of the drug still held.

FORM 4 (FOR SECTION 103)

First-Aid Register

Institution and location ....
Drug[1].............................Strength[1]...............................Form[1]...........................

Date[2]	Name and Address[3]	Dealing[4]	In[5]	Out[5]	Balance[6]	Remarks	Counter signature[7]	Signature[8]

1. One drug, 1 strength, 1 form only per page of register.
2. Date of dealing.
3. Name and address of supplier, or person to whom the drug is administered (if the latter is ascertainable).
4. Nature of dealing—whether receipt, administration, surrender, loss or theft.
5. Quantity of the drug coming in or going out.
6. Quantity of the drug still held.
7. If the drug is disposed of—countersignature of the drug inspector who authorised the disposal.
8. Signature of the person making the entry in the register.

FORM 5 (FOR SECTION 109)

DRUGS OF DEPENDENCE INVENTORY

Pharmacy: Pharmacy Stamp
Address: ....
....
Name of outgoing pharmacist:..
Name of incoming pharmacist:..

Drug	Form	Strength	Quantity stated in register	Actual quantity held	Discrepancy

.... Date: . . . / . . . / . . .
(Signature of outgoing pharmacist conducting inventory)
                                             Inventory *Correct/*Incorrect
                                             * Chief Health Officer notified

.... Date: . . . / . . . / . . .
(Signature of incoming pharmacist checking inventory)
*Incoming pharmacist to delete where inapplicable

Appendix Five

CLIENT RIGHTS

(List of consumer rights adapted from the Queensland *Code of Patients' Rights*)

Access to High Quality Treatment, Services and Care

The right:
- to safe, appropriate, and timely health care when needed, and to acute care in emergencies.
  - to the provision of services subject to these limitations:
  - equitable distribution of health resources according to need, and priority given to acute and emergency services;
  - the provider's incapacity to treat the consumer or sincere conscientious objections;
  - the provider's clinical judgment that treatment is futile or that risks outweigh benefits;
  - private providers' right to decide whom they will treat (subject to client's other rights); and
  - the consumer's access to other qualified providers);
- to continuity of care according to need, including co-operation among the providers involved in the client's diagnosis, treatment, care and support;
- to treatment and care of the highest assured quality and technical standard practicable;
- to relief from suffering and to humane palliative care;
- to die with dignity; and
- a fair, open and ethical process in the provision of treatment in limited supply, based on clinical criteria and without unlawful discrimination.

Provision of Information

The right:
- to information necessary to make informed decisions about health care. This information will normally include:
  - the possible or likely nature of the illness;
  - the proposed approach to investigation, diagnosis and treatment;
  - what the proposed approach entails;

- the expected benefits, common side effects and material risks of any intervention, including any significant long term physical, emotional, mental, social, sexual, or other outcome which may be associated with a proposed intervention;
- whether a proposed procedure is conventional or experimental;
- who will undertake the intervention;
- other options for investigation, diagnosis and treatment;
- the degree of uncertainty of any diagnosis or the therapeutic outcome;
- the likely consequences of not having the proposed treatment, or any treatment at all; and
- (in advance) the time and costs involved

▮ ..... to communicate with the health care provider in a form and language suitable for the client;
▮ ..... to retain a copy of this information;
▮ ..... to ask questions, and to be given complete, direct and honest answers, about all matters;
▮ ..... to be informed of the name and qualifications of any person providing care, and to be introduced to the person who is primarily responsible for your care or support;
▮ ..... to information about the health care system, services and facilities; and
▮ ..... to choose whether to be treated as a public or private patient in a public hospital, and to receive an explanation of what this decision means.

Self-Determination and Consent

The client has a right:
▮ ..... to make independent choices and decisions about health care;
▮ ..... to accept or refuse treatment, before any intervention takes place (unless provided by law);
▮ ..... to halt an intervention or treatment, and to a careful explanation of the implications of refusing or halting such an intervention;
▮ ..... to decide:
- to choose to leave the condition untreated;
- to change the decision at any time;
- to refuse admission or to leave a health care facility regardless of the client's condition or against medical advice (except as provided by law);
- to refuse or withdraw consent to a procedure;
- to refuse to participate in research and experiments; or
- to refuse life-prolonging treatment or to receive only palliative care.

▮ ..... to decide:
- whether or not to take part in student training;
- who will be present, during any examination or procedure;
- to seek information, advice and treatment from other health workers; or
- to seek a second opinion.

▮ ..... to express a wish whether to donate organs or tissues (before or after death);
▮ ..... to authorise another person to make decisions on his or her behalf in the event of incapacity, or the appointment of a legally authorised representative if someone has not been authorised;
▮ ..... to choose, who, if anyone, should be informed about the client's health care.

> Parents and guardians have rights on behalf of a child or ward except where this is overridden by law, provided they also respect the child's right to be consulted as they grow older and acquire an increasing capacity to make decisions on their own behalf. [Comment: but see Chapter 5 regarding children and consent.]

Services Free from Discrimination and Exploitation

Clients have the right:
- ..... to receive health services regardless of ethnic or national origin, culture, disability, age, gender or sexuality;
- ..... to receive health services free from exploitation, assault or abuse including financial abuse, deception or fraud by any health care provider, institution or social care facility; and
- ..... to receive health care free from any unwelcome, or exploitative conduct of a sexual nature or any unsolicited act of physical intimacy or request for sexual favours either directly or by connotation.

Privacy and Respect

Clients have the right:
- ..... to be treated with dignity, courtesy, and due consideration of their background, needs and wishes; and
- ..... to physical facilities that ensure reasonable privacy for examinations or treatments, and personal sensitivity on the part of health providers, especially with necessary access to the unclothed body.

Confidentiality and Access to Records

Clients have the right:
- ..... to access personal health records (except when prohibited by law);
- ..... to be informed about the nature and location of their health records;
- ..... to maintenance of confidentiality of identifying personal information from anyone without consent unless disclosure is required or authorised by law;
- ..... to know who has or may have access to personal health records within the bounds of confidentiality, and to place reasonable restrictions on access by others;
- ..... to participate in recording and keeping personal information including:
  — receiving an explanation of the meaning and purpose of recorded information; and
  — having information amended and the client's comments attached; and

■.....nominating in writing another person who may receive personal information.

Access to Complaints Mechanisms and Support Systems

The client has the right:
- ■.....to reasonable access to family, relatives and friends for support during care;
- ■.....to access an advocate of the client's choice during the course of care and treatment;
- ■.....to comment on or complain about health care without reprisal and to have a complaint about health care dealt with promptly and fairly;
- ■.....to have any complaint of sexual abuse dealt with in a sensitive manner consistent with established practice for such complaints;
- ■.....to be told about and have access to procedures for the redress of any grievance about the provision of health services, and to seek compensation for injuries or illness resulting from care; and
- ■.....to seek information, advice and advocacy, including legal advice and representation (in a form and language accessible to the client) in making a complaint or in seeking redress for an injury or damage resulting from health care.

INDEX

[References are to paragraph numbers]

Aboriginal people
customary law, [1.56]
provision for some recognition by courts, [1.56]
establishment of Aboriginal and Torres Strait Islander Social Justice Commissioner, [18.18]
legal principles applying to, [1.56]
registration of Aboriginal health workers, [13.2]

Abortion
consent, [5.72], [5.83]
child, of, without parental consent, [5.36]
criminal law and child destruction, [14.73], [14.187]–[14.188]
definition, [14.73]
unlawful, [14.157]
legislation, [1.2], [14.155], [14.159]
Australian Capital Territory, [14.176]
English precedent, [14.158]
New South Wales, [14.165]
Northern Territory, [14.162]
Queensland, [14.171]
South Australia, [14.160]
Victoria, [14.164]
Western Australia, [14.172]
rights of foetus, [14.182]–[14.185]
rights of third parties, [14.186]
termination, stage of pregnancy, [14.181]
who may carry out, [14.177]–[14.180]
wrongful life action, [6.157]

Accidents and injuries
action by clients, [12.1]–[12.3]
advising insurer of health facility, [12.3]
injuries to health carers, [12.4]–[12.6], [12.32]
injury, defined, [12.29]
cases, [12.29]–[12.32]
lack of full and frank disclosure, [12.2]
liability of occupiers for accidents on their property — *see* **Occupiers**
negligence — *see* **Negligence**
prompt reporting, [12.2]

safe working environment — *see* **Workplace safety**
occupational health and safety — *see* **Occupational health and safety**
rate of industrial accidents in Australia, [12.18]

Actions — *see* **Litigation**

Acts Interpretation Acts
dominant and mandatory rule, [3.29], [3.33]
effects of, [3.28]

Administrative Appeals Tribunal (AAT)
appeals relating to registration and practice, [2.78], [13.23]
jurisdictions, [13.23]
re-hearings, [13.24]
complaints from decisions, [2.78]
decisions, review on merit, [2.79]
establishment, [2.56]
jurisdiction, [2.47], [2.62]
review of government and administrative policy, [2.79]

Administrative law
administrative decisions, [2.68]
AAT, [2.78], [2.79]
complaints, [2.72]
judicial review, [2.74]–[2.76]
orders a court can make in reviewing, [2.76]
decision-making functions, [2.68]
disciplinary action, [2.70]
ombudsman, [2.77]
purpose of, [2.71], [2.72]
quasi-judicial power, [2.69]
tribunals — *see* **Tribunals**

Advance directives
access to, [5.117]
advantages, [5.100], [5.102]
autonomy, [5.99], [5.103]
disadvantages, [5.102], [5.104]
psychiatric treatment not included, [5.105]–[5.106]
legal force, [5.101]

Advance directives — *continued*
  legislation giving effect to
    Australian Capital Territory, [5.115]
    Northern Territory, [5.110]
    Queensland, [5.113], [5.114]
    South Australia, [5.109]
    Victoria, [5.111], [5.112]
  provision for intentions and wishes, [5.100]
  Qumsieh's case, [5.108]
  recording of, [5.117]
  refusal of treatment agreed to in directive, [5.116]
  triggering event for, [5.107]

Aged care
  Aged Care Act, [18.73]
  complaints mechanism, [18.73]
  Department of Community Services and Health, [18.74]
  discrimination and special considerations, [18.73]–[18.74]
  Hostels Standards Review Panel, [18.74]
  inspection of hostels, [18.74]
  quality care principles, [18.73]
  user rights principles, [18.73]

AIDS — *see* **HIV/AIDS**

Alcohol
  contractual capacity of intoxicated person, [10.63]

Alternative dispute resolution (ADR)
  tribunals, [2.53]
    appropriateness of, [2.54]

Anti-Discrimination Board, [18.36]

Anti-discrimination tribunals, [2.63]

Appeal
  adverse judgment, from, [3.6]
  District courts, to, [2.20]
  High Court, [2.26]
    special leave, [2.27]
  intermediate courts, to, [2.20]
  Magistrates court, from, [2.19], [2.20], [2.21], [2.25]
    Local Court (NSW), [2.10]
  Privy Council, abolition of Australian appeals to, [2.29]
  retrial, [2.34]
  Supreme Court, [2.22]
    federal law, under, [2.25]
  unreasonable finding, basis for appeal, [2.34]

Appellant, [3.6]

Appellate jurisdiction, [2.33], [2.34]

Applicant, [3.4], [3.5], [3.22]

Applications, [3.22]

Artificial conception
  artificial insemination, [17.46]
    common law, [17.47]
    legislation, [17.48]–[17.54]
  assisted conception and reproductive technology — *see* **Reproductive technology**
  recording of parentage in register, [15.2]

Assault
  action against health carer for, [4.10], [4.19]
    checklist, when self-defence is a valid defence, [14.63]–[14.64]
  apprehension of, [4.19]
  assault and battery distinguished, [4.23]
  assault and battery in health care, [14.3], [14.4]
  defences to action, [4.56], [14.43]–[14.67]
  definition, [4.19]
  domestic violence, [16.81], [16.85]
  medical treatment without consent, [4.2], [4.19]
  threats by health carers, [4.19]–[4.21], [4.79]
  trespass to the person, [4.10], [4.17], [4.18]

Australian Hospital Care Study, [6.4]

Australian Industrial Relations Commission, [2.67]

Australian law
  common law — *see* **Common law**
  indigenous customary law — *see* **Customary law**
  sources of, [1.18]
  statutory law — *see* **Legislation**

Australian Medical Association
  Code of Ethics, [7.56]

Automatism
  defence to criminal charge, [14.50]–[14.58]
  definition, [14.51]–[14.52]

Autonomy — *see also* **Consent**
   client's wishes, [4.3], [4.6], [4.8], [4.48]
   duty of care, conflict with, [4.7]
   good communication, need for, [4.4]
   human rights principle of dignity, autonomy and integrity, [18.4]
   legal right to, [4.3], [4.6], [4.7]
      breaches, [4.8]
      person unable to make health care decisions, [5.99]–[5.117], [5.170]
      pregnant woman, [4.139]

Bailment
   act of bailment, [9.4]
   bailee, [9.2]
      involuntary, [9.14]
   bailor, [9.2]
   categories, [9.10]
      bailment for reward, [9.11]
      gratuitous bailment, [9.12]
   common law, [9.4]
   definition, [9.2]
   involuntary bailment, [9.16]
   negligence, available remedy, [9.4]

Barristers
   functions, [3.12]
   negotiated settlement, [3.13]

Battery
   action against health carer, [4.10], [4.19]
      damage need not be caused, [4.23]
      intention, [4.24], [4.32]
      patient unaware of battery, [4.26], [4.39]–[4.40]
   assault and battery distinguished, [4.23]
   defences to an action, [4.56]
      best interests of client, [4.75], [5.100]
      defence of another and of property, [4.79]–[4.81]
      emergencies, [4.58]–[4.64]
      emergency services, [4.65]
      necessity, [4.68]–[4.74]
      self-defence, [4.76]–[4.78]
      statutory power to use force, [4.82]
      suicide attempts, [4.66]–[4.67]
   definition, [4.22]
   implications for health carers, [4.27], [4.32]
      blood transfusion, [4.29]–[4.31], [4.47], [4.136]
      deep sleep treatment, [4.27]–[4.29]
      ossiculectomy without consent, [4.24], [4.25]
      presumption of consent, [4.32]–[4.34], [4.58]
      spinal anaesthetic for surgical treatment, [4.39]–[4.40]
      threats, [4.20]
      transplantation, removal of human tissue for, [17.28]
   trespass to person, [4.10], [4.17], [4.18]

Bioethics, [1.2]

Birth
   notification of, [15.2]
      checklist for health carers, [15.11]
      failure to notify, [15.3], [15.8]
      homebirths, [15.5]–[15.7]
      parentage, [15.2]
      recording of father's name, [15.4]
      requirements in New South Wales, [15.7]–[15.8]
      requirements in Victoria, [15.5]–[15.6]
      responsibility for notification, [15.3], [15.5]–[15.7]
      stillbirths, [15.2], [15.9]–[15.11], [15.16]
      time limit, [15.3], [15.5], [15.7]

Blood and tissue tests
   consent issues, [4.155]–[4.158]
      alcohol content, [4.156]
      criminal suspects, [4.157]
   DNA tests, [4.158], [17.12]
   statutory provisions for taking blood and tissue, [17.9], [17.10]
      circumstances where permitted, [17.9]
      health carers involved in collection of specimens, [17.12]
      time limits, [17.11]
      urine samples, [17.10]

Blood donations
   authorisation to collect, [17.7]
   consent, [17.5]
   giving of blood by live donor, [17.1]
      adults, [17.5]
      caution where blood testing for serious disease diagnosis, [17.18]
      children, [17.8]
      statutory declaration required of blood donor, [16.33], [17.7], [17.17]
   place, [17.6]
   Red Cross Centre, [17.6]

Blood donations — *continued*
  statutory provisions for taking blood, [17.9]
    indemnity against liability for contraction of blood-borne diseases, [17.7], [17.18]
  tissue donations — *see* **Human tissue transplants**

Blood transfusions
  consent issues, [4.136]
    adults, [17.13]
    adult's refusal, [17.14]
    child, [5.4]–[5.12], [17.16]
    emergency or necessity, [17.15]
    Qumsieh's case, [5.108], [17.14]
    T's case, [4.29]–[4.31], [4.47]
  HIV/AIDS virus, [16.32], [16.33], [17.17]
    blood testing on admission to facilities, [17.18]
    statutory declaration required of blood donor, [16.33], [17.7], [17.17]

Breach of confidence
  actions available, [7.59]
  breach of contract, [7.60]
  confidential information — *see* **Confidential information**
  defamation — *see* **Defamation**
  equitable remedy, [7.65]
  negligence — *see* **Negligence**
  tort of, [7.59], [7.63]–[7.64]
    action in negligence, [7.67]

Breach of contract — *see also* **Contract**
  elements of, [7.60]
  remedies for, [10.102]
    common law remedy, [10.103]–[10.104]
    damages, [10.103]–[10.104]
    equitable remedies, [10.105]–[10.108]
    injunction, [10.107]–[10.108]
    specific performance, [10.106]

Breach of the peace, [1.39]

Burdekin Report, [5.184]

Causation
  actual harm caused to plaintiff by defendant, [6.159]–[6.163]
  "but for" test, [6.159], [6.160], [6.164]
  common sense approach, [6.165]–[6.171]
  remoteness of damage, [6.164]

Certiorari, [2.31]

Child
  consent to blood donation, [17.8]
  consent to health care, [5.55]
    blood transfusion in different States, [5.4]–[5.12]
    common law principle of consent, [5.2]
    emergencies, [5.4]–[5.12], [5.37], [5.41]
    guardian or third parties, [5.40]–[5.43], [5.45]–[5.55]
    informed consent, [5.20]–[5.21]
    Marion's Case, [5.17]–[5.21], [5.27], [5.30], [5.38], [5.58]
    mature minor, [5.3], [5.23], [5.28], [5.30], [5.37]–[5.39]
    non-urgent treatment, [5.13]–[5.16]
    parens patriae, [5.16], [5.18], [5.22], [5.28], [5.31]
    special medical treatment, [5.14]
    statutory exceptions, [5.13]–[5.15]
    sterilisation, [5.14], [5.17]–[5.19], [5.21]–[5.22]
    therapeutic treatment, [14.76]
    when child can consent, [5.23]–[5.27]
    when parents do not have power to consent, [5.20]
    where child abused or neglected, [5.44]–[5.45]
  consent to removal of tissue from child
    non-regenerative tissue, [17.25]
    regenerative tissue, [17.22], [17.23]
    summary of legislative provisions, [17.23]
  contractual capacity, [10.54]–[10.61]
  Convention on the Rights of the Child, [18.12], [18.15]
  criminal law and child destruction, [14.73], [14.187]–[14.188]
  Declaration of the Rights of the Child, [18.12], [18.14]
  definition, [5.2], [14.71]
    born alive, [14.72]
  detention, power of medical personnel, [5.45]
  notification of birth — *see* **Notification**
  refusal of medical treatment, [5.28]–[5.33]
    anorexia nervosa cases, [5.28]–[5.32]

Index | 681

Child — *continued*
refusal of medical treatment — *continued*
consideration of child's wishes,
[5.35]–[5.36]
mature minor, [5.37]–[5.39]
South Australia, [5.15]
right to contraceptive advice and
measures, [5.23]–[5.27], [5.36]
sexually transmitted disease, [16.26]

Child abuse
basic legal principle, [16.61]
care of abused child, [16.80]
statutory provisions for taking
blood and tissue, [17.9]
child in need of care or maltreated,
[16.62]
neglect, [5.44]–[5.45], [16.62]
evidence of abuse, [16.79]
interpretation of terms
adverse environment, [16.62]
child's behaviour, [16.62]
in bad company, [16.79]
maltreatment and abuse, [16.62]
moral danger, [16.79]
neglect, lack of care, [16.62]
mandatory reporting, [15.1], [16.1],
[16.71]
Australian Capital Territory, [16.72]
New South Wales, [16.73]
Northern Territory, [16.74]
objective evidence of abuse, [16.79]
offence for failure to report, [16.71]
Queensland, [16.75]
South Australia, [16.76]
Tasmania, [16.77]
Victoria, [16.78]
moral danger, [16.79]
protection from defamation, [16.63],
[16.70], [16.71]
voluntary reporting, [16.63]
Australian Capital Territory, [16.64]
New South Wales, [16.65]
objective evidence of abuse, [16.79]
Queensland, [16.66]
South Australia, [16.67]
Tasmania, [16.68]
Victoria, [16.69]

Child welfare
child abused or neglected, where,
[5.44]–[5.45]
in need of care, [5.46]
legislative provisions, [5.46]–[5.55]
Australian Capital Territory, [5.47]
New South Wales, [5.48]–[5.49]
Northern Territory, [5.50]
power of medical personnel, [5.45]
power of minister or director, [5.46]
Queensland, [5.51]
South Australia, [5.52]
Tasmania, [5.53]
Victoria, [5.54]
Western Australia, [5.55]
parental responsibility, [16.61]
withdrawing treatment to newborn
infants, [14.133]–[14.144]

Children's Court, [2.18]

Civil law
civil action, [3.2], [4.23]
main steps, [3.21]
negligence, [6.13]
claim of damage and compensation,
[3.4]
claim to certain rights and privileges,
[3.4]
costs, [3.10]
damages — *see* **Damages**
definition, [1.13]
judge, role of, [3.5]
litigation — *see also* **Litigation**
monetary limits, [2.20]
terms used, [3.4], [3.5]

Client access to records
common law, [7.112]
federal government arrangements,
[7.113]
freedom of information, [7.113],
[7.119]
ground for refusal, [7.116]
guardian of child, [7.114]
High Court ruling, [7.111]
legislation, [7.113], [7.119]
amendment to *Privacy Act* 1988,
[7.117]
Australian Capital Territory, [7.115]
private health sector, changes for,
[7.51]–[7.52], [5.117]
rights, [7.115]
considerations by health carers,
[7.119]
improved quality of records, [7.118]
X-rays and pathology reports, [7.111],
[7.112]

Client injury — *see* **Accidents and
injuries**

Codes of ethics
A Code for Nurses: Ethical Concepts
Applied to Nurses, [19.12]
British Medical Association Code of
Ethics, [19.11]

Codes of ethics — *continued*
  International Code of Medical Ethics, [19.12]
  principles, [19.12]–[19.14]

Colonial history
  background to law, [1.20], [1.21]
  Colonial Laws Validity Act 1865, [1.21]

Commissions
  activities of, [2.64]
  Australian Industrial Relations Commission, [2.67]
  health care complaints commissions, [2.65]
  Human Rights and Equal Opportunity Commission, [2.66]
  mandate of, [2.64]
  request for information, [7.109]

Committal hearing
  Magistrates Court role, [2.14]
  pleading guilty to indictable offence, [2.17]

Common law
  Australian law, source of, [1.17]
  bailment, [9.4]
  criminal law principles — *see* **Criminal law principles**
  equity, effect of, [1.45]
    principles of, [1.45], [1.46]
  establishment, effect of, [1.44]
  historical background, [1.11], [1.37]–[1.44]
  legal system of, [1.11], [1.12]
  meaning of term depends on context, [1.12], [1.47]
  medical treatment without consent, [4.18]
  principles applied when determining the reason for decision, [3.48]–[3.55]
  protection of human rights, [1.62], [3.43]
  "purpose" or "mischief" rule, [3.29]
  scope for change, [1.57]
    where no precedent or legislation, [1.55], [3.56]–[3.69]
  stare decisis, [1.44], [1.54], [1.57]
  statutory law and equity, inter-relationship with, [1.48], [1.49], [3.43]

Communication
  autonomy, [4.4]
  confidential information — *see* **Confidential information**
  defamation — *see* **Defamation**
  medical records — *see* **Medical records**
  preventable adverse events, [6.8]

Compensation
  damages — *see* **Damages**
  percentage of claims not acted upon, [3.8]
  victims of crime — *see* **Victims of crime**
  workers' compensation — *see* **Workers' compensation**

Compensation Court (New South Wales), [2.38]

Competence
  definition, [4.43]
  fluctuating and reversible loss of, [4.48]
  incompetence — *see* **Incompetence**
  rights of competent person at law, [4.42]
    absolute right of competent person to refuse treatment, [4.18]
  capacity for consent, [4.44], [4.52]
  understanding, [4.14], [4.49]–[4.54], [4.84]

Complaints
  AAT decision, complaint of, [2.78]
  administrative decision, complaint of, [2.72]
  discrimination, [18.71]
    aged, [18.73]
    people with disability, [18.72]
    remedies under federal legislation, [18.78]–[18.80]
    sexual harassment, [18.71]
  health care complaints bodies, [2.65], [18.22], [18.32], [18.33]
    Australian Capital Territory, [18.25]
    causes of complaints, [18.23]
    conciliation, [18.33]
    functions and powers, [18.23]–[18.24], [18.32], [18.33]
    immunity from legal action, [18.24]
    independent complaints units, [18.22]–[18.24]
    investigation of complaints, [18.23]
    New South Wales, [18.26]
    Northern Territory, [18.27]
    protection from reprisals, [18.24]
    Queensland, [18.28]
    referral of matters, [18.33]
    statutory mechanisms, [18.22]
    Tasmania, [18.29]
    Victoria, [18.30]

Index | 683

Complaints — *continued*
health care complaints bodies — *continued*
Western Australia, [18.31]
Human Rights Commission — *see*
Human Rights and Equal Opportunity Commission
privacy complaints [7.53]

Complementary Medicines Evaluation Committee, [8.34]

Confidential information
breach of confidence — *see* **Breach of confidence**
changes for private health sector, [7.49]–[7.50], [5.117]
new guidelines about client information, [7.51]–[7.52]
client access to records — *see* **Client access to records**
complaints [7.53]
defamation — *see* **Defamation**
definition, [7.41]
disclosure, [7.40], [7.41], [7.109]
disclosure allowed, [7.70]
agreement, [7.71]
checklist, [7.110]
compulsion by law, [7.72]
HIV-positive client, [7.83]–[7.88]
interest of party concerned, [7.81]
public interest, [7.74]
relatives, [7.82]
electronic technology, impact of, [7.43]
guidelines and administrative instructions, [7.56], [7.109]
OECD *Guidelines for the Security of Information Systems*, [7.57]
health carer, [7.40]
best interests of clients, [7.60]
duty of confidentiality, [7.44]–[7.45], [7.109]
relationship with client, not privileged, [7.46]–[7.47]
legislation, [7.58]
privacy — *see* **Privacy**
professional coincidental relationship privilege, [7.47]
sexual assault communication privilege, [7.47]
sexually transmitted diseases, [16.25]–[16.26]

Consent
basic legal requirements, [4.5], [4.9]–[4.16]
child — *see* **Child**
client's consent, [4.2]
presumption of consent, [4.32]–[4.34], [17.4]
revocation, [4.32], [17.27]
client's wishes, [4.3], [4.4], [4.6], [4.7], [4.53], [14.76]
competent person — *see* **Competence**
incompetent person — *see* **Incompetence**
forms — *see* **Consent forms**
general consent, [4.11], [4.15]
informed consent, [4.12], [4.16], [4.51], [4.53], [4.122]
child, [5.20]–[5.21]
electroconvulsive therapy, [5.186]–[5.192]
expression, interpretation of, [4.84]–[4.86]
information required — *see* **Information**
refusal of courts to recognise doctrine as basis for action, [4.121]
lawful consent, elements needed for, [4.13], [4.35]–[4.55]
minor — *see* **Minor**
patients' rights, [4.6], [4.8]
absolute right to refuse treatment, [4.18], [14.78]
checklist when client refuses treatment, [14.80]–[14.81]
written consent, [4.41], [4.122]
person with mental illness — *see* **Mental illness**
psychiatric patients — *see* **Psychiatric patients**
reasonable disclosure, [4.4]
proper and in patient's interests, [4.51]
signed statements to avoid potential negligence claims, [4.135]
specific consent, [4.35], [4.55]
specific situations, [4.136]–[4.158]
transplants, human tissue for — *see* **Human tissue transplants**
treatment without consent — *see* **Trespass to the person**
understanding by client of proposed procedure, [4.14], [4.49]
broad nature and effects, [4.11], [4.15], [4.49]
material risks, [4.12], [4.16]
verbal or implied, [4.127]
voluntary consent, [4.35], [4.36]
misrepresentation as to nature of treatment, [4.38]
misrepresentation as to need for treatment, [4.37]

Consent forms
awareness of need for, [4.127], [4.132]
checklist, [4.134]
legal implications, [4.128]
  anomolies, [4.129]
  legal rules, [4.131]
  liability, [4,135]
signature of client, [4.127], [4.130]
specific to procedure, [4.133]

Consent to Medical Treatment and Palliative Care Act (South Australia) 1995, [14.101], [14.105], [14.120]–[14.121]

Constitution
federal legislative powers, [1.24], [1.27]
  concurrent powers, [1.26]
  specific matters, [1.25]
foreign affairs power, [1.30]–[1.32], [18.11]–[18.12]
function of, [1.23]
national referendum needed to change, [1.34], [1.35]
prevalence of federal law over State laws, [1.19], [1.28]
State Constitutions, [1.23], [1.36]
State legislative powers, [1.23], [1.24]
  referral of powers, [1.28]
statutory interpretation, [1.29]
  foreign affairs power, [1.30]–[1.32], [18.11]–[18.12]
  major function of High Court, [1.29]
  power vested in federal government, [1.29]–[1.32]
Territories, legislating for, [1.33]

Contingency fee, [3.10]

Contract — *see also* **Contracts to provide health care services**
checklist for valid contract, [10.3]
  invalid contract, [10.66]
contractual relationship between health carer and Health Insurance Commission, [10.1]
deeds, [10.36]
  limitation period, [10.37]
definition, [10.3]
discharge of contracts, [10.96]
  agreement, [10.98]
  election upon breach, [10.100]
  frustration, [10.99]
  performance, [10.97]
  stipulated condition occurs, [10.101]
elements of contract, [10.3]
  acceptance must be in full, [10.28]–[10.30]
  agreement that contract not legally binding, [10.12]
  bilateral contracts, [10.20]–[10.21]
  conditions in offer, [10.14], [10.24]
  consideration, [10.34]–[10.35]
  gratuitous offers, [10.23]
  intention to create legal relationship, [10.4]–[10.11]
  offer and acceptance, [10.13], [10.17], [10.26]–[10.30]
  offers can be oral, in writing or implied, [10.16]–[10.19], [10.38]
  parties, identification of, [10.33]
  past consideration, [10.35]
  person unaware of details in offer, [10.14]
  privity of contract, [10.27], [10.35]
  simple contract, [10.34]
  time limit for acceptance, [10.26]
  unilateral contracts, [10.22]
  withdrawal of offer, [10.15], [10.31]
health care contract, [10.45]
  actions for breach, [10.46], [10.47]
  agreement, who it is with, [10.47]
  compensation, [10.46]
  diagram of possible contracts, [10.47]
  harm, [10.46]
  terms, [10.47]–[10.52]
health facility undertakings, [10.1]
invalid contracts, [10.66]–[10.95]
liability in contract, [10.2]
  liability in negligence distinguished, [10.2]
overview, [10.1]
principles applying to offers, [10.16]–[10.19]
practitioner undertakings, [10.1]
remedies for breach of contract, [10.102]
  common law remedy, [10.103]–[10.104]
  damages, [10.103]–[10.104]
  equitable remedies, [10.105]–[10.108]
  injunction, [10.107]–[10.108]
  specific performance, [10.106]
terms of, [10.41]
  benefits of contracts in writing, [10.40]
  implied, [10.1], [10.42]–[10.44]
  importance of taking time to read, [10.41]
unenforceable agreement, [10.66]
  duress, [10.76]

Contract — *continued*
unenforceable agreement — *continued*
fraud, [10.83]–[10.84]
illegal or against public policy, [10.89]–[10.91]
mistake, [10.71]–[10.75]
misrepresentation, [10.67]–[10.70]
surrogacy contracts, [10.92]–[10.95]
unconscionable contracts, [10.85]–[10.88]
undue influence, [10.77]–[10.82]
who can make a contract, [10.53]
intoxicated person, [10.63]
minors, [10.54]–[10.61]
persons of "unsound mind", [10.62]–[10.64]
unincorporated bodies, [10.65]
writing, in, [10.16], [10.38]–[10.44]
contracts which must be, [10.39]

Contracts to provide health care services
employee or independent contractor determining the difference, [11.2]–[11.9]
health carer as independent contractor, [11.10]
partnership, [11.15]
principal and agent, [11.12]–[11.14]
relationships, other, [11.10]
employment, contract of, [11.1]
implied terms of employment, [11.16]
common law, [11.16]–[11.48]
common law right to discipline employees, [11.44]–[11.48]
statutes, enterprise agreements and industrial awards, [11.49]–[11.102]
implied undertakings by employee, [11.16]
carrying out lawful and reasonable order of employer, [11.16]
disclosure of information to employer, [11.33]
employer's property, accounting for, [11.32]
faithful to employer's interests, [11.27]–[11.31]
reasonable care taken when carrying out orders, [11.25]–[11.26]
refusing to work, [11.19]–[11.24]
role in maintaining safety in workplace, [11.34]–[11.35]
implied undertakings by employer, [11.36]
competent staff, provision of, [11.42]
payment of wages, [11.37]
safe place of work, provision of, [11.38]–[11.41]
safe system of work, provision of, [11.43]
industrial relations — *see* **Industrial relations**
service, contract of, [11.1]

Convention on the Rights of the Child, [18.12], [18.15]

Coroner
Coroner's Court, [2.18], [15.18]–[15.19], [15.74]
coronial hearings, [2.13]
examination of the body, [15.45]
postmortem examination — *see* **Postmortem**
inquests — *see* **Coroner's inquest**
inquiry into cause of fires, [15.18]
legislation, [15.19]
reporting of death to, [15.28], [15.38]
health carers reporting requirements, [15.44]
person finding body, [15.40]
person with knowledge of death, [15.39], [15.40]
Queensland, [15.40]
South Australia, [15.41]
Victoria, [15.42]
Western Australia, [15.43]
role of, [15.17], [15.20]–[15.24]
facts of case, [15.45]

Coroner's inquest
determination of death, [15.18], [15.20]
death in custody, [15.23]
determination, [15.20]
publicising unsafe products or practices, [15.22]
recommendations, [15.21]
referral to Director of Public Prosecutions, [15.20]
referral to registration board, [15.24]
reports, [15.23]
discretion to hold inquest, [15.25]–[15.26]
trial or royal commission, where, [15.27]

Coroner's inquest — *continued*
  evidence, [15.54]
    answering questions, [15.64]–[15.67]
    depositions of witnesses, [15.57], [15.62]
    directions, [15.54]
    disposition of body, [15.50]
    hearsay, [15.57]
    incriminating evidence, [15.70]–[15.73]
    medical records and reports, availability of, [15.61]–[15.62]
    perjury, [15.63]
    preparation of health carer's formal statement, [15.52]
    rules of evidence, [15.55], [15.68]–[15.69]
    summons to appear, [15.59]–[15.62]
  examination of the body — *see* **Postmortem**
  findings, [15.20]–[15.21], [15.24], [15.74]
    cases, [15.76]–[15.83]
    disappearances, [15.74], [15.84]
    result of inquest, [15.74]
  grounds for holding an inquest, [15.26]
    list of mandatory or discretionary categories in different jurisdictions, [15.26]
  health carer's preparation for inquest
    account of events, [15.51]
    cross-examination by lawyers, [15.58], [15.64]–[15.67]
    disposition of body, [15.50]
    giving testimony under oath, [15.57], [15.62], [15.70]–[15.73]
    preparation of formal statement, [15.52]
  procedure, [15.63]
    jury, where, [15.53], [15.74]
  purpose of, [15.18], [15.20]
  request by relative or another, [15.26], [15.29]
    Australian Capital Territory, [15.30]
    New South Wales, [15.31]
    Northern Territory, [15.32]
    Queensland, [15.33]
    South Australia, [15.29]
    Tasmania, [15.34]
    Victoria, [15.35]
    Western Australia, [15.36]
  when held, [15.18], [15.25]–[15.37]

Costs
  legal advice, [3.10]
  litigation, [3.10]
  threat of, [3.7]

County courts, [2.20]

Courts
  definition, [2.2]
  District Court — *see* **District Court**
  English courts — *see* **English courts**
  Federal, [2.6], [2.7], [2.8]
    diagram of system, [2.7]
    geographical, [2.4], [2.5]
    reporting of cases in, [2.85]
  Federal Magistrates Court, [2.6], [2.43]
  High Court — *see* **High Court**
  judicial decisions from other countries, [2.83]
  judicial review of administrative decisions, [2.74]–[2.76]
  jurisdiction, [2.3]–[2.29]
    appellate, [2.33], [2.34]
    original, [2.32]
    scope of, [2.31]
  Local Courts — *see* **Local Court**
  Magistrates Court — *see* **Magistrates Court**
  power to make orders, [2.2], [2.76]
  Privy Council, [2.29], [2.30]
  reason for decision, [3.48]–[3.55]
  rules of the court, [2.35], [3.28]–[3.46]
    "purpose" or "mischief" rule, [3.29]
  specialist courts, [2.36]
    Compensation Court (NSW), [2.38]
    Drug Court (NSW), [2.37]
    Family Court, [2.39]–[2.42]
    Federal Magistrates Court, [2.43]
  State, [2.9]–[2.25]
    diagram of State and Territory court system, [2.9]
    geographical, [2.4], [2.5]
    reporting of cases in, [2.86]
    three tiers in mainland States, [2.9], [2.10], [2.20], [2.22]
    two tiers in Tasmania and Territories, [2.9], [2.10], [2.22]

Criminal law
  action, [3.2], [3.7], [14.1]
    main steps, [3.18]
  common law, [14.5]
  compensation, [3.3], [14.1]
  criminal negligence, [14.151]
    degree of culpability, [14.152]
    manslaughter, [14.152]–[14.154]
  defences to criminal charge, [14.43]–[14.44], [14.49]
    automatism, [14.50]–[14.58]
    diminished responsibility, [14.48]

Criminal law — *continued*
  defences to criminal charge — *continued*
    duress, [14.59]–[14.60]
    insanity, [14.45]–[14.47]
    McNaghten rules, [14.46]–[14.47]
    provocation, [14.65]–[14.67]
    self-defence, [14.60]–[14.64]
  forensic evidence — *see* **Forensic evidence**
  offences, [3.20]
    relevant to health carers, [14.4], [14.68], [14.196]
  principles — *see* **Criminal law principles**
  prosecution by State, [3.3]
  summary offences, [3.19]
  victims of crime — *see* **Victims of crime**

Criminal law principles
  any act must be voluntary, [14.20]–[14.19]
    status offences, [14.24]
    strict liability, [14.23]
  common law, [14.5]
  criminal offences established prior to charge, [14.6]–[14.9]
  guilt must be personal, not vicarious, [14.26]–[14.32]
    accomplices to crime, [14.32]
    delegation, [14.31]
    liability through incitement, [14.30]
    liability through others, [14.29]
  ignorance of law no excuse, [14.38]
  intention to commit an act, [14.14]–[14.19]
  precise act must have been committed, [14.33]–[14.37]
  presumption of innocence, [14.39]–[14.41]
    exceptions, [14.42]
  there must be an act, [14.10]–[14.13]
    failure to act, [14.11]
    omission, [14.11]

Customary law
  features of Aboriginal customary law, [1.56]
  international and indigenous, [1.16]
  principles applying to Aboriginal people, [1.56]
  source of law in Australia, [1.18]

Damages
  amount of compensation, [6.141], [6.158]
  causation — *see* **Causation**
  definition, [6.141]
  dependants may sue, [6.149]
  general damages, [6.144]
    court considerations, [6.145]
  harm, [6.146]
    economic harm, [6.148]
    physical harm, [6.147]
    psychological harm, [6.150]–[6.156]
  liability for, [6.140]
  losses claimed, [6.142]
  nervous shock — *see* **Nervous shock**
  quantified, [6.149]
  specific damages, [6.143]
  wrongful life, [6.157]

Death
  brain-death, [14.150], [17.30]
  compensation, [12.58]
  coronial inquiries — *see* **Coroner's inquest**
  disappearances, [15.74], [15.84]
  definitions, [17.30]
  euthanasia — *see* **Euthanasia; Voluntary euthanasia**
  examination of the body — *see* **Postmortem**
  notification of, [15.12]
    failure to notify, [15.15]
    notifying the appropriate person, [15.14]
    perinatal deaths, [15.16]
    registrar, reporting to, [15.14]
    reporting of death to coroner, [15.28], [15.38]–[15.44]
    responsibility for notification, [15.13]
    time limits, [15.14]

Decision making
  addressing ethical principles, [19.2]
  applying ethical principles in decision making, [19.16]
  ascertain legal obligations, [19.19]–[19.24]
  best ethical option, determination of, [19.29]–[19.34]
  investigate and communicate facts and reasons for action, [19.17]–[19.18]
  legal obligations to client, [19.25]
  legal obligations to employer and colleagues, [19.26]–[19.28]
  probability of harm, [19.25]
  end-of-life decision making, [14.82]–[14.84]

Decision making — *continued*
  government decision-making
    functions, [2.68]
  overview, [19.1], [19.2]
  process, [19.3]
    consideration of consequences,
      [19.42]–[19.47]
    identifying the issue, [19.3]
    implications for health carers,
      [19.63]
    steps in process, [19.44]

Declaration of Human Rights, [1.59],
  [18.6]

**Declaration of the Rights of Disabled
  Persons**, [18.12], [18.14]

**Declaration on the Rights of Mentally
  Retarded Persons**, [5.63],
  [18.12], [18.14]

Declaration of the Rights of the Child,
  [18.12], [18.14]

Declarations
  definition, [3.23]
  dying declarations, [7.28]
  statutory declarations, [7.13]

Defamation
  action, [7.90]
    elements of, [7.94]
  compensation for damaged
    reputation, [7.100]
  defamatory comments
    allegations of guilt in victim of
      crime cases, [14.194]
    medical records, [7.111]
  defamatory material, [7.96]
  defamatory statement, [7.95]
    reference to the subject, [7.99]
    subject of, [7.93]
  defences, [7.101]
    absolute privilege, [7.103]
    fair comment, [7.107]
    justification, [7.102]
    qualified privilege, [7.104]
  definition, [7.89]
  examples, [7.91]–[7.92]
  implication, [7.97]
  legislation, [7.90]
    differences between jurisdictions,
      [7.89]
  oral, [7.89]
  publication, [7.98]
  reference to the subject, [7.99]
  reputation, [7.90]
    compensation for damaged, [7.100]

Defences
  absolute defences, [6.203]
    expiration of limitation period,
      [6.204]–[6.206]
    no breach of duty, [6.208]–[6.210]
    no causation, [6.211]
    no cause due to intervening factor,
      [6.213]–[6.217]
    no duty of care, [6.207]
  action in negligence, [6.202]
  criminal charge, to, [14.43]–[14.44],
    [14.49]
    automatism, [14.50]–[14.58]
    diminished responsibility, [14.48]
    duress, [14.59]–[14.60]
    insanity, [14.45]–[14.47]
    McNaghten rules, [14.46]–[14.47]
    provocation, [14.65]–[14.67]
    self-defence, [14.60]–[14.64]
  limitation period, [6.204]–[6.206]
  partial defences, [6.218]
    contributory negligence, [6.220]
    joint liability, [6.222]
    voluntary assumption of risk,
      [6.219]
  "reasonable person test", [10.2]

Defendant, [3.4], [3.5], [3.6]

Delegated legislation, [1.19]

Dental services
  code of ethics of Australian Dental
    Association, [19.12]
  federal government regulation of,
    [1.35]

Detention
  action of false imprisonment, [4.159],
    [4.161]
    cases, [4.161]–[4.173]
  child, power of medical personnel,
    [5.45]
  definition, [4.161]
  freedom to leave hospital,
    [4.184]–[4.186]
  lawful restraint, [4.160]
  mentally ill patients — *see* **Mental
    illness**
  restraint and seclusion — *see*
    Restraint
  trespass to person, [4.10]

Diminished responsibility
  defence to criminal charge, [14.48]
    infanticide, [14.73]
    manslaughter, [14.73]

Disability
   complaints, [18.72]
   conciliation, [18.78]–[18.79]
   litigation, [18.80]
   definition, [18.72]
   Disability Discrimination Act, [18.72], [18.78], [18.91]
   discrimination, [18.72]

Disciplinary action
   disciplinary boards, [2.49], [13.2], [13.7], [13.25]
   grounds for, [13.27], [13.31], [13.53]–[13.107]
      conduct demonstrating inadequate knowledge, [13.73]–[13.76]
      coroner's finding of breach, [15.24]
      failure to properly assess and treat injuries, [13.61]–[13.68]
      improper or unethical conduct, [13.77]–[13.80]
      intimate relations with clients or past clients, [13.58]–[13.61]
      lack of mental or physical fitness, [13.28], [13.107]
      overuse of drugs or alcohol, [13.30]
      provision of drugs to addicts, [13.53]
      surgery carried out in non-orthodox fashion, [13.54]–[13.57]
   procedures, [13.25]
      checklist for health carers, [13.112]
   purpose of, [13.26]
   registration boards — *see* **Registration boards**
   reprimand, [13.110]
   suspension or cancellation of registration, [13.25], [13.108]–[13.112]
   unprofessional conduct and misconduct — *see* **Professional misconduct**

Disclosure
   client access to records — *see* **Client access to records**
   confidential information, of, [7.40], [7.41], [7.109]
   changes in legislation, [7.51]–[7.52]
   checklist, [7.110]
   compulsion by law, [7.72]
   guidelines for health carers, [7.109]
   HIV/AIDS client, [7.83]–[7.88], [16.38]
   interest of party concerned, [7.81]
   privacy principles, [7.86]
   public interest, [7.74]
   relatives, [7.82]
   consent and reasonable disclosure, [4.4]
   proper and in patient's interests, [4.51]
   contracts, disclosure of information to employer, [11.33]
   defamation — *see* **Defamation**
   disclosure allowed, [7.70]
   agreement, [7.71]
   privacy — *see* **Privacy**
   private health sector, changes to, [7.51]–[7.52]
   reporting accidents and injuries, lack of full and frank disclosure, [12.2]

Discrimination
   complaints procedure, [18.71], [18.72], [18.73]
   conciliation, [18.78]–[18.79]
   litigation, [18.80]
   which legislation to use, [18.90]–[18.91]
   definitions and interpretation, [18.34], [18.35]
   direct discrimination, [18.36]
   exceptions to wrongful discrimination, exceptions, [18.42]
   indirect discrimination, [18.37]–[18.39]
   disability, [18.72]
   definition, [18.72]
   Disability Discrimination Act, [18.52], [18.53], [18.91]
   federal legislation, [18.40]
   Aged Care Act, [18.73], [18.91]
   controversial exception, [18.75]–[18.76]
   Disability Discrimination Act, [18.72], [18.91]
   Equal Opportunity for Women in the Workplace Act, [18.93]
   employment discrimination, [18.41]–[18.42]
   exceptions in employment provisions, [18.51]
   Human Rights and Equal Opportunity Act, [18.41]–[18.49], [18.91]
   Racial Discrimination Act, [18.52]–[18.53], [18.91]
   remedies, [18.78]–[18.80]
   Workplace Relations Act, [18.50]
   HIV/AIDS, [16.39]
   education of medical staff, [16.42]
   effect of anti-discrimination legislation on health carer, [16.41]

Discrimination — *continued*
HIV/AIDS — *continued*
human rights considerations, [18.41]
legislation to prohibit, [16.40]–[16.41]
Human Rights Commission, [18.40], [18.76]–[18.77], [18.91]
cases involving, [18.43]–[18.49], [18.54]–[18.59], [18.77]
measures to achieve equality, [18.75]–[18.76], [18.93]
racial discrimination, [18.52]
cases, [18.54]–[18.58]
definition, [18.52]
International Convention on the Elimination of all Forms of Racial Discrimination, [18.52], [18.53]
Racial Discrimination Act, [18.52], [18.53], [18.91]
sex discrimination, [18.59]
cases, [18.60]–[18.62], [18.65]–[18.66], [18.68], [18.69]–[18.70]
complaints procedure, [18.71]
definition, [18.59]
International Convention on the Elimination of all Forms of Discrimination against Women (CEDAW), [18.59]
male employees, [18.69]–[18.70]
obligations of employers, [18.65]–[18.66]
reproductive technology, access to, [17.68]
Sex Discrimination Act, [18.59], [18.60], [18.77], [18.78]
sexist harassment, [18.67]–[18.68]
sexual harassment, [18.65]
special considerations for the aged, [18.73]
Aged Care Act, [18.73]
Department of Community Services and Health, [18.74]
Hostels Standards Review Panel, [18.74]
inspection of hostels, [18.74]
quality care principles, [18.73]
State and Territory legislation, [19.92]
Australian Capital Territory, [18.82]
exceptions, [18.51], [18.92]
New South Wales, [18.83]
Northern Territory, [18.84]
Queensland, [18.85]
South Australia, [18,86]
Tasmania, [18.87]
Victoria, [18.88]
Western Australia, [18.89]

Diseases — *see* **Notifiable disease**

Dispute resolution
alternative — *see* **Alternative dispute resolution (ADR)**
civil or criminal actions, [3.2], [3.7]
negotiation, [3.7]–[3.9], [3.13]
out-of-court settlements, [3.8]
before court judgment, [3.13]
without prejudice, [3.9]

District Court
appeal from magistrates court, [2.20], [2.21]
functions of, [2.20]
trials, [2.21]

Domestic violence
arrest of offender by police, [16.86], [16.88]
breach of protection order, [16.97]
assault, [16.81], [16.85]
criminal nature of, [16.81]
definition, [16.83]
gun laws, [16.99]
health carers dealing with, [16.82]
access and entry issues, [16.98]
where no legal obligation to report, [16.82]
immediate assistance
detention without warrant, [16.81], [16.86]
emergency accommodation, [16.81]
power of police to enter, search and seize weapons, [16.81], [16.99]
prosecution, [16.86]
proof of event, problems with, [16.87]
protection of victims, [16.83], [16.84], [16.86]
Commonwealth legislation, [16.89]
state and territory legislation, [16.90]
protection orders, [16.86]
chart showing who may seek and be protected by, [11.92]
conditions for granting by court, [16.94]
considerations for granting by court, [16.95]
effect of domestic violence order, [16.96], [16.97]
injunction to restrain person, from magistrates court, [16.90]
injunction under *Family Law Act* 1975, [16.89]
lawyer not required for, [16.93]

Domestic violence — *continued*
protection orders — *continued*
New South Wales, [16.91]
non-molestation order restricting access, [16.98]
serving of, [16.97]
provocation, [16.81], [16.87]

Donation of blood — *see* **Blood donations**

Donation of human tissue — *see* **Human tissue transplants**

Drug Court (New South Wales), [2.37]

Drugs
administration, [8.18]
complexity of legislation, [8.19]
definition, [8.18]
errors in, [8.2]–[8.4], [8.52]–[8.64]
procedural directions, [8.9], [8.68]
register kept, [8.18]
breach of duty of care, [8.1]
criminal law, [8.37]
disciplinary action, [8.38]
destruction of drugs, rules for [8.24]–[8.26]
dispensing drugs, [8.13]
drug order forms, [8.28]
verbal orders, [8.29]
drug schedules, [8.7]–[8.8]
emergencies, [8.30]–[8.32]
illegal or illicit drugs, [8.11]
negligence, [8.39]
consent, [8.40]
failure to check drugs, [8.55]
failure to check for adverse effects, [8.65]–[8.67]
giving drug in wrong site, [8.61]–[8.64]
giving drug to wrong patient, [8.60]
giving wrong dose, [8.57]–[8.59]
giving wrong drug, [8.52]–[8.54]
reasonable care, [8.40]
telephone order, [8.48]–[8.49]
transcribing drug orders, [8.50]–[8.51]
unclear order, [8.41]–[8.47], [8.53]
non-scheduled drugs, [8.33]–[8.35]
Complementary Medicines Evaluation Committee, [8.34]
nurse practitioners, [13.18]
New South Wales, [13.20]
Victoria, [13.21]
oral orders, [8.29]–[8.32], [8.53]
opiates, [8.31]
outdated, [8.71]
telephone, [8.48]–[8.49]
possession of drugs, [8.15]
prescription of drugs, [8.16]
drugs of addiction, [8.27]
offence, [8.17]
professional misconduct cases
failure in drug administration, [13.93]–[13.94]
intention of practitioner, [13.98]–[13.100]
provision of drugs to addicts, [13.53]
prohibition and controls, [8.10]
protocols checklist, [8.68]–[8.70]
re-packaging drugs, [8.36]
regulation of, [8.9]–[8.16]
restricted drugs, [8.12], [8.31]
standing orders, [8.68]
checklist, [8.68]–[8.70]
statutory law, [8.5], [8.39]
Therapeutic Goods Act 1989, [8.6], [8.34]
storage and recording of drugs, [8.20]–[8.23]
supplying drugs, [8.14]
suspension or cancellation of registration for overuse, [13.30]
uniform classification of, [8.7]
vicarious liability, [8.9]

Duress
defence to criminal charge, [14.59]–[14.60]

Duty of care — *see also* **Professional negligence**
health carer, [6.13], [6.174]
nature or amount of harm, [6.29]–[6.30]
occupier's, [6.62]
psychological harm, issue of, [6.51]–[6.53]
question of law, [6.31]–[6.32]
reasonable foreseeability, [6.22]–[6.29]
policy, as, [6.33]
rescuers, owed to, [6.49]–[6.50]
stranger, [6.43]–[6.48]
third persons, to, [6.39]–[6.42]
unborn, to, [6.54]–[6.61]
when one assumes duty, [6.37]–[6.38]

Dying declarations, [7.28]

Emergencies
  consent for medical treatment in, [4.58]–[4.64], [4.110]
    blood transfusion, [17.15]
    child, [5.4]–[5.12], [17.16]
    person with mental illness — *see* **Mental illness**
  removal of tissue, [17.28]
  hospitals, [6.123], [6.133]–[6.134]
    accidents and other incidents, [6.135]
    adequate follow-up on discharge, [6.131]–[6.134]
    checklist of considerations on patient leaving hospital, [6.134]
    client's property in emergency admissions, [9.25]–[9.26]
    liability of clinic, [6.134]
    liability of doctor, [6.134]
    oral orders for drugs, [8.30]–[8.32]
    proper assessment and diagnosis, [6.125]
    reasonable care, [6.129]–[6.130]
    treatment by hospital, [6.134]
    triage nurses, [6.126], [6.133]–[6.134]
  standard of care, [6.75]–[6.77], [6.114]–[6.139]

Emergency services
  refusal of consent by competent person, [4.65]
  standard of care, [6.75]–[6.77], [6.114]
    ambulance, paramedics and rescue workers, [6.115]–[6.122]
    hospitals — *see* **Emergencies**
    scene of accident, [6.135]

Employee
  contract generally — *see* **Contract**
  contracts with employers — *see* **Contracts to provide health care services**
  discrimiation — *see* **Discrimination**
  indemnity insurance, [6.196]
  International Convention Concerning Discrimination in Respect of Employment and Occupation, [18.14]
  power of employers to discipline, [11.44]–[11.48]
  vicarious liability
    in course of employment, [6.197]
    legislation to protect, [6.199]–[6.201]
    tests to determine employment, [6.182]
    who is, [6.181]

  workers' compensation — *see* **Workers' compensation**
  workplace safety — *see* **Workplace safety**

Employers
  contracts to provide services — *see* **Contracts to provide health care services**
  disclosure of health carer's HIV/AIDS status to, [16.58]
  discrimination — *see* **Discrimination**
  ownership of medical records, [7.111]
  power to discipline employees, [11.44]–[11.48]
  request for information by, [7.109]
  vicarious liability, [6.198]
    right to require contributions to compensation, [6.199]
  workplace safety, [12.9]
    guidelines for, [12.11]
    interpretation in handling issues, [12.10]
    provisional improvement notice, [12.15]
    responsibilities, [12.7], [12.9]
    written plan, [12.11]

English courts
  Court of Appeals, [2.81]
  House of Lords, [2.80]
  negligence law, relevance to, [2.82]

Equal Opportunity for Women in the Workplace Act, [18.93]

Equal opportunity tribunals, [2.63]

Equity
  principles of, [1.45], [1.46]
    origins of, [1.45]
  statutory law and common law, inter-relationship with, [1.48], [1.49]

Error of law
  appeal, [3.6]
  judicial review, [2.75]

Ethical and moral rules
  concept of, [1.1], [19.6]–[19.9]
  euthanasia, [14.74]–[14.76]
  examples of past and current breaches, [19.8]
  relationship to law, [1.2], [19.11]

Ethics
  applying ethical principles in decision making, [19.16]
  ascertain legal obligations, [19.19]–[19.24]
  best ethical option, determination of, [19.29]–[19.34]
  investigate and communicate facts and reasons for action, [19.17]–[19.18]
  legal obligations to client, [19.25]
  legal obligations to employer and colleagues, [19.26]–[19.28]
  probability of harm, [19.25]
  bioethics, [1.2]
  codes of ethics, [19.12]
    A Code for Nurses: Ethical Concepts Applied to Nurses, [19.12]
    British Medical Association Code of Ethics, [19.11]
    International Code of Medical Ethics, [19.12]
    principles, [19.12]–[19.14]
  decision making process, [19.2], [19.6]
  consideration of consequences, [19.42]–[19.47]
  steps in process, [19.44]
  definitions, [19.4]–[19.7]
  ethical dilemmas, surgical examples, [19.48]–[19.57]
    cardiac arrest, [19.52]–[19.54]
    errant anaesthetist, [19.50]–[19.51]
    light excuse, [19.48]–[19.50]
    unfortunate removals, [19.54]–[19.58]
  ethical (duty) statements, [19.35]
    differentiation from other statements, [19.36]
    duty statement, [19.40]–[19.41]
    expressive statement, [19.37]
    prescriptive statement, [19.39]
    value statement, [19.38]
  health carer, implications for, [19.63]
  legal and ethical considerations, [19.55]–[19.62]
    mandatory use of incident reports, [19.61]
  issue of ethics, [19.3], [19.8]
  past and current transgressions, [19.8]

Euthanasia
  active euthanasia, [14.74]
  civil negligence, where, [14.74]
  definition, [14.74]
  homicide, where, [14.74], [14.75]
  legal considerations
    assisting a "good death", [14.77]
  duty of care, [14.74], [14.76]
  principle of "sanctity of life", [14.76], [14.102]
  voluntary euthanasia — see **Voluntary euthanasia**
  passive euthanasia, [14.74]
  prohibition of, [1.2]
  theological considerations, [14.103]–[14.104]

Extradition, [2.5]

False imprisonment — see **Detention; Restraint**

Family Court
  counselling and advising role, [1.40]
  functions and principles of, [2.39]
  informality of procedures, [1.41]
  lawyers in, [1.42]
  orders for sterilisation of children, [5.213]
  parens patriae jurisdiction, [5.16], [5.18]

Federal funding
  provisions, [1.35]

Federal Magistrates Court
  establishment of, [2.6], [2.43]
  family law matters, [2.43]
  federal court system diagram, [2.7]
  function, [2.43]
  human rights and discrimination — see **Discrimination**
  mandate, [2.43]

Federation
  Australian Constitution, [1.22], [1.23]
  legal arrangements, [1.22], [1.23]

Feudalism, [1.37]

Foreign affairs power
  interpretation, [1.30]
  narrow, [1.31]
  wider view, [1.32]

Forensic evidence
  consent, [14.189], [14.195]
  patients allegedly the perpetrators of crime, [14.195]
  victims of crime, [14.191]–[14.192]
    confidentiality, [14.194]
    hospital procedures, [14.191]
    involvement in potential criminal cases, [14.193]

Forensic evidence — *continued*
  victims of crime — *continued*
    obligation to report serious crime, [14.191]
    useful evidence, retaining of, [14.192]

Guardian
  appropriate person, [5.85]
  child's medical record, access to, [7.114]
  donation of blood by child, [17.8]
  guardianship boards and tribunals, purpose of, [5.91]
  guardianship where person unable to give consent, [5.84]
    disagreement, where, [5.92]
  mental illness, [5.207]
  notification of sexually transmitted disease of child, [16.26]
  orders, [5.91]
    grounds for guardianship/management orders, diagram, [5.85]
  plenary powers, [5.86]
  summary of legislative provisions for consent to removal and use of regenerative tissue from child, [17.23]
  wishes of person, [5.87], [5.92]

Guilt
  jury to determine whether guilty as charged, [2.16]
    guilty of lesser offence, [2.16]
  "not guilty" verdict, [2.15]
  pleading guilty to indictable offence, [2.17]

Gun laws, [16.99]

Health care complaints commissions
  Australian Capital Territory, [18.25]
  functions of complaints bodies, [18.23], [18.32]
    conciliation, [18.33]
    investigation of complaints, [18.23]
    protection from reprisals, [18.24]
    referral of matters, [18.33]
  immunity from legal action, [18.24]
  independent complaints units, [18.22]–[18.24]
  New South Wales, [18.26]
  Northern Territory, [18.27]
  powers, [18.23]–[18.24], [18.32], [18.33]
    dealing with complaints, [2.65], [18.22], [18.33]
    restrictions where negligent treatment, assault or battery, [18.32]
  Queensland, [18.28]
  statutory mechanisms, [18.22]
  Tasmania, [18.29]
  Victoria, [18.30]
  Western Australia, [18.31]

Health care funding
  federal government power, [1.35]

Health care institutions
  contracts to provide services — *see* **Contracts to provide health care services**
  liability for accidents on property, [12.62], [12.64]
  withholding treatment, [4.6], [14.75], [14.79]
    withdrawing treatment to newborn infants, [14.133]–[14.144]

Health carer
  client consent, [4.4], [4.6], [4.8], [4.25]
    conflict with duty of care, [4.7]
    incompetent persons, [5.88]–[5.89]
    trespass to the person, [4.10], [4.17], [4.18]
  collection of forensic evidence, [14.189]–[14.194], [14.195]
  custody of client's property — *see* **Property**
  duty of confidentiality, [7.44]–[7.47], [14.194]
  ethical decision making, [19.63]
    dealing with dilemmas, [19.16]–[19.34]
    legal and ethical considerations, [19.55]–[19.62]
    mandatory use of incident reports, [19.61]
  expanded health care practice, [6.136]–[6.139]
  human rights — *see* **Health consumers' rights**
  indemnity insurance, [6.196]
  liability, [6.2], [6.3]
    assault — *see* **Assault**
    battery — *see* **Battery**
    consent of child, [5.14]
    learners and inexperienced, [6.99]–[6.105]

Health carer — *continued*
liability — *continued*
negligence — *see* **Professional negligence**
risk of, [4.8], [4.25], [5.88]–[5.89]
list of legal obligations, [1.3]
list of legal rights, [1.3]
negligence — *see* **Professional negligence**
questioning role
checklist for situation causing concern, [6.110]
directions by superior, [6.106]–[6.113]
responsibilities of employers and employees, [6.174]
where incapable of reasonable care, [6.172]–[6.176]
registration — *see* **Registration**
disciplinary action *see* **Disciplinary action**
restraining patients — *see* **Restraint**
self-defence, [4.76]–[4.78]
statutory power to use force, [4.82]
vicarious liability of — *see* **Vicarious liability**

Health consumers' rights
absolute right to refuse medical treatment, [4.18], [14.78]
checklist when client refuses treatment, [14.80]–[14.81]
informed consent issues in Australian courts, [4.51]
refusal in United Kingdom, [4.53]
administratively established rights, [18.2]–[18.4]
Australian Hospitals Association circular, [18.3]
dignity, autonomy and integrity, principle of, [18.4]
hospital's bill of rights, [18.1]
Queensland Health Complaints Commissioner, list of client's rights, [18.3]
charters of patients' rights, [4.20]
common law rights, [18.2]
complaints — *see* **Complaints**
confidentiality — *see* **Confidential information**
consent — *see* **Consent**
Consumers Health Forum of Australia, [18.19]
recommendations, [18.20]
disregard of wishes, [4.53]
health carers, implications for, [18.94]–[18.101]

Human Rights Commission — *see* **Human Rights and Equal Opportunity Commission**
international conventions, under, [18.9], [18.10], [18.12]
domestic application, [18.13], [18.14]
list of rights, [18.14], [18.17]
quality of life issues, [14.126]–[14.132]
do not resuscitate orders, [14.147]–[14.150]
life support, [14.145]–[14.146]
withdrawing treatment to newborn infants, [14.133]–[14.144]
right to privacy — *see* **Privacy**
right to reasonable care — *see* **Negligence**
suicide, [14.78]–[14.80]
attempts, [4.66]–[4.67]
terminally ill patient, [14.76]–[14.89]
checklist to law relating to treatment, [14.150]
coma, [14.150]
end-of-life decision making, [14.82]–[14.84]
"locked-in" state, [14.110]–[14.112], [14.150]
New South Wales guidelines, [14.124]
pain relief, [14.90]–[14.104]
patient's requests, [14.87]
persistent vegetative state, [14.106]–[14.110], [14.150]
voluntary euthanasia — *see* **Voluntary euthanasia**
withholding or withdrawing treatment, [14.75], [14.79]–[14.81]
threats by health carers, [4.19]–[4.21], [4.79]
Trade Practices legislation, [18.21]
victims of crime — *see* **Victims of crime**

Health Insurance Commission
contractual relationship with health carer, [10.1]

Hearsay evidence, [7.25]–[7.26], [7.28]

Henry II, [1.39], [1.40]

High Court
appeals, [2.26]
special leave, [2.27]
costs, [2.26]
hierarchy, [2.26]

High Court — *continued*
  jurisdiction, [2.28]
  video conference technology, [2.26]

Hippocratic Oath, [4.1], [7.56], [19.12]

HIV/AIDS
  blood-borne disease
    blood suppliers' indemnity against liability for contraction of, [17.7], [17.18]
    statutory declaration required of blood donor, [16.33], [17.7], [17.17]
  disclosure of client's confidential information, [7.83]–[7.88], [16.38]
    checklist of privacy principles, [7.86]
    dilemma for health carer, [7.83], [16.5]
    disclosure of identity, [16.38]
    government instrumentalities, [7.87]
    partner notification, [7.83], [7.87], [7.88]
    police with valid warrant, [7.85]
    special consideration for confidentiality of, [7.86]
  disclosure of health carer's HIV/AIDS status, [16.58]
    negligence action, [16.59]
    no legal requirement, [16.59]
    recommendation of Legal Working Party of the Intergovernmental Committee on AIDS, [16.58]
  discrimination, [16.39], [18.96]–[18.99]
    cases compared, [18.97]–[18.100]
    education of medical staff, [16.42]
    effect of anti-discrimination legislation on health carer, [16.41]
    health carers, implications for, [18.94]–[18.96]
    human rights considerations, [18.41]
    legislation to prohibit, [16.40]–[16.41]
  National Health and Medical Research Council (NHMRC)
    infection control guidelines, [16.44]
    recommendations on child immunisation, [16.57]
  National HIV/AIDS strategy, [16.28]

  notifiable disease, [16.5], [16.8], [16.9], [16.14]
    AIDS, concern about, [16.27]
    categories and interpretations, [16.29]
    compulsory examination, [16.43], [16.45]
    legal requirements, [16.28]–[16.31]
    obligations of medical practitioner, [16.30]–[16.31]
    stages of disease, [16.28]–[16.29]
    testing, [16.32]
  public health issues, [16.4]–[16.5]
    blood testing on admission to facilities, [16.44]
    blood transfusions [16.32], [16.33]
    caution where blood testing for diagnosis, [17.18]
    HIV-infected syringes, [16.36]
    safe sex practices, [16.31]
    semen donation, [16.34]
  public health legislation
    compulsory medical tests and treatment, [16.43], [16.45]
    detention, [16.45]–[16.47]
    needle exchange, [16.48]–[16.56]
    Tasmania, [16.46]
  spreading of disease, [16.35], [16.41]
    legislation to prohibit, [16.36]–[16.37], [16.46]
    malicious infection, [16.36]
    offences and penalties, [16.36]–[16.37]
  tests, [16.32], [16.45]
    blood test on admission to facilities, [16.44]
    caution where blood testing for diagnosis, [17.18]
    discrimination cases, [18.96]–[18.100]
    HIV positive serum tests, [16.29]
    legislation for counselling and information, [16.32]
    regenerative tissue, [17.23]
  workplace safety, [12.13]

Homicide
  definition, [14.68]
  euthanasia, [14.74]–[14.76]
  infanticide, [14.73]
    child born alive, [14.72]
  manslaughter, [14.70]
  murder, [14.69]
  principle of "sanctity of life", [14.76]–[14.77], [14.102]
  spreading of disease, [16.35], [16.41]
  suicide, [14.78]

Hospitals
  contracts to provide services — *see* **Contracts to provide health care services**
  custody of client's property — *see* **Property**
  emergency care, [6.123], [6.133]–[6.134]
    accidents and other incidents, [6.135]
    adequate follow-up on discharge, [6.131]–[6.134]
    checklist of considerations on patient leaving hospital, [6.134]
    client's property in emergency admissions, [9.25]–[9.26]
    liability of clinic, [6.134]
    liability of doctor, [6.134]
    oral orders for drugs, [8.30]–[8.32]
    proper assessment and diagnosis, [6.125]
    reasonable care, [6.129]–[6.130]
    treatment by hospital, [6.134]
    triage nurses, [6.126], [6.133]–[6.134]
  ethics — *see* **Ethics**
  privacy guidelines, [7.57], [7.109]
  rights of patients — *see* **Health consumers' rights**
  vicarious liability, [6.179], [6.183]
    case of negligence in nursing care, [6.187]–[6.193]
    procedural directions for handling drugs, [8.9]

Human rights
  application to any person, [18.5]
    summary of rights applicable in Australia, [18.14]
  Burdekin Report, [5.184]
  common law protection of, [1.62], [3.43], [5.183], [18.2]
  definition, [18.2], [18.15]
  domestic law, [18.13]
    Human Rights Commission — *see* **Human Rights and Equal Opportunity Commission**
  health carers, implications for, [18.94]–[18.101]
  health consumers' rights — *see* **Health consumers' rights**
  international law, [18.5]
    complexity of, [18.7]
    Convention on the Rights of the Child, [18.12], [18.15]
    Declaration of Human Rights, [1.59], [18.6]
    Declaration of the Rights of Disabled Persons, [18.12], [18.14]
    Declaration of the Rights of Mentally Retarded Persons, [18.12], [18.14]
    Declaration of the Rights of the Child, [18.12], [18.14]
    enforcement, [18.8], [18.9]
    foreign affairs power, [18.11]–[18.12]
    international conventions, [18.9]–[18.10]
    International Convention Concerning Discrimination in Respect of Employment and Occupation, [18.14]
    International Court of Justice, [18.8]
    International Covenant on Civil and Political Rights, [2.71], [18.10], [18.12], [18.14]
    International Covenant on Social, Economic and Cultural Rights, [18.12]
    ratification, [18.9]
    reservations to specific clauses, [18.9]
  mentally ill persons — *see* **Mental illness**
  overview, [18.1], [18.5]
  referendum, [1.34]
  what is a right, [18.2]
    administratively established rights, [18.2]–[18.4]
    statute-based rights, [18.2]

Human Rights and Equal Opportunity Commission
  criticism of legislation for mental health care, [5.141]
  definition of human rights, [18.15]
  discrimination in employment — *see* **Discrimination**
  establishment of, [18.14], [18.40]
  Federal Court and unconciliated matters, [18.41A]
  function and responsibilities, [2.66], [18.14], [18.41], [18.41A]
  complaints, [18.13], [18.14]
  human rights guaranteed under international conventions, [18.14],
  powers, [18.16], [18.41], [18.41A]
    enforcement, [18.17], [18.41A]
    limitations, [18.17], [18.75]
  principles for health carers treating patients allegedly the perpetrators of crime, [14.196]

Human Rights and Equal Opportunity Commission — *continued*
  racial discrimination — *see* **Racial discrimination**
  unlawful discrimination — *see* **Discrimination**

Human Rights and Equal Opportunity Commission Act 1986
  amendments, [18.41A]
  effects of, [5.63], [14.196], [18.13]–[18.17], [18.91]
  employment discrimination, [18.40]–[18.51]
  establishment of Aboriginal and Torres Strait Islander Social Justice Commissioner, [18.18]

Human tissue transplants
  blood and tissue testing — *see* **Blood and tissue tests**
  blood donations — *see* **Blood donations**
  blood transfusions — *see* **Blood transfusions**
  consent issues, [17.3], [17.4], [17.5], [17.13], [17.16]
    donation from dead donor, [17.32]–[17.35]
    emergencies, [17.28]
    non-regenerative tissue, [17.24]–[17.25]
    person other than operating surgeon, [17.26]
    regenerative tissue, [17.20]–[17.22]
    revocation, [17.27]
    summary of legislative provisions for children, [17.23]
    therapeutic treatment, [17.28]
  controls for tissue donation, [17.4]
  criminal offence of maiming, [17.3]
  definition of "tissue", [17.1]
    exclusions, [17.1]
    non-regenerative, [17.1]
    regenerative, [17.1]
  donations from dead donors, [17.2], [17.29]
    artificial respiration and life support, [17.29], [17.31]
    consent, [17.32]–[17.35]
    controls for tissue donation, [17.4], [17.29], [17.31]
    definitions of "death", [17.30]
    no available next of kin, [17.35]
    postmortems and anatomical examinations — *see* **Postmortem**
    senior available next of kin, [17.34]
  donations from live donors, [17.1], [17.19]–[17.28]
  non-regenerative tissue
    adults, [17.24]
    children, [17.25]
    definition, [17.1]
    parents, [17.25]
  postmortems and anatomical examinations, [17.36]
    consent for, [17.37]
    responsibility of designated officer of health facility, [17.38]
    stipulation of conditions by coroner, [17.36]
  preserving tissues for donation, [17.29]
  prohibition in trading in tissue, [17.1]
  regenerative tissue
    adults, [17.20]
    certificate for removal of, [17.20], [17.21]
    children, [17.22], [17.23]
    definition, [17.1]
    summary of legislative provisions for consent from child, [17.23]
    testing for HIV/AIDS antibodies, [17.23]
  storage and use of ova, spermatozoa and foetal tissue, [17.19]
  therapeutic purpose, [17.3], [17.5]
    therapeutic treatment, [17.28]
  transplantation legislation, [17.1]
  valid consent, [17.1]

Immunisation, [16.57]

Impairment
  definition, [18.41]
  impairment due to drugs, [5.64]

Incompetence
  child — *see* **Child**
  definition, [5.1], [5.63]
  persons legally incapable of consent to health care, [5.1]
    Alzheimer's disease, [5.67]
    chronic dementia, [5.67]
    chronic incapacity, [5.66]–[5.67]
    impairment due to drugs, [5.64]
    intellectual disability, [5.66], [5.93]–[5.98]
    mental illness — *see* **Mental illness**
    other legal obligations, [5.93]–[5.98]
    temporary incapacity, [5.62]–[5.65], [5.135]

Incompetence — *continued*
  responsibilities of health carers, [5.88]–[5.89]
    property, when client becomes incompetent, [9.29]
    psychiatric patients, [5.208]–[5.210]
    resuscitation case, [5.56]–[5.61]
    role of court, [5.56]
    special medical procedures, [5.83], [5.87]
    spouse or relatives, consent of, [5.71]–[5.72]
    exceptions, [5.73]–[5.80]
    who can give consent for impaired person, [5.68]–[5.83]
      advance directives — *see* **Advance directives**
      diagram, [5.69]
      guardian — *see* **Guardian**
      power of attorney — *see* **Power of attorney**

Indictable offence
  committal hearing, pleading guilty at, [2.14], [3.20]
  main steps, [3.20]
  right to trial before jury, [2.14], [3.20]

Industrial relations
  arbitration, [11.56]
  bans, [11.57]–[11.60]
  conciliation, [11.55]
  disputes
    anti-discrimination, [11.89]
    industrial action, [11.73]–[11.75]
    resolution of disputes, [11.55]–[11.62]
  enterprise agreements, [11.49]
  generally, [11.50]
    development of mechanisms, [11.53]
    effect of subsequent conduct of parties, [11.51]
    industrial relations law, [11.52]
  implied terms of employment, [11.16]
  industrial agreements
    Australian Workplace Agreements (AWAs), [11.76]–[11.78]
    certified agreements, [11.71]
    non-award agreements, [11.70]
  industrial awards, [11.49]
    allowable matters, [11.67]–[11.69]
  legislation, [11.49]–[11.50]
    commonwealth, [11.63]–[11.69]
    states and territories, [11.63]–[11.69], [11.92]–[11.102]
  Workplace Relations Act, [11.65]–[11.69], [11.71]–[11.73], [11.79]–[11.82]
  minimum wages, [11.90]
  parental leave and family leave, [11.91]
  strikes, [11.57]–[11.60]
  termination of employment, [11.61]–[11.62], [11.79]–[11.80]
  unfair dismissal, [11.62], [11.83]–[11.88]
  unlawful, [11.81]–[11.82], [11.89]

Information
  client access to records — *see* **Client access to records**
  client request, [7.109]
  confidential information — *see* **Confidential information**
  disclosure — *see* **Disclosure**
  informed consent, required for, [4.83], [4.89]–[4.102]
    answering questions, [4.114]–[4.119]
    checklist, [4.122]–[4.125]
    implications for health carers, [4.108]
    material risk, [4.103]–[4.107]
  lack of information as ground for negligence, [4.85], [4.87]–[4.88]
  medical records — *see* **Medical records**
  plaintiff to prove that ignorance affected decision, [4.120]
  request by court or commission, [7.109]
  request by media, [7.109]
  request by other health professional, [7.109]
  request by police, [7.109]
  request by relative, [7.109]
  statutory requirements, [4.93]
  therapeutic privilege, [4.8], [4.109]–[4.119]
  when client does not want to know, [4.125]–[4.126]

Injuries
  accidents — *see* **Accidents and injuries**
  definition, [12.29]
  failure to properly assess and treat injuries, [13.61]–[13.68]
  workplace safety — *see* **Workplace safety**

Innocence
  presumption of innocence, [1.61]

Innocence—*continued*
  proof of, [2.15]–[2.18]
    term "non guilt", [2.15]

Insanity
  defence to criminal charge, [14.45]–[14.47]
  McNaghten rules, [14.46]

International Convention Concerning Discrimination in Respect of Employment and Occupation, [18.14]

International Convention on the Elimination of all Forms of Discrimination against Women (CEDAW), [18.59]

International Convention on the Elimination of all Forms of Racial Discrimination, [18.52], [18.53]

International Covenant on Civil and Political Rights, [2.71], [18.10], [18.12], [18.14]

International Covenant on Social, Economic and Cultural Rights, [18.12]

Internet, [1.19]

Islamic law, [1.15]

Judge
  functions and task, [3.15]
  independence of client, undermining of, [4.8]

Jurisdiction of courts—*see* **Courts**

Jurisprudence
  study of [1.4]
  theories, [1.7]

Jury
  District Court trials, [2.21]
  function and task, [3.14]
  Magistrates Court, [2.13], [2.14], [2.16]

Law
  basic understanding of, [1.4]
  classifications, [1.5]
  consequences for breach of, [1.1]
  legal responsibilities and rights of health carers, [1.3]
  legal theory, [1.6]
  natural law, [1.7]
  positive law, [1.8]
  procedural law, [1.5]
  relationship to ethical principles, [1.2]
  sources for Australian law, [1.18]–[1.57]
  substantive law, [1.5]

Law reports
  reporting of legal cases, [2.84]
    Federal Courts, [2.85]
    State Courts, [2.86]

Legal aid, [3.10]

Legal reasoning, [3.25]

Legal structure, [2.1]

Legal systems
  basic principles, [1.58]
    erosion of, [1.63]
    natural justice, principles of, [1.59]
    presumption of innocence, [1.61]
    protection of human rights, [1.62]
    rule of law, [1.60]
  civil law, [1.13]
  common law, [1.11], [1.12], [1.17]
    origins, [1.37]–[1.44]
  customary law, [1.16]
  Islamic law and some Eastern legal systems, [1.15]
  overview, [1.10]
  socialist law, [1.14]

Legal theory, [1.6]

Legislation
  delegated, [1.19]
  diagram of different levels, [1.19]
  repeal or amendment of, [1.36]
  statutes, [1.19]
  statutory interpretation—*see* **Statutory interpretation**
  where no precedent or legislation, [1.55], [3.56]–[3.69]

Litigation
  civil and criminal actions, [3.2], [3.7]
  costs, [3.10]
    threat of expenses, [3.7]
  discrimination complaint, [18.80]

Litigation — *continued*
incidence of medical litigation, [3.8]–[3.9], [6.7]
damages — *see* **Damages**
negotiation — *see* **Dispute Resolution; Negotiation**

Local Court — *see* **Magistrates Court**

Magistrates Court
appeals from, [2.19]
  federal law, under, [2.25]
  Local Court (NSW), [2.10]
committal hearing, [2.14]
coronial hearing, [2.13]
function and title varies between States, [2.10]
guilt — *see* **Guilt**
hierarchy, [2.12]
jury, [2.13], [2.14]
  determination of guilty as charged, [2.16]
matters dealt with, [2.11]
summary decisions, [2.13]

Mandamus, [2.31]

Manslaughter
criminal negligence, [14.152]–[14.154]
diminished responsibility, [14.73]
homicide, [14.70]

Medical negligence — *see* **Professional negligence**

Medical records
client access to records — *see* **Client access to records**
confidential information — *see* **Confidential information**
coroner's inquest, availability at, [15.61]–[15.62]
functions, [7.6]–[7.7]
  protection of health carers, [7.9]–[7.27], [7.39]
incident reports, [7.29]–[7.33]
  checklist, [7.37]
  evidence, as, [7.34]–[7.39]
  reporting a serious accident, [7.38]–[7.39]
legislation, [7.58]
ownership of, [7.2]–[7.5], [7.111]
reports, requirements for
  adequate and accurate, [7.14]
  contemporaneous, [7.9]
  errors not obliterated, [7.20]–[7.21]
  evidence, as, [7.25]–[7.28]
  legible and clear, [7.19]
  objective, [7.16]–[7.18]
  rewritten at later date, not, [7.22]
  treatment orders, not transcribed, [7.23]
  written on behalf of another, not, [7.24]
statutory declarations, [7.13]

Medical research
consent issues, [4.150]–[4.154]
liability of practitioner, [6.139]
privacy, [7.48]
  request for information, [7.109]
protocols and guidelines, [6.139], [7.48]
registers for epidemiological research, [16.11]
registration boards, [13.10]
  statistical information, collection of, [13.13]

Medical services
federal government regulation of, [1.35]

Medicare
contractual relationship, [10.1], [10.46]

Mental health tribunals or boards, [2.49]

Mental illness
certification, [5.147]–[5.150]
contractual capacity, [10.62], [10.64]
definitions, [5.143]–[5.145]
  behaviour not regarded as mental illness, [5.146], [5.150]
  mental disorder, [5.145]
  psychiatric illness, [5.145], [5.149], [5.174]
  unsound mind, [10.62]
emergency detention and treatment, [5.159], [5.169]
  Australian Capital Territory, [5.161]
  danger to themselves or others, [5.169]
  habeas corpus, [5.159]
  issue of certificates, [5.160]
  lawful detention, [5.159]
  New South Wales, [5.162]
  orders for treatment — *see* orders for treatment *below*
overview, [5.142]
rights — *see* protection of person's rights *below*
South Australia, [5.165]

Mental illness — *continued*
  emergency detention and treatment — *continued*
    Tasmania, [5.166]
    Victoria, [5.167]
    Western Australia, [5.168]
  guardianship, [5.207]
  health carers, implications for health carers, [5.182]–[5.185], [5.206]–[5.210]
  international human rights relevant to health carer
    Declaration on the Rights of Mentally Retarded Persons, [5.63], [18.12]
    Principles for the Protection of Persons with Mental Illness and the Improvement of Mental Health Care, [5.140], [18.12]
  involuntary patients — *see* emergency detention and treatment *above*
  mental illness or mental disability, distinguished, [5.151]
  natural justice, [5.59], [5.177]
  orders for treatment, [5.152]–[5.154], [5.170]–[5.174], [5.185]
    appeal, [5.173]
    community care, [5.178]–[5.179]
    electroconvulsive therapy, [5.186]–[5.192]
    evidence, careful consideration of, [5.171]
    mental illness or dysfunction must be established, [5.175]–[5.177]
    psychiatric illness, [5.174], [5.175]–[5.177]
    psychiatric surgery, [5.186], [5.193]–[5.198]
    representation at hearing, [5.172]
  person unable to give consent, [5.61]
  Principles for the Protection of Persons with Mental Illness and the Improvement of Mental Health Care, [5.140], [18.12]
  protection of person's rights, [5.139]–[5.218]
    Burdekin Report, [5.184]
    care should be neither unnecessary or excessive, [5.181]
    common law protection of, [5.183], [5.199]
    Declaration on Rights of Mentally Retarded Persons, [5.63]
    guardianship, [5.207]
    implications for health carers, [5.182]–[5.185]
    period of treatment or detention is set, [5.180]
    statement of rights, [5.140]
    restraints on person with, [4.181], [5.204]–[5.206]
    detention — *see* emergency detention and treatment *above*
    statutory legislation in Victoria, [4.191], [5.205]
    Western Australia, [5.206]
  sterilisation of persons with, [5.211]–[5.220]
    provisions, [5.211]
  voluntary patients, [5.155]–[5.158], [10.64]

Midwifery
  practice of, [3.46]

Minor — *see also* **Child**
  contractual capacity, [10.53]–[10.61]
  definition, [5.2]
  mature minor, [5.3], [5.23], [5.28], [5.30]
    disagreement with parents, [5.37]–[5.39]

Mischief rule, [3.29]

Murder, [14.69]

National Health and Medical Research Council (NHMRC)
  ethical guidelines on assisted reproductive technology, [17.39], [17.59]
  further requirements, [17.60]
  infection control guidelines, [16.44]

National Occupational Health and Safety Commission, [12.12]

Natural justice, principles of, [1.59], [2.75]

Natural law, [1.7], [1.59]

Necessity, [4.68]–[4.74], [4.110]

Negligence
  absence of consent, [4.10], [6.1]
  action in negligence, [4.12]
    cases, [4.49], [4.51]
    damages — *see* **Damages**
    defences — *see* **Defences**
    lack of information as ground for, [4.85], [4.87]–[4.88]
  claims for compensation, percentage resolved out of court, [3.8]

Index | 703

Negligence — *continued*
  criminal negligence, [14.151]
    degree of culpability, [14.152]
    manslaughter, [14.152]–[14.154]
  difference between negligence and incompetence, [6.3]
  informed consent, [4.51]
  malpractice — *see* **Professional negligence**
  meanings, [3.32]
  professional negligence — *see* **Professional negligence**
  relevance of English courts to, [2.82]
  vicarious liability — *see* **Vicarious liability**

Negotiation
  avoiding litigation, [3.7]
    negotiated settlement by barristers, [3.13]
    out-of-court settlements, [3.8]
    without prejudice, [3.9]

Nervous shock
  cases, [6.151]–[6.155]
  definition, [6.150]
  legislative provisions, [6.156]
  relatives eligible for damages, [6.156]

Notifiable disease
  AIDS — *see* **HIV/AIDS**
  authorities, powers of, [16.22], [16.45]
  blood borne disease
    blood suppliers indemnity against liability for contraction of, [17.7], [17.18]
    statutory declaration required of blood donor, [16.33], [17.7]
  cancer, [16.10]
    definition, [16.10]
    epidemiological research, [16.11]
    types of cancers included, [16.11]
  contagious disease, [16.4]
    sexually transmitted disease — *see* **Sexually transmitted disease**
  definitions, [16.6]
    dangerous disease, [16.6]
    notifiable disease, [16.4], [16.6], [16.8]
    reportable disease, [16.6], [16.7]
    transmissible diseases, [16.9]
  disclosure where carer has notifiable disease, [16.58]–[16.60]
    no legal requirement, [16.59]
  fumigation of property, [16.22]
  government gazette, [16.7]
  immunisation, [16.57]
  infectious diseases, [16.4], [16.8], [16.9], [16.27]
    control by state, [16.45]–[16.47]
    examples of infectious and transmissible diseases, [16.9]
  information to be provided, [16.21]
  inspection of premises, [16.22]
  jurisdictions, different classifications in, [16.7], [16.12]
    New South Wales, [16.13]–[16.14]
    Queensland, [16.15]
    South Australia, [16.16]
    Victoria, [16.17]
    Western Australia, [16.18]
  public health issues, [16.3]–[16.5]
    AIDS — *see* **HIV/AIDS**
  public health legislation
    authorities, powers of, [16.22], [16.45]
    compulsory medical tests and treatment, [16.45]
    detention, [16.45]–[16.47]
    needle exchange, [16.48]–[16.56]
    other measures to control infection, [16.57A]
  regulation of, [16.4]
    freedom of individual issues, [16.5]
  reporting to the state, [15.1], [16.1]
    role of health worker, [16.20]
  who must report
    Australian Capital Territory, [16.19]
    New South Wales, [16.13]–[16.14]
    Queensland, [16.15]
    South Australia, [16.16]
    Tasmania, [16.19]
    Victoria, [16.17]
    Western Australia, [16.18]

Notification
  matters which must be reported to the state, [15.1], [16.1]
  births — *see* **Birth**
  child abuse — *see* **Child abuse**
  death — *see* **Death**
  diseases — *see* **Notifiable disease**
  domestic violence — *see* **Domestic violence**
  HIV/AIDS — *see* **HIV/AIDS**

Nurses
  emergency facilities, triage nurses, [6.126], [6.133]–[6.134]
  ethics — *see* **Ethics**
  professional misconduct
    counselling case, [13.71]–[13.80]
    failure in drug administration, [13.93]–[13.94]

Nurses — *continued*
  professional misconduct — *continued*
    meaning of "in the practice of nursing", [13.69], [13.70]
  registration, governing Acts in various jurisdictions, [13.2]
  registration of nurse practitioners, [13.18]
    New South Wales legislation, [13.19], [13.20]
    offences, cancellation and suspension, [13.22]
    poisons and therapeutic goods, [13.20], [13.21]
    Victoria, [13.21]
  unprofessional conduct
    Australian Capital Territory, [13.48]
    New South Wales, [13.34]
    Northern Territory, [13.50]
    Queensland, [13.37]
    South Australia, [13.38]
    Tasmania, [13.39]
    Victoria, [13.41]
    Western Australia, [13.43]–[13.44]

Obiter dicta, [3.49], [3.50]

Occupational health and safety
  employers, [12.9]
    guidelines for, [12.11]
    interpretation in handling issues, [12.10]
    provisional improvement notice, [12.15]
    responsibilities, [12.7], [12.9]
    written plan, [12.11]
  inspectors and investigators, [12.17]
    default notices, [12.15]
  legislation, [12.7], [12.15]–[12.16]
    codes of practice, [12.11]
    National Occupational Health and Safety Commission Act 1985, [12.12]
  National Occupational Health and Safety Commission, [12.12]
  safe workplace, [12.8]–[12.17]
    inspection, [12.17]
    joint staff-management committees, [12.13]
  workers, [12.11]
    health and safety representatives, [12.13], [12.15]–[12.16]
    immediate threat to health and safety, [12.14]
    victimisation, [12.16]
  workers' compensation — *see* **Workers' compensation**
  Worksafe Australia, [12.12]

Occupiers
  definition, [12.63]–[12.65]
  liability for accidents on their property, [12.62]–[12.65]
    duty of care, [12.64], [12.69]
    injuries by dogs and other animals, [12.77]–[12.78]
  rights, [12.73]–[12.76]
  standard of care, [12.66]
  warning notices, [12.68], [12.72]

Ombudsman, [2.77]

Original jurisdiction, [2.32]

Palliative care
  Consent to Medical Treatment and Palliative Care Act 1995 (SA), [14.101], [14.120]–[14.121]
  Northern Territory, [14.122]
  summary to law relating to withholding or withdrawing treatment, [14.150]
  treatment of terminally ill patients — *see* **Health consumers' rights**

Parens patriae
  consent for health care of adult legally incapable of consent, [5.56], [5.58]
  consent for health care of child, [5.16], [5.18], [5.22], [5.28], [5.31]

Paternalism, [4.1], [4.6], [4.47], [4.121], [7.113]

Patient's rights — *see* **Health consumers' rights**

Plaintiff, [3.4], [3.5], [3.6]

Positive law, [1.8]
  political or ideological basis for laws, [1.9]

Postmortem
  coroner's order, [15.46]
    overruled by court, [15.48]–[15.49]
  examination of the body, [15.45]
  exhumation, warrant for, [15.49]
  objection by next of kin, [15.47]–[15.48]

Postmortem — *continued*
   request for, [15.46]
     appeal, [15.46]
   transplantation, removal of human tissue for, [17.36]
     consent for postmortem examination, [17.37]
     responsibility of designated officer of health facility, [17.38]
     stipulation of conditions by coroner, [17.36]
     use of bodies and body parts obtained in, [17.36]

Power of attorney
   concept, [5.118]
   enduring power, [5.119]–[5.131]
   medical agent
     appointment, [5.132]
     obligations and powers, [5.134]
     revocation of appointment, [5.138]
   ordinary power, [5.118]
   role of health carers, [5.136]
     differences of opinion, [5.137]
     transitory incapacity of client, [5.135]
   witness, [5.132]
     role of witness, [5.133]

Practice of medicine
   meaning of "in the practice of", [13.69], [13.70]
   cases, [13.69]–[13.80]

Precedent
   court hierarchy, [1.50]
     decisions, when binding, [1.51]
     following precedent established by earlier and higher courts, [1.54]
   effect on judgment, [1.52], [3.45]
   law reporting, [2.84]
   legal reasoning, [3.25]
   persuasive precedent, [1.51], [1.53], [2.83]
     Privy Council, [2.30]
   stare decisis, [1.44], [1.54]
   where no precedent or legislation, [1.55], [2.83], [3.56]–[3.69]

Pregnant woman
   consent issues, [4.137]–[4.140]
   cases, [4.141]–[4.149]

Presumption of innocence
   principle of criminal law, [1.61], [14.39]–[14.41]
   exceptions, [14.42]
     diminished responsibility, [14.48]
     insanity, [14.45]–[14.47]
     McNaghten rules, [14.46]–[14.47]

Preventable adverse events
   Australian Hospital Care Study, [6.4]
   communication, [6.8]
   denial and cover up, [6.9]
   incident monitoring scheme, [6.6]
   Quality in Australian Health Care (QAHCS), [6.5]
   risk management, [6.6], [6.8]

Prima facie case, [2.14]

Principles for the Protection of Persons with Mental Illness and the Improvement of Mental Health Care, [5.140], [18.12]

Privacy — *see also* **Confidential information**
   Commonwealth Privacy Commissioner, [7.48], [7.51]
     new privacy code, [7.53]
   complaints [7.53]
   confidentiality guidelines
     health carers, [7.109]
     private health sector, changes for, [5.117], [7.51]–[7.52]
   obligations on client and health carer, [7.40]
   right to, [7.42], [18.1]
   statutory provisions, [7.48]–[7.55]
     changes for private health sector, [7.49]–[7.53]

Privy Council
   abolition of Australian appeals to, [2.29]
   decisions no longer binding, [2.30]
   function, [2.29]
   persuasive precedent, [2.30]

Procedural law
   diagram, [1.5]

Professional indemnity arrangements
   blood suppliers' indemnity against liability for contraction of blood-borne diseases, [17.7], [17.18]
   Compensation and Professional Health Indemnity in Health Care, [3.8]
   review of, [8.3]

Professional misconduct
   concepts of, [13.31]–[13.51]
     Australian Capital Territory, [13.45]–[13.48]
     New South Wales, [13.32]–[13.34]
     Northern Territory, [13.50]
     Queensland, [13.36]–[13.37]

Professional misconduct — *continued*
concepts of — *continued*
South Australia, [13.38]
Tasmania, [13.39]
Victoria, [13.40]–[13.41]
Western Australia, [13.42]–[13.44]
disciplinary action for — *see*
Disciplinary action
failure to properly assess and treat injuries, [13.61]–[13.68]
fitness to practice, [13.28], [13.107]
general guidelines, [13.91]–[13.94]
improper or unethical conduct, [13.77]–[13.80]
intention of practitioner, [13.95]–[13.106]
intimate relations with clients or past clients, [13.58]–[13.61]
meaning of "in the practice of", [13.69], [13.70]
cases, [13.69]–[13.80]
meaning of "incompetence" and "recklessness", [13.85]–[13.87]
meaning of "infamous conduct in a professional respect", [13.81]–[13.84]
provision of drugs to addicts, [13.53]
specific provisions, [13.31]–[13.51]
surgery carried out in non-orthodox fashion, [13.54]–[13.57]
unprofessional behaviour must be related to professional practice, [13.88]–[13.94]

Professional negligence
causation — *see* **Causation**
damages — *see* **Damages**
defences — *see* **Defences**
definition, [6.11]–[6.12]
duty of care, [6.13]–[6.21]
assuming of, when, [6.37]–[6.38]
nature or amount of harm, [6.29]–[6.30]
occupier's, [6.62]
psychological harm, issue of, [6.51]–[6.53]
question of law, [6.31]–[6.32]
reasonable foreseeability, [6.22]–[6.29], [6.33]
rescuers, owed to, [6.49]–[6.50]
stranger, [6.43]–[6.48]
third persons, to, [6.39]–[6.42]
unborn, to, [6.54]–[6.61]
health carers, relevance to, [6.2], [6.9], [6.10]
difference between negligence and incompetence, [6.3]
incidence of medical litigation, [3.8]–[3.9], [6.7]
learners and inexperienced health carers, [6.99]–[6.105]
malpractice, [6.2]
preventable adverse events — *see* **Preventable adverse events**
standard of care, [6.63]
anticipation of patient's actions, [6.85]–[6.86]
checklist for reasonable standard of care, [6.68]
cirumstances, relevance of, [6.68], [6.75]–[6.77]
different accepted practices, [6.87]–[6.89]
emergencies, [6.75]–[6.77]
evidence of reasonable practice [6.79]
examples of courts' approach, [6.69]–[6.74]
knowledge and practice issues, [6.79]–[6.85]
magnitude of harm, [6.96]
objective test, [6.66]–[6.67]
other limiting factors, [6.90]–[6.91]
person suffering from specific disability, [6.93]–[6.95]
probability of harm, [6.92], [19.25]
procedure manuals, directives, policies and protocols, [6.79]
social utility of activity principle, [6.97]–[6.98]
statutory law, [6.78]
tort of negligence, [6.63]–[6.65]
vicarious liability — *see* **Vicarious liability**

Professional organisations
disciplinary action — *see* **Disciplinary action**
registration — *see* **Registration**
registration board — *see* **Registration board**
self-regulatory system, [13.1], [13.3]

Proof
burden of proof, [3.16]
standard of proof, [3.17]

Property
criminal law and, [14.1]
forms of theft or fraud, [14.4]
custody of client's property, [9.1]
bailment — *see* **Bailment**
entrusting property to another, [9.2]

Property — *continued*
custody of client's property — *continued*
health carers — *see* recommended procedures for health carers *below*
legal aspects for health carers, [9.5]–[9.9]
liability for goods, [9.31]–[9.34]
negligent handling of goods, [9.9]
ownership and possession, [9.2], [9.6]–[9.8]
reasonable care, [9.1], [9.15]
reasons for, [9.3]
wrongful interference, [9.6]–[9.8]
defence of property, in action for battery, [4.79]–[4.81]
fumigation of property where notifiable disease, [16.22]
liability of occupiers for accidents on their property — *see* **Occupiers**
recommended procedures for health carers
best rule: leave it at home, [9.18]
care of valuables, [9.20], [9.26]
careful recording, [9.19]
checklist on admission and transfer, [9.37]
handing property to relatives, [9.22]
witnessed documentation, [9.26]
witnessing by third person, [9.21], [9.26]
special considerations
emergency admissions, [9.25]–[9.26]
exemption clauses, [9.31]–[9.34]
money, [9.24]
possessions kept with client, [9.27]
transfer of client, [9.28], [9.37]
valuable possessions, [9.23]
when client becomes incompetent, [9.29]
when client dies, [9.30]
unclaimed belongings
common law, [9.35]
statute law, [9.36]–[9.37]

Provocation
defence to criminal charge, [14.65]–[14.67]
domestic violence, [16.81]

Psychiatric patients — *see also* **Mental illness**
electroconvulsive therapy, consent to, [5.186]
Australian Capital Territory, [5.187]
informed consent, [5.186]–[5.192]
New South Wales, [5.189]
South Australia, [5.190]
Victoria, [5.191]
Western Australia, [5.192]
non-psychiatric care, consent to, [5.199]
legislation, [5.200]
New South Wales, [5.201]
non-urgent treatment, [5.201]
urgent treatment, [5.201]
Victoria, [5.202]
Western Australia, [5.203]
psychiatric illness
definition, [5.145]
implications for health carers, [5.208]–[5.210]
medication, [5.174]
mild psychiatric illness, case, [5.175]–[5.177]
psychiatric surgery, consent to, [5.186], [5.193]–[5.198], [19.8]
Australian Capital Territory, [5.194]
New South Wales, [5.195]
Northern Territory, [5.193]
Queensland, [5.193]
South Australia, [5.196]
Tasmania, [5.193]
Victoria, [5.197]
Western Australia, [5.198]

Quality in Australian Health Care (QAHCS), [6.5]–[6.6]

Queensland Health Complaints Commissioner, [18.3]

Racial discrimination
conciliation, [18.78]–[18.79]
litigation, [18.80]
definition, [18.52]
International Convention on the Elimination of all Forms of Racial Discrimination, [18.52], [18.53]
Racial Discrimination Act, [18.52], [18.78], [18.91]
areas covered, [18.53]
cases, [18.54]–[18.58]

Ratio decidendi, [3.48], [3.50]

Rationes decidendi, [3.48]

Referendum
changing the constitution, [1.34]
human rights referendum, [1.34]

Referendum — *continued*
referendum giving federal
government new powers in
medical area, [1.34]
funding of medical and dental
services, [1.35]

Registrar of Births Deaths and Marriages, [15.2]

Registration
appeals, [2.78], [13.23], [13.112]
  AAT, [2.78], [13.23], [13.112]
  finding advice for, [13.24]
  jurisdictions, [13.23]
  re-hearings, [13.24], [13.112]
governing Acts, [13.2]
  Aboriginal health workers, [13.2]
  chiropractors, [13.2]
  dentists, [13.2]
  medical practitioners, [13.2], [13.16]
  nurses, [13.2], [13.18]–[13.22]
  occupational therapists, [13.2]
  opticians, [13.2]
  optometrists, [13.2]
  osteopaths, [13.2]
  pharmacists, [13.2]
  physiotherapists, [13.2]
  podiatrists, [13.2]
  psychologists, [13.2]
  radiographers, [13.2]
  speech therapists, [13.2]
jurisdiction, [13.2]
  mutual recognition, [13.4]–[13.6]
nurse practitioners, [13.18]
  New South Wales legislation, [13.19]
  poisons and therapeutic goods, [13.20], [13.21]
  Victoria, [13.21]
offences, cancellation and
  suspension, [13.22], [13.15]
  disciplinary action — *see*
  Disciplinary action
purpose of registration, [13.12]
register, maintenance of, [13.11]
registerable health professions, [13.2]
registration board or council — *see*
  Registration boards
requirements for eligibility, [13.3], [13.12]
  good health and character,
    applicant must be, [13.14]
  payment of fee, [13.13]
  renewal, [13.11], [13.13]
self-regulatory system, [13.1]

suspension or cancellation, [13.25], [13.108]–[13.111]
temporary registration, [13.15]
  conditional, [13.17]
  provisional, [13.15]
  special events, [13.15], [13.16]
  visiting health professionals, [13.15], [13.16]

Registration boards
AAT appeals, [2.78], [13.23], [13.112]
composition, [13.8]
functions and powers, [2.68], [13.7], [13.24], [13.108]
  codes of practice, [13.10]
  inquiries, [13.108]
  removal of ineligible person, [13.111]
  reprimand, [13.110]
  research, [13.9]
  standard of education and practice, [13.9]
  statistical information, collection of, [13.13]
  suspension or cancellation — *see*
    Disciplinary action
health carers
  checklist for disciplinary
    procedures, [13.112]
  coroner's finding of breach, [15.24]
  legal advice, [13.109]
  right to appear in person at
    inquiries, [13.108]
legislation, [13.2], [13.3]
purpose of, [13.3]
re-hearing, [13.24], [13.112]
refusal decision, review of, [13.23]
website for provisions, [13.108]

Rehabilitation
Declaration of the Rights of Disabled
  Persons, [18.12]
workers, of, [12.22], [12.24]

Reproductive technology
access and eligibility for treatment, [17.68]–[17.71]
artificial insemination, [17.46]
  common law, [17.47]
  legislation, [17.48]–[17.54]
clinics performing other reproductive
  technology procedures, [17.55]
  accreditation, [17.59]
  National Health and Medical
    Research Council (NHMRC), [17.59], [17.60]
  prohibited procedures, [17.62], [17.66], [17.67]

Reproductive technology — *continued*
  clinics performing other reproductive technology procedures — *continued*
    regulating bodies, [17.57]–[17.58]
    regulation of procedures, [17.61]–[17.67]
    super-ovulation therapy, [17.56]
  definitions and terminology, [17.40]
    assisted conception, [17.41]
    conception, [17.41]
    GIFT, [17.42]
    in vitro fertilisation, [17.41], [17.64]
    PROST, [17.41]
    TEST, [17.41]
    ZIFT, [17.41]
  ethical considerations, [17.39]
    NHMRC ethical guidelines on assisted reproductive technology, [17.39], [17.59], [17.60]
    research and experimentation issues, [17.43], [17.56]
  Infertility Treatment Authority, [17.63]
  parentage, [17.44]
    donor of gametes, [17.45]
    identity of donor, [17.45]
    need for accurate recording of genetic origins of children, [17.46]
  record keeping, [17.75]–[17.79]
  research issues, [17.43], [17.56]
  storage and use of gametes, zygotes and embryos, [17.72]–[17.74]
  surrogacy agreements, [17.80]
    Australian Capital Territory, [17.87]–[17.88]
    dispute between birth and substitute parents, [17.89]
    Family Law Act 1975, [17.89]
    general national policy, [17.81]
    legislation, [17.82]–[17.89]
    Queensland, [17.84]
    South Australia, [17.83]
    Tasmania, [17.85]
    Victoria, [17.82]
    Western Australia, [17.86]
  who are the parents, [17.44]–[17.45]

Research — *see* **Medical research**

Respondent, [3.4], [3.5], [3.6]

Restraint
  chemical, [4.188]
    definition, [4.176]
  definition, [4.175]
  freedom to leave hospital, [4.184]–[4.186]
  lawful restraint, [4.160]
  least restrictive means, [4.187]
  mentally ill patients — *see* **Mental illness**
  no damage required for action, [4.182]
  policy considerations
    checklist for, [4.190]
    written, [4.189]
  reasonable grounds, [4.183]
  studies of hospital practice, [4.177]–[4.180]

Rights — *see also* **Health consumers' rights; Human rights**

Rogers v Whitaker
  case, [4.98], [4.100], [4.107], [4.109], [4.110]
  effect of, [4.111], [4.114]–[4.115]

Rule of law, [1.60]

Self-defence
  charge of assault, [14.63]–[14.64]
  charge of murder, [14.63]–[14.64]
    High Court requirements, [14.63]
  defence to criminal charge, [14.60]
    case, [14.62]
    checklist, [14.63]–[14.64]
    domestic violence, [16.81]

Sex discrimination
  cases, [18.60]–[18.62], [18.65]–[18.66], [18.68], [18.69]–[18.70]
  complaints procedure, [18.71]
  conciliation, [18.78]–[18.79]
  definition, [18.59]
  International Convention on the Elimination of all Forms of Discrimination against Women (CEDAW), [18.59]
  male employees, [18.69]–[18.70]
  Sex Discrimination Act, [18.59], [18.60], [18.77], [18.78], [18.91]
  imputations, [18.60]
  reproductive technology, access to, [17.68]
  sexual harassment, [18.65]
    obligations of employers, [18.65]–[18.66]
    sexist harassment, [18.67]–[18.68]

Sexual assault
  dealing with victims of, [14.189]–[14.196]

Sexual assault — *continued*
  evidence of the offence, [14.189]–[14.190]
    collection of forensic evidence, [14.191]–[14.192]
  health carer considerations
    confidentiality, [14.194]
    consent, [14.189], [14.195]
    hospital procedures, [14.191]
    involvement in potential criminal cases, [14.193]
    obligation to report serious crime, [14.191]
    useful evidence, retaining of, [14.192]
  patients allegedly the perpetrators of crime, [14.195]
    obligations of health carers, [14.196]
  victim impact statements, [3.3]

Sexual harassment
  prohibition in workforce, [18.65]
    obligations of employers, [18.65]–[18.66]
    sexist harassment, [18.67]–[18.68]

Sexually transmitted diseases
  confidentiality, [16.25]
  examples of, [16.9], [16.23]
  HIV — *see* **HIV/AIDS**
  notification, [15.1], [16.1], [16.23]
  offence to place others at risk, [16.24]
  public health issues, [16.4]–[16.5]
  regulation of, [16.4]
    differences between jurisdictions, [16.8], [16.23], [16.24]
    freedom of individual, [16.5]
    New South Wales, [16.24]
    Queensland, [16.24]
    South Australia, [16.24]
    Victoria, [16.24]

Social Security Appeals Tribunal, [2.62]

Socialist law, [1.14]

Solicitors, [3.11]

Standard of care — *see also* **Professional negligence**
  checklist for reasonable standard of care, [6.68]
  cirumstances, relevance of, [6.68], [6.75]–[6.77]
  different accepted practices, [6.87]–[6.89]
  emergencies, [6.75]–[6.77]
  emergency care, [6.114]–[6.139]
  evidence of reasonable practice [6.79]
  examples of courts' approach, [6.69]–[6.74]
  expanded health care practice, [6.136]–[6.139]
  foreseeable harm, [6.70]
    anticipation of patient's actions, [6.85]–[6.86]
    magnitude of harm, [6.96]
    more good than foreseeable harm, [6.97]–[6.98]
    other limiting factors, [6.90]–[6.91]
    person suffering from specific disability, [6.93]–[6.95]
    probability of harm, [6.92], [19.25]
  knowledge and practice issues, [6.79]–[6.85]
  learners and inexperienced health carers, [6.99]–[6.105]
  objective test, [6.66]–[6.67]
  overview, [6.63]
  procedure manuals, directives, policies and protocols, [6.79]
  questioning of superior's instructions, [6.106]–[6.113]
    checklist for situation causing concern, [6.110]
  social utility of activity principle, [6.97]–[6.98]
  statutory law, [6.78]

Stare decisis, [1.44], [1.54], [1.57]

Statutory declarations
  definition, [7.13]
  health carer's formal statement at coroner's inquest, [15.52]

Statutory interpretation
  ambiguity, [1.29], [3.27]
  checklist, [3.46]
  Constitution, of, [1.29]
    foreign affairs power, [1.30]–[1.32], [18.11]–[18.12]
    major function of High Court, [1.29]
    power vested in federal government, [1.29]–[1.32]
  courts, by, [1.29], [3.28]
    effect on precedent, [3.45]
    favouring of citizen rather than State, [3.42]
    further problems, [3.30]
    golden rule, [3.35]–[3.36]
    literal rule, [3.32]–[3.34]
    presumptions of interpretation, [3.38]–[3.44]

Statutory interpretation — *continued*
  courts, by — *continued*
    purpose rule, [3.28], [3.30], [3.33]
    purposive rule, [3.28], [3.30]
    statute to be read as a whole, [3.37]
    statutes not retrospective, [3.44]
  definitions, [3.31]
  useful publications, [3.46]

Statutory law — *see also* **Legislation**
  common law and equity,
    inter-relationship with, [1.48], [1.49]
  statutes, [1.19]
    legal reasoning, [3.25]

Sterilisation
  special medical treatment, [5.83]
    child, [5.14], [5.211]–[5.213]
    mental illness, cases of, [5.211]–[5.220]

Stillbirths
  definition, [15.9]
  notification of, [15.10]
    failure to give notice, [15.11]
    false information, [15.11]
    parentage, [15.2]
    perinatal deaths, [15.16]

Substantive law
  diagram, [1.5]

Suicide
  attempts, [4.66]–[4.67]
  definition, [14.78]
  end-of-life decision making, [14.82]–[14.84]
  health carer
    checklist when client refuses treatment, [14.80]–[14.81]
    making means of suicide available, [14.78]
    patient's requests, [14.87]
    withholding of life-saving treatment, [14.79]–[14.81]

Supreme Court
  appeals, [2.24]
    federal law, under, [2.25]
  general jurisdiction, [2.23]
  hierarchy, [2.22]

Surrogacy
  agreements, [17.80]
  surrogacy contracts, [10.92]–[10.95]
  dispute between birth and substitute parents, [17.89]
  general national policy, [17.81]
  legislation, [17.82]–[17.89]
    Australian Capital Territory, [17.87]–[17.88]
    Family Law Act 1975, [17.89]
    Queensland, [17.84]
    South Australia, [17.83]
    Tasmania, [17.85]
    Victoria, [17.82]
    Western Australia, [17.86]
  procedures, classification of, [17.42]

Technology
  electronic technology, impact of, [7.43]
  reproductive technology — *see* **Reproductive technology**
  video conference technology in High Court, [2.26]

Territories, [1.33]

Test cases, [1.55]
  change in common law, [1.57]
  where no precedent or legislation, [1.55]

Therapeutic Goods Act 1989, [8.6]

Therapeutic privilege — *see also* **Consent**
  definition, [4.109], [4.110]
  information, withholding of, [4.109]
  judgments, [4.8], [4.109]–[4.119]

Tissue — *see also* **Human tissue transplants**
  definition, [17.1]

Torts
  breach of confidence, [7.59], [7.63]–[7.64]
  classification of tort law, [1.5]
  meaning, [1.38], [6.2]
  negligence, [1.38], [6.2], [6.63]–[6.65]

Trade Practices legislation, [18.21]

Transplants — *see* **Human tissue transplants**

Trespass to the person — *see also* **Consent**
  action in, [4.11], [4.18]
  assault — *see* **Assault**
  battery — *see* **Battery**
  medical treatment without consent, [4.10], [4.17], [4.18]

Trespass to the person — *continued*
negligence — *see* **Negligence**
unlawful restraint or detention — *see* **Detention; Restraint**

Tribunals — *see also* **Administrative law**
adjudicative tribunals, [2.49]
alternative dispute resolution (ADR), [2.53]
 appropriateness of, [2.54]
 model in New South Wales, [2.55]
anti-discrimination tribunals, [2.63]
appeal bodies, as, [2.44], [2.68]
commissions, [2.64]–[2.67]
Commonwealth Administrative Appeals Tribunal — *see* **Administrative Appeals Tribunal (AAT)**
courts, difference from, [2.46]
decisions by, [2.44]
equal opportunity tribunals, [2.63]
investigative tribunals, [2.50]
jurisdiction, [2.47]
powers, [2.45]
review tribunals, [2.51]
 referral of matters, [2.52]
Social Security Appeals Tribunal, [2.62]
specialist divisions, [2.47], [2.55], [2.58]
specialist tribunals, [2.47], [2.61]–[2.68]
types, [2.48]
Victorian Civil and Administrative Tribunal (VCAT), [2.59]
Western Australian Administrative Review Tribunal, [2.60]

United Nations Conventions and Declarations
Convention on the Elimination of all Forms of Discrimination [1.32]
Convention on the Rights of the Child, [18.12], [18.15]
Declaration of Human Rights, [1.59], [18.6]
Declaration of the Rights of Disabled Persons, [18.12], [18.14]
Declaration on the Rights of Mentally Retarded Persons, [5.63], [18.12], [18.14]
Declaration of the Rights of the Child, [18.12], [18.14]
enforcement, [18.8], [18.9]
 International Court of Justice, [18.8]
International Convention Concerning Discrimination in Respect of Employment and Occupation, [18.14]
International Convention on the Elimination of all Forms of Discrimination against Women (CEDAW), [18.59]
International Convention on the Elimination of all Forms of Racial Discrimination, [18.52], [18.53]
International Covenant on Civil and Political Rights, [2.71], [18.10], [18.12], [18.14]
International Covenant on Social, Economic and Cultural Rights, [18.12]
Principles for the Protection of Persons with Mental Illness and the Improvement of Mental Health Care, [5.140], [18.12]
ratification, [18.9]
UNESCO Convention Concerning the Protection of the World Cultural and Natural Heritage, [1.30]

Unlawful detention — *see* **Detention; Restraint**

Unprofessional conduct — *see* **Professional misconduct**

Vaccines, [16.57]

Verdict
"not guilty", [2.15]

Vicarious liability
agent, [6.194]
 health carers as, [6.194]–[6.196]
definition, [6.177]
drugs, [8.9]
employee, [6.181]
 legislation to protect, [6.199]–[6.201]
 tests to determine employment, [6.182]
employers, [6.198]
 right to require contributions to compensation, [6.199]
employment, in course of, [6.197]
establishing existence of, [6.180]

Vicarious liability — *continued*
  hospitals and health care facilities, [6.179], [6.183]
    negligence in nursing care, [6.187]–[6.193]
  indemnity and contribution, [6.199]
  indemnity insurance, [6.196]
  principle, [6.178], [14.26]–[14.32]
    accomplices to crime, [14.32]
    delegation, [14.31]
    liability through incitement, [14.30]
    liability through others, [14.29]

Victims of crime
  compensation in criminal cases, [3.3], [14.1]
  evidence of the offence, [14.189]–[14.190]
    collection of forensic evidence, [14.191]–[14.192]
  health carer considerations
    confidentiality, [14.194]
    consent, [14.189], [14.195]
    hospital procedures, [14.191]
    involvement in potential criminal cases, [14.193]
    obligation to report serious crime, [14.191]
    useful evidence, retaining of, [14.192]
  patients allegedly the perpetrators of crime, [14.195]
    obligations of health carers, [14.196]
  victim impact statements, [3.3]

Victorian Civil and Administrative Tribunal (VCAT)
  establishment, [2.59]
  jurisdiction, [2.47]
    appealling registration board decision, [13.23]

Video conference technology
  High Court, in, [2.26]

Voluntary euthanasia
  checklist to law relating to treatment, [14.150]
  double effect, [14.90], [14.113]
    cause of death, [14.95]
    intention, [14.99]
  extraordinary measures, [14.102], [14.113]
    definitions, [14.103]–[14.104]
  legislation, [14.85], [14.116]
    Australian Capital Territory, [14.123]
    Northern Territory, [14.85]–[14.89], [14.122]
    South Australia, [14.101], [14.105], [14.120]–[14.121]
    Victoria, [14.117]–[14.119]
  quality of life issues, [14.126]–[14.132]
    do not resuscitate orders, [14.147]–[14.150]
    life support, [14.145]–[14.146]
    withdrawing treatment to newborn infants, [14.133]–[14.144]
  removal of life-sustaining machinery, [14.75], [14.79]–[14.82], [14.110]–[14.112]
  terminally ill patient, [14.76]–[14.89]
    brain death, [14.150]
    coma, [14.150]
    end-of-life decision making, [14.82]–[14.84]
    "locked-in" state, [14.110]–[14.112], [14.150]
    New South Wales guidelines, [14.124]
    pain relief for, [14.90]–[14.104]
    persistent vegetative state, [14.106]–[14.110], [14.150]
  withholding or withdrawing treatment, [14.75], [14.79]–[14.81], [14.133]
    checklist to law relating to, [14.150]
    patient's requests, [14.87]

Western Australian Administrative Review Tribunal, [2.60]

Women
  Equal Opportunity for Women in the Workplace Act, [18.93]
  health service discrimination case, [18.76]–[18.77]
  International Convention on the Elimination of all Forms of Discrimination against Women (CEDAW), [18.59]

Women's Electoral Lobby, [18.36]

Worker
  definition, [12.26]

Workers' compensation
  administration of claims, [12.21]

Workers' compensation — *continued*
  application for, [12.55]
    reporting of all injuries, [12.57]
  common law claim, [12.61]
  compensation, [12.58]
    death, [12.58]
    incapacity, [12.59]
    payments, [12.60]
  court interpretation, [12.24]
  employees covered, [12.25]–[12.28]
  events covered, [12.33]–[12.54]
    accommodation, [12.49]
    activities during breaks, [12.36]
    activities incidental to
      employment, [12.35]
    assault at work, [12.54]
    harm and employment,
      connection of, [12.33]
    journeys, [12.42]
    sporting and other activities,
      [12.46]
    statutory extensions, [12.45]
    travel to classes and conferences,
      [12.53]
  legislation, [12.19], [12.24]
    changes, [12.19]
    limitations, [12.21]
  liability of occupiers for accidents on
    their property — *see* **Occupiers**
  no fault schemes, [12.20]
  rehabilitation, [12.22], [12.24]
  serious injury cover, [12.18]

Workplace safety
  definition, [12.8]
  employers, [12.9]
    guidelines for, [12.11]
    interpretation in handling issues,
      [12.10]
    provisional improvement notice,
      [12.15]
    responsibilities, [12.7], [12.9]
    written plan, [12.11]
  injuries to health carers, [12.4],
    [12.32]
    common law, [12.4]–[12.5]
    safe working environment,
      [12.4]–[12.6]
    statute law, [12.6]
  injury, defined, [12.29]
    cases, [12.29]–[12.32]
  inspectors and investigators, [12.17]
    default notices, [12.15]
  joint staff-management committees,
    [12.13]
  rate of industrial accidents in
    Australia, [12.18]
  workers, [12.11]
    health and safety representatives,
      [12.13], [12.15]–[12.16]
    immediate threat to health and
      safety, [12.14]
    victimisation, [12.16]
  workers' compensation — *see*
    Workers' compensation

Worksafe Australia, [12.12]